ESTUARINE ECOLOGY

ESTUARINE ECOLOGY

JOHN W. DAY, JR.
Louisiana State University
Baton Rouge, Louisiana

CHARLES A. S. HALL
State University of New York
Syracuse, New York

W. MICHAEL KEMP
University of Maryland
Cambridge, Maryland

ALEJANDRO YÁÑEZ-ARANCIBIA
Universidad Nacional Autónoma de México
México D.F., México

WILEY

A WILEY-INTERSCIENCE PUBLICATION
JOHN WILEY & SONS
New York • Chichester • Brisbane • Toronto • Singapore

Library of Congress Cataloging in Publication Data:

Estuarine ecology / John W. Day, Jr. . . . [et al.].
    p.   cm.
  "A Wiley-Interscience publication."
  Includes bibliographies and index.
  ISBN 0-471-06263-4
  1. Estuarine ecology. I. Day, John W.

QH541.5.E8E849 1987
574.5'26365--dc19   87-27031
                                  CIP

Printed in the United States of America

10 9 8 7 6 5 4 3

CONTRIBUTORS

ROBERT R. CHRISTIAN, Department of Biology, East Carolina University, Greenville, North Carolina 27858

JOHN W. DAY, JR., Department of Marine Sciences and Coastal Ecology Institute, Center for Wetland Resources, Louisiana State University, Baton Rouge, Louisiana 70803

LINDA A. DEEGAN, Department of Forestry and Wildlife Management, University of Massachusetts, Amherst, Massachusetts 01003

CHARLES A. S. HALL, College of Environmental Science and Forestry, State University of New York, Syracuse, New York 13210

W. MICHAEL KEMP, Horn Point Environmental Laboratories, University of Maryland, Cambridge, Maryland 21613

BJÖRN KJERFVE, Department of Geology, University of South Carolina, Columbia, South Carolina 29208

ERIC KIVIAT, Hudsonia Institute, Bard College, Annandale, New York 12504

ALEJANDRO YÁÑEZ-ARANCIBIA, Instituto de Ciencias del Mar y Limnología, Universidad Nacional Autónoma de México, 04510 México, D. F., México

To Carolyn and Jason

This is a textbook for a course in estuarine ecology, designed to introduce students to the function and structure of estuarine ecosystems. It is designed for upper level undergraduates or for an introductory graduate course. We have tried to include extensive literature citations so that the book might also serve as general reference for estuarine scientists and as a source book for persons involved in the management and protection of estuaries. Our major objective in writing this book is to treat estuarine ecology in a concise and coherent manner for the beginning student.

The book is divided into six sections. The first introduces the reader to estuaries and estuarine ecology via excursions through three estuarine systems in which we have considerable experience. These are the North River, Massachusetts; Barataria Bay, Louisiana; and the Laguna de Términos, Mexico. In this section we introduce the reader to some of the background, definitions, theory, and issues of estuarine ecology. The second section of the book deals with physical and chemical aspects of estuaries. The nature of estuarine ecosystems is to a great extent determined by a complex and dynamic physical, geological and chemical environment. Therefore, a basic understanding of these topics is essential for a full comprehension of estuarine ecology.

The next three sections treat the detailed ecology of estuaries. These sections deal with estuarine primary producers, microbial ecology and organic detritus, and estuarine consumers. In these chapters we follow the flow of organic matter from production by plants, to processing and cycling by microbes, and then through the various consumer levels. In these discussions we develop detailed information on estuarine organisms and processes such as taxonomy, physiology, life histories, ecological role, growth, and relationships to abiotic factors.

The final section treats human interaction with estuaries in terms of fisheries and environmental impacts. This is a subject of increasing importance as human societies continue to exploit and pollute estuarine systems with increased intensity.

Our motivation for writing this book grew out the frustration each of us has experienced in teaching introductory classes in estuarine science without an appropriate textbook. While there are a number of good books now available in the related fields of marine and coastal ecology, none of these is sufficiently comprehensive to satisfy requirements for our own courses. The field of *estuarine ecology* is an infant science which has undergone explosive growth during the last two decades. This growth has been accompanied by a rapid proliferation in the published literature of estuarine research. While it is beyond the scope of our objectives to create an exhaustive compendium of that literature here, we have attempted to integrate and summarize the key information in this expanding field of science. We present numerous examples of data from this literature to highlight both those conceptual generalizations which are widely accepted and those which are centerpieces for hotly debated controversies. From the outset of this project, we recognized that there would necessarily be omissions in a book written over several years in this dynamic climate of change. It is our hope, however, that this book will serve, at least, as a starting point in the essential intellectual maturation processes which are presently underway in the estuarine sciences.

JOHN W. DAY, JR.
CHARLES A.S. HALL
W. MICHAEL KEMP
ALEJANDRO YÁÑEZ-ARANCIBIA

Baton Rouge, Louisiana
Syracuse, New York
Cambridge, Maryland
México D.F., México
May 1988

■ ACKNOWLEDGMENTS

Since estuarine ecology is such a dynamic science, we depended heavily on many of our colleagues in writing this book. Through discussions, suggestions, and review of different chapters, many estuarine ecologists helped shaped this book. Among those who were particularly helpful were William Odum, Wiley Kitchens, Charles Hopkinson, Richard Wetzel, Edward Kuenzler, Robert Twilley, Irving Mendelssohn, Walter Sikora, James Gosselink, Eugene Turner, Robert Costanza, Don Baltz, Walter Boynton, Court Stevenson, George Helz, Bill Dennison, Tom Malone, Michael Roman, Bruce Peterson, Patricia Sánchez-Gil, Francisco Flores-Verdugo, W. Wolff, Robert Howarth, Don Heinle, Leonard Bahr, and Scott Nixon. We acknowledge the intellectual stimulation of Howard and Eugene Odum. Their work, as well as that of their students and colleagues, is richly represented throughout this book. This book could not have been finished without the help of Suzanne Hautot, Kandy Simoneaux, and Anne Slater who dealt with countless details involved in its production.

CONTENTS

ESTUARINE ECOLOGY

INTRODUCTION AND OVERVIEW

OFFPRINTS FROM: ESTUARINE ECOLOGY
Edited by John W. Day Jr., Charles A. S. Hall., Dr. W. Michael Kemp, and Alejandro Yáñez-Arancibia
Copyright © 1989 by John Wiley & Sons, Inc.

▬ 1

Background, Theory, and Issues

INTRODUCTION

We begin this description of estuaries and their functions by defining estuaries very broadly as that portion of the earth's coastal zone where there is interaction of ocean water, fresh water, land, and atmosphere. Large estuarine zones are most common on low-relief coastal regions, including especially the broad coastal plains of, for example, Europe and the east coast of North America. They are much less common on uplifted coastlines like the Pacific edge of North and South America. We wish to begin our assessment as broadly as possible to include all portions of the earth that interact at the edge of the sea, for all of these regions affect what goes on in the smaller-scale regions sometimes more narrowly defined as estuaries proper.

From the vantage point of an orbiting satellite several of the most basic attributes of estuaries are observable. Plumes of sediment-laden water float seaward on the ocean surface from the largest rivers, such as the Amazon, the Nile, and the Mississippi. Color differences among various water masses, representing waters of different histories and different biotic richness, are often apparent. Coastal waters in areas with significant riverine input and broad shelf areas generally appear more greenish-brown than the deep blue waters adjacent to many other coastlines. There are also atmospheric features of importance to estuaries obvious from space. Clouds commonly form directly over the edges of continents as one manifestation of the atmospheric "thermal engine" that maintains the freshwater cycle on which estuaries depend. At the altitude of a satellite the dense human populations that have proliferated in coastal zones during the last century are hardly visible during the day. Exceptions include the lake formed by the Aswan Dam on the Nile River, and the deltaic plain of the Yangtze River, which has been almost totally converted from wetland to agriculture. At night, many of the estuaries of the world are outlined by the lights of the dense human populations that live along them.

The two most recent geological epochs, collectively named the Holocene, could be called the age of the estuary, for estuaries are abundant today even though they are geologically tenuous. All present day estuaries are less than 5000 years old, representing the time since sea level peaked near its present level following the last ice age. Human populations have flourished during this same time period, in no small measure as a result of exploiting the rich estuarine resources. Many "cradles of civilization" arose in deltaic and riparian (riverside) areas where natural biota was abundant and where flooding cycles produced the rich bottomland soils and readily available freshwater supplies on which agriculture "took root." Early centers of civilization that developed in estuarine or deltaic environments include those of the Tabascan lowlands of Mexico, and the valleys of the Nile, Tigris—Euphrates, Yellow, and Indus Rivers.

Let us now continue our aerial survey of estuaries, but this time at a much lower altitude, about 1000 m, in a light airplane following the course of a river in the southeastern United States from its headwaters to the ocean. The headwater river is narrow with rapids and falls, but changes near the coast to a larger meandering form with broad marshy areas where the actual edge of the river is not always clearly evident. The water color changes from clear to yellowish-brown as the river picks up silt. As the river water nears the coast tidal currents become apparent and, as we move seaward, the influence of the tidal currents becomes greater and greater.

Along the banks of the estuary, fresh and brackish water marsh plants grow at the edges of embayments. Among these marshes a variety of wading birds may be observed stalking their prey at the water's edge. Where the water is shallow and relatively clear, dark-colored patches indicate the presence of submerged grass beds.

As we travel seaward, the tidal influence becomes more important and the intertidal zone becomes more extensive. Brown mud flats come into view, as well as greenish-gray oyster reefs fringing the banks or dotting the mud flats. Various birds such as oyster catchers feed on the reefs, along with an occasional raccoon. The mud flats are peppered with mud snails, and just beneath the surface are teeming communities of small worms and crustaceans. Various shore birds are feeding at the water's edge, and skimmers fly along in quiet areas, plowing a furrow in the water with their lower bill as they fish for silversides and other small fish.

The mouth of the estuary takes the form of a broad sound that opens up behind a barrier island. The sound is shallow, and we can see porpoises herd schools of juvenile menhaden, followed by gulls trying to get in on the action. Crab pot bouys and fishing boats are much in evidence. On either side of the barrier island are narrow passes with visible eddies and strange wave patterns, indicating rapid and complex currents.

Along the ocean beach a number of shrimp boats raise long spiraling muddy plumes of sediment as they drag their trawls along the bottom. A kilometer or so offshore of the tidal passes the water color changes from dark brownish-green to a lighter, less turbid green. Further offshore it is a darker and bluer color.

On the landward side of most such barrier islands are found flat intertidal areas colonized by salt marsh plants. The highest part of the island includes some live oak trees, stunted on the ocean side. The beach may include a series of dunes, the farthest from the ocean covered with vegetation, the nearer dunes less and less vegetated. The seaward side of the dune closest to the ocean has much less vegetation because the wave energy from storms makes it difficult for any plants to survive.

In summary, from many elevations estuaries can be seen as complex, dynamic, and biotically rich environments dominated by physical forces. Their study requires a consideration and knowledge of geology, hydrology, chemistry, physics, and biology. Ideally we can integrate our knowledge gained through these specific disciplines using what we call systems science. This book is an introduction to the specifics of estuarine science and their integration into a coherent view of estuaries as ecosystems. We will show how estuaries are different from one another and how they are similar, and why we need to to preserve them while enhancing their value to civilizations.

We will begin by describing a very generalized estuary, to provide the reader with an introduction to the geology, physics, chemistry, and biology of estuaries. This is done with a certain danger—for, as the rest of the book will show, estuaries are characterized as much by difference as by similarity.

Nevertheless, in this first chapter we attempt to describe a generalized estuary. But before we proceed further, let us attempt to define an estuary.

1.1 DEFINITIONS, TERMS, OBJECTIVES

1.1.1 Definitions of Estuary and of Ecology, and Difficulties in Applying the Standard Definitions to Real Estuaries

The term estuary comes from the Latin *aestus,* meaning heat, boiling, or tide. Specifically, the adjective *asetuarium* means tidal. Thus the *Oxford Dictionary* defines estuary "as the tidal mouth of a great river, where the tide meets the current." *Webster's Dictionary* is more specific: "a passage, as the mouth of a river or lake where the tide meets the river current; more commonly, an arm of the sea at the lower end of a river; a firth. (b) in physical geography, a drowned river mouth, caused by the sinking of land near the coast."

Perhaps the most widely quoted definition of an estuary in the scientific literature is given by Pritchard (1967): "An estuary is a semi-enclosed coastal body of water which has a free connection with the open sea and within which sea water is measurably diluted with fresh water derived from land drainage." Certainly one of the most characteristic attributes of most coastal areas is the action of the tide. Pritchard's definition makes no specific mention of tide, although the mixing of sea water and fresh water implies this. There are, however, many nontidal seas, such as the Mediterranean, where fresh and salt water mix.

There are also estuaries in semiarid regions which may not receive any fresh water for long periods; and sometimes, as in the Pacific coast of California and Mexico, Western Australia, and several parts of Africa, the estuary may become blocked by longshore sand drift, so that it is ephemerally isolated from the sea. In other regions the tidal limit, sometimes with a tidal bore, may reach 100 km or more above the limits of salt water intrusion. So Pritchard's definition of estuary will exclude many coastal areas where estuarine ecology is studied today.

In an attempt to address these limitations of Pritchard's definition, Fairbridge (1980) gave a more comprehensive definition of an estuary:

> An estuary is an inlet of the sea reaching into a river valley as far as the upper limit of tidal rise, usually being divisible into three sectors; (a) a marine or lower estuary, in free connection with the open sea; (b) a middle estuary subject to strong salt and fresh water mixing; and (c) an upper or fluvial estuary, characterized by fresh water but subject to daily tidal action. The limits between these sectors are variable, and subject to constant changes in the river discharge.

Fairbridge's definition also excludes some coastal geomorphic features such as lagoons, deltas, and sounds and also nontidal estuaries. The distinctions between these different terms is treated in detail in Chapter 2, but characteristic estuarine ecosystems have developed in all these coastal systems. Therefore, when we use the terms estuary or estuarine in this book, unless specifically stated otherwise, we mean it in a general ecological sense rather than any specific narrower geological sense. All of the definitions of estuaries given above reflect, for the most part, physical and geological characteristics of estuaries. But why is this so? The people who first defined and classified estuaries were geologists and physical oceanographers, because in many respects the most salient features of estuaries are physical and geomorphic. And the ecosystems which exist in estuaries are physically dominated. We can illustrate this point by comparing an estuarine ecosystem with a tropical forest ecosystem. A visitor to a rain forest is immediately struck by the richness of the vegetation. If the visitor stays in the forest for some time he or she will notice that it rains a lot and the temperature is warm. If the visitor is a careful observor, he or she will perhaps learn about the soils of the forest. But the most striking characteristic is the vegetation. Rain forests are biologically dominated systems and have been described primarily by their biological characteristics.

In contrast, the visitor to an estuary cannot escape noticing the impact of abiotic characteristics. These include the rise and fall of the tide, complex water movements, high turbidity levels, and different salt concentrations. The nature of land forms such as beaches, barrier islands, mud flats, and deltas and the geometry of the basin are also very noticeable. There are, of course, outstanding biotic characteristics of estuaries such as salt marshes, submerged grass beds, and oyster reefs. But, in general, one has to look carefully to obtain even a general idea of the biological structure of estuaries.

The visibility of the abiotic attributes of estuaries reflect the fact that estuaries are, to a large degree, physically dominated ecosystems. To begin to understand what an estuarine ecosystem is and how it functions, an estuarine ecologist must have a good understanding of the geology, physical oceanography, and chemistry of estuaries. Thus one of the basic functions of Chapters 2 and 3 is to form a physical basis which will lead to an understanding of the biotic processes, for in estuaries the physical and biotic processes are tightly linked.

Before we go further it is necessary to define ecology, since this book is about estuarine ecology. Usually ecology is defined as the study of the relation of organisms or groups of organisms to each other and to their environment. Margalef (1968) gives a definition of ecology which is, perhaps, more appropriate to the way we will approach estuarine ecology. He stated "ecology is the study of systems at the level in which individuals or whole organisms can be considered as elements of interaction, either among themselves, or with a loosely organized environmental matrix. Systems at this level are called ecosystems, and ecology is the biology of ecosystems." Thus, in this book, we will consider the environmental matrix of estuaries, the interactions among specific organisms and the environment, and the structure and functioning of whole estuarine ecosystems.

1.2 VIEWS OF THREE ESTUARIES

Now that we have an idea of what estuaries are, we will travel to several real estuarine systems so that we can obtain first-hand knowledge of what these systems look like and of some of the processes that affect them. Our choices reflect an effort to give an impression of the range of conditions that exist in estuarine systems based upon estuaries in which we have personally worked.

1.2.1 North River, Massachusetts

Our trip up the North River estuary begins with the launching of a canoe near the sea, 2 hours before high tide in August. We take along an oxygen meter, a thermometer, and a refractometer (a device for measuring salinity). The North River at this point is about 200 m wide, and looks almost like a strongly flowing, clear, fresh-water river running through a broad meadow (Fig. 1.1). Closer examination shows that the grass is *Spartina alterniflora*, a flowering grass from about a half meter to a meter high that is characteristic of many temperate intertidal estuarine environments. Later, as the tide comes in, the grass meadows themselves flood so that the river grows from 200 to more than 2000 m wide, and the meadow begins to look like a large, grassy lake. A kilometer away, ocean waves can be seen breaking against the sandbar at the mouth of the estuary.

The August water is cold, clear, and salty, for it is mostly water that has just moved in from the adjacent ocean. Our instruments tell us that the water has a

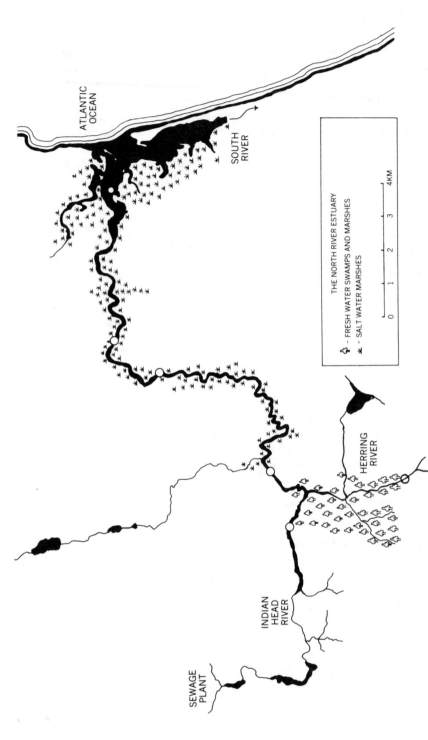

Figure 1.1 The North River estuary in Massachusetts, showing salt and freshwater marshes. Boston is located about 50 km to the north.

temperature of 16°C and a salinity of 32 parts per thousand (ppt). The oxygen concentration of 9 ppm is about the value expected for seawater in equilibrium with the atmosphere. We decide to use the inflowing tide to help us move upstream to look at the interior portions of the estuary, so we shove off and paddle with the current away from the sea. Immediately we are impressed with the huge mussel beds in the channel and the fish of all sizes which are abundant, often swirling at the water's surface. Clearly life is abundant and rich here.

As we travel upstream our route becomes very tortuous, for the narrow river meanders back and forth through a 2-km-wide marsh area. Fish life remains abundant, and sometimes large schools of silverside (*Menidia* sp.), alewive (*Alosa pseudoharengus*), mumichog (*Fundulus heteroclitus*), and other small fish can be seen moving with the current or, occasionally, jumping to escape predators. There are many boats moored here, for the North River is a popular area for boating, swimming, and fishing. There are also many houses along the low hills that line the estuary, for the region has been a popular place to live, first by the Massasoit Indians, and later by European settlers. In the 1800s the North River was an important site for ship building.

As we travel further upstream the meadow area becomes narrower and the *Spartina* appears somewhat taller and bushier. We are surprised that the tide is still coming in, for it has been two and a half hours since we departed and high tide was supposedly a half hour ago. The salinity is 21 ppt, about 2/3 as salty as the sea. Since there is no appreciable salt in the water coming in from the freshwater rivers at the head of the estuary we know that about 1/3 of the water under our canoe is derived from the rivers and about 2/3 from the ocean, and that these two water masses are mixing in this section of the river. As we progress further upstream, still with the tidal current, the channel narrows to 50 m wide, the vegetation begins to change from *Spartina alterniflora* to *Spartina patens,* a different species of marsh grass often found in slightly fresher salt water. The refractometer shows that the salinity has decreased to 10 ppt, the oxygen meter shows that oxygen is only 3 ppm, considerably lower than nearer the sea, and the water has become less clear, almost tea-colored. Even now the tide is still flowing inward, more than 2 hours after the predicted high tide at the mouth, reflecting the fact that high tide occurs progressively later as we move further from the coast, so that at this time water is flowing seaward at the mouth while it is flowing landward here some 15 km from the sea. Finally we reach the two major freshwater rivers above the tidal influence. One drains from a heavily settled region of the suburbs of Boston and is somewhat choked with algae. The other, draining mostly natural swamps with fewer people living nearby, is crystal clear. Both branches have many fish, though, and we remark about how such a lush natural area can exist within the boundaries of a major metropolitan region. The marsh vegetation here is characterized by wild rice, cattails, and rushes.

All along our trip we have noticed that the marsh along the river was flat and covered with vegetation, but that the vegetation changed abruptly to forest where low hills emerged from the edge of the marsh. This configuration is typical of many estuaries in the Northeastern United States and is called a "drowned river valley morphology," in that what we see now was once a more or less V-shaped river valley that was "drowned" as the sea level rose following the last glacial retreat. As the sea level rose marsh plants were able to grow increasingly inland, where they trapped sediments and, upon dying, added their own remains to the valley floor. (This subject is covered in more detail in Chapter 2.)

1.2.2   Barataria Bay, Louisiana

We begin our trip to the Barataria Estuary in early April at Grand Isle, one of the barrier islands that separates Barataria Bay from the Gulf of Mexico (Fig. 1.2). Jean Lafitte, the pirate who helped Andrew Jackson at the Battle of New Orleans, used Grande Isle as a base, and as we travel up the estuary we follow a route similar to that used by Lafitte in the early 19th century on his way to New Orleans. Because Barataria Bay is much larger than the North River Estuary, we use an outboard motor boat. In addition to the food and drink brought by both pirates and estuarine ecologists, we take along an oxygen meter, a Secchi disc (a device used to measure water clarity), a refractometer, and a trawl for fish.

As we pull away from the dock into Barataria pass, we pass a conglomeration of shrimp boats, oyster boats, pleasure craft, and work boats which serve the oil industry. Several kilometers across the pass stand the ruins of Fort Jefferson on Grande Terre, the next island. There are a number of dolphins surfacing in the pass and hundreds of shore birds on the far shore. Out in the Gulf numerous offshore oil rigs are visible. Geologists tell us that this oil was formed millions years ago in an environment very similar to the one we see today, and undoubtedly, oil is forming today slowly from the rich plant life of the bay. Even though we are near the Gulf of Mexico, the salinity here is only 25 ppt. This reflects not so much the input of landward rivers as the effect in this part of the Gulf of Mexico of water that originated from the Mississippi River, which empties into the Gulf about 50 km southwest of Grand Isle. The pass is deep; over 50 m in places, but most of Barataria Bay is between 1 and 2 m deep.

As we head north from Grand Isle, we see mostly a broad expanse of open water with no salt marsh, but dotted with a few islands covered with low shrubby growth of black mangroves, *Avicenia germinians*. In the tropics this species grows into trees up to 25–30 m high, but here it is at the northernmost extent of its range and seldom grows more than a few meters tall before being killed by a freeze. Some of these islands began as oyster reefs that were annhilated by predators which moved into this area with the higher salinity water that was one result of the flood-control levees that have been built along the Mississippi River. A few brown pelicans (*Pelicanus occidentalis*), the Louisiana state bird, live on some of the islands. These few birds represent an attempt to reestablish this species in Louisiana using pelicans imported from Florida. The large populations formerly present here were eliminated by pesticide poisoning.

In the middle of lower Barataria Bay, the water is greenish and very turbid (less than 1 m visibility as measured with a Secchi disc), the salinity is 20 ppt, and the oxygen is 7.5 ppm, which is near equilibrium with the atmosphere. The

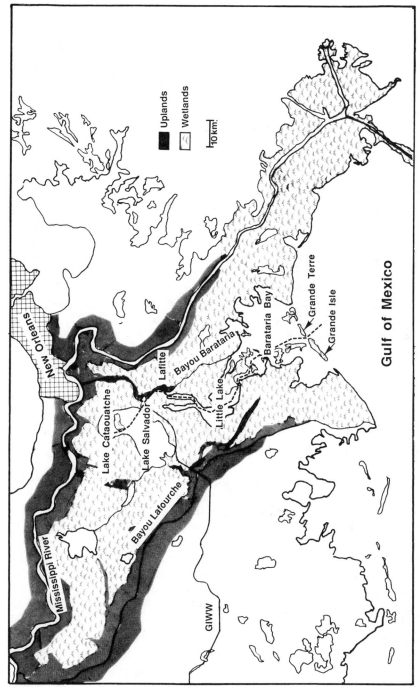

Figure 1.2 The Barataria Bay estuary in southern Louisiana. The dashed line is the route of the trip discussed in the text.

11

depth is 1.8 m and the water column is well mixed from top to bottom. A short trawl sample yields over 100 anchovies (*Anchoa mitchelii*), numerically the most abundant fish in this estuary. There are also a number of croaker (*Micropogonias undulatus*), hardhead catfish (*Arius felis*), and spot (*Leiostomus xanthurus*) as well as a few speckled trout (*Cynoscion nebulosus*), several blue crabs (*Callinectes sapidus*), and a few other species. The numerous small juvenile and larval fish are very noticeable. Spring is the time when these immature forms are most abundant, and many of the developing young migrate into the estuary after having been spawned out in the Gulf.

As we continue heading away from the Gulf, the salt marsh is visible as a thin line on the horizon. For as far as we can see there is no high land. Later, as we approach the marsh, there is a very dense stand of marsh grass *Spartina alterniflora,* the same grass that was so abundant in North River. The tide is rising and has reached the level of the marsh sediments. We raise the motor and paddle the boat 20–30 m up a small tidal channel. Along the edge of the marsh there are numerous fiddler crabs (probably of the genus *Uca*) scurrying about, and the tidal channel is full of fishes swimming rapidly as we disturb them. A number of mullet (*Mugil cephalus*) are jumping and one actually lands in the boat, adding to our planned supper. Oxygen here is only 1.8 ppm, and the bottom is very soft and muddy. We leave the boat to walk in the marsh. The grass near the water's edge is very dense and over a meter tall, and it is difficult walking. There is a strong hydrogen sulfide (rotten egg) smell as our walking disturbs the anoxic sediments. Several types of snails are very abundant on the grass stalks, and when the grass is parted beneath our feet we see occasional clumps of mussels. About 50 m from the water the grass is much less dense and the animals are much less abundant. We walk back to the boat and push off. As we leave we wave to an oyster boat making wide, slow circles as oysters are dredged and brought aboard.

As we travel, we cannot help but notice the many platforms in the water where oil wells are located. Additionally, there are many dredged channels in the marsh. Some of these are for navigation, but most were made by the petroleum industry for pipelines and for access to drilling rigs located in the marsh. The dredged canals are generally lined with "spoil" material along both sides. These straight and deep man-made canals are a striking contrast to the natural tidal channels which are shallow and twisting. Recent studies have shown that these channels are contributing significantly to erosion of the marshes.

As we travel further from the Gulf there is more marsh and less open water. We have taken a number of salinity readings and the water is gradually becoming fresher. At the lower end of a lake (named Little Lake) the salinity is only 8 ppt, the water depth is 1.0 m, and the water color has changed from greenish to brownish-green. We make another stop in the marsh. The dominant species here has changed to *Spartina patens,* a species characteristic of lower salinity waters. When we walk on the marsh it is much more spongy.

A little further on we stop to eat lunch on an oak-covered island of shells about 1 m high and 1–2 hectares in extent. The oaks are hung with Spanish moss. This mound is composed primarily of shells of the brackish water clam *Rangia cuneata* and was built a thousand years ago by native Americans who used the *Rangia* for food and the mound as a base for their homes. Such mounds are common in Louisiana's wetlands, indicating extensive Indian presence in these coastal regions. Mixed in with the shells are numerous pottery fragments, some with intricate markings.

In the distance is a long elevated ridge lined with oaks and cypress. This ridge is called Bayou L'Ours and it is an abandoned channel where a channel of the Mississippi River flowed only about 700 years ago. We know that it is slowly sinking into the marsh along with the rest of the Mississippi deltaic plain. The river that once flowed in this channel probably provided the sediments that initially formed the marshland around our island.

In Little Lake, a trawl sample yields many of the same species we found earlier. Anchovies are still the most abundant species, although there are also blue crabs, shrimp, croakers, spot, and menhaden. For the first time there are a few freshwater catfish. We leave Little Lake and travel through Bayou Rigolettes to the town of Lafitte, bordering Bayou Barataria. Lafitte is a picturesque town. Along the water there are many different types of boats—oyster, shrimp, oil, fishing, and yachts—for this town makes its livelihood from the water, as does much of southern Louisiana. In the streets French is heard along with English, reflecting Louisiana's French heritage.

We continue northward up Bayou Barataria, cross the muddy Intracoastal Waterway, and enter Lake Salvador. This is a large lake a little over 3 m deep. In the shallow water along the shore there are grass beds. Anchovies, spot, and croaker are still common, but freshwater catfish are more common and there are a few freshwater shad. The salinity is 3 ppt and the oxygen is 7.5 ppm.

We pass into Lake Cataouatche. The marsh is composed mainly of bulltongue (*Sagitaria* sp.) and is referred to as "intermediate" marsh because it is characterized by species from both fresh and salt water. Although the salinity is similar to Lake Salvador, the water is an intense green and the oxygen concentration is 14 ppm during the day due to dense phytoplankton populations which grow as a result of nutrient enrichment from runoff. The skyline of New Orleans rises in the distance, reminding us of the source of many of the nutrients leading to the heavy phytoplankton growth.

1.2.3 Laguna de Terminos, Mexico

The Laguna de Terminos is a large tropical estuary in Mexico, bordering the southern Gulf of Mexico (Fig. 1.3). It receives drainage from the Palizada River, a distributary of the Usamacinta River, which is part of the largest river system in Mexico and an important avenue of trade for thousands of years. The first large regional civilization in the New World, the Olmecs, and later the Maya lived along its course. Our trip is in December, after it is has already turned cold in most temperate estuaries, but it is warm here. The seasons here are determined much more by seasonal rains than by temperature. December is toward

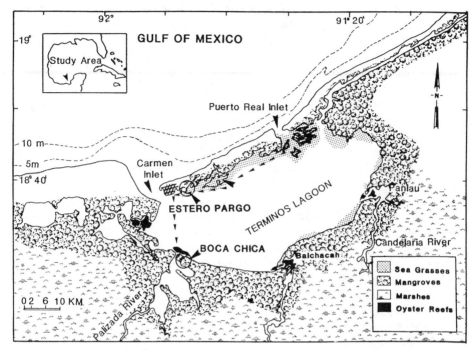

Figure 1.3 Laguna de Terminos in the state of Campeche, Mexico. The dashed line is the route of the trip discussed in the text.

the end of the wet season; rains and river flow reached their peak in October. The dry season begins in January or February and lasts until June. Storms called nortes, caused by cold fronts which have moved across the United States and the Gulf of Mexico, are possible in December, but it is sunny and warm for our trip. Nortes cause rains, high winds, and frigid temperatures (to natives of the area) as low as 18°C.

We launch the boat at Puerto Real, on the eastern end of the island of Carmen and a popular bathing beach for people who live on the island. As we move into the 4-km-wide pass, the tide is rising and water is flowing into the lagoon. The water is transparent; we can clearly see the bottom at 4 m where there are patches of turtle grass (*Thalassia testudinum*). There is a 1-m swell rolling in from the Gulf.

As we move into the lagoon the depth becomes shallower, the grass more abundant, the swell is diminished, and the water is calm. This shallow area is part of a flood-tide delta which is forming as suspended material swept in from the Gulf settles with the slower currents. The salinity here is about full sea water, 35 ppt, but at the end of the dry season it may be as high as 38 or 39 ppt. The sediments are sandy and firm.

We pull a trawl through an area of grass and sand flats. As in Barataria Bay and even, occasionally, more northern estuaries, the most numerous fish is the anchovy. Most of the other individual fish species are different from those in temperate estuaries, but estuarine ecologists know by their morphology, behavior, feeding habits, and migration patterns that they are very similar "ecologically" to fish in the temperate estuaries. For example, there are bottom-feeding flounders, planktivorous herringlike fishes, and predacious jacklike fishes.

Beyond the inlet delta the water depth increases to about 3 m, which is characteristic of most of the lagoon. The southern shore is not visible from this point. When the expedition of Juan de Grijalva and Juan Diaz, the Spanish explorers, arrived at this inlet in 1518, they named it Boca de Terminos (Last Inlet) because they could not see the far shore and thought that the white Yucatan Peninsula was an island.

We travel in a westerly direction about a kilometer from Carmen Island. The water is greenish here, the salinity is 28 ppt and the Secchi depth is 1.5 m. Between us and the mangrove and palm-lined shore are more submerged grass beds. About midway to the island, an arc of low, linear islands extends about 2 km into the lagoon. This is a relic delta like the one forming at Puerto Real. There was an active inlet here when the Spanish arrived in this area, but it has since filled in and closed.

Nearer the western end of the island, the grass beds have become thinner and the turbidity has increased. We enter Estero Pargo, a 5-km tidal channel lined with a mangrove swamp where the water is clear but stained brown. Along the shore is a dense mangrove stand with many arching prop roots composed almost entirely of red mangrove (*Rhizophora mangle*). The submerged portion of many of the roots are covered with oysters.

We leave Estero Pargo and continue to the end of the island where the city of Ciudad del Carmen is located. This is an old city and it was an important mahogany port when the American explorer John Stevens passed through here in the 1830s. As we pass close to Manigua Beach we see people swimming, smell fish cooking, and hear the distinctive sound of tropical Latin music. Moving into Carmen Inlet, the fishing fleet comes into view. There are many small sleek fishing skiffs with outboard motors and hundreds of large offshore shrimp trawlers. There are also numerous support boats associated with the developing offshore oil industry. Except for the music and the clear water it is reminiscent of Barataria Bay.

We cross Carmen Inlet and head for Boca Chica, the mouth of the Palazida River. The water becomes fresher and more turbid as we cross the lagoon. About 3 km from the mouth of the river salinity is 5 ppt and the Secchi depth is 30 cm. There are extensive oyster reefs at the mouth and as the water flows over them standing waves are formed. The water is completely fresh now but the salinity can get as high as 15 ppt during the dry season. Red mangroves line the river here, but inside the swamp it is almost completely dominated by black mangroves (*Avicennia germinans*). The trees here are 15-20 m high as compared with 6-7 m at Estero Pargo. As we leave the swamp, we pass the house of a woodcutter who is making charcoal from mangrove wood.

A striking thing about Laguna de Terminos is that with the exception of Ciudad del Carmen, it is almost completely undeveloped. Nowhere in the United States or Europe is there such a large estuarine system (about 2500 km^2) in such a pristine condition. Even so, Terminos is heavily used by fishermen and new oil discoveries in the region may produce considerable development.

After these short journeys, we begin to have a better feeling about what estuarine ecosystems are. Tides, river flows, and other physical forces are extremely important. Complex and sometimes strong water movements caused by the ebb and flow of the tide, river currents, and winds are common. There is evidence of rapid geological changes. In areas with strong currents or waves there are coarse sediments such as sand, while in quiet areas the sediments are soft and often smell of hydrogen sulfide. In the intertidal zone there are marsh grasses, mangroves, and oyster and mussel reefs. Birds and fishes are very abundant. Human activity is also highly visible both in terms of use of the estuary and impact on it.

1.3   FIVE VIEWS OF A GENERALIZED ESTUARY

Our trips have given us a casual view of three particular estuaries. It is now time to discuss estuaries in a more systematic and scientific manner, and we will do this through five views of a generalized estuary, emphasizing common characteristics among these divergent systems.

1.3.1   Top View

Our first view of a generalized estuary is from above (Fig. 1.4). At one end there is a river entering a large bay and at the other end a barrier island separating the bay from the ocean. Wave energy along the ocean beach is high and there is a wide sandy beach. On the beach there is little immediate evidence of life other than a few birds. Studies have shown, however, that there is an abundant and diverse community of tiny organisms living among the sand grains on the beach. The wave energy is very important to these organisms because the waves pump water containing oxygen and food constantly through the sand while carrying away waste products. The beach is an area of very high physical energies and the sediments are completely oxidized. This is an example of the importance of physical processes in determining the biotic characteristics of the estuarine environment.

In the tidal pass the water is still clear and the salinity high. The wave activity is somewhat reduced but currents are still strong. At the entrance to the pass the sediments are still sandy and completely oxidized, but beyond the influence of strong currents reducing conditions appear a few tens of centimeters below the sediment surface. The biota is abundant and diverse in the pass, and, as contrasted to the beach, epifauna becomes abundant. The pass is often the deepest part of the estuary.

As we move through the estuary, there are distinct changes in depth, physical

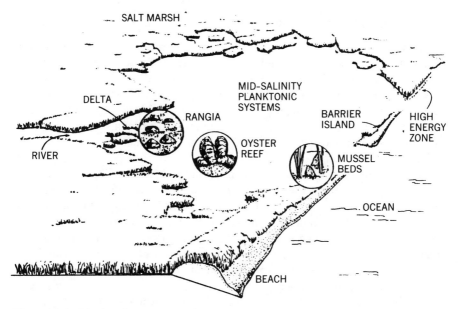

Figure 1.4 Idealized top view of a typical estuary showing some of the major subsystems.

energy levels (current and turbulence), water clarity, salinity, biota, chemical concentrations, oxidizing and reducing conditions in the sediments, and so on. In intertidal and subtidal areas with significant currents there are often worm flats or mollusc beds. These filter feeding organisms depend on currents to transport oxygen and food and carry away wastes.

In shallow subtidal waters of somewhat reduced currents where light reaches the bottom, submerged marine meadows or seagrass beds often occur. Water clarity is high and sediments are finer, partially as a result of the grass's ability to trap sediments. The reduced zone of the sediments extends to within a centimeter or less of the surface. In high-salinity tropical waters these submerged grass beds are often dominated by turtle grass, *Thalassia testudinum,* and in the temperate zone by eel grass, *Zostera marina.* In lower-salinity waters (less than 5 ppt) genera such as *Ruppia, Potamogeton,* and *Valisneria* are common.

In this typical estuary, the salinity decreases steadily from the ocean to the river. The high-salinity area of the estuary (30–35 ppt) is called polyhaline, middle salinities around 15 ppt constitute the mesohaline, and the very low-salinity region (0–5 ppt) is called the oligohaline zone.

Bordering the estuary in areas of mild to sluggish currents are intertidal wetlands where salt marshes occur in the temperate zone and mangrove swamps occur in the tropics. These are areas of turbid waters and highly reducing and very fine sediments. The vegetation has very high growth rates and the animals tend to be deposit feeders.

1.3.2   Cross-Section View

A cross-section view of the estuary (Fig. 1.5) illustrates a number of vertical as well as horizontal attributes of estuarine ecosystems. Such vertical gradients are important in determining the nature of these ecosystems. Perhaps the most obvious is the intertidal zone which is alternately flooded and exposed. In the intertidal zone there may be salt marsh or mangrove wetlands, algal beds, sand or mud flats, or reefs of oysters, mussels, or clams. Most organisms that live in the intertidal zone have developed special adaptations, which are discussed in numerous places in this book.

A second important vertical gradient is that of light. The lighted zone in an aquatic system is called the *euphotic* zone, while the zone with no light is the *aphotic* zone. Obviously photosynthesis occurs only in the euphotic zone. Where light reaches the bottom plants can live attached to the bottom. Estuarine water clarity tends to be much greater near the ocean, so both rooted and planktonic plants can generally photosynthesize in greater depths than in lower-salinity regions. Animals that live in the aphotic zone are dependent on food being transported in from somewhere else.

Another extremely important gradient for biological and chemical processes in estuaries is that from oxidizing (where oxygen is present) to reducing (where oxygen is absent) conditions. An oxidizing environment is also called *aerobic* and a reducing one *anaerobic* or *anoxic*. The estuarine water column is normally aerobic, but estuarine sediments usually are anaerobic a short distance below the sediment surface. The amount of oxygen in the sediments is related both to the rate oxygen moves into the sediments and the rate at which it is consumed. In areas with high physical energies, such as waves or strong currents, there are well-sorted coarse sediments which are oxidized. The physical energy serves both to replenish the oxygen to the sediments and to wash out finer materials which, for several reasons, consume oxygen rapidly. The opposite condition exists in areas of fine sediments. There the currents are too weak to sort the sediments or replenish oxygen rapidly and in some cases (such as highly reduced marsh soils), anaerobic conditions persist to the sediment surface. Since most estuaries are underlain by fine sediments, the reduced zone is widespread.

The activities of the biota, including the construction of burrows by organisms such as worms and fiddler crabs, facilitate the movement of water and oxygen through sediments. Many plants that grow in reduced conditions, including *Spartina*, actively pump oxygen into the soil and create a thin oxidized zone around their roots.

1.3.3   Longitudinal Section

The longitudinal section (Fig. 1.6) demonstrates some of the attributes that result from the mixing of fresh and sea water. Salinity gradually increases from fresh water to that of the sea. The isohalines (lines of equal salinity) also show that salinity increases with depth. This salinity distribution results from the den-

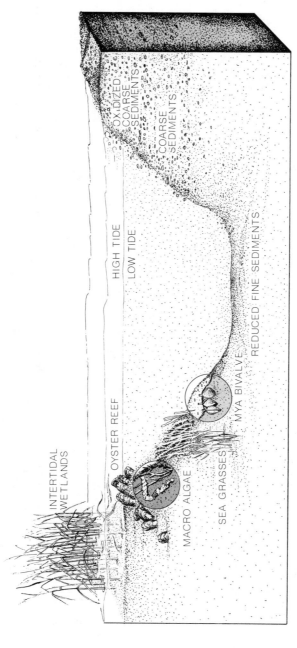

Figure 1.5 Idealized cross section through a typical estuary indicating the vertical distribution of several important components. The vertical scale is exaggerated.

INTERTIDAL WETLANDS

OYSTER REEF

HIGH TIDE

LOW TIDE

MACRO ALGAE

SEA GRASSES

MYA BIVALVE

REDUCED FINE SEDIMENTS

OXIDIZED COARSE SEDIMENTS

COARSE SEDIMENTS

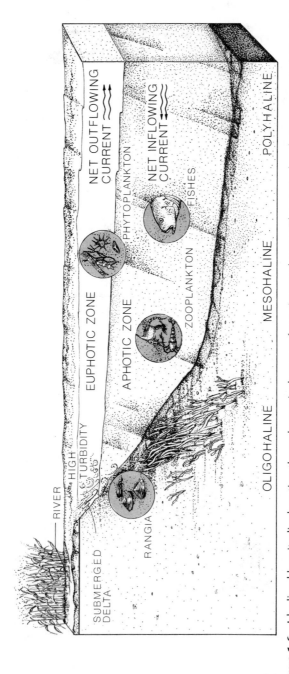

Figure 1.6 Idealized longitudinal section through a typical estuary from river to the sea. The vertical scale is exaggerated. The darker area near the sediment surface indicates an oxidized zone.

sity difference between salt and fresh water. Fresh water from the river tends to flow above the salt water because it is less dense. As the fresh water flows to the sea, deeper salt water mixes with it and it becomes saltier. This causes more salt water to move in on the bottom. This results in a net outflow to the sea at the surface and a net inflow of salt water on the bottom. This circulation pattern, and the resulting salinity distribution, is a general feature that is developed in many estuaries with significant river input, and will be discussed in more detail in Chapter 2.

We again see the euphotic and aphotic zones, but the depth of the euphotic zone decreases toward fresh water due to increasing turbidity. The most turbid water occurs at salinities from 1 to 5 ppt, and this "turbidity maximum," is a result of several physical and chemical changes which occur as the river and sea water mix. These changes will be addressed in Chapter 3.

Because this transect is through the deep part of the estuary, there are fine sediments and reducing conditions occur below the sediment surface along the entire transect. At the mouth of the river note the "platform" of riverine sediments which have settled out of the water where the river enters the estuarine bay.

Organisms that occur in the water column include phytoplankton, zooplankton, and fishes. Benthic animals include infauna such as polychaete worms, amphipods, and the very small meiofauna. Of special note is the dense bed of the clam, *Rangia cuneata,* in the oligohaline region. The diversity of benthic organisms along this transect changes from salt water to fresh and we will discuss this in more detail later in this chapter as well as in Chapter 9.

1.3.4   A Typical Estuarine Food Web

Thus far our observations of the typical estuary have been of the structure and, as such, have been rather static. We now discuss some more dynamic aspects of the estuary by considering typical estuarine food web (Fig. 1.7). This also will allow a more detailed consideration of some of the organisms which live in estuaries. For illustrative purposes, we will compare estuarine and marine systems.

We begin by listing several terms using definitions derived from E.P. Odum (1971). The transfer of food energy from the source in plants through a series of organisms eating one another is referred to as a *food chain,* or, more properly, *food web,* for food chains interconnect with one another. The word *trophic* is used interchangably with food, and trophic dynamics refers to the pattern of food consumption as it occurs and changes over time.

The trophic dynamics of estuaries tend to be complex. Figure 1.7 illustrates a number of important characteristics of estuarine trophic dynamics. First, there are almost always several different types of primary producers in estuaries, including salt marsh plants, mangroves, submerged sea grasses, and benthic algae. By contrast, the open ocean has only phytoplankton. There are other important distinctions between the open sea and estuaries. For example, in the sea practically all phytoplankton are consumed alive. A food web that begins with

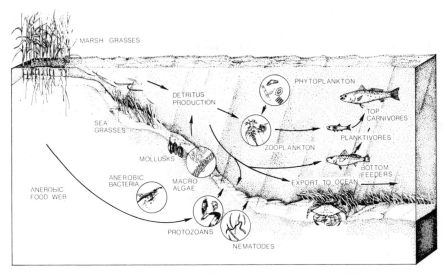

Figure 1.7 The food web of a typical estuary showing some of the major trophic groupings.

consumption of live plants is called a *grazing food web*. In estuaries many important plants are not heavily grazed, but die and begin to decompose before being consumed. This decomposing material is called *organic detritus* and the food web it supports is called a *detrital food web*. Organic detritus is an important food in estuaries and much of Chapter 7 is devoted to this subject.

Nevertheless, the part of the estuarine food web that is often the most readily recognizable to students is the grazing web based on phytoplankton. These small plants are eaten by zooplankton which are then eaten by small planktivorous fish. In this example they are herring, but in other estuaries these fish may be anchovies or sardines. The zooplankton also are eaten by larvae of larger fish. At the top of the food web are larger carnivores such as bluefish.

An extremely important characteristic of estuarine food webs is the role of the bottom. First, a variety of plants grow on the bottom in shallow waters (e.g., marsh grasses, sea grasses, and benthic algae). Second, there are important flows of food and inorganic nutrients from the water column to the bottom as well as in the opposite direction. Benthic animals such as oysters, clams, and mussels are filter feeders, that is, they remain in one place and concentrate food that flows past them in the water currents. There are other benthic organisms which live in areas of weak currents. They move over and through the sediments and take food from the sediment itself. These are called deposit feeders and include worms, amphipods, and a host of other small organisms. There are a large number of nonbottom-dwelling organisms which feed on the bottom. These include a variety of invertebrates, fish, and birds. In fact, the majority of fish species found in estuaries have adaptations for bottom feeding.

All of this flow of food energy from phytoplankton, detritus, and through the bottom converges upon a group of top carnivores which are generalist feeders on a wide variety of organisms. These top carnivores include many birds and fish such as sea gulls, sea trout, striped bass, and flounder.

In summary, estuarine trophic dynamics are characterized by a variety of primary producers, grazing and detrital food chains, a high degree of interaction between the water column and bottom, a complex food web, and a large number of generalist top feeders.

1.3.5 An Estuarine Energy-Flow Diagram

Thus far we have discussed visible aspects of estuarine ecosystems. We can see an oyster reef and a salt-marsh and a sample taken from the bottom. We can watch a trout eat an anchovy and, if we have a microscope, we can even observe a zooplankter ingesting a phytoplankton cell. But important processes go on which are not visible. We cannot see sunlight interacting with nitrogen during photosynthesis. Nor can we watch phosphorus flowing out of bottom sediments and being moved into surface waters by currents. It is very difficult to measure organic detritus flowing out of a marsh, much less visibly observe it. Nevertheless, an understanding of these and other processes is essential if we are to begin to comprehend how estuaries work. Thus in this section we want to use an energy-flow diagram (Fig. 1.8), both to present systematically some of the concepts we have discussed and to conceptualize some of these invisible processes. To do this we use the symbols developed by H.T. Odum (1971, 1983).

The diagram illustrates the grazing and detrital food webs we discussed in the last section. It shows the importance of tidal currents in transporting detritus out of the marsh and in moving phytoplankton to benthic filter feeders. The dynamics of nutrient cycling are important and complex in estuaries. Our diagram shows both input of nutrients and organic matter from the river as well as recycling from both sediment and water-column organisms. Again the importance of currents in transporting nutrients is illustrated. Finally the diagram shows that there is an interaction of sunlight and inorganic nutrients during primary production by phytoplankton, and that plankton produce oxygen which is subsequently used by animals.

There are, of course, many interactions and details left out of this energy diagram as well as the preceeding views of estuaries. Throughout this book we will endeavor to fill in as much detail as possible as develop a fuller general understanding of estuaries. At this point, however, you should have a good foundation to begin a more in-depth study of estuaries. In the next section we discuss a classification of estuarine ecosystems.

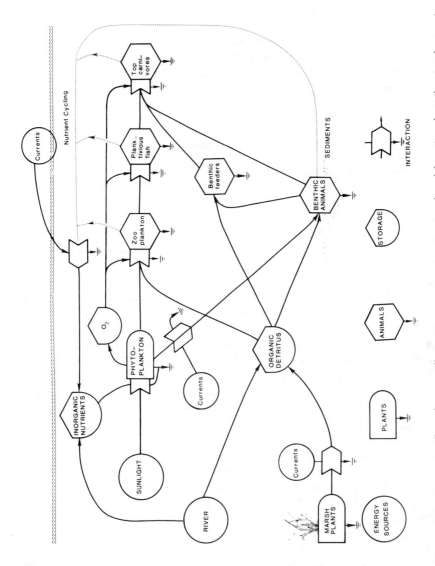

Figure 1.8 An energy-flow diagram illustrating some major structural and functional attributes of estuaries.

1.4   ESTUARINE HABITAT TYPES

The previous two sections demonstrated that there is a high diversity of habitat types within estuarine systems. This is due to two reasons. First, from an abiotic point of view, there is a high diversity of physical habitats. These include beaches, passes, intertidal and shallow subtidal flats, deeper areas, and deltas. Second, the biota has fully exploited these different areas to make the biological habitat diversity even higher. For example in the intertidal zone there may be salt marshes, tide pools, algal flats, mud flats, oyster reefs, and mussel beds. Oyster reefs and mussel beds in turn have created new types habitat by changing the physical environment. Subtidal areas can include seagrass beds, sandy shoals, soft muddy bottoms, or mollusc beds. Some of the more important biotic habitats are described in Table 1.1.

1.5   ECOLOGICAL CHARACTERIZATION AND CLASSIFICATION

1.5.1   Characterization of the Ecosystem

We have defined estuary and ecology, but because they are so variable, it is difficult to define estuarine ecosystems, except as those ecosystems that have developed and persist in estuaries. We can easily describe, however, the abiotic factors that are most important in determining the specific nature of estuarine ecosystems as well as the salient ecological characteristics of these ecoystems.

The physical environment (climate, geomorphology, presence or absence of water, salt, etc.) is the primary determinant of the type of ecosystem that will develop in a particular location. The constancy and regularity, or the lack thereof, of the physical environment is an important attribute of physical conditions that influence the biota. That is, the biota is most importantly determined by the degree of change, rather than the absolute level, of such factors as microclimate, water movement, chemical cycling, and physical structure.

Both abiotic factors and the biota itself can reduce the degree of fluctuation in the physical environment. Tropical rain forests and coral reefs are examples of ecosystems where the ambient physical environment is greatly modified by the biota. Alpine lichen-herb and sandy beach ecosystems are stongly impacted by physical inputs and are relatively unaffected by the biota. Estuarine ecosystems are intermediate between these extremes, but are still strongly physically dominated.

The following abiotic features are important in determining the specific nature of estuaries:

1. The degree to which they are protected and hence buffered to a degree from direct oceanic forces.
2. The quantity of fresh water input along with the amount of associated dissolved and suspended materials.

TABLE 1.1 Characteristics of Common Estuarine Habitats

Habitat	Physical Characteristics	Biological Characteristics
A. High Physical Energy Areas	Tidal passes and beaches; strong currents and or waves; often clear water; coarse sediments such as sand; well oxidized water column and sediments; generally high salinities.	Benthos dominated by filter feeders; high diversity and biomass; high rates of metabolism supported by current transport of food; heterotrophic; motile organisms mostly transient.
B. Mid-estuarine systems 1. Middle Salinity Plankton-Nekton System	Strong to moderate turbulence (waves and currents); salinity 10–25 ppt; oxygenated water column; bottom deeper than euphotic zone; medium water clarity.	Grazing food chain of phytoplankton, zooplankton, fishes; diatoms, dinoflagellates and nannoplankton common phytoplankters; copepods and meroplankton important zooplankters; relatively high rates of primary production with strong seasonal pulse in temperate zone disappearing in the tropical; balanced community metabolism; intermediate diversity.
2. Deep Benthos	Sluggish currents; fine sediments; no light on bottom; reducing conditions just below sediment surface; water column normally oxygenated.	Deposit feeders dominate (worms and amphipods); low density and biomass; heterotrophic with relatively low metabolic rate; low diversity.
C. Shallow Littoral Areas 1. Submerged Grassbeds	Moderate to strong currents; bottom within euphotic zone; oxygenated water column; sediment reduced just below surface; sediments range from sandy to fine.	High salinity grassbeds dominated by eel grass (Zostera) in temperate zone and by turtle grass (Thalassia) in tropics; high rates of gross primary productivity; community net productive; detrital food chain important; direct grazing increases in tropics; both deposit feeders and filter feeders important in benthos; high biomass, low diversity; complex chemical cycling; important nursery and feeding area for migratory species; high epiphytic community.

2. Algal Mats	Shallow, clear, often hypersaline water; sediments sandy to fine silts: highly reduced below mat; large oxygen changes due to metabolic activity.	Blue-green algal mats; extremely productive, P/R close to one; low consumer diversity.
D. Wetlands	Sluggish currents; intertidal wetlands act as sediment traps, sediments generally very soft often with peats; strong reducing conditions in sediments sometimes to sediment surface; often low oxygen in water column; complex chemical cycling; wetlands occur from fresh to marine salinities and from the arctic to the tropics.	Saline wetlands characterized by marshes (*Spartina*) in temperate zone and mangrove swamps (*Rhizophora*) in tropics; freshwater wetlands swamp or marsh; freshwater areas have higher producer diversity; high rates of gross primary production and net production; detrital food chain important; high biomass of both producers and consumers; low diversity; deposit feeders most common; important nursery and feeding area for migratory species.
E. Reefs, Worm, and Clam Flats	More or less constant currents—moderate to strong; intertidal or subtidal; oxygenated water column; reduced sediments; reef structure often amplifies currents; intermediate salinities for oysters; sediments for molluscs flats normally oxygenated; oyster reefs normally in fine, soft sediments, others in firmer sediments of sand or shell.	High biomass; low diversity; relatively high food supplies in water column; filter feeders predominate; high rates of metabolism; heterotrophic; often exploited commercially; *Crassostrea* and *Ostrea* common genera of oysters; oysters epifaunal, flats populated by infauna organisms.
F. Oligohaline	Located at river mouth-estuary boundary; highly variable salinity; water contains high levels of suspended solids and nutrients; high sedimentation rates, high turbidity, "nutrient trap"	Low species diversity; very high biomass; high rates of metabolism; heterotrophic; filter feeders dominate; *Rangia cuneata* and *Mya arenaria* very common in south and north temperate, respectively; heavily used by migrating fishes.

3. The water circulation patterns as determined by riverine and tidal currents and geomorphology. Tides are particularly important, for they exert a profound influence on estuarine circulation and biochemical and biological processes.

4. The depth of the estuary. Where estuaries are shallow there is a stronger interaction between the water column and the bottom. This allows, for example, for nutrients released from the bottom to be used by phytoplankton in the surface waters.

5. The sharpness and pattern of the gradient in salinity from the sea to fresh water. This salinity variation has a pronounced inpact on water circulation as well as on many biological processes.

6. The rate of geomorphological change as determined by various physical energies that move sediments.

Most estuarine ecosystems are open, variable systems dominated and subsidized by physical processes, resulting in large exchanges of biotic and nonbiotic materials, including water, salt, nutrients, sediments, and organisms, with neighboring systems. The exchange of organisms over millions of years has resulted in a rich genetic heritage, and the biota is derived from marine, fresh-water, and terrestrial sources. Over time periods of hundreds to thousands of years deltas grow and erode and barrier islands shift. On a shorter time scale there is a high degree of variability in estuaries. Salinity changes with tide and river flow, water levels fluctuate so that the intertidal region is subjected to wetting and drying and extremes of temperature. But estuarine organisms have developed physiological and behavioral patterns to deal with the dynamic environment, and many are able to modify the physical environment. Many organisms use the intense and variable physical energies as subsidies, as, for example, in the case of an oyster reef "using" the flow of tides to exploit phytoplankton produced elsewhere. Nevertheless, such an ever-changing world imposes considerable potential stress on estuarine organisms for the large changes in salinity, temperature, and so on can be deleterious, even lethal, for estuarine organisms. The relative importance of physical forces as subsidies or stresses forms the basis for the estuarine classification discussed in the next section.

1.5.2   Functional Classification of Estuarine Ecosystems

In Chapter 2, several estuarine classification schemes based on physical and geomorphic characteristics are presented. These definitions help us to understand the origin and physical nature of estuaries and can be used as the beginnings of an estuarine classification system. We need from the standpoint of estuarine ecology, however, a classification system that leads to a better understanding of estuaries as ecosystems.

Odum and Copeland (1972) proposed a "functional" system for understanding and classifying coastal ecosystems based on an energetic analysis. We like their approach because it is a true esosystem classification addressing both biotic and abiotic properties and it recognizes the large importance of energy. Their idea is that the status of an ecosystem is a balance between energies that build structure and order and stresses that cause a loss of structure and order. The former are called energy sources or *ordering energies* and the latter energy stresses or *disordering energies*. This idea is shown diagramatically in Figure 1.9A. We want to emphasize that energy sources and stresses are not always mutually exclusive categories of energies, but rather that a particular energetic force affects organisms relative to the ecosystem (or part of an ecosystem) in question. A few examples will illustrate this point. Moving water can be either an energy source or stress in estuarine ecosystems. Moderate currents are a source of energy for seagrass beds because they transport organic matter and nutrients to the beds and wastes away. If the currents become very strong with high waves, however, the grass bed may be destroyed. In the latter case, the hydraulic energy is a stress. But the same strong waves are an energy source for tiny animals living among the sand grains on a beach because the waves pump oxygen and food through the sand. Likewise, heat from the sun is an energy source for a marsh because it increases the rate of metabolism. But the intense heat of a fire will destroy a marsh.

The distinction between energy source and energy stress is the central concept in this classification system. Whether an energy input is ordering or disordering depends on the particular system or subsystem in consideration and it is the balance between the two that is important. If energy sources are greater then stresses, the system will build structure and maintain order. However if stresses are greater, there will be a loss of structure and order.

There are three general categories of energy sources for estuarine ecosystems: (1) the mechanical energy of moving water, (2) sunlight, and (3) organic and inorganic fuels imported into estuaries (Fig. 1.9B). Moving water does work, such as by connecting trophic components in the bottom and surface waters, bringing food to filter feeders, recycling nutrients, and removing wastes. Organisms in effect "save" their own energy by using the water current energy. The energy of sunlight drives photosynthesis of plants, which in turn supports estuarine food chains. Sun energy also supplies heat and thus produces thermal gradients in estuarine ecosystems. Supplementary organic and inorganic fuels are imported into estuaries via rivers, terrestrial runoff, and the sea. The organic matter is an added food to that produced in estuaries and the inorganic compounds such as nitrogen can increase photosynthesis by providing needed materials.

There are three general categories of stress energies for estuarine ecosystems: (1) stress due to energy diverted from the system, (2) that due to microscale random disordering, and (3) stress due to forced losses within the system (Fig. 1.9C). Stress caused by energy diverted refers to energy that could be a source but is, for some reason, lost. For example, turbidity caused by natural conditions or human activities lowers the amount of light energy that enters the water column and thus the photosynthesis of deeper submerged plants. For another,

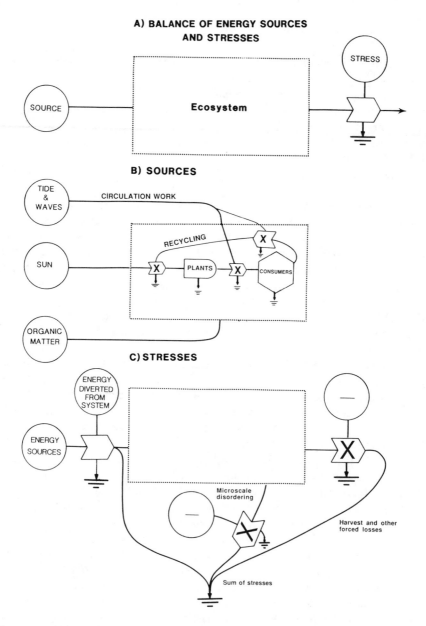

A) BALANCE OF ENERGY SOURCES AND STRESSES

STRESS

SOURCE

Ecosystem

B) SOURCES

TIDE & WAVES

CIRCULATION WORK

RECYCLING

SUN

PLANTS

CONSUMERS

ORGANIC MATTER

C) STRESSES

ENERGY DIVERTED FROM SYSTEM

ENERGY SOURCES

Microscale disordering

Harvest and other forced losses

Sum of stresses

Figure 1.9 Energy-flow diagrams illustrating how ordering and disordering energies are related in estuarine ecosystems. The status of an ecosystem results from a balance between energy sources, which build structure and order, and energy stresses, which cause a loss of structure and order (A). For estuaries there are three main kinds of energy sources: sunlight, moving water such as tides and waves, and organic and inorganic materials (B). Three general kinds of energy stresses are energy diverted from the system, microscale or entropic disordering, and harvest and other forced losses (C). See text for further discussion. (Figures from Odum and Copeland 1974, used by permission.)

when a marsh is impounded, the energy of tidal currents is eliminated and marsh productivity normally is lowered. A dam or river also can reduce the input of water and organic and inorganic matter entering an estuary. When the Aswan Dam was constructed in Egypt, the amount of river-borne material entering the estuary was drastically reduced and the sardine fishery in the eastern Mediterranean that depended on the material collapsed.

The second kind of stress on estuarine ecosystems and their inhabitants is that due to microscale random disordering of the kind described by the second law of thermodynamics. This stress is the inevitable tendency of order and complexity to degrade into disorder. If an animal does not eat for a relatively short period of time, it dies because food is the potential energy source it uses to maintain its internal order against this constant tendency toward disorder. The struggle against random disorder is a problem for all living creatures, and particularly for estuarine organisms, because much of the ordering energy available for estuarine organisms must be used to compensate for the large environmental variability. Human activity can aggravate the problem for estuarine organisms, for example, by the introduction of toxins, which tend to increase physiological "disorder" and thus make it even more difficult for an organism to cope with natural variability.

The last type of stress is forced loss. This means that potential energy within the system is removed before it can be used to do work. For example, the constant seaward flow of the rivers and the action of the tides flush material out of estuaries. Thus the water movement can be a stress as well as an energy source, and, most often, it is both. Human activities such as fishing and wetland destruction are also ways in which potential energy can be lost from an ecosystem.

Many estuarine organisms have evolved various behavioral and physiological adaptations to cope with the stresses in estuaries that would kill most other aquatic organisms (Vernberg and Vernberg 1972, 1976). In doing so they have become better able to exploit the available energy sources. These adaptations also allow organisms to use as an energy source energies that would be stressful to most other organisms. For example, the small animals that live among the sand grains on a beach would be destroyed by the full force of the waves if they were not adapted to them, and meanwhile they use the oxygen and food which the waves pump through the sand. The *Rangia* clam of the oligohaline zone is adapted to high siltation rates, periodic low oxygen, and extremely variable salinity, and thus is able to live where it can use the large input of organic matter from the river without much predation or competition from other filter feeders. Many other examples of this type of adaptation will be discussed throughout the book.

Because different estuarine systems and subsystems have characteristic energy stresses and sources, the biota of these various areas have adapted to these energies in different ways. These different energies and adaptations serve as the basis for the functional classification system of Odum and Copeland (Fig. 1.10). For most estuarine ecosystems, stress energies are moderate and similar so that the changing temperature and sunlight regime with latitude becomes the most

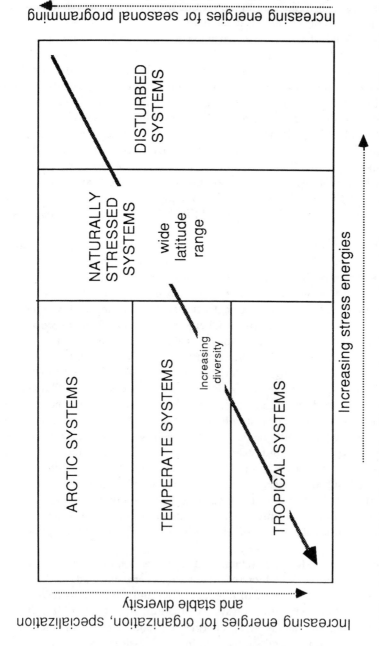

Figure 1.10 A functional classification of coastal ecosystems based on important energy sources and stresses. (From Odum and Copeland 1974, used by permission.)

important factor determining the characteristics of these systems. Tropical, temperate, and arctic estuarine ecosystems are conveniently distinguished. Solar energy input is highest and most regular in the tropics, but because of higher temperatures there is more thermal disordering to overcome, so that organisms there have higher energy requirements. Seasonal changes become more distinct in higher latitudes and the productivity of the system is concentrated into shorter periods of time, hence seasonal "programming" of activities and migratory species become more important. In the arctic, ice and extreme cold are important stress energies.

When stress energies become large, either naturally or because of human activity, the adaptations to them are in a sense similar over a wide latitudinal range. Thus in these circumstances, the estuarine ecosystem can be classified according to the characteristic stress. Sedimentary deltas, hypersaline lagoons, and beaches are examples of these types.

1.6 ESTUARIES AND ESTUARINE ECOSYSTEMS IN A GEOLOGICAL CONTEXT

It is interesting to note that practically all of the estuaries discussed in this book did not exist 10,000–15,000 years ago and that they will cease to exist in the near geological future. The world's present estuaries were formed when sea level rose after the last glaciation. Since that time, they have been progressively infilled and will continue to be. Thus present estuaries will, for the most part, cease to exist because they will fill up or because sea level will change again. Other estuaries will continue to exist at the edge of the sea, wherever it exists. At times like the present, when sea level is high enough to flood the edge of the continents, estuaries are widespread. When sea level was low enough so that the edge of the sea was on the continental slopes, as during the height of the glaciers, total estuarine area was small. The situation we see along the western coast of the Americas is the rule when sea level is low.

Of course the species and the types of biological communities that presently exist in estuaries have certainly existed for much longer periods of time. And rivers have always flowed into the sea, whether it was higher or lower than at present. Estuarine ecosystems, with their characteristic species composition and adaptations have moved back and forth with the edge of the sea. Therefore, even though particular estuaries are relatively short-lived, estuarine organisms and estuarine ecosystems are very old.

1.7 HIGH PRODUCTIVITY: AN ESTUARINE FOCAL POINT

One of the things that makes the study of estuarine ecology so exciting at this time is the lively discussion surrounding many of our ideas about what makes estuaries the way they are. In this section we will outline some of these issues, so that we have them in mind as we address the information in each chapter. The following discussion summarizes some current thinking about estuarine production. Perhaps we will view the idea very differently in 20 years.

The first idea is that estuaries are productive. One of the most widely held beliefs by both estuarine scientists and others familiar with estuaries is that they are very productive per unit area. Sometimes this means that the plants that exist in estuaries are very productive. At other times it means that more organic matter is produced in estuaries than is used there or that estuaries are very productive of fish.

1.7.1 Reasons for High Estuarine Primary Productivity: The Classic View

What are the reasons for the supposed high productivity of estuaries? C.L. Schelske and E.P. Odum in a well-known paper entitled "Mechanisms maintaining high productivity of Georgia estuaries" (Schelske and Odum 1962) stated that the estuaries of Georgia were among the most productive natural ecosystems in the world. They listed several reasons for this high productivity: (1) three types of primary production units (marsh grass, benthic algae, and phytoplankton), which insure maximum utilization of light at all seasons; (2) ebb and flow of water movements resulting from tidal action; (3) abundant supplies of nutrients; and (4) rapid regeneration and conservation of nutrients due to the activity of microorganisms and filter feeders. A number of these ideas have been discussed earlier in this chapter.

Now let's examine these points in more detail and consider the evidence on which they are based. There are, indeed, several distinct groups of primary producers in estuaries, many of which have high rates of primary production. A more general statement is that there is a diversity of sources of the organic matter. In Georgia there are three important producer groups: salt marsh grass, phytoplankton, and benthic algae. In other estuaries submerged sea grasses, mangrove swamps, and macroalgae may be important. Epiphytic algae grow on most surfaces in the euphotic zone. There is also input of organic matter from rivers and upland runoff.

The high primary production measurements in Georgia and elsewhere led Schelske and Odum to the conclusion that "estuaries are among the most productive natural ecosystems in the world." In Chapters 4, 5, and 6 on estuarine primary production, we consider the factors controlling productivity and try to determine whether all estuaries actually do have extremely high rates of productivity relative to other ecosystems. Another reason for high productivity in Georgia estuaries, according to Schelske and Odum, is that there is significant year-round production. This has been shown to be the case for a number of estuaries in lower latitudes, but it is not true in higher latitude estuaries, which are also often very productive.

Organic detritus from a variety of plant sources is abundant in many, if not most, estuaries. Many scientists have argued that organic detritus is an important food source. Most estuaries have an extensive autotrophic community, and there is often a surplus of organic matter available to consumers all year as organic detritus. The dynamics of orgainc detritus in estuaries has been the subject of a tremendous amount of research and controversy over the past several decades. In Chapter 7 on organic detritus and microbial ecology, we will consider the question of availability of organic matter.

Tidal action was considered to be an important factor contributing to high productivity. E.P. Odum once defined estuaries as "tidally subsidized fluctuating water level ecosystems." Others have expanded upon this to include high levels of physical energy, including wind, waves, and riverine currents as well as tides. These factors produce very complex water movements in estuaries. In much of this book we consider the nature of these physical factors, how they affect ecological processes, and how important they really are in ecological dynamics.

There are abundant supplies of nutrients in Georgia estuaries. Nutrient concentrations in estuaries are almost always higher than in the ocean and often higher than in freshwater systems. Schelske and Odum believed that most of these nutrients came from within the estuary and that they were responsible for the high levels of production. Some workers have emphasized the importance of rivers as sources of nutrients while others have not. Later, we will discuss these two questions.

The final factor considered important was the rapid regeneration and conservation of nutrients. Since most estuaries are relatively shallow and well mixed, there is a persistent intermingling of water and the bottom. This means that food in the water is available to organisms on the bottom and that nutrients released by benthic organisms are mixed throughout the water column. Some have argued that the combination of benthic regeneration and a shallow, well-mixed water column are the most important factors producing high estuarine productivity. The relative importance of different sources of nutrients is a topic of much discussion by estuarine ecologists and we will deal with it in detail in Chapter 3.

As we indicated in the previous paragraphs, the factors listed by Schelske and Odum are not unequivocally accepted 20 years after their proposal. These issues have been the inspiration and focus of much research since then and are still a source of inspiration and controversy today.

1.7.2 Other Important Hypotheses about Estuarine Ecology

A number of other important hypotheses about estuarine function have been proposed and questioned and help to unify the study of estuaries. They are interrelated, but we will separate them for the sake of clarity.

1. Intertidal wetlands are important to estuarine productivity because they (a) produce large quantities of organic detritus which is an important source of energy in estuaries, and (b) serve as an important nursery to the

young of many marine and estuarine species. Many important chemical reactions take place in wetlands and thus estuarine chemistry is regulated by wetlands.

2. Organic detritus is exported from wetlands and serves as a very important food source for a wide variety of estuarine consumers. Recent evidence suggests that we may have to reexamine the importance of organic detritus.

3. Estuaries, especially those with extensive wetlands, support rich fisheries. There is considerable evidence showing both functional and empirical relationships between wetlands and fisheries. For example, the abundance of wetlands in estuarine regions is strongly correlated with regional fish catch. Very few fish are absolutely estuarine dependent, however, and some have argued that the evidence is weak for estuary—fishery coupling, particularly wetland—fishery coupling. We consider this issue in Chapters 10 and 12.

1.8   HOW WE WILL PROCEED THROUGH THE BOOK

The remainder of the book is designed to systematically carry the reader through the science of estuarine ecology. Chapters 2 and 3 introduce estuarine physical oceanography, geomorphology, and chemistry. A knowledge of these subjects is essential to a good understanding of the ecology of estuaries, because so much of the biology is related to such factors as water movement, sediment distribution, and chemical gradients. The two chapters are designed to both introduce the subjects and to put the information in the context of ecological processes.

The next three sections of the book cover various aspects of the ecology of organisms that live in estuaries. Section III deals with estuarine plants and primary production. In Chapters 4, 5, and 6 we cover, respectively, phytoplankton, intertidal wetlands, and seagrasses of estuaries. In each chapter, the composition and distribution of the plants is discussed, and spatial and seasonal patterns of productivity and factors regulating productivity are analyzed. Chapter 7 is about estuarine microbial ecology and organic detritus. The sources, transport, and utilization of organic detritus are topics which have generated considerable research and discussion over the last 2 to 3 decades and we try to capture some of this excitement. In Section V there are several chapters that cover the animals in estuaries. We cover zooplankton, benthos, nekton, and wildlife in Chapters 8, 9, 10, and 11, respectively. We discuss topics such as compositon and distribution of the communities, rates of secondary production, food habits, and factors regulating these communities.

The final two chapters include a discussion of the way humans have interacted with coastal systems. We cover interactions of people with estuaries in terms of fisheries and human impacts in Chapters 12 and 13.

GENERAL REFERENCES

Note: The references listed here include both those cited in Chapter 1 and a bibliography of general literature on estuarine ecology.

ACIESP, 1987. Ecossistemas Costeiros. Costa Sul Sudeste Brasileira: Sintese dos Conhecimentos. Preceedings International Symposium Cananeia April 11–16, 1987. Academia de Ciancias do Estado de Sao Paulo, Brasil. Publ. ACIESP 54(1) 459 pp., 54(2) 425 pp., 54(3) 363 pp.

Aston, S.R., 1980. Nutrients, dissolved gases, and general biogeochemistry in estuaries. In: Olausson, E. and I. CATO (Eds.), Chemistry and Biogeochemistry of Estuaries. Wiley-Interscience, New York, pp. 233–262.

Ayala-Castañares, A. and F.B. Phleger (Eds.), 1969. Coastal Lagoons, A Symposium. Mem. Simp. Intern. Lagunas Costeras UNAM-UNESCO, Mexico Nov. 28–30, 1967. Universidad Nacional Autónoma de México, 686 pp.

Bahnick, J., 1972. Estuary Studies. Training Manual, U.S. Environmental Protection Agency. Office of Waters Programs, Washington, 80 pp.

Bakus, G.J., 1969. Energetics and feeding in shallow marine waters. Int. Rev. Gen. Exp. Zool., 4:275–369.

Barnes, R.S.K., 1974. Estuarine Biology. Edward Arnold, London, 77 pp.

Barnes, R.S.K. (Ed.), 1977. The Coastline: Ecology, Physiography and Management, Wiley-Interscience, John Wiley and Sons Inc., London, 356 pp.

Barnes, R.S.K. and J. Green (Eds.), 1972. The Estuarine Environment. Applied Science, London, 133 pp.

Barnes, R.S.K., 1980. Coastal Lagoons: The Natural History of a Neglected Habitat. Cambridge University Press, Cambridge, 106 pp.

Barnes, R.S.K. and K.H. Mann (Eds.), 1980. Fundamentals of Aquatic Ecosystems. Blackwell Scientific Publications, Oxford, 230 pp.

Beccasio, A.D., G.W. Weissberg, A.E. Redfield (Eds.), 1980. Atlantic Coast Ecological Inventory: User's Guide and Information Base. Washington, DC, Biological Services Program, U.S. Fish and Wildlife Service, FWS/OBS-80/51, 163 pp.

Beccasio, A.D., J.S. Isakson, A.E. Redfield (Eds.), 1981. Pacific Coast Ecological Inventory: User's Guide and Information Base. Washington, DC, Biological Services Program, U.S. Fish and Wildlife Service, FWS/OBS-81-30, 159 pp.

Beccasio, A.D., N. Fotheringham and A.E. Redfield (Eds.), 1982. Gulf Coast Ecological Inventory: User's Guide and Information Base. Washington, DC, Biological Services Program, U.S. Fish and Wildlife Service, FWS/OBS-82/55, 191 pp.

Bechtel, T.J. and B.J. Copeland, 1970. Fish species diversity indices as indicators of pollution in Galveston Bay, Texas. Contrib. Mar. Sci., 15:103–132.

Bird, E.C.F., 1969. Coasts. Series on Systematic Geomorphology. Vol. 4. Massachusetts Institute of Technology, Cambridge, 246 pp.

Bryan, C.F., P.J. Zwank, and R.H. Chabreck (Eds.), 1985. Proceedings of the Fourth Coastal Marsh and Estuary Management Symposium. Louisiana State University Printing Office, Baton Rouge, 241 pp.

Burton, J.D. and P.S. Liss (Eds.), 1976. Estuarine Chemistry. Academic, London, 229 pp.

Chabreck, R.H. (Ed.), 1973. Proceeding of the Second Coastal Marsh and Estuary Management Symposium. Louisiana State University Division of Continuing Education, Baton Rouge, 316 pp.

Chao, L.N. and W. Kirby-Smith (Eds.), 1985. Proceeding of the International Symposium on Utilization of Coastal Ecosystems: Planning, Pollution and Productivity. Nov. 21-27, 1982. Editora da FURG, Rio Grande, Brasil, 496 pp.

Clark, J.R., 1977. Coastal Ecosystem Management (A Technical Manual for the Conservation of Coastal Zone Resources). Wiley Interscience, New York, 864 pp.

Clark, J.R. (Ed.), 1985. Coastal Resources Management: Development Case Studies. Renewable Resources Information Series, Coastal Management Publication No. 3. National Park Service, USDI, and U.S. Agency for International Development, Washington, 749 pp.

Clough, B.F. (Ed.), 1982. Mangrove Ecosystems in Australia: Structure, Function and Management. Australian National University Press, Canberra, 302 pp.

Cronin, L.E. (Ed.), 1975. Estuarine Research. Volume 1, Chemistry, Biology and the Estuarine System. Academic, New York, 738 pp.

Cronin, L.E. (Ed.), 1975. Estuarine Research. Volume 2, Geology and Engineering. Academic, New York, 587 pp.

Cross, R. and D. Williams (Eds.), 1981. Proceeding of the National Symposium on Freshwater Inflow to Estuaries. U.S. Fish and Wildlife Service, Office of Biological Services, Washington, FWS/OBS-81/04, Vol. 1., 526 pp., Vol. 2, 528 pp.

Dame, R.F. (Ed.), 1979. Marsh Estuarine Systems Simulation. The Belle W. Baruch Library in Marine Science No. 8. University of South Carolina Press, Columbia, 260 pp.

Darnell, R.M., 1961. Trophic spectrum of an estuarine community based on studies of Lake Pontchartrain, LA. Ecology, 42(3):553-568.

Darnell, R.M., 1967. Organic detritus in relation to the estuarine ecosystem. In G.H. Lauff (Ed.), Estuaries. American Association for the Advancement of Science, Washington, Publ. No. 83, pp.376-382.

Day, J.H. (Ed.), 1981. Estuarine Ecology with Particular Reference to Southern Africa. A.A. Baldema, Rotterdam, 412 pp.

Day, J.W., D.D. Culley, R.E. Turner, and A.J. Mumphrey (Eds.), 1979. Proceedings Third Coastal Marsh and Estuarine Management Symposium. Louisiana State University, Division of Continuing Education. Baton Rouge, 512 pp.

Day, J.W., W.G. Smith, P.R. Wagner, and W. C. Stowe. 1973. Community Structure and Carbon Budget of a Salt Marsh and Shallow Bay Estuarine System in Louisiana. Center for Wetland Resources, Louisiana State University, Baton Rouge, Publication No. LSU-SG-72-04, 80 pp.

Day, J.W. and A. Yáñez-Arancibia, 1982. Coastal lagoons and estuaries: ecosystem approach. Ciencia Interamericana, Organization of American States, Washington, D.C., 22:11-26.

Douglas, P. and R.H. Stroud (Eds.), 1971. A Symposium on the Biological Significance of Estuaries. Sport Fishing Institute, Washington, D.C., 144 pp.

Dunbar, M.J. (Ed.), 1979. Marine Production Mechanisms. International Biological Programme Rept. 20. Cambridge, 338 pp.

Dyer, K.R., 1973. Estuaries: A Physical Introduction. Wiley-Interscience, New York, 140 pp.

Emery, K.O., R.E. Stevenson, and J. Hedgpeth, 1957. Estuaries and Lagoons. I. Physical and chemical characteristics. II. Biological aspects. III. Sedimentation in estuaries, tidal flats and marshes. In: J.W. Hedgpeth (Ed.), Treatise on Marine Ecology and Paleoecology. Geol. Soc. America, Mem. 67, 1:673-748.

Fairbridge, R. 1980. The estuary: Its definition and geodynamic cycle. In E. Olausson and I. Cato (Eds.), Chemistry and Biochemistry of Estuaries. Wiley, New York, pp. 1-35.

Fenchel, T.M. and R.J. Riedl, 1970. The sulfide system: a new biotic community underneath the oxidized layer of marine sand bottoms. Mar. Biol., 7(3):255-268.

Ferguson Wood, E. and R.E. Johannes (Eds.), 1975. Tropical Marine Pollution, Elsevier Oceanography Series 12, Elsevier, New York, 192 pp.

Flint, R.W. and N.N. Rabalais (Eds.), 1981. Environmental Studies of a Marine Ecosystem: South Texas Outer Continental Shelf. University of Texas Press, Austin, 240 pp.

Folch Guillen, R. (Ed.), 1977. El Sistemes Naturals del Delta del de'l Ebre. Institució Catalana D Historia Natural. Edita l'Institut D Estudis Catalans, Barcelona, Vol. 8, 326 pp.

Fore, P. and R.D. Peterson (Eds.), 1980. Proceedings of the Gulf of Mexico Coastal Ecosystem Workshop. U.S. Fish and Wildlife Service, Albuquerque, NM, FWS/OBS-80/30, 214 pp.

Gierloff-Emden, H.G., 1976. La Costa del El Salvador: Monografía Morfológica Oceanográfica. Ministerio de Educación, Dirección de Publicaciones, San Salvador, 285 pp.

Goldberg, E.D., 1976. The Health of the Oceans. The UNESCO Press, Paris, 172 pp.

Goldberg, E.D., 1978. Biogeochemistry of Estuarine Sediments. Proceeding of a UNESCO/SCOR Workshop, Melreux, Belgium. UNESCO, Paris, 294 pp.

Gosner, K.L., 1971. Guide to the Identification of Marine and Estuarine Invertebrates (Cape Hatteras to the Bay of Fundy). Wiley-Interscience, New York, 693 pp.

Gosselink, J., E.P. Odum, and R.M. Pope, 1974. The value of the tidal marsh. Center for Wetland Resources, Louisiana State University, Baton Rouge, 30 pp.

Green, J., 1968. The Biology of Estuarine Animals. University of Washington Press Biological Series, Seattle, 401 pp.

Hall, C. and J. Day, 1977. Ecosystem Modeling in Theory and Practice. Wiley-Interscience, New York, 684 pp.

Hamilton, P. and K. MacDonald (Eds.), 1980. Estuarine and Wetland Processes with Emphasis on Modeling. Plenum Press, New York, 654 pp.

Hasler, A.D. (Ed.), 1975. Coupling of Land and Water Systems. Springer-Verlag, New York.

Johnston, J.B. and L.A. Barclay (Eds.), 1978. Contributed Papers on Coastal Ecological Characterization Studies. Fourth Biennial International Estuarine Research Federation Conference; Mt. Pocono, PA, 2-5 Oct. 1977. Office of Biological Services, U.S. Fish and Wildlife Service. FWS/OBS-77/37, 66 pp.

Kapetsky, J.M., 1982. Consideraciones para la Ordenación de las Pesquerías de Lagunas y Esteros Costeros. FAO Documento Técnico de Pesca 218, FAO, Rome, 50 pp.

Kennedy, V.S. (Ed.), 1980. Estuarine Perspectives. Academic, New York, 600 pp.

Kennedy, V.S. (Ed.), 1982. Estuarine Comparisons. Academic, New York, 710 pp.

Kenedy, V.S. (Ed.), 1984. The Estuary as a Filter. Academic, New York, 600 pp.

Kennish, M.J. and R.A. Lutz (Eds.), 1984. Ecology of Barnegat Bay, New Jersey. Lecture Notes on Coastal and Estuarine Studies. Springer-Verlag, New York, 396 pp.

Kjerfve, B. (Ed.), 1978. Estuarine Transport Processes. The Belle W. Baruch Library in Marine Science No. 7. University of South Carolina Press, Columbia, 332 pp.

Kjerfve, B. (Ed.), 1988. Hydrodynamics of Estuaries. CRC Press Inc., Boca Raton, Fla, Vol. I, 160 pp., Vol. II, 144 pp.

Lankford, R.R., 1977. Coastal lagoons of Mexico: Their origin and classification. In: Wiley, M.L. (Ed.), Estuarine Processes. Academic, New York, 2:182-215.

Lankford, R.R., 1978. Man's use of coastal lagoon resources. In: Charnock, H. and G.E.R. Deacon (Eds.), Advances in Oceanography. Plenum Press, New York, pp. 245-253.

Lasserre, P., 1979. Coastal lagoons. Sanctuary ecosystems, cradles of culture, targets for economic growth. Nat. Resour., 15(4):1-21.

Lasserre, P. and H. Postma (Eds.), 1982. Coastal Lagoons. Proceedings of the International Symposium on Coastal Lagoons. Bordeaux, France 8-14 Sep. 1981. Oceanologica Acta, Vol. Spec. 5(4):462 pp.

Lasserre, P., H. Postma, J. Costlow, and M. Steyaert (Eds.), 1981. Coastal lagoons research: present and future. II. Proc. UNESCO/IABO Seminar Duke Univ. Mar. Lab., Baufort, NC, Tech. Paper Mar. Sci. UNESCO, 33:1-300.

Lauff, G.H. (Ed.), 1967. Estuaries. American Association for the Advancement of Science, Washington, D.C., Publ. No. 83, 757 pp.

Leatherman, S.P. (Ed.), 1979. Barrier Islands from the Gulf of St. Lawrence to the Gulf of Mexico. Academic, New York. 325 pp.

Livingston, R.J. (Ed.), 1979. Ecological Process in Coastal and Marine Systems. Plenum, New York, 548 pp.

Long, S.P. and C.F. Mason, 1983. Saltmarsh Ecology. Blackie and Son Limited, Glasgow, 160 pp.

Longhurst, A.R., 1978. Ecological models in estuarine management. Ocean Management, 4:287-302.

Lugo, A.E. and G.L. Morris, 1982. Los Sistemas Ecológicos y la Humanidad. Organización de los Estados Americanos (OEA), Washington, Serie de Biología, Monogr. 23, 82 pp.

MacLeish, W.H. (Ed.), 1976. Estuaries. Oceanus, Vol. 19, No. 5. Woods Hole Oceanographic Institution, MA, 74 pp.

MacNae, W., 1968. A general account of the fauna and flora of mangrove swamps and forests in the Indo-West-Pacific region. Adv. Mar. Biol., 6:70-270.

Mann, K.H., 1982. Ecology of Coastal Waters: A Systems Approach. University of California Press, Los Angeles, 322 pp.

Margalef, R. 1968. Perspectives in Ecological Theory. Univ. Chicago Press, Chicago.

McCarty, P.L. and R. Kennedy (Eds.), 1967. Proceedings of the National Symposium on Estuarine Pollution, Stanford University Press, Los Angeles, 850 pp.

McDowell, D.M. and B.A. O'Conner (Eds.), 1977. Hydraulic Behaviour of Estuaries. Wiley-Interscience, New York, 292 pp.

McLusky, D.S., 1981. The Estuarine Ecosystem. Blackie and Son Limited, Glasgow, 150 pp.

McRoy, P.C. and C. Helfferich (Eds.), 1977. Seagrass Ecosystems: A Scientific Perspective. Marcel Decker, New York, 314 pp.

Mee, L.D., 1979. Chemistry in coastal lagoons. In: Riley, J.P. and R. Chester (Eds.), Chemical Oceanography. Academic, New York, pp. 441–410.

Mitsch, W.J. and J.G. Gosselink, 1986. Wetlands. Van Nostrand Reinhold Co., New York, 539 pp.

Muus, B.J., 1967. The Fauna of Danish Estuaries and Lagoons: Distribution and Ecology of Dominating Species. Meddelelser fra Danmarks Fisheri- og Havundersogelser N.S., 5(1):1–316.

Newsom, J.D. (Ed.), 1968. Proceeding of the First Coastal Marsh and Estuary Management Symposium. Louisiana State University, Division of Continuing Education, Baton Rouge, 250 pp.

Nielson, B. and L. E. Cronin (Eds.) 1980. Estuaries and Nutrients. Humana Press, Clifton, N.J., 644 pp.

Nihoul, J.C.J. (Ed.), 1975. Modelling of Marine Systems. Elsevier Scientific Publishing Co., Amsterdam, 272 pp.

Nihoul, J.C.J. (Ed.), 1978. Hydrodynamics of Estuaries and Fjords. Proceedings of the 9th International Liege Colloquium on Ocean Hydrodynamics. Elsevier, New York, 546 pp.

Nixon, S.W., 1980. Between coastal marshes and coastal waters, a review of twenty years of speculation and research on the role of salt marshes in estuarine productivity and water chemistry. In: Hamilton, P. and K.B. Mac Donald (Eds.), Estuarine and Wetland Processes. Plenum Publishing Corp., New York, pp. 437–525.

Nixon, S.W., 1982. Nutrient dynamics, primary production and fisheries yields of lagoons. In: Lasserre, P. and H. Postma (Eds.), Coastal Lagoons. Oceanologica Acta. Vol. Spec. 5(4):357–372.

Odum, E.P., 1969. The strategy of ecosystem development. Science, 164:262–270.

Odum, E.P., 1971. Fundamentals of Ecology. W. B. Saunders, Philadelphia, 574 pp.

Odum, H.T. 1971. Environment, Power, and Society. Wiley-Interscience, New York, 331 pp.

Odum, H.T. 1983. Systems Ecology. Wiley-Interscience, New York, 664 pp.

Odum, H.T. and B.J. Copeland, 1972. Functional classification of coastal ecological systems of the United States. In: B. W. Nelson (Ed.), Environmental of Coastal Plain Estuaries. Geol. Soc. Amer., Mem. 133, 9–25.

Odum, H.T., B.J. Copeland and E.A. McMahan, 1974. Coastal Ecological Systems in the United States (4 vol., aprox. 2000 p.). Publication Department of the Conservation Foundation, Washington D.C.

Officer, C.B., 1976. Physical Oceanography of Estuaries and Associated Coastal Waters. Wiley-Interscience, New York, 465 pp.

O'Kane, J.P., 1980. Estuarine Water-Quality Management. Pitman Advanced Publishing Program, Boston, 755 pp.

Olausson, E. and I. Cato (Eds.), 1980. Chemistry and Biogeochemistry of Estuaries. Wiley-Interscience, New York, 452 pp.

Perkins, E.J., 1974. The Biology of Estuaries and Coastal Waters. Academic, London, 678 pp.

Pillay, T.V.R. (Ed.), 1972. Coastal Aquaculture in the Indo-Pacific Region. FAO Fishing News (Books) Ltd. The Whitefriars Press, London, 498 pp.

Pomeroy, L.R. and R.G. Wiegert (Eds.), 1985. The Ecology of a Salt Marsh. Springer-Verlag, New York, 271 pp.

Pritchard, D. 1967. Observations of circulation in coastal plain estuaries. In: G. Lauff (ed.), Estuaries. American Association for the Advancement of Science. Publ. No. 83, Washington, D. C., pp. 37–44.

Ranwell, D.S., 1972. Ecology of Salt Marshes and Sand Dunes. Cox and Wyman, Great Britain, 258 pp.

Reid, G. and R.D. Wood, 1976. Ecology of Inland Waters and Estuaries. Van Nostrand, New York, 485 pp.

Remane, A. and C. Schlieper, 1971. Biology of Brackish Water. Wiley- Interscience, New York, 372 pp.

Salm, R.V. and J.R. Clark, 1984. Marine and Coastal Protected Areas: A Guide for Planners and Managers. State Printing Co., Columbia, SC., 302 pp.

Schelske, C.L. and E.P. Odum, 1962. Mechanisms maintaining high productivity in Georgia estuaries. Proc. Gulf Caribb. Fish. Inst., 14:75–80.

Schubel, J.R. (Ed.), 1974. The Estuarine Environment, Estuaries and Estuarine Sedimentation. American Geological Institute, Washington, D.C., 150 pp.

Sinha, E. and B. McCosh, 1974. Coastal–Estuarine and Nearshore Processes: An Annotated Bibliography. Ocean Engineering Information Service, La Jolla, CA, Water Resources Scientific Information Center, U.S. Dept. of the Interior, 218 pp.

Smith, R.F., A.H. Swartz, and W.H. Massman (Eds.), 1966. A Symposium on Estuarine Fisheries. American Fisheries Society Special Publication No. 3, 150 pp.

Snedaker, S.C. and C.D. Getter, 1985. Coastal Resources Management Guidelines. Renewable Resources Information Series, Coastal Management Publication No. 2. National Park Service, USDI, and U.S. Agency for International Development, Washington, 205 pp.

Steele, J.H. (Ed.), 1970. Proceedings of a Symposium on Marine Food Chains. Oliver and Boyd, Edinburg, 552 pp.

Stevenson, L.H. and R.R. Colwell (Eds.), 1975. Estuarine Microbial Ecology. The Belle W. Baruch Library in Marine Science No. 1. University of South Carolina Press, Columbia, 250 pp.

Teal, J.M., 1962. Energy flow in the salt marsh ecosystem of Georgia. Ecology, 43(4):614–624.

Tippie, V.K. and D.A. Flemer (Eds.), 1983. Chesapeake Bay: A Profile of Environmental Change. U.S. Environmental Protection. Agency, Washington, Vol. 1, 200 pp., Vol. 2, Appendices.

Turner, R.E. (Coordinator), 1982. Oceanography of the Mississippi River Bight. Contributions in Marine Science, 25:107–198.

UNESCO (Ed.), 1980. Estudoio Científico y Impacto Humano en el Ecosistema de Manglares. Memorias del Seminario Organizado por UNESCO en Colombia, Cali 27 nov.–1 dic., 1978. UNESCO Montevideo, 406 pp.

United Nations, 1981. River Inputs to Ocean Systems. Proceeding of a Review Workshop held at FAO, Rome, 26–30 March, 1978, SCOR Working Group No. 46. Joint Copyright UNEP-UNESCO, 384 pp.

Valiela, I., 1984. Marine Ecological Processes. Springer-Verlag, New York, 546 pp.

Vantine, M. and S.C. Snedaker, 1974. A Bibliography of the Mangrove Literature. International Symposium on the Biological Management of Mangroves, Honolulu, Hawaii, 100 pp.

Vernberg, F.J. (Ed.), 1978. Physiological Ecology of Marine Organisms. The Belle W. Baruch Library in Marine Science No. 3. University of South Carolina Press, Columbia, 398 pp.

Vernberg, W.B. and F.J. Vernberg, 1972. Environmental Physiology of Marine Animals. Springer-Verlag, New York.

Vernberg, W.B. and F.J. Vernberg, 1976. Physiological adaptations of estuarine animals. Oceanus, 19(5):48–54.

West, R.C., N.P. Psuty, and B.G. Thom, 1985. Las Tierras Bajas de Tabasco en el Sureste de Mexico. Gobierno del Estado de Tabasco, Instituto de Cultura de Tabasco Villahermosa, Mexico, 409 pp.

Wiley, M.L. (Ed.), 1977. Estuarine Processes. Volume 1, Uses, Stress and Adaptation to the Estuary. Academic, New York, 541 pp.

Wiley, M.L. (Ed.), 1977. Estuarine Processes. Volume 2, Sediments and Transfer of Materials in the Estuary. Academic, New York, 428 pp.

Wiley, M.L. (Ed.), 1978. Estuarine Interactions. Academic, New York, 604 pp.

Whittaker, R.H., 1975. Communities and Ecosystems, 2nd ed., Macmillan, New York.

Wright, F.F., 1974. Estuarine Oceanography. American Geological Institute, McGraw-Hill, New York, 76 pp.

Yáñez-Arancibia, A., 1978. Taxonomia, Ecologia y Estructura de las Comumidades de Peces en Lagunas Costeras con Bocas Efimeras del Pacifico de Mexico. Centro Cienc. del Mar y Limnol. Univ. Nal. Autón. México Publ. Esp. 2, 306 pp.

Yáñez-Arancibia, A., (Ed.), 1985. Fish Community Ecology in Estuaries and Coastal Lagoons: Towards an Ecosystem Integration. UNAM/PUAL/ICML, México D.F., 654 pp.

Yáñez-Arancibia, A., 1986. Ecologia de la Zona Costera—Análisis de Siete Tópicos. AGT Editor, S.A. Mexico City, 189 pp.

Yáñez-Arancibia, A., and J.W. Day (Eds.), 1988. Ecology of Coastal Ecosystems in the Southern Gulf of Mexico: The Terminos Lagoon Region. Editorial Universitaria, México, D.F., 450 pp.

Yáñez-Arancibia, A. and P. Sánchez-Gil, 1988. Ecología de Recursos Demersales Marinos. Fundamentos en Costas Tropicales. AGT Editor, S.A., México City, 230 pp.

PHYSICAL CONSIDERATIONS

▬ 2

Estuarine Geomorphology and Physical Oceanography[1]

2.1 INTRODUCTION

To understand the processes affecting the distribution and cycles of particulates, pollutants, nutrients, and organisms in estuaries, it is insufficient to focus solely on the biological and chemical aspects of the processes. Equally important are the water movements and other hydrodynamic aspects of coastal systems, including circulation patterns, stratification, mixing and flushing, as well as a careful consideration of the time scales of these processes. When hydrodynamic changes occur quickly relative to biological, geological, and chemical transformations, they become the dominant controlling factors of many ecological processes in estuaries (Officer 1980), and it is now widely recognized that a thorough understanding of the marine ecology of estuaries requires a comprehensive knowledge and integration of the physical processes affecting the system. This chapter is aimed at organizing, classifying, and describing some of these important physical characteristics and processes. The terminology will be that of a shallow-water oceanographer and, hopefully, this chapter will encourage future marine ecologists to use physical terms more precisely and consistently than has sometimes been the case in the past.

2.2 GLACIATION CYCLES

Present-day estuaries are geologically ephemeral coastal features. They formed during the last interglacial stage as sea level rose 120 m from 15,000 years ago to

[1] By B. Kjerfve.

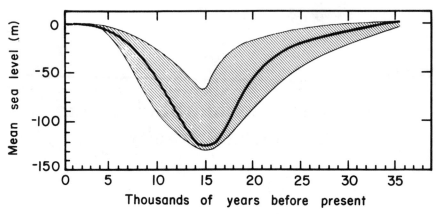

Figure 2.1 The variation of mean sea level for the past 35,000 years based on data from the Atlantic continental shelf of the United States: the solid line is the mean sea level and the dashed area is the envelope of all values (modified after Milliman and Emery 1968).

the present level, which was reached approximately 5000 years ago (Milliman and Emery 1968; Fig. 2.1.). Such glaciation and deglaciation events have occurred regularly during the past few million years, causing shifts in the position of the coastlines worldwide. The locations of estuaries have shifted accordingly.

Presently, estuaries are common coastal features, constituting as much as 80–90% of the coasts along the east and Gulf coasts of North America, but as little as 10–20% along the United States' Pacific coast (Emery 1967). Typically, estuaries are more abundant on coasts with broad flat continental margins than on coasts with narrow, steep continental margins (Schubel and Hirschberg 1978).

During glaciation periods, a considerable fraction of the world's oceans were frozen into continental glaciers, and sea level was much lower than now. Coastlines were then located on what is now the continental slope, and estuaries were both smaller and rarer. During interglacial periods, the glaciers melted, sea level rose world wide, and estuaries became large and abundant (Schubel and Hirschberg 1978).

The present situation of high sea level and extensive estuaries has existed for only 10–20% of the time during the past million years, for once formed, estuaries quickly fill with sediments and essentially disappear. The sediment sources are river-borne terrestrial materials from the eroding continents and net up-estuary movement of sand-sized materials from the continental shelf (Meade 1969). From a geological viewpoint, the time scale of this infill is extremely short. Emery and Uchupi (1972) estimated that if sea level remained constant and all sediments were deposited into today's U.S. estuaries, these would be filled within 9500 years, even if the load of the Mississippi River, which is half the nation's total, was not counted. But all estuaries obviously do not infill at this rapid rate, so that estuaries of various stages of geological development exist around the shorelines of the world (Schubel and Hirschberg 1978). One major reason is that the sea level has been rising for the past 10,000 years. Another is that coastal erosional forces remove sediments from estuaries.

2.3   FROM LAGOONS TO DELTAS

The type and rate of geologic development of estuaries depend not only on glaciation cycles and local variabilities in sediment supply, but also on a combination of other factors including climatic variability, regional and local geology, and variability in marine energy inputs, particularly waves and tides impinging on the coast.

According to the scheme of Davies (1973), there is a continuum of estuarine types (Fig. 2.2). At one end of the spectrum exist lagoons produced by marine (wave) action, found typically behind a barrier, and characterized by sand-sized sediments. Good examples of this type of environment are the lagoons of the southern Texas and Mexican Gulf coasts (Lankford 1976). At the opposite end of the spectrum lie deltas. They are produced by river processes rather than by marine activities. They typically protrude into a receiving basin and are characterized by fine-grained silty sediments from terrestrial run off. In between lagoons and deltas lie estuarine lagoons, estuaries, and estuarine deltas, representing a mixture and gradation of the two extreme coastal environments. Presumably, a decrease in wave energy, coupled with an increase in river sediments, would shift a particular system from the lagoon extreme toward a delta

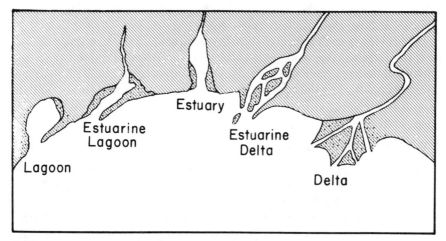

Figure 2.2   Schematic representation of the continuum of inlet types from lagoons to deltas (modified from Davies 1973).

extreme. Estuaries have probably shifted in such a fashion throughout geologic time as climates have changed.

2.4   DEFINITION

2.4.1   A New Definition

The existing definitions of estuaries are neither satisfying nor useful to the modern problems of estuarine ecologists or to the diversity of environments considered above. Thus I propose a new functional definition, one that I hope will be helpful to those who work with the spectrum of estuarine types, including lagoons, river mouths, and deltas. An estuarine system is a coastal indentation that has a restricted connection to the ocean and remains open at least intermittently. The estuarine system can be subdivided into three regions:

(a) A *tidal river zone* a fluvial zone characterized by lack of ocean salinity but subject to tidal rise and fall of sea level.

(b) A *mixing zone* (the estuary proper) characterized by water mass mixing and existence of strong gradients of physical, chemical, and biotic quantities reaching from the tidal river zone to the seaward location of a river-mouth bar or ebb-tidal delta.

(c) A *nearshore turbid zone* in the open ocean between the mixing zone and the seaward edge of the tidal plume at full ebb tide.

This definition differs considerably from those previously proposed in that it recognizes and includes a nearshore marine component, estuarine in character, which should be considered in the treatment of the physical or chemical dynamics, or ecology, of the estuarine system as a whole. Thus our definition of estuaries includes the adjacent coastal waters.

Dionne (1963) and Fairbridge (1980) chose to subdivide the mixing zone into an upper and lower region somewhat arbitrarily, and Hansen and Rattray (1965) subdivided the same zone into three dynamic regions. Such subdivisions can, of course, be made when the need arises, depending on the particular applications or local conditions.

2.4.2   Dynamic Boundaries

It should be recognized that the boundaries of the three zones listed above are dynamic. They will change positions continuously, on time scales from shorter than a tidal cycle, to annual cycles, to geologic time scales. The landward extent of the tidal river zone moves downriver with increasing fresh water discharge, and as the tidal amplitude changes from spring to neap tide. Similarly, the interface between the tidal river and mixing zones will oscillate over the tidal cycle and move seaward with increasing river runoff. The interface between the mixing and nearshore zones changes much more slowly, since it is defined by the edge of the land, usually only on time scales longer than the seasonal cycle and most dramatically over thousands of years. A severe storm, however, could breach a barrier island or reef (see Hayes 1978) and thus dramatically relocate this interface overnight. The seaward boundary of the nearshore zone will change positions depending on the stage of the tide, river discharge, and prevailing oceanographic and meteorologic conditions.

In a given system, all zones may not be present. For example, lagoons in arid or semiarid coastal regions with a small tidal range may not exhibit a tidal river zone. An example of such a system is Cancun Bay, Mexico, on the Caribbean side of the Yucatan Peninsula. A given estuarine/lagoon system may not exhibit a mixing zone, as defined, if the river discharge is very large. In that case, the tidal river could border directly on the nearshore zone, so that fresh water leaves the river mouth with no mixing with salt water and the estuarine mixing processes would actually take place within the nearshore zone. Examples of such systems are the Amazon River (Gibbs 1970) and many large rivers at flood stage. Finally, the nearshore zone may be nonexistent in lagoons such as Cancun Bay, where the tidal range is small and there is lack of fresh water and sediment discharge. A particular estuary can in theory go through cycles so that the system alternately consists of one, two, or three of the defined zones on a seasonal basis.

2.4.3   Some Exceptions

Because an estuary is defined as "a coastal indentation," semi-enclosed inland seas such as the Baltic and the Mediterranean systems in their entirety are not included in the definition, nor are estuary-like systems that connect to large lakes rather than to an ocean (e.g., the Sea of Azov, which adjoins the Black Sea).

The large hypersaline (300 ppt) lagoons on the eastern shore of the Caspian Sea may be expected to exhibit processes similar to those operating in coastal lagoons (see Klenova 1968). Because these inland lagoons are emptied of water by severe wind action for half the year, the dynamics and ecology of the Caspian Sea systems are very different from the typical coastal lagoon. Some western Australia coastal salt flats/lagoons that flood probably behave similarly.

2.4.4   Water Balance

Pritchard (1952) proposed a classification of estuaries based on their water balance. He gives three classes: (a) positive estuaries, where the combined fresh water input from rivers, ground water, and rainfall exceeds evaporation; (b) neutral estuaries, with a balance between evaporation and freshwater input; and (c) negative or inverse estuaries, where the evaporation exceeds the combined freshwater input.

Most readers would think that "estuary" means what Pritchard calls a positive estuary, and that a coastal lagoon means a negative estuary. Depending on the hydrologic cycle, a system could change seasonally from being positive to negative or vice versa. The neutral estuary is not an important stage, but represents a temporal transition of a system between positive and negative stages.

Although it may at times be useful to think of coastal systems in terms of the water balance, this means of classifying an estuary is no longer in common use. With the exception of lagoons in arid or semiarid regions, most estuaries are positive. In fact, the traditional definition of an estuary (Cameron and Pritchard 1963; Pritchard 1967) as "a semi-enclosed coastal body of water with a free connection with the open sea within which sea water is measurably diluted by fresh water from land drainage" defines an estuary as a positive estuary. It certainly represents the estuarine system most commonly studied. It is, however, a much too restrictive definition in that it excludes negative estuaries, the tidal river, or nearshore zones. Using this definition, a system does not remain an estuary during high run-off conditions when the mixing zone disappears, as in the case of the Mississippi River flood or the Amazon River at all times.

2.5 GEOMORPHIC CLASSIFICATION

2.5.1 Estuarine Types

It is more useful to classify estuaries according to their geomorphology. Each geomorphic type exhibits at least a somewhat similar dynamic behavior in terms of water circulation and mixing. Estuaries can be divided into four main groups (Pritchard 1952b; Dyer 1973): (a) coastal plain estuaries, (b) lagoons (or bar-built estuaries), (c) fjords, and (d) tectonically caused estuaries.

2.5.2 Coastal Plain Estuaries: Classical

Coastal plain estuaries have been studied most extensively, because they are the most common type in regions where studies began. They formed during the last eustatic sea level rise, when river valleys became increasingly more flooded by the melting glaciers. Thus they exhibit the geomorphic characteristics of river channels and flood plains and are sometimes called "drowned river valley estuaries." The typical cross section of a classical coastal plain estuary consists of a V-shaped channel, seldom deeper than 20 m, bordered by broad shallow flats (Figs. 2.3 and 2.4). Coastal plain estuaries vary greatly in size up to that of the Chesapeake Bay, some 25 km long and on the average 25 km wide, the largest U. S. coastal plain estuary. Other good examples of large coastal plain estuaries are Delaware Bay and Charleston Harbor, South Carolina. Others have been described by Officer (1976) and Dyer (1973).

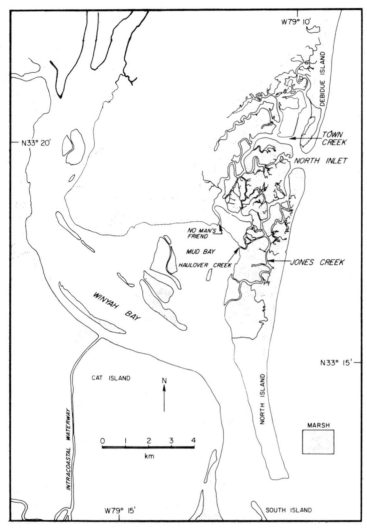

Figure 2.3 Examples of coastal plain estuaries: Winyah Bay and North Inlet, South Carolina. Winyah Bay is a classical coastal plain estuary, whereas the North Inlet system is a coastal plain salt-marsh estuary.

2.5.3 Coastal Plain Salt Marsh Estuaries

Another kind of coastal plain estuary, the salt marsh estuary or salt marsh creek, is found commonly along much of the U. S. East coast, particularly from Cape Fear, North Carolina to Cape Canaveral, Florida. It is characterized by the lack of a major river source but has a well-defined tidal drainage network, dendrit-

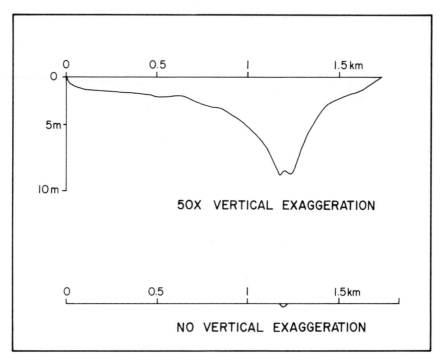

Figure 2.4 Cross-sectional profiles of an arbitrary coastal plain estuary, showing the same section in 50 times vertical exaggeration (top) and without any vertical exaggeration (bottom). Coastal plain estuaries have very wide and shallow cross sections. When these sections are presented with vertical exaggeration (which is most often the case), this gives a misleading impression.

ically intersecting the extensive coastal salt marshes. These estuary-marsh systems are usually interconnected. Water and material exchange between the system and the coastal ocean occur through narrow, tidal inlets, which continuously change their configurations, sometimes dramatically, on time scales of less than 10 years (see Brunn 1978). Although these systems formed in a manner similar to lagoons, they have infilled to a much greater extent and now consist primarily of subaerial or intertidal salt marsh. The estuary proper consists of the drainage channels. These typically occupy less than 20% of the system area and resemble dynamically the classical coastal plain estuary. The size of the estuary is proportional to the size of the marsh drained. The typical cross section usually exhibits two deep channels separated by a shallow region. Channel depths seldom exceed 10 m, although it is known that localized, deep scour holes in excess of 25 m commonly occur at the junction of tidal creeks (Kjerfve et al. 1979).

2.5.4 Lagoons

Whether salt marsh estuaries are classified as "coastal plain estuaries" or "lagoons" is rather unimportant and certainly arbitrary. Lagoons, in my mind, exhibit a larger fractional area of open water compared with, for example, southeastern salt marsh estuaries. Whereas lagoons are oriented parallel to the coast, coastal plain estuaries are most often oriented normal to the coast (Fairbridge 1980) (Fig. 2.5). Lagoons have a less well-drained subaqueous drainage channel network and are uniformly shallow, often less than 2 m deep, over large expanses. The physical processes of lagoons are mostly wind-dominated, whereas diffuse fresh water inflow and tide tend to dominate salt marsh systems, at least in the southeast. Nevertheless, the origin of lagoons is similar to that of the southeastern salt marsh estuaries (Lankford 1976).

During the interglacial stage, 80,000 years ago, the Pleistocene shoreline stabilized some 6 m above the present mean sea level, leading to the formation of a narrow raised ridge system parallel to the coast. The ridge is most commonly a sand barrier, as in the case of Laguna de Terminos, Mexico, or a coral reef barrier, as in the case of the Belize barrier reef lagoon on the Caribbean side of the Yucatan Peninsula. Then, during the lowered level of the last glacial period, atmospheric and fluvial processes eroded much of that earlier coast. As sea level

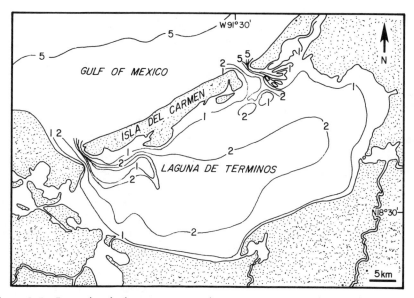

Figure 2.5 Example of a lagoon, Laguna de Terminos, Campeche, Mexico. Isobaths in meters are drawn and indicate that the lagoon for most parts is only 2 m deep (modified after Gierloff-Emden 1977).

again rose to its present level, extensive areas behind the remnants of the raised ridge flooded, while marine and atmospheric processes maintained and re-shaped the barrier ridge (Lankford 1976). Sedimentation processes then caused the systems to infill differentially, and the estuary shapes were further modified by climate and vegetation.

True lagoons are common on all continents, and are far more prominent than the sparse literature implies. In North America, for example, they fringe the Gulf of Mexico and are abundant on the Pacific coast of Mexico. The physical characteristics and dynamics of a few have been described by Lankford (1976), Castanares and Phelger (1979), and Collier and Hedgepeth (1950). But, other studies of lagoons are rare; several have been studied in other countries: the Coorong in South Australia (Noye 1973, Noye and Walsh 1976); St. Lucia la-goon in South Africa (Orme 1974, Orme and Loeher 1974); and those of south-eastern Australia (Bird 1967).

2.5.5   Fjords: Classical

Fjords also owe their origin to the glaciation cycle. During the advance of conti-nental glaciers, tongues of the leading ice edge scoured out many river valleys in latitudes above 45° (Fairbridge 1980; Dyer 1979). Where the ice edge reached its most seaward extent, on what was then a portion of the continents, a steep rock bar usually had formed seaward of the leading ice edge. It was there for two reasons. First, the ice had not yet been able to scour it away, in part because the ice began to float upon the salt water. Second, scoured material from the basin was pushed forward by the advancing glacier and deposited at the leading ice edge. When the glaciers retreated, the rock bar remained to provide spectacular relief at the seaward edge of the basin itself. Whereas the present water depth over the sill generally varies from 10 to 90 m, the depth of the interior fjord basin often exceeds 800 m. The overdeepened portion of the basin commonly extends several hundred kilometers inland. A further geomorphic characteristic of fjords and glacially carved inlets is their U-shaped cross-sectional form, due to the gla-cier scour.

Fjords and glacial inlets are common in both hemispheres where there has been glacial activity. They are particularly spectacular on coasts that serve as leading edges of tectonic plate margins, called subducted coasts. Good examples are the fjord inlets of southern Chile (Pickard 1971), Alaska, British Columbia (Fig. 2.6) (Pickard 1956), and New Zealand. Fjords also occur on the present or formerly glaciated coasts of Norway, Spitsbergen, Greenland, and Graham Land in Antarctica (Fairbridge 1980). A useful treatment of the oceanographic features of Norwegian fjords is that of Saelen (1967).

2.5.6   The Fjord-Like Fjärd

Closely related to fjords are fjärds (Swedish) or firths (Scottish). These occur commonly in southern Sweden, eastern Canada and New England, and Scot-

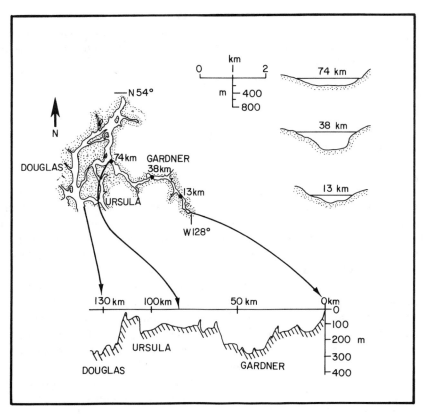

Figure 2.6   Example of a fjord, the Gardner system in British Columbia, Canada (modified after Pickard 1956).

land, where the continental relief is less spectacular and the continental shelf more extensive compared with a subducted margin coast (Fairbridge 1980). Fjärds or firths also formed as a result of glacier scour but do not exhibit the overdeepened basin or the U-shaped profile. Water depths are much shallower than for fjords, usually on the order of tens of meters. The shallow water depth, particularly in the case of Swedish fjärds, is due at least partially to the quick isostatic rebound of the continent, a response to the cessation of ice loading. This uplift rate has been measured as high as 15 m per 1000 years.

2.5.7   Tectonically Caused Estuaries

The fourth and final geomorphic classification category occurs on tectonically active coasts. These are the estuaries caused by faulting, graben formation, landslide, or volcanic eruption. The best and most extensively studied estuary in this group is San Francisco Bay (see Officer 1976; Conomos 1979). Tectonically caused estuaries exhibit much variability and different ones may behave oceanographically similarly to coastal plain estuaries, fjords, or lagoons, depending on the local constraints. In summary we see that estuaries are formed by specific physical processes. The extensive nature of estuaries today is due in large part to the extensive glaciation of 10,000 years ago.

2.6   CIRCULATION

2.6.1   Estuarine Circulation

Estuarine water circulation is a physical process that affects or controls many ecological processes. For example, the residence time of a given parcel of water in an estuary is a function of the circulation patterns, and the ratio of the residence time of the water to the biogeochemical turnover rate indicates the degree to which the hydrodynamics dominate or modify estuarine processes.

Thus computation of fluxes of dissolved constituents such as nutrients, pollutants, and salt, as well as of particulate materials such as sediments, detrital matter, and plankton, requires knowledge of the circulation. It is common to simulate estuarine physical processes with rather complex mathematical equations. But reasonable formulations for such equations usually can be achieved only after making several simplifying assumptions, and these assumptions depend very much on the assumptions we make about circulation. Very often the complexity of the real systems makes it difficult for us to produce realistic results from our simplified models. Also, the estuarine bathymetry is a function of the circulation, and in turn the circulation depends on the bathymetry (Kjerfve 1978). Thus care must be exercised in using estuarine hydrodynamic information. As will be shown, just because the circulation causes water to move in a certain direction does not necessarily mean that dissolved and particulate constituents will move in the same direction.

Estuarine circulation normally is defined as the residual water movement, meaning that short-term effects are averaged out. Because water motions occur on a continuum of time scales, it is critical to choose the appropriate time duration over which to estimate these residual currents. Thus our computations of circulation depend greatly on the averaging time scale used. As most of the current variability usually occurs with a tidal periodicity, the estuarine circulation is usually calculated as the residual water movement after the currents are averaged over one, two, or numerous complete tidal cycles. It is important to realize that the circulation can never be determined from a single set of instantaneous measurements, but represents a calculated quantity that requires systematic measurements over an extended time period for its determination (Kjerfve 1979).

The time-averaged currents that make up the circulation vary depending on location in the estuary and the particular depth at which an estimate is made. It is common practice to refer to these time-averaged currents as net currents, tidal currents, tidal residuals, or nontidal flows.

2.6.2 Types of Estuarine Circulation

The energy that drives estuarine circulation is derived from either solar heating or gravitational attraction between the moon and sun, on the one hand, and the ocean waters on the other.

Solar heating differentials also cause wind, rainfall, and ocean water temperature differences. The rainfall, in particular, affects estuaries by the energy and mass associated with fresh water inflow from rivers, and these are major processes driving estuarine circulation. Estuarine circulation is also driven by wind stress on the estuarine water surface, a second major force driving estuarine processes.

Gravitational attraction on the sea by the moon and the sun is a third important process driving the estuarine circulation, which is responsible for the regular rise and fall of the tide and the more complex oscillatory water currents.

Although wind waves generated within the estuary or swells propagating into the estuary from the ocean could conceivably cause or alter circulation, such waves are normally not very important. But variability in the nearshore current structure has a modifying effect on the estuarine circulation and may drive the circulation in some cases, as will be discussed later.

Two other factors are important in determining the circulation—estuarine geometry and bathymetry (i.e., curvature and friction effects). Both effects are capable of modifying the circulation significantly, but they differ from the driving forces in that they are passive, that is, these factors alter the flow pattern only when currents already exist. Similarly both the existence of an ice cover on high-latitude estuaries and human activities in estuaries (e.g., dredging, channelization, damming, and diversion) can alter induced circulation patterns.

The three main driving forces are each responsible for a particular circulation type, respectively: (a) gravitational circulation (due to fresh water runoff), (b) tidal circulation, and (c) wind-driven circulation. Each type is discussed in more detail below. Although a given estuary usually is dominated by one circulation type, this may change temporarily. Also, two or all three circulation types could, in fact, be operating simultaneously in the same estuary. This makes for a situation difficult to interpret easily.

2.6.3 Gravitational Circulation

Circulation induced by density and elevation differences between fresh water runoff and salt water is called gravitational circulation. The less dense fresh water runoff has a tendency to remain primarily in the surface layer of an estuary (Fig. 2.7). The effect of tide and wind, however, is to mix the water column, causing a vertical exchange between fresher surface waters and saltier water from below. This mixing process explains the existence of longitudinal and verti-

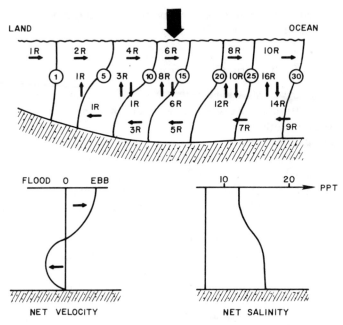

Figure 2.7 Schematic representation of the net circulation in the mixing zone of a partially mixed estuary. Horizontal and vertical water volume exchanges are expressed in units of river flow R. Isopleths of salinity (isohalines) in parts per thousand are superimposed in the circulation, indicating the change of net salinity profiles (and thus stratification) from the tidal river zone to the nearshore zone (modified after Dyer 1979).

cal salinity and density gradients in the estuary. These may be reinterpreted in terms of time-averaged pressure gradients, which can be related directly to the gravitational circulation.

The pressure surfaces tilt seaward in the less dense surface layer, causing a net outflow. In the salty and dense bottom layer they tilt up-estuary, driving the flow landward. Somewhere in mid water column, the pressure surfaces become horizontal. A horizontal surface is called an equipotential surface and represents an arbitrary surface on which gravitational forces are constant. At the depth where the pressure surface becomes an equipotential surface, the net flow or circulation vanishes, that is, a level of no net motion, which for a given cross section may slope slightly across the section because of the earth's rotation (Pritchard 1952b and 1956) or a bend in the channel (Stewart 1957). The result is that the surface of such estuaries is characterized by net seaward flows and the bottom is characterized by landward flows.

The resulting circulation is called the "classical" estuarine gravitational circulation, and it has been described by Pritchard (1956), Pritchard and Kent (1956), and Dyer (1973), and has been represented in an elegant mathematical solution by Rattray and Hansen (1962) and Hansen and Rattray (1965). Their "simularity solution" for the estuarine circulation still represents the state of the art of our theoretical understanding of the physical dynamics of estuaries.

Much more water takes part in the gravitational circulation than was introduced as fresh water runoff. For example, if the river discharge into the Chesapeake Bay estuary is R units (measured in m^3/s), and the surface outflow at the mouth is 25 R units (Schubel and Pritchard 1972), there must be a net inflow and subsequent outflow of 24 R units (on the average) of water from the bottom layer of the adjacent ocean. This is a difficult concept to grasp, but has great ecological significance, relating to, for example, the computation of residence times and the reproductive patterns of fishes.

Although gravitational circulation in estuaries is related primarily to the salinity distribution, the temperature distribution can drive the circulation just as well under certain conditions. In shallow estuaries, salinity alone usually determines the water density (see Kjerfve 1979), because the fresh water inflow provides a source of less dense water that mixes with dense ocean water only slowly. Usually, there is no equally effective temperature source or sink which could create as large a density difference. An exception to this generality may be found in certain arctic or subarctic estuaries where chilly, and thus relatively dense, fresh water debouches into a less cold ocean. In this case, the temperature structure may be as important as the salinity in driving the gravitational circulation of the estuary. Pickard and Trites (1957) showed that a number of Britsh Columbia inlets had this characteristic.

Similarly, temperature effects can be of importance in driving indirectional gravitational circulation in lagoons that receive little or no fresh water runoff. Heating by the sun of a shallow lagoon causes high evaporation and, therefore, superelevated salinities in interior lagoons with restricted passages to the ocean. Whereas the ocean salinity is 35ppt, lagoons commonly have salinities in excess of 90ppt (Noye 1973), and sometimes much higher. This is especially true during the summer in arid or semiarid regions. Collier and Hedgepeth (1950) suggested that this process sets up an inverse estuarine circulation, with oceanic inflows in a surface layer and outfow of denser salty lagoon waters in a bottom layer.

It is somewhat questionable whether this hypothesis actually reflects many estuaries. Lagoons are often very shallow, open, and exposed to the wind, and thus tend to be well mixed vertically by the wind. This mixing would inhibit the development of a two-layered vertical circulation, inverse or otherwise. Differences in time-averaged salinities would probably be manifested more often across the entrance to such systems rather than between incoming and outgoing waters. Thus winds, tides, and/or basin geometry are more important as driving or modifying factors in lagoon systems than is gravitational circulation.

It has been proposed that the Coriolis effect can modify the classical estuarine circulation (Pritchard 1952a). If this is true the surface net outflow would be stronger along the right side of an estuary in the Northern hemisphere, looking downstream. Similarly, the net bottom inflow would be strongest along the opposite side. It is rather questionable whether the Coriolis effect is generally significant in this respect. Channel curvature, bottom friction, or the flow of a major portion of the fresh water to one side of the estuary are probably of significantly greater importance.

2.6.4   Tidal Circulation

In the absense of density gradients and wind stress, the estuarine circulation is driven by tidal currents. This type of circulation often is referred to as tidal pumping. It may seem curious that tidal currents, which are largely oscillatory, produce a nontidal flow, but the tidal waves interact with the bathymetry in nonlinear, complex ways. Because the estuarine bathymetry varies, the interactions between tidal currents and bathymetry are seldom identical at two locations in an estuary. This is manifested by slight differences in the strength of maximum ebb and flood currents, and in the duration of ebbing and flooding tidal flows. The resultant spatial distribution of currents, both horizontally and with depth, is called the tidal circulation due to the tidal pumping.

Tidal circulation is particularly pronounced in estuaries with a shallow water depth and a large tidal range. Examples of such systems are North Inlet, South Carolina (Fig. 2.8) (Kjerfve and Proehl 1979) and the Bay of Fundy (Tee 1976). Tidal and gravitational circulations probably coexist in many systems, although this has received only scant attention. The salt-balance studies by Fischer (1972), Dyer (1974), and Murray et al. (1975) point to the likelihood of the simultaneous and equal importance of these two circulation mechanisms in many estuaries. In fact, in most shallow systems with a tidal range of approximately 2 m or greater and a moderate to high river inflow, neither tidal nor gravitational circulation can be ignored.

For tidal pumping to exist a nonlinear interaction between the tide and estuarine boundaries is required. This comes about because variable cross-sectional width, differences in water depth, existence of tidal flats, and channel curvature cause large spatial velocity gradients. The time-average tidal currents are often systematically ebb-directed on one side of an estuarine cross section and flood directed on the other (Kjerfve 1978; Kjerfve and Proehl 1979). The cause is the boundary interaction rather than the Coriolis effect. Oppositely directed net currents in a cross-section, that is, the existence of tidal pumping, does not imply a net loss or gain of water in the long term. Still, this circulation could on the average systematically export or import water-borne constituents.

The innermost basin of the Bay of Fundy on the Canadian Atlantic coast experiences the largest tidal range in the world, on the average approximately 12 m. Tee (1976) developed a numerical hydrodynamic model for the Minas Basin of the Bay of Fundy. The computer solutions showed that tidal pumping drives net currents and the circulation, explained by the importance of nonlinear inertial effects. Simulated net tidal currents were measured up to 0.76 m/s. The time-averaged tidal circulation manifested itself as large horizontal eddies with diameters on the order of 20 km—the width of the estuary. The sense of rotation

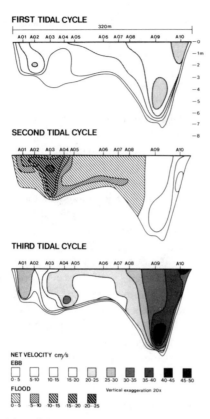

Figure 2.8 Example of the tidal circulation (pumping) in a North Inlet, South Carolina, cross section. Isopleths of net velocity (isotachs) are expressed in cm/s and indicate that the deep channel is mostly prone to net ebb flow. When net flood flow occurs, it is found in the secondary channel. There is considerable variation from tidal cycle to tidal cycle (modified after Kjerfve and Proehl 1979).

(i.e., cyclonic or anticyclonic) of these eddies was not attributed to the Coriolis effect but to particular coastal geometry (Tee 1976).

2.6.5 Wind-Driven Circulation

As implied previously, wind-driven circulation is thought to be particularly important in lagoons. Large expanses of open water, shallow water depths, a small tidal range, and low fresh water inflows are the conditions that favor dominance of wind-driven circulation. This type of circulation has not been studied well. First, it is often masked by gravitational and tidal circulations. Second, the wind is highly variable over a range of periods from minutes to weeks. A particularly important wind variance component is associated with frontal passages, with periods typically from 3 to 9 days. The duration over which estuarine currents must be averaged to yield a picture of the wind-driven circulation is therefore very long, a multiple of the frontal passage cycle (see Weisberg 1976a, Weisberg and Sturges 1976) (Fig. 2.9). This usually makes it impractical and much too costly to measure.

There are several empirical studies, however, that point to a major response of the time-averaged estuarine flow to wind forcing. Weisberg (1976b) found that approximately 48% of the current variability in the Narragansett Bay was related to metereological variability on time scales longer than 2 days. Similarly, Cannon (1978) and Holbrook et al. (1980) showed that even deep currents in inlets and fjords are correlated well with meteorological events. Water surface slopes as large as 4×10^{-5} radians (i.e., slopes of 0.4 m per 10 km distance) were attributed to 10 m/s wind forcing in a Louisiana bar-built estuary (Kjerfve 1973), and Smith (1977) found significant water exchange between Corpus Christi Bay, Texas and the Gulf of Mexico due to meteorological forcing. The wind tides of the Texas lagoons are well known (Collier and Hedgpeth 1950; Copeland et al. 1968). During winter northers, water piles up in the south ends of the lagoons and a seiche (back and forth sloshing of the water) develops, having a period on the order of a few hours, or approximately equal to twice the length of the lagoon divided by the square root of the product of gravity and the average water depth. The ecological significance of these wind tides can be very large, as a minute change in water level could expose hundreds of square kilometers of mud flats or inundate an equally large area of coastal salt marshes and grass lands. These studies obviously do not provide the final answers to the dynamics of the wind-driven circulation, but at least indicate the likely importance of the wind as a mechanism driving the estuarine circulation. This becomes very

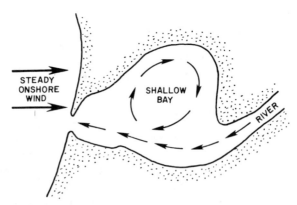

Figure 2.9 Schematic representation of the horizontal wind-driven circulation in a lagoon system (modified after Fischer et al. 1979).

obvious in shallow lagoons, but may be equally important in partially mixed estuaries such as Narragansett Bay or deep fjords.

Theoretical solutions of the hydrodynamic equations indicate that a steady, along-estuary wind stress will significantly augment the gravitational circulation (Rattray and Hansen 1962, Hansen and Rattray 1965) (Fig. 2.10). The effect of a down-estuary wind would be to increase the net surface ebb flow and at the same time increase the net inflow at depth. On the other hand, in the case of a steady wind blowing into the estuary, the resulting net surface current may be flood-directed, a midlayer would experience net ebb flow, and the net bottom-flow would be much reduced and flood-directed.

2.6.6   Circulation Modes

Traditionally most estuaries were thought to have a two-layered circulation with net outflow in the surface layer and net inflow in the bottom layer. There was, however, early evidence for the existence of significant deviations from this conceptual model. But the inconsistent data were initially not reported in the literature, for such periods of "nontraditional" circulation were thought of as being just "unusual events" (Pritchard 1978).

A recent study of the currents in the Potomac estuary, Virginia, put the classical two-layered estuarine circulation in a reasonable perspective. Elliott (1976) installed recording current meters at three depths on a vertical mooring for 1 year. After analysis of the data, Elliott defined six circulation modes (Fig. 2.11). These represent six separate states of the same partially mixed estuary:

1. Classical circulation: surface outflow and bottom inflow.
2. Reverse circulation: surface inflow and bottom outflow.

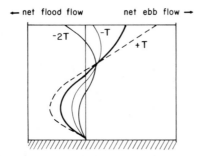

Figure 2.10   Schematic representation of the vertical gravitational circulation (heavy line) in a partially mixed estuary without wind stress. The dashed line represents the vertical circulation profile with the wind stress acting down-estuary with a magnitude of T. The other two lines represent the vertical net velocity profile with the wind stress acting up-estuary of magnitude T and 2T (modified after Rattray and Hansen 1962).

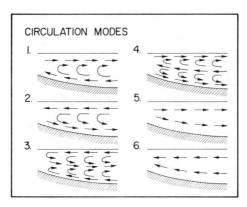

Figure 2.11 Schematic representation of the six circulation modes found (Elliott 1976) to exist in a partially mixed estuary.

3. Three-layered circulation: surface and bottom inflow and outflow at middepth.
4. Reverse three-layered circulation: surface and bottom outflow and inflow at middepth.
5. Discharge circulation: outflow at all depths.
6. Storage circulation: inflow at all depths.

The most common of these circulation modes was the classical estuarine circulation. In the Potomac it occurred 43% of the time and lasted for an average of 2.5 days. The storage circulation occurred 22% of the time with an average duration of 1.6 days. Next followed reverse circulation for 21% of the time and with an average duration of 1.6 days; the reverse three-layered circulation for 7% of the time and an average of 1.5 days; discharge circulation for 6% of the time and an average duration of 1.3 days; and finally three-layered circulation for 1% of the time and an average duration of 1.0 day. Also, the classical estuarine circulation pattern is usually followed by either discharge or reverse circulation. Discharge circulation is most commonly followed by reverse circulation, which in turn is followed most often by the classical circulation mode.

Estuarine circulation is obviously not a simple matter. Estuaries are seldom in steady state, but rather exhibit complex temporal as well as spatial variabilities. Elliott's (1976) study focused on the vertical-longitudinal aspects of the circulation. Had lateral flow variabilities also been included in the analysis, still more complexity would undoubtedly have arisen. The detailed current measurements in an estuarine cross section by, for example, Kjerfve and Proehl (1979), indicate the great lateral variability that can exist in the flows.

2.6.7 Far-Field Effects

Several independent factors are believed to be responsible for altering the circulation from one mode to the next. Changing wind stress, variations in the river discharge, and the varying tidal range due to the fortnightly spring-neap cycle are all likely agents causing temporal changes in the circulation. Another less obvious factor is the influence that the behavior or "climate" of the coastal waters may have on the estuarine circulation, the slowly varying mean sea level at the location of the estuary, and the exchange of water and materials.

Coupling between the coastal ocean and the estuary occurs on many time scales. Estuarine tides, for example, are for the most part forced by ocean tides at the mouth. Similarly, the synoptic (large-scale) wind stress, acting on the coastal ocean surface, is often of far greater importance than the local wind stress on the estuarine water surface in imparting water accelerations. This is especially true in the case of narrow, branching, and winding estuaries.

The meteorological forcing of coastal and shelf waters by moving atmospheric pressure systems and wind-stress fields generates long waves that propagate along the coast. These can be either (1) Kelvin waves, (2) continental shelf waves, or (3) coastal trapped waves (Mysak and Hamon 1969, LeBlond and Mysak 1976, Gill 1982), each with their own characteristics (cf., Gill 1982). These long waves have periods from 2 to 15 days and wave lengths on the order of 1000 km. They travel parallel to the coast, on the continental shelf, at speeds from 0.1 to 1.0 m/s (Brooks and Mooers 1977). Their wave height decreases

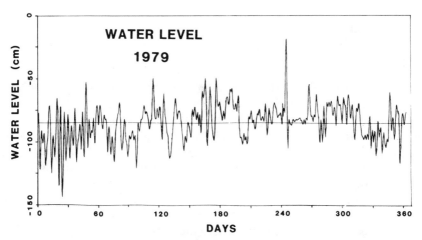

Figure 2.12 Estuarine manifestation of nonlocal forcing is readily visible in a tidal record after appropriate smoothing. This year-long water-level time series from North Inlet, South Carolina was filtered to remove fluctuations with periods shorter than approximately 2 days (modified after Kjerfve et al. 1982).

exponentially away from the coast. The wave heights may be as great as 0.8 m at the coastline and in estuaries (Kjerfve et al., 1982).

Long waves on the continental shelf are forced by either the synoptic meteorological conditions (i.e. wind and pressure) or what is known as "free-propagation," meaning that probably they were generated by a distant weather system. Long waves on the continental shelf are possibly the most dramatic, important, and commonly occurring form of far-field forced events in estuaries, although the estuarine sea level and possibly even the circulation may be influenced more by the wind-generated wave activity at the mouth of the estuary. For example, when high ocean waves of long period either break at or impinge on an estuarine entrance, wave momentum is radiated or transferred into the estuary. The result is a significantly raised estuarine water level compared with times of little or no oceanic wave action (Thomson and Hamon, 1979).

There are several ecological implications of these long-period estuarine events of nonlocal origin, for although they are most usually detected by analysis of tidal records, they produce significant low-frequency water flows and material transports. Tidal innundation of marshes and adjacent flats is considerably more extensive during the passage of a long wave crest compared with the passage of a trough for the same tidal conditions. Thus when one is making measurements of tidal transports or budgets, it is imperative to account for the nonlocal events with periods of a few days. Otherwise, the transport/budget estimates run the risk of being severely biased. Also, long waves produced on the shelf influence estuaries through long-periods of up-estuary-down-estuary oscillations of the turbidity maximum zone and the salinity fields.

2.7 ESTUARINE MIXING

2.7.1 Mixing Processes

Estuaries represent regions where salt water mixes with waters derived from land drainage. *Mixing* is the process whereby a water parcel or water mass is diluted by, or redistributed within, other water masses. The mixing process is either *advective* or *dispersive*. The distinction between the two is rather arbitrary, however, depending on the choice of an averaging time. Mixing on a longer time scale is called advection, and short-term mixing is called dispersion. The estuarine circulation movements are generally the most important mixing mechanism, but smaller-scale advective and dispersive processes may operate simultaneously and must be considered for the mixing to be characterized properly.

Water molecules from the ocean versus those from runoff sources cannot be differentiated easily. Thus it is usually impractical to determine mixing by use of isotopic ratios of stable and radioactive hydrogen or oxygen atoms within water molecules. Rather, the distribution in time and space of dissolved (and sometimes suspended) material in estuaries is used as a measure of the mixing. The dissolved substance can be naturally occurring (e.g., salt) or introduced for the purpose of an investigation (e.g., dyes or radioisotopes). The estuarine salinity distribution is the most commonly used indicator of mixing for three reasons: (1) salinity is a conservative constituent, that is, the salt concentration essentially is not altered by biogeochemical processes but only by mixing processes—dispersion and advection—and, to a lesser degree, by local rainfall, evaporation, and freezing; (2) most of the estuarine salt is derived from one source, the ocean (whereas oceanic salinities are approximately 35 ppt, most land runoff has a salinity less than 0.6 ppt); (3) salinity is easy and inexpensive to determine (see Kjerfve 1979) and does not require great precision because of large temporal and spatial salt gradients within most estuaries. However, in systems that receive little fresh water runoff or that exhibit multiple ocean entrances, salinity is not a good mixing indicator and it may be necessary to introduce a suitable tracer substance to determine the mixing.

Dispersive mixing may be defined as the scattering of water parcels or particles dissolved in the estuary. It is due to the combined effect of several processes, including (1) tidal sloshing, (2) shear effects, (3) eddy (or turbulent) diffusion, (4) molecular diffusion, and (5) tidal trapping (or chopping). By the theoretical decomposition of the flux of a dissolved constituent, Bowden (1963) showed how the first four effects contribute to the dispersive mixing. The contribution of trapping has been described by Pritchard (1969).

Diffusion within the water refers to the random scattering of water parcels or particles by either random molecular or eddy (turbulent) motions. Molecular diffusion is always several orders of magnitude less than eddy diffusion in estuaries and can be ignored. Bowden (1963) showed that eddy diffusion also is negligible in most estuarine situations, compared with the sloshing and shear effects, at least with respect to net dispersive mixing over one or more tidal cycles. *Sloshing,* which refers to the time-averaged flux of particles by oscillatory tidal currents, is usually the dominant longitudinal mixing process. When attempting to determine the mass transport of a substance by time averaging the product of estuarine velocity and particle concentration (meaning there is generally some material left behind at one place or another), the integral seldom vanishes because of phase differences between current and concentration time representations (see Kjerfve 1975). Thus particles are systematically scattered or transported in one direction over a tidal cycle, causing longitudinal mixing by the sloshing mechanism. The *shear effect* is mixing over a tidal cycle due to systematic covariations of velocity and particle concentration over the estuary. In other words, shear results from different velocities of parallel currents. This can be in three dimensions: (1) depth (vertical shear, Bowden 1963); (2) width (lateral shear, Fischer et al. 1979); or (3) cross section (cross-sectional shear, Hansen and Rattray 1965). It is an important mixing effect. Whereas vertical shear was considered most important earlier, it is now clear that lateral shear is equally important (Dyer 1974, Fischer 1976, Murray et al. 1975, Rattray and Dworski 1980). Finally, tidal trapping occurs when water is temporarily trapped within shoreline indentations and branching channels. As the tidal current oscillates past these shoreline features, the trapped water parcels and particles are released into the flow and replaced by new water and particles. The net effect is one of longitudinal dispersion (Okubo 1973, Fischer et al. 1979).

2.7.2   The Forces That Cause Mixing

The energy required to mix estuaries is derived from several sources: (1) tidal forcing; (2) wind stress; (3) wave motions other than tides; and (4) river runoff. All effects, of course, ultimately are driven by energy from solar heating or gravitational attractions, as was the case with respect to circulation.

Tidal forcing is usually the most important cause of mixing in estuaries. Interaction between tidal currents and estuarine boundaries generates turbulence and causes large-scale mixing such as tidal pumping (advective mixing) and dispersive effects (i.e., sloshing, shear, and trapping). Direct wind mixing is usually of lesser importance in estuaries unless the tidal range is small or the estuary consists of large open areas or is shallow, as in the case of many lagoons. The wind is usually responsible for the generation of surface waves, internal waves, basin seiches, and Langmuir wind rows/cells. Each of these wave types at times enhances mixing in estuaries significantly.

Finally, rivers represent a source of buoyancy and also cause mixing. The density difference between river and ocean drives the gravitational circulation, which is a form of advective mixing. Pressure gradients occur because of sloping isopycnals (usually isohalines) and control the direction of mean density-driven (baroclinic) flow, often resulting in the classical estuarine circulation pattern (i.e., gravitational circulation). The estuary is then mixed advectively by a net seaward surface-layer flow and a net landward flow in a bottom layer, and in some cases, by winds. In view of the previous discussion of circulation, this picture of estuarine behavior is obviously quite simplified. Sometimes lagoons and other shallow estuaries are mixed completely in the vertical direction by wind or bottom turbulence. Even in lagoons, though, the horizontal differences in density due to freshwater input can still drive an internal circulation and are thus instrumental in mixing.

The degree of mixing is by no means steady. The same estuary may at times mix quickly and completely because of a frontal passage or strong winds and at times slowly and imcompletely because of lack of winds. Similarly, variations in tidal range have a profound effect on vertical mixing in the Chesapeake Bay (Haas 1977). During neap tides with a small tidal range, tidal energy is limited, and the water column becomes stratified vertically because of denser bottom waters and a less dense surface layer. This represents stable stratification and inhibits vertical mixing. During spring tides, the tidal range and maximum currents are increased, and a sufficient level of tidal energy is available to break down the vertical density stratification. The result is an enhancement of vertical mixing, allowing nutrients and food particles in the bottom layer to mix up into the photic surface zone and enhance production and, in addition, force oxygen-rich surface waters to the bottom, replenishing oxygen. Thus Chesapeake Bay and similar estuaries can be expected to alternate between being stratified (limited vertical mixing) and well-mixed (effective vertical exchange) on the fort-nightly spring-neap tide cycle (Haas 1977).

2.7.3 Mixing Diagrams

As a dissolved or suspended constituent is transported into an estuarine region, it is subjected to advective and dispersive mixing processes as well as changes in salinity. The end result is often that various constituents will settle out within the estuary, making the system act as a material sink. This is largely the case with fine-grained sediments from river sources as well as sand-sized sediments from the coastal ocean (Meade 1969). Thus an important question to ask is whether a dissolved or suspended constituent mixes conservatively within the estuary ver-sus whether it is added to or subtracted from the water column. It would mix conservatively if the material concentration changes proportionately to the change in salinity. Salinity is a conservative constituent, and if a material con-centration is plotted linearly against salinity, it too would be conservative. Such a plot of salinity against a material concentration is referred to as a mixing dia-gram. Systematic deviation of a measured estuarine concentration from a straight line in a mixing diagram is interpreted to imply nonconservative behav-ior of the constituent. This would then usually imply that the estuary is a sink or a source for a given constituent.

However, extreme care must be exercized in using a mixing diagram. The transformation from distance along the estuary to salinity assumes (1) one-di-mensional (longitudinal) mixing; (2) quasi steady state; and (3) that all data are averaged over one or more complete tidal cycles (Officer 1979; Officer and Lynch 1981; Loder and Reichard 1981). These assumptions are seldom met in the strict sense and thus deviations from a straight line in a mixing diagram may not necessarily mean non-conservative behavior. In particular, it is well known (Loder and Reichard 1981; Officer and Lynch 1981) that temporal variations in either the riverine or oceanic material concentrations can cause non-linear mix-ing curves in spite of a constituent behaving conservatively. Corrections can be made, with difficulty, for this problem if sufficient data are available. The idea of mixing diagrams is developed further in Chapter 3, which also contains some examples in the figure.

2.7.4 Dynamic Classification

Rather that classifying estuaries according to geomorphic characteristics, Pritchard (1955) proposed a useful classification scheme based on circulation and stratification. The three basic estuarine types are A (highly stratified), B (partially mixed), and C (well mixed). The C type may be subdivided into C1 (vertically homogeneous with laterally reversing net flow) and C2 (vertically and laterally homogeneous).

The highly stratified type A estuary is exemplified by the lower Mississippi River. The density (or salinity) stratification is extremely sharp, so that pure fresh and pure salt water are virtually adjacent, and vertical salt exchange occurs as a function of the breaking of internal waves along the mid-depth pynocline. The type A estuary usually exhibits a low tidal range, which cannot break down the vertical stratification, and a moderate to great amount of fresh water input.

The partially mixed estuary, type B, is exemplified by the Chesapeake Bay estuarine system. The vertical salt gradient has the shape of the cotangent curve with time-averaged salinity differences from 2–10 ppt between surface and bottom waters. The classical estuarine circulation (i.e., a well-developed gravitational circulation), would be typical for the type B system, which for the most part would be a coastal plain estuary or a fjärd or shallow fjord system. These systems are characterized by a moderate to large tidal range and moderate fresh water inflow.

The well-mixed estuary, finally, is exemplified by North Inlet, South Carolina. Tidal mixing is intense because of a large tidal range and little fresh water influx. Accordingly, there are no vertical density (or salinity) gradients. The net circulation is either everywhere seaward (C2), or with one side flowing in and the other side flowing seaward in cross section. In the latter case, tidal pumping is the dominant circulation mode.

Pritchard (1955) suggested further that in managing estuaries, it would be possible to change the circulation and mixing characteristics of a particular estuary from A toward C or from C toward A. By dredging an estuary and thus making it deeper, the estuary can be expected to alter its characteristics from A to B or B to C. Similarly, by widening a channel, the characteristics of that section can be expected to change toward a B or a C type if all other parameters are held constant. The damming of rivers leading into an estuary can likewise change the estuarine dynamics because of the change in buoyant mixing. The greater the discharge, the more likely is the A-type estuary because of a well-developed vertical stratification. With decreasing river input the type A may become a type B, and the type B a type C.

2.7.5   Circulation—Stratification Diagram

Hansen and Rattray (1965) proposed an improvement on the dynamical classification of estuaries by a dimensionless circulation—stratification diagram (Fig. 2.13). By plotting a stratification parameter versus a circulation parameter, they managed to describe a continuum of estuaries and show how a given estuary may change over a season.

The stratification parameter is simply the ratio of the salinity difference between bottom and surface layers and the depth-averaged salinity. Each of these salinities are first averaged over one or more complete tidal cycles. The circulation parameter is likewise a ratio between the net surface flow and the fresh water flow. The net surface flow is taken as a representative value across an estuarine section to smooth out lateral effects and with the assumption of a steady state. Thus changes in water level from beginning to end of a tidal cycle

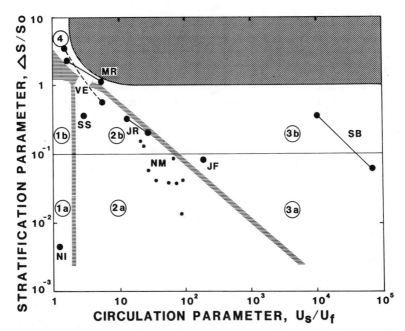

Figure 2.13 Estuarine classification diagram (Hanson and Rattray 1965) according to nondimensional stratification and circulation parameters. MR, Mississippi River; VE, Vellar Estuary, India; NI, North Inlet, SC; SS, South Santee, SC; JR, James River, VA; NM, Narrows of Mersey, UK; JF, Straits of Juan de Fuca, WA; and SB, Silver Bay, AK.

are averaged out. The fresh water flow is simply the steady fresh water discharge divided by the cross-sectional area.

Hansen and Rattray (1965) found that most estuaries could be grouped into four regions on their diagram. Class 1 estuaries are either lagoons or bar-built estuaries. Class 1a is vertically mixed and includes North Inlet, whereas 1b exhibits more of a vertical stratification. Both, however, have a total lack of gravitational circulation. Upstream salt mixing takes place by longitudinal dispersion mechanisms alone. Most estuaries studied fall into class 2, which overlaps with coastal plain and partially mixed estuaries. Again, this type was subdivided into a well-mixed (2a) and a weakly stratified (2b) subclass. This class is characterized by a reasonably well-developed gravitational circulation and longitudinal mixing by both dispersive and advective mechanisms.

Class 3 estuaries, on the other hand, are dominated by advective mixing processes, with dispersive effects playing a negligible role. Most systems in this class show moderate to strong stratification and are further characterized by a well-developed gravitational circulation. This class includes most fjord and some fjärd estuaries and a number of estuarine straits.

Class 4 estuaries, finally, coincide with Pritchard's (1955) type A, the strongly stratified system. Vertical mixing is limited and the gravitational circulation is weak or nonexistent.

Hansen's and Rattray's (1965) classification represents an improvement over previous classification schemes in that it allows a direct comparison of estuarine dynamics and mixing processes between systems. This, in turn, makes it possible to generalize to some degree about different estuaries. With this basic background in the physics of estuaries it is now possible to consider the chemistry and biology of estuaries, which are very much influenced by these basic physical properties.

REFERENCES

Bird, E.C.F., 1967. Coastal lagoons of southeastern Australia. In J.N. Jennings and J.A. Mabbutt (Eds.), Land Form Studies from Australia and New Guinea. Cambridge University Press, London, pp. 365–385.

Boon, J.D., III, 1975. Tidal discharge asymmetry in a salt marsh drainage system. Limnol. Oceanogr., 20:71–80.

Bowden, K.F. 1963. The mixing processes in a tidal estuary. Int. J. Air Water Poll., 7:343–356.

Brooks, D.A. and C.N.K. Mooers, 1977. Wind-forced continental shelf waves in the Florida current. J. Geophys. Res., 82:2569–2576.

Brunn, P., 1978. Stability of Tidal Inlets Theory and Engineering. Elsevier, Amsterdam.

Cameron, W.M. and D.W. Pritchard, 1963. Estuaries. In M.N. Hill (Ed.), The Sea. Wiley, New York, Vol. 2, pp. 306–324.

Cannon, G.A. (Ed.), 1978. Circulation in the Strait of Juan de Fuca: Some recent oceanographic observations. NOAA Technical Report ERL 399-PMEL 29, 49 pp.

Castanares, A.A. and F.B. Phleger (Eds.), 1969. Coastal Lagoons, A Symposium. Universidad Nacional Autonoma de Mexico. Ciudad Universitaria, Mexico 20, D.F., 686 pp.

Collier, A. and J.W. Hedgpeth, 1950. An introduction to hydrography of tidal waters of Texas. Publ. Inst. of Mar. Sci., 1:125–194.

Conomos, T.J. (Ed.), 1979. San Francisco Bay: The urbanized estuary. Pacific Division of the American Association for the Advancement of Science, San Francisco, 493 pp.

Copeland, B.J., J.H. Thompson, Jr. and W.B. Ogletree, 1968. Effects of wind on water levels in the Texas Laguna Madre. Texas J. Sci., 20:196–199.

Davies, J.L., 1973. Geographical Variation in Coastal Development. Hafner, New York.

Dionne, J.C., 1963. Towards a more adequate definition of the St. Lawrence estuary. Z. Geomorphol., 7:36–44.

Dyer, K.R., 1973. Estuaries: A Physical Introduction. Wiley, New York.

Dyer, K.R., 1974. The salt balance in stratified estuaries. Estuarine Coastal Mar. Sci., 2:273–281.

Dyer, K.R., 1979. Estuaries and estuarine sedimentation. In K.R. Dyer (Ed.), Hydrography and Sedimentation in Estuaries. Cambridge University Press, London, pp. 1–18.

Elliott, A.J., 1976. A study of the effect of meteorological forcing on the circulation in the Potomac estuary. Special Report 56, Chesapeake Bay Institute, The Johns Hopkins University, Baltimore, MD.

Emery, K.O., 1967. Estuaries and lagoons in relation to continental shelves. In G.H. Lauff (Ed.), Estuaries. American Association for the Advancement of Science, Washington, D.C., 83:9–11.

Emery, K.O. and E. Uchupi, 1972. Western North Atlantic Ocean: Topography, rocks, structure, water, life and sediments. American Association of Petroleum Geologists, Mem. 17, Tulsa, Oklahoma.

Fairbridge, R.W., 1980. The estuary: Its definition and geodynamic cycle. In E. Olausson and I. Cato (Eds.), Chemistry and Biochemistry of Estuaries. Wiley, New York. pp. 1–35.

Fischer, H.B., 1972. Mass transport mechanisms in partially stratified estuaries. J. Fluid Mech., 53:671–687.

Fischer, H.B., E.J. List, R.C.Y. Koh, J. Imberger, and N.H. Brooks, 1979. Mixing in Inland and Coastal Waters. Academic, New York.

Fischer, H.B. 1977. Mixing and dispersion in estuaries. pp. 107–133. In M. van Dyke, W. Vincinti, and J.V. Wehausen (Eds.). Annual Review of Fluid Mechanics. Academic, New York, Vol. B, pp. 107–133

Gibbs, R.J., 1970. Circulation in the Amazon River estuary and adjacent Atlantic Ocean. J. Mar. Res., 28:113–123.

Gierloff-Emden, H.G., 1977. Orbital Remote Sensing of Coastal and Offshore Environments. A Manual of Interpretation. Walter de Gruyter, Berlin, 176 pp.

Gill, A.E. 1982. Atmosphere—Ocean Dynamics. Academic, New York, 662 pp.

Haas, L.W. 1977. The effect of the spring—neap tidal cycle on the vertical salinity structure of the James, York, and Rappahannock rivers, Virginia, U.S.A. Estuarine Coastal. Mar. Sci., 5:485–496.

Hansen, D.V. and M. Rattray, Jr., 1965. Gravitational circulation in straits and estuaries. J. Mar. Res., 23:104–122.

Hayes, M.O., 1978. Impact of hurricanes on sedimentation in estuaries, bays and lagoons. In M.L. Wiley (Ed.), Estuarine Interactions. Academic, New York. pp. 323–346.

Holbrook, J.R., R.D. Muench, D.G. Kachel, and C. Wright, 1980. Circulation in the Straight of Juan de Fuca: Recent oceanographic observations in the eastern basin. NOAA Technical Report ERL412-PMEL33, 42 pp.

Kjerfve, B., 1973. Dynamics of the water surface in a bar-built estuary. Ph.D. Dissertation, Louisiana State University, 91 pp.

Kjerfve, B. 1975. Velocity averaging in estuaries characterized by a large tidal range to depth ratio. Estuarine Coastal. Mar. Sci., 3:311–323.

Kjerfve, B., 1978. Bathymetry as an indicator of net circulation in well-mixed estuaries. Limnol. Oceanogr., 23: 814–821.

Kjerfve, B., 1979. Measurements and analysis of water current, temperature, salinity and density. In K.R. Dyer (Ed.), Hydrography and Sedimentation in Estuaries. Cambridge University Press, United Kingdom. pp. 186–216.

Kjerfve, B. and H.N. McKellar, Jr., 1980. Time series measurements of estuarine material fluxes. In V. Kennedy (Ed.), Estuarine Perspectives. Academic, New York, pp. 341–357.

Kjerfve, B. and J.A. Proehl, 1979. Velocity variability in a cross section of a well-mixed estuary. J. Mar. Res., 37:409–418.

Kjerfve, B., C.C. Shao, and F.W. Stapor, Jr., 1979. Formation of deep scour holes at the junction of tidal creeks: An hypothesis. Mar. Geol., 33:M9–M14.

Klenova, M.V., 1968. Caspian Sea. In R.W. Fairbridge (Ed.), The Encyclopedia of Geomorphology. Reinhold, New York, pp. 109–116.

Lankford, R.R., 1976. Coastal lagoons of Mexico; their origin and classification. In M.L. Wiley (Ed.), Estuarine Processes, Vol. II. Academic, New York, pp. 182–215.

LeBlond, P.H. and L.A. Mysak, 1978. Waves in the Ocean. Elsevier, New York, 602 pp.

Loder, T.C. and R.P. Reichard, 1981. The dynamics of conservative mixing in estuaries. Estuaries, 4(1):64–69.

Meade, R.H., 1969. Landward transport of bottom sediments in estuaries of the Atlantic coastal plain. J. Sediment. Petrolo., 39:222–234.

Milliman, J.D. and K.O. Emery, 1968. Sea levels during the past 35,000 years. Science, 162:1121–1123.

Murray, S.P., D. Conlon, A. Siripong, and J. Santoro, 1975. Circulation and salinity distribution in the Rio Guayas estuary, Ecuador. In L.E. Cronin (Ed.), Estuarine Research, Vol. II Academic, New York, pp. 345–363.

Murray, S.P. and A. Siripong, 1978. Role of lateral gradients and longitudinal dispersion in the salt balance of a shallow, well-mixed estuary. In B. Kjerfve (Ed.), Estuarine Transport Processes. University of South Carolina Press, Columbia, SC. pp. 113–124.

Mysak, L.A. and B.V. Hamon, 1969. Low-frequency sea level behavior and continental shelf waves off North Carolina. J. Geophys. Res., 74:1397–1405.

Noye, B.J., 1973. The Coorong-past, present and future. Publication 38, Department of Adult Education, The University of Adelaide, South Australia.

Noye, B.J. and P.J. Walsh, 1976. Wind-induced water level oscillations in shallow lagoons. Aust. J. Mar. Freshwater Res., 27:417–430.

Officer, C.B., 1976. Physical Oceanography of Estuaries and Associated Coastal Waters. Wiley, New York.

Officer, C.B., 1979. Discussion of the behavior of nonconservative dissolved constituents in estuaries. Estuarine Coastal Mar. Sci., 9(10):91–94.

Officer, C.B., 1980. Box models revisited. In P. Hamilton and K.B. McDonald (Eds.), Estuarine and Wetland Processes with Emphasis on Modeling. Plenum, New York.

Officer, C.B. and D.R. Lynch, 1981. Dynamics of mixing in estuaries. Estuarine Coastal. Shelf Sci., 12:525–533.

Okubo, A. 1973. Effect of shoreline irregularities on streamwise dispersion in estuaries and other embayments. Neth. J. Sea Res., 6:213–224.

Orme, A.R. 1974. Estuarine sedimentation along the Natal Coast, South Africa. Technical Report 5, Office of Naval Research Contract N00014-69-A-0200-4035, Task NR 388-102, 53 pp.

Orme, A.R. and L.L. Loeher, 1974. Remote sensing of subtropical coastal environments,

Natal, South Africa. Technical Report 3, Office of Naval Research, Contract N00014-69-A-0200-4035, Task NR 388-102, 89 pp.

Pickard, G.L., 1956. Physical features of British Columbia inlets. Trans. R. Soc. Can. L, III:47-58.

Pickard, G.L., 1971. Some physical oceanographic features of inlets of Chile. J. Fish. Res. Board Can. 28:605-616; 1077-1106.

Pickard, G.L. and R.W. Trites, 1957. Fresh water transport determination from the heat budget with applications to British Columbia inlets. J. Fish. Res. Board Can., 14:605-616.

Pritchard, D.W., 1952a. Estuarine hydrography. In Advances in Geophysics, Vol. I Academic, New York, pp. 243-280.

Pritchard, D.W., 1952b. Salinity distribution and circulation in the Chesapeake Bay estuarine system. J. Mar. Res., 11:106-123.

Pritchard, D.W. 1955. Estuarine circulation patterns. Proc. Am. Soc. Civ. Eng., 81:717/1-717/11.

Pritchard, D.W., 1956. The dynamic structure of a coastal plain estuary. J. Mar. Res., 15:33-42.

Pritchard, D.W., 1967. What is an estuary: Physical viewpoint. In G.H. Lauff (Ed.), Estuaries. American Association for the Advancement of Science, Publication 83, Washington, D.C., pp. 3-5.

Pritchard, D.W., 1969. Dispersion and flushing of pollutants in estuaries. Proc. Am. Soc. Civ. Eng., J. Hydraul. Div., 95:115-124.

Pritchard, D.W., 1978. What have recent observations obtained for adjustment and verification of numerical models revealed about the dynamics and kinematics of estuaries? In B. Kjerfve (Ed.), Estuarine Transport Processes, University of South Carolina Press, Columbia, SC, pp. 1-9.

Pritchard, D.W. and R.E. Kent, 1956. A method for determining mean longitudinal velocities in a coastal plain estuary. J. Mar. Res., 15:81-91.

Rattray, M., Jr. and J.G. Dworski, 1980. Comparison of methods for analysis of the transverse and vertical circulation contributions to the longitudinal advective salt flux in estuaries. Estuarine Coastal Mar. Sci., 11:515-536.

Rattray, M., Jr. and D.V. Hansen, 1962. A simularity solution for circulation in an estuary. J. Mar. Res., 20:121-133.

Saelen, O.H., 1967. Some features of the hydrography of Norwegian fjords. In G.H. Lauff (Ed.), Estuaries. American Association for the Advancement of Science, Washington, DC, pp. 63-70.

Schubel, J.R. and D.J. Hirschberg, 1978. Estuarine graveyards, climatic change and the importance of the estuarine environment. In M.L. Wiley (Ed.), Estuarine Interactions. Academic, New York, pp. 285-303.

Schubel, J.R. and D.W. Pritchard, 1972. The estuarine environment. J. Geol. Educ., 20:60-68.

Smith, N.P., 1977. Meteorological and tidal exchanges between Corpus Christi Bay, Texas, and the northwestern Gulf of Mexico. Estuarine Coastal Mar. Sci., 5:511-520.

Stewart, R.W., 1957. A note on the dynamic balance for estuarine circulation. J. Mar. Res., 16:34-39.

Tee, K.T., 1976. Tide-induced residual current, a 2-D nonlinear, numerical model. J. Mar. Res. 34:603–628.

Thompson, R.O.R.Y. and B.V. Hamon, 1980. Wave set-up of harbor water level. J. Geophys. Res., 85:1151–1152.

Wang, D.P. and A.J. Elliott, 1978. Non-tidal variability in the Chesapeake Bay and Potomac River: Evidence for non-local forcing. J. Phys. Oceanogr., 8:225–232.

Weisberg, R.H., 1976a. A note on estuarine mean flow estimation. J. Mar. Res., 34:387–394.

Weisberg, R.H., 1976b. The non-tidal flow in the Providence River of Narragansett Bay: A stochastic approach to estuarine circulation. J. Phys. Oceanogr., 6:721–734.

Weisberg, R.H. and W. Sturges, 1976. Velocity observations in the West Passage of Narragansett Bay: A partially mixed estuary. J. Phys. Oceanogr., 6:345–354.

— **3**

Estuarine Chemistry[1]

3.1 Introduction

The existence and rate of activity of biological communities in estuarine (and other) environments is largely a function of the physical and chemical processes that transport and transform materials and energy to, within, and among individual organisms. Nevertheless we rarely see the direct results of most chemical reactions, even those that are the very basis for life in the estuary. Some reactions leave a visual trace as color changes, bubble formation, or precipitation of solids; however, most changes in concentration of various compounds over time and space can be discerned only through meticulous measurement with instruments. In this chapter we discuss some important aspects of the chemistry of estuaries.

A fundamental concept of ecology is that energy enters the biosphere principally in the form of sunlight, and is transformed to energy-rich organic substances via photosynthesis and chemosynthesis. This organic matter is the fuel for most biotic activities, and as the energy in these substances is used it is dissipated into heat. As this occurs the chemicals that are the building blocks for the biotic material in nature are taken up and released as organic matter is created and destroyed. The complex chemical compounds of life are transformed by organisms, but the constituent chemical elements are conserved as they are transferred between organisms and their environment, and one organism's wastes become another's nutrients. Hence energy flows through an estuarine ecosystem from sunlight to organic matter to heat, while the chemical constituents of or-

[1]Written primarily by W.M. Kemp.

ganisms are continually cycled among organisms, water, sediments, and atmosphere.

The aquatic environment is a very special one in that water is an excellent solvent, for the polar nature of water renders it capable of dissolving a wide variety of salts. In addition, water's relatively high density compared to air allows some solid materials to float or be suspended readily, and enables rooted plants to stay upright without rigid stalks or stems. Since estuaries are, by definition, the sites where rivers meet the sea, the exact nature of the chemical processes occurring in an estuary depends on the quantity and kind of materials transported by the fresh and salt water sources, the different chemical reactions that occur in fresh versus salt water, and the residence time of river water in the estuary.

Chemical approaches are being used increasingly in the study of estuarine ecology. For example, the energy flow through benthic ecosystems has been shown to depend heavily on microbially mediated chemical processes such as sulfate reduction and denitrification. The topics we have chosen to include in this chapter reflect both classical and recent approaches to the description of both aquatic and marine chemistry (e.g., Riley and Chester, 1971). Our approach draws on basic principles of aquatic chemistry and attempts to demonstrate their application to estuarine problems. The remainder of the chapter is divided into four sections, the first of which deals with the chemical composition of fresh and seawater, and the chemical processes involved in their mixing. The second section considers the major oxidation—reduction reactions which determine energy flow and chemical dynamics in sediments, and the final two sections cover metabolic gases and cycling of biologically important nutrients.

Before plunging into the details of estuarine chemistry, we will examine briefly a few common chemical changes in the three estuaries we explored in Chapter 1. Dissolved oxygen (DO) and inorganic nitrogen have been measured in these estuaries and we will consider some spatial and temporal patterns of these chemical species. Near the mouth of the North River, DO and NO_3^- can change considerably over a 24 hour period. Much of the change is due to physical forces: changing water masses due to the rise and fall of the tide. For example, on the rising tide oceanic water relatively high in oxygen but low in nitrogen is often encountered. On the falling tide water draining from fringing marshes is low in oxygen but has high levels of ammonia. In eutrophic Lake Cataouatche in the Barataria Basin, marked change in oxygen over 24 hours is due primarily to biological activity. Phytoplankton photosynthesis raises the DO during the day, while community respiration lowers it at night. Oxygen levels are generally lower in lower salinity regions of estuaries, and this is the case for North River, Barataria Bay, and Laguna de Terminos. Normally these lower-oxygen regions are produced by high rates of oxygen consumption by rich biotic communities.

There is considerable variability in the concentration of inorganic nitrogen in estuaries. In the North River, NO_3^- levels can be ten times higher at the head of the estuary compared to the mouth. Similar patterns exist for Barataria Basin and the Laguna de Terminos. There are also striking seasonal patterns, with

NO_3^- levels in North River and Barataria Bay much higher in winter and spring due to fresh water runoff. In Laguna de Terminos, the highest NO_3^- levels occur during the fall, which is the time of highest river discharge. During the period of high river flow, NO_3^- decreases with increasing salinity in all three estuaries and this can be explained primarily by dilution with seawater. During periods of peak phytoplankton growth, NO_3^- often disappears completely. These changes in oxygen and nitrogen are a result of both physical and biological processes occuring not only in the water column, but also in fringing wetlands and the sediments. We will consider these and many other processes in the remainder of the chapter.

3.2   THE ESTUARINE MIXING BOWL

3.2.1   Composition

The composition of river water in terms of species and amounts of dissolved substances varies widely across the continents. Seawater, however, is remarkably uniform in terms of its major dissolved constituents no matter where in the world it is measured. The salts dissolved in river water arise from two primary sources: precipitation-derived salts in rain originally derived from sea spray and wind-eroded terrestrial dust and, of greater overall significance, the products of rock weathering. The most important constituents of seawater are chloride, sodium, sulfate, and magnesium, but for global average river water, they are bicarbonate, calcium, silicon, and sulfate (Table 3.1). The majority of biotically important compounds entering an estuary are from riverine sources (e.g., silicon, iron, nitrogen, and phosphorus); however, others crucial to estuarine chemistry are derived predominantly from the sea (e.g., sulfate and bicarbonate). Many of the metals entering estuaries from rivers are transported primarily in particulate form. For example, about 95% of the iron and manganese carried by the Yukon and Amazon Rivers is associated with particulate matter (Burton 1976).

As river water mixes with sea water during its retention in an estuarine basin, the dissolved and particulate constituents may behave conservatively (i.e., the concentrations are changed only by dilution) or they may undergo marked transformations in response to physical, chemical, and biotic processes. Many of the most important reactions are transformations between dissolved and particulate forms. These processes include (1) adsorption or desorption upon particle surfaces; (2) coagulation, flocculation, and precipitation; and (3) biotic assimilation or excretion. Biotic processes can readily alter the chemical composition of estuarine waters, and this will be discussed further in subsequent sections.

3.2.2   Behavior of Dissolved Ions: Adsorption and Flocculation

Direct adsorption of dissolved ions to estuarine silts is particularly important for highly charged anions such as phosphate (PO_4^{3-}). For example, Jitts (1959)

TABLE 3.1 Estimated Composition of Dissolved Constituents in World Wide Average Sea and River Water[a]

		Sea Water		River Water	
Constituent		Concentration (mg/l)	Rank	Concentration (mg/l)	Rank
		Major Ions[b]			
Chloride	$(Cl-)$	19,340	1	8	5
Sodium	$(Na+)$	10,770	2	6	6
Sulfate	(SO_4^{2-})	2,712	3	11	4
Magnesium	(Mg^{2+})	1,294	4	4	7
Calcium	(Ca^{2+})	412	5	15	2
Potassium	(K^+)	399	6	2	8
Bicarbonate	(HCO_3^-)	140	7	58	1
Bromide	(Br^-)	65	8	—	—
Strontium	(Sr^+)	9	9	—	—
		Trace Elements mg/l			
Boron	(B)	4,500	1	10	15
Silicon	(Si)	(5,000)	2	13,100	3
Fluoride	(F)	1,400	3	100	12
Nitrogen	(N)	(250)	4	230	11
Phosphorus	(P)	(35)	5	20	13
Molybdenum	(Mo)	11	6	1	18
Zinc	(Zn)	5	7	20	14
Iron	(Fe)	3	8	670	9
Copper	(Cu)	3	9	7	17
Manganese	(Mn)	2	10	7	16
Nickle	(Ni)	2	11	0.3	19
Aluminum	(Al)	1	12	$(400)^b$	10

[a]After Nicol 1960, Burton 1976, and Liss 1976. Designations, major ions, and trace elements are with respect to sea water, and separate rankings are given for sea water in both designations, while a single combined ranking is used for river water.
[b]Median values given in parentheses.

showed that 80-90% of the PO_4^{3-} entering an Australian estuary during runoff periods could be trapped in that estuarine basin, depending on the iron and organic matter contents of those silts. Both *flocculation* (e.g., coalescing of colloidal particles less than 1 mm into larger aggregates) and *adsorption* (the "sticking of chemical ions on particles") appear to be a function of salinity, and therefore these processes vary along the estuarine salinity gradient. Suspended silts, clays, and colloidal humic acids, which are transported into an estuary via river flow, tend to carry negative electrovalent charges (Duinker 1980). In fresh water, repulsion between the negatively charged particles dominates, so that stable suspensions are formed. But with increasing salinity, the interparticle forces become attractive, so that when particles collide they agglomerate into flocs which may settle to the bottom. The destabilization of the once stable suspensions is thought to occur from the neutralization of the negative charges on the suspended materials as they enter increasingly saline waters with higher ionic strength, which allows the attractive van der Waals forces to dominate as particles continue to collide. This process of flocculation as a result of change in charge has been shown to occur between 0 and 5 ppt salinity (Duinker 1980, Stumm and Morgan 1972), and this process coupled with estuarine circulation patterns provides an important mechanism for entrapping chemicals entering estuaries into estuarine sediments.

Two essentially different approaches have been used to investigate the physical and chemical removal of dissolved and particulate substances from river (or sea) water during estuarine mixing. These are the *reactant* and the *product* approaches (Sholkovitch 1976, Liss 1976, Burton 1976, Duinker 1980). The reactant approach compares the *observed* distribution of a given dissolved constituent entering the estuary with that *predicted* from the simple mixing of river and seawater while assuming that the constituent is conserved (i.e., the total amount is unchanged). This technique is most useful when the concentrations of the constituent are markedly different at the two end members of the mixing zone (i.e., river and sea). The conservative index of mixing most commonly used in this method is salinity, where the riverine salinity is markedly lower than that of the oceanic source. Thus a plot of the constituent concentration versus salinity (called a mixing diagram) will yield a straight, sloping line if the constituent behaves conservatively in the estuary, while convex or concave lines indicate that the estuary is acting as a net source or sink, respectively, for that constituent (Fig. 3.1a–c). Several mixing diagrams for various dissolved constituents and estuaries are provided as examples in Fig. 3.1. In these examples we find evidence of the estuary acting as a sink for iron, phosphate, and, during the summer, for silicon and nitrate (Figs. 3.1d, e, f, h). Internal sources of ammonium are apparent in the summer (Fig. 3.1i). In winter, silicon and nitrate behave conservatively (Figs. 3.1f, h). Manganese exhibits very complex behavior.

There are two basic assumptions (Boyle et al. 1974) involved in using the reactant approach: (1) the concentration and flux of the constituent at the riverine end member are constant over the mixing time; and (2) there are only two significant end-member sources of the constituent (i.e., no tributaries). It has been demonstrated recently by analytical modeling (Loder and Reichard 1981) that changing concentrations of riverine input can result in a curved mixing diagram even if the constituent behaves conservatively. In addition, the method has been criticized by Sholkovitch (1976) because it provides no insight into the mechanism of removal nor to the nature of the product removed (e.g., suspended particulates or bottom sediments).

In the alternative product approach developed by Sholkovitz (1976), river water is mixed with varying amounts of seawater to yield a series with salinities

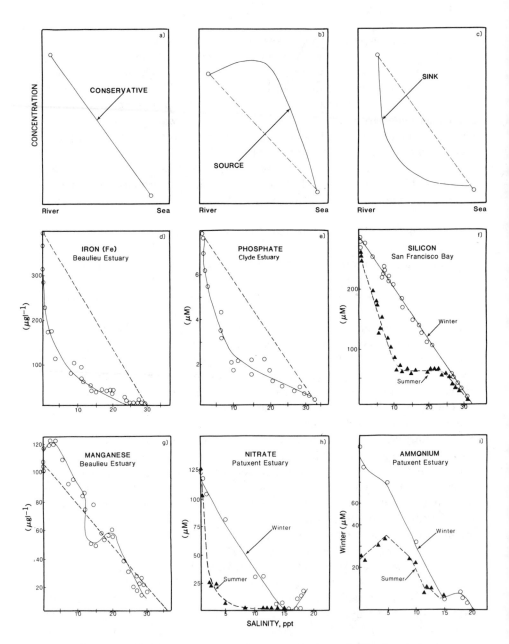

Figure 3.1 Mixing diagrams. The top three panels show idealized patterns for conservative mixing (a), and when an estuary acts as a source (b) or a sink (c) for a particular material. See text for discussion of individual estuaries. Data for San Francisco Bay from Peterson et al. (1975); for the Beaulieu Estuary, used with permission from P. Liss (1976); for the Clyde Estuary, used with permission from D. MacKay and T. Leatherland (1976); both from Estuarine Chemistry, Copyright: Academic Press Inc. (London) Ltd.; for the Patuxent Estuary, used with permission from D. Flemer (unpublished).

from about 0–30 ppt. The concentration of various constituents is measured in the flocculent material that results from these mixtures. It has been shown that metals such as Fe, Mn, Al, and P typically are removed rapidly from solution by flocculation between 0 and about 18 ppt (Fig. 3.2). The removal appears to be closely associated with flocculation of humic acids and hydrous iron oxides. While this method is very useful in quantifying the removal of dissolved substances by this one mechanism, it is obviously inappropriate for estimating overall behavior of any substance for which other mechanisms, such as sediment-water interactions, are important. Thus a combination of reactant and product approaches can be especially useful.

3.3   REDOX REACTIONS AND THE CHEMISTRY OF ESTUARINE SEDIMENTS

3.3.1   Oxidation—Reduction Reactions

Much of the particulate organic matter carried to an estuary by rivers, as well as that produced *in situ* by phytoplankton, seagrass, and marshes, eventually comes to rest on the sediment surface. This material provides the primary energy source (which can be viewed chemically as *electron donors*) for organisms living in the environment. The respiratory processes of these organisms are essentially oxidation—reduction (redox) reactions involving a variety of oxidizing agents (*electron acceptors*). Such redox reactions are defined as the transfer of electrons from one material to another, and much of the energy flow in estuarine sediments is regulated by the availability of suitable electron acceptors. Oxygen gas (O_2) is the most important electron acceptor in the biosphere, but, at the bottom of a deep estuarine water column, far from the atmospheric source of oxygen, supplies of this oxidant may be exhausted, especially when stratification reduces the rate of replenishment from above. Thus as we move down into sediments, oxygen is rapidly depleted and other electron acceptors, such as sulfate (SO_4^{2-}), become significant. The major product of sulfate reduction is hydrogen sulfide, which gives salt marsh soils their characteristic pungent smell.

Both solid and liquid phases of various substances exist in estuarine sediments, where aqueous solutions fill the interstices or pores between adjacent sediment particles. Many redox reactions are relatively slow, and this, combined with incomplete mixing or insufficient diffusion, tends to keep such reactions away from chemical equilibrium. The primary mechanism by which ions move within sediments is molecular diffusion, although disturbances by burrowing animals and rising gas bubbles may facilitate this process. In general, conditions are more oxidized near the sediment—water interface and more reduced deeper in the sediments. The term *redox potential* (E_h) refers to the relative degree of oxidation and reduction in a chemical environment, and higher values indicate more oxidized conditions (see Apendix 3.1). Superimposed upon the major vertical redox gradients are microscopic gradients, where markedly different redox

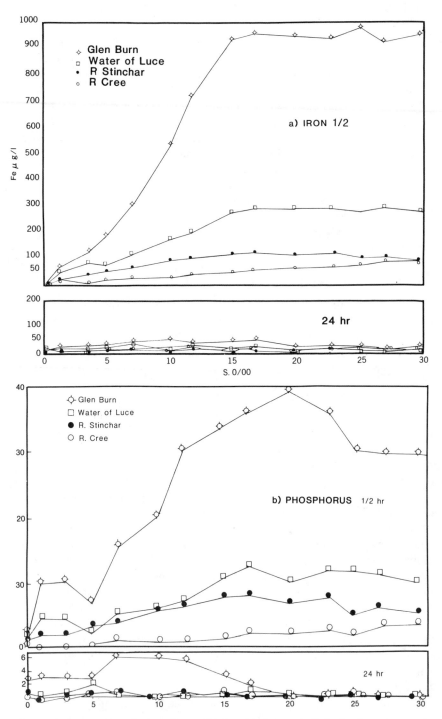

Figure 3.2 Iron (a) and phosphorus (b) flocculation vs. salinity for four river waters, showing the effect of increasing salt content in removing materials from fresh waters. Flocculant concentrations are given for 1/2 hr and 24 hr after mixing with sea water. From Sholkovitch (1976).

conditions may exist in close proximity. All chemical reactions influence the redox potential of the environment, and these reactions are, in turn, affected by existing redox conditions (i.e., the relative quantity of potential electron donors and acceptors). Many redox processes are not coupled directly because of spatial separations and kinetic considerations. Thus we see that estuarine sediments are extremely dynamic chemical systems.

Redox potential is the term commonly used to indicate the relative availability (or activity) of electrons in a particular chemical environment. Because there are no free electrons *per se* in the environment, every oxidation that occurs must be accompanied by a reduction. As the result of electron transfers in redox reactions, the oxidation states of reactants and products change. The oxidation state (or number) of a given atom represents the charge that it would have if the ion or molecule of which it is a part were to dissociate from other atoms in a constituent molecule.

3.3.2 Vertical Gradients in Sediments

There is a predictable sequence of respiratory chemical processes, so that different strata in the sediments are characterized by different electron acceptors (Fig. 3.3). Generally, oxygen is the most important oxidizing agent at the surface,

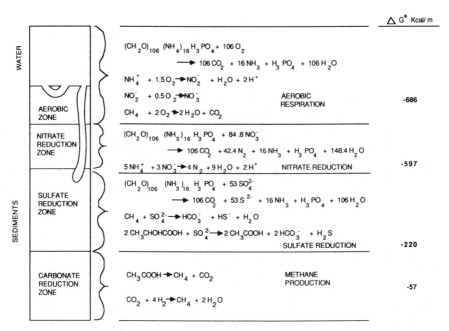

Figure 3.3 Observed sequence of mircobially mediated reactions in estuarine sediment, including stoichiometric decomposition equations (Martens 1978).

while somewhere in the 0–4 cm depth region nitrate (NO_3^-) is the preferred electron acceptor, followed by sulfate (SO_4^{2-}) and carbonate (mostly CO_2) over the
next 10–50 cm. The depth where free oxygen disappears and hence E_h goes to
zero is called the *redox discontinuity layer,* RDL (Fig. 3.4*a*). Most of the biological energy flux in estuarine sediments is confined to these four zones, and this
sequence follows the respective free-energy yields for these four redox reactions
(Fig. 3.3). Aerobic respiration will predominate as long as oxygen remains, since
the other three processes are strictly anaerobic. The remainder of this sequence
can be explained in terms of the relative abilities of mediating organisms to compete for organic and other reduced substrates such as H_2. However, other factors
such as end-product (e.g., H_2S) toxicity may be involved as well (Martens 1978).
Further discussion of the specific respiratory processes will be given
subsequently.

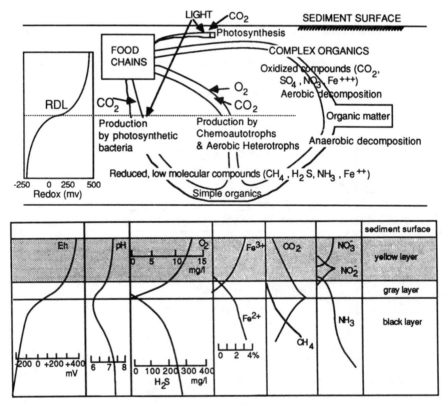

Figure 3.4 Schematic representation of energy flow and some major microbial processes (a), and vertical profiles of E_h, pH, and several chemical species (b) in estuarine
sediments in the vicinity of the redox potential discontinuity (RDL) layer (from Fenchel
and Riedl 1970).

The relative importance of these and other processes occurring in estuarine sediments to the flow of ecological energy for a generalized estuary is suggested in Fig. 3.4a. Here, we see that microbial heterotrophic production in both the aerobic and anoxic zones provides food for benthic invertebrates. Some of the reduced respiratory products (e.g., H_2S, NH_4^+, CH_4) also serve as energy sources for chemoautotrophic bacteria that refix carbon into organic matter, some of which enters estuarine food chains (see Chapter 7).

3.4 DIAGENESIS

The overall transformation of particulate material deposited on estuarine sediments is often referred to as diagenesis ("early" diagenesis refers to processes occurring in the upper portion of the sediments). The rates and results of diagenetic processing can be investigated by examining vertical profiles of particulate materials and establishing a time—depth relationship by measuring sediment deposition rates. Diagenetic chemical processes are understood more readily, however, by studying the liquid phase (pore waters) in temporal and spatial dimensions. This is because the changes in concentrations of ions and compounds as a result of diagenesis tend to be relatively large in pore waters compared with the changes in particulate materials (Presley and Trefry 1980).

Some typical vertical profiles of E_h, pH and various dissolved chemical species are given in Fig. 3.4b for a hypothetical estuarine sediment. The vertical zonation of the four respiratory processes discussed above are evident in terms of distributions of O_2, NO_3^-, H_2S, and CH_4, although the zonation is blurred somewhat by diffusive transport. The resulting large and continual reduction in E_h and smaller changes in pH are evident here. Various metals such as iron (Fe) also serve as electron acceptors, resulting in changes in oxidation number. To some extent the vertical zonation is apparent as changes in color the of the mud, largely due to oxidation and reduction of iron. By examining a cut-away box core of these sediments, one can see that the upper few centimeters (or less) are colored brown from iron oxides and hydroxides. This is related to the process that makes iron anchors brown with rust. The deepest part of the mud core is shaded black from the reduced species, ferrous sulfide (FeS) and pyrite (FeS_2), while the region in between is greyish colored from other iron–sulfur compounds. The critical plant nutrients nitrogen (as NH_4^+) and phosphorus (as PO_4^{3-}) are released in the oxidation of organic matter both aerobically and anaerobically (SO_4^{2-} reduction), and these processes will be discussed below.

3.4.1 Measuring Diagenesis

Knowledge of the vertical profiles in pore-water concentrations of various ions can be used to calculate rates of diagenetic chemical transformations. Simple one-dimensional (depth) diagenetic models are often used to estimate the vertical flux of a given constituent,

$$\frac{\delta C}{\delta t} = D \frac{\delta^2 C}{\delta x^2} - \omega \frac{\delta C}{\delta x} + R(C) \qquad (1)$$

where C is the concentration of the constituent (such as NH_4), x is the depth dimension, t is time ($\delta C/\delta t$ = flux of C at any point along x), D is the diffusion coefficient, ω is the rate of deposition of sediment particles, and $R(C)$ is the net rate of all chemical reactions influencing C (Berner 1980). The first term on the right-hand side represents simple Fickian diffusion while the second indicates advective transport of C. Coupled redox reactions can be considered together by developing separate equations for each species involved and considering all relevant reactions. However, the equations can also be simplified by making assumptions such as steady state ($\delta C/\delta t = 0$), or that advection is unimportant. Often the flux of a substance across the sediment-water interface is of interest, and this can be estimated (assuming no advection and steady-state conditions) by integrating Eq. 1.

$$\text{flux} = \frac{\delta C}{\delta t} = D\left(\frac{\delta c}{\delta x}\right)_{x=0} \qquad (2)$$

Unfortunately, recent attempts to compare fluxes of NH_4^+, PO_4^{3-}, and other species estimated by diagenetic modeling with those measured directly have indicated that modeling may underestimate the actual flux by a factor of 2 to 20 (e.g., Kemp et al. 1982). The discrepancy may be due to (1) rapid remineralization at the surface which is not reflected in pore water profiles, (2) the acceleration of advection by methane bubbles, or (3) increased diffusion by bioturbation (the disruption of sediments by animal burrowing). The effects of bioturbation (Fig. 3.5a) on diffusion can be incorporated into these models by experimentally measuring D with and without burrowing animals; because bioturbation can increase $\delta C/\delta x$ (Fig. 3.5b). Recent experiments showed that the addition of the polychaete *Nereis virens* to estuarine sediments increased the ammonia evolving from sediments from 2 to 71 μmol NH_4^+ $m^{-2}h^{-1}$ (Henriksen et al. 1981). Here, comparison of simple models to actual observations has led to insights concerning the mechanism regulating diagenesis.

3.5 ANAEROBIC ENERGY FLUX: THE SULFUR CYCLE

We have shown that much of the biological energy fixed in estuarine photosynthesis is deposited on the sediments, and that much of this organic energy is utilized anaerobically by bacteria. The energy is used for bacterial production, some of which is passed on to invertebrates and fish via detrital food chains. Some of the energy is stored temporarily in reduced chemical ions and compounds through electron transfer in redox reactions, and some of the energy of these reduced compounds is passed on to food chains. Comprehensive measurements in estuarine muds and salt marsh peat has shown that much of the energy

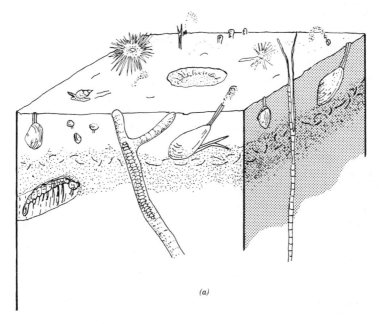

(a)

Figure 3.5a Schematic representation of major burrowing fauna from a sediment locality in Long Island Sound indicating the degree to which animals can alter the sediment structure (from Aller 1980, Berner 1980).

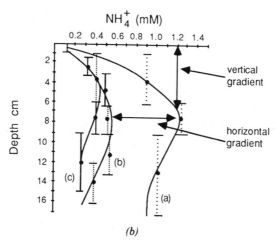

(b)

Figure 3.5b NH_4^+ concentration in pore water from two concentric sample intervals around one arm of an *A. ornata* burrow and from 30 cm away from burrow axis. a = 0.5–1.5 cm radial interval from burrow axis; b = 1.5–3.75 cm radial interval; c = surrounding sediment 30 cm from axis (After Aller and Yingst 1978). Each bar represents the depth interval over which the sample was taken. Note that NH_4^+ concentrations are higher near the oxygenated environment of the burrow.

flowing through these ecosystems is modulated through anaerobic microbial metabolism, especially that of the sulfur cycle.

By far the most abundant electron acceptor (or oxidizing agent) in most estuaries is sulfate (SO_4^{2-}), which is reduced to sulfide (S^{2-}). This is accomplished through two main pathways, assimilatory and dissimilatory (Fig. 3.6). *Assimilatory* reduction involves the uptake and biochemical incorporation of SO_4^{2-} into organic molecules (e.g., the amino acids methionine and cystine); sulfide is released through subsequent aerobic mineralization of these compounds (desulfuration). In estuarine muds the *dissimilatory* reduction is more important and it occurs as sulfate diffuses down into the anoxic zones, where organisms such as *Desulfovibrio* use it to oxidize organic substrates, producing elemental sulfur. Some of the sulfide may be trapped in the sediments by precipitation with metal ions such as iron, but much of it remains dissolved and diffuses to the aerobic surface strata. Here it is oxidized immediately back to SO_4^{2-} either spontane-

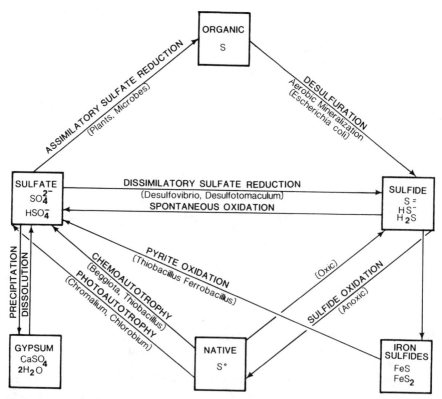

Figure 3.6 Transformations within the sulfur cycle in estuarine systems. Names in parentheses are organisms that carry out particular reactions.

ously (without biological mediation) or through catalysis by chemoautotrophic (in oxic sediments) or photoautotrophic (in anoxic sediments) bacteria, refixing organic carbon. A portion of the pyrite (FeS_2) formed in precipitation will be reoxidized to SO_4^{2-}, and other reactions with sediment minerals such as gypsum also occur.

These processes profoundly alter the sediment environment, and the influence of total sulfide concentration on sediment redox potential is evident in the data of Fig. 3.7. Here simultaneous measurements of sulfide, E_h and pH were taken by Fenchel (1969) in sediment and water environments containing decomposing seaweeds. The lines in Fig. 3.7a represent the predicted E_h based on chemical equilibrium calculations at a given sulfide level with no other redox reaction occurring. The general agreement between measured and calculated values for the observed range in pH suggest the dominant influence of sulfides on E_h.

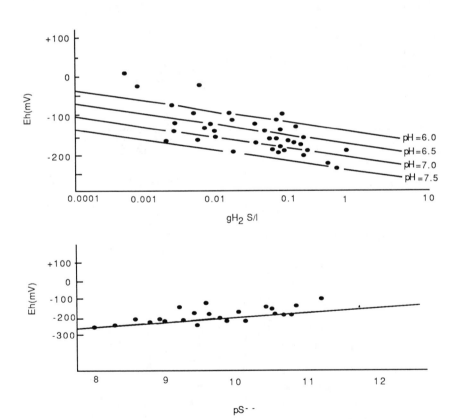

Figure 3.7 (a) The relationship betweeen H_2S contents and E_h in interstitial water (closed circles) and the theoretical values of E_h at different pH values (solid line). (b) The relation between E_h and pS in interstitial water (closed circles) and the theoretical relation between E_h and pS (solid line). From Fenchel 1969.

In most estuarine sediment environments both aerobic respiration and sulfate reduction generally appear to follow seasonal temperature cycles as shown in Fig. 3.8a. However, not all of the oxygen uptake by these sediments is attributable to aerobic respiration by both bacteria and invertebrates. In fact, Jørgensen (1977) estimated that in a Danish fjord (4–12 m depth) about 50% of the total sediment oxygen demand was due to sulfide oxidation. But there is a 1–2 month

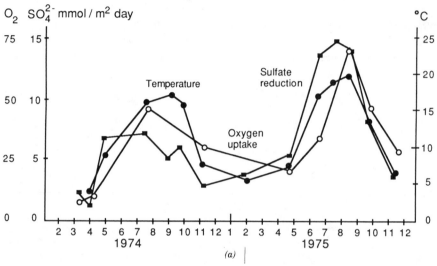

Figure 3.8a Seasonal variation in rate of sulfate reduction within upper 10 cm of the sediment, and dark oxygen uptake rate and temperature at the sediment surface in a Danish fjord (averages of all stations). From Jørgensen (1977).

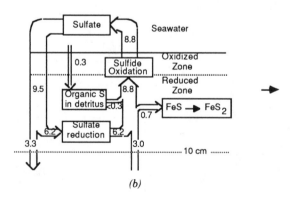

Figure 3.8b Sulfur cycle of the sediment. Figures indicate transfer rates in mmol Sm^{-2} d^{-1}, calculated as weighted averages over 2 yr for all stations. From Jørgensen (1977).

lag between peak sulfate reduction and peak oxygen consumption (Fig. 3.8a), because some of the oxygen uptake is due to the oxidation of previously reduced sulfur. Jørgensen developed an annual budget of sulfur cycling in this fjord (Fig. 3.8b), which shows that sulfide oxidation is large and nearly balances sulfate reduction. Precipitation of ferric sulfide (FeS) and pyrite (FeS_2), which can dominate oxygen uptake in other estuarine muds, are less important here. But there are currently few quantitative data to tell us how important autotrophic sulfide oxidation is in refixing organic carbon. We do know, however, that chemoautotrophic bacteria such as *Beggiatoa* are capable of rapid growth and bacterial mats of up to 4 g dry wt/m^2 have been measured in this Danish estuary.

It now appears that roughly half the total respiration in many estuarine sediments is associated with sulfate reduction. Recent measurements of sulfate reduction in a salt marsh peat in Massachusetts suggest that an actual majority of the organic matter fixed in photosynthesis is channeled into the sulfur cycle (Howarth and Teal 1979, 1980).

While sulfate reduction is probably important in most estuarine sediments, it is not always the dominant respiratory pathway. For example, in shallow (0.5 m) Danish estuarine sediments, it was found that only about 10–30% of the respiratory energy flux was associated with sulfur, and aerobic respiration was dominant in both winter and summer (Fig. 3.9, Sørensen et al. 1979). Anaerobic respiration via NO_3^- reduction (denitrification) was substantially less important than that via sulfur in the energy budget of these sediments for the warmer months. In winter, however, when NO_3^- concentrations are relatively high and commmunity metabolism is limited by low temperatures, NO_3^- reduction contributed over 20% to the total metabolism of the sediments. In this system, as in most estuarine sediments, denitrification and sulfate reduction are spatially separate, with denitrification occurring closer to the sediment surface. Denitrification is of further importance in terms of cycling the essential plant nutrient nitrogen.

In most estuarine environments another anaerobic process that contributes to sediment metabolism is methane production from reduction of carbon dioxide or acetate. This process, however, is considerably less important than either sulfate reduction or aerobic respiration because, just as the presence of oxygen precludes sulfate reduction, the presence of SO_4^{2-} inhibits CH_4 production (Martens and Berner 1977). There are exceptions, however. Some estuarine sediments experiencing rapid rates (10 cm/yr) of organic matter deposition, such as those of Cape Lookout Bight, North Carolina (Martens and Klump 1980), produce substantial amounts of CH_4 (summer rates of 320 mmol $m^{-2}h^{-1}$, Martens and Klump 1980). Only a small percentage (~1%) of this CH_4 is reoxidized by chemoautotrophic bacteria (Iversen and Blackburn 1981, Sansone and Martens 1978). Salt marsh peats may also produce CH_4 at relatively high rates comparable to those at Cape Lookout Bight (e.g., Lipschultz 1981); however, even these rates are only 1–2% of sulfate reduction rates reported for a New England marsh ecosystem (Howarth and Teal 1979).

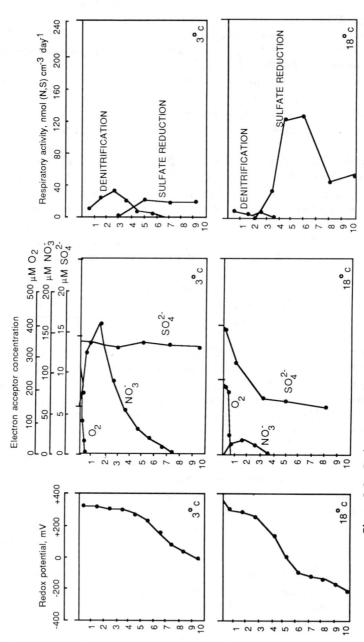

Figure 3.9 Redox potentials, concentrations of oxygen, nitrate, and sulfate, and activity of denitrification and sulfate reduction during winter (3°C) and summer (18°C) in Randers Fjord, Denmark (from Sørensen et al. 1979).

3.6 METABOLIC GASES

A number of important substances in estuarine ecosystems occur primarily as gases, including oxygen (O_2), carbon dioxide (CO_2), nitrogen (N_2), methane (CH_4), hydrogen sulfide (H_2S), ammonia (NH_3), and nitrous oxide (N_2O). These gases are reactants and products in various key metabolic processes involving estuarine organisms, and in this section we discuss various physical and chemical factors affecting the behavior of these gases, focusing on O_2 and CO_2. We dealt with H_2S and CH_4 in the previous section in relation to sediment diagenesis, while N_2, NH_3, and N_2O will be discussed subsequently with nutrient cycling.

3.6.1 Atmospheric Composition and Physical Factors

Over 99% of the earth's atmosphere is comprised of two gases, N_2 and O_2. Carbon dioxide is also relatively abundant, at 0.034%. Table 3.2 gives the eleven most abundant atmospheric gases. Five of these, the noble gases (Ar, Ne, He, Kr, and Xe), behave conservatively in estuarine and other environments. Their nonreactive chemical nature makes them excellent tracers to compare with other gases to detect transformations of the latter. Thus, for example, the departure of N_2: Ar ratios from atmospheric proportions (83.6:1) provides an index of relative rates of net N_2 fixation and denitrification.

The concentrations of gases that can occur in estuarine water depends in part on their respective solubilities, which can be expressed in terms of their Bunsen coefficient (α). This is the volume of the pure gas at 1 atm pressure (of that gas) that can be dissolved in a unit volume of water at standard temperature and pressure. The solubility of a gas in an estuary is also a function of pressure, salinity, and temperature. The effect of pressure is dictated by Henry's law, where the solubility of a gas (C_s, ml/l) is directly proportional to the partial pressure (P) it exerts in the gaseous phase,

TABLE 3.2 Proportions of Nonvariable Gases in the Atmosphere[a]

Gas	Partial Pressure (atm)	Gas	Partial Pressure (atm)
N_2	0.7808	Kr	1.14×10^{-6}
O_2	0.2095	Xe	8.7×10^{-8}
CO_2	0.000340	H_2	5×10^{-7}
Ar	0.00934	CH_4	2×10^{-6}
Ne	1.82×10^{-5}		
He	5.24×10^{-6}	N_2O	5×10^{-7}

[a]From Riley and Chester 1965.

$$C_S = 1000\alpha(P) \tag{3}$$

The presence of dissolved ions (salinity, S) in estuarine water lowers the solubility of atmospheric gases according to the following:

$$ln(\alpha) = b_1 - b_2 S \tag{4}$$

The solubility of gases also decreases with elevated temperature

$$ln(\alpha) = K(1/T) \tag{5}$$

where K is a coefficient characteristic of the particular physical attributes of that system and T is absolute temperature. Whereas P is relatively constant, salinity and temperature vary continually in an estuary.

The transfer of a gas between the atmosphere and the water in an estuary is a dynamic process driven by the turbulence in the air and water bodies, the departure of the water from saturation conditions, and the molecular diffusion coefficient for the particular gas. Gas flux (dQ/dt, mg m^{-2}h^{-1}) across the air–water interface is given by

$$\frac{dQ}{dt} = A(D)(1/d_z)(C - C_s) \tag{6}$$

where A is the surface area, d_z is the thickness of a hypothetical film separating gas and liquid, D is the molecular diffusivity, and C is the aqueous gas concentration. The term d_z is inversely proportional to water turbulence and wind speed. In practice, it is often convenient to combine (AD/d_z) into a single gas transfer coefficient (K_D), which is measured empirically, and to consider departure from saturation in terms of "saturation deficit" ($S_c = (C - C_s/C_s)$. Equation 6 then becomes

$$\frac{dQ}{dt} = K_D S_c \tag{7}$$

For dissolved oxygen, values of K_D range from about 0.1 to 2.5 mg O$_2$ m^{-2}h^{-1} atm^{-1} with lower values typical of shallow salt ponds and high ones occurring in turbulent or windy conditions. Although diffusion coefficients (D) do not vary greatly for different atmospheric gases, the actual flux (dQ/dt) for a given partial pressure can be very different because of variations in solubilities. For example, the mass transfer between air and water for O$_2$ would be twice that for N$_2$, while for CO$_2$ it would be 70 times the N$_2$ flux.

3.6.2   The Carbon Dioxide System

The behavior of carbon dioxide in estuarine and other natural waters is markedly different from that of other gases in that it reacts with the water itself. In doing so the CO_2-water system establishes a chemical equilibrium (see below) which in turn imparts special properties to the aquatic system. Before discussing the carbon dioxide system we shall review some pertinent concepts of aquatic chemistry.

In a sense, the chemical composition of the ocean is the result of a great acid-base titration, where acids have leaked from the earth's interior and bases have been released by weathering of primary rock (Sillen 1961). Acid-base reactions involve the transfer of one or more protons (hydrogen ions, H^+), and these transfers generally occur rapidly. Acids are often defined according to the Bronsted-Lowry theory as substances that can donate a proton, while bases are substances that can accept protons in a chemical reaction. A measure of the relative acidity or basicity of a solution is provided by pH.

$$pH = -\log[H^+] \tag{8}$$

where pH ranges from 0 to 14 in aqueous environments, and pH $= 7$ is considered neutral. The relative strength of an acid or base depends on the tendency for proton donation and acceptance in the same system, and in aquatic systems the solvent H_2O is used as the "standard" base or acid.

An important approximation used to describe chemical reactions in nature is the concept of chemical equilibrium. In chemical equilibria reactants and products are interchangeable, and concentrations of each remain constant with time. In natural systems equilibria exist only ephemerally, and are continually disrupted by exchanges with regions outside the site of the reaction. Nevertheless the relative concentrations of reactants and products in acid-base reactions at equilibrium can be illustrated conveniently using diagrammatic presentations of reactant-product concentration versus pH. We will describe the CO_2-water equilibrium discussed below in terms of one such diagram.

When CO_2 is allowed to equilibrate with water a sequence of equilibrium reactions is established. The equations for these chemical reactions are

$$CO_2 \text{ (gas)} + H_2O \rightleftharpoons CO_2 \text{ (solute)} + H_2O \tag{9}$$

$$CO_2 \text{ (solute)} + H_2O \rightleftharpoons H_2CO_3 \tag{10}$$

$$H_2CO_3 \rightleftharpoons HCO_3^- + H^+ \tag{11}$$

$$HCO_3^- \rightleftharpoons CO_3^{2-} + H^+ \tag{12}$$

The arrows in both directions for each equation indicate that the equilibrium concentrations and the direction of the reaction vary depending on the relative concentrations of substances on the left and right sides of each equation. The first reaction (Eq. 9) is simply a solution equilibrium. The processes of hydration and dehydration (Eq. 10) are slow first-order reactions, but they can be stimulated biochemically by the presence of the enzyme carbonic anhydrase. Once the carbonic acid (H_2CO_3) is formed, it undergoes nearly instantaneous ionizations or dissociations (Eqs. 11 and 12). Since these two reactions involve the release of protons (H^+), and since all four reactions are interconnected, the relative balance among species in this system is controlled by pH.

The quantitative nature of equilibrium reactions such as these can be described in terms of dissociation constants, which are the ratio of concentrations of products to concentrations of reactants. Thus for the CO_2-water system the dissociation of H_2CO_3 (Eqs. 11 and 12) is defined by two constants:

$$K_1' = \frac{[H^+][HCO_3^-]}{[H_2CO_3]} \tag{13}$$

$$K_2' = \frac{[H^+][CO_3^{2-}]}{[HCO_3^-]} \tag{14}$$

where the brackets indicate concentration and the primes indicate that these are apparent K's since chemical activities are not considered. Strictly speaking, Eqs. 13 and 14 should be expressed in terms of chemical activity, which is related to concentration, interactions among ions and other factors. For our purposes we consider concentration to be the dominant factor determining activity, but the interested student is encouraged to consult other sources (e.g., Stumm and Morgan 1972) for further explanation. The importance of pH in controlling CO_2 equilibrium species is illustrated in Fig. 3.10, where the percentage of total CO_2 (TCO_2) as H_2CO_3, HCO_3^- and CO_3^{2-} is shown at various pH's. Thus, in seawater at its normal pH range of 7.8-8.3, HCO_3^- is by far the dominant form of TCO_2. The dissociation constants are also illustrated here as the intersections of H_2CO_3/HCO_3^- and HCO_3^-/CO_3^{2-} curves, respectively, where $pK' = -\log K'$.

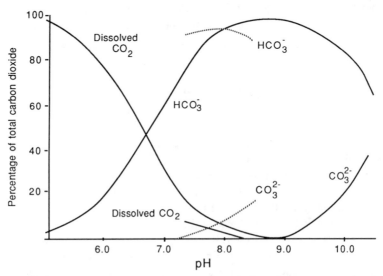

Figure 3.10 Percentages of dissolved carbon dioxide, bicarbonate ion, and carbonate ion as a function of pH at 0°C. Solid line is distilled water; dotted line is sea water (Cl = 20‰) (from Riley and Chester 1971).

3.6.3   Calculating Carbon Species

Only two variables in the CO_2-water system (Eqs. 9–12) can be measured directly—TCO_2 and CO_2 (solute). All others must be estimated indirectly from pH measurements and relationships such as Fig. 3.10 and Eqs. 13 and 14. In equilibrium systems such as this one, concentrations of various species shift in accordance with Eqs. 13 and 14 whenever a given species is added or removed from the aqueous environment. Thus an addition of CO_2 (as from respiration) will cause the equilibrium to change with the consequence of more protons $[H^+]$ being released, and consequently the pH declines. However, in estuarine waters with considerable TCO_2 some of the effect of adding this acid (CO_2) is absorbed by the formation of intermediate species (H_2CO_3, HCO_3^-), producing a reduced response of pH compared to what would occur in pure water. This "buffering effect" is very important in sea water, where pH rarely occurs outside the range of 7.8 to 8.3. In estuaries there is somewhat less TCO_2, owing to river water dilution; however, the effect is still strong and pH is generally between 7.5 and 8.8. In estuarine and marine sediments this buffering effect may be swamped by the typically high concentrations of acids such as NH_4^+ and HS^-. The buffering capacity (B) of an estuarine oceanic system dominated by dissolved CO_2 is defined by

$$B = \frac{d(TCO_2)}{d(pH)} \tag{15}$$

On a geological time scale, the pH of the sea may also be controlled by equilibria involving suspended clay minerals, where cation exchange sites in the crystalline lattice structure provide a means of buffering against sharp increases or decreases in $[H^+]$.

The general alkaline nature of oceanic and estuarine water is due to the presence of bicarbonate, carbonate, and borate ions. These ions, along with hydroxyls (OH^-), are regarded as bases because they are able to accept protons. The term "alkalinity" is used in natural waters to describe the degree to which the water accepts protons, and it is defined as the sum of concentrations of four ions (HCO_3^-, CO_3^{2-}, BO_3^{2-}, OH^-) minus $[H^+]$. In the pH range 5.5–8.5 the OH^- and H^+ terms can be ignored. As a first approximation, the concentration of borate $[BO_3^{2-}]$ can also be ignored for pH > 8.0, and the term "carbonate alkalinity" is often used to describe the summed concentrations of the remaining ions. Alkalinity is generally conservative in its behavior with respect to salinity, since TCO_2 is so large compared with rates of CO_2 production and consumption, and also relative to precipitation reactions involving CO_3^{2-}.

Carbonate reacts readily with calcium in estuaries to form various crystals of calcium carbonate, $CaCO_3$. Two crystalline forms are common, calcite (rhombohedral) and the unstable aragonite (orthorhombic), the latter form being substantially less soluble. Various organisms accelerate the precipitation of $CaCO_3$, and various species sequester different crystalline and chemical forms of this precipitate. The precipitate is used by many benthic invertebrate organisms to form the shells or tests which protect them from predators and environmental rigors. Molluscs, bryozoans, corals, sponges, foraminifera, echinoderms, and ostracods as well as several species of algae all secrete $CaCO_3$ for their hard parts. Organisms such as oysters accelerate $CaCO_3$ precipitation by various mechanisms, including enzymatic processes and local increases in CO_2 which shift the equilibrium toward CO_3^{2-}. Magnesium is commonly enriched in the shells of such organisms, where it is found as $MgCO_3$.

3.6.4   Biological Effects on O_2 and CO_2 Concentrations

While CO_2 is the fourth most abundant gas in the earth's atmosphere, only 2% is stored there compared to the quantity dissolved in the oceans. This in turn is dwarfed by the carbon stored in rocks, carbonate sediments, and living and dead organic matter. The concentration of CO_2 in the atmosphere is increasing now at a rate of about 0.3% per year because of the burning of fossil fuels and plant biomass. However, there is currently a debate among meteorologists, oceanographers, and ecologists as to the ultimate sources and sinks of global CO_2 (e.g., Broecker et al. 1980, Detwiler and Hall 1988). This is of particular importance in light of the so-called "greenhouse effect," whereby the temperature of earth's atmosphere could increase owing to increased absorption of back-radiation by CO_2. The consequences of such a trend could be a melting of the polar ice caps and would lead to the destruction or at least movement of present-day estuaries. The interested student is encouraged to consult Broecker et al. (1980) and Detwiler and Hall (1988) for further explanation of this problem. It is of critical importance to understand the carbonate system of aquatic systems to understand how change in atmospheric chemistry will ultimately affect climate.

Temporal and spatial variations in concentrations of O_2 and dissolved CO_2 can be used to estimate rates of biological production and consumption of organic matter in aquatic ecosystems. Since dissolved CO_2 cannot be measured directly, it is necessary to estimate it by measuring pH and applying theoretical relationships between pH, alkalinity, and TCO_2, or by empirically calibrating TCO_2 with pH via titration (Beyers et al. 1963). Diel changes in pH and oxygen can then be used to indicate production and consumption, where daytime increases in oxygen and pH (decreases in CO_2) represent photosynthetic production, and decreases at night provide a measure of community respiration (Fig. 3.11, Hall and Moll, 1975).

Oceanographers have utilized spatial and seasonal distributions of oxygen in relation to physical variables such as velocity, temperature, and salinity to infer rates of biotic production and (especially) consumption. In relatively "stagnant" water masses virtually disconnected from the atmosphere by vertical density stratification, long-term changes in oxygen versus conservative tracers of water masses such as salinity can be used to estimate consumption. When oxygen concentrations depart from conservative mixing in deeper waters it also provides an approach for estimating indirectly *apparent oxygen utilization* (AOU), a measure of respiration.

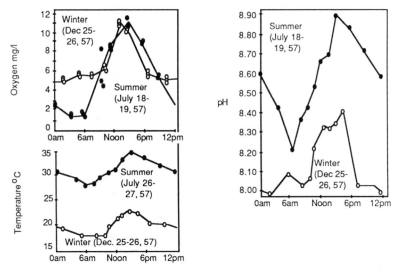

Figure 3.11 Diurnal oxygen, pH, and temperature variations at Redfish Bay, Texas. Closed circles show summer data for July 18–19, 1957. Open circles are winter data for December 5–6, 1957 (from Park et al. 1958).

Such techniques are less useful in estuarine waters because of the dynamic nature of physical circulation. Interpretation of these data for inferring biological processes involves various assumptions and corrections for gas transfer across the air-water interface, and these have been discussed extensively (e.g., Odum 1959, Beyers and Odum 1959, Kemp and Boynton 1980). In many estuarine environments physical processes move water masses extensively and hence can dominate observed diel variations in oxygen (or pH) at any one place, complicating interpretation. This was indicated for the North River in the beginning of the chapter. An example of the relative contributions of horizontal dispersion (H), vertical diffusion (D_z), air-water transfer (D_e) production (P), and respiration (R) on diel budgets of oxygen at a station (6 m) in Chesapeake Bay is provided in Fig. 3.12. Here we see that biological processes accounted for 43–69% of observed inputs to and outputs from a water column in June and September, while horizontal dispersion exerted a similar influence (11–53%). Normally upstream-downstream methods (see Hall and Moll 1975) could correct for this, but this is not well developed in estuaries.

An important environmental problem in vertically stratified estuaries is that bottom waters often go anoxic during summer conditions. The rate of oxygen depletion can be used to estimate respiratory consumption given sufficient knowledge of physical circulation. In coastal plain estuaries such as Chesapeake Bay and its tributaries, there is some indirect evidence that increased inputs of organic matter and plant nutrients from human activities have contributed to increasing the spatial and temporal extents of bottom water anoxia. An example

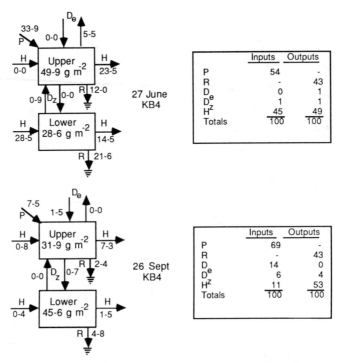

Figure 3.12 Summaries of oxygen budgets for a station in upper Chesapeake Bay on June 27 and September 26, 1977. Oxygen exchanges are given in g O_2d/L and relative contributions to the budget are given as percentages. P = production, R = respiration, D_e = air-water transfer, D_z = vertical diffusion, H = horizontal dispersion. Used with permission from Kemp and Boynton, 1980, Estuarine and Coastal Shelf Science. Copyright: Academic Press Inc. (London) Ltd.

of this increasing anoxia trend is provided in Fig. 3.13, where conditions in bottom waters low in or devoid of oxygen have spread up the estuary during the early summer.

3.7   THE AUTOTROPHIC NUTRIENTS

The importance of nutrient fluxes in controlling the primary and secondary production of estuaries is becoming increasingly apparent now, and as more and more information is developed, perceptions of the relative roles of various transformation pathways are being modified and refined.

Among the most important chemical elements in the functioning of estuarine ecosystems are the autotrophic nutrients which serve as raw materials for the primary production of organic matter. The nutritional requirements of algae

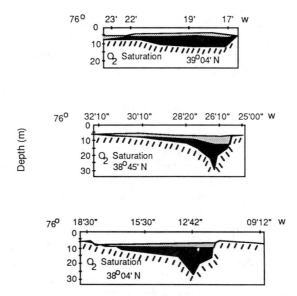

Figure 3.13 Summer oxygen saturation on three transects accross Chesapeake Bay. White = greater than 20% saturation, gray = 0–20% saturation, black = H$_2$S present. From Taft et al. (1980).

and other estuarine autotrophs are numerous, and although variable among different species, these include C, N, P, Si, S, K, Mg, Na, Ca, Fe, Mn, Zn, Cu, B, Mo, Co, V, and the vitamins thiamin, cyanocobalamin, and biotin (Hutchinson 1967). The first four of these are utilized most heavily in algal growth, although silicon is used only by diatoms. Since carbon is extremely abundant in estuarine waters, and the minor nutrients (sulfur to biotin in the list) are generally in adequate supply, nitrogen (N), phosphorus (P), and silicon (Si) are most likely to be found in insufficient quantities relative to algal requirements. Therefore, this section deals primarily with N, P, and Si, the so-called macronutrients.

Concentrations of these nutrients in estuaries are constantly changing in time and space due to inputs and outputs from river flows and oceanic exchange as well as biological uptake and regeneration. These nutrients are constantly cycling between organic and inorganic forms, as well as among different organic components in the food chain. It is axiomatic in ecology to think of nutrients (materials) being cycled in the biosphere while energy flows through it (from photons to organic matter to heat), and it is often the case that nutrient cycles can control energy flux. At the scale of a given ecosystem such as one estuary, nutrients and energy are both cycled within and passed through the system. Thus nutrient transformations and cycles are fundamental to an understanding of estuarine ecology.

Prior to the mid-1960s most information concerning estuarine nutrients was derived from measurements of spatial and temporal concentration distribution patterns. Within the last two decades, however, the development and use of radioactive and stable isotopic tracer techniques as well as other methods has enabled the measurement of rates of nutrient transformations among various chemical species between and within organic and inorganic forms.

3.7.1 Nutrient Forms and Distributions

The nutrients nitrogen, phosphorus, and silicon occur in estuarine environments in many forms which can be described in terms of oxidation state, solid-liquid-gas phase, chemical structure, or the analytical methods used for detection. The forms of nitrogen are most diverse. The oxidation state ranges from nitrate (NO_3^-, $+5$) to ammonium (NH_4^+, -3), and compounds exist in all states in between (Webb 1981). Organic nitrogen is highly reduced (-3) in cell protoplasm and in such compounds as urea and amino acids. Inorganic phosphorus occurs most often as the phosphate ion (PO_4^{3-}) in an oxidation state of $+5$. While there are 3 structural configurations of phosphate (ortho, para, meta), the elemental composition is the same. Various organic phosphorus compounds occur at the same oxidation state in cellular materials and dissolved in the external environment. Silicon is present in estuaries in three principle forms: detrital quartz; aluminosilicate clays, and dissolved silicon. As with phosphorus, silicon occurs primarily in one oxidation state ($+4$), and the dissolved species is predominantly as silicic acid (H_4SiO_4).

Prior to discussing specific transformations and cycles of these nutrients we will examine how aqueous concentrations of selected nutrient species can vary at several scales in time and space. Much of this discussion will focus on nitrogen and phosphorus, because relatively fewer data are available for silicon. Seasonal cycles of NO_3^-, NH_4^+, and PO_4^{3-} in surface water samples for four very different estuaries are shown in Fig. 3.14. Some patterns related to internal cycling are quite similar among the four systems, even though they range from a river-dominated coastal plain estuary (Patuxent) to a coastal lagoon with little fresh water input (Chincoteague). For example, the mid-summer peak in PO_4^{3-} concentrations appearing in each estuary is probably the result of temperature-regulated respiratory regeneration and changes in sediment redox conditions. On the other hand, NO_3^- levels, which exhibit winter maxima in the river-influenced systems are controlled largely by external inputs to the estuary via land runoff. Concentrations of NH_4^+ are highest in the estuaries receiving major inputs of sewage (e.g., Patuxent and Narragansett); however, seasonal patterns seem to be more a function of the relative balance between phytoplankton uptake and benthic regeneration. Diel cycles of PO_4^{3-} and NO_3^- are occasionally evident owing to light-regulated uptake by phytoplankton, which produce low concentrations in the late morning and early afternoon and relatively high values late at night. Little evidence is available for daily cycles of NH_4^+.

We have already indicated (in effect) some of the possible spatial patterns of dissolved inorganic nutrients along the main axis of estuaries by plotting concen-

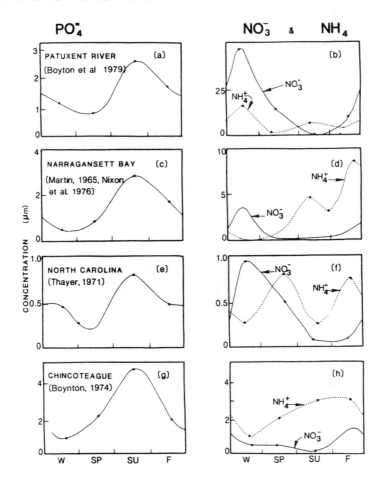

Figure 3.14 Some typical seasonal patterns of PO$_4$, NO$_3$, and NH$_4$ for (a, b) the Patuxent River, Maryland (from Boynton et al. 1979), (c, d) Narrangansett Bay, Rhode Island (from Martin 1965, Nixon et al. 1976), (e, f) a North Carolina sound (from Thayer 1971), and (g, h) Chincoteague Bay, Virginia (from Boynton, 1974).

tration versus salinity in mixing diagrams (Fig. 3.1). We saw a variety of these longitudinal profiles, where higher concentrations of NH$_4^+$, NO$_3^-$, PO$_4^{3-}$, and H$_4$SiO$_4$ generally occurred at the riverine end, with some evidence of net uptake or remineralization along the axis. When concentrations are graphed on a time-space map with distance from the head-of-tide to the mouth as the Y axis and months of the year on the X axis, we begin to see interactions between temporal and spatial patterns. Data are presented in this fashion for the Pamlico River estuary, North Carolina (Fig. 3.15), and upon close examination some interesting relations emerge. For example, a region of high PO_4^{3-} appears at 20–30 km during the mid-late summer period, thereby suggesting a definite locus of phosphorus regeneration. Concentrations of NH_4^+ exhibit both upstream and downstream gradients (October–November), probably representing river input and subsequent uptake and some internal recycling (August–September). NO_3^- occurs at high levels throughout the estuary during fall and winter (due to riverine input) with a zone of rapidly declining concentrations which migrates from 30 to 40 km in March to 5 km in July (due to biological uptake).

3.7.1.1 Patterns with Depth. We illustrated in a previous section vertical profiles of nutrient concentrations in the pore waters of estuarine sediments (Figs. 3.4 and 3.5). There was a general trend of increasing concentrations of NH_4^+ and PO_4^{3-} with depth because of relatively slow upward diffusion of these ions toward the sediment-water interface. Nitrate may exhibit peak concentrations at intermediate to near-surface depths (0-5 cm) due to nitrification in the sediments, or it may decrease from the surface into the sediments where levels are high in the water above, with high rates of NO_3^- reduction (to NH_4^+ or N_2) occurring in the sediments.

In deeper estuaries vertical profiles of NH_4^+ and PO_4^{3-} in the overlying water column often follow similar trends of increasing concentration with depth. This occurs when sediments are a significant source of recycled nutrients and vertical dispersion is reduced by density stratification (Fig. 3.16). When such stratification is broken down by major mixing events and mixing rates exceed regeneration rates, any trace of these gradients is lost. Nitrate and nitrite may exhibit any of a number of trends in the vertical dimension, for nitrification can occur in the water column as well.

3.7.2 Chemical Kinetics: The Key to Rates and Fluxes

To understand the cycle of nutrients in estuarine ecosystems that leads to the patterns discussed above, it is essential to examine the rates of biochemical transformations resulting from the metabolism of bacteria, algae, protozoa, and metazoan invertebrates. These transformations (e.g., between organic and inorganic forms or between various oxidation-reduction states) result in fluxes of nutrients between major components of the ecosystem, such as between sediment and water, which ultimately influence energy flow. A key to measuring and interpreting rates and fluxes is to understand the basic concepts of chemical kinetics. Therefore, we review briefly some important ideas in the field of chemical kinetics in Appendix 3.2.

3.7.3 Nutrient Assimilation

Dissolved inorganic salts (and some organic forms) of N, P, and Si are incorporated into particulate organic matter primarily via the assimilative processes of

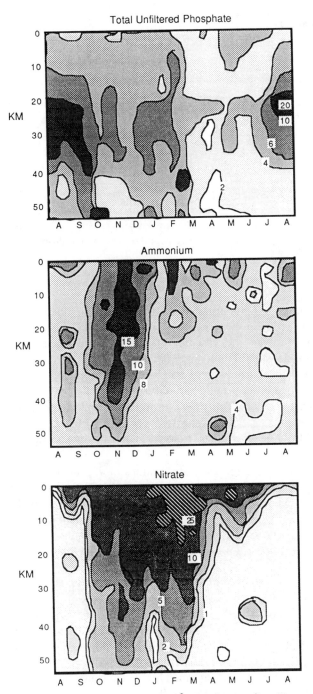

Figure 3.15 Isopleths of NO_3^-, NH_3, and PO_4^{3-} for the Pamlico River estuary, North Carolina, from August 1971 through August 1972, concentrations in mg at/l. The Y-axis is the distance (Km) from the river end of the transect (from Hobbie et al. 1975).

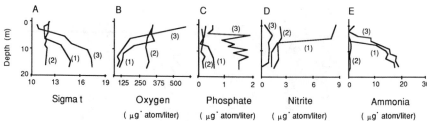

Figure 3.16 Depth profiles of (A) sigma t, (B) oxygen, (C) phosphate, (D) nitrite, and (E) ammonia for 10 August, 23 August, and 29 August 1978 in the York River estuary to show the effects of mixing. On 10 August the water column was stratified; the water was mixed on 23 August and by 29 August, it had restratified (from Webb and D'Elia 1980).

autotrophic photosynthetic organisms. We discuss the kinetics of nutrient uptake and assimilation elsewhere (see Chapter 4), and the general relations are similar for macroalgae and vascular plants. In most estuarine environments competition for assimilable nutrients is intense among various plant and algal species and ecological groups, and also between bacteria and algae. In general, an organism with a lower kinetic half-saturation coefficient (K_s) for a given nutrient will have a greater affinity for that nutrient, and therefore will have competitive advantage over other organisms when the nutrient is in short supply. Organisms with larger K_s values, however, can take greater advantage of high levels of nutrients.

Table 3.3 gives some representative values of K_s for different autotrophic groups. We can see that K_s values for NH_4^+ and NO_3^- in phytoplankton range from about 0.1–2.6 μM, while for PO_4^{3-}, K_s is only about one-half to one-tenth of that for the nitrogen ions. From the limited experimental data available for PO_4^{3-}, it appears that the nutrient kinetic parameters for benthic microalgae are close to those for phytoplankton (both are single-celled organisms). It turns out that these K_s values are similar to ambient concentrations of the respective nutrients during the summer period of peak growth in many temperate estuaries (e.g., Fig. 3.14), although concentrations of NO_3^-, NH_4^+, and PO_4^{3-} are commonly observed to be less than 0.3, 0.1, and 0.05 μM, respectively. Only when nutrient concentrations are near or below these levels would we expect nutrient uptake to limit the rate of primary productivity.

In general, macrophytic (multicellular) plants appear to have much higher K_s values; that is, they saturate at much higher concentrations. Presumably, this is the result of limitations at sites other than the loci of biochemical reaction, for example, in the transport of ions across epidermal surfaces. The high K_s values for macrophytes do not result in as severe a nutrient limitation as would be ex-

TABLE 3.3 Summary of Some Nutrient Uptake Kinetic Parameters for Representatives of Various Autotrophic (Plant) Groups

Autotrophic Group	Maximum[a] Uptake, V_m (d^{-1})	Half-Saturation[b]		References
		Chemical Species	K_s (μM)	
Phytoplankton	0.8–3.0	NO_3^-	0.4–2.6	Eppley et al. (1969)
		NH_4^+	0.1–2.0	Parsons et al. (1977)
		PO_4^{3-}	0.05–0.2	Furnas et al. (1976)
Seagrasses	0.04–0.10	$(NH_4^+)_{leaf}$	101	Iizumi et al. (1982)
		$(NH_4^+)_{root}$	30–100	Kemp et al. (1984)
				Thursby & Harlin (1982)
Marsh grass	0.02–0.08	NO_3^-	9	Morris (1980)
		NH_4^+	4	
Marcroalgae	0.05–0.14	NO_3^-	5	Fortes & Luning (1980)
		NH_4^+	4	Topinka & Robbins (1976)
Benthic microalgae	1.0–1.8	PO_4^{3-}	0.1	Admiraal (1977)

[a]It is assumed that V_m is the same for all chemical species since the elemental composition remains relatively constant.
[b]These values are meant only to represent general trends.

pected, because these plants live rooted in or attached to the sediments, where (as we have discussed earlier) ambient nutrient concentrations are generally 10–1000 times those in the euphotic zone of deeper (>10 m) estuarine water columns (see Figs. 3.4 and 3.14). Even for sea grasses that can assimilate nutrients either through leaves in the near-bottom waters or through roots buried in the sediments, differences in K_s for leaf versus root uptake seem to correspond reasonably well to the respective ambient concentrations. These findings mean, of course, that plants have adapted to the average nutrient concentrations they generally have encountered.

3.7.4 Nutrient Regeneration Via Decomposition

Organic matter resulting from the excretion, defecation, and death of living organisms is subjected to enzymatic decomposition by microorganisms (bacteria and fungi). Microorganisms obtain energy in this process, and the elements composing the organic matter are released in dissolved inorganic form if the decomposition process is complete. In this case nutrients are released in the same relative proportions as the organic matter from which they were derived. The overall general decomposition reaction can be described by

$$106\ CH_2O + 16\ NH_3 + H_3PO_4 + 106\ O_2$$

$$\rightarrow 106\ CO_2 + 16\ NH_3 + H_3PO_4 + 106\ H_2O \quad (16)$$

According to the relations given above, the decomposition of phytoplankton will produce 16 atoms of nitrogen, and 106 atoms of carbon while consuming 212 (or 276 if NO_3^- is the final nitrogen form) atoms of oxygen for every atom of phosphorus released (Redfield et al. 1963). Silicon is released by dissolution of diatom tests (skeletons)—rather than microbially mediated decompostition—in the proportions $Si:P = 15:1$; however, recent studies (e.g., D'Elia et al. 1983) have suggested that enzymatic processes may be involved. In fact, a variety of observations in field and laboratory conditions (Fig. 3.17) indicated release of nitrogen (as NH_4^+ only; not NO_3^-), silicon, and phosphorus in approximate proportions of $16:16:1$ by atom.

In the estuarine environment, microbially mediated decomposition occurs in the water column as planktonic debris falls toward the bottom. However, the relatively shallow water depths (e.g., 2-20 m) and rapid settling rates result in fairly short residence times for detrital material in estuarine waters. Therefore, most of the microbial regeneration of nutrients probably takes place on or in the sediments. As we discussed earlier, substances other than O_2 can serve as terminal electron acceptors (oxidizing agents) in the decomposition of organic matter and subsequent release of nutrients. Most of the sediment regeneration of NH_4^+, SiO_2, and PO_4^{3-} results from either O_2 or sulfate respiration, the former being thermodynamically favored, and the latter ion being more abundant in sediment pore waters. The preference for oxygen, and the fact that recently deposited organic material is usually more readily metabolized, result in exponentially decreasing rates of NH_4^+ regeneration with depth in sediments (e.g., Blackburn 1979, Aller and Yingst 1980). About nine times more NH_4^+ was released by O_2 respiration than sulfate reduction in a North Sea estuary in Belgium (Vanderborght et al. 1977). In some oceanic waters anamously low O:N ratios (compared with Redfield proportions of 6.6:1) can be explained in terms of SO_4^{2-} reduction (Redfield et al. 1963). By contrast, Nixon (1981) summarized measurements of net NH_4^+ regeneration versus O_2 consumption from several estuarine sediments. This data shows an overall deficiency in atoms of nitrogen released compared with atoms of oxygen used. A regression line drawn through these data yielded an O:N ratio of 12 (Fig. 3.18).

The overall rates of nutrient regeneration from sediments can be measured directly by observing changes in concentrations of nutrients in circulated water under chambers placed in situ on the sediment surface (e.g., Hale et al. 1978, Zeitschel 1980). The rates of nutrient regeneration measured from estuarine sediments are relatively large; annual mean values range from about 20-300 μmol m^{-2} h^{-1} for NH_4^+ and 0-40 μmol $m^{-2}h^{-1}$ for PO_4^{3-} (Fig. 3.19). From 20 to 200% of the respective nutrient demands for phytoplankton assimilation in overlying waters can be supplied by benthic decomposition of organic matter, indicating the large potential importance of benthic regeneration for plankton. In temperate estuaries seasonal patterns of benthic nutrient regeneration generally exhibit strong summer maxima which correlate well with water temperature (Fig. 3.20). The effects of temperature on these processes tend to produce an Arrhenius type expression (Fig. 3.21), although the large scatter in such data

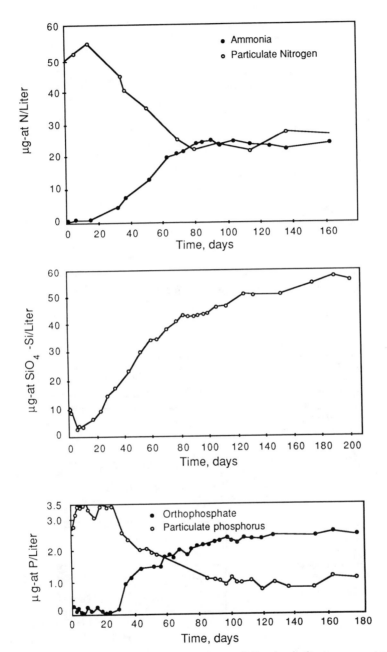

Figure 3.17 Changes in phosphorus, nitrogen, and dissolved silicate concentrations due to decomposition of phytoplankton (from Grill and Richards 1964).

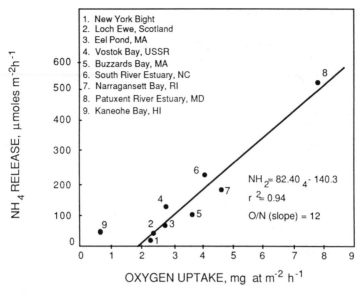

Figure 3.18 The relationship between oxygen uptake and ammonia release by the sediments in a variety of coastal marine systems during summer (from Nixon 1981).

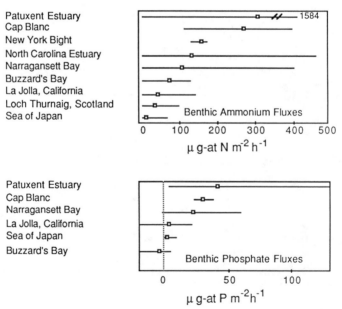

Figure 3.19 Comparative benthic fluxes (annual mean and range) of ammonium and dissolved inorganic phosphate from selected estuarine and coastal ecosystems (from Boynton et al. 1980).

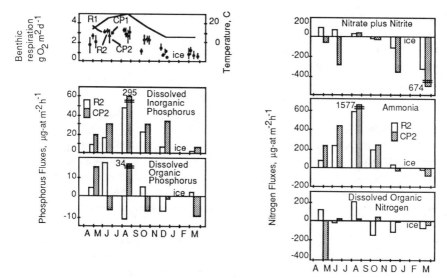

Figure 3.20 Seasonal estimates of benthic respiration rate and flux rates of dissolved phosphorus and nitrogen in the Patuxent Estuary, 1978–1979. R1, R2, CP1, and CP2 are different stations (from Boynton et al. 1980).

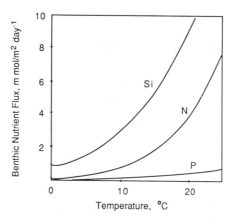

Figure 3.21 Benthic regeneration of nutrients versus temperature. Data from three major bottom communities in Narragansett Bay over an annual cycle were used to fit the empirical equations (after Kremer and Nixon 1978).

suggest processes other than simple temperature kinetics. For example, a portion of the NH_4^+ released in decomposition may be oxidized to NO_3^- before leaving the sediments. Phosphate regenerated in decomposition reacts rapidly with iron and manganese oxides and hydroxides to form insoluble precipitates in oxidized environments. Once sediments are sufficiently reduced to become anaerobic, soluble forms of $Fe(Mn)-PO_4^{3-}$ complexes are produced, and phosphate is released to the water (Callender 1982). This may lead to a sharp summer peak in PO_4^{3-} regeneration unrelated to temperature.

It might be expected that planktonic debris decomposing on estuarine floors would release N, Si, and P in the proportions of phytoplankton cells (16:15:1). Nixon (1981), however, summarized values of benthic nutrient regeneration for 12 different estuaries where N:P ranged from 2 to 20 with a mean of about 8.4, or half that expected. While the full explanation of this discrepancy awaits further study, Nixon and his colleagues suggest that some of the recycled NH_4^+ is oxidized to NO_3^- (nitrification) and subsequently reduced to N_2 (denitrification) which is lost as a gas, producing a lower N:P ratio from sediment release (see discussion below). As we discussed earlier the atomic ratio of dissolved inorganic N:P in the water during the summer is typically far less than the 16:1 proportion needed for phytoplankton growth, and Nixon (1981) has hypothesized that this is the consequence of the low N:P ratio in benthic nutrient regeneration. On the other hand, several studies (e.g., Callender and Hammond 1982) have shown that although the ratios of N:Si:P regeneration in sediments differ along the salinity gradient of estuaries, they are, nevertheless, generally similar to the algal cell proportions. Dissolution of siliceous minerals is directly proportional to salinity, so that is more rapid in marine waters. It had been suggested by some (e.g., Officer and Ryther 1980) that dissolution rates for particulate silicon in diatom skeletons are slow compared with microbially mediated regeneration of nitrogen and phosphorus from dead algal cells, so that midsummer shifts in algal species domination from diatoms to flagellates may result from silicon limitation due to relatively slow regeneration. However, recent measurements of benthic nutrient regeneration indicate that summer rates of silicon recycling are comparable to those for nitrogen (Callender and Hammond 1982, D'Elia et al. 1983).

3.7.5 Nutrient Regeneration via Excretion

A portion of the nutrients assimilated by phytoplankton and other microbes in estuarine water columns is regenerated from particulate to dissolved form as dead algae sink through the water column. While some of this water-column (or planktonic) regeneration results from bacterial decomposition of the dead plankton cell, much of it arises from excretion by zooplankton (and perhaps phytoplankton themselves). Nitrogen and phosphorus are excreted in the form of ammonium and dissolved organic nitrogen compounds (urea, uric acid, amino acids), and as phosphate and dissolved organic phosphorus. Metazoan zooplankton excrete through gills and antennal glands, while protozoa excrete them across cell walls as a means of waste removal and to achieve ionic and acid-base balance. It is unlikely that silicon is excreted by zooplankton to any significant extent; however, bacterial degradation of diatom skeletons may be enhanced when they are packed in zooplankton fecal pellets.

Rates of nitrogen and phosphorus excretion have been measured using two principal techniques. The first involves measuring temporal changes of nutrient concentration in filtered water containing individual zooplankters. This method allows simultaneous measurement of excretion of various nutrient forms, and it facilitates relating excretion rates to organism characteristics. However, this method does not allow in situ observations, and interpretation is confounded by simultaneous uptake. The second method employs isotopic tracers, either the radioactive isotopes of phosphorus (^{33}P or ^{32}P) or the relatively heavy mass isotope of nitrogen (^{15}N). This approach requires more sophisticated analytical equipment (liquid scintillation counters and mass spectrometers), but has provided a means for measuring rates as they occur in nature.

In general, nutrient excretion rates are directly proportional to respiration rates for zooplankton. Typical atomic ratios of C:N:P for zooplankton metabolism are about 30:9:1, indicating that oxidation of food (presumably phytoplankton with a ratio of 106:16:1) is incomplete (Satomi and Pomeroy 1965, Harrison 1980). In general, nutrient excretion rates are a function of temperature according to the Arrhenius relation. Excretion is also influenced by zooplankton feeding rate, increasing somewhat from normal levels under both starvation and at very high feeding rates. Excretion rates per unit weight of zooplankton are inversely proportional to the size of individual zooplankton (Johannes 1964), as they are for respiration (Fig. 3.22). Thus it would be expected that smaller microzooplankton (< 100 μm) would contribute more to total excretion than predicted by biomass proportions. Recent measurements of NH_4^+ excretion by size fractions indicated that organisms associated with particulates < 35 μm account for most of the release in nature (Fig. 3.23). This is generally consistent with the findings of Harrison (1978, 1980), who reported that the smaller (1–35 μm) size organisms accounted for most of the NH_4^+ excretion on the southern California coast and the PO_4^{3-} excretion in Bedford Basin, Nova Scotia. In the Chesapeake Bay, however, samples associated with very small-size groups (< 10 μm) were progressively less important (Glibert 1982).

The relative significance of planktonic excretion as a recycling mechanism to supply the nutrient demand for phytoplankton assimilation seems to vary seasonally and in an inshore-offshore direction. Whereas planktonic nutrient regeneration may be more significant in support of "recycled" production, "new" production is related more to inputs from land and benthic regeneration (Kemp and Boynton 1984; see Chapter 4). Water-column nutrient regeneration seems to be more important in deep coastal and oceanic waters (Harrison 1980); however, even in shallower waters (8–10 m) planktonic regeneration of N and P is important (Fig. 3.24). Based on the limited number of measurements upon which Fig. 3.23 was based it would appear that zooplankton excretion in Chesapeake Bay waters can provide all of the NH_4^+ needed for phytoplankton assimila-

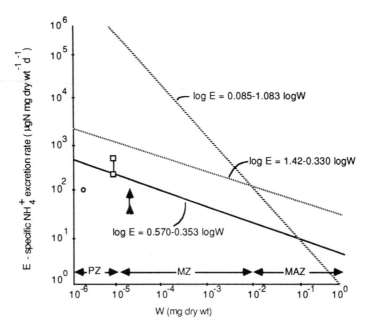

Figure 3.22 Biomass-excretion rate relationships for zooplankton. Solid line, temperate/tropical species; dashed line, calculated assuming dry wt = 100 × particulate phosphorus, NH_4^+-excretion = 10 × P-excretion; broken dashed line, PZ = protozoans; MZ = metazoans; MAZ = macrozooplankton; triangles = oligotrophic microzooplankton; squares = eutrophic microzooplankton; circles = protozoan excretion based on gross assimilation efficiency (from Harrison 1980).

tion. Boynton et al. (1980) and Callender and Hammond (1982), however, have shown that most of the phytoplankton requirements can also be met by benthic nutrient regeneration in these waters. Therefore, where these two sources of regenerated nutrients exceed algal demand, as appears to be the case in many estuaries, other nutrient sinks, such as bacterial assimilation of N and P may be more important than previously thought (e.g., Wheeler and Kirchman 1986, see Chapter 4).

3.7.6 Nitrogen Fixation

The next several sections emphasize the nitrogen cycle. This cycle is complicated and difficult to "digest" when one first learns about it. Perhaps it can be better understood if you remember that some reactions, such as fixation, are done to get nitrogen for structural synthesis, but others are energy reactions where organisms use ammonia for a fuel or nitrate for an oxidizing agent or electron acceptor.

As we discussed earlier the gaseous form of elemental nitrogen (N_2) comprises some 78% of the atmosphere, although N_2 is relatively insoluble in water, it still

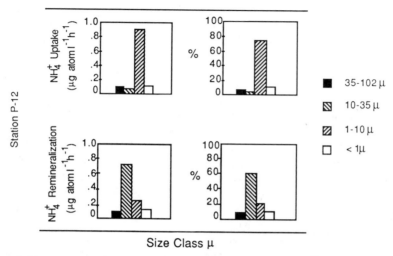

Figure 3.23 NH$_4^+$ uptake rate and NH$_4^+$ remineralization rate for various plankton size fractions at a station sampled in the Chesapeake Bay. Left, actual rates; right, percent of total activity represented by each fraction. (from Glibert 1982)

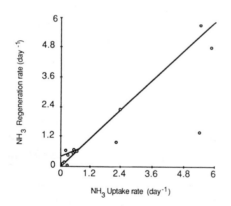

Figure 3.24 Turnover rates of ammonia pool in photic zone samples taken from enclosed water column experiments. Ordinate: turnover rate calculated from regeneration through amino acid degradation; abscissa: turnover rate calculated from ammonia uptake due to photosynthesis (from Hollibaugh et al. 1980).

dissolves sufficiently so that nitrogen deficiencies would never limit photosynthesis if N$_2$ were available for phytoplankton assimilation. However, most plants cannot use N$_2$ directly and only a select few procaryotic organisms (bacteria and blue-green algae) are capable of "fixing" N$_2$ into the inorganic salt ammonium. Nitrogen fixation proceeds by the following energy-intensive anaerobic reaction:

$$N_2 + 3H_2 \rightarrow 2NH_3 \qquad\qquad (17)$$

which requires 147 kcal/mole. Since this process is inhibited by oxygen (which inactivates the enzyme nitrogenase), it can occur in blue-green algae only within special organelles referred to as heterocysts, within which anoxic conditions are maintained.

A considerable variety of bacteria and blue-green algae are capable of N_2 fixation. Bacterial genera mediating N_2 fixation in estuarine and coastal environments include *Clostridium, Azobacter,* and the ubiquitous *Pseudomonas.* Heterocystous blue-greens include *Calothrix* sp., *Dicothrix* sp., and *Trichodesmium* (formerly *Oscillatoria* sp.) The oceanic forms of *Trichodesmium* do not possess heterocysts, and most utilize some other mechanism to separate nitrogenase from photosynthetically produced O_2 (Fogg 1978). One blue-green species, *Richelia intracellularis,* occurs inside diatom cells and has been reported to be rather abundant in the ocean.

Nitrogen fixation can be measured either indirectly by the acetylene reduction technique or directly by use of ^{15}N-labelled N_2 and mass spectrometry. Acetylene acts as a substitute substrate for nitrogenase and is reduced to ethylene at a rate that is thought to be quantitatively analogous to nitrogen reduction, which can be measured by gas chromatography. In lakes and other fresh water systems N_2 fixation may represent a major component in the overall nitrogen budget, and this pathway commonly contributes 30–80% of the total annual nitrogen income for an entire water body (Horne 1978). Elemental nitrogen fixation seems to be a natural process which may accelerate lake eutrophication. Natural nitrogen fixation is enhanced by the experimental addition of phosphates (without adding nitrogen) to lakes. In other words such phosphorus additions have resulted in 5–10-fold enhancement of N_2 fixation, and this fixation supplied about 50% of the nitrogen needed for phytoplankton assimilation in this treated system (Lean et al. 1978). Conversely, N_2 fixation is inhibited by high concentrations of NH_4^+ in lakes.

In estuarine and coastal waters, however, N_2 fixation tends to be relatively unimportant for overall nitrogen budgets except in specialized environments. For example, the fixation rates for various coastal systems summarized in Table 3.4 indicate that this process rarely supplies more than 5% of the local autotrophic demand for nitrogen assimilation. There are exceptions, however. In tropical marine seagrasses, epiphytic blue-green and bacterial populations colonizing plant leaves as well as bacteria in sediments commonly contribute 20–50% of the NH_4^+ needed for seagrass production. Nitrogen fixation has also been found important in salt marshes (Valiela and Teal 1979).

The reason for the generally low importance of N_2 fixation in estuaries compared with lakes is uncertain. Many estuaries are characterized by relatively high NH_4^+ concentrations, and NH_4^+ inhibition may be a factor. But coastal waters containing low concentrations of NH_4^+ still have little N_2 fixation. There has been some suggestion that the physical turbulence characterizing these waters may constitute sufficient stress to destroy the structure of delicate heterocysts

TABLE 3.4 Summary of Nitrogen Fixation Rates and Associated Effect on Assimilative Demand for Selected Estuarine and Coastal Ecosystem

Ecosystem Dominant Sp. (N$_2$-Fixing Organisms)	N$_2$ Fixation (mg Nm^{-2}d^{-1})	Assimilative Demand Satisfied (%)	References
Salt Marsh			
Spartina alterniflora			
(Blue-green algae)	5–45	1–5	Carpenter et al. 1978
(Sediment bacteria)	80	15	Jones 1974
			Whitney et al. 1975
Seagrass			
Thalassia testudinum			
(Epiphytes)	4–150	3–100	Capone 1983
(Sediment bacteria)	20–80	15–50	
Zostera marina			
(Epiphytes)	0–0.1	0–0.5	Capone 1983
(Sediment bacteria)	0.2–6	0.5–5	
Myriophyllum spicatum			
(Epiphytes and sediments)	3	2	Lipschultz et al. 1979
Estuarine shallows			
(Sediment bacteria)	0.5–10	1–5	Brooks et al. 1971
Coastal shelf			
(Planktonic blue-greens)	0.01–1.3	1–5	Carpenter & Price 1977
(Bacteria on *Sargassum*)	0.01	1	Carpenter 1972

(Fogg 1978). Another possibility, suggested by Howarth and Cole (1985), is that the high concentrations of sulfate in seawater compared to freshwater may inhibit the ability of nitrogen-fixers to obtain sufficient quantities of molybdenum needed for synthesis of nitrogenase. Evidently, sulfate, which is chemically similar to molybdate, causes competitive inhibition of molybdate assimilation. Relatively lower concentrations of organic matter in seawater may also contribute to reduced N$_2$ fixation. Higher levels of dissolved organics allow for formation of low-oxygen micro-environments in which nitrogen fixation can occur (Paerl et al. 1987).

3.7.7 Nitrification and Denitrification

Two additional key processes in the cycling of nitrogen in estuarine ecosystems are nitrification and denitrification. *Nitrification* is the oxidation of ammonium to nitrate, and it occurs only under aerobic conditions. Only a few heterotrophic organisms oxidize NH$_4^+$; instead, the vast majority of nitrification in natural environments occurs through an autotrophic pathway by organisms that use energy obtained from the transformation (Billen 1975). Nitrifying bacteria use NH_4^+ as an energy source to fix carbon dioxide into cellular organic matter similar to the use of sulfide as an energy source by chemoautotrophic sulfur bacteria (as discussed earlier). The overall process involves two major steps, the first (Eq. 18) is mediated by bacteria of the genus *Nitrosomonas* (a few other species are also capable of this metabolic pathway, e.g., *Nitrocystis* sp.) and the second is carried out by *Nitrobacter* spp. (Eq. 19).

$$NH_3 + 3/2\ O_2 \rightarrow HNO_2 + H_2O \tag{18}$$

$$HNO_2 + 1/2\ O_2 \rightarrow HNO_3 \tag{19}$$

The first of these yields 66 kcal/mole while the second produces only 17.5 kcal/mole (Delwich 1970).

The second step (Eq. 19) in this coupled reaction tends to be the slower (and therefore rate-limiting) process. Temperature influences this process in a manner similar to other microbially mediated reactions; however, sediment nitrification rates are relatively high in cooler months because of greater O_2 availability. Values of K_s for the second step of nitrification appear to be between 25 and 750 μM with 150 μM being a typical value (Painter 1970, McLaren 1976). Thus nitrifying bacteria have a relatively low affinity for NH_4^+ compared with (for example) microalgae, for which K_s is on the order of 1.0 μM (Table 3.3). In addition, nitrification is limited to relatively oxidized conditions ($E_h > 200$ mV, Billen 1975), so that it will not occur deep within estuarine sediments. Nitrification is measured as increases in NH_4^+ or decreases in NO_3^- or CO_2 incorporation in the presence of the specific nitrification inhibitor N-serve. It is also measured more directly using ^{15}N-labelled NH_4^+ substrate and monitoring $^{15}N\text{-}NO_3^-$ production.

The maximum rates of nitrification measured in estuaries have been in the water column directly below sewage outfalls, where NH_4^+ concentrations can reach 150 μM. Here, sufficient levels of NH_4^+ combined with high concentrations of O_2 provide an ideal circumstance for nitrification. However, where NH_4^+ is below about 5 μM (more typical of nonpolluted estuaries), nitrification rates tend to be negligible in the water column. Nevertheless, nitrification does occur at moderate rates in the upper most part (0–1 cm) of estuarine sediments, typically at rates of about 50 μg atoms m^{-2}h^{-1} (Table 3.5) compared with common benthic NH_4^+ regeneration rates of about twice that (Fig. 3.19). Nitrification rates in sea grass sediments may be slightly higher (Table 3.5) than in nonvegetated muds because of the aerating effect of photosynthetically produced O_2, which leaks from plant roots into sediment pore waters (Iizumi et al. 1980). Seasonal cycles of nitrification in estuarine sediments have not been well defined, and data from two Danish fjords suggest two different patterns (Fig. 3.25a). The better defined cycle (Kysing Fjord) exhibits highest rates in the winter and fall and reduced values in summer. This may be due to greater competition for NH_4^+ and more reduced E_h conditions during the summer (Jenkins and Kemp 1984).

Denitrifying bacteria use NO_3^- as an electron acceptor to oxidize organic matter anaerobically, releasing N_2 gas by the following reaction:

TABLE 3.5 Summary of Nitrification and Denitrification Rates in Various Estuarine Ecosystems

Ecosystem	Nitrification	Denitrification	References
	\multicolumn{2}{c}{(μg atoms m^{-2}h^{-1})}		
Salt marsh	60	110	Kaplan et al (1979)
Spartina alterniflora			
Seagrass	20–120	20–90	Iizumi & Hattori (1980)[a]
Zostera marina,			Shenton (1982)
Potamogeton perfoliatus			
Estuarine water	0–5000	0	Billen (1975)
			Elkins
Estuarine sediment	10–115	10–300	Billen (1978)
			Sorenson (1978)
			Oren & Blackburn (1979)
			Nishio et al. (1982)
			Seitzinger et al. (1980)
			Henriksen et al. (1981)
			Hansen et al. (1981)

[a]Assumes bulk density of sediments at 1 g/cm^3, and rates limited to upper 20 cm of sediment.

$$5\ C_6H_{12}O_6 + 24\ HNO_3 \rightarrow 30\ CO_2 + 42\ H_2O + 12\ N_2 \qquad (20)$$

which yields 570 kcal/mole (Delwiche 1970). Numerous bacteria are capable of denitrification metabolism, and many of these, such as *Pseudomonas denitrificans,* are facultative anaerobes able to exist with or without oxygen. Denitrifiers can also produce nitrous oxide (N_2O) from NO_3^- via the pathway, which is actually the first step in the overall reaction as given in Eq. 20,

$$C_6H_{12}O_6 + 6\ HNO_3 \rightarrow 6\ CO_2 + 9\ H_2O + 3\ N_2O \qquad (21)$$

which generates 545 kcal/mole (Delwiche 1970). Nitrous oxide, which is also produced as an intermediate in nitrification under certain conditions, is (like N_2) unavailable for phytoplankton assimilation. Anthropogenic acceleration of N_2O production could result in a general heating of the earth's atmosphere because N_2O reacts with, and breaks down, atmospheric ozone (O_3), which normally helps maintain the earth's heat balance (McElroy et al. 1978). Denitrification can be measured directly as total N_2 production from degassed sediments. However, since N_2 is very abundant naturally, long incubations (4–10 days) are needed to obtain significant changes in N_2 concentration. The process can also be measured indirectly as N_2O production in the presence of acetylene which inhibits the reduction of N_2O to N_2.

Denitrifying bacteria seem to have a much greater affinity for NO_3^- than nitrifying bacteria have for NH_4^+ (K_s values are commonly 10–50 μM) (Billen 1978, Koike and Hattori 1978). Some of the NO_3^- reduction occurring in estuarine sediments produces NH_4^+ as the reduced nitrogen species rather than N_2 or N_2O.

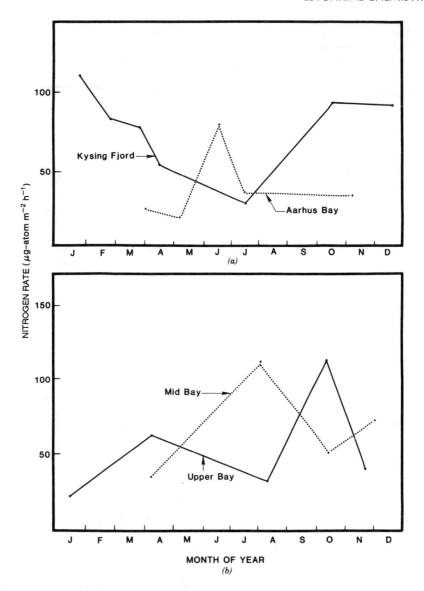

Figure 3.25 (a) Nitrification rates for estuarine sediments in Denmark (from Hansen et al. 1981), and (b) denitrification rates for estuarine sediments in Narragansett Bay, Rhode Island (from Seitzinger 1982).

In general, rates of NO_3^- reduction to NH_4^+ are similar to rates of denitrification to N_2 (Koike and Hattori 1978). Denitrification in many estuarine sediments appears to be limited by NO_3^- availability much of the time. Various studies have demonstrated that denitrification potential remains high throughout most of the year, and that NO_3^- addition will stimulate the reaction (Jenkins and Kemp 1984).

The NO_3^- substrate used in denitrification in estuarine sediments is made available from two principal sources. First, when NO_3^- levels are high in overlying water, such as can occur from land runoff, or from nitrification in the water, NO_3^- may diffuse into anaerobic regions of the sediments where denitrification occurs. Second, nitrification may occur in the upper sediment layers with NO_3^- diffusing the relatively short distance to just below the redox discontinuity layer (RDL) or to anoxic microsites above the RDL associated with sediment particles. In the latter case, nitrification and denitrification are intimately coupled so that little or no NO_3^- leaves the sediments. In the former case, large fluxes of NO_3^- from water to sediments may be observed (Fig. 3.26), particularly in regions where extensive agricultural fertilization in surrounding watersheds has led to increasing rates of nitrogen runoff and elevated estuarine concentrations of NO_3^- (Kemp et al. 1982).

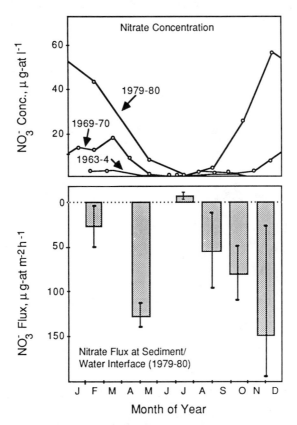

Figure 3.26 Exchange of nitrate across the sediment-water interface and the concentration of nitrate in the overlying water during 3 different years in the upper Patuxent River estuary, Maryland. Note that high uptake generally occurred when water column concentrations were high (from Kemp et al. 1982).

Broadly speaking, estuarine denitrification rates are similar to or perhaps slightly higher than nitrification rates, where values of 50–100 μg-atom m^{-2} h^{-1} have been commonly reported (Table 3.5). These are also similar to NH_4^+ regeneration rates in the sediments. Particularly, high rates (200–300 μg-atom m^{-2} h^{-1}) occur in estuaries receiving heavy inputs of NO_3^- (Nishio et al. 1982). Seitzinger (1982) measured denitrification in the sediments of large microcosms treated with various levels of nitrogen loading and found that a 10-fold increase in loading resulted in a five fold increase in mean denitrification rates (Fig. 3.27). Measurements of seasonal patterns of denitrification presently are limited to work in Narragansett Bay, Rhode Island. Two stations were characterized by distinctly different patterns, neither of which is particularly strong (Fig. 3.25b). These data do not distinguish between denitrification of NO_3^- produced in situ versus NO_3^- from runoff, and such a distinction might help explain these trends. However, the general magnitude of these rates has been used to account for the anomalously low (compared with Redfield proportions) N : P ratios in sediment nutrient regeneration (Seitzinger et al. 1980), implying that denitrification may contribute significantly to the relative availability of N and P for phytoplankton assimilation.

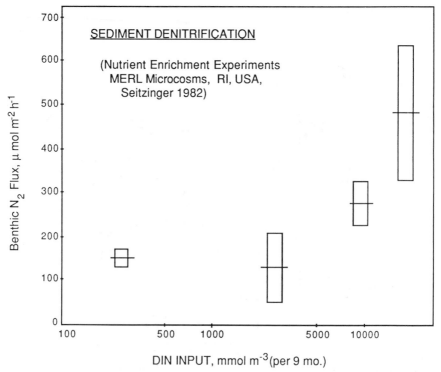

Figure 3.27 Sediment denitrification as a function of increasing input of dissolved inorganic nitrogen (DIN) input in estuarine microcosms (from Seitzinger 1982).

3.7.8   Synthesis: Estuarine Nutrient Cycles

We have now discussed most of the major transformation processes and chemical forms of the three major plant nutrients (N, P, and Si) as they relate to estuaries. In this final section we will synthesize briefly this information into conceptual models of the system whereby these nutrients are received, cycled, and deposited or discharged in an estuarine environment. All of these processes collectively determine the patterns of chemicals such as those given briefly at the beginning of this chapter.

The cycle of phosphorus utilization, transformation, and regeneration is relatively simple compared with that of nitrogen (Fig. 3.28). Phosphorus enters the estuary either from weathering of soil and rock and subsequent runoff, or from point-source discharges such as sewage treatment plants. Operationally, it is common to define three major forms of phosphorus which are distinguished as much by analytical criteria as by chemical nature. Dissolved inorganic phosphorus (DIP) is assimilated by algae and bacteria into cellular organic matter. Some of this particulate organic phosphorus (POP) is excreted (or released in cell lysing) either as DIP or as dissolved organic phosphorus (DOP), which can be decomposed by bacterial action releasing DIP. These processes also occur in the sediments; however, on the estuarine floor the ratio of regeneration to assimilation is far greater than it is in the euphotic zone. The relative importance of bacteria in regeneration of inorganic salts (DIP) is larger in the sediments than in the water column. Materials dissolved in sediment pore waters are exchanged via diffusion and some advective pumping by infauna with the overlying medium.

Three (mostly) inorganic particulate forms of phosphorus are important in estuarine sediments. Dissolved inorganic phosphorus, and possibly DOP, is involved in complexing reactions with metal (such as Fe and Mn) oxides and hydroxides to form insoluble precipitates under aerobic conditions, but these are redissolved when redox becomes sufficiently reduced. This is a crucial chemical interaction which strongly influences the seasonal availability of DIP for algal assimilation. At a much slower, but still significant, rate DIP participates in precipitation reactions to form various minerals such as apatite, which is important in some animal skeletons. The highly charged phosphate anion PO_4^{3-} is also readily sorbed onto the surfaces of charged clay (and detrital organic) particles. Since these sorption-desorption processes are truly first-order equilibrium reactions, they (in effect) provide a buffering mechanism for DIP. At high concentrations of DIP, PO_4^{3-} is sorbed onto particles, while at lower concentrations DIP is released into the water, thus maintaining moderate ambient concentrations (Jitts 1959). In general, these processes occurring in estuarine sediments are not well understood empirically. While there is evidence that they exert a profound effect on phosphorus cycling, an exact description of their quantitative significance awaits further study.

The silicon cycle in estuarine ecosystems can be reasonably portrayed in even simpler terms than for phosphorus (Fig. 3.29). While silicon is the crystalline

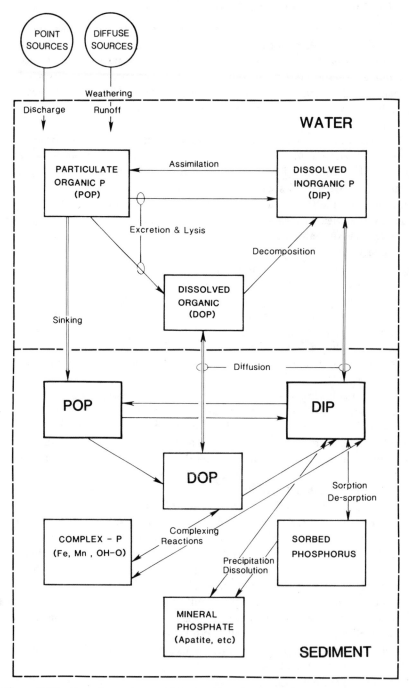

Figure 3.28 Transformations within the phosphorus cycle in estuarine systems.

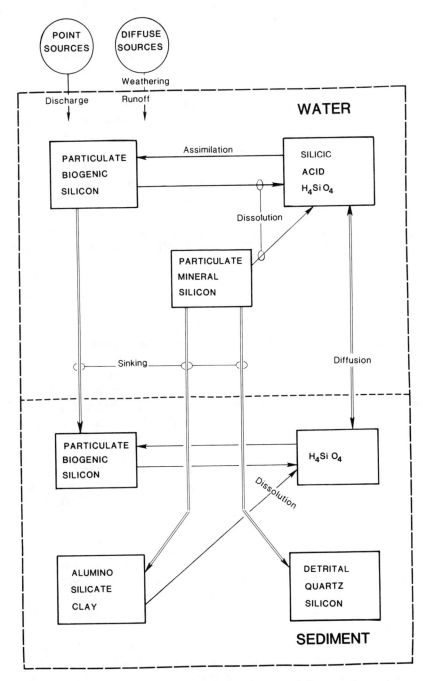

Figure 3.29 Transformations within the silicon cycle in estuarine systems.

base of all clay minerals (each of which is different) as well as quartz, it occurs in dissolved form primarily as silicic acid. The crystalline form of biogenic silica (e.g., diatoms tests or animal skeletons) is markedly different from that of clay minerals and thus should be considered separately. Silicon enters estuaries via runoff water containing the products of weathering, and from sewage discharges where N : Si : P atom ratios are about 5.4 : 2.5 : 1.0 (Garside et al. 1976). Silicon is assimilated by diatoms at a rate similar to that for nitrogen. Once incorporated into particulate mineral form, it returns to solution primarily through the physical-chemical process of dissolution. The role of enzyme catalysis in regenerating dissolved silicon is presently uncertain and deserves further study. While some have argued that this dissolution process is relatively slow, others have shown empirically that silicon regeneration rates are comparable to those for nitrogen, and that regeneration rates appear to be most rapid in the upper (0-4 cm) sediment strata (Vanderborght et al. 1977).

The estuarine nitrogen cycle is clearly the most intricate of the three major plant nutrient cycles (Fig. 3.30). There are three important dissolved inorganic salts (which are interconvertible through redox reactions); there are two major gaseous forms which are produced by and are substrates for metabolic processes; there are a host of soluble organic salts of nitrogen including urea, uric acid, and all amino acids.

Nitrogen enters estuaries from point and diffuse sources on the land, atmospheric diffusion, upwelling deep oceanic waters, and biological fixation. Dissolved inorganic and organic salts are assimilated by phytoplankton (and bacteria), which preferentially take up NH_4^+. Small amounts of NH_4^+ enter the ecosystem via nitrogen fixation, while large quantities leave via denitrification in sediments. The compound NO_3^- enters via runoff and is produced in water and upper sediment strata (0-1 cm) by nitrification. Both sources are important in providing substrates for denitrification. Nitrogen is regenerated, largely as NH_4^+, from metazoan excretion in (especially) the water column and by bacterially-mediated decomposition of organic matter in the water column and the sediments. The NH_4^+ concentrations are "buffered" to an extent by sorption-desorption reactions with particulate matter, especially clays and humic material, having high cation-exchange capacity.

Many aspects of the nitrogen cycle are not yet well understood. For example, we still do not have contemporaneous measurements of sediment and water-column regeneration rates over long enough periods to compare relative contributions of each. Circumstantial evidence suggests that bacterial uptake or some other loss mechanism for regenerated NH_4^+ must be important at certain times. There are insufficient measurements of any of the major nitrogen transformation processes to describe (much less explain) adequately spatial and temporal patterns within an estuary. We need more experimental work to explain the factors controlling relative availability of dissolved inorganic forms of N, Si, and P as they change in time and space, and there is as yet no satisfactory explanation of the relative unimportance of nitrogen fixation in estuaries.

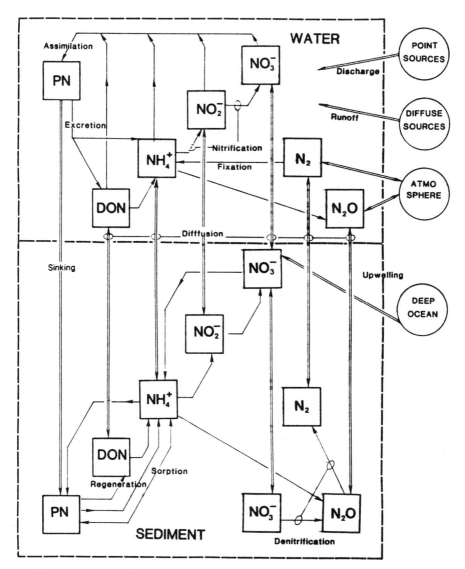

Figure 3.30 Transformations within the nitrogen cycle in estuarine systems.

From preliminary budgets it appears that NH_4^+ regeneration, nitrification, and denitrification are all important processes in several coastal sediment nitrogen budgets (Table 3.6). There is a direct relationship apparent here between NH_4^+ regeneration and denitrification. Since these two processes are not directly linked, it is most likely that both are related through nitrification, as well as by direct input of dissolved inorganic nitrogen (ultimately NO_3^-) to the overlying

TABLE 3.6 Comparison of Major Nitrogen Fluxes in the Sediments of Four Coastal and Estuarine Ecosystems

| Coastal Ecosystem | Nitrogen Fluxes (μg atoms $m^{-2}h^{-1}$) | | | | References |
	Deposition	NH_4^+ Regen	Nitrification	Dentrification	
Patuxent River	19.2	11.2	1.7	3.2[a]	Boynton et al. (1980)
Narragansett Bay	—	7.6	2.8	2.4	Seitzinger et al. (1980)
North Sea Coast	—	5.4	3.5	1.2	Billen (1978)
Sluice Dock	—	6.7	4.5	2.1	Vanderborght et al. (1977)

[a]Assumes 50% of NO_3^- reduction is denitification.

water (Kemp et al. 1982). Similar nitrogen balances were developed for three other stations along the Patuxent, and in general NH_4^+ regeneration appears to be from between 60 and 100% of the rate of nitrogen deposition onto the sediments (Boynton et al. 1979). On the other hand, the same study revealed that DIP regeneration was only about 10–30% of particulate phosphorus deposition rates.

At the scale of any entire estuary, it appears that for Narragansett Bay, relative cycling rates (regeneration/input) for the three elements are Si > P > N (Nixon 1981). There are insufficient data to assess this trend for other estuaries; however, phosphorus seems to be cycled more rapidly (relative to input) than nitrogen in the Patuxent as well (Boynton et al. 1979). The ratio of regeneration to input (R : I) for nitrogen ranges from about 0.7 for Narragansett and for the Chowan River, North Carolina (Stanley and Hobbie 1981) to 6.6 for Charlestown Lagoon (Nixon and Pilson 1983). For phosphorus R : I ranges from 1.1 in Narragansett to 5.5 for the Patuxent, while R : I for silicon was estimated to be 7.4 for Narragansett Bay. In any case, the rates of regeneration tend to equal or exceed rates of input for all three nutrients, further emphasizing the importance of nutrient recycling processes. All in all, while substantial advances have been made in our understanding of nutrients in estuaries, it is evident that much is to be done. The following chapters examine biotic processes in more detail. The reader should keep in mind, however, that all of the plants and most of the animals are routinely and profoundly influenced by their chemical environment.

APPENDIX 3.1   EXPLANATION OF REDOX POTENTIAL

By convention the term pE is used as a measure of relative electron (e^-) activity,

$$pE = -\log[e^-] \tag{22}$$

This is analogous to the use of pH as a measure of proton activity (see Section 3.6.2). The free energy involved in electron transfer is also related to pE

$$pE = -\frac{\Delta G}{n\,2.3RT} \tag{23}$$

where ΔG is Gibbs free energy, n is the number of molecules, R is the universal gas constant, and T is absolute temperature. The energy gained in transferring 1 mole of electrons from an oxidant to hydrogen gas (H_2) is used as a measure of the redox potential, and is called E_h (in volts). The direct relation between redox potential and the activity of oxidants (ox) and reductants (red) is given by the Nernst equation

$$E_h = E_h^\circ + \frac{2.3RT}{nF} \log \frac{[ox]}{[red]} \tag{24}$$

where E_h° is a constant representing E_h at specified conditions of temperature and pressure and F is the Faraday coefficient. Thus pE and E_h are related directly

$$pE = \left(\frac{F}{2.3RT}\right)E_h \qquad (25)$$

and E_h is measured electrochemically as an electromotive force associated with the oxidizing intensity of a sediment or water system. The variable pE is inferred from E_h measurements; however, the former is more commonly used (as is the case for pH) because it is convenient, dimensionless, and on a logarithmic scale.

Since much of the chemistry of aquatic systems, including estuarine muds, can be described in terms of acid-base and redox reactions, the activity of protons and electrons (pH and E_h conditions, respectively) in a given environment largely dictate the kinds of compounds (or ions) and microorganisms which can exist there. This can be illustrated graphically by calculating the species of a given element that will be most abundant as a function of various levels of pH and E_h. Such an analysis for three sulfur species is given in Fig. 3.31a, where lower values of both E_h and pH favor the reduced form (H_2S for which the oxidation state of sulfur is -2). The chemosynthetic sulfur bacteria of the genus *Thiobacillus*, which oxidize H_2S and $S°$ to SO_4^{2-}, can exist only at the upper limit of stability for the reduced substances they metabolize (Fig. 3.31a). In fact, the broad E_h-pH region (Fig. 3.31b) within which all biological metabolism is contained (Bass Becking et al. 1960) lies between the lower limits for H_2 and oxygen. Superficial estuarine muds occupy relatively narrow E_h (-300 and $+600$) and pH (5 and 10) conditions.

APPENDIX 3.2 CHEMICAL KINETICS

Broadly speaking, chemical kinetics is the study of the rates of chemical reactions and the mechanisms by which they occur. Whereas a given set of chemical species will tend toward a particular equilibrium distribution that can be explained by thermodynamic considerations, chemical kinetics describes the rate at which the system will move toward that condition, for reaction rates observed at the level of aqueous ecosystems are generally explained at the atomic-molecular level. Our review is drawn largely from two sources (Mortimer 1971, Brezonik 1972).

The rate at which a reaction proceeds is a function of the number of collisions between reacting molecules and the energy of such collisions. For two colliding molecules to react successfully, they must first form a transitory intermediate called an "activated complex." The kinetic energy of the molecular collision must exceed a threshold level, referred to as the "activation energy," for the activated complex to form. For many reactions there exist one or more special substances, known as catalysts, which increase the rate of reaction without being consumed in the process. Catalyzed reactions proceed through a different mechanism (i.e., different intermediates) than do non catalyzed reactions, and the

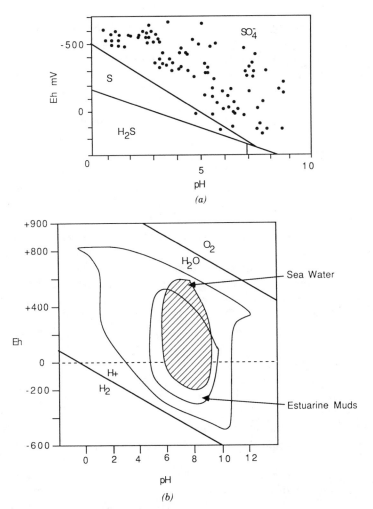

Figure 3.31 (a) Values for E_h and pH in active cultures of Thiobacillus (squares) on sulfur and the thermodynamic stability of different species of sulfur at various values of pH and E_h (lines). From Bass Becking and Wood (1955). (b) Approximate "areas" of E_h and pH for sea water and estuarine muds. The larger "envelope" designates E_h-pH limits for natural environments studied by Bass Becking et al. (1960). Used by permission, copyright by The University of Chicago.

activation energy required for the catalyzed pathway is lower. A large variety of catalysts, known as enzymes, are utilized in biochemical reactions (see discussion below).

At the level of an ecosystem, reaction rates are generally dependent on the concentrations of reacting solutes or the partial pressure of reacting gases. The rate of any one-step reaction (or for any stage in a multistep reaction) can be derived from the stoichiometrically balanced chemical equation (i.e., where the number of atoms and the number of electrons are equal on both sides of the equation). For example, in the simple hypothetical reaction of substance A with the diatomic molecule B_2 to form AB, we can write the following equation

$$2A + B_2 \rightarrow 2AB \tag{26}$$

The reaction rate, or rate of loss of A, can be described by the following

$$\text{rate} = \frac{dA}{dt} = k[A]^2[B] \tag{27}$$

where brackets indicate concentration and k is the rate constant. This rate expression is predicted by the so-called "law of mass action," where the reaction rate at any time is proportional to the concentrations of reactants, each of which is raised to a power corresponding to the number of molecules of that reactant in the balanced equation. Thus the square of the concentration of A in Eq. 27 indicates that two molecules of A are required to react with one of B_2.

The number of exponents of the concentrations appearing in the rate equation determines the order of the reaction. In the example given above, the reaction is second order with respect to A, first order relative to B, and third order overall. In reality reaction rates may not follow the mass-action law strictly, and rate equations must be determined experimentally. Fractional orders of reaction may characterize multistep reactions involving several rate equations, and rates may be zero order with respect to a given reactant, indicating that the process is controlled elsewhere. The overall rate of a particular reaction is determined by the slowest step in a multiple stage process. In addition, since the stoichiometric composition of final products of a chemical reaction are fixed, the relative concentrations of reacting substances must be in proportions similar to the composition of the product substances for them to influence the reaction rate significantly. If the concentration of reactant A in Eq. 27 is greatly in excess of that needed to react with the existing concentration of reactant B, the process will not be effected by the concentrations of A. Then the concentration of B, the "rate limiting substance," will determine the reaction rate.

Most biological reactions are mediated by enzymes that have very specific protein catalysts. Such enzymatic reactions, which are important in estuarine nutrient cycling, may also be limited by the availability of the enzyme. In such cases, the rate will be linearly proportional to the quantity of substrate (which interacts with the enzyme) until the rate of substrate processing exceeds the enzymatic capacity, at which point the reaction rate is insensitive to the quantity of the substrate. In this case the rate plotted against substrate concentration yields a rectangular hyprobola form, and the rate equation is often described in terms of the Michelis—Menten expression (see Chapter 4).

The rate of any chemical reaction is increased with elevated temperature resulting from more rapid motion of the interacting molecules and a higher probability of molecular collision. The "rate constant" (C) for any chemical reaction generally increases with temperature according to the Arrhenius equation

$$C = A[e^{-E_a/RT}] \tag{28}$$

where A is a constant characteristic of the reaction, E_a is the energy of activation, R is the universal gas constant (1.987 cal/mole K), and T is absolute temperature. The term in brackets in Eq. 28 represents the fraction of molecules having energy $> E_a$, and this can be derived from knowledge of the molecular energy distribution. Graphing ln C versus $(1/T)$ will produce a straight line (Arrhenius plot) for reactions following this expression, with the Y intercept equal to (ln A) and the slope $= (-E_a/R)$. The relative increase in rates in response to a 10°C rise in temperature is often referred to as a Q_{10}. For many biological processes about a doubling of rates occurs with a 10°C increase between 0 and 30°C, thus indicating a $Q_{10} = 2$. Biological reactions also exhibit an inverse relationship to temperature at very high T, resulting from the break down (or denaturing) of enzymatic protein. Hence all such reactions have an optimum temperature (T_{opt}) beyond which protein denaturing effects outweigh the Arrhenius effect. For an organism the metabolic response to temperature is the summation of effects on numerous internal biochemical process; however, the Arrhenius equation still describes temperature effects on metabolism reasonably well for $T < T_{opt}$. Other expressions have been derived to describe the relation at or beyond T_{opt}.

REFERENCES

Admiraal, W. 1977. Influence of various concentrations of orthophosphate on the division rate of an estuarine benthic diatom, *Navicula arenaria,* in culture. Mar. Biol. 42:1-8.

Aller, R.C. and J.Y. Yingst, 1978. Biogeochemistry of tube-dwellings: a study of the sedentary polychaete *Amphitrite ornata* (Leidy). J. of Mar. Res., 36(2):201-254.

Aller, R.C., 1980. Diagenetic processes near the sediment water interface of Long Island Sound. I. Decomposition and nutrient element geochemistry (S, N, P). Adv. in Geophysics, 22:237-350.

Aller, R.C. and J.Y. Yingst, 1980. Relationships between microbial distributions and the anaerobic decomposition of organic matter in surface sediments of Long Island Sound, USA. Mar. Biol., 56:29-42.

Baas Becking, L., and E. Wood, 1960. Biological processes in the estuarine environment. I. Ecology of the sulphur bacteria. Proc. Konink. Nederland Akad. v. Wetenschappen, Ser. B, Vol. 56:160-181.

Baas Becking, L., I. Kaplan, and D. Moore, 1960. Limits of the natural environment in terms of pH and oxidation-reduction potentials. J. Geology, 68(3):243-284.

Berner, R.A., 1980. Early Diagenesis A Theoretical Approach. Princeton University Press, New Jersey, 241 pp.

Billen, G., 1975. Nitrification in the Scheldt Estuary (Belgium and the Netherlands). Estuarine Coastal Mar. Sci., 3:79-89.

Billen, G., 1978. A budget of nitrogen recycling in North Sea sediments off the Belgian Coast. Estuarine Coastal Mar. Sci., 7:127-146.

Blackburn, H.T., 1979. Method for measuring rates of NH_4^+ turnover in anoxic marine sediments, using a ^{15}N-NH_4^+ dilution technique. Appl. Environ. Microbiol., 37(4):760–765.

Boyle, D., R. Collier, A. Dengler, J. Edmond, A. Ng, and R. Stallard, 1974. On the chemical mass-balance in estuaries. Geochim. Cosmochim. Acta, 38:1719–1728.

Boynton, W., 1974. Phytoplankton production in Chincoteague Bay, MD. MS Thesis, University of North Carolina, Chapel Hill, N.C., 142 p.

Boynton, W., W. Kemp, C. Osborne, and K. Kaumeyer, 1979. Community metabolism and nutrient dynamics of the Patuxent Estuary interacting with the Chalk Point Power Plant. Interim Report, Maryland Power Plant Siting Program, Chesapeake Biological Laboratory, Solomons, Maryland.

Boynton, W.R., W.M. Kemp, C.G. Osborne, 1980. Nutrient fluxes across the sediment water interface in the turbid zone of a coastal plain estuary. In V.S. Kennedy (Ed.), Estuarine Perspectives. Academic, New York, pp. 93–109.

Brezonik, P.L., 1972. In L.L. Ciaccio, (Ed.), Water Pollution Handbook, Vol. III.

Brooks, R., P. Brezonik, H. Putnam, and M. Keirn, 1971. Nitrogen fixation in an estuarine environment: The Waccasassa on the Florida coast. Limnol. Oceanogr., 16:701–710.

Broecker, W., T. Peng, and R. Engh, 1980. Modeling the carbon system. Radiocarbon, 22:565–598.

Burton, J.D., 1976. Basic properties and processes in estuarine chemistry. In J.D. Burton and P.S. Liss (Eds.), Estuarine Chemistry. Academic, New York, pp. 1–31.

Byers, R.J., J. Larimen, H.T. Odum, R.B. Parker, and N. Armstrong, 1963. Instructions for the determination of changes in carbon dioxide concentrations from changes in pH. Publ. Inst. Mar. Sci., Univ. Texas, 9:454–489.

Callender, E., 1982. Benthic phosphorus regeneration in the Potomac River Estuary. In P.G. Sly (Ed.), Proceedings Second International Symposium on Sediment/Fresh Water Interaction. Junk, The Hague, The Netherlands.

Callender, E. and D.E. Hammond, 1982. Nutrient exchange across the sediment-water interface in the Potomac River estuary. Estuarine Coastal Shelf Sci., 15:395–413.

Capone, D., 1983. Benthic nitrogen fixation. In E. Carpenter and D. Capone (Eds.), Nitrogen in the Marine Environment. Academic Press, New York, pp. 105–137.

Carpenter, E.J., 1972. Nitrogen fixation by a blue-green epiphyte on pelagic Sargassum. Science, 178:1207–1208.

Carpenter, E.J., and C. Price, 1977. Nitrogen fixation, distribution, and production of *Oscillatoria* (*Trichodesmium*) spp. in the western Sargassum and Caribbean Seas. Limnol. Oceanogr., 22:60–72.

Carpenter, E.J., C.D. Van Raalte, and I. Valiela, 1972. Nitrogen fixation by algae in a Massachusetts salt marsh. Limnol. Oceanogr., 7:318–327.

Carpenter, E.J., C. Van Raalte, and I. Valiela, 1978. Nitrogen fixation by algae in a Massachusetts salt marsh. Limnol. Oceanogr. 23:318–327.

D'Elia, C., D. Nelson, and W. Boynton, 1983. Chesapeake Bay nutrient and plankton dynamics: III. The annual cycle of dissolved silicon. Geochim. Cosmochim. Acta, 47:1945–1955.

Delwiche, C.C., 1970. The nitrogen cycle. Sci. Am., 223(3):137–146.

Detwiler, P. and C.A.S. Hall, 1988. Tropical forests and the global carbon cycle. Science, 239:42–47.

Duinker, J.C., 1980. In E. Olausson and I. Cato (Eds.), Chemistry and Biogeochemistry of Estuaries. Wiley, New York, pp. 121–145.

Eppley, R., J. Roger, and J. McCarthy, 1969. Half-saturation constants for uptake of nitrate and ammonia by marine phytoplankton. Limnol. Oceanogr., 14:912–920.

Fenchel, T., 1969. The ecology of marine microbenthos IV. Structure and function of the benthic ecosystem, its chemical and physical factors and the microfauna communities with special reference to the ciliated protozoa. Ophelia, 6:1–182.

Fenchel, T.M., and R.J. Riedl, 1970. The sulfide system: a new biotic community underneath the oxidized layer of marine sand bottoms. Marine Biology, 7:255–268.

Fogg, G.E., 1978. Nitrogen fixation in the oceans. Environmental role of nitrogen-fixing blue-green algae and a symbiotic bacteria. Ecol. Bull. (Stockholm), 26:11–19.

Fortes, M.D. and K. Luning, 1980. Growth rates North Sea macroalgae in relation to temperature, irradiance and photoperiod. Helgolander Meeresunters. 34:15–29.

Furnas, M., G. Hitchcock, and T. Smayda, 1976. Nutrient-phytoplankton relationships in Narragansett Bay during the 1974 summer bloom. In M. Wiley (Ed.), Estuarine Processes. Academic Press, New York, Vol I, pp. 118–134.

Garside, C., T.C. Malone, O.A. Roels, B.A. Sharfstein, 1976. An evaluation of sewage-derived nutrients and their influence on the Hudson estuary and New York light. Estuarine Coastal Mar. Sci., 4:281–289.

Glibert, P.M., 1982. Regional studies of daily, seasonal and size fraction variability in ammonium remineralization. Mar. Biol., 70:209–222.

Grill and Richard, 1964. Nutrient regeneration from phytoplankton decomposing in seawater. J. Mar. Res., 22:51–69.

Hansen, J.I., K. Henriksen, T.H. Blackburn, 1981. Seasonal distribution of nitrifying bacteria and rates of nitrification in coastal marine sediments. Microbial Ecology, Vol. 7 Springer-Verlag, New York, pp. 297–304.

Hall, C. and R. Moll, 1975. Methods of assessing aquatic primary production. In H. Lieth and R. Whittaker (Eds.), Primary Production of the Biosphere, Springer-Verlag, New York, pp. 19–53.

Harrison, W.G., 1978. Experimental measurements of nitrogen remineralization in coastal waters. Limnol. and Oceanogr., 23(4):684–694.

Harrison, W.G., 1980. Nutrient regeneration and primary production in the sea. In P.G. Falkowski (Ed.), Primary Productivity in the Sea. Plenum, New York, pp. 433–460.

Henriksen, K., J.I. Hansen, T.H. Blackburn, 1981. Rates of nitrification, distribution of nitrifying bacteria, and nitrate fluxes in different types of sediment from Danish waters. Mar. Biol., 61:299–304.

Hobbie, J., B. Copeland, and W. Harrison, 1975. Sources and fates of nutrients of the Pamlico River estuary, North Carolina. In L. Cronin (Ed.), Estuarine Research. Academic Press, New York, Vol. I, pp. 287–302.

Hollibaugh, J.T., A.B. Carruthers, J.A. Fuhrman and F. Azam, 1980. Cycling of organic nitrogen in marine plankton communities studied in enclosed water columns. Marine Biology 59:15–21.

Horne, A.J., 1978. In R. Mitchell (Ed.), Water Pollution Microbiology, Wiley, New York, Vol. 2, pp. 1-28.

Howarth, R.W. and J. Cole, 1985. Molybdenum availability, nitrogen limitation, and phytoplankton growth in natural waters. Science, 229:653-656.

Howarth, R.W. and J.M. Teal, 1979. Sulfate reduction in a New England salt marsh. Limnol. Oceanogr., 24(6):999-1013.

Howarth, R.W. and J.M. Teal, 1980. Energy flow in a salt marsh ecosystem: The role of reduced inorganic sulfur compounds. Am. Nat., 116(6):862-872.

Hutchinson, E.G., 1967. A Treatise on Limnology. Wiley, New York, p. 1,115

Iizumi, H., and A. Hattori, 1982. Growth and organic production of eelgrass (*Zostera marina* L.) in temperate waters of the Pacific coast of Japan. III. The kinetics of nitrogen uptake. Aq. Bot., 12:245-256.

Iizumi, H., A. Hattori, and P. McRoy, 1980. Nitrate and nitrite in interstitial waters of eelgrass beds in relation to the rhizosphere. J. Exp. Mar. Biol. Ecol., 47:191-201.

Iversen, N., and T.H. Blackburn, 1978. Seasonal rates of methane oxidation in anoxic marine sediments. Appl. Environ. Microbiol., 41:1295-1300.

Jenkins, M., and W. Kemp, 1984. The coupling of nitrification and denitrification in two estuarine sediments. Limnol. Oceanogr., 29:609-619.

Jitts, H.R., 1959. The adsorption of phosphate by estuarine bottom deposits. Aust. J. Mar. Freshwater Res., 10:7-21.

Johannes, R.E., 1964. Uptake and release of dissolved organic phosphorus by representatives of a coastal marine ecosystem. Limnol. Oceanogr., 9:224-234.

Jones, K., 1974. Nitrogen fixation in a salt marsh. J. Ecol., 62:553-565.

Jorgensen, B.B., 1977. The sulfur cycle of a coastal marine sediment. Limnol Oceanogr., 22(5):814-832.

Kaplan, W., I. Valiela, and J.M. Teal, 1979. Denitrification in a salt marsh ecosystem. Limnol. Oceanogr., 24(4):726-734.

Kemp, W.M. and W.R. Boynton, 1980. Influence of biological and physical processes on dissolved O_2 dynamics in an estuarine system: Implications for measurement of community metabolism. Estuarine Coastal Mar. Sci., 11(4):407-431.

Kemp, W.M., R. Wetzel, W. Boynton, C. D'Elia, and J. Stevenson, 1982. Nitrogen cycling and estuarine interfaces: some current research directions. In V. Kennedy (Ed.), Estuarine Interactions. Academic Press, New York, pp. 209-230.

Kemp, W.M., W. Boynton, R. Twilley, J. Stevenson, and L. Ward, 1984. Influences of submersed vascular plants on ecological processes in upper Chesapeake Bay. In V. Kennedy (Ed.), The Estuary as a Filter. Academic Press, New York, pp. 367-394.

Klump, J.V. and C.S. Martens, 1981. Biogeochemical cycling in an organic rich coastal marine basin. II. Nutrient sediment-water exchange processes. Geochim. Cosmochim. Acta, 45(1):101-121.

Koike, I. and A. Hattori, 1978a. Denitrification and ammonia formation in anaerobic coastal sediments. Appl. Environ. Microbiol., 35(2):278-282.

Koike, I. and A. Hattori, 1978b. Simultaneous determinations of nitrification and nitrate reduction in coastal sediments by a ^{15}N dilution technique. Appl. Environ. Microbiol., 35(5):853-857.

Kremer, J. and S. Nixon, 1978. A Coastal Marine Ecosystem, Simulation and Analysis. Springer Verlag, New York, Ecological Studies 24, 217 p.p.

Lean, D.R.S., C.F.H. Liao, T.P. Murphy, and D.S. Painter, 1978. The importance of nitrogen fixation in lakes. Environmental role of nitrogen-fixing blue-green algae and a symbiotic bacteria. Ecol. Bull. (Stockholm), 26:41-51.

Lipschultz, F., 1981. Methane release from a brackish intertidal salt-marsh embayment of Chesapeake Bay, Maryland. Estuaries, 4:143-145.

Lipschultz, F., J.J. Cunningham, J.C. Stevenson, 1979. Nitrogen fixation associated with four species of submerged angiosperms in the central Chesapeake Bay. Estuarine Coastal Mar. Sci., 9:813-818.

Liss, P., 1976. Conservative and non-conservative behavior of dissolved constituents during estuarine mixing. In J. Burton and P. Liss (Eds.), Estuarine Chemistry. Academic Press, New York, pp. 93-130.

Loder, T. and R. Reichard, 1981. The dynamics of conservative mixing in estuaries. Estuaries, 4:64-69.

MacKay, D. and T. Leatherland, 1976. Chemical properties in a estuary receiving major inputs of industrial and domestic wastes. In J. Burton and P. Liss (Eds.), Estuarine Chemistry. Academic Press, New York, pp. 185-218.

Martens, C.S., 1978. Some of the chemical consequences of microbially mediated degradation of organic materials in estuarine sediments. Biogeochemistry of Estuarine Sediments. UNESCO, Paris, pp. 266-278.

Martens, C. and J. Klump, 1980. Biogeochemical cycling in Cape Lookout Bight. I. Methane sediment-water exchange processes. Geochim. Cosmochim. Acta, 44:471-490.

Martin, J., 1965. Phytoplankton-zooplankton relationships in Narragansett Bay. Limnol. Oceanogr., 10:185-191.

McElroy, M.B., J.W. Elkins, S.C. Wofsy, C.E. Kolb, A.P. Duran, and W.A. Kaplan, 1978. Production and release of N_2O from the Potomac estuary. Limnol. Oceanogr., 23(6):1168-1182.

McLaren, A.D., 1976. Rate constants for nitrification and denitrification in soils. Radiation and Environmental Biophysics, Vol. 13. Springer-Verlag, New York, pp. 43-48.

Morris, J., 1980. The nitrogen uptake kinetics of *Spartina alterniflora* in culture. Ecology, 61:1114-1121.

Mortimer, C., 1971. Chemical exchanges between sediments and water in the Great Lakes—Speculations on probable regulating mechanisms. Limnol. Oceanogr., 16:387-404.

Nicol, J., 1960. The Biology of Marine Animals. John Wiley & Sons, Inc., New York, p. 699.

Nishio, T., I. Koike, and A. Hattori, 1982. Denitrification, nitrate reduction, and O_2 consumption in coastal and estuarine sediments. Appl. Environ. Microbiol., 43(3):648-653.

Nixon, S.W., 1981. Remineralization and nutrient cycling in coastal marine ecosystems. In B. J. Neilson and L. E. Cronin (Eds.), Estuaries and Nutrients. Humana, New Jersey, pp. 111-138.

Nixon, S.W. and M.E.Q. Pilson, 1983. Nitrogen in estuarine and coastal marine ecosystems. In E.J. Carpenter and D.G. Capone (Eds.), Nitrogen in the Marine Environment. Academic, New York. pp. 565-646.

Nixon, S., C. Oviatt, and S. Hale, 1976. Nitrogen regeneration and the metabolism of coastal marine bottom communities. In J. Anderson and A. Macfadyen (Eds.), The Role of Terrestrial and Aquatic Organisms in Decompostion Processes. Blackwell Scientific Publications, London, pp. 269-283.

Officer, C.B. and J.H. Ryther, 1980. The possible importance of silicon in marine eutrophication. Mar. Ecol. Prog. Ser., 3:83-91.

Oren, A. and T.H. Blackburn, 1979. Estimation of sediment denitrification rates at in situ nitrate concentrations. Appl. Environ. Microbiol., 37(1):174-176.

Paerl, H.W., K.M. Crocker and L.E. Prufert, 1987. Limitation of N_2 fixation in coastal marine waters: Relative importance of molybdenum, iron, phosphorus, and organic matter availability. Limnol. Oceanogr. 32:525-536.

Park, K., D. Hood, and H.T. Odum, 1958. Diurnal pH variation in Texas bays, and its application to primary production estimation. Publ. Institute Mar. Sci, U. Texas, 5:47-64.

Parsons, T., M. Takahashi, and B. Hargrave, 1977. Biological Oceanographic Processes. Second Edition. Permagon Press, New York, 332 p.

Peterson, D., J. Conomos, W. Broenkow, and E. Scrivani, 1975. Processes controlling the dissolved silica distribution in San Francisco Bay. In L. Cronin (Ed.), Estuarine Research. Academic Press, New York, Vol. I, pp. 153-187.

Presley, B.J. and J.H. Trefry, 1980. Sediment-Water interactions and the geochemistry of interstitial waters. In E. Olausson and I. Cato (Eds.), Chemistry and Biogeochemistry of Estuaries. Wiley, New York, pp. 187-226.

Redfield, A.C., B.H. Ketchum, and F.A. Richards, 1963. The influence of organisms on the composition of sea-water. In N.M. Hill (Ed.), The Sea, Vol. 2. Wiley-Interscience, New York, pp. 26-77.

Riley, J., and R. Chester, 1971. Introduction to Marine Chemistry. Academic Press, New York, 465 p.

Sansone, F. and C. Martens, 1978. Methane oxidation in Cape Lookout Bight, North Carolina. Limnol. Oceanogr., 23:349-355.

Satomi, M. and L.R. Pomeroy, 1965. Respiration and phosphorus excretion in some marine populations. Ecology 46:877-881.

Seitzinger, S., 1982. The importance of denitrification and nitrous oxide production in the nitrogen dynamics and ecology of Narragansett Bay, Rhode Island. Ph.D. Thesis, University of Rhode Island, Kingston, RI.

Seitzinger, S., S. Nixon, M.E.Q. Pilson, and S. Burke, 1980. Denitrification and N_2O production in near-shore marine sediments. Geochim. Cosmochim. Acta, 44:1853-1860.

Shenton, M.A., 1982. Nitrifying and denitrifying activity in the sediments of estuarine littoral zones. MS Thesis, University of Maryland, College Park, 51 p.

Sholkovitch, E., 1976. Flocculation of dissolved organic inorganic matter during mixing of river water and sea water. Geochim. Cosmochim. Acta., 40:831-845.

Sillen, L., 1961. AAAS Publ. 67, Washington, D.C., pp. 549.

Sorensen, J., 1978a. Capacity for denitrification and reduction of nitrate to ammonia in a coastal marine sediment. Appl. Environ. Microbiol., 36:139-143.

Sorensen, J., 1978b. Denitrification rates in a marine sediment by the acetylene inhibition technique. Appl. Environ. Microbiol., 35:301-305.

Sorensen, J., B.B. Jorgensen, and N.P. Revsbech, 1979. A comparison of O_2, nitrate, and sulfate respiration in coastal marine sediments. Microb. Ecol., 5:105–115.

Stanley, D.W. and J.E. Hobbie, 1981. Nitrogen recycling in a North Carolina coastal river. Limnol. Oceanogr., 26(1):30–42.

Stumm, W. and J.J. Morgan, 1972. Aquatic Chemistry—An Introduction Emphasizing Chemical Equilibria in Natural Waters. Wiley-Interscience, New York, p. 583.

Taft, J., W. Taylor, E. Hartwig, and R. Loftus, 1980. Seasonal oxygen depletion in Chesapeake Bay. Estuaries, 3:242–247.

Thayer, G., 1971. Phytoplankton production and the distribution of nutrients in a shallow, unstratified estuarine system near Beaufort, NC. Chesapeake Sci., 12:240–253.

Thursby, G. and M. Harlin, 1982. Leaf-root interactions in the uptake of ammonia by Zostera marina. Mar. Biol., 72:109–112.

Topinka, J. and J. Robbins, 1976. Effects of nitrate and ammonium enrichment on growth and nitrogen physiology in Fucus spiralis. Limnol. Oceanogr., 21:659–654.

Valiela, I. and J. Teal, 1979. The nitrogen budget of a salt marsh. Nature, 280:652–656.

Vanderborght, J.P., R. Wollast, and G. Billen, 1977. Kinetic model of diagenesis in disturbed sediments. Part 2. Nitrogen diagenesis. Limnol. Oceanogr., 22(5):794–803.

Webb, K.L., 1981. Conceptual models and processes of nutrient cycling in estuaries. In B.J. Neilson and L.E. Cronin (Eds.), Estuaries and Nutrients. Humana, New Jersey, pp. 25–46.

Webb, K. and C. D'Elia, 1980. Nutrient and oxygen redistribution during a spring neap tidal cycle in a temperate estuary. Science, 207:983–985.

Whitney, D., G. Woodwell, and R. Howarth, 1975. Nitrogen fixation in Flax Pond: a Long Island salt marsh. Limnol. Oceanogr. 20:640–643.

Zeitzschel, B., 1980. Sediment water interactions in nutrient dynamics. In K. Tenore and B. Coull (Eds.), Marine Benthic Dynamics. University of South Carolina Press, Columbia, pp. 195 -218.

ESTUARINE PLANTS AND PRIMARY PRODUCTION

OFFPRINTS FROM: ESTUARINE ECOLOGY
Edited by John W. Day Jr., Charles A. S. Hall., Dr. W. Michael Kemp, and Alejandro Yáñez-Arancibia
Copyright © 1989 by John Wiley & Sons, Inc.

▬ 4

Estuarine Phytoplankton

4.1 DISTRIBUTION AND TAXONOMIC COMPOSITION

4.1.1 Composition

Phytoplankton are tiny, single-cell algae that drift about with the motion of the water. They are the most ubiquitous group of autotrophic organisms—occurring in all estuarine waters and contributing substantially to overall primary production. They provide a major, direct food source for animals in the water column and in the sediments. Generally, the dominant groups are diatoms and dinoflagellates, while other important groups include cryptophytes, chlorophytes (green algae), and chrysophytes (blue-green algae). The species composition of a given phytoplankton community is a function of various environmental factors including salinity, turbidity, nutrients, turbulence, and depth. Representative species of estuarine phytoplankton are depicted in Fig. 4.1 for five major groups. As you can see in this figure, estuarine phytoplankton vary widely in size and shape.

A convention has evolved over the years of separating phytoplankton into two categories of size based on whether they will be retained on a standard screen (20 μm mesh; Malone 1980b). Those retained are called *netplankton* (or *microplankton*) while those passed are referred to as *nanoplankton*. A third group, the *ultraplankton* or *picoplankton* (diameter <2 μm), is sometimes considered distinct (Dussart 1965). Nanoplankton are generally numerically dominant in most estuaries, although netplankton comprise a major part of the biomass. As one moves from the estuary to the ocean, the phytoplankton tend to be domi-

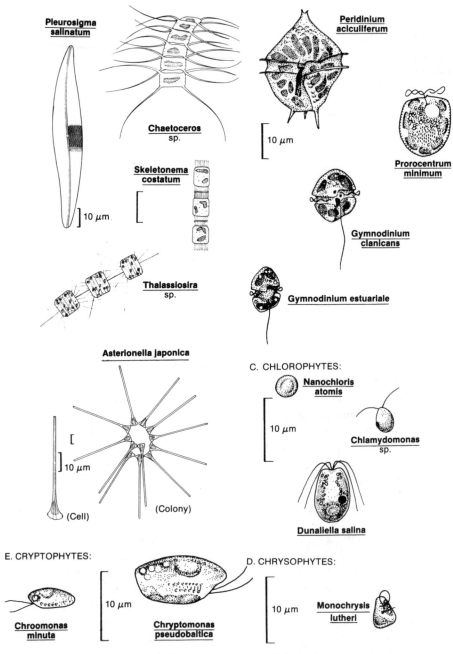

A. DIATOMS:

Pleurosigma salinatum

Chaetoceros sp.

Skeletonema costatum

Thalassiosira sp.

Asterionella japonica

(Cell) (Colony)

10 μm

B. DINOFLAGELLATES:

Peridinium aciculiferum

10 μm

Prorocentrum minimum

Gymnodinium clanicans

Gymnodinium estuariale

C. CHLOROPHYTES:

Nanochloris atomis

10 μm

Chlamydomonas sp.

Dunaliella salina

E. CRYPTOPHYTES:

Chroomonas minuta

Chryptomonas pseudobaltica

10 μm

D. CHRYSOPHYTES:

10 μm

Monochrysis lutheri

Figure 4.1 Representatives of five major groups of phytoplankton occurring in estuaries (after Campbell 1973, with permission of the author).

nated increasingly by smaller forms (Malone 1980a). For example, Yentsch and Ryther (1959) reported that only 2–10% of the diatoms and small flagellates of the Gulf of Maine were retained by a standard plankton net.

The annual pattern of species composition of netplankton in a temperate coastal-plain estuary is exemplified in the data of Smayda (1957) for Narragansett Bay, Rhode Island (Fig. 4.2). In this case, the dominant phytoplankton population is that of the diatom *Skeletonema costatum*. This one species represents about 81% of the annual mean total numerical abundance of phytoplankton cells, with major blooms occurring during late summer and winter. Dominance by a single species has been reported for other temperate estuaries, where, for example, *S. costatum* comprised more than 80% of the total in both Block Island Sound (Riley 1951) and the James River (Marshall 1967). Smayda's data for Narragansett Bay also demonstrate the overall importance of diatoms and dinoflagellates to the netplankton, a pattern that also occurs in lower Chesapeake Bay, where diatoms comprised 70% of the total number of species and dinoflagellates 26% (Marshall 1967). In Sandy Hook Bay, New Jersey the two groups constituted 60 and 22% of the total species of the net plankton, respectively (Kawamura 1962).

4.1.2 Spatial and Temporal Patterns in Temperate Estuaries

One example of the changes in phytoplankton species composition encountered while moving from lower to higher salinity along an estuarine axis is indicated in Fig. 4.3 for the Pamlico River, North Carolina. Here we see that dinoflagellates dominate samples from low-salinity areas. Diatoms and occasional chlorophytes, cyanophytes, and cryptophytes are of secondary importance. This pattern also was reported by Matthiessen (1960) for an oligohaline salt pond in Massachusetts. Seaward, in the midsalinity region, diatoms and dinoflagellates are about equally important, with the former dominating in winter and spring and the latter more significant during the summer. This seasonal trend appears to be common in many temperate estuaries, including lower Chesapeake Bay (Patten et al. 1963), Long Island Sound (Riley and Conover 1967), the lower Hudson River (Malone 1977), and a small estuary on Long Island (Carpenter and Dunham 1985). As such, it may reflect changing conditions of temperature, insolation, water-column stability, and nutrient availability, and different abilities of various species to exploit changing conditions. Summer species (dinoflagellates) have higher light optima, shorter generation times, and they are motile. Winter forms (diatoms) have lower light optima, longer generation times, and greater capacity for energy storage, but they require mixing to remain suspended (Smayda 1980). In addition, diatoms tend to sink from surface waters (often en masse) as their growth rates decline in summer (Smetacek 1985). In some very shallow systems such as the Dutch Wadden Sea, blooms of diatoms and flagellates tend to alternate over the whole growing season, with three peaks of both groups occurring between April and September (Cadée 1986).

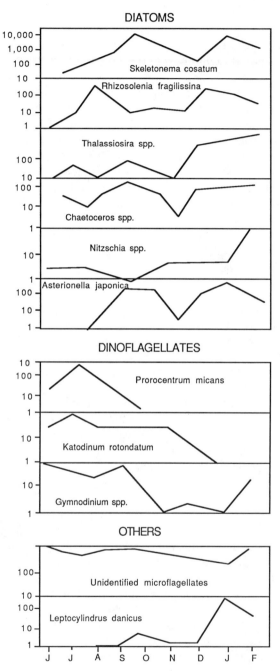

Figure 4.2 The annual pattern of species composition of the netplankton in Narragansett Bay, Rhode Island (from Smayda 1957). Units are number of cells per ml.

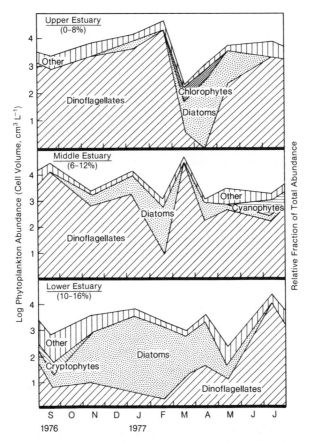

Figure 4.3 Seasonal changes in the total net phytoplankton abundance (as cell volume) from upper to lower estuary (salinity range given) in the Pamlico River, North Carolina (from Kuenzler et al. 1979). Total cell volume (uppermost line in each panel) is given as logarithm, while relative fraction of total comprised by each taxonomic group is depicted as an arithmetic percent of the total. (a) Upper estuary, 0–8%; (b) middle estuary, 6–12%; (c) lower estuary, 10–16%.

As salinity approaches full strength, phytoplankton communities resemble more closely oceanic ones. For example, Hopkins (1966) found that the dominant phytoplankton species of St. Andrews Bay, Florida, an embayment with marine salinities, were two marine diatoms common in the Gulf of Mexico (*Chaetoceros* sp. and *Rhizosolenia* sp.).

4.1.3   Arctic and Tropical Patterns

From the evidence available, the taxonomic composition of arctic phytoplankton appears to be somewhat different from that of temperate estuaries. For example,

Bursa (1963) observed that diatoms accounted for only 34% of the population in Elson Lagoon (Alaska), while dinoflagellates comprised a mere 4% of the numerical abundance, and small green flagellates made up the remainder. A distinct assemblage of diatoms also can be found growing in arctic sea ice. The most common genera here are *Navicula* and *Pinnularia* where salinities are from 18 to 40 (Apollonio 1961, Bunt 1963, Meguro et al. 1967, McRoy 1968).

Relatively stable and characteristic plankton associations occur in shallow waters along tropical and subtropical coasts where the ecosystem is not subjected to regular seasonal light and temperature pulses. With less controlling influence from seasonal factors, more complicated biological interactions develop than in temperate systems. On a landward transet starting offshore of the Puerto Rican coast, Margalef (1962) described the deeper, stratified offshore regions as resembling blue-water oligotrophic conditions while inshore waters were vertically well mixed. Diatoms, which dominated in the well-mixed areas, were replaced by dinoflagellates in the shallow quiescent waters influenced by inputs from surrounding mangrove and seagrass communities. A remarkable example of such a bay is Bahia Fosforescente in Puerto Rico where continual blooming of the dinoflagellate *Pyrodinium bahamence* causes an impressive bioluminescence (Seliger et al. 1970).

Phytoplankton of tropical blue water coasts are characterized by high diversity and increasing importance of nanoplankton as compared to temperate areas (Marsh 1974). In the tropics there is a higher diversity of dinoflagellate species, but not diatoms which, however, flourish in colder regions (Wood 1965). Nanoplankton tend to become relatively more important over netplankton in the oligotrophic waters at lower latitudes. For example, Miller and Moore (1935) reported that nanoplankton were about 1000 times more abundant than netplankton in oligotrophic tropical waters of the Florida Straits.

4.2   PATTERNS OF PRODUCTION AND ABUNDANCE

Phytoplankton productivity is a major source of primary food-energy for most estuarine ecosystems throughout the world. Photosynthesis by these autotrophic organisms proceeds, as with all green plants, by the conversion of the light energy of solar photons into biological energy with the fixation of carbon dioxide, the splitting of the water molecule, and the production of carbohydrates and oxygen. Phytoplankton photosynthesis is measured in a number of ways, including (1) rate of oxygen production (Gaarder and Gran 1927), (2) rate of CO_2 uptake or associated alkalinity-pH changes (Beyers and Odum 1960), (3) rate of incorporation of a radioactive carbon (^{14}C) into particulate matter (Steeman-Nielsen 1956), and (4) rate of increase of particulate matter (Ryther and Menzel 1965). Not all of these methods yield exactly the same information and it is sometimes difficult to compare results from various methods (Hall and Moll 1975; Peterson 1980). However, recent experiments comparing productivity measurements as ^{14}C incorporation and oxygen evolution have observed almost identical rates for the two methods (Williams et al. 1979, 1983). Nevertheless, it is necessary to compare the various measurements to understand the general patterns of estuarine productivity.

The seasonality of overall phytoplankton abundance changes from the tropics to higher latitudes. This is illustrated in an idealized way for standing stocks of phytoplankton and zooplankton for coastal systems of different latitudes (Fig. 4.4). In the arctic the populations follow the strong seasonal peak in sunlight. Temperate systems often show spring and fall phytoplankton peaks, and there is little predicable seasonality for the tropical systems, when higher production may be associated with patterns of river flow (Flores-Verdugo et al. 1987). These latter two patterns may be true for some estuaries, but factors such as river discharge, rainfall, nutrient availability, and cloud cover make the patterns for lower latitudes much more variable.

4.2.1 Total Productivity

Mean daily rates of primary production for selected estuarine systems are given in Fig. 4.5a. Rates range from near zero to 4.8 $gCm^{-2}d^{-1}$. The average for all estuarine systems is about 0.70 $gCm^{-2}d^{-1}$. (256 $gCm^{-2}yr^{-1}$.), a value substantially higher than the 100 $gCm^{-2}yr^{-1}$ reported by Ryther (1963) for coastal areas and on the same order as Ryther's value of 300 $gCm^{-2}yr^{-1}$ estimated for upwelling areas. Despite the large range in location, freshwater input, physical morphology, insolation and other factors, highest rates tend to occur when water temperatures are at annual maxima. This is especially true for well-mixed estuaries. This pattern has been interpreted by some investigators to indicate that

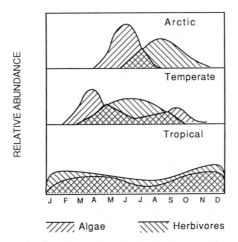

Figure 4.4 Idealized graph of possible phytoplankton and zooplankton standing stocks over an annual cycle for coastal systems of different latitudes (after Cushing 1959).

temperature strongly influences nutrient recycling processes and planktonic growth rates which are, in turn, important factors for maintaining high photosynthetic rates (e.g., Williams 1966, Flemer 1970, Thayer 1971).

While high production rates often occur in summer in moderately and highly stratified systems, the pattern is not as consistent as in nonstratified systems. Factors such as nutrient exhaustion in the euphotic zones, deep mixing of plankton (Riley 1946), and dispersion of phytoplankton stocks (Welch et al. 1972) have been invoked to explain these patterns. Depth is an important factor for nonstratified estuaries, where generally the most productive systems in this group are shallow (mean depth < 3 m). This question of seasonality of production is addressed further in the next section (4.2.2).

Concentrations of phytoplankton chlorophyll *a* (the main photosynthetic pigment, which is an index of biomass) appear to be greatest in high-river-flow nonstratified systems (Fig. 4.5*b*). Such estuaries generally receive the greatest nutrient inputs, which are converted to phytoplankton biomass. It should be noted that while the geographic coverage for the data summarized here is quite broad, there is a distinct lack of information for tropical systems.

The majority of phytoplankton photosynthesis in estuaries appears to be contributed by nannoplankton. In the marine-influenced Beaufort Channel, netplankton constituted at times as much as about 40% of the total productivity; however, on an annual basis nannoplankton production was almost 80% of the total (Williams and Murdoch 1966). McCarthy et al. (1974) found that nannoplankton comprised almost 90% of the annual production in both upper and lower Chesapeake Bay. They found little difference in the ratio of net- to nannoplankton production along the salinity gradient, although there was some indication that netplankton were more important in the most riverine stations.

4.2.2   Seasonal and Spatial Patterns of Productivity

In temperate latitudes, peak seasonal phytoplankton production occurs most often in the summer, with seasonal cycles corresponding roughly to the peaks in solar radiation and temperature (Fig. 4.6). This is not always the case, however, as illustrated by the high values from February through April for Narragansett Bay, Rhode Island. In the tropics, the strong seasonal patterns of solar radiation and temperature are lacking, and thus production seasonality is more variable. In Terminos Lagoon, Mexico, peak production and chlorophyll values occur in the fall, during the time of highest river discharge (Day et al. 1982).

Seasonal peaks in productivity may not be associated with increases in phytoplankton biomass. For example, seasonal and spatial patterns of phytoplankton productivity and chlorophyll *a* in a temperate estuary are illustrated for the Pamlico River in Fig. 4.7 (Kuenzler et al. 1979). It can be seen that a strong peak in photosynthesis occurred throughout the estuary in late summer, and in the upper estuary in late winter and early spring of 1977. The winter/spring peak was accompanied by an increase of phytoplankton biomass (chlorophyll *a*) which moved down-bay beyond the actual point of the productivity peak. On the

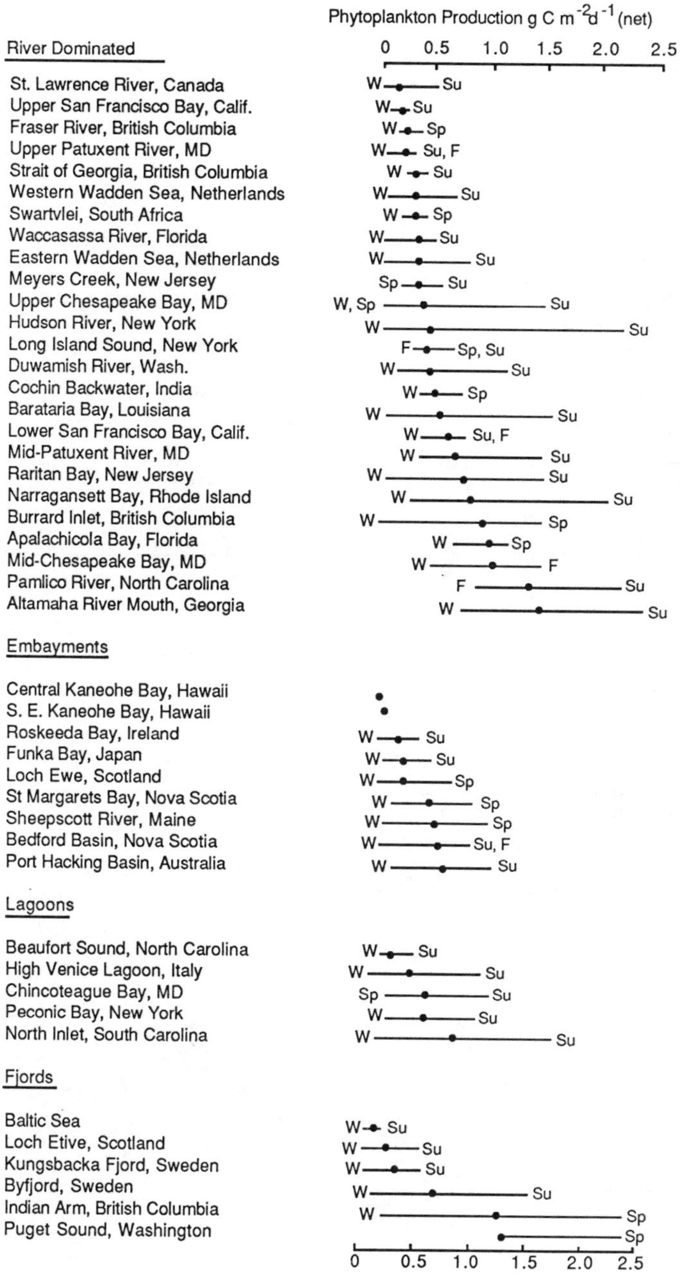

Phytoplankton Production g C m^{-2}d^{-1} (net)

(a)

Figure 4.5a Summary of average daily phytoplankton production rates (solid dot) in 45 estuarine systems. Horizontal bars indicate annual ranges. Season in which maximum and minimum rates occured is also indicated (W, winter; Sp, spring; Su, summer; F, fall).

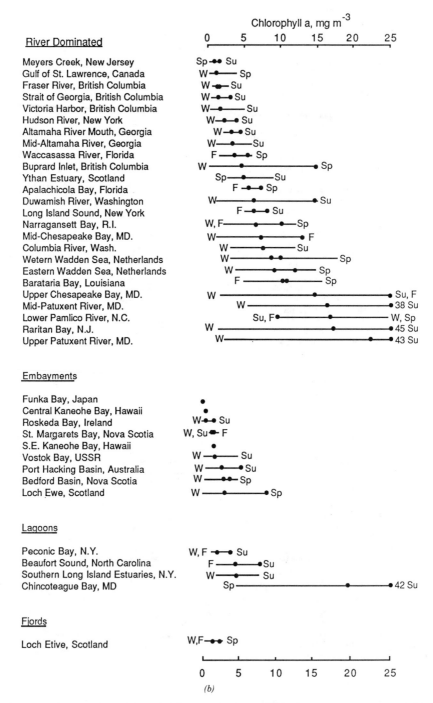

Figure 4.5b Summary of chlorophyll a concentrations in 39 estuarine systems. Annual ranges and seasons in which maximum and minimum concentrations occurred are indicated as in Fig. 4.5a. Solid dots indicate chlorophyll a concentrations at time of maximum production. (From Boynton et al. 1982)

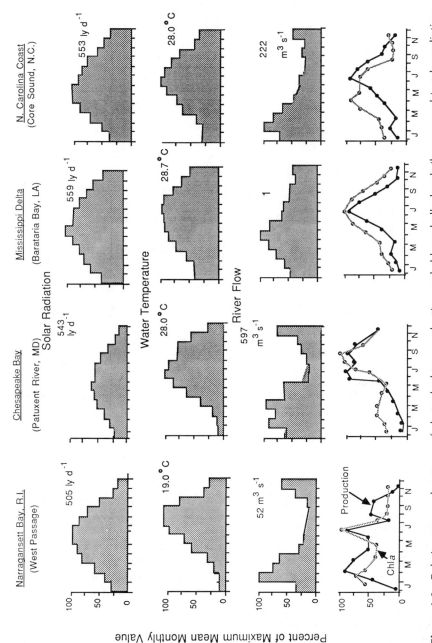

Figure 4.6 Relative seasonal patterns of phytoplankton production and chlorophyll a levels (lower panels), solar radiation, water temperature, and river flow for four estuarine systems. Maximum mean monthly values are given (redrawn from Nixon 1981).

157

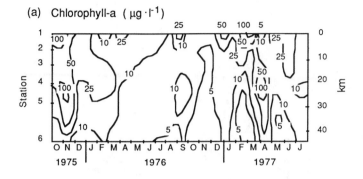

(a) Chlorophyll-a (μg · l⁻¹)

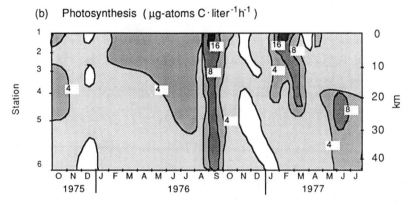

(b) Photosynthesis (μg-atoms C · liter⁻¹h⁻¹)

Figure 4.7 Seasonal and longitudinal distributions of phytoplankton, chlorophyll a, and photosynthesis in Pamlico River estuary. Stations 1, 4, and 6 correspond to upper, middle, and lower estuary, respectively, in Fig. 4.3 (redrawn from Kuenzler et al. 1979).

other hand, the summer production maximum was not accompanied by an increase in chlorophyll *a*, presumably because of higher respiration and grazing rates occurring during the warm season.

This general pattern, of highest production in summer and highest chlorophyll levels in spring, has been reported for other estuaries such as Long Island Sound (Riley 1946). There are, however, numerous variations on this basic theme. For example, Flemer (1970) consistently found a single annual period of maximum productivity in late summer throughout the upper and middle Chesapeake Bay. Chlorophyll *a* levels were not as pronounced down-bay, but even there relatively high values were observed into the autumn with peaks lagging photosynthesis by about 2 months. Only a very slight winter/spring bloom was evident in Beaufort Sound, North Carolina, a shallow, high-salinity embayment (Thayer 1971). There was a single, marked seasonal peak in photosynthesis occurring in July with a mid-spring maximum of chlorophyll *a* apparent during a period of lower but increasing photosynthesis. In the nearby deeper Beaufort Channel, Williams and Murdoch (1966) reported a broad summer period of maximum productivity (June through September), with chlorophyll *a* peaks occurring especially in late winter but to a lesser degree in late spring and fall.

In summary, timing and location of phytoplankton blooms are regulated by a balance between physical circulation, light conditions, nutrient availability and grazing in a given estuary. Extended periods of stratification from early spring through late summer allow for a long phytoplankton growing season (Sinclair et al. 1981). Turbidity conditions in winter can, however, affect the timing of the phytoplankton peaks in the following spring (Cadée 1986a). Seasonal, or more frequent, shifts in stratification and cross-channel circulation may also markedly affect phytoplankton growth (Malone et al. 1986). In many shallow systems, the dominant summertime phytoplankton blooms may be driven by temperature-regulated nutrient recycling from sediment processes (Kemp and Boynton 1984). In other relatively deep estuaries dominated by spring runoff and associated inputs of nutrients, summer phytoplankton production tends to be reduced relative to spring, and benthic recycling of nutrients is less important (Malone and Chervin 1979).

In partially stratified estuaries, regions of maximal phytoplankton biomass and production tend to occur just seaward of the turbidity maximum. Here, we find an interface between areas of high nutrients but turbid water (landward) and low nutrient levels but clearer water (seaward) (Kemp et al. 1982; Fisher et al. 1986). The exact location of this "chlorophyll maximum" will vary from year to year with changes in riverflow (Malone et al. 1980; Cloern et al. 1983; Filardo and Dunstan 1985; Pennock and Sharp 1986). Local regions of patches of water with very high phytoplankton abundance can occur within estuaries in association with tidal and topographic fronts or interfaces between different water masses (Seliger et al. 1981; Tyler 1984) and distributions of turbulent eddies (Denman and Platt 1975; Therriault et al. 1978). In these "chlorophyll patches," phytoplankton distribution is controlled largely by physical circulation (Platt 1972).

Boynton et al. (1983) found that there was much more variation in volume-based than area-based primary production over a wide range of aquatic ecosystems, including estuaries. One reason is that more oligotrophic ecosystem had a deeper light penetration and hence more volume with net photosynthenis.

4.3 FACTORS REGULATING PHYTOPLANKTON PHOTOSYNTHESIS

Numerous factors regulate the magnitude, seasonal pattern, and species composition of phytoplankton photosynthesis, including light, temperature, nutrients, physical transport processes, and herbivory. As suggested by Boynton et al. (1982, 1983), these factors affect phytoplankton assemblages at both the ecological scale and individual cells. At the ecological scale, environmental factors influence phytoplankton through species selection. In addition, adaptation to these changing environmental conditions is regulated at the physiological scale by intracellular biochemical mechanisms, including changes in enzyme and pigment concentrations providing near-optimal response for specific species. The relative signficance of these factors apparently varies from one system to the next and it is our purpose now to compare the importance of these factors.

4.3.1 Light

One of the most important variables controlling phytoplankton photosynthesis is photosynthetically active radiation, PAR, or light in the range of wavelengths from 400–700 nm, which provides the predominant source of energy for these autotrophic organisms. The overall importance of light in regulating phytoplankton photosynthesis is apparent on a geographic scale for lakes and reservoirs where, for example, Brylinsky and Mann (1973) found light to be the single best predictor of phytoplankton production for a large sample of lakes throughout the world. Similiar relationships have yet to be demonstrated for estuaries, probably owing to local differences in nutrient availability and physical circulation.

Phytoplankton photosynthetic response to light can be demonstrated with a photosynthesis—irradiance (P-I) curve. Photosynthetic response to increasing irradiance (starting at total darkness) is, at first, linearly proportional. The relative rate of photosynthesis, however, starts to diminish at higher light levels, until eventually a response plateau is reached, where increases in light promote no further increase in productivity. At very high irradiance levels, photosynthesis may begin to decrease because of light inhibition (associated with photochemical destruction of pigments). The response plateau may be very broad, so that inhibitory conditions occur only at extremely high light levels, or it may be a narrow peak. A generalized response curve (Fig. 4.8a) can be described in terms of (Parsons et al. 1979): the y intercept, the initial positive slope (alpha), the peak or light-saturated photosynthetic rate (P_{max}), the irradiance where net photosynthesis is zero (I_c); the irradiance where alpha intersects P_{max} (I_k) and the irradiance at which initial inhibition is evident (I_i). The actual shape of P-I curves for specific algal assemblages depends on the light conditions in which the cells are growing (e.g. Fig. 4.8b and c).

Light is reflected, absorbed, and refracted by dissolved and suspended substances in the water and by the water itself. The extent to which light is attenuated at a given depth of water is determined by the clarity of that water. The distribution of light with depth in the water column can be described by the Beer-Lambert expression (Parsons et al. 1979):

$$I_z = I_o(e^{-K_T z}) \tag{1}$$

where I_z is the light at any depth z, I_o is the light at the top of the water column, and K_T is the diffuse downwelling irradiance attenuation coefficient. This coef-

a) Generalized P - I Response Curve

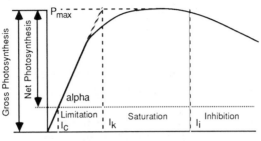

Irradiance   (Light intensity)

Example P - I   Response Curves

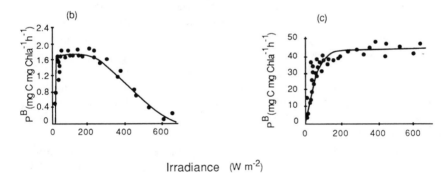

Irradiance   (W m^{-2})

Figure 4.8   (a) General curve relating photosynthesis to light intensity. Curves illustrating photosynthetic response by different algae with different light adaptations: (b) adaptation to low light with inhibition beginning at about 300 Ws/m^2; (c) adaptation to high light with no inhibition (from Platt and Gallegos 1980).

ficient characterizes the clarity of the water, and typically it ranges from 0.1 to 3.0/m for coastal waters. Lorenzen (1970) has shown that

$$K_T = K_w + K_c + K_d + K_p \qquad (2)$$

where K_w, K_c, K_d, and K_p are, respectively, the attenuation coefficients attributable to water, chlorophyll a, dissolved substances, and nonalgal particulate matter. Thus phytoplankton themselves diminish the amount of light available to them. In a typical estuarine water column K_c may comprise from 5 to 50% of

K, while K_w represents less than 5%. A traditional measure of turbidity is the depth at which a white circular disk (referred to as a *Secchi disk*) will just disappear from sight. This Secchi depth (Z_s) is inversely related to the combined extinction coefficient (K) by the following:

$$K = c/Z_s \qquad (3)$$

where the coefficient c varies from about 1.4 to 1.8 in estuarine waters (Poole and Atkins 1929, Holmes 1970, Keefe et al. 1976).

Phytoplankton, when incubated in bottles at a series of depths, exhibit characteristic patterns of photosynthetic rate with depth in relation to the vertical distribution of ambient light. Often phytoplankton incubated in bottles at the water surface display a pronounced light inhibition with maximum phytosynthetic rates occurring somewhat below the surface (Fig. 4.9b). In more turbid waters no surface inhibition will be evident owing to the rapid attenuation of light with depth (Fig. 4.9a). Marra (1978a,b), however, suggested that cells are, in fact, adapted to fluctuating light regimes and that vertical mixing enhances phytoplankton production by providing flashes of relatively bright light. Algal cells are able to maximize photosynthesis by rapidly acclimating to changing light by varying their photosynthetic pigment composition and enzyme concentrations, with response times of one hour or less (Falkowski 1980, Fig. 4.10a). At low irradiance, higher initial P-I slope (alpha) allows cells to use limited light more efficiently, yielding higher photosynthetic rates at a given irradiance level. Marra (1980) also showed that algal cells rotated through a vertical series of depths often had significantly greater photosynthetic production, even though the total light available was the same in both cases (Fig. 4.9b). Similarly Platt and Gallegos (1980) developed a model simulating phytoplankton photoadaptation to demonstrate that a mixed-water column generated about 20% more photosynthesis than a static system (Fig. 4.10b).

On the other hand, extreme vertical mixing in an estuarine water column can cause reduced photosynthesis by transporting cells below the depth at which there is sufficient light to maintain their growth. The depth at which gross photosynthetic rate (P) is just equal to algal respiration rate (R) is referred to as the *compensation depth* (D_c) (Fig. 4.11). Below this level a given cell cannot survive because there is insufficient light for it to produce as much energy as the cell requires for its own base respiration. This D_c is often approximated by the depth at which 1% of surface irradiance is available (e.g., Flemer 1970) or as 2.5 times the Secchi depth (Parson et al. 1979). Since algal cells are continually mixed through the water column, however, D_c is not as important as the *critical depth* (D_{cr}), to which an entire phytoplankton population or assemblage can be mixed while still maintaining a balance between integrated (over time and depth) photosynthesis (P_I) and integrated respiration (R_I), i.e. an average algal cell can be mixed from surface to D_{cr} and still maintain a positive energy balance. At D_{cr}, the vertically integrated photosynthesis equals vertically integrated respiration or $P_I = R_I$ (Fig. 4.11a). However, if the depth to which the upper layer of a water column is mixed (D_m) exceeds D_{cr}, as can occur in a nonstratified estu-

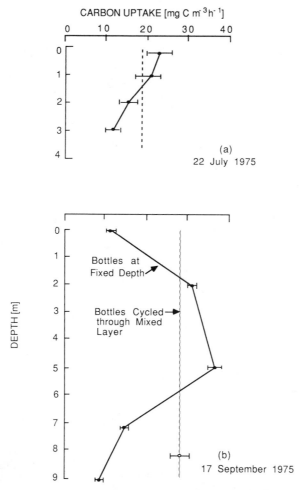

Figure 4.9 Variations in phytoplankton production with incubations at different depths in a coastal water column on two different dates (Marra 1980). Production (carbon uptake) for algal cells incubated in bottles at fixed depths is indicated by filled circles and solid lines, while mean production for cells in bottles rotated vertically through the water column at the same time is indicated by open circles and dashed line.

ary, assemblages of nonmotile plankton will not be able to develop net photosynthesis and growth (Fig. 4.11*b*). Hence, for deep and/or turbid coastal waters the light regime in the top layer of a stratified system is often more favorable for phytoplankton photosynthesis than in a vertically well-mixed system.

The early work of Riley (1942) showed a positive relationship between water-column stability (as indicated by the inverse of mixed-layer depth) and plankton

(a)

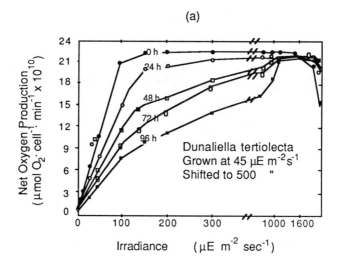

(b)

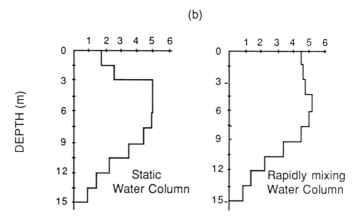

Figure 4.10   (a) Photosynthetic response of *Dunaliella tertiolecta* at different light intensities and after different times—after being shifted to 500 μE/m² s after being grown at 45 μE/m² s (from Falkowski 1980). (b) Photosynthesis in a mixed-water column compared with a static water column (from Platt and Gallegos 1980).

production at George's Bank. Sverdrup (1953) later derived an elegant formulation to estimate D_{cr}, where in most instances D_{cr} can be approximated as the ratio of irradiance at the surface (I_o) to that at compensation depth (I_c) divided by the light attenuation coefficient, $D_{cr} = (I_o/I_c)/K$. Several investigations (e.g., Parsons et al. 1966) have compared critical depth with depth of the mixed layer to predict or reconstruct geographic patterns of phytoplankton productivity in the ocean. Similarly, Ragotzkie (1960) observed that no net phytoplankton

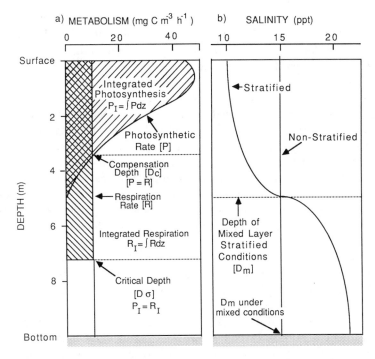

Figure 4.11 (a) Vertical profiles of phytoplankton photosynthesis and respiration in relation to compensation depth and critical depth. (b) Effect of stratification and mixing on the depth of the mixed layer and its relation to the critical depth. See text for further explanation.

productivity occurred in the estuarine waters near Sapelo Island, Georgia when D_{cr} was less than the mixed depth (which was identical to the mean depth of the water column in this shallow, well-mixed system). More recently, Wofsy (1983) has developed the concept of "optical depth" (OD) which is equal to the product of diffuse PAR attenuation coefficient (K_T, Eq. 1) and the depth of the upper mixed layer (D_m). Optical depth is, thus, also related to the ratio of D_m to Secchi disk depth (OD $= 1.7 D_m/Z_s$). The optical depth, which measures the proportion of the upper mixed layer containing more than one-third of the surface irradiance, varies over a relatively narrow range of 4 to 8 for eutrophic estuaries. For all such estuaries, a strong positive relation was found between depth of the mixed layer and Secchi depth ($D_m = 0.2 + 2.3Z_s$). The implication of this is that phytoplankton growth and abundance in those estuaries not limited by nutrients is adjusted such that PAR attenuation due to cells results in irradiance at the bottom of the mixed layer being 1% of that at the water surface. This "homeostatic" adjustment of phytoplankton biomass results in efficient use of light by the algal community, and often leads to conditions where light is not limiting.

In estuaries containing high concentrations of suspended sediments, the relationship between D_m and Z_s changes. Pennock (1985), for example, has shown that peak abundance of phytoplankton along the length of the Delaware estuary generally occurs downstream of the suspended sediment maximum. Significant development of algal standing stocks, however, only occurs in this estuary when occasional development of stratification in the water column reduces D_m, which otherwise coincides with the overall water depth (Pennock 1985). Delaware Bay has a relatively high OD compared to Chesapeake Bay, which is more stratified, so that phytoplankton growth in the former system (deeper mixed depth and more turbid) appears to be more generally light limited (Harding et al. 1986). Cole and Cloern (1984) have shown that phytoplankton net production is directly proportional to the ratio of photic zone depth to water column depth for the weakly stratified San Francisco Bay. This relation again emphasizes the importance of vertical mixing in regulating the availability of light for phytoplankton growth.

On the temporal scale of an annual cycle, the effect of light in temperate latitudes is marked, where for example it has been demonstrated that the initiation of winter-spring diatom blooms is keyed to increasing light intensities for Long Island Sound and Narragansett Bay (Riley 1967, Hitchcock and Smayda 1977, Nixon et al. 1979, see also Fig. 4.6). Over diel cycles light obviously controls photosynthetic fixation of carbon, where none occurs in the dark. Diel patterns of nitrate and ammonium uptake for coastal phytoplankton communities dominated by the dinoflagellate *Gonyaulax* sp. have also been reported, with highest uptake occurring in late morning (MacIsaac and Dugdale 1972). Fisher et al. (1982) reported some effect of reduced light on ammonium uptake, but this effect was relatively minor compared to diel cycles of carbon assimilation. Kuenzler et al. (1979) also observed only a weak relationship between light and inorganic nitrogen assimilation, either with depth (and attendent light) or over a diel cycle.

4.3.2 Nutrients

Phytoplankton assimilate inorganic dissolved nutrients (and a few selected organic forms) and transform these materials into the organic matrix of their cells through internal enzymatic processes. The transport of nutrient elements across the algal cell wall is, in part, a result of simple Fickian diffusion, which is driven by the difference between intracellular and external concentrations. This simple diffusion may be facilitated by internal cellular enzymes that actively transport nutrients into the cell (e.g., Taft et al. 1975). At low concentrations, phytoplankton uptake of a particular nutrient exhibits a linear relationship to the concentration of that nutrient in the aqueous medium. As external concentrations increase further, however, the uptake rate ceases to increase with higher concentrations, and nutrient uptake becomes saturated. At this point, the overall process of nutrient assimilation essentially becomes limited at some step other than uptake.

Phytoplankton require a diverse array of mineral nutrients for sustenance and growth, including N, P, Si, Mo, Zn, Mn, Ca, as well as carbon dioxide and several vitamins such as B-12. Generally, the most important are the so-called "macronutrients" (carbon, nitrogen, phosphorus, and silicon). These elements, along with hydrogen and oxygen, comprise the largest portion of estuarine phytoplankton cells. Of these macronutrients, nitrogen is available in the widest assortment of forms and it undergoes the most complicated biogeochemical cycling (see Chapter 3 for further details).

Sustained algal primary production requires a continuing availability of the basic input factors for photosynthesis (particularly light, inorganic carbon, nitrogen, phosphorus, and silicon). Phytoplankton uptake and productivity can be related to the availability of each of these substances individually in terms of a rectangular hyperbolic response curve as shown in Fig. 4.12 (see Appendix 4.1 for further explanation). Usually, the concentration of one or more of these substances is less than its "saturation level," and it is thereby a potential limiting factor for algal photosynthesis and growth.

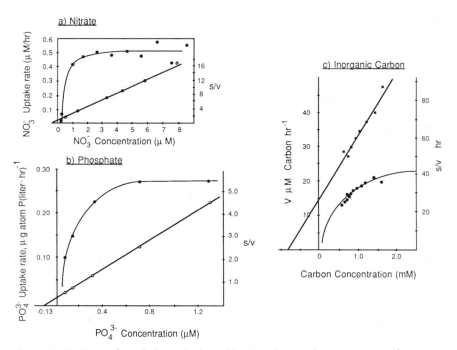

Figure 4.12 Examples of phytoplankton kinetic relations for nutrient uptake versus substrate concentration for: (a) nitrate (Furnas et al. 1978); (b) phosphate (Taft et al. 1975); (c) inorganic carbon (Loftus et al. 1979). Curved lines are rectangular hyperbola for uptake, while straight lines are for ratio of substrate to uptake (see appendix 4.1 for further explanation).

As explained in introductory chemistry courses, the overall rate of a chemical reaction can be described by the rate of the slowest step (Le Chatelier's principle). Similarly, overall phytoplankton growth is determined by its response to the single factor that is least available (or most limiting) for its existence (Leibig's Law of Limiting Factors). Transient periods may occur when algal growth is limited by more than one factor. The replenishment rates for these substances tend to be different, so that a single ingredient will eventually be most limiting. This process must be viewed as a dynamic one, where limiting-factor status may fluctuate from one substance (or condition) to another, sometimes over brief intervals of time and space.

It is, nevertheless, convenient to relate the proportions in which nutrients are found in the composition of algal cells to the relative proportions in which these elements are available in the external estuarine environment. In the classic paper describing the chemical composition of sea water and plankton cells Redfield et al. (1963) demonstrated a remarkably consistent atomic proportion in the elemental composition of oceanic algae. These "Redfield Ratios" of atomic weights of the elements $C:N:Si:P$ are on the order of $106:16:15:1$. Others have demonstrated that estuarine plankton also are characterized by a similar elemental composition (Parsons et al. 1961). In estuarine and coastal environments, however, ratios of dissolved inorganic $N:P$ in the water can range from <1.0 to over 200 (Fig. 4.13). During the season of peak phytoplankton production, $N:P$ in estuarine water tends to be less than the ratio of $16:1$ observed for cellular constituents of estuarine plankton (Fig. 4.13). Thus, because the estuarine environment has less nitrogen available per unit of phosphorus than algal cells require for their structure, it is often concluded that nitrogen is the more limiting nutrient for estuarine photosynthesis.

There are several possible exceptions to this view of nutrient limitation. External concentrations of more than one nutrient may be below their respective "saturation" values. This might create a condition of "multiple" limiting nutrients, where an addition of more than one nutrient element would result in a linear proportional increase in algal uptake and growth (e.g., McCarthy et al. 1975). Futhermore, nutrient uptake rates, for kinetic studies, should be expressed on a per unit cell or cellular enzyme basis to be theoretically consistent (e.g. Brezonik 1972). Thus, although nutrient concentrations greater than kinetic saturation levels may not cause increased uptake per algal cell, they can result in increased abundance of cells as long as nutrient inputs and recycling rates are sufficiently high to avoid nutrient depletion (Caperon et al. 1971).

Ratios of $N:P$ in both algae and the water column vary over the course of an annual cycle and along the estuarine salinity gradient. For the Pamlico River estuary, North Carolina Kuenzler et al. (1979) show that ratios of dissolved inorganic $N:P$ in the water ranged over a factor of 30 while algal $N:P$ varied by a factor of only 3 (Fig. 4.14). Lowest values of dissolved inorganic $N:P$ occured in the summer, and the ratio was generally highest in the upper estuary. Only during the spring in the uppermost reaches did the algal and environmental ratios approach one another.

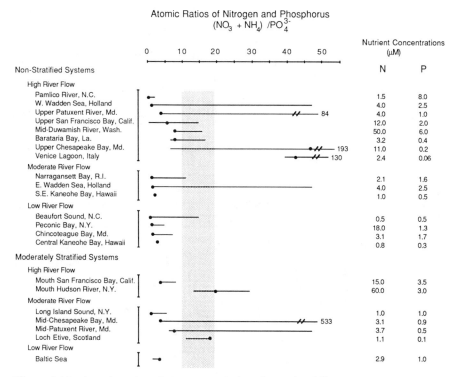

Figure 4.13 Atomic ratios of nitrogen and phosphorus for different estuarine systems. The solid line is the range and the closed circle and the values on the right are average values. The shaded area is the approximate range of N:P ratios for living plankton (from Boynton et al. 1982).

In various "bioassay" experiments in which nitrogen and phosphorus were added to estuarine water separately it has generally been observed that nitrogen-enriched incubations exhibited enhanced photosynthesis or population growth, while phosphorus enrichment gave a varied, but always smaller response (Ryther and Dunstan 1971, Thayer 1974, Goldman et al. 1973). The results of a typical experiment are presented in Fig. 4.15. Note the fact that addition of both N and P resulted in the greatest response, indicating a multiple nutrient limitation. D'Elia et al. (1985) used large continuous culture systems for phytoplankton in an estuarine tributary of Chesapeake Bay to examine seasonal variations in the relative importance of N vs. P limitations for growth. Although P limitation was more important during winter, N limitation prevailed through most of the main phytoplankton growing season. Phytoplankton compete with bacteria for inorganic nutrients, so that other conditions favoring bacterial growth can exacerbate algal nutrient limitation (Rhee 1972, Thayer 1974, Remsen et al. 1972). Recent studies using pre-filtration and specific inhibitors revealed that bacterial

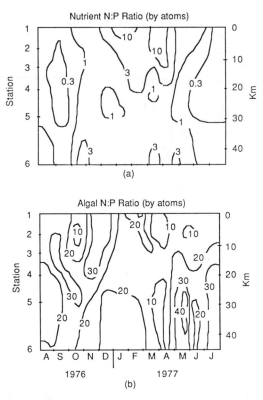

Figure 4.14 Seasonal distributions of ratios of nitrogen to phosphorus along the length of the Pamlico River estuary. (a) Ratio of dissolved inorganic nitrogen (ammonium plus nitrate) to dissolved inorganic phosphorus. (b) Ratio of N:P for phytoplankotn tissue. Figure redrawn from Kuenzler et al. (1979). See Figures 4.7 and 4.3 for production, chlorophyll, plankton composition, and salinity for this area.

uptake accounted for >75% of the total ammonium assimilation in estuarine waters (Wheeler and Kirchman 1986).

While nitrogen is the macronutrient that most often limits production of estuarine phytoplankton in general, Smith (1984) and Smith et al. (1986) have provided geochemical and mass balance data and arguments to suggest that, ultimately, P will limit production in coastal marine systems. Recent reports of inorganic N:P ratios in mesohaline Chesapeake Bay water also indicate a deficiency of P even during summer (Boynton and Kemp 1985; Malone et al. 1986), so that this issue remains an open question. Futhermore, diatom productivity may be often limited (both seasonally and annually) by the availability of silicon in the form of silicates (Officer and Ryther 1981). The seasonal sequence of late spring-early summer diatom blooms giving way to late summer-early fall flagel- late-dominated blooms seems to be common to many temperate estuaries (Figs.

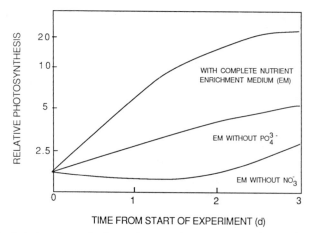

Figure 4.15 Relative phytoplankton photosynthetic response to added nutrients compared with a control (indicated by a value of 1, from Thayer 1974).

4.2 and 4.3, Margalef 1958, Pratt 1965, and Smetacek 1980). Officer and Ryther (1981) suggest that this pattern results from diatom utilization of the bountiful nutrient supplies (including silicon) built up over the winter, followed by depletion of silicon, which is regenerated more slowly than nitrogen and phosphorous. It has been suggested that the relatively slow rate of silicon recycling might result from the fact that silicon is incorporated into diatom tests or skeletal materials, which have little or no nutritional value for grazers. Officer and Ryther (1981) cite four estuarine systems for which there is significant evidence of silicon limitation: San Francisco Bay, the Hudson estuary, the Potomac estuary; and Narragansett Bay. Recent evidence (D'Elia et al. 1983) indicates that silicon dissolution rates may be comparable to nitrogen regeneration rates in middle-to-high salinity waters of the Potomac Estuary. Therefore the argument of Officer and Ryther (1981) may hold only for low-salinity waters.

Uptake of a given nutrient by estuarine phytoplankton can deviate from strict rectangular hyperbolic kinetic responses to concentrations (Fig. 4.12). It has been shown for both coastal and freshwater plankton that nutrient uptake can proceed at rates far in excess of those needed for algal growth (e.g., Ketchum 1939, 1967). This so-called "luxury consumption" of a given nutrient occurs for certain algal species when that nutrient exists in excess abundance compared to the other macronutrients.

Coastal and estuarine phytoplankton exhibit distinct patterns of preference for the various compounds of nitrogen available to them. Typically, the more chemically reduced forms are preferred, because energy is required to convert oxidized nitrogen to the most reduced inorganic form, ammonium, before cellular incorporation into amino acids. In Chesapeake Bay mixed phytoplankton assemblages preferred nitrogen forms in the following order NH_4^+ > urea >

$NO_2^- > NO_3^-$ (McCarthy et al. 1977). While urea is more reduced than ammonium, its organic form presumably renders it somewhat less available. A relative preference index (RPI) can be defined as the uptake rate of a given nitrogen compound per unit available external concentration divided by the uptake rate of all other nitrogen forms per unit of their available concentration. Kuenzler et al. (1979) observed a similar relationship between NO_3^- and NH_4^+ in the Pamlico River estuary. Concentrations of NH_4^+ in excess of 2 μm appeared virtually to inhibit all NO_3^- uptake, while nitrate exerts no influence on NH_4^+ uptake. Although Carpenter and Dunham (1985) reported similar patterns of phytoplankton preference for different nitrogen species, high ambient concentrations of NO_3^- in a small Long Island estuary resulted in nitrate being the dominant form of nitrogen assimilated by phytoplankton over an annual cycle.

4.3.3 Temperature

In a comprehensive review article, Eppley (1972) noted that temperature response curves for phytoplankton growth and photosynthesis were similar for most algal species studied, with relatively rapid declines in production at temperatures in excess of their optima. Goldman (1977) showed that temperature optima for five coastal phytoplankton species all fell in the range of 20 to 25°C (Fig. 4.16a–e), as a mixed assemblage of these species in lieu of severe competitive interaction (Fig. 4.16f). Moreover, it appears that cellular nitrogen content is inversely related to the temperature-regulated growth of these algal populations, possibly indicating relatively greater effects of temperature on carbon versus nitrogen metabolism. For the numerous studies reviewed by Eppley (1972), physiological temperature optima occurred over a wide range (10–40°C) for different species. The range of adaptation to changing temperature is, however, limited for each species, and occurs on time scales of about a day. Yentsch (1974) and Yentsch et al. (1974) reported that mixed assemblages of phytoplankton from a given temperate coastal environment exhibited temperature responses similar to those for pure cultures, regardless of the ambient temperature from which they were sampled. Temperature evidently exerts a selective force for populations whose temperature optima coincide with local environmental conditions. Temperature acclimatization for a given assemblage is thus limited. More recently, Karentz and Smayda (1984) reported that maximum abundances for 30 algal species in Narragansett Bay occurred at temperatures 3–14°C lower that their respective optimum growth temperatures observed in laboratory cultures. These findings suggest that seasonal succession of phytoplankton species in nature, while affected by temperature, is more directly controlled by other factors.

4.3.4 Herbivory

The importance of zooplankton grazing on phytoplankton stocks as a mechanism for regulating productivity has been an issue of some debate for the last several decades. Steeman-Nielsen (1958b), for example, argued that the com-

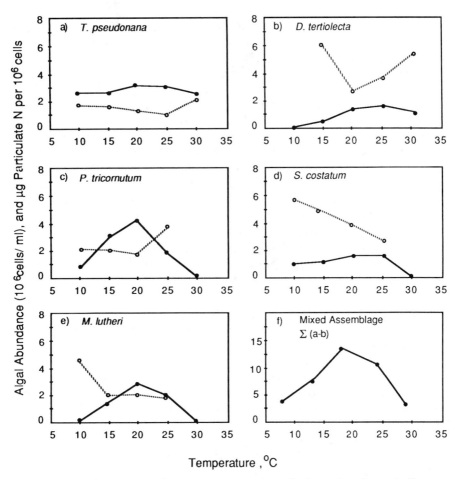

Figure 4.16 Effects of growth temperature on phytoplankton abundance (cell numbers, solid lines) and on nitrogen content of cells (dashed lines) for five species (a–e) grown in continuous culture (Goldman 1979) and for a hypothetical mixed assemblage (f) of these populations (a simple arithmetic sum of the separate cultures, a–e) (from Goldman 1979).

monly observed seasonal patterns of more or less coincidental peaks in phytoplankton and zooplankton abundance supported the hypothesis that grazing maintained algal populations in a steady-state balance the level of which was determined by the limitations of other environmental conditions (i.e., light, nutrients, temperature). In contrast, Cushing (1959) utilized a simple predator-prey model to conclude that grazing did, indeed, affect the magnitude and timing of phytoplankton stocks, and that a lag between peak abundances of phytoplankton and zooplankton populations could be observed consistently, especially in colder climates (see Fig. 4.4). Extremely high population densities of zooplankton in both lakes and estuaries are a relatively common occurrence, and in many cases the energy needed to support associated herbivory must be explained either in terms of tightly coupled turnover rates (Cushing 1976) or organic carbon sources other than phytoplankton (Heinle and Flemer 1975).

In estuaries such as Chesapeake and Narragansett Bays, high suspension-feeding rates of ctenophores and medusae on zooplankton may serve to keep the zooplanton grazing in balance (Heinle 1974, Kremer 1979). Recent studies have reported inverse relationships between abundances of herbivorous crustacean and gelatinous zooplankton from field observations and direct relationships between ctenophore abundance and phytoplankton chlorophyll a (Lindahl and Hernroth 1983; Feigenbaum and Kelly 1984). Walsh (1976) has speculated that, in the sea, the relatively low productivity in offshore divergence zones compared with coastal upwellings may be attributable to higher grazing pressures in the former area, since nutrient regimes are similar in both. While zooplankton herbivory may be an important control on phytoplankton productivity for certain seasons in certain environments (e.g., Martin 1970), it is not likely to be a severe limitation overall (e.g., Oviatt et al. 1979). This topic is covered in more detail in Chapter 8.

In certain shallow coastal environments suspension feeding by benthic macrofauna can reduce phytoplankton abundance significantly (Cloern 1982; Officer et al. 1982). For several estuarine systems, it has been shown that a single dominant suspension-feeding bivalve population was capable of filtering the entire overlying water column in 1–4 days (Cohen et al. 1984; Nichols 1985; Doering et al. 1986). Such grazing rates can reduce phytoplankton standing stocks by a factor of four or more. In certain environments, however, benthic filtration can also reduce overlying populations of herbivorous zooplankton as well, thereby partially ameliorating the effects on phytoplankton (Carlson et al. 1984).

4.3.5   River Flow Effects

Seasonal and interannual variations in river flow can influence phytoplankton production and taxonomic distribution in an estuarine system through several mechanisms, including: (1) changing inputs of nutrients from watershed to estuary; (2) changing rates of dilution or advection of algal cells out of the estuary; (3) changing light availability through stratification, gravitational circulation, and longitudinal positioning of turbidity maximum. Annual means of phytoplankton production and abundance have been significantly correlated to riverine nutrient inputs or mean concentrations for several estuarine systems (Cadée 1986b; Boynton et al. 1982). In addition, there is evidence that a massive delivery of nutrients to Chesapeake Bay during Hurricane Agnes in 1972 was reflected in elevated productivity not only during that year, but during the following year (Boynton et al. 1982), suggesting a mechanism of retention and recycling of nutrients within the estuary as well (Kemp and Boynton 1984). On the other hand, high river flow can lead to low phytoplankton abundance when growth rates are less than rates of advective removal of cells. For example, Welsh et al. (1972) attributed reduced phytoplankton abundance during high flow years in the Duwamish River estuary of Oregon to wash-out of algal cells. Seasonally, this also occurs in the lower Hudson River estuary during spring (Malone and Chervin 1979); however, in this case river-driven gravitational circulation also induces transport of diatoms into the estuary from offshore to seed the spring bloom (Malone et al. 1980).

As mentioned earlier, river flow can also control the location of the region of maximum phytoplankton production within an estuary. Under summer-fall low-flow conditions, Filardo and Dunstan (1985) found peak chlorophyll a concentrations occurring in the brackish regions of the James River estuary. With increasing river flow, a portion of this algal biomass was transported downstream, and highest phytoplankton growth was centered in the lower estuary with a markedly different species composition. In northern San Francisco Bay, gravitational circulation tends to concentrate algal cells in the oligohaline reaches, and the strength of river input regulates the longitudinal position of these algal assemblages (Cloern et al. 1983). Since this bay is relatively turbid, phytoplankton growth is light-limited, and blooms can occur only when river flows position the algal stock adjacent to a broad reach of shallow flats where water depths are less than the Sverdrup critical depth (see Section 4.3.1). Similar effects of river discharge on phytoplankton growth have been reported for Delaware Bay (Pennock 1985). In this case, however, the appearance of phytoplankton blooms in the lower bay depends on the development of vertical stratification (such that mixing depth is less than critical depth) which is, in turn, dependent on river discharge (Pennock and Sharp 1986). In Fourleague Bay, Louisiana, Randall and Day (1987) reported that phytoplankton production in the lower bay was approximately twice that of the turbid upper bay which was close to the mouth of the Atchafalaya River. Because of the turbidity introduced by the river, peak production occurred in September and October at both stations.

SUMMARY

Phytoplankton production is the major source of autochthonous organic matter (produced in the system) in most estuarine ecosystems. These tiny algal cells are well adapted to the rich but rigorous conditions of the estuarine environment. The role of phytoplankton net production in the particulate organic carbon budget of Chesapeake Bay is described in the data provided by Biggs and Flemer (1972), which is summarized in Fig. 4.17. It can be seen that the organic carbon budget in the turbid upper estuary is dominated by the input from river flow, and phytoplankton sources comprise less than 10% of the total inflow. On the other hand, the clearer waters of the middle bay are far less influenced by river input and phytoplankton production provides some 97% of the total source. Although inputs from marshes and submerged macrophytes were not considered

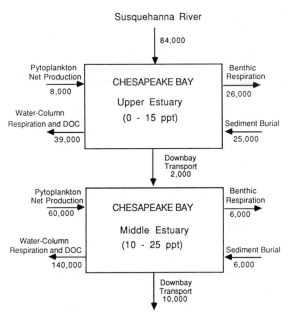

Figure 4.17 The relative importance of phytoplankton production and riverine input to the organic caarbon budget of Chesapeake Bay (from Biggs and Flemer 1972).

in this budget, the general pattern would not be affected significantly by including them.

One of the few estuarine systems for which full annual cycles of physical variables and nutrient concentrations are available for comparison with phytoplankton biomass and production estimates is the lower Hudson estuary (Malone 1977, Fig. 4.18). These data illustrate seasonal trends of physical variables typical for mid-latitude estuarine systems, with summer peaks of temperature and irradiance and minimum salinities. Maximum stratifications is in winter-spring. Phosphate and dissolved inorganic nitrogen (mostly ammonium) concentrations generally follow the temperature cycle, indicating the importance of recycling sources (as discussed in Chapter 3), while silicate concentrations are inversely related to salinity, possibly reflecting riverine sources. Annual maxima of phytoplankton productivity and mean chlorophyll *a* occur in late summer; however, netplankton (mostly diatoms), which dominate in early spring, sink into bottom waters. It is difficult to determine the relative importance of light, temperature, or nutrients in regulating phytoplankton production, since all exhibit annual maxima in late summer. Evidently, incipient stratification in late winter is essential for initiating the spring diatom bloom, and depletion of surface silicate concentrations does not appear to be involved in the late spring decline in diatom abundance.

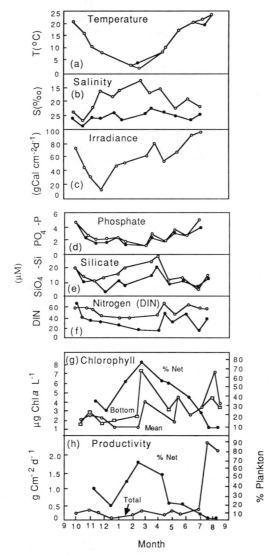

Figure 4.18 Representative annual cycles of (a) temperature, (b) salinity, (c) irradiance (mean for euphotic zone), (d) phosphate, (e) silicate, (f) dissolved inorgnic nitrogen (DIN); (g) chlorophyll a, (h) productivity for the lower Hudson River estuary (from Malone 1977). For panels (a), (b), (d), (e), and (f), solid circles indicate bottom water, while open circles are for surface water. Chlorophyll a (g) water column means are indicated by open circles and solid lines, while bottom water values are given as squares and % net plankton chlorophyll a is given by solid circles. Total productivity (h) is indicated by open circles and as % net plankton is given as dashed line.

177

The relative influence of environmental factors on estuarine phytoplankton production varies from one estuary to another. However, a model for seasonal changes in factors regulating production in temperate estuaries is given in Riley's (1967) description of Long Island Sound (Fig. 4.19). The spring flowering of phytoplankton chlorophyll and net photosynthesis, which typifies temperate estuaries, can be explained as the result of a balance between vernal availability of light to fuel photosynthesis and heat to stabilize the water column but sufficiently low temperatures to maintain a reduced respiratory drain. This bloom is initiated in midwinter (January–March) in shallow coastal systems (20–30 m), while in deeper waters the flowering may begin much later (April–May). This high level of production terminates in spring or early summer as the result of some combination of zooplankton grazing, depletion of nutrients, and reduced water clarity. Nutrient limitation is probably the most important mechanism. Summer productivities are variable, but may reach substantial proportions if there is a high availability of recycled nutrients. In most deeper systems an autumnal flowering is generated in much the same way as occurs in temperate lakes. Thermal cooling of surface layers and reduced river input cause a brief period of water-column instability and a resulting mixing up of bottom waters, which allows release of sediment nutrients to the euphotic zone. After restabilization and reduced vertical mixing, sufficient nutrients and light are available for a surge in productivity. Similar turnover events may be generated throughout the year via strong wind (and tidal) mixing.

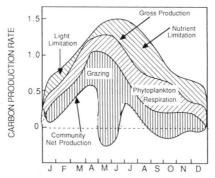

Figure 4.19 Idealized seasonal pattern of gross phytoplankton production (second line from top), and net community production (lower line). Also indicated are differences between potential (upper line) and actual gross production due to light limitation in winter and nutrient limitation in summer and fall, as well as losses in actual gross production due to phytoplankton respiration and grazing by zooplankton (after Riley 1946).

APPENDIX 4.1   THE KINETICS OF NUTRIENT UPTAKE

The kinetic descriptions of phytoplankton nutrient uptake versus concentration have been extensively studied (McCarthy 1980), and these relationships have proved very useful in understanding and predicting algal response to a given nutrient regime. The shape of the response function is similar to a rectangular hyperbola (Fig. 4.20a), which can be described by the following equation:

$$V = V_m \left[\frac{S}{K_s + S} \right] \tag{4}$$

where V is the velocity of nutrient uptake (properly expressed per cell or enzyme unit) at a given concentration of nutrient (S), V_m is the maximum uptake rate which is approached as the process becomes saturated, and K_s is the concentration of nutrients at which uptake is 0.5 V_m. The general form of this expression was derived by Monod for bacterial growth and by Michaelis and Menton for enzyme-catalyzed reactions (Yentsch 1974).

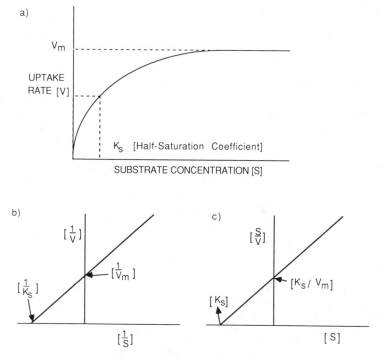

Figure 4.20 (a) Rectangular hyperpola describing Michaelis-Menten kinetic relation between nutrient substrate concentration (S) and uptake (V). Two algebraic transformations, (b) and (c), used for estimating kinetic coefficients (V_m and K_s) from experimental data.

Two methods are commonly used for estimating graphically the coefficents for this equation from experimental data, and both involve simple algebraic transformations. In the first (referred to as the Lineweaver-Burke plot), Eq. (4) is inverted and rearranged in the form

$$\frac{1}{V} = \left[\frac{K_s}{V_m}\right]\frac{1}{S} + \left[\frac{1}{V_m}\right] \tag{5}$$

and $1/V$ is plotted against $(1/S)$, with $(1/V_m)$ becoming the y intercept and $(1/K_s)$ the x intercept (Fig. 4.20b).

The second transformed version of the Michaelis-Menten expression is derived simply by multiplying Eq. (5) by (S) to obtain

$$\frac{S}{V} = \left[\frac{1}{V_m}\right]S + \left[\frac{K_s}{V_m}\right] \tag{6}$$

and (S/V) is plotted against (S), with (K_s/V_m) becoming the y intercept and K_s the x intercept (Fig. 4.20c).

REFERENCES

Apollonio, S., 1961. The chlorophyll content of arctic sea-ice. Arctic, 14(3):197–199.

Bellis, V., 1974. Medium salinity plankton systems. In H.T. Odum, B.J. Copeland, E.A. McMahan (Eds.), Coastal Ecological Systems of the United States. Cons. Found., New York, pp. 358–396.

Beyers, R.J., and H. Odum, 1960. Differential filtration with strong acids or bases vs CO_2 water for productivity studies. Limnol. Oceanogr., 5:228–230.

Biggs, R.B., and D.A. Flemer, 1972. The flux of particulate carbon in an estuary. Marine Biology, 12:11–17.

Boynton, W.R., and W.M. Kemp, 1985. Nutrient regeneration and oxygen consumption by sediments along an estuarine salinity gradient. Mar. Ecol. Prog. Ser., 23:45–55.

Boynton, W.R., W.M. Kemp, and C.W. Keefe, 1982. A comparative analysis of nutrients and other factors influencing estuarine phytoplankton production. In V.S. Kennedy (Ed.), Estuarine Comparisons. Academic Press, New York, pp. 69–90.

Boynton, W., C.A.S. Hall, P.G. Falkowski, C.W. Keeje, and W.M. Kemp, 1983. Photoplankton Productivity in Aquatic Ecosystems. Encyclopedia of Plant Physiology 12D. 305–327.

Brezonik, P.L., Chemical kinetics and dynamics in natural water systems. In L.L. Ciaccio (Ed.), Water and Water Pollution Handbook. Vol. III. 1972. Marcel Dekker, New York, pp. 831–913.

Brylinsky, M. and K.H. Mann. 1973. An analysis of factors governing productivity in lakes and reservoirs. Limnol. Oceanogr., 18(1):1–14.

Bunt, J.S. 1963. Diatoms of antarctic sea ice as agents of primary production. Nature, 199:1255–1257.

Bursa, A.S. 1963. Phytoplankton on coastal waters of the Arctic Ocean at Point Barrow, Alaska. Arctic, 16(4):239–262.

Cadée, G.C., 1986a. Recurrent and changing seasonal patterns in phytoplankton of the westernmost inlet of the Dutch Wadden Sea from 1969 to 1985. Marine Biology, 93:281-289.

Cadée, G.C., 1986b. Increased phytoplankton primary production in the marsdiep area (Western Dutch Wadden Sea) Netherlands Journal of Sea Research, 20(2/3):285-290.

Campbell, P.H. 1973. Studies on brackish water phytoplankton. I. The phytoplankton of Gates Creek with emphasis on the taxonomy and ecology of estuarine phytoflagellates. PhD Thesis, University of North Carolina, Chapel Hill, 407 pp.

Caperon, J., S. Scatell, and G. Grasnick, 1971. Phytoplankton kinetics in a subtropical estuary: eutrophication. Limnol. Oceanogr., 16:599-607.

Carlson, D.J., D.W. Townsend, A.L. Hilyard, and J.F. Eaton, 1984. Effect of an intertidal mudflat on plankton of the overlying water column. Can J. Fish Aquat. Sci., 41:1523-1528.

Carpenter, E.J. and S. Dunham, 1985. Nitrogenous nutrient uptake, primary production, and species composition of phytoplankton in the Carmans River estuary, Long Island, New York. Limnol. Oceanogr., 30(3):513-526.

Cloern, J.E., 1982. Does the benthos control phytoplankton biomass in south San Francisco Bay. Mar. Ecol. Prog. Ser., 9:191-202.

Cloern, J.E., A.E. Alpine, B.E. Cole, R.L.J. Wong, J.F. Arthur, and M.D. Ball, 1983. River discharge controls phytoplankton dynamics in the northern San Francisco Bay estuary. Est., Coastal and Shelf Sci., 16:415-429.

Cohen, R.R.H., P.V. Dresler, E.J.P. Phillips, and R.L. Cory, 1984. The effect of the Asiatic clam, *Corbicula fluminea*, on phytoplankton of the Potomic River, Maryland. Limnol. Oceanogr., 29(1):170-180.

Cole, B.E. and J.E. Cloern, 1984. Significance of biomass and light availability to phytoplankton productivity in San Francisco Bay. Mar. Ecol. Prog. Ser., 17:15-24.

Cushing, D.H., 1959. The seasonal variation in oceanic production as a problem in population dynamics. J. Conseil Exp. Mer., 24:455-464.

Cushing, D.H., 1976. Grazing in Lake Erken. Limnol. Oceanogr., 21:349-346.

Day, J.W., R.H. Day, M.T. Barreiro, F. Ley-Lou, and C.J. Madden, 1982. Primary production in the Laguna de Terminos, a tropical estuary in the Southern Gulf of Mexico. Oceanologica Acta, N° SP, pp. 269-275.

D'Elia, C.F., D.M. Nelson, W.R. Boynton, 1983. Chesapeake Bay nutrient and plankton dynamics: III. The annual cycle of dissolved silicon. Geochimica Cosmochimica Acta, 47:1945-1955.

D'Elia, C.F., J.G. Sanders, and W.R. Boynton, 1986. Nutrient enrichment studies in a coastal plain estuary: phytoplankton growth in large-scale, continuous cultures. Can. J. Fish. Aquat. Sci., 43:397-406.

Denman, K.L. and T. Platt, 1975. Coherences in the horizontal distributions of phytoplankton and temperature in the upper ocean. Mémoires Société Royale des Sciences de Liége, 8: 19-30.

Doering, P.H., C.A. Oviatt, and J.R. Kelly, 1986. The effects of the filter-feeding clam *Mercenaria mercenaria* on carbon cycling in experimental marine mesocosms. J. Mar. Research, 44:839-861.

Dussart, B.H., 1965. Les different categories de plancton. Hydrobiologia, 26:72-74.

Eppley, R.W., 1972. Temperature and phytoplankton growth in the sea. Fish. Bull., 70:1063–1085.

Falkowski, P.G., 1980. Light-shade adaptation in marine phytoplankton. In P.G. Falkowski (Ed.), Primary Productivity in the Sea. Plenum, New York, pp. 99–120.

Feigenbaum, D. and M. Kelly, 1984. Changes in the lower Chesapeake Bay food chain in presence of the sea nettle *Chrysaora quinquecirrha* (Scyphomedusa). Mar. Ecol. Prog. Ser., 19:39–47.

Filardo, M.J. and W.M. Dunstan, 1985. Hydrodynamic control of phytoplankton on low salinity waters of the James River estuary, Virginia, U.S.A. Est., Coastal and Shelf Sci., 21:653–667.

Fisher, T.R., P.R. Carlson, and R.T. Barber, 1982. Carbon and nitrogen primary productivity in three North Carolina estuaries. Est., Coastal and Shelf Sci., 15:621–644.

Fisher, T.R., L.W. Harding, Jr., D.W. Stanley, and Larry G. Ward, 1988. Phytoplankton, nutrients, and turbidity in the Chesapeake, Delaware, and Hudson estuaries. Est. Coastal Shelf Sci. 27:61–93

Flemer, D.A. 1970. Primary production in the Chesapeake Bay. Chesapeake Sci., 11:117–129.

Flores-Verdugo, F.J., J.W. Day, and R. Briseño-Dueñas, 1987. Structure, litter fall, decomposition, and detritus dynamics of mangroves in a Mexican coastal lagoon with an ephemeral inlet, Mar. Ecol. Progr. Ser., 35:83–90.

Furnas, M.J., G.L. Hitchcock, and T.J. Smayda, 1978. Nutrient-phytoplankton relationships in Narragansett Bay during the 1974 summer bloom. Estuarine Processes, Vol. 1.

Gaarder, T. and H.H. Gran, 1927. Investigation of the production of plankton in the Oslo fjord. Rapp. Proc. Verb., Cons. Int. Explor Mer, 42:1–8.

Goldman, J.C., 1979. Temperature effects on steady-state growth, phosphorus uptake, and the chemical composition of a marine phytoplankton. Microbial. Ecol., 5:153–166.

Goldman, J.K. Tenore, and D. Stanley, 1973. Inorganic nitrogen removal from wastewater: effect on phytoplankton growth in coastal marine waters. Science, 80:955–956.

Harding, L.W., Jr., B.W. Meeson, and T.R. Fisher, Jr., 1985. Photosynthesis patterns in Chesapeake Bay phytoplankton: short- and long-term responses of P-I curve parameters to light. Mar. Ecol. Prog. Ser., 26:99–111.

Harding, L.W., Jr., B.W. Meeson, and T.R. Fisher, Jr., 1986. Phytoplankton production in two east coast estuaries: photosynthesis-light functions and patterns of carbon assimilation in Chesapeake and Delaware Bays. Est., Coastal and Shelf Sci., 23:773–806.

Hall, C.A.S. and R. Moll, 1975. Methods of assessing aquatic primary productivity. In H. Lieth, and R.H. Whitaker (Eds.), Primary productivity in the biosphere. Springer-Verlag, New York, pp. 19–26.

Heinle, D.R., 1974. An alternative grazing hypothesis for the Patuxent Estuary. Chesapeake Sci., 15:146–150.

Heinle, D.R. and D.A. Flemer, 1975. Carbon requirements of a population of the estuarine copepod, *Eurytemora affinis*. Mar. Biol., 31:235–247.

Hitchcock, G.L. and T.J. Smayada, 1977. The importance of light in the initiation of the 1972-1973 winter-spring diatom bloom in Narragansett Bay. Limnol. Oceanogr., 22:126-131.

Holmes, R.W., 1970. The secchi disk in turbid coastal waters. Limnol. Oceangr., 15(5):688-694.

Hopkins, T.L. 1966. The plankton of the St. Andrew Bay System, Florida. Univ. Tex. Inst. Mar. Sci. Pub. 11:12-64.

Kawamura, T. 1966. Distribution of phytoplankton populations in Sandy Hook Bay and adjacent areas in relation to hydrographic conditions in June 1962. U.S. Fish Wildl. Serv. Tech. Paper No. I. 37 p.

Karentz, D. and T.J. Smayda, 1984. Temperature and seasonal occurance patterns of 30 dominant phytoplankton species in Narragansett Bay over a 22-year period (1959-1980). Mar. Ecol. Prog. Ser., 18:277-293.

Keefe, C., D.Flemer, and D.H. Hamilton, 1976. Seston distribution in the Patuxent River estuary. Chesapeake Science, 17(1):56-59.

Kemp, W.M. and W.R. Boynton, 1984. Spatial and temporal coupling of nutrient inputs to estuarine primary production: the role of particulate transport and decomposition. Bull. Mar. Sci., 35(3):522-535.

Kemp, W.M., R.L. Wetzel, W.R. Boynton, C.F. D'Elia, and J.C. Stevenson, 1982. Nitrogen cycling and estuarine interfaces: some current soncepts and research directions. V.S. Kennedy (Ed.), Estuarine Comparisons. Academic Press, New York, pp. 209-230.

Ketchum, B.H., 1939. The absorption of phosphate and nitrate by illuminated cultures of Nitzschia closterium. Am. J. Bot., 26:399-407.

Ketchum, B.H., 1967. Phytoplankton nutrients in estuaries. In G. Lauff (Ed.), Estuaries. American Association for the Advancement of Sciences Publication Number 83, Washington, DC, pp. 329-335.

Kremer, P., 1979. Predation by the ctenophore Mnemiopsis leidyi in Narragansett Bay, R.I. Estuaries, 2:97-105.

Kuenzler, E.J., D.W. Staley, and J.P. Koenings, 1979. Nutrient kinetics of phytoplankton in the Pamlico River, North Carolina. Water Resources Research Institute, Raleigh, NC. Report No. UNC-WRRI-79-139.

Lindahl, O. and L. Hernroth, 1983. Phyto-zooplankton community in coastal waters of western Sweden-An ecosystem off balance? Mar. Ecol. Prog. Ser., 10:119-126.

Loftus, M.E., A.R. Place, and H.H. Seliger, 1979. Inorganic carbon requirements of natural populations and laboratory cultures of some Chesapeake Bay phytoplankton. Estuaries, 2(4):236-248.

Lorenzen, C.J., 1972. Extinction of light in the ocean by phytoplankton. J. Cons. int. Explor. Mer., 34(2):262-267.

MacIsaac, J.J. and R.C. Dugdale, 1972. Interactions of light and inorganic nitrogen in controlling nitrogen uptake in the sea. Deep-Sea Research, 19:209-232.

Malone, T.C., 1980a. Size-fractionated primary productivity of marine phytoplankton. In P.G. Falkowski (Ed.), Primary Productivity in the Sea. Plenum, New York, pp. 301-320.

Malone, T.C., 1980b. Algal Size. In: I. Morris (Ed.), The Physiological Ecology of Phytoplankton. Blackwell, Oxford.

Malone, T.C. and M.B. Chervin, 1979. The production and fate of phytoplankton size fractions in the plume of the Hudson River, New York Bight. Limnol. Oceanogr., 24(4):683–696.

Malone, T.C., P.J. Neale and D. Boardman, 1980. Influences of estuarine circulation on the distribution and biomass of phytoplankton size fractions. In V. Kennedy (Ed.), Estuarine Perspectives. Academic Press, New York, pp. 249-262

Malone, T.C., W.M. Kemp, H.W. Ducklow, W.R. Boynton, J.H. Tuttle, and R.B. Jonas, 1986. Lateral variation in the production and fate of phytoplankton in a partially stratified estuary. Mar. Ecol. Prog. Ser., 32:149-160.

Marra, J., 1980. Vertical mixing and primary production. In: P.G. Faikowski (Ed.), Primary Productivity in the Sea. Plenum Press, New York.

Marra, J., 1978a. Effect of short-term variations in light intensity on photosynthesis of a marine phytoplankter: A laboratory simulation study. Mar. Biol., 46:191-202.

Marra, J., 1978b. Phytoplankton photosynthetic response to vertical movement in a mixed layer. Mar. Biol., 46:203-208.

Marsh, J.A., 1974. Tropical inshore plankton system. In H.T. Odum, B.J. Copeland, and E.A. McMahan (Eds.), Coastal Ecological Systems of the United States I. Conservation Foundation Publ., Washington, D.C. pp.488-513.

Marshall, H.G. 1967. Plankton in James River estuary, Virginia: I. Phytoplankton in Willoughby Bay and Hampton Roads. Chesapeake Sci., 8(2):90-101.

Matthiessen, G.C., 1960. Observations on the ecology of the soft clam, *Mya arenaria*, in a salt pond. Limnol. Oceanogr., 5(3):291-300.

Margalef, R., 1958. Temporal succession and spatial heterogeneity in phytoplankton, In Buzzati-Traverso (Ed.), Perspectives in Marine Biology. Univ. of California Press, Berkeley, pp. 323-347.

Margalef, R., 1962. Communidades Naturales. Publicacion Especial; Institute Biologia Marina Universidad de Puerto Rico, Mayaguez, 469 p.

Martin, J.H., 1970. Phytoplankton-zooplankton relationships in Narragansett Bay. IV. The seasonal importance of grazing. Limnol. Oceanogr., 15:413-418.

McCarthy, J.J., W.R. Taylor, and M.E. Loftus, 1974. Significance of nannoplankton in the Chesapeake Bay estuary and problems associated with the measurement of nannoplankton productivity. Marine Biology, 24:7-16.

McCarthy, J.J., W.R. Taylor, and J.L. Taft, 1977. Nitrogenous nutrition of the plankton in the Chesapeake Bay. 1. Nutrient availability and phytoplankton preferences. Limnol. Oceanogr., 22(6):996-1011.

McCarthy, J.J., 1980. Nitrogen and phytoplankton ecology. In I. Morris (Ed.), The Physiological Ecology of Phytoplankton. Blackwell, Oxford, pp. 191-233.

McRoy, C.P. 1968. The distribution and biogeography of *Zostera marina* (eelgrass) in Alaska. Pacific Sci., 22(4):507-513.

Meguro, H., K. Ito and H. Fukushima, 1967. Ice flora (bottom type) a mechanism of primary production in polar seas and the growth of diatoms in sea ice. Arctic, 20:114-133.

Miller, S.M. and H.B. Moore, 1953. Significance of nannoplankton. Nature, 171:1121.

Nichols, F.H., 1985. Increased benthic grazing: An alternative explanation for low phytoplankton biomass in northern San Francisco Bay during the 1976-1977 drought. Est., Coastal and Shelf Sci., 21:379-388.

Nixon, S.W., 1981. Freshwater inputs and estuarine productivity. In R.D. Cross and D.L. Williams (Eds.), Proceedings of the National Symposium on Freshwater Inflow to Estuaries. U.S. Fish and Wildlife Service, Office of Biological Services, FWS/OBS-81/04, Washington, D.C., Vol. 1, pp. 31-57.

Nixon S.W., C.A. Oviatt, J.N. Kremer, and K. Perez, 1979. The use of numerical models and laboratory microcosms in estuarine ecosystem analysis: Simulations of a winter phytoplankton bloom. In R.F. Dame (Ed.), Marsh-Estuarine Systems Simulation. University of South Carolina Press, Columbia, pp. 165-188.

Officer, C.B. and J.H. Ryther, 1980. The possible importance of Silicon in marine eutrophication. Mar. Ecol. Prog. Ser., 3:83-91.

Officer, C.B., T.J. Smayda, and R. Mann, 1982. Benthic filter feeding: A natural eutrophication control. Mar. Ecol. Prog. Ser., 9:203-210.

Oviatt, C.A., S.W. Nixon, K.T. Perez, and B. Bucklay, 1979. On the seasonal nature of perturbations in micoorcosm experiments. In R.F. Dame (Ed.), Marsh-estuarine Systems Simulation. University of South Carolina Press, Columbia, pp. 143-164.

Parsons, T.R., K. Stevens, and J.D.H. Strickland, 1961. On the chemical composition of eleven species of marine phytoplankton. J. Fish. Res. Bd., Canada, 18:1001-1016.

Parsons, T.R., M. Takahashi, and B. Hargrave, 1979. Biological Oceanographic Process, 2nd Edition. Pergamon, New York. pp.

Patten, B.C., R.A. Mulford, and J.E. Warinner. 1963. An annual phytoplankton cycle in the lower Chesapeake Bay. Chesapeake Sci. 4(1):1-20.

Pennock, J.R., 1985. Chlorophyll distributions in the Delaware Estuary: regulation by light-limitations. Est., Coastal Shelf Sci., 21:711-725.

Pennock, J.R. and J.H. Sharp, 1986. Phytoplankton production in the Delaware Estuary: temporal and spatial variability. Mar. Ecol. Prog. Ser., 34:143-155.

Peterson, B.J., 1980. Aquatic primary productivity and the ^{14}C-CO_2 method: A history of the productivity problem. Ann. Rev. Ecol. Syst., 11:359-386.

Platt, T., 1972. Local phytoplankton abundance and turbulence. Deep-Sea Res., 19:183-188.

Platt, T. and C.L. Gallegos, 1980. Modelling primary production. In P. Falkowski (Ed.), Primary Production in the Sea, Plenum, New York. pp. 339-362.

Poole, H.H. and W.R.G Atkins, 1929. Photo-electric measurements of submarine illumination throughtout the year. J. Mar. Bibl. Assoc. UK, 16:297-324.

Pratt, D.M., 1965. The winter-spring diatom flowering in Narragansett Bay. Limnol. Oceanogr., 10:173-184.

Ragotzkie, R.A., 1960a. Plankton productivity in estuarine waters of Georgia. Publ. Inst. Mar. Sci., University of Texas, 6:146-159.

Ragotzkie, R.A., 1960b. Marine marsh, In Encyclopedia of science and Technology. McGraw-Hill, New York, pp. 217-218.

Randall, J.M. and J.W. Day, Jr., 1987. Effects of river discharge and vertical circulation on aquatic primary production in a turbid Louisiana (USA) estuary. Netherlands J. Sea Research, 21(3)231-242.

Redfield, A.C., B.H. Ketchum, and F.A. Richards, 1963. The influence of organisms on the composition of sea-water. In N.M. Hill (Ed.), The Sea. Wiley-Interscience, New York, 2:26-77.

Remsen, C.C., E.J. Carpenter, and B.W. Schroeder, 1972. Competition for urea among estuarine microorganisms. Ecology, 53:921-926.

Rhee, G.-Yull, 1972. Competition between an alga and an aquatic bacterium for phosphate. Limnol. Oceanogr., 17(4):505-514.

Riley, G.A., 1942. The relationship of vertical turbulence and spring diatom flowerings. J. Mar. Res., 5:67-87.

Riley, G.A., 1946. Factors controlling phytoplankton population on George's Bank. J. Mar. Res., 6:54-73.

Riley, G.A., 1967. The plankton of estuaries. In G. Lauff (Ed.), Estuaries. American Association for the Advancement of Science, Publication Number 83, Washington DC, pp. 316-326.

Riley, G.A. and S.M. Conover, 1967. Phytoplankton of Long Island Sound, 1954-55. Bull. Bingham Oceanogr. Coll., 19(2):5-34.

Ryther, J.H., 1963. Geographical variations in productivity. In M.N. Hill (Ed.), The Sea, Vol II. Wiley-Interscience, New York, pp. 347-380.

Ryther, J.H. and Dunstan, 1971. Nitrogen, phosphorus, and eutrophication in the coastal marine environment. Science, 171:1008-13.

Ryther, J.H. and D.W. Menzel, 1965. Comparison of the 14C technique with direct measurement of carbon fixation. Limnol. Oceanogr., 10:490-492.

Seliger, H.H., J.H. Carpenter, M. Loftus, and W.D. McElroy, 1970. Mechanisms for the accumulation of high concentrations of dinoflagellates in a bioluminescent bay. Limnol. Oceanogr. 15:234-245.

Seliger, H.H., K.R. McKinley, W.H. Biggley, R.B. Rivkin, and K.R.H. Aspden, 1981. Phytoplankton patchiness and frontal regions. Marine Biology, 61:119-131.

Sinclair, M., D.V. Subba Rao, and R. Couture, 1981. Phytoplankton temporal distributions in estuaries. Oceanologica Acta, 4(2):239-246.

Smayda, T.J., 1957. Phytoplankton studies in lower Narragansett Bay. Limnol. Oceanogr., 2(4):342-359.

Smayda, T.J., 1980. Phytoplankton species succession. In I. Morris (Ed.), The Physiological Ecology of Phytoplankton, Blackwell, Oxford, pp. 483-570.

Smetacek, V., 1980. Annual cycle of sedimentation in relation to plankton ecology in western Kiel Bight. Ophelia, 1:65-76.

Smetacek, V., 1985. Role of sinking in diatom life-history cycles: ecological evolutionary and geological significance. Marine Biology 84:239-251.

Smith, S.V., 1984. Phosphorus versus nitrogen limitation in the marine environment. Limnol. Oceanogr., 29(6):1149-1160.

Smith, S.V., W.J. Wiebe, J.T. Hollibaugh, S.J. Dollar, S.W. Hager, B.E. Cole, G.W. Tribble, and P.A. Wheeler, 1987. Stoichiometry of C, N, P, and Si fluxes in a temperate-climate embayment. J. Mar. Res. 45:427-460.

Steeman-Nielsen, E., 1952. The use of radioactive carbon for measuring organic production in the sea. J. Cons. Int. Explor. Mer, 18:117-140.

Steeman-Nielsen, E,. 1958. The balance between phytoplankton and zooplankton in the sea. J. Cons. Explor. Mer, 23:178-188.

Stross, R.G. and J.R. Stottlemeyer, 1966. Primary production in the Patuxent River. Chesapeake Sci., 6:125-140.

Sverdrup, H.U., 1953. On conditions for the vernal blooming of phytoplankton. J. Cons. Explor. Mer, 18:287-295.

Taft, J.L., W.R. Taylor, and J.J. McCarthy, 1975. Uptake and release of phosphorus by phytoplankton in the Chesapeake Bay estuary, USA. Marine Biology, 33:21-32.

Thayer, G.W., 1971. Phytoplankton production and the distribution of nutrients in a shallow unstratified estuarine system near Beaufort, NC. Chesapeake Sci., 12:240-253.

Thayer, G.W., 1974. Identity and regulation of nutrients limiting phytoplankton production in the shallow estuaries near Beaufort, N.C. Oecologia (Berl.), 14:75-92.

Therriault, J., D.J. Lawrence, and T. Platt, 1978. Spatial variability of phytoplankton turnover in relation to physical processes in a coastal environment. Limnol. Oceanogr., 23(5):900-911.

Tyler, M.A., 1984. Dye tracing of a subsurface chlorophyll maximum of a red-tide dinoflagellate to surface frontal regions. Marine Biology, 78:285-300.

Walsh, J.J., 1976. Herbivory as a factor in patterns of nutrient utilization in the sea. Limnol. Oceanogr., 21:1-13.

Welch, E.B., R.M. Emery, R.I. Matsuda, and W.A. Dawson, 1972. The relationship of algal growth in an estuary to hydrographic factors. Limnol. Oceanogr., 17:734-737.

Wheeler, P.A. and D.L. Kirchman, 1986. Utilization of inorganic and organic nitrogen by bacteria in marine systems. Limnol. Oceanogr., 31(5):998-1009.

Williams, R.B., 1966. Annual phytoplanktonic production in a system of shallow temperate estuaries. In H. Barnes (Ed.), Some Contemporary Studies in Marine Sciences. George Allen and Unwin, London, pp. 699-717.

Williams, R.B. and M.B. Murdoch, 1966. Phytoplankton production and chlorophyll concentration in the Beaufort channel, North Carolina. Limnol. Oceanogr., 11:73-81.

Williams, P.J., R.C.T. Raine, and J.R. Bryan, 1979. Agreement between the ^{14}C and oxygen methods of measuring phytoplankton production: reassessment of the photosynthetic quotient. Oceanologica Acta, 2(4):411-416.

Williams, P.J., K.R. Heinemann, J. Marra, and D.A. Purdie, 1983. Comparison of ^{14}C and O_2 measurements of phytoplankton production in oligotrophic waters. Nature, 305:49-50.

Wood, E.J.F., 1965. Marine Microbial Ecology. Reinhold, New York. 243 p.

Wofsy, S.C., 1983. A simple model to predict extinction coefficients and phytoplankton biomass in eutrophic waters. Limnol. Oceanogr., 28(6):1144-1155.

Yentsch, C.S., 1974. Some aspects of the environmental physiology of marine phytoplankton: A second look. Oceanogr. Mar. Biol. Ann. Rev., 12:41-75.

Yentsch, C.S., C.M. Yentsch, L.R. Strube, and I. Morris, 1974. Influence of temperature on the phytosynthetic efficiency in natural populations of marine phytoplankton. In J.W. Gibbons and R.R. Sharitz (Eds.), Thermal Ecology. USAEC Conference Series CONF-730505. NTIS, Springfield, VA, pp. 508-517.

Yentsch and Ryther, 1959. Relative significance of net phytoplankton and nanoplankton in the waters of vineyard sound. J. Cons. Perm. Int. Explor. Mer., 24:231-238.

OFFPRINTS FROM: ESTUARINE ECOLOGY
Edited by John W. Day Jr., Charles A. S. Hall., Dr. W. Michael Kemp. and Alejandro Yáñez-Arancibia
Copyright © 1989 by John Wiley & Sons, Inc.

5

Intertidal Wetlands: Salt Marshes and Mangrove Swamps

Intertidal wetlands are a common feature of most estuaries and are widely distributed in estuarine systems over the world. Numerous studies of intertidal salt marshes and mangrove swamps show that they are among the most productive plant communities in the world and are often a large proportion of the total area of estuaries. In addition they are important to other components of estuarine ecosystems because they (1) provide a food source to both estuarine and coastal ocean consumers, (2) serve as habitat for large numbers of both young and adult estuarine organisms, and (3) regulate important components of estuarine chemical cycles. Since an understanding of the ecology of estuarine wetlands is fundamental to understanding these characteristics, we will discuss in this chapter the composition, distribution, and productivity of salt marshes and mangrove swamps and the factors that affect productivity. As mentioned above, intertidal wetlands generally are composed either of salt marshes or mangrove swamps. The mangrove community occurs along tropical shores and is made up of tree species, while salt marshes are grass communities found principally in the temperate zone. The two communities are ecologically analogous in that their physical location, ecological processes, and trophic contribution to the overall estuarine ecosystem are very similar. We now consider these two communities in more detail. Recently, there have been several reviews of intertidal wetland communities (Pomeroy and Wiegert 1981, Clough 1982, Odum et al. 1982, 1984, Zedler 1982, Josselyn 1983, Nixon 1982, Gosselink 1984, Stout 1984, Mitsch and Gosselink 1986, Teal 1986, Dijkema 1987).

5.1   COMPOSITION AND CLASSIFICATION OF INTERTIDAL WETLANDS

5.1.1   Salt Marshes

Salt marshes are beds of intertidal rooted vegetation which are alternately inundated and drained by the tides. Salt marshes occur principally along temperate and boreal coasts (Fig. 5.1), but occasionally form in the tropics on salt flats not occupied by mangroves. There is an almost constant interaction between water and marsh. This is facilitated by a complex network of channels through which water, suspended and dissolved material, and organisms pass. Grasses are normally the dominant primary producer, although sometimes low, shrubby vegetation replaces grasses. In addition many types of algae grow on the plants and on the surface of the mud.

The appearance of salt marshes differs along different coasts. Along the Southeastern and Gulf of Mexico coasts of the United States, for example, marshes are often dense and robust. By contrast, high-latitude coastal areas generally support short, sparse stands of marsh. In an attempt to explain this variability Chapman (1960) divided salt marshes into nine broad groups based on physiognomy, floristic composition, and geographic distribution (Table 5.1). He also listed over 600 species of plants that grow in salt marshes throughout the world. Species diversity is lowest in the arctic and generally increases toward

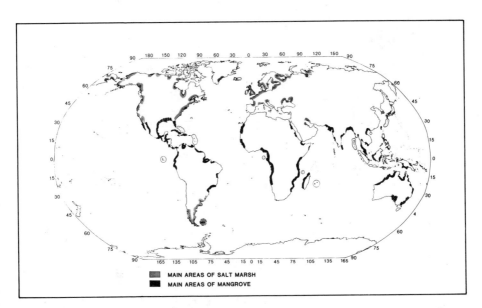

Figure 5.1   Worldwide distribution of salt marshes and mangrove swamps (after Chapman 1960).

TABLE 5.1 Worldwide Classification of Salt Marshes Based on Geographic Distribution, Floristic Composition, and Physiognomy.[a]

Group	Geographic Distribution	Dominant Plants	Important Controlling Parameters
Arctic	Greenland, Iceland, and artic coasts of North America, Scandinavia, and Russia	*Puccinellia phryganodes Carex* sp.	Ice, extreme low temp.
Northern Europe	Iberian peninsula north to Norway and southwestern Sweden	*Puccinellia maritima* *Juncus gerardii* *Salicornia* sp. *Spartina*	Sufficient precipitation Salinity Substrate Moderate climate
	West coast of Great Britain, Scandinavia	*Festuca rubra* *Agrostis stolonifera*	Coast with a high proportion of sand
	Coasts of Baltic Sea	*Carex paleacea* *Juncus bufonius* *Desmoschoenus bottnica* *Scirpus* sp.	Low salinity
	Along English Channel and other muddy coasts	*Spartina townsendii*	Muddy coasts
Mediterranian	Along Mediterranean coasts	Much low shrubby vegetation *Arthrocnemum* *Limonium* also *Juncus* and *Salicornia*	Arid to semi arid Rocky to sandy coasts Generally high salinity Moderate temperatures
Eastern North America	Temperate Atlantic and Gulf of Mexico coasts of North America	*Spartina Alterniflora* *Spartina patens* *Juncus roemerianus* *Distichlis spicata* *Salicornia* *Puccinellia maritima* at higher latitudes	Sufficient precipitation Generally muddy coasts and moderate climate Broad development of marshes

Western North America	Temperate Pacific coasts of North America	*Spartina gracilis* *Spartina foliosa* *Distichlis* *Frankenia* *Salicornia*	Arid in south to high precipitation in north Rugged coasts Limited marsh development
Sino-Japanese	Temperate Pacific coasts of China, Japan, Russia, and Korea	*Triglochin maritima* *Limonium japonicum;* also *Zoysia macrostachya* *Salicornia*	Rugged, uplifting coast Limited marsh development Moderate precipitation
South America	South America coasts too cold for mangroves	Unique species of *Spartina* *Limnonium* *Distichlis* *Juncus* *Heterostachys* and *Allenrolfea;* also *Salicornia*	Rugged coasts Geographic isolation
Australia	South Australia, New Zealand, Tasmania	*Hemichroa* *Arthrocnemetum* *Salicornia*	Rainfall Geographic isolation
Tropical	Saline flats not occupied by mangroves	*Salicornia* *Limonium* *Spartina brasiliensis*	Salinity

[a] After Chapman (1960).

lower latitudes. A number of genera are broadly distributed and are a major component of the flora in many areas (Fig. 5.2). *Puccinellia* is common along northern coasts where ice and extremely low temperatures occur in winter. *Spartina, Juncus,* and *Distichlis* are common along nonrocky temperate coasts of Europe, Asia, and North and South America. *Limonium* is found along rugged coasts. *Salicornia* has the broadest distribution; it is found in the upper intertidal marshes in practically all areas because of its ability to withstand dessication and salinity stress.

The most extensive development of salt marshes occurs in areas of abundant rainfall, muddy to sandy coasts, and moderate climate. The broadest development occurs along the east and west coasts of the north Atlantic and the Gulf of Mexico. Here there is sufficient rainfall evenly spread through the year, gentle coastal slopes, and muddy to sandy sediments. The largest single area of coastal marshes is in the delta of the Mississippi River, where almost 40% of coastal salt marshes (approx. 2×10^6 ha) of the "lower 48" states occur.

5.1.2 Mangrove Swamps

Low-lying tropical and subtropical coasts often are bordered by dense thickets or forests called mangrove swamps. These swamps occur generally between 25°N and 25°S latitude; on the east coast of Africa, in Australia, and in New Zealand they extend 10–15° further south; and in Japan they reach about 7° further north (Kuenzler 1974). In the United States, black mangrove shrubs occur along the northen coast of the Gulf of Mexico at 29°N. "Mangrove plants are typically adapted to fixation in loose, wet soils, a dominantly saline habitat, and periodic submerged tides. They exhibit different degrees of viviparity of the fruits and seed and typical xeromorphic adaptations, and have respiratory roots" (Davis 1940). Mangroves reach their maximum growth in brackish waters, although they occur from hypersaline to fresh waters.

Mangroves are a group of halophytic species from 12 genera in 8 different families (Waisel 1972, Lugo and Snedaker 1974).

Avicenniaceae	Myrsinaceae
Avicennia sp.	*Aegiceras* sp.
Chenopodiaceae	Plumbaginaceae
Suaeda monoica	*Aegialitis* sp.
Combretaceae	Rhizophoraceae
Laguncularia sp.	*Rhizophora* sp.
Lumnitzera sp.	*Bruguiera* sp.
Meliacene	Sonneratiaceae
Conocarpus sp.	*Sonneratia* sp.
Xylocarpus sp.	

Fewer than 10 species are found in the new world and a total of 36 have been described from the Indo-West-Pacific area (Macnae 1968).

It is important to distinguish between two meanings of mangrove. The first

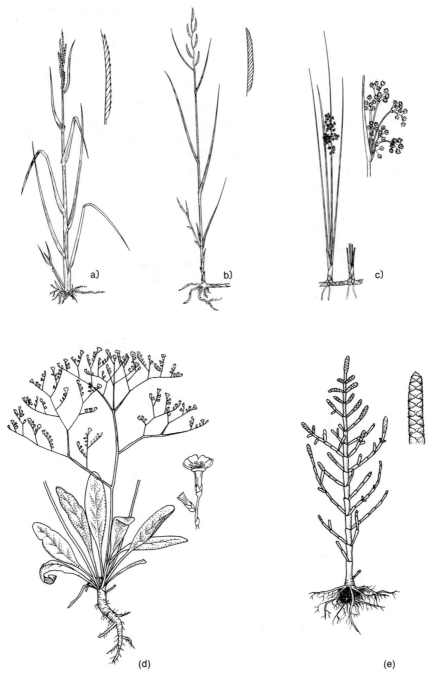

Figure 5.2 Several common species of salt marsh plants. (a) *Spartina alterniflora,* (b) *Spartina patens,* (c) *Juncus roemerianus,* (d) *Linonium carolinianum,* (e) *Salicornia bigelouii.*

refers to a group of plant species and the second to the whole swamp association. For example, Schimper (1903) defined mangrove to include the formation of plants below the high-tide mark, and the term tidal forests is a common synonym for mangrove forest. "True" mangrove species, however, occur in only part of the intertidal zone, and they may occur in subtidal to supratidal areas (Lugo and Snedaker 1974).

Lugo and Snedaker (1974) classified mangrove forests in south Florida into six types (Fig. 5.3). Four species of mangrove (*Rhizophora mangle, Avicennia germinans, Laguncularia racemosa,* and *Conocarpus errecta*) occur in varying mixtures. The first three are most common in the new world and they are shown in Figure 5.4. The formation and physiognomy of these types appear to be controlled strongly by local patterns of tides and terrestrial surface drainage.

This classification seems generally applicable to mangrove forests; however, local variation occurs. Bordering the Laguna de Terminos, Mexico, for example, there are fringe forests and riverine forests. The fringe forest is dominated by *R. mangle* and there is no apparent zonation pattern. In the riveine forest, *A. germinans* is the dominant with *R. mangle* growing only directly adjacent to the streams (Day et al. 1987).

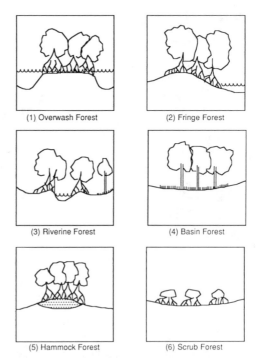

Figure 5.3 The six mangrove community types (from Odum et al. 1982 as modified from Lugo and Snedaker 1974).

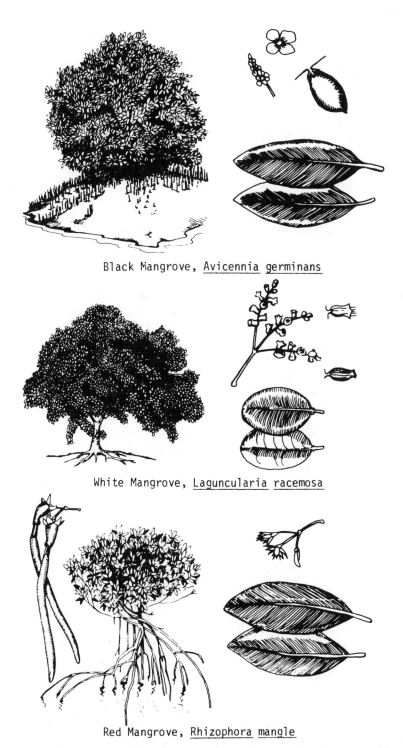

Black Mangrove, <u>Avicennia germinans</u>

White Mangrove, <u>Laguncularia racemosa</u>

Red Mangrove, <u>Rhizophora mangle</u>

Figure 5.4 Three species of Florida mangroves with propagules, flowers, and leaves (from Odum et al. 1982).

5.2   ZONATION OF MANGROVE SWAMPS AND SALT MARSHES

Observations of intertidal wetlands in many different areas of the world reveal similar spatial patterns of distribution of plants. Often the distribution takes the form of bands or zones of different associations of plants that are similar from one location to another. Such zonation provides insight into how different plants deal with and alter environmental gradients of the intertidal zone. In this section we will describe zonation of intertidal plants in estuaries and discuss the factors responsible for this zonation.

Zonation occurs at several different spatial scales. At the broadest level there is *latitudinal scale zonation,* where climate plays the major role in affecting distributional patterns. At an intermediate scale, there is *coastal drainage basin zonation,* where mean water salinity and coastal morphology are important in determining zonation patterns. Finally, *local zonation* occurs along tidal creeks as a result of elevation changes and variation in tidal water exchanges as one moves closer to, or further from, a tidal creek. In addition, some worldwide zonation occurs as a result of geographic isolation (e.g., the unique vegetation assemblages of Australian and South American salt marshes). And in all wetlands there is local "patchiness" caused by adjustment of plants to various types of small scale heterogeneity. We now consider zonation at these spatial scales (latitudinal, drainage basin, and local) in somewhat more detail.

5.2.1   Latitudinal Zonation

On a broad latitudinal scale, zonation of intertidal wetlands is affected primarily by climate. As indicated earlier, mangroves grow in the tropics and temperate regions to about 30°N. Salt marshes are present along north temperate coasts from about 30°N up to about 65°N latitude. Above this latitude ice and extremes of temperature prevent marsh formation. On the Atlantic coast of North America, there is no aboveground winter biomass higher than about 38°N latitude due to ice scour (Turner 1976). Therefore, ice first affects biomass in the winter at about 40°N and then prevents marsh growth altogether at latitudes above about 65°N.

Within this general temperature gradient, rainfall plays an important role. Where seasonal moisture deficits exist in tidally flooded land, barren flats may exist among emergent wetlands. Under conditions of extreme or prolonged dryness, there may be little or no vegetation in the tidal zone. These points are illustrated by patterns of wetland distribution around the Gulf of Mexico.

The Gulf of Mexico extends from the tropics in the south to the temperate zone in the north, and includes a large variation in temperature and rainfall (Fig. 5.5). Annual rainfall exceeds 1500 mm along the north central and southern coasts. Arid areas with less than 1000 mm occur on the northwestern Yucatan Peninsula near Progresso and in the western Gulf between Tampico and Galveston. These temperature and rainfall gradients affect the distribution of intertidal vegetation. Mangroves occur along the tropical and semitropical

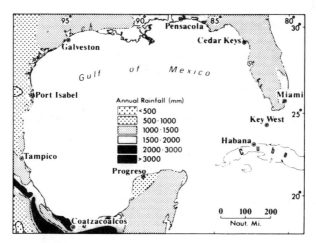

Figure 5.5 Average annual rainfall (mm) along Gulf of Mexico coast (from Smith and Monte 1975).

coasts south of Cedar Keys in Florida and generally south of Port Isabel, Texas. With the exception of a few isolated, scrubby stands of black mangrove in the Mississippi deltaic plain, mangroves are absent from the northern Gulf Coast, which is dominated by salt marshes.

In high rainfall areas, intertidal wetlands tend to cover the entire tidal plain. Thus the Gulf areas with the broadest development of intertidal vegetation are the salt marshes of the Mississippi River deltaic plain and the mangrove swamps surrounding the Laguna de Terminos and in the delta of the Grijalva River. In the arid areas, intertidal vegetation generally occurs only on the more frequently flooded parts of the intertidal zone. The higher parts of the tidal plain are barrens devoid of higher plant life. Halophytes such as *Salicornia* often grow in a narrow zone between the barrens and wetland vegetation growing in the lower tidal plain. Macnae (1968) has shown similar patterns for the Queensland coast mangrove communities, where the changes in rainfall regions are rapid over short distances along the coast.

In summary, at a broad geographic scale, climatic factors such as temperature and rainfall are the principal determinants of intertidal wetland distribution. Where freezes occur more than once or twice a year, salt marshes replace mangroves. At high latitudes extremely low temperatures and ice stress prevent the formation of marshes. When rainfall is low, intertidal vegetation is restricted to the lower tidal plain or absent.

5.2.2   Zonation at the Level of the Coastal Drainage Basin

If we travel from the sea inland, we find for most estuaries progressively diminishing tidal influence until at some point there is no longer a tide. Within this area affected by the tide, there is generally also a salinity gradient. Obviously, near the sea the mean salinity is near that of the sea. As sea water mixes with fresh water, the salinity decreases moving inland, until a point is reached where there is always fresh water. Tidal and salinity dynamics are complex and many different patterns can be observed. For example, in arid areas, hypersaline conditions often exist in coastal bays and lagoons. In very small estuarine systems with little freshwater input, such as the "inlets" of South Carolina or Flax Pond, New York, the salinity of the entire estuary area may be essentially that of the adjacent sea. But, for most estuarine systems, there is a gradient in mean salinity from near that of sea water to the coast to fresh water some distance from the coast.

Now, what do we see if we observe intertidal vegetation along this salinity gradient? In typical estuaries, there are broad vegetation zones which are closely related to the salinity gradient. Nearest the coast, the intertidal community is dominated by salt marshes or mangrove swamps (depending on the latitude). The composition of this community changes with decreasing salinity until the community is composed entirely of freshwater vegetation. This vegetational zonation has been described for many locations, and we include several examples.

In the Barataria Basin, Louisiana, there are several broad vegetation zones (Fig. 5.6). Nearest the coast there is a band of saline marsh, with zones of brackish marsh, fresh marsh, and swamp forest progressively further inland. The diversity is lowest in the saline marshes and highest in the fresh marsh (Table 5.2), a pattern which holds for most estuaries. Similar patterns exist for the marshes of the Chesapeake Bay. In the tropical Laguna de Terminos an analogous zona-

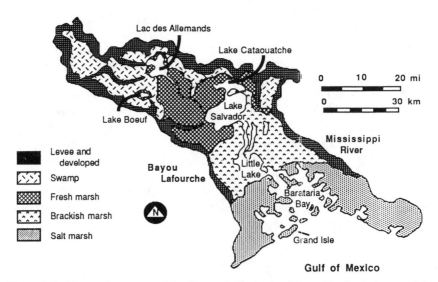

Figure 5.6 Vegetation zones of the Barataria Basin, Louisiana. The basin is one of the subestuaries of the Mississippi Delta (from Conner and Day 1987).

TABLE 5.2 Major Species of Grasses in Different Marsh Types in the Barataria Basin[a]

Marsh Type/Species	% of total	Number of Species Comprising Greater than 1% of Total
Saline marsh		6
Distichlis spicata	10.0	
Juncus roemerianus	14.9	
Spartina alterniflora	62.8	
Spartina patens	7.8	
Brackish marsh		7
Distichlis spicata	29.0	
Spartina alterniflora	9.0	
Spartina patens	45.8	
Intermediate marsh		8
Bocopa monniere	24.0	
Pluchea camphorata	16.8	
Spartina pateus	42.0	
Fresh marsh		14
Eleocharis sp.	12.3	
Panicum hemitomon	41.4	
Sagittaria falcata	17.4	

[a]From Chabreck (1970).

tion occurs, but with mangroves bordering the lagoon. Inland of the mangroves are fresh marshes with such plant genera as *Typha*. The importance of salinity also is evident in the distribution of plant species in the Baltic Sea (Fig. 5.7). In polyhaline waters *Scirpus parvulus* is the most common emergent, while *Phragmites communis* is found in mesohaline to oligohaline waters.

5.2.3 Local Zonation Patterns

The striking patterns of marsh zonation that occur along tidal creeks have attracted the attention of wetland scientists for many years. These zones are a result of differences in reproduction and growth and in differential response to environmental gradients encountered from low to high water. Some of the most important factors are elevation, drainage, and soil type. Tidal exchange and soil type are important in determining the oxidation-reduction state of the soil and the level of hypersaline conditions in the high marsh. In both salt marshes and mangrove swamps there is often a distinct elevation gradient from the water's edge up to the upland boundary, and often a streamside levee. In the high marsh, salt pans (areas of hypersalinity) often form. Examples of zonation

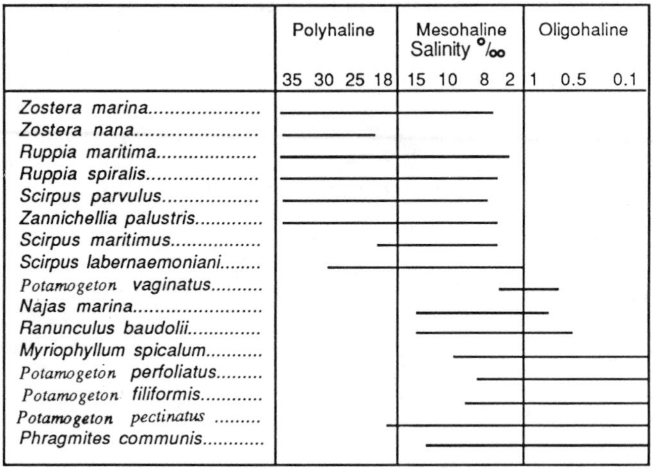

	Polyhaline	Mesohaline Salinity ‰	Oligohaline
	35 30 25 18	15 10 8 2	1 0.5 0.1
Zostera marina......................			
Zostera nana........................			
Ruppia maritima....................			
Ruppia spiralis.....................			
Scirpus parvulus...................			
Zannichellia palustris.............			
Scirpus maritimus.................			
Scirpus labernaemoniani........			
Potamogeton vaginatus..........			
Najas marina.......................			
Ranunculus baudolii..............			
Myriophyllum spicalum...........			
Potamogeton perfoliatus.........			
Potamogeton filiformis............			
Potamogeton pectinatus			
Phragmites communis............			

Figure 5.7 The salinity distribution of several species of marsh and submerged plants around the Baltic Sea (from Zenkevitch 1963).

across this gradient for marshes in New England and Georgia are given in Fig. 5.8*a* and 5.8*b*.

Often the different species of mangrove also occur in distinct zones owing to differences in rooting and growth of seedlings and to differential plant response to the various environmental gradients encountered from low to high water. Davis (1940) recognized this zonal pattern in southwest Florida and attributed it to differences in elevation, tidal coverage, and soil type (Fig. 5.9).

The characteristic zonation patterns observed in Florida swamps also exists in many other estuaries, although the species may be different (Kuenzler 1974). For example, in Australia *Avicennia marina* occurs adjacent to the sea while *Rhizophora stylosa* usually forms the second succeeding band (Macnae 1967). The subterranean root mat and countless emergent pneumatophores of *Avicennia* are capable of holding the surface sediments firm, but *Rhizophora* seedlings sooner or later germinate in the shade of the *Avicennia* and eventually crowd them out (Macnae 1967). Further inland, *Rhizophora* usually borders along stream banks. In East Africa, there are sharply defined zones with *Sonneratia alba* nearest the open water, then *Rhizophora mucronata,* then *Ceriops candolleana,* and finally *Avicennia marina* nearest the high ground (Walter and Steiner 1936).

A number of authors have proposed schemes for zonation of mangroves. Macnae (1968) reviewed several proposed for the Indo-West-Pacific region; Davis (1940) classified the mangroves of the new world; and de la Cruz (1969) compared zonation stands in the eastern and western hemispheres.

From these kinds of studies Davis (1940), Watson (1928), and others classified different mangrove species as "pioneer" or "climax" species, inferring that

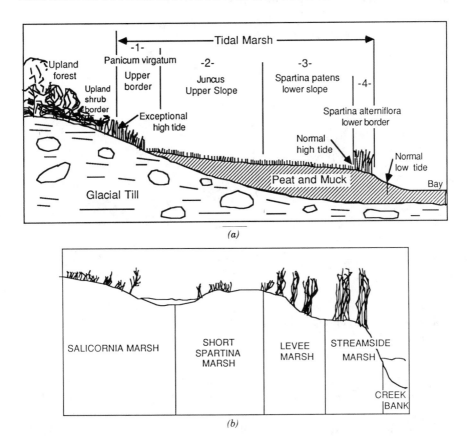

(a)

(b)

Figure 5.8 Zonation of vegetation in typical North American salt marshes. (a) New England salt marsh. Mosquito ditches with their accompanying levees, together with pannes, complicate this upland to bay sequence with variations that may occupy the major part of the marsh surface (From ''Vegetation of the Wequetequock-Pawcatuck tidal marshes, Connecticut'' by W.R. Miller and F.E. Egler, Ecological Monographs, 1950, 20, 143–172. Copyright © by the Ecological Society of America, reprinted by permission). (b) Georgia salt marsh (From ''Energy Flow in the salt marsh ecosystem of Georgia'' by J.M. Teal, Ecology, 1962, 43, 614–624. Copyright © by The Ecological Society of America. Reprinted by permission).

each zone represents a stage in a succession leading via soil accumulation to a terrestrial forest (Richards 1952). Other authors have put forward the view that zonation is a response of the mangrove ecosystem to external forces rather than a temporal sequence induced by the plants themselves. This concept of a steady-state landscape as it applies to mangroves is supported by the work of Thom (1967) and Egler (1952). Thom (1967) demonstrated that the zonation and struc-ture of mangrove forests in Tabasco, Mexico are responsive to eustatic changes in sea level, and that mangrove zones can be viewed as steady-state zones migrat-

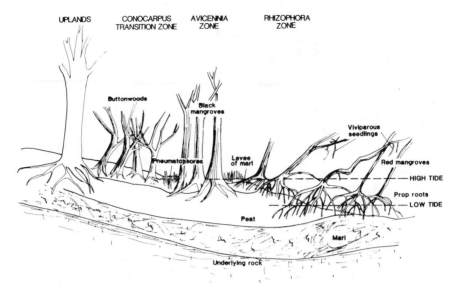

Figure 5.9 Zonation pattern of mangroves in southwest Florida. Adaptations include viviparous seedlings, proproots of red mangroves and pneumatophores of black mangroves (after Davis 1940).

ing toward or away from the sea, depending on its level. He postulated that mangrove zones were responsive to geomorphological changes in the regions where they grow. He considered substratum and water regime to be the important factors controlling zonation, and that each species, within its tolerance range to salinity, finds its place in the environmental gradient created by the regimes of substratum and water flow. According to Thom, salinity is simply a competition eliminator and not the determining factor in zonation.

Thus it appears plausible that the zonation of mangroves may not necessarily represent a successional sequence and that mangrove areas may not invariably accumulate soil. Instead, the "zonation" of mangroves may be a result of all the external sources acting on a locality. Perhaps in periods of decreasing tidal energy or the lowering of sea level, mangroves advance toward the sea, but when the flushing action of water is high or when the sea rises, the zones migrate inland. Both Lugo (1980) and Snedaker (1982) concluded that zonation patterns in mangroves represent steady state adjustments rather than successional stages. In a simular manner, Mitsch and Gosselink (1986) reviewed marsh zonation patterns and concluded that the zones were not necessarily the result of succession.

5.3 SALT MARSH PRODUCTIVITY

The rates of and the factors affecting the productivity of salt marshes have been studied extensively; much more so than those for mangroves. For this reason, we will first review marsh productivity and then cover mangroves. The majority of the existing studies are for *Spartina alterniflora*, although there is considerable information available for other species (Turner 1976, Mitsch and Gosselink 1986). One reason that the productivity of salt marshes has been examined so thoroughly is that it is often remarkably high—higher than for most other ecosystem types. Another reason is that there is considerable evidence that salt marsh production forms the basis of important estuarine food chains.

Most of the existing productivity values are for net production calculated from changes in live and dead plant biomass over an annual cycle. The data of such studies often look more or less like the examples in Fig. 5.10. Since most salt marshes are located in temperate climates, the live biomass increases during the growing season (spring until fall), then flowers and dies. As the grass dies live biomass decreases and dead organic material increases. In the spring, the quantity of dead grass decreases as it decomposes. In lower latitude marshes, such as in Louisiana and Georgia, there is some growth year round and live material is present at all times. In the Atlantic coast marshes of the United States above about 38°N latitude there is no vegetation left on the marsh during winter because of the ice that freezes around the dead grass and shears it off during tidal action (Turner 1976). This is shown for a salt marsh in Massachusetts in Figure 5.10*f*.

But all salt marsh plants do not necessarily have seasonal patterns like that of *S. alterniflora*. For example, in Louisiana the live biomass of *S. patens* (Fig. 5.10) or *Juncus roemerianus* does not change in any regular manner. In addition to these seasonal differences in marsh grass biomass, in practically all marshes studied there are distinct differences in both live and dead biomass between streamside and inland marsh locations, due to such factors as variations in tidal flooding, nutrient chemistry, and oxygen content of the soil. All of these factors will be treated in more detail in Section 5.4. The point here is that it is important to sample a number of areas carefully.

There may be quite a large variation in maximum biomass attained (one index of productivity) at different locations, both within the same marsh and among different marshes. Turner's review gives the following ranges of maximum dry biomass: streamside, 682–3018 g/m^2; inland, 259–782 g/m^2; marsh average, 300–923 g/m^2. If the data is averaged by state, however, there is a general increase in maximum standing crop from the Gulf of Mexico to New England (Table 5.3). Productivity values calculated from data on changes in marsh grass biomass range from less than 200 to greater than 6000 g dry wt/m^2 yr.

The exchange of CO_2 between marsh plants and the atmosphere has also been used to measure production (Blum et al. 1978, Houghton and Woodwell 1980). This technique allows the examination of daily and even hourly dynamics of marsh grass production. Figure 5.11 shows CO_2 exchange between a marsh and the atmosphere during the summer in New York when productivity was high. There is a net uptake of atmospheric CO_2 during the day when the plants are photosynthesizing and a net release at night when there is only respiration. The height of the tide also affects the rate of CO_2 exchange with the atmosphere.

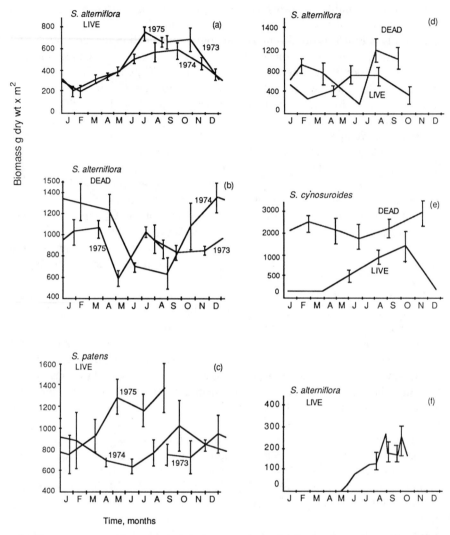

Figure 5.10 Seasonal patterns of aboveground marsh biomass from several locations. For coastal Louisiana salt marshes data is presented for live (a) and dead (b) *Spartina alterniflora* and live *S. patens* (c) over a two year period (from Aboveground production of seven marsh plant species in coastal Louisiana, Hopkinson, Gosselink, and Parrondo, Ecology, 1978, 59, 760–769. Copyright © by the Ecological Society of America, reprinted by permission); live and dead biomass for *S. alterniflora* (d) and *S. cynosuroides* (e) for coastal Georgia (from Schubauer and Hopkinson 1984); and for live *S. alterniflora* (f) from Massachusetts (adapted from Valiela et al. 1976).

TABLE 5.3   Variations in Average Marsh End-of-Season (Peak) Standing Live Biomass[a]

Location	Biomass (g dry wt/m²)
Texas	756
North Florida	701
Louisiana	643
Georgia	762
North Carolina	497
Chesapeake Bay Area	431
New England	418
Average All Sites	620

[a]Adapted from Turner (1976).

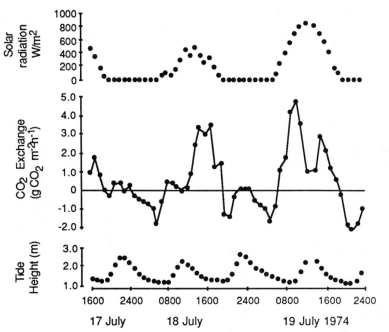

Figure 5.11   Solar radiation, atmospheric CO_2 exchange, and tide height for Flax Pond on 17–19 July 1974 (from The Flax Pond ecosystem study: exchanges of CO_2 between a salt marsh and the atmosphere, Houghton and Woodwell, Ecology, 1980, 61, 1434–1445. Copyright © by the Ecological Society of America, reprinted by permission).

When the tide is high, more of the plant is covered and CO_2 exchange is with the water rather than the atmosphere. Therefore, photosynthetic uptake from the air during the day and respiratory release at night are both lower during the time of high tide. This does not necessarily mean that photosynthesis or respiration are lower, for some of the CO_2 exchange is with the water. But it does mean that the data must be interpreted with care.

5.3.1 Belowground Production

Belowground production of marsh plants has been reported much less often than aboveground production primarily because it is much more difficult to measure. In contrast with aboveground vegetation, it is often very difficult to distinguish live roots and rhizomes from dead and to determine distinct seasonal patterns. Good et al. (1982) discussed a number of problems associated with belowground productivity measurements. Productivities estimates for *S. alterniflora* range from 0.5 to 6.2 kg/m^2yr (Good et al. 1982). The ratio of aboveground to belowground biomass for *S. alterniflora* ranges from 0.3 to 48.9 with most values being higher than 1 (Good et al. 1982), indicating that belowground biomass is almost always considerably greater than aboveground. Reported values for belowground production for *S. alterniflora* for several sites are presented in Table 5.4.

TABLE 5.4 Published Values of Above- and Belowground Net Productivity for *Spartina alterniflora* (Adapted from Schubauer and Hopkinson 1984).

Sampling Locale	Height Form	Net primary production (g dry mass m^{-2} yr^{-1}) Above	Below
Nova Scotia	Not reported	803	1051[1]
Massachusetts	Not reported	420	3500[2]
New Jersey	Short	500	2300[3]
North Carolina	Short	650	460[4]
	Tall	1300	500[4]
Georgia	Short	1350	2020[5]
	Tall	3700	2110[5]
	Medium	2840	4780[6]

[1]Livingstone and Patriquin 1981.
[2]Valiela et al. 1976.
[3]Smith et al. 1979.
[4]Stroud and Cooper 1968, Stroud 1976.
[5]Gallagher and Plumley 1979, Gallagher et al. 1980.
[6]Schubauer and Hopkinson 1984.

5.3.2 The Effect of Measurement Method on Productivity Results

As indicated above, there is a high degree of variability among marsh grass productivity values reported in the literature. This is partially a result of the different methods used. Our purpose here is not to evaluate these different techniques in detail, but to suggest that the method must be known when considering different productivity values. It is also important to understand that different methods tell you different things.

The most commonly used production methods involve the harvest of live and dead grasses, done most simply by the harvest of peak end-of-season live standing material. Live material is continually dying, however, so that this end-of-season technique is an underestimate. More sophisticated methods include determining the changes in both live and dead standing crop at regular intervals and the use of techniques to estimate the loss of both dead and live material between sampling dates (Wiegert and Evans 1964). Other techniques include different types of tagging to measure the increase in height, diameter, and number of leaves as well as the disappearance of individual plants and leaves (Hopkinson et al. 1978, 1980).

As an example, Hopkinson et al. (1980) found that different techniques for measuring annual net production of salt marsh plants in Louisiana gave highly variable results (Fig. 5.12). A comparison of these different methods is available in a number of articles (Turner 1976; Kirby and Gosselink 1976; Hopkinson et al. 1978, 1980; Linthurst and Reimold 1978; and Shew et al. 1981). It is gener-

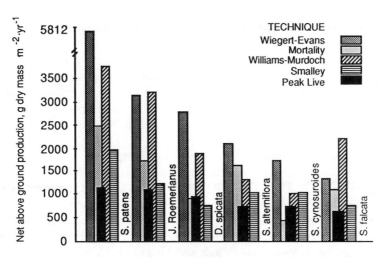

Figure 5.12 Estimates of annual aboveground production calculated from several widely used techniques (from Hopkinson, Gosselink, and Parrondo, production of coastal Louisiana marsh plants calculated from phenometric techniques, Ecology, 1980, 61, 1091–1098. Copyright © by the Ecological Society of America, reprinted by permission).

ally considered that techniques which take into consideration changes in both live and dead standing material between sampling dates give the most accurate estimates of production. The net production calculated from gas-exchange measurements, as described above, has generally been in fairly close agreement with harvest techniques (Teal 1962, Young 1974, Houghton and Woodwell 1980).

5.4   FACTORS AFFECTING MARSH PRODUCTION

A variety of factors influence the productivity of wetland plants. Most of these are due to changes in the physical or chemical environment, including solar radiation, temperature, tides, nutrient concentrations, soil type, drainage, oxygen concentration, and pH. The individual plant species present in the marsh can also affect productivity, because some plants have growth rates that are intrinsically higher than others. Some of these factors cause a difference in productivity over a latitudinal range while others operate at the local level. In this section we shall consider each of these factors separately, although obviously they act together. Therefore, we also will examine how some of these factors interact.

5.4.1   Solar Radiation, Temperature, and Evapotranspiration

The energy of solar radiation affects photosynthesis in several direct and indirect ways. Solar energy directly energizes plant pigments so that the electromagnetic energy of light is converted into chemical potential energy. Solar radiation affects plants indirectly because changes in radiation lead to changes in temperature, and temperature directly affects the rate of metabolic processes. Heat energy is used to evaporate water and vascular plants obtain essential nutrients as a result because nutrients are moved from the soil to the leaves in replacement water. Evapotranspiration, as this process is called, is temperature dependent. Plants change their activity in response to changes in solar inputs, for example as day length increases or decreases.

Solar radiation, temperature, and evapotranspiration act together to produce differences in marsh production over a latitudinal gradient (Fig. 5.13). This production gradient is not unexpected in view of our knowledge of other species. Geographic variations in the growth of plants with similar physiology, litterfall, and net ecosystem production are closely correlated to those factors which measures of latitude integrate, especially temperature and sunlight (Fogg 1973, Bray and Gorham 1964, Rosenzweig 1968, and Turner 1976).

In contrast to upland plants, wetland vegetation is rarely water limited, and the actual evapotranspiration is nearly the same as potential evapotranspiration (PE), which is closely related to temperature. Thus, Turner (1979) was able to derive simple relationships between productivity of *Spartina alterniflora* and ei-

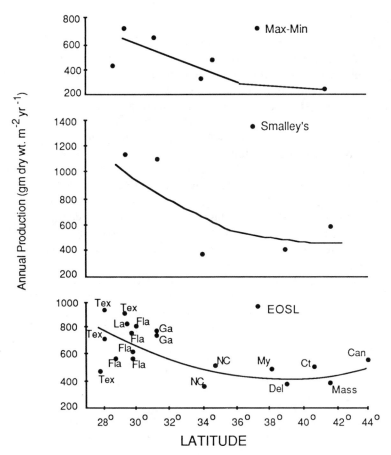

Figure 5.13 The relationship between latitude and annual production estimates of *S. alterniflora*. Top: Max-min method; Middle: Smalley's method; bottom: EOSL estimates (from Turner 1976).

ther PE or air temperature. The relationships were valid for averaged marsh production over a wide latitudinal range, but not for sites within a marsh.

Low winter temperatures and the presence of ice affect the winter minimum biomass found on the marsh. Along the Atlantic and Gulf coasts of North America the minimum winter biomass decreases gradually between a latitude of 28°N and 35°N. Above 38°N the presence of ice generally prevents any winter biomass (Turner 1976).

In summary, sunlight, temperature, and solar radiation are interrelated and together lead to differences in marsh productivity over a wide latitudinal gradient, as indicated in Fig. 5.13. The scatter of the points, however, is indicative that other factors are important. These are discussed in the following sections.

5.4.2   Tide

The tide is one of the unique attributes of estuaries, and E. P. Odum (1969, 1971, 1974) called estuaries fluctuating water level ecosystems which are *subsidized* by tidal action. Differences in marsh production which apparently are related in some way to tidal effects have been identified over broad areas with different tidal ranges as well as between streamside and inland marshes at many different sites. Steever et al. (1976) reported a strong correlation between tidal range and the peak standing crop of *S. alterniflora* along the Connecticut coast unrelated to the changes in climatic and edaphic factors. When they plotted data from various areas along the Atlantic coast with tide ranges between 0.5 and 2.5 m, a relationship was evident for all areas (Fig. 5.14). In addition, they found that a "gated" marsh at Westport, Connecticut had a lower peak standing crop than a nearby marsh where tidal exchange was not restricted. Steever et al. (1976) concluded that the "data strongly suggest that the 'energy subsidy' provided by tidal action is a significant factor in the standing crop production of *S. alterniflora.*"

Spartina alterniflora production is not positively influenced by tidal action over an infinite range, for at very high tidal ranges, the tide may become a stress. This is demonstrated in the Bay of Fundy where the tide range exceeds 10 m and

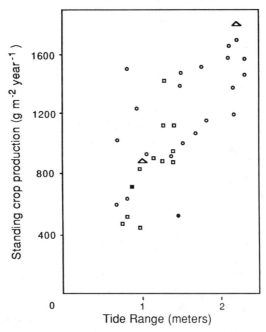

Figure 5.14   Production of intertidal *S. alterniflora* vs. mean tide range for various Atlantic coastal marshes: o, Long Island Sound; □, Narragansett Bay; ●, North Carolina; ■, New Jersey; △ Sapelo Island, Georgia (from Steever et al. 1976).

intertidal *S. alterniflora* is only 10–20 cm high. In addition, coastal Louisiana has a low tide range (0.3 m) and very high productivity. This information and the scatter of points in Fig. 5.14 indicate that still more factors are important in determining marsh productivity.

Tidal subsidies may also operate on a smaller scale. In almost all marshes there is a striking difference between streamside and inland marshes. Turner (1979) showed that the difference between peak streamside and inland biomass was greater with greater tidal range. Much of the difference between streamside and inland marshes is related to the movement of water in the two areas. At low tide water drains almost completely from the streamside marsh surface. In inland marshes there is often incomplete drainage, leading to ponding and high salt levels during periods with high evaporation (Odum 1980). There are also differences in subsurface water movement in streamside and inland marshes. Riedeburg (1975) injected a dye 24 cm below the surface in streamside and inland marshes in Georgia. Dye moved freely, both vertically and horizontally in the streamside marsh sediments, while there was very little movement of the dye in the inland marsh.

Another important factor in the drainage of marsh soils is the percolation rate (the rate at which water flows through the sediment surface into the deeper sediments). In a Massachusetts salt marsh, Howes et al. (1981) found that the relative percolation of water into sediments was inversely related to grass height. The barrier to water movement in the top 2 cm of the sediment was greatest where tall *Spartina* grows. They hypothesized that fine sediments probably filled the sediment pores, forming a relatively impermeable layer on the surface. In addition, they found that the subsurface sediments of the streamside region drained much more rapidly at low tide than inland sediments. Thus the combination of a relatively impermeable surface and well-drained sediments leads to high *Spartina* growth in the streamside zone (Fig. 5.15). The situation in the inland marsh is just the opposite. Water flows freely through the surface, but the soils drain very poorly and growth of *Spartina* is less. It is interesting that they also found tall *Spartina* in a narrow zone bordering the upland. Here the water table is depressed because of the elevation of the site (Fig. 5.15). They concluded that *Spartina* grows well where the root zone is not water logged. Many other factors that affect *Spartina* growth at the local level also are related to the differences in flooding and drainage. We shall examine these next.

5.4.3 Factors Affecting Marsh Productivity at the Local Level

A number of factors affect the growth of salt marsh plants within a local area. These include nutrient levels (such as the concentration of N, P, and Fe), the pH and E_h of the soil, waterlogging and drainage of the soil, oxygen levels, sediment type, soil salinity, and rainfall. These factors are interrelated and affect plant growth and in turn are affected by it. Mendelssohn and McKee (1982) provide a review of these factors. Since nutrients are one of the most important factors limiting plant growth, we begin our discussion with this subject.

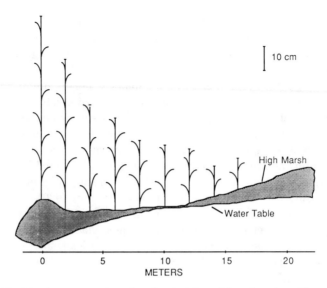

Figure 5.15 Marsh cross section showing heights of *Spartina alterniflora,* marsh surface contour, and low-tide water table (Howes et al. 1981).

Studies over a wide geographic range have shown that the addition of inorganic nitrogen (but not inorganic phosphorus) increases the growth of *S. alterniflora.* Areas where this has been shown include Massachusetts (Valiela and Teal 1974), Delaware (Sullivan and Daiber 1974), North Carolina (Broome et al. 1975, Mendelssohn 1979), Georgia (Gallagher 1975, Haines and Dunn 1976), and Louisiana (Patrick and DeLaune 1976, Buresh et al. 1980). The results shown in Table 5.5 for a Louisiana marsh are typical of the effects that have been reported. In this study, nitrogen addition increased fall aboveground biomass by twenty-three percent.

TABLE 5.5   Effect of Added Nitrogen and Phosphorus on Height, Aboveground Biomass, and Belowground Biomass of *Spartina alterniflora* in a Louisiana Salt Marsh. [a]

| | Aboveground | | |
Treatment	Plant height cm	Biomass kg/m^2	Belowground biomass
Nitrogen, 200 kg/ha	64*	1.36*	6.32
Phosphorus, 200 kg/ha	52	1.03	
Control	51	1.06	5.49

[a]The grass was harvested in late September, four months after application (from Buresh et al. 1980).
*Significantly higher than control.

These results show clearly that the plant macronutrient that most limits *Spartina* growth is nitrogen. However, other studies show that additional factors affect nitrogen uptake by plants. For example, in both Louisiana and Georgia marshes, nitrogen addition gave a greater response in inland marshes than it did in streamside marshes (Buresh et al. 1980). These and other studies in Louisiana, North Carolina, and Massachusetts have shown that ammonia levels were higher in inland marsh soils although *Spartina* growth was less (Buresh et al. 1980, Mendelssohn 1979, Valiela and Teal 1974, 1979). Thus higher nitrogen does not necessarily mean greater plant growth. Some other factors can help explain these results.

The amount of oxygen present in marsh soils is an important factor affecting plant growth. Maximum growth of *S. alterniflora* occurs in oxygenated soils (Morris 1979) and the H_2S produced in anaerobic sediments inhibits respiration and nutrient uptake (Mitsui 1965). Marsh soils, however, are almost completely anaerobic. How then does *Spartina* achieve such high growth? The answer to this question is a function both of the metabolism of *Spartina* and the drainage characteristics of marshes.

It has been known for some time that atmospheric oxygen moves in some fashion to the roots of *Spartina*, producing a thin oxidized layer around the roots (Teal and Kanwisher 1960). Apparently, the healthier a plant is, the better able it is to move oxygen to its roots. In a Massachusetts study, the E_h of the sediments was much higher in tall *Spartina* and much lower in areas devoid of grass (see Fig. 5.16). Negative values reflect anaerobic conditions and values above +100 mv indicate the presence of free oxygen.

The results in Fig. 5.16 reflect both metabolic "pumping" of oxygen by *Spartina* as well as better drainage of the sediments. Well-drained sediments have higher oxygen levels because the air spaces can hold atmospheric oxygen, and streamside marshes generally have the best drainage (see Fig. 5.15). Similar results have been shown for *S. alterniflora* in North Carolina (Mendelssohn and Seneca 1980). Fertilization can also increase the E_h of the sediments indirectly by increasing the productivity and hence the oxygen pumping capacity of the plants. Howes et al. (1981) showed that fertilized inland marsh sites had higher E_h values from the sediment surface to a depth of 30 cm. The relation appears reciprocal, for it has been reported that aeration increased the growth response of *Spartina* to nitrogen additions (Linthurst and Blum 1980, Linthurst and Seneca 1981). Recent results suggest that water taken up by roots and lost via evapotranspiration during photosynthesis may be very important in lowering the water table and thus leading to increases air entry and soil oxidation (Dacey and Howes 1984, Morris and Whiting 1985). Some of these interrelations of nutrient uptake, soil oxidation, and soil drainage is shown graphically in Fig. 5.17.

In highly reduced sediments *S. alterniflora* does not conduct enough oxygen to the roots for complete aerobic respiration and evidences several metabolic adaptations to anoxia (Mendelssohn et al. 1981). If flooding conditions and the degree of anoxia are not too severe, relatively nontoxic end products such as malate will tend to accumulate and alcoholic fermentation is not stimulated.

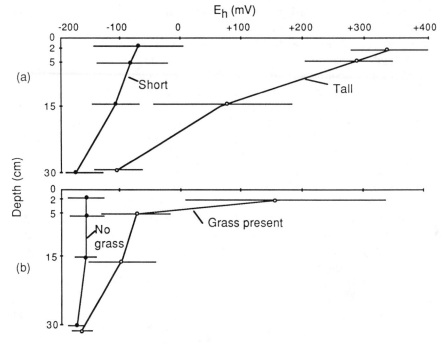

Figure 5.16   (a) Profiles of E_h in sediment with tall and short stands of *S. alterniflora*. (b) Profiles of E_h in an area devoid of vegetation and in nearby clumps of *S. alterniflora* expanding into bare area (from Howes et al. 1981).

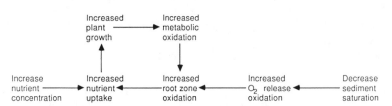

Figure 5.17   Summary of positive interactions of sediment oxidation, nutrient concentration, and plant growth (Howes et al. 1981).

The end products can then be utilized by the *Spartina* when aerobic conditions reoccur. But with more severe and prolonged flooding with resultant anoxia, alcoholic fermentation is stimulated and toxic ethanol is produced, which is lost from the roots by diffusion into the surrounding pore water. This represents a significant loss of energy to the plants and can lead to a decline in growth (Mendelssohn et al. 1981). Anaerobic metabolism in combination with sulfide toxicity appears to be associated with reduced growth of *S. alterniflora*. These conditions are partially the cause of the short or inland form of *Spartina* and may be a cause of dieback in these marshes.

Salinity is also an important determinant of salt marsh growth. Adams (1963) reported that *S. alterniflora* and *Distichlis spicata* are salt obligates and that *S. patens* is a faculative halophyte. Adams (1963) also reported that soil salinities of 70 ppt prevented the establishment and survival of most salt marsh species. On the other hand, *S. alterniflora* grown in fresh water becomes chlorotic. Mooring et al. (1971) found the best growth at 10 ppt salinity. Linthurst (1980) reported that although growth of *S. alterniflora* was less at 30 and 40 ppt, growth at these salinities was stimulated by aeration and nitrogen additions. At high salinities, osmotic stress (resulting in reduced water uptake) or cell membrane damage are likely to limit growth. Membrane permeability changes can reduce the influx of necessary nutrients and/or cause leakage of nutrients from the roots to the surrounding substrate. Increased permeability may also decrease the effectiveness of any selective ion uptake mechanisms in addition to increasing the potential for losses of needed oxygen from the roots (Linthurst 1980).

Halophytes seem to deal with osmotic stress by selectively concentrating preferred ions while making metabolic adaptations to the high concentrations of ions. In addition, these plants have the capacity for salt removal via salt glands and a mechanism in the roots for slowing the inward penetration of toxic ions (Waisel 1972). The result of this process is readily observed as the salt deposits found on the tips of *Spartina alterniflora*.

Rainfall is an indirect factor in regulating plant growth. We noted earlier that in arid areas, large portions of the intertidal zone were devoid of vegetation. This is almost certainly due to high sediment salinity resulting from excess evapotranspiration. In addition low rainfall does not deliver new nutrients to the plants either directly or indirectly via upland runoff, as is the case where rain is abundant.

The pH of the soil affects plant growth. Linthurst (1980) reported that the growth of *Spartina* was optimal at pH 6 in comparison to a pH of either 4 or 8. The pH also affects the response of plants to variations in salinity (Linthurst and Blum 1980).

The nature of the soil in marshes affects the growth of marsh plants. Fine-grained clay and silty clay soils have higher nutrient levels than sandy soils and support greater growth of marsh grasses. For example, Smart and Barko (1978) grew several species of marsh grasses on sandy, clay, and silty clay soils. The concentration of nitrogen in the three soil types were 0.3, 3.2, and 5.2 g N/kg and 0.05, 1.94, and 1.64 g P/kg, respectively. In almost all cases marsh grass growth was much higher on clay and silty clay soils, probably owing to their higher nutrient concentration. Soil density also appears to effect growth. Soil density is highest in streamside marsh soils because of the input of mineral sediments during high tide. DeLaune et al. (1979) found in Louisiana that the aboveground standing crop of *S. alterniflora* was correlated with soil density. This correlation was apparently a result of the association of this property with the content of mineral matter in the soil. They also found that the input of nutrients with new sediments was the most important source of "new" nutrients for the salt marsh. Since the sedimentation rate is much higher on streamside marshes, this is an important factor causing higher productivity there compared with marshes further inland.

Some recent studies indicate that the age of a plant stand affects its productivity (Smart 1986, Bertness 1987). These finding suggest that as a marsh ages, there is increasing belowground biomass, especially of refractory organic materials. Nutrients become tied up with this biomass as organic nutrients and are less available for plant growth.

Herbivory can also affect the growth of marsh grasses, although studies have shown that direct herbivory is very low. The highest reported value is about 5% of net aboveground production (Teal 1962).

A final major factor which is partly responsible for the high productivity of salt marshes is that many species of salt marsh plants have the C_4 biochemical pathway of photosynthesis. C_4 plants have, as a group, higher levels of production than most other plants (C_3 plants). The designation refers to the number of carbon atoms in the initial product of photosynthesis, which for C_3 plants is phosphoglyceric acid and for C_4 plants, oxaloacetic acid. The details of the biochemistry of the two pathways can be found elsewhere (Zelitch 1971, Mitsch and Gosselink 1986). The response of these two types of plants to different environmental parameters is of interest here. C_4 plants have much higher light and temperature saturation levels than C_3 plants. For example, the summer temperature optimum for *S. alterniflora* (a C_4 plant) is 30–35°C while that for *Juncus roemerianus* (a C_3 plant) is 25°C (Giurgevick and Dunn 1978, 1979). This means that as temperature or light rises, the photosynthesis rate for C_3 plants levels off earlier than for C_4 plants. There is also less water transpired per unit photosynthesis in C_4 plants. This could be important in limiting salt build-up on the leaf surface when transpiring salty estuarine water. Most C_3 plants exhibit levels of photorespiration which are higher relative to photosynthesis than C_4 plants. For example, photorespiration for *S. alterniflora* is 11–40% of photosynthesis while that for *Juncus roemerianus* is 54% (Giurgevick and Dunn 1978, 1979). Since many salt marsh species (including *Spartina* sp. and *Distichlis* sp.) are C_4 plants, this leads to generally high marsh productivity.

5.5 MANGROVE PRODUCTIVITY

Mangrove swamps have not been studied as intensively as salt marshes, but similar patterns are evident in both the levels of production and the factors that control production. Litter production values have been most often reported (see Brown and Lugo 1982 and Odum et al. 1982 for recent reviews of mangrove productivity). Production rates for mangrove swamps can be among the highest for forest ecosystems. There is a gradient from high productivity in riverine forests to low values in scrub forests (Table 5.6) and litterfall seems to be strongly correlated with forest structure (Fig. 5.18, from Twilley 1985, see also Table

TABLE 5.6 Structural Characteristics, Primary Productivity, Respiration, and Litter Fall for Different Types of Mangrove Wetlands in the New World Tropics.

Parameter	Riverine	Basin	Fringe	Scrub
		Mangrove Wetland Type		
Structural Characteristics[1]				
Mean canopy height (m)	17.7	9.0	8.2	1.0
Stem density (No. ha^{-1})	1760	3580	5930	25032
Basal area (m^2 ha^{-1})	41.3	18.5	17.9	0.6
Primary Productivity[2] (g org. matter m^{-2}d^{-1})				
Gross primary productivity	24.0	18.0		2.8
Total plant respiration	11.4	12.4		4.0
Net primary productivity	12.6	5.6		0
Litter fall (g m^{-2} yr^{-1})[3]	1170	730	906	120

[1]From Pool et al. (1977) and Brown and Lugo (1982).
[2]From Brown and Lugo (1982), based on CO_2 gas exchange methods.
[3]From Brown and Lugo (1982), Twilley et al. (1986), and Day et al. (1987).

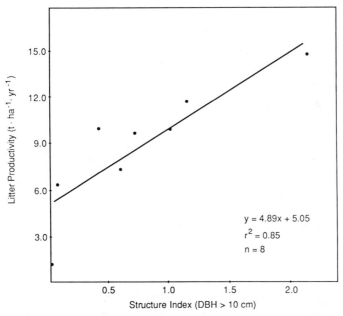

Figure 5.18 Relationship among structural indexes of mangrove forests and their litter productivity estimates for several sites in the Caribbean and south Florida (from Twilley 1985).

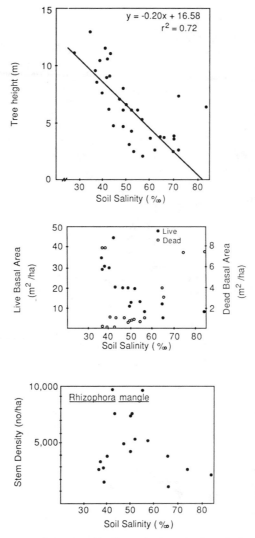

Figure 5.19 Response of structural indices of salt water forested wetlands to increase in soil water salinity for several sites in Puerto Rico (Cintron et al. 1978).

5.6). Average total litterfall ranges from 120 g dry mass/m²yr for scrub forests to 1170 for riverine forests. Along this gradient from riverine to scrub forests, freshwater and nutrient input decrease, and salt content of the soils increases. The correlation between forest structure and litterfall does not always hold, however. For example, Flores-Verdugo et al. (1986) reported very high litterfall in a small coastal lagoon in Mexico which had poorly developed forest structure.

They attributed the high litterfall to high riverine input and the simple structure to frequent hurricanes.

The factors that control mangrove productivity are generally similar to those for salt marshes. The most notable difference is that there is not any latitudinal gradient in mangrove production because mangroves occur entirely within the tropical zone and there is little latitudinal gradient in sunlight or temperature. The higher productivity of riverine compared with scrub forests (Table 5.6) reflects different flooding regimes, lower salinity, higher nutrient levels, and lower H_2S levels. Two factors that have been shown to affect mangrove production are nutrient levels and soil salinity (Brown and Lugo 1982). As with salt marshes, increasing nutrient outputs increases productivity. Pool et al. (1975) reported that increasing freshwater turnover resulted in higher litter production for mangroves, apparently a result of both increased nutrient input and lowered soil salinity stress. A number of workers have shown that increased nutrient availability is related to higher productivity in mangroves (Onuf et al. 1977, Snedaker and Brown 1981, Brown and Lugo 1982, Boto et al. 1984). Cintrón et al. (1978) found that with increasing salinity the values of a number of structural and productivity parameters decreased. These included litterfall, tree density, basal area (total cross-sectional area of trunks), and tree height (Fig. 5.19). Above a soil salinity of about 70-80 ppt very few mangroves survive. Nickerson and Thibodeau (1985) reported that the distributions of Avecennia and Rhizophora were closely correlated with the amount of hydrogen sulfide in the soil. They found that when compared with with vegetation distant from the streamside, vegetation fringing streams was taller, more robust and grew in soils with lower hydrogen sulfide. This suggests that the concentration of hydrogen sulfide is an important factor regulating both primary productivity and forest structure in mangroves. One reason riverine mangroves are highly productive is that the concentration of SO_4 is much lower and thus H_2S would also be lower.

REFERENCES

Adams, D.A., 1963. Factors influencing vascular plant zonation in North Carolina salt marshes. Ecology, 44:445-456.

Bertness, M.D., 1987. Peat accumulation and the success of marsh plants. Ecology, 69:703-713.

Blum, U., E. Seneca, and L. Stroud, 1978. Photosynthesis and respiration of *Spartina* and *Juncus* salt marshes in North Carolina: some models. Estuaries, 1:228-238.

Boto, K., J. Bunt, and J. Wellingon, 1984. Variations in mangrove forest productivity in northern Australia and Papua New Guinea. Estuarine Coast. Mar. Sci., 19:321-329.

Bray, J. and E. Gorham, 1964. Litter production in forests of the world. Advances in Ecological Research, 2:101-157.

Broome, S.W., W.W. Woodhouse, and E.D. Seneca, 1975. The relationship of mineral nutrients to growth of *Spartina alterniflora* in North Carolina. II. The effects of N, P, and Fe fertilizers. Soil Sci. Am. Proc., 37:301-307.

Brown, S. and A.E. Lugo, 1982. A comparison of structural and functional characteristics of saltwater and freshwater forested wetlands. In B. Gopal, R. Turner, R. Wetzel, and D. Whigham (Eds.), Wetlands Ecology and Management. Proceedings of the First International Wetlands Conference, New Dehli. National Institute of Ecology and International Scientific Publications, New Delhi, India. Sept. 1980, pp. 109–130.

Buresh, R.J., R.D. DeLaune, and W.H. Patrick, Jr., 1980. Nitrogen and phosphorous distribution and utilization by *Spartina alterniflora* in a Louisiana Gulf Coast Marsh. Estuaries, 3(2):111–121.

Chabreck, R.H., 1970. Vegetation and size of hydrologoic units along the Louisiana coast. Cooperative Wildlife Research Unit, School of Forestry, Louisiana State Univ., Baton Rouge.

Chapman, V.J., 1960. Salt Marshes and Salt Deserts of the World. Interscience, New York, 392 pp.

Cintron, G., A.E. Lugo, D.J. Pool, and G. Morris, 1978. Mangroves of arid environments in Puerto Rico and adjacent islands. Biotropica, 10:110–121.

Clough, B.F., 1979. Mangrove ecosystems in Australia. Australian National Univ. Press, Canberra, 302 pp.

Conner, W. and J. Day, 1987. The ecology of the Barataria Basin, Louisiana: An estuarine profile. U.S. Fish and Wildlife, Biol. Rept. 85(7.13). 165 pp.

Dacey, J.W. and B.L. Howes, 1984. Water uptake by roots controls water movement and sediment oxidation in short *Spartina* marsh. Science, 224:487–489.

Davis, J.H., 1940. The ecology and geologic role of mangroves in Florida. Carnegie Institution, Washington, Publ. No. 517, pp. 303–412.

Day, J., W. Conner, F. Ley-Lou, R. Day, and A. Machado Navarro. 1987. The productivity and compositon of mangrove forests, Laguna de Términos, Mexico. Aquat. Bot., 27:267–284.

de la Cruz, A., 1969. Mangroves-tidal swamps of the tropics. Sci. Rev., 10:9–16.

DeLaune, R.D., R.J. Buresh, and W.H. Patrick, Jr., 1979. Relationship of soil properties to standing crop biomass of *Spartina alterniflora* in a Louisiana marsh. Estuarine Coastal Mar. Sci., 8:477–487.

Dijkema, K., 1987. Geography of salt marshes in Europe. Z. Geomorph. N.F., 31:489–499.

Egler, F., 1952. Southeast saline Everglades vegetation, Florida, and its management. Veg. Acta Geobot., 3:213–265.

Flores-Verdugo, F.J. Day, and R. Briseño-Dueñas, 1986. Structure, litterfall, decomposition, and detritus dynamics of mangroves in a Mexican coastal lagoon with an ephemeral inlet. Mar. Ecol. Prog. Ser., 35:83–90.

Fogg, G.E., 1973. The Growth of Plants, 2nd ed. Penguin, Baltimore, MD, 290 pp.

Gallagher, J.L., 1975. Effect of an amonium nitrate pulse on the growth and elemental composition of natural stands of *Spartina alterniflora* and *Juncus roemerianus*. Am. J. Bot., 62:644–648.

Gallagher, J.L. and F. Plumley, 1979. Underground biomass profiles and productivity in Atlantic coastal marshes. Am. J. Bot., 66: 156–161.

Gallagher, J.L., R. Reimhold, R. Linthurst, and W. Pfeiffer, 1980. Aerial production, mortality, and mineral accumulation-export dynamics in *Spartina alterniflora* and *Juncus roemerianus* plant stands in a Georgia salt marsh. Ecology, 61:303–312.

Good, R., N. Good, and B. Frasco, 1982. A review of primary production and decomposition dynamics of the belowground marsh component. In V. S. Kennedy (Ed.), Estuarine Comparisons. Academic Press, New York, pp. 139–157.

Gosselink, J., 1984. The ecology of delta marshes of coastal Louisiana: a community profile. U.S. Fish and Wildlife Service. Rept. No. FWS/OBS-84/09. Washington, 134 pp.

Giurgevich, J. and E. Dunn, 1978. Seasonal patterns of CO_2 and water vapor exchange of *Juncus roemerianus* Scheele in a Georgia salt marsh. Am. J. Bot., 65:502–510.

Giurgevich, J. and E. Dunn, 1979. Seasonal patterns of CO_2 and water vapor exchange of the tall and short forms of *Spartina alterniflora* Loisel in a Georgia salt marsh. Oecologia, 43:139–156.

Haines, B.L. and E.L. Dunn, 1976. Growth and resource allocation responses of *Spartina alterniflora* Loisel to three levels of NH_4-N, Fe, and NaCl in solution culture. Bot. Gazette, 137:224–230.

Hopkinson, C., G. Gosselink, and R. Parrondo, 1978. Aboveground production of seven marsh plant species in coastal Louisiana. Ecology, 59(4):760–769.

Hopkinson, C., G. Gosselink, and R. Parrondo, 1980. Production of coastal Louisiana marsh plants calculated from phenometric techniques. Ecology, 61(5):1091–1098.

Houghton, R.A. and G.M. Woodwell, 1980. The flax pond ecosystem study: Exchanges of CO_2 between a salt marsh and the atmosphere. Ecology, 61(6):1434–1445.

Howes, B.L., R.W. Howarth, J.M. Teal, and I. Valiela, 1981. Oxidation-reduction potentials in a salt marsh: Spatial patterns and interactions with primary production. Limnol. Oceanogr., 26(2):350–360.

Josselyn, M., 1983. The ecology of San Francisco Bay tidal marshes: a community profile. U.S. Fish and Wildlife Service. Rept. No. FWS/OBS-83/23. Washington, 102 pp.

Kirby, C.J. and J.G. Gosselink, 1976. Primary production in a Louisiana Gulf Coast *Spartina alterniflora* marsh. Ecology, 57(5):1052–1059.

Kuenzler, E. J., 1974. Mangrove swamp systems. In H. T. Odum, B. J. Copeland, and E. A. McMahon (Eds.), Coastal Ecological Systems of the United States. The Conservation Foundation, Washington, Vol. 1, pp. 346–372.

Kurz, H. and K. Wagner, 1957. Tidal-marshes of the Gulf and Atlantic coasts of northern Florida and Charleston, SC: Fla. State Univ. Stud., v. 24, pp.1–168.

Linthurst, R., 1980. An evaluation of aeration, nitrogen, pH and salinity as factors affecting *Spartina alterniflora* growth: a summary. In V. Kennedy (Ed.), Estuarine Perspectives. Academic Press, New York, pp. 235–247.

Linthurst, R.A. and U. Blum, 1980. Growth modifications of *Spartina alterniflora* Loisel by the interactions of pH and salinity under controlled conditions. J. Exp. Mar. Biol. Ecol., 55:207–218.

Linthurst, R.A. and R.J. Riemold, 1978. An evaluation of methods for estimating the net aerial primary productivity of estuarine angiosperms. J. Appl. Ecol., 15:919–931.

Linthurst, R.A. and E. Seneca, 1981. Aeration, nitrogen and salinity as determinants of *Spartina alterniflora* Loisel. growth response. Estuaries, 4:53–63.

Livingstone, D. and D. Patriquin, 1981. Below growth of *Spartina alterniflora* Loisel: Habit, functional biomass, and nonstructural carbohydrates. Estuarine Coastal Shelf Sci., 12:579–588.

Lugo, A., 1980. Mangrove ecosystems: successional or steady state? Biotropica, 12:65–72.

Lugo, A. and S. Snedaker. 1974. The ecology of mangroves. Ann. Rev. Ecol. and Syst., 5:39–64.

Macnae, W., 1967. Zonation within mangroves associated with estuaries in North Queensland. In G. Lauff (Ed.), Estuaries. AAAS Publ. 83, Washington, pp. 432–441.

Macnae, W., 1968. A general account of the fauna and flora of mangrove swamps and forests in the Indo-West-Pacific region. Advan. Mar. Biol. 6:73–270.

Margalef, R., 1962. Comunidades naturales. Publicacion especial. Instituto de Biologia Marina Universidad de Puerto Rico, Mayaguez, 469 pp.

Mendelssohn, I.A., 1979. Nitrogen metabolism in the height forms of *Spartina alterniflora* in North Carolina. Ecology, 60:574–584.

Mendelssohn, I. A. and K. L. McKee, 1982. Sublethal stresses controlling *Spartina alterniflora* productivity. In B. Gopal, R. Turner, R. Wetzel, and D. Whigham (Eds.), Wetlands: Ecology and Management. International Scientific Publications. Jaipur, India, pp. 223–242.

Mendelssohn, I. A. and K. L. McKee, 1988. *Spartina alterniflora* die-back in Louisiana: time-course investigation of soil waterlogging effects. J. Ecol., 76:509–521.

Mendelssohn, I. A. and E. D. Seneca., 1980. The influence of soil drainage on the growth of salt marsh cordgrass *Spartina alterniflora* in North Carolina. Estuarine Coastal Mar. Sci., 11:27–40.

Mendelssohn, I. A., K. L. McKee, and W. H. Patrick., 1981. Oxygen deficiency in *Spartina alterniflora* roots: Metabolic adaptation to anoxia. Science, 214:439–441.

Miller, W. and F. Egler, 1950. Vegetation of the Wequetequock-Pawcatuck tidal marshes. Ecol. Monogr., 20:143–172.

Mitsch, W. and J. Gosselink. 1986. Wetlands. Van Nostrand Reinhold, New York, 539 pp.

Mitsui, S., 1965. Dynamic aspects of nutrient uptake. In The Mineral Nutrition of the Rice Plant. Symposium Proceedings International Rice Research Institute, 1964. John Hopkins University, Baltimore, MD, pp. 53–62.

Mooring, M.T., A.W. Cooper, and E.D. Seneca, 1971. Seed germination response and evidence for height ecophenes in *Spartina alterniflora* from North Carolina. Am. J. Bot., 58:48–55.

Morris, J.T., 1979. The nitrogen uptake kinetics and growth response of *Spartina alterniflora*. PhD Thesis, Yale University, New Haven, CT.

Morris, J.T. and G.J. Whiting, 1985. Gas advection in sediments of a South Carolina salt marsh. Mar. Ecol. Prog. Ser., 27:187–194.

Nickerson, N.H. and F.R. Thibodeau, 1985. Association between pore water sulfide concentrations and the distribution of mangroves. Biogeochemistry, 1:183–192.

Nixon, S., 1982. The ecology of New England high salt marshes: a community profile. U.S. Fish and Wildlife Service. Rept. No. FWS/OBS-81/55. Washington, 70 pp.

Odum, E.P., 1969. The strategy of ecosystem development. Science, 164:262–269.

Odum, E.P., 1971. Fundamentals of Ecology, 3rd ed. Saunders, Philadelphia, 574 pp.

Odum, E.P., 1974. Halophytes, energetics and ecosystems. In R.J. Reimold and W.H. Green (Eds.), Ecology of Halophytes. Academic, New York, pp. 599–602.

Odum, E.P., 1980. The status of three ecosystem-level hypotheses regarding salt marsh estuaries: tidal subsidy, outwelling, and detritus-based food chains. In V. Kennedy (Ed.), Estuarine Perspectives. Academic, New York, pp. 485–495.

Odum, W. E., C. McIvor, and T. Smith, 1982. The ecology of the mangroves of south Florida: a community profile. U.S. Fish and Wildlife Service, Office of Biological Services. Rept. No. FWS/OBS-81/24. Washington, 144 pp.

Odum, W. E., T. Smith, J. Hoover, and C. McIvor, 1984. The ecology of tidal freshwater marshes of the United States east coast: a community profile. U.S. Fish and Wildlife Service. Rept. No. FWS/OBS-83/17. Washington, 177 pp.

Onuf, C., J. Teal, and I. Valiela, 1977. The interactions of nutrients, plant growth, and herbivory in a mangrove ecosystem. Ecology, 58:514–526.

Patrick, W.H., Jr. and R.D. DeLaune, 1976. Nitrogen and phosphorous utilization by *Spartina alterniflora* in a salt marsh in Barataria Bay, Louisiana. Estuarine Coastal Mar. Sci., 4:59–64.

Pomeroy, L. and R. Wiegert (Eds.), 1981. The Ecology of a Salt Marsh. Springer-Verlag, New York, 271 pp.

Pool, D.J., A.E. Lugo, and S. Snedaker, 1975. Litter production in mangrove forests in southern Florida and Puerto Rico. In G. Walsh, S. Snedaker, and J. Teas (Eds.), Proceedings of the International Symposium on Biology and Management of Mangroves. Institute of Food and Agriculture Science, Univ. of Florida, Gainesville, pp. 213–237.

Pool, D.J., S. Snedaker, and A.E. Lugo, 1977. Structure of mangrove forests in Florida, Puerto Rico, Mexico, and Costa Rica. Biotropica, 9:195–212.

Richards, P., 1952. The Tropical Rain Forest: an Ecological Study. Cambridge Univ. Press, Cambridge, 450 pp.

Riedeburg, C., 1975. The intertidal pump in a Georgia salt marsh. MS Thesis, Univ. of Georgia, Athens, 81 pp.

Rosensweig, M.L., 1968. Net primary production of terrestrial communities: Prediction from climatological data. Am. Nat., 102:67–14.

Schimper, A., 1903. Plant Geography on a Physiological Basis. Oxford Univ. Press, Oxford, 839 pp.

Schubauer, J. and C. Hopkinson, 1984. Above- and belowground emergent macrophyte production and turnover in a coastal marsh ecosystem, Georgia. Limnol. Oceanogr., 29(5):1052–1065.

Shew, D.M., D.A. Linthurst, and E.D. Seneca, 1981. Comparison of production computation methods on a southeastern North Carolina *Spartina alterniflora* salt marsh. Estuaries, 4(2):97 -109.

Smart, M., 1986. Intraspecific competition and growth form differentiation of the salt marsh plant, *Spartina alterniflora* Loisel. Ph.D. Dissertation, Univ. of Delaware, Newark, 283 pp.

Smart, R.M. and J.W. Barko, 1978. Influence of sediment, salinity and nutrients on the physiological ecology of selected salt marsh plants. Estuarine Coastal Mar. Sci., 7:487–495.

Smith, K., R. Good, and N. Good, 1979. Production dynamics for above- and below-ground components of a New Jersey tidal marsh. Estuarine Coastal Mar. Sci., 9:189–201.

Smith, W. and J. Monte. 1975. Marshes: The wet grasslands. Geoscience and Man, Louisiana State Univeristy, Baton Rouge, 20:27–38.

Snedaker, S., 1982. Mangrove species zonation: why? In D. Sen and K. Rajpurohit (Eds.), Tasks for Vegetation Science, Vol. 2. Junk, The Hague, pp. 111–125.

Snedaker, S., and S. Brown, 1981. Water quality and mangrove ecosystem dynamics. EPA, Office of Research and Development, Gulf Breeze, Florida, EPA-600/4-81-022, 80 p.

Steever, E.Z., R.S. Warren, and W.A. Wiering, 1976. Tidal energy subsidy and standing crop production of *Spartina alterniflora*. Estuarine Coastal Mar. Sci., 4:473–478.

Stout, J., 1984. The ecology of irregularly flooded salt marshes of the northeastern Gulf of Mexico: a community profile. U.S. Fish and Wildlife Service. Biol. Rept. 85(7.1). Washington, 98 pp.

Stroud, L. M., 1976. Net primary production of belowground material and carbohydrate patterns in two height forms of *Spartina alterniflora* in two North Carolina marshes. PhD Thesis, North Carolina State University, Raleigh, 140 pp.

Stroud, L.M. and W. Cooper, 1968. Color infra-red aerial photographic interpretation and net primary productivity of regularly flooded North Carolina marsh. North Carolina Water Resources Research Institute Report No. 14, 86 pp.

Sullivan, M.J., and F.C. Daiber, 1974. Response in production of cord grass, *Spartina alterniflora*, to inorganic nitrogen and phosphorous fertilizer. Chesapeake Sci., 15(2):121–124.

Teal, J.M., 1962. Energy flow in the salt marsh ecosystem of Georgia. Ecology, 43:614–624.

Teal, J., 1986. The ecology of regularly flooded salt marshes of New England: a community profile. U.S. Fish and Wildlife Service. Biol. Rept. 85(7.4). Washington, 61 pp.

Teal, J.M. and J. Kanwisher, 1960. Gas exchange in a Georgia salt marsh. Limnol. Oceanogr., 6:388–399.

Thom, B., 1967. Mangrove ecology and deltaic morpohology: Tabasco, Mexico. J. Ecol. 55:301–343.

Turner, R.E., 1976. Geographic variations in salt marsh macrophyte production: A review. Contrib. Mar. Sci., 20:47–68.

Turner, R.E., 1979. A simple model of the seasonal growth of *Spartina alterniflora* and *Spartina patens*. Contrib. Mar. Sci., 22:137–147.

Twilley, R., 1982. Litter dynamics and organic carbon exchange in black mangrove (*Avicennia germinas*) basin forests in a southwest Florida estuary. PhD Dissertation, Universtiy of Florida, Gainsville.

Twilley, R., 1985. An analysis of mangrove forests along the Gambia River estuary: Implications for the management of estuarine resources. International Programs Report No. 6, Great Lakes and Marine Waters Center, University of Michigan, Ann Arbor, 75 pp.

Twilley , R., A. Lugo, and C. Patterson-Zucca, 1986. Litter production and turnover in basin mangrove forests in southwest Florida. Ecology, 67:670-683.

Valiela, I. and J.M. Teal, 1974. Nutrient limitation in salt marsh vegetation. In R.J. Riemold and W.H. Green (Eds.), Ecology of Halophytes. Academic, New York, pp. 547-563.

Valiela, I. and J.M. Teal, 1979. The nitrogen budget of a salt marsh ecosystem. Nature, 280:652-656.

Valiela, I., J.M. Teal, and N.Y. Persson, 1976. Production and dynamics of experimentally enriched salt marsh vegetation: Belowground biomass. Limnol. Oceanogr., 21:245-252.

Waisel, Y. 1972. Biology of Halophytes. Academic Press, New York, 395 pp.

Walter, H. and M. Steiner, 1936. Die Okologie der Ost-Afrikanischen Mangroven. Z. Bot., 65-193.

Watson, J., 1928. Mangrove forests of the Malay Peninsula. Malayan Forest Records 6. Fraser & Neave, Ltd., Singapore, 275 pp.

West, R.C., 1966. The natural vegetation of the Tabascan lowlands, Mexico: Rev. Geograf., v. 64, pp. 108-122.

Wiegert, R. and F. Evans, 1964. Primary production and the disappearance fo dead vegetation on an old field in southeastern Michigan. Ecology, 45:49-63.

Young, D., 1974. Studies of Florida Gulf Coast salt marshes receiving thermal discharges. In J. Gibbons and R. Sharitz (Eds.), Thermal Ecology. USAEC Publication CONF-730505, pp. 532-550.

Zedler, J., 1982. The ecology of southern California coastal salt marshes: a community profile. U.S. Fish and Wildlife Service. Rept. No. FWS/OBS-81/54. Washington, 110 pp.

Zelitch, I., 1971. Photosynthesis, Photorespiration, and Plant Productivity. Academic, New York.

Zenkevitch, L. 1963. Biology of the Seas of the USSR. Interscience, New York, 955 p.

▬ 6

Estuarine Seagrasses[1]

Beneath the water surface in shallow estuarine sediments, there are often dense communities of vascular plants. Worldwide there are more than 50 species capable of inhabiting this submerged saline environment, a relatively small number compared with the number of plant species in other environments (den Hartog 1970). Those species occurring in full-strength sea water are referred to as *seagrasses* although these monocotyledenous flowering plants are not related to true grasses. These marine angiosperms belong to 2 major botanical families, *Potamogetonaceae* and *Hydrocharitaceae*, and to 12 genera, 9 of which are in the former family (den Hartog 1970). While there are no true estuarine species of submerged vascular plants, a wide variety of both marine and freshwater plants can be found in brackish waters. Growth forms of seagrass are generally linear or elliptic, while freshwater species exhibit considerably greater morphological diversity (den Hartog 1970). Several common estuarine submerged plants (or macrophytes) are depicted in Fig. 6.1. Perhaps the most common and certainly the most extensively studied seagrasses in the temperate and tropical regions are eelgrass, *Zostera* spp., and turtlegrass, *Thalassia testudinum*, respectively. Other marine species such as *Halodule* spp. also dominate certain coastal shallows. One species, *Ruppia maritima* (Wideongrass), can be found across the entire estuarine salinity gradient from near fresh to full sea water and in temperate and tropical waters. Certain freshwater aquatic macrophytes penetrate the saline environment to varying degrees, including the ribbon-leaf *Vallisneria americana, Elodea canadensis, Myriophyllum spicatum,* and *Potamogeton perfoliatus.*

[1]Written primarily by W. M. Kemp.

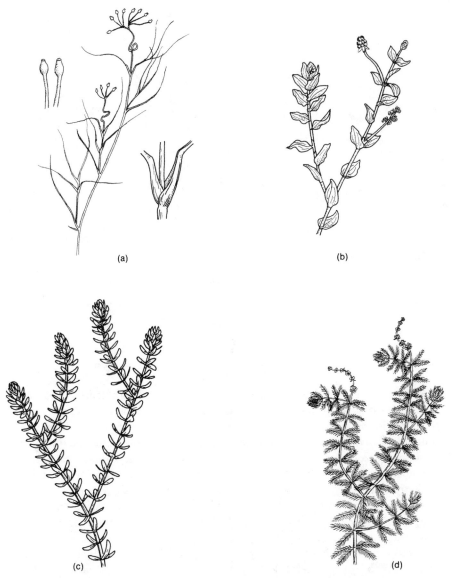

(a)

(b)

(c)

(d)

Figure 6.1 Examples of common "seagrasses" that occur in estuarine systems. (a) *Ruppia maritina*, (b) *Potamogeton perfoliatus*, (c) *Elodea canadensis*, (d) *Myriophyllum spicatum*, (e) *Thalassia testudinum*, (f) *Vallisneria americanum*, (g) *Halodule wrightii*, (h) *Zostera marina*. (Hotchkiss 1967)

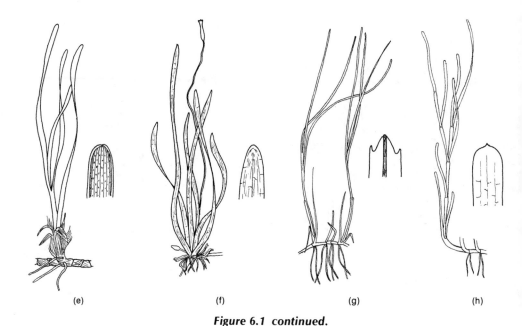

(e)   (f)   (g)   (h)

Figure 6.1 continued.

6.1   SPATIAL DISTRIBUTIONS

These estuarine seagrasses are distributed along various gradients in space and time, including geographic, vertical, seasonal, and longitudinal (that is, along the estuarine salinity gradient). The observed distribution of a given species is a function of environmental conditions including light, temperature, salinity, substrate, waves and currents, nutrients, and availability of seed. Estuarine grasses are most common in soft sediments of semisheltered areas where depth and turbidity conditions allow sufficient light.

On a broad geographic scale we find that the common eelgrass *Zostera* and its subgenus *Zosterella* are widely distributed in the temperate zones of North America, Europe, and Asia, as well as the south temperate coasts of Australia (den Hartog 1970, Fig. 6.2). This pattern was modified markedly in the decade of 1935–1945 by the general decline of eelgrass in Europe and North America. The so-called "wasting disease" associated with this phenomenon has been ascribed to, among other causes, a general increase in summer temperatures (Rasmussen 1977). The distribution of the tropical seagrass *Thalassia testudinum* is considerably narrower (den Hartog 1970), confined to North American and Afro-Asian tropical zones. In the latter region it is found in association with *Cymodocia,* which is a dominant speices along the Mediterranean coastal margins.

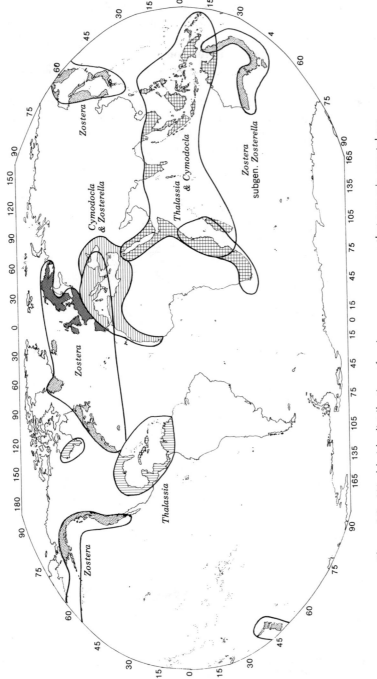

Figure 6.2 Worldwide distribution of major seagrass genera that occur in coastal systems. (from Mann 1972 after den Hartog 1970)

The vertical zonation of estuarine grasses is controlled primarily by interactions between light availability and wave action and secondly by substrate type and nutrient supply. Den Hartog (1970) developed a scheme to classify the depth distribution of major seagrasses in relation to growth form. For example, *Zostera* can be found throughout the inter- and subtidal zones, while *Thalassia* is confined to the upper sublittoral depths. The depth distribution of *Zostera marina* biomass reflects a balance between light and wave effects, with maximum standing crop occurring just below mean low water as exemplified for the slightly turbid waters of a California coastal lagoon (Fig. 6.3). The overriding importance of light conditions on depth zonation of eelgrass is suggested by the data of

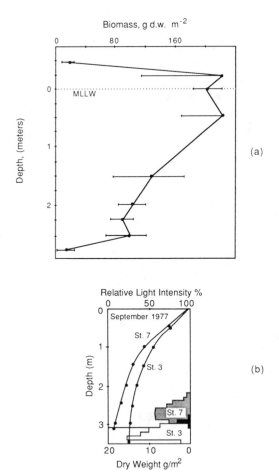

Figure 6.3 Depth distribution of *Zostera marina* (a) in a California coastal lagoon (from Backmon and Barliotti 1976) and (b) in Odawa Bay, Japan (from Mukai et al. 1980). Note that at station 3 with clearer water the maximum *Zostera* biomass occurs at a greater depth.

Mukai et al. (1980) for the relatively clear water of Odawa Bay, Japan where maximum biomass is found at depths corresponding to 20–30% surface irradiance for two stations having markedly different turbidities. Vertical distributions of leaf area index (LAI, the horizontally oriented area of leaves per unit surface area of sediments) for seagrasses such as *Zostera* generally follow those of biomass, ranging from 1–5 m^2/m^2 (Aioi 1980, Wetzel and Penhale 1983).

Seagrasses are affected by water depth and they can reciprocally influence the nature and depth of their own sediment bed through the trapping and binding suspended particulates associated with damping wave and tidal energy (e.g., Burrell and Schubel 1977). Transects across macrophyte beds often reveal a thick layer of highly sorted, organically rich, fine-grained materials concentrated at the center of the grass bed for both eelgrass (Fig. 6.4*a–c*) and turtle-grass (Fig. 6.4*d–f*) communities. Peak standing crop and density of grasses along this transverse axis also tend to occur in the central area where wave action is reduced and ample nutrients in organic sediments may enhance seagrass growth (Zieman 1975).

Along the land-sea axis of an estuary the relative distribution and abundance of seagrasses may be influenced by relative availabilities of nutrients (higher at the riverine end) and light (water clarity higher at the ocean end). Patterns of species distributions also are affected by salinity tolerances along this land-sea axis. Hence we find the true seagrasses dominating at the oceanic end of the salinity gradient, and freshwater macrophytes most abundant in the oligo- and mesohaline regions. As mentioned previously, *Ruppia maritina* occurs throughout the salinity range. The relative effects of salinity on growth of several macrophytes are illustrated in Fig. 6.5*a*, where increasing salinity from zero caused a steady decline in growth for *Vallisneria* to about 8 ppt, where it virtually ceased to occur, while *Potamogeton* exhibited peak growth at 7 ppt and a marked deline at 13 ppt. Eelgrass and turtle grass have broad regions of tolerance from 15–40 ppt, with peak growth occurring at about 30 ppt (Fig. 6.5*b*).

6.2 PRODUCTION AND STANDING CROP

Seagrass production has been the subject of considerable attention since early in this century (e.g., Peterson 1918). It has been suggested by numerous investigators that seagrass meadows are among the most productive aquatic ecosystems known (Mann 1972, McRoy and McMillan 1977, Zieman and Wetzel 1980). Seagrasses support the growth of higher organisms through their contribution to detrital food chains (Petersen 1918, Fenchel 1970), by providing complex physical habitats which shelter invertebrates and juvenile fish from predators, and by creating a substrate for growth of rich epiphytic communities (Carr and Adams 1973, Adams 1976, Stoner 1980). By trapping suspended material and taking up nutrients and other dissolved substances (Burrell and Schubel 1977, Patriquin 1972; Ward et al. 1984), seagrass may help to increase the clarity and general quality of estuarine waters.

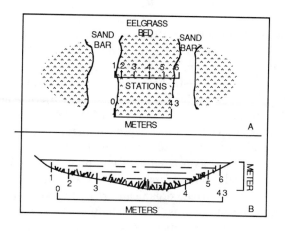

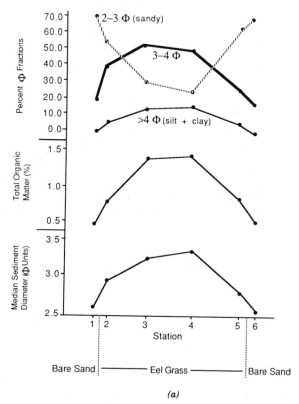

Figure 6.4a Pictorial representation of study area at Sandy Point. (A) Transect across *Zostera* bed situated between sand bars showing positions of sampling locations. (B) Cross-section of the transect. Reproduced by permission of the University of South Carolina Press from Orth (1977a).

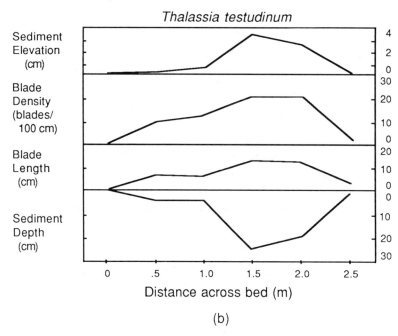

Figure 6.4b Transects across a *Thalassia* bed off Key Largo, Florida (from Zieman 1975) showing horizontal gradients in various sediment and plant characteristics.

Standing crops of seagrass populations may exceed 1000 g dry wt m^{-2} for subtropical *Thalassia* populations and for north temperate and arctic communities of *Zostera* (Zieman and Wetzel 1980), and peak biomass values are generally in excess of 100 g dry wt m^{-2}. Productivities range from about 1 to 15 g C m^{-2} day^{-1}, with relatively high daily rates occurring over the full latitudinal distribution (Table 6.1, Zieman and Wetzel 1980). Annual rates tend to be greatest in the tropics and subtropics, where growing seasons may extend over the entire annual cycle, but high rates can still occur in high altitudes (McRoy and McMillan 1977). Macrophyte biomass values tend to be somewhat lower in more brackish waters, with values greater than 500 g dry wt m^{-2} rarely reported. In contrast to biomass, daily productivities for estuarine communities of freshwater plants can rival those reported for coastal marine seagrasses (Kemp et al. 1984).

On a diel cycle, seagrass productivity patterns tend to follow the daily irradiance cycle, with peak values occurring between late morning and early afternoon. A typical diel cycle of dissolved oxygen and in a water column containing an estuarine eelgrass population is presented in Fig. 6.6 (Nixon and Oviatt 1972). Diel patterns of O_2 and CO_2 (total dissolved inorganic carbon) in seagrass beds tend to be mirror images of each other where pH decreases during the day with lowered concentration of carbon dioxide resulting from plant photosynthesis (Smith 1981 See also Fig. 3.11). Recently, some investigators have reported

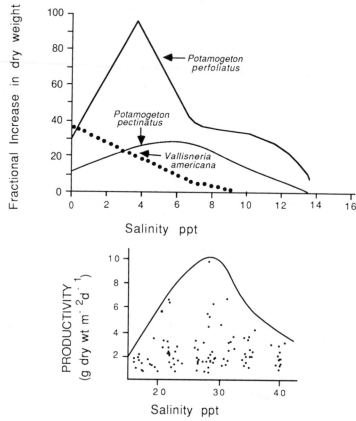

Figure 6.5 (a) Growth of *Potamogeton* and *Vallisneria* along a salinity gradient (redrawn from Bourn 1932) (b) Scattergram of productivity (gm dry wt/m² day) as a function of salinity (redrawn from Zieman 1975).

midafternoon depressions of production in seagrass communities, and they suggest the possibility of short-term nutrient and/or inorganic carbon limitation (Wetzel and Penhale, 1983).

There are three conventional techniques employed for estimating seagrass production: (1) determining changes in concentrations of metabolic gases (e.g., oxygen) in the water surrounding the plants; (2) measuring the incorporation of ^{14}C-labeled inorganic carbon from water enclosed around seagrass leaves; and (3) observing temporal increases in plant biomass or elongation of marked leaves. Concern has been raised that oxygen production might underestimate photosynthesis because some oxygen molecules are stored or cycled in the plant's internal lacunal (gas space) systems (e.g., Hartman and Brown 1967, Zieman and Wetzel 1980). However, recent experiments have shown that for most of these plants this problem is transient and unimportant relative to the overall

TABLE 6.1   Representative Seagrass Productivities[a]

Species	Location	Productivity (gC/m^2 day)
Cymodocea nodosa	Mediterranean	5.5–18.5
Halodule wrightii	North Carolina	0.5–2.0
Posidonia oceanica	Malta	2.0–6.0
Syringodium filiforme	Florida	0.8
	Texas	
Thalassia testudinum	Texas	0.6–9.0
	Florida (east coast)	0.9–16.0
	Cuba	0.6–7.2
	Puerto Rico	2.5–4.5
	Jamaica	1.9–3.0
	Barbados	0.5–3.0
	Bermuda	5.6 (leaves)
		7.2 (total plant)
Zostera marina	Denmark	2.0–7.3
		0.9–3.2 (leaves)
		0.5 (rhizomes)
	Rhode Island	0.4–2.9
	North Carolina	0.2–1.7
	Washington	0.7–4.0
	Alaska	3.3–8.0

[a]From Zieman and Wetzel (1980).

metabolic rate (Westlake 1967, Sand-Jensen et al. 1982, Kemp et al. 1986). The ^{14}C technique of Wetzel (1964) may underestimate productivity because it assumes that inorganic carbon is taken up exclusively from the water column, and $^{14}CO_2$ similarly may be stored and recycled within the lacunal gas space (Wium-Andersen 1971, Penhale and Thayer 1980, Sondergaard 1979). While the leaf marking techniques (Zieman, 1975; Sand-Jensen, 1975; Patriquin, 1973) may be the least ambiguous estimators of seagrass production (Zieman and Wetzel 1980), the technique suffers from an inability to measure short-term (hours) rates for total plant production, because experiments generally must be conducted over periods of 8–12 days to allow for significant emergence of new leaves. In addition, production estimated by marking techniques does not measure losses associated with excretion, sloughing, and herbivory. While several studies have shown the three methods do provide generally similar values of productivity (e.g., Bittaker and Iverson 1976, Capone et al. 1979, Kemp et al. 1986), we can conclude that each measures something slightly different from the others and each is appropriate for a particular experimental situation.

Annual patterns of seagrass production have been studied for a variety of estuarine and coastal communities. In temperate latitudes productivity tends to follow the seasonal cycle of solar radiation, with maxima often occurring in late

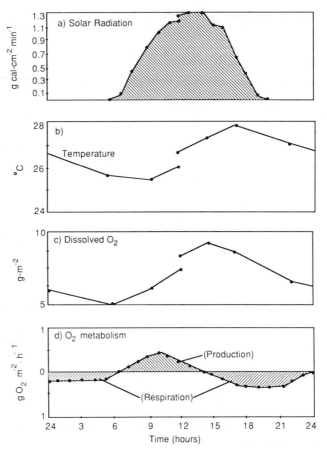

Figure 6.6 Typical diel cycle of (a) solar radiation, (b) temperature, (c) dissolved oxygen over an eelgrass, *Zostera marina*, bed in Narragansett Bay, and (d) estimated rates of net apparent O_2 production and respiration (Nixon and Oviatt 1972).

spring to early summer. An example of this annual course for an estuarine eelgrass population in Denmark is provided in Fig. 6.7. The biomass cycle shown in this figure lags 2–3 months behind productivity, with maximum values coinciding approximately with temperature. While similar seasonal sequences have been observed in various other seagrass populations (e.g., Zieman 1975), other patterns have been reported as well. For example, in North Carolina, Penhale (1977) observed that the major biomass peak occurred in early spring, while the seasonal productivity maximum occurred in summer, when temperature was highest. The growth pattern apparent in the data of Fig. 6.7 reflects an early spring sprouting of numerous shoots with maximum *turion* (leaf bundle) density in April, followed by peak leaf and rhizome biomass in mid to late summer, and flowering throughout the late spring and early summer. This temporal sequence is almost identical to that reported for other eelgrass populations (e.g., Aioi 1980).

At the end of the growing season (and to some extent throughout the year) much of the plant material dies and begins to decay. During decomposition much of the N, P, C, and other elements which are tied up in seagrass biomass are released back to the environment in a dissolved form. A part of the chemical energy associated with plant structure, as well as a portion of the elemental composition, are incorporated into microbial and animal biomass through the detritus food chain (see Chapter 7). The grazing activity of macroinvertebrates increases the rate of decay significantly, and facilitates the transfer of energy to secondary consumers.

Large quantities of oxygen are utilized in the respiratory processes associated with decomposition. Seagrass decay is rapid compared with that of salt marsh plants, with half-lives (the time required for loss of 50% of original material) of 1 month compared with 7 months for marsh grasses. Thus the chemical energy and nutrients incorporated in seagrass are transferred to heterotrophic organisms effectively and quickly. Decompostion of algal material occurs even more quickly, however, which may place such a large demand on O_2 levels such that consumption may exceed reaeration rates, leading to anoxic conditions. Thus seagrass may be a particularly favorable source of detritus, representing a balance between rapid energy utilization by consumer organisms and slow oxygen consumption (Twilley et al. 1986). This topic is covered in much more detail in Chapter 7.

The contribution of seagrass production to estuarine carbon budgets can range from negligible to almost 50% of the total production within an estuary. For example, the combined production of seagrass and their epiphytes generate almost 45% of the total carbon fixed in Beaufort Sound, North Carolina. Prior to the widespread decline of submerged macrophytes in Chesapeake Bay between 1965 and 1980, estuarine seagrasses comprised almost one-third of the total production, whereas under present conditions seagrass contribution is less than 5% (Kemp et al. 1984).

6.3 FACTORS AFFECTING SEAGRASS PRODUCTION

6.3.1 Irradiance

The specific responses of seagrass photosynthesis to light are similar to those discussed previously for phytoplankton (Chapter 4). Photosynthesis versus irradiance ($P - I$) curves typically exhibit an initial linear response with a gradually decreasing slope until saturation is achieved, after which a plateau may occur with no photosynthetic response to increased irradiance. For seagrass photosynthetic inhibition at extremely high light levels is rare. An example of such a $P - I$ curve for *Zostera marina* in Alaska is given in Fig. 6.8. Numerous measurements of $P - I$ relations have been reported for a variety of submerged vascular plants, and these relations generally exhibit a remarkable similarity. For exam-

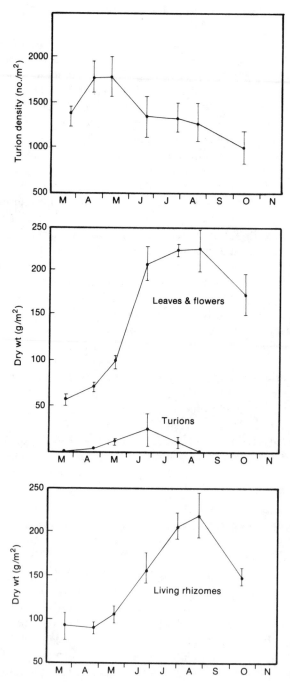

Figure 6.7 *Zostera marina* production and population characteristics in Vellerup Vig, Denmark (from Sand-Jensen 1975).

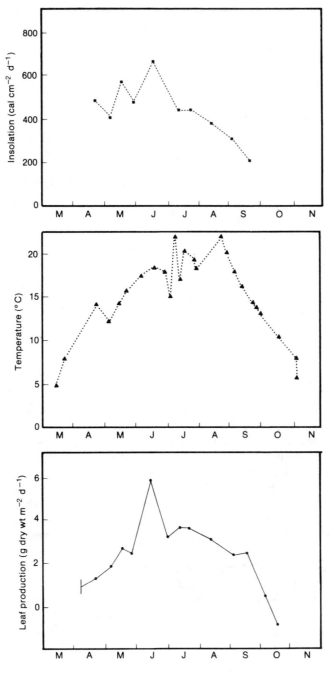

Figure 6.7 continued.

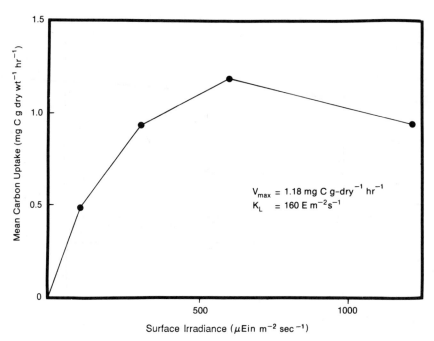

Figure 6.8 Uptake of inorganic carbon by *Zostera marina* at different light intensities (from McRoy 1974).

ple, Williams and McRoy (1982) have shown similar light responses for the production of six seagrass species growing in different regions from 10 to 50°N latitude.

In some shallow estuarine systems, particularly where oceanic influence is greater than riverine, light conditions are maintained above saturation levels (ca. 400-600 μEin m^{-2}sec^{-1}), beyond which increased light will not produce increased photosynthesis, such that light is not limiting (e.g., Penhale 1977, Capone et al. 1979). In more turbid estuarine systems, however, availability of light appears to be crucial to the production and survival of seagrasses (e.g., Backman and Berilotti 1976, Congdon and McComb 1979, Wetzel and Penhale 1983, Bulthuis 1983). Within limits, submerged macrophytes can adapt to varying light regimes via morphological (e.g., leaf elongation and canopy development) and biochemical (e.g., altered pigment composition) mechanisms (Spence 1975, Bowes et al. 1977, Wiginton and McMillan 1979). While such adaptations allow maintenance of relatively high production under suboptimum light conditions, the range of adaptation is limited (Dennison and Alberte 1982, 1984).

6.3.2 Nutrients

The accessibility of dissolved nutrients (nitrogen, phosphorus, and carbon) represents another important factor governing the production of seagrass. In general seagrasses can utilize both free carbon dioxide (CO_2) and bicarbonate (HCO_3^-) although they have greater affinity for CO_2 (Allen and Spence 1981; Sand-Jensen and Gordon 1984). Although seagrasses are capable of obtaining some of the required inorganic carbon via root uptake, this mechanism appears limited for most marine plants, at least (Wetzel and Penhale 1979). Carbon limitation is more likely to be important in the low-salinity regions of the estuary where reduced carbonate buffering can allow conditions of high pH and low inorganic carbon concentrations. For example, Adams et al. (1978) demonstrated that carbon limitation may be common in many lacustrine communities of the macrophyte *Myriophyllum spicatum* (which occurs commonly in brackish environments, as well). It is evident in Fig. 6.9 that below about 100 mg CO_2/l (27 mg C/l) photosynthesis of *M. spicatum* is a linear function of carbon concentration. Such low concentrations are typical of those found in brackish estuarine waters. Thus limited availability of inorganic carbon may influence production of estuarine macrophytes, especially where reduced turbulence limits diffusion of CO_2 between leaves and surrounding water.

The response of seagrass nutrient uptake to changes in nutrient concentrations generally follows the typical hyperbolic relationship we have seen for phytoplankton (Chapter 4). There is a marked difference between phytoplankton and seagrass nutrient assimilation, however, in that the seagrasses are capable of deriving their nitrogen and phosphorus from two sources: (1) the water column via leaves and (2) sediment interstitial waters via roots and rhizomes (Iizumi and Hattori 1982; Thursby and Harlin 1982, 1984; Short and McRoy 1984). In general it appears that leaf uptake of ammonium saturates at concentrations typical of estuarine seasonal maxima (10–20 μM), while root uptake does not become saturated until the much higher concentrations common in interstitial waters (Fig. 6.10). Thus the two nitrogen uptake modes seem adjusted to the ambient

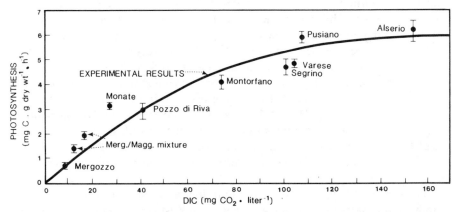

Figure 6.9 Ambient photosynthesis of *Myriophyllum spicatum* and dissovled inorganic carbon for 10 sampling stations. Mean and standard errors are shown for 10 replicates from each experiment. Solid line represents results of photosynthetic response experiments for varied concentrations of DIC (from Adams et al. 1978).

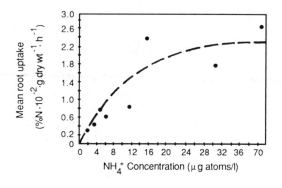

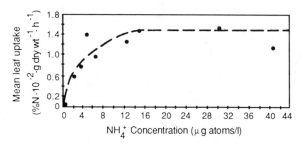

Figure 6.10 Rate of root and leaf acculation of $^{15}NH_4^+$ by *Carex aqualitis* as a function of ammonium concentration (from McRoy and Alexander 1975).

nutrient condititons which they experience. When there are sufficiently high concentrations of nitrogen in the water, leaf uptake may dominate; however, when inorganic nitrogen is depleted in the water, root uptake is the only route. This dual uptake scheme allows a more constant nitrogen availability.

Current information suggests that phosphorus is assimilated predominantly through the roots. McRoy et al. (1972) have shown not only that phosphorus is taken up mostly via roots, but also that it is excreted from the leaves to the overlying water (Fig. 6.11). Denny (1972) showed that growth of *Potamogeton* is enhanced in nutrient-rich muddy sediments compared with sand, and hypothesized that the ratio of root-to-leaf structure in aquatic macrophytes may reflect the relative importance of interstitial versus water-column nutrient sources (Fig. 6.12).

The potential for N and P, rather than inorganic carbon, to limit seagrass production is particularly great at higher salinity estuarine and coastal environments. For example, Patriquin (1972) estimated that water-column concentrations represent less than 0.3 and 3.0 days supply of the N and P, respectively, demanded by photosynthetic uptake of seagrasses in the West Indies. Sediment

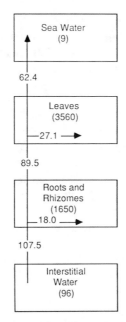

Figure 6.11 Net daily movement of phosphorus (mg/m^2) in an eelgrass stand. Amount of phosphorus (mg/m^2) in each compartment is in parentheses (from McRoy et al. 1972).

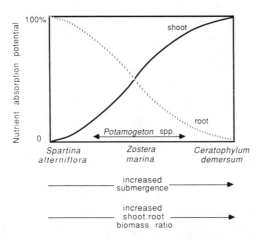

Figure 6.12 A schematic diagram of factors which could contribute towards a tendency for root or shoot nutrient absorption. The taxa are arranged in a linear order of shoot absorption potential but their actual position on the x-axis is arbitrary. (Adapted from Denny 1972).

pore-waters, on the other hand, contain some 10 and 500 days worth of N and P uptake, respectively. This suggests that nitrogen may be less available (more limiting) than phosphorus for seagrass production in these waters, and Patriquin (1972), in fact, found a far stronger correlation between leaf growth versus sediment nitrogen supply than for leaf growth versus phosphorus supply (Fig. 6.13).

Even in the relatively nutrient-rich estuarine waters of lower Chesapeake Bay, Orth (1977b) demonstrated a rapid and positive growth response by *Z. marina* to in situ applications of commercial fertilizer (containing both N and P), indicating nutrient limitation (Fig. 6.14). Similar responses of increased seagrass growth with fertilization have been observed for populations in Narragansett Bay (Harlin and Thorne-Miller 1981) and western Australia (Bulthuis and Woelkerling 1981). Particulate organic matter trapped in seagrass bed sediments from external waters may provide an important source of nutrients to support new plant growth (Kemp et al. 1984). Rapid decomposition of this organic material in seagrass sediments results in regeneration of nutrients (Iizumi et al. 1982; Kenworthy et al. 1982) available for plant uptake. Oxygen released by healthy plant roots to the sediment may result in nitrogen loss by causing enhanced nitrification and denitrification (see Chaper 3; Iizumi et al. 1980). At night, when oxygen is depleted in the rhizosphere, seagrass roots may use anaerobic metabolic pathways (Pregnall et al. 1984). However, under conditions of extreme oxygen depletion, seagrass roots may be exposed to toxic metabolites from bacterial respiration, this creating a stressful environment for the plants (Penhale and Wetzel 1983).

A considerable portion of this seagrass nitrogen demand may be provided, on the other hand, via nitrogen fixation by bacteria and blue-green algae on seagrass leaves and in their sediments. It appears that most of the nitrogen fixation occurs in the epiphytic community (Capone and Taylor 1977). McRoy and Goering (1974) reported that nitrogen fixed by epiphytes can be transferred to and absorbed by the seagrass host. While nitrogen fixation may provide consid-

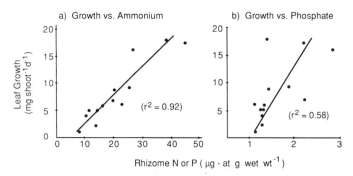

Figure 6.13 *Thalassia testudinum*. Relation of leaf growth to (a) rhizome water-soluble ammonium nitrogen and (b) water-soluble phosphorus (Patriquin 1972).

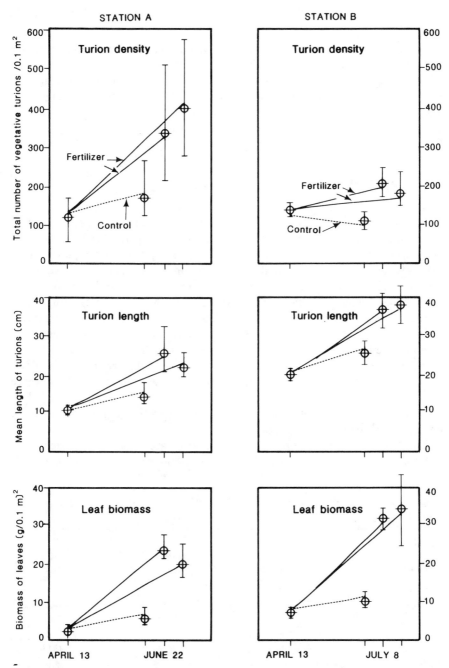

Figure 6.14 Effects of the addition of two different fertilizers (5-10-10 and 10-10-10) to sediments on growth of eelgrass, *Zostera marina* ($\bar{x} \pm$ 95% confidence interval). Station B was a monospecific stand of eelgrass; Station A was a mixed stand of eelgrass and *Puppia maritima* (Orth 1977b).

erable inputs of nitrogen to some seagrass systems (e.g., Patriquin and Knowles 1977, Goering and Parker 1972, Capone et al. 1979), it is far less important in other environments (e.g., McRoy et al. 1973). As seen in Table 6.2 the proportion of nitrogen requirements of seagrasses met by nitrogen fixation range from about 1 to about 100%, with fixation least important in lower salinity parts of estuaries, where ambient nitrogen concentrations tend to be higher (See Chapter 3).

6.3.3   Epiphytic Growth

A characteristic component of seagrass ecosystems is the community of algae, bacteria, protozoa, and invertebrates attached to the plant leaves. This attached community, which is variously referred to as epiphytes, periphytion, or aufwuch associations, is a normal part of healthy seagrass systems and typically comprises 10–50% of the combined seagrass-epiphyte production and standing stock (e.g., Penhale 1977). Seagrass and the epiphytes may be closely connected so that they exchange both nutrients and carbon (McRoy and Goering 1974, Penhale and Smith 1977), or they may be loosely attached with little direct interaction (e.g., Kalff and Cattaneo 1979). Various investigators have, however, demonstrated that extensive epiphytic colonization directly reduces the light available to seagrass leaves (e.g., Wium-Anderson and Borum 1980) and can inhibit directly the saturated photosynthetic response to light by 25% or more (Sand-Jensen 1977, Penhale and Smith 1977, see Fig. 6.15). Sand-Jensen (1977) has indicated that the uptake of inorganic carbon by the seagrass itself can be reduced significantly by epiphytic growth.

The growth of epiphytic organisms can be stimulated by nutrient enrichment. Cattaneo and Kalff (1979) reported strong correlations between lacustrine nutri-

TABLE 6.2   Comparison of Nitrogen-Fixation Rates Associated with Seagrass Communities.*

Seagrass or Macrophyte	Location	N_2-Fixation (mgN m^{-2}d^{-1})	Fraction (%) N-Required for Plant Growth
Thalassia	Florida		
testudinum	Sediments	0–13	0–23
	Epiphytes	11–28	20–50
	Barbados		
	Sediments	27–137	100+
Zostera	Long Island Sound		
marina	Sediments	2–17	3–28
	Epiphytes	0	0
Myriophyllum	Chesapeake Bay		
spicatum	Epiphytes	3	2

*After Lipschultz et al. (1979) and Capone (1983).

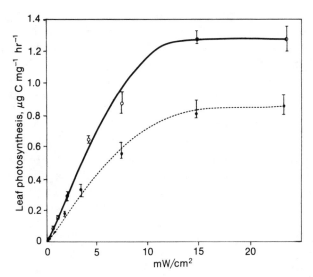

Figure 6.15 Photosynthesis of *Zostera* leaves with epiphytes (●, broken line) and without epiphytes (○, solid line) as a function of light intensity. Each value represents mean ± SE of four samples (from Sand-Jensen 1977).

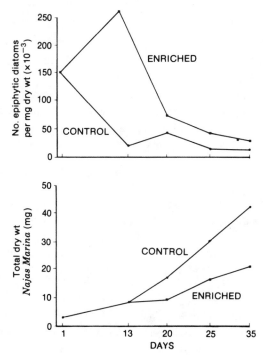

Figure 6.16 Effects of enrichment on biomass of *Najas marina* and epiphytic algae in experimental tanks (from Philips et al. 1978).

ent concentrations and epiphytic colonization and growth. Nutrient enrichment of freshwater (Phillips et al. 1978) and estuarine systems (Kemp et al. 1983, Twilley et al. 1985, Borum 1985) may be responsible for observed declines of submerged macrophyte populations where increased epiphyte and phytoplankton growth results light available for the macrophytes. Nutrient additions to experimental macrophyte systems resulted in increased growth of phytoplankton and epiphytes with reduced biomass of host macrophytic populations (Kemp et al. 1983, Fig. 6.16). Some evidence suggests that allelopathic (antibiotic) substances excreted by seagrasses may help to keep epiphytic growth under control (Harrison and Chan 1980) under healthy conditions. In low nutrient environments seagrasses have a competitive edge over epiphytes and phytoplankton because they have access to sediment interstitial nutrients.

The role of seagrass communities as animal habitats and their influence on the overall ecology of estuaries is considered in Chapters 7 and 10 (see also Boynton and Heck 1982, Kemp et al. 1984, Stoner and Lewis 1985).

REFERENCES

Adams, M.S., P. Guilizzoni, and S. Adams, 1978. Relationship of dissolved inorganic carbon to macrophyte photosynthesis in some Italian lakes. Limnol. Oceanogr., 23(5):912-919.

Adams, S.M., 1976. Feeding ecology of eelgrass fish communities. Trans. Am. Fish Soc., 105:514-519.

Aioi, K., 1980. Seasonal changes in the standing crop of eelgrass (*Zostera marina* L.) in Odawa Bay, Central Japan. Aquat. Bot. 8:343-354.

Backman, T.W. and D.C. Berilotti, 1976. Irradiance reduction: Effects on standing crops of the eelgrass *Zostera marina* in a coastal lagoon. Mar. Biol., 34:33-40.

Barko, J.W. and R.M. Smart, 1981. Comparative influences of light and temperature on the growth and metabolism of selected submersed freshwater macrophytes. Ecol. Monogr., 51:219-235.

Beer, S. and Y. Waisel, 1979. Some photosynthetic carbon fixation properties of seagrasses. Aquat. Bot., 7:129-138.

Bittaker, H.F. and R.L. Iverson, 1976. *Thalassia testudinum* productivity: a field comparison of measurement methods. Marine Biology, 37:39-46.

Borum J. and S. Wium-Andersen, 1980. Bismass and production of epiphytes on eelgrass (*Zostera marina* L.) in the Oresund, Denmark. Ophelia (Suppl. 1):57-64.

Borum, J., 1985. Development of epiphytic communities on eelgrass (*Zostera marina*) along a nutrient gradient in a Danish estuary. Marine Biology 87:211-218.

Bourn, W.S. 1932. Ecological and physiological studies on certain aquatic angiosperms. Boyce Thompson Inst. Plant Res. Rep. 4:425-496.

Bowes, G., T.K. Van, L.A. Garrard, and W.T. Haller, 1977. Adaptation to low light levels by Hydrilla. J. Aquat. Plant Management., 15:32-35.

Boynton, W.R. and K. Heck, 1982. Ecological role and value of submerged macrophyte communities: a scientific summary. In E.G. Macalaster, D.A. Barber and M. Kaspar, eds. Chesapeake Bay Program technical studies. U.S. Enivronmental Protection Agency, Washington, D.C., pp. 429-502.

Buesa, R.J., 1975. Population biomass and metabolic rates of marine angiosperms on the northwestern Cuban shelf. Aquat. Bot., 1:11-23.

Bulthuis, D.A., 1983. Effects of in situ light reduction on density and growth of the seagrass *Heterozostera tasmanica* (Martens ex Aschers.) den Hartog In Western Port, Victoria, Australia. J. Exp. Mar. Biol. Ecol., 67:91-103.

Bulthuis, D.A. and Wm.J. Woelkerling, 1981. Effects of in situ nitrogen and phosphorus enrichment of the sediments on the seagrass *Heterozostera tasmanica* (Martens ex Aschers.) den Hartog In Western Port, Victoria, Australia. J. Exp. Mar. Biol. Ecol., 53:193-207.

Burrell, D.C. and J.R. Schubel, 1977. Seagrass ecosystem oceanography In C.P. McRoy and C. Helfferich (Eds.), Seagrass Ecosystems. Marcel Dekker, New York, pp. 195-227.

Capone, D.G., P. Penhale, R.S. Oremland, and B.F. Taylor, 1979. Relationship between productivity and $N_2(C_2H_2)$ fixation in a *Thalassia testudinum* community. Limnol. Oceanogr., 21:117-125.

Carr, W.E.S. and C.A. Adams, 1973. Food habits of juvenile marine fishes occupying seagrass beds in the estuarine zone near Crystal River, Florida. Trans. Am. Fish Soc., 102:511-540.

Cattaneo, A. and J. Kalff, 1979. Primary production of algae growing on natural and artifical aquatic plants: A study of interactions between epiphytes and their substrate. Limnol. Oceanogr., 24(6):1031-1037.

Cole, B.S. and D.W. Toetz, 1975. Utilization of sedimentary ammonia by Potamogenu. nodosus and Scirpus. Verh. Int. Ver. Limnol., 19:2765-2772.

Congdon, R.A. and A.J. McComb, 1979. Production of Ruppia: Seasonal changes and dependence on light in an Australian estuary. Aquat. Bot., 6:121-132.

Conover, J.T., 1967. The importance of natural diffusion gradients in the metabolism of benthic marine plants. Bot. Mar.,

den Hartog, C., 1970. The sea-grasses of the world. North-Holland, Amsterdam, 275 p.

den Hartog, C., 1977. Structure, function and classification in seagrass communities. In C.P. McRoy and C. Helfferich (Eds.), Seagrass Ecosystems. Marcel Dekker, New York, pp. 89-121.

Dennison, W. and R.S. Alberte, 1985. Role of daily light period in the depth distribution of *Zostera marina* (eelgrass). Mar. Ecol. Progr. Ser., 25:51-61.

Drew, E.A., 1979. Physiological aspects of primary production in seagrasses. Aquat. Bot., 7:139-150.

Fenchel, T., 1970. Studies on the decomposition of organic detritus derived from turtlegrass, *Thalassia testudinum*. Limnol. Oceanogr. 15:14-20.

Ginsburg, R.N. and H.A. Lowenstorn, 1958. The influence of marine bottom communities on the depositional environment of sediments. J. Geol., 66:310-318.

Goering, J.J. and P.L. Parker, 1972. Nitrogen fixation by epiphytes on sea grasses. Limnol. Oceanogr., 17:320-323.

Harlin, M.M. and B. Thorne-Miller, 1981. Nutrient enrichment of seagrass beds in a Rhode Island coastal lagoon. Marine Biology 65:221-229.

Hotchkiss, N., 1967. Underwater and floating-leaved of the United States and Canada. Bur. Sport Fish. Wildl. No. 44, Washington, DC, 124 p.

Iizumi, H., A. Hattori, and C.P. McRoy, 1980. Nitrate and nitrate in interstitial waters of eelgrass beds in relation to the rhizosphere. J. Exp. Mar. Biol. Ecol., 47:191-201.

Iizumi, H. and A. Hattori, 1982. Growth and organic production of eelgrass (*Zostera marina* L.) in temperate waters of the Pacific coast of Japan. III. The kinetics of nitrogen uptake. Aquatic Botany, 12:245-256.

Iizumi, H., A. Hattori, and C.P. McRoy, 1982. Ammonium regeneration and assimilation in eelgrass (*Zostera marina*) beds. Marine Biology, 66:59-65.

Jacobs, R.P.W.M., C. den Hartog, B.F. Braster, and F.C. Carriere, 1981. Grazing of the seagrass *Zostera noltii* by birds at Terschelling (Dutch Wadden Sea). Aquat. Bot., 10:241-259.

Jupp, B.P. and D.H.N. Spence, 1977. Limitations on macrophytes in a eutrophic lake, Loch Leven. J. Ecol., 65:175-186.

Keefe, C.W., D.A. Flemer, D.H. Hamilton, 1976. Seston distribution in the Patuxent River estuary. Chesapeake Sci., 17:56-59.

Kemp, W., R. Twilley, J. Court Stevenson, W. Boynton, and J. Means, 1983. The decline of submerged vascular plants in upper Chesapeake Bay: Summary of results concerning possible causes. Mar. Technol. Soc. J., 17:78-89.

Kemp, W., W. Boynton, R. Twilley, J. Court Stevenson, and L. Ward, 1984. Influences of submersed vascular plants on ecological processes in upper Chesapeake Bay. In V.S. Kennedy (ed.), The Estuary as a Filter, Academic Press, New York. pp. 367-394.

Kemp, W., M. Lewis, and T. Jones, 1986. Comparison of methods for measuring production by the submersd macrophyte, *Potamogeton perfoliatus* L., Limnol. Oceanogr., 31:1322-1334.

Kenworthy, W., J. Zieman, and G. Thayer, 1982. Evidence for the influence of seagrasses on the benthic nitrogen cycle in a coastal plain estuary near Beaufort, North Carolina (USA). Oecologia, 54:152-158.

Lewis, M.R., 1980. An investigation of some homeostatic properties of model ecosystems in terms of community metabolism and component interactions. MS Thesis, University of Maryland, College Park, 150 pp.

Mann, K.H., 1972. Macrophyte production and detritus food chains in coastal waters. Mem. Ist. Ital. Idrobiol., 29(Suppl.):353-383.

McRoy, C.P. 1974. Seagrass productivity: Carbon uptake experiments in eelgrass, *Zostera marina*. Aquaculture, 4:131-137.

McRoy, C.P. and V. Alexander, 1975. Nitrogen kinetics in aquatic plants in arctic Alaska. Aquat. Bot., 1:3-10.

McRoy, C.P. and R.J. Barsdate, 1970. Phosphate adsorption in eelgrass. Limnol. Oceanogr., 15:6-13.

McRoy, C.P. and J.J. Goering, 1974. Nutrient transfer between the seagrass *Zostera marina* and its epiphytes. Nature, 248:173-174.

McRoy, C.P. and C. McMillan, 1977. Production ecology and physiology of seagrasses. In C.P. McRoy and C. Helfferich (Eds.), Seagrass Ecosystems: A Scientific Perspective. Marcel Dekker, New York, pp. 53-87.

McRoy, C.P., R.J. Barsdle, M. Nebort, 1972. Phosphorus cycling in an eelgrass ecosystem. Limnol. Oceanogr., 17:58–67.

McRoy, C.P., J.J. Goering, and B. Choney, 1973. Nitrogen fixation associated with seagrasses. Limnol. Oceanogr., 18:998–1002.

Mukai, H., K. Aioi, and Y. Ishida, 1980. Distribution and biomass of eelgrass (*Zostera marina* L.) and other seagrasses in Odawa Bay, Central Japan. Aquat. Bot., 8:337–342.

Neinhuis, P.H. and B.H.H. DeBree, 1977. Production and ecology of eelgrass (*Zostera marina* L.) in the Corevelingen estuary, The Netherlands, before and after the closure. Hydrobiology, 52:55–66.

Neinhuis, P.H. and B.H.H. DeBree, 1980. Production and growth dynamics of eelgrass (*Zostera marina*) in brackish Lake Grevelingen (The Netherlands). Neth. J. Sea Res., 14:102–118.

Neinhuis, P.H. and E.T. VanIerland, 1978. Consumption of eelgrass, *Zostera marina* by birds and invertebrates during the growing season in Lake Grevelingen (SW Netherlands). Neth. J. Sea Res., 12:180–194.

Nichols, D.S. and D.R. Keeney, 1976. Nitrogen nutrition of Myriophyllum spicatum: Uptake and translocation of ^{15}N by shoots and roots. Freshwater Biol., 6:145–154.

Odum, H.T., 1967. Biological circuits and marine systems of Texas. In T.A. Olson and F.J. Burgess (Eds.), Pollution and Marine Ecology. Wiley-Interscience, New York, pp. 99–157.

Orth, R.J., 1977a. The importance of sediment stability in seagrass communities. In B.C. Coull (Ed.), Ecology of Marine Benthos. University South Carolina Press, Columbia, pp. 281–300.

Orth, R. J., 1977b. Effect of nutrient enrichment on growth of eelgrass *Zostera marina* in the Chesapeak Bay, Virginia (USA). Marine Biology 44:187–194.

Patriquin, D.G. 1972. The origin of nitrogen and phosphorus for growth of the marine angiosperm, *Thalassia testudinum*. Mar. Biol., 15:35–46.

Patriquin, D.G., 1973. Estimation of growth rate, production and age of the marine angiosperm, *Thalassia testudinum,* Konig. Caribbean J. Sci., 13:111–123.

Patriquin, D.G. and K. Knowles, 1972. Nitrogen fixation in the rhizosphere of marine angiosperms. Mar. Biol., 16:49–58.

Penhale, P.A., 1977. Macrophyte-epiphyte biomass and productivity in an eelgrass (*Zostera marina* L.) community. J. Exp. Mar. Biol. Ecol., 26:211–224.

Penhale, P.A. and G.W. Thayer, 1980. Uptake and transfer of carbon and phosphorus by eelgrass (*Zostera marina* L.) and its epiphytes. J. Exp. Mar. Biol. Ecol., 42:113–123.

Penhale, P. and R. Wetzel, 1982. Structural and functional adaptations of eelgrass (*Zostera marina* L.) to the anaerobic sediment environment. Can. J. Bot. 61:1421–1428.

Peterson, C.G.J., 1918. The sea bottom and its production of fish food: A survey of the work done in connection with valuation of Danish waters from 1883–1917. Reports Danish Biolological Station Number 25, Copenhagen.

Phillips, G.L., D. Eminson, and B. Moss, 1978. A mechanism to account for macrophyte decline in progressively eutrophicated freshwaters. Aquat. Bot., 4:103–126.

Pregnall, A., R. Smith, T. Kursar, and R. Alberte, 1984. Metabolic adaptation of *Zostera marina* (eelgrass) to diurnal periods of root anoxia. Marine Biology 83:141-147.

Rasmussen, E., 1977. The wasting disease of eelgrass (*Zostera marina*) and its effects on environmental factora and fauna. In C.P. McRoy and C. Helfferich (Eds.), Seagrass Ecosystems. Marcel Dekker, New York, pp. 1-51.

Sand-Jensen, K., 1975. Biomass, net production and growth dynamics in an eelgrass (*Zostera marina* L.) population in Vellerup Vig. Denmark. Ophelia 14:185-201.

Sand-Jensen, K., 1977. Effects of epiphytes on eelgrass photosynthesis. Aquat. Bot., 3:55-63.

Sand-Jensen, K. and D. Gordon, 1984. Differential ability of marine and feshwater macrophytes to utilize HCO_3^- and CO_2. Marine Biology 80:247-253.

Sand-Jensen, K., C. Prahl, and H. Stokholm, 1982. Oxygen release from roots of submerged aquatic macrophytes. Oikos 38:349-354.

Short, F. and C. McRoy, 1984. Nitrogen uptake by leaves and roots of the seagrass *Zostera marina* L. Botanica Marina 27:547-555.

Smith, S.V., 1981. Marine macrophytes as a global carbon sink. Science, 211:838-840.

Spence, D.H.N., 1975. Light and plant response in freshwater. In G.C. Evans, R. Bainbridge, and O. Rackham (Eds.), Light as an Ecological Factor. Blackwell, Oxford, pp. 93-133.

Stoner, A.W., 1980. The role of seagrass biomass in the organization of benthic macrofuanal assemblages. Bull. Mar. Sci., 30:537-551.

Stoner, A. and F. Lewis, 1985. The influence of quantitative and qualitative aspects of habitat complexity in tropical sea-grass meadows. J. Exp. Mar. Biol. Ecol., 94:19-40.

Thayer, G.W., S.M. Adams, and M.W. LaCroix, 1975a. Structural and functional aspects of a recently established *Zostera marina* community. In L.E. Cronin (Ed.), Estuarine Research. Academic, New York, pp. 518-540.

Thayer, G.W., D.A. Wolfe, and R.B. Williams, 1975b. The impact of man on seagrass systems. Am. Sci., 63:288-296.

Thursby, G. and M. Harlin, 1982. Leaf-root interaction in the uptake of ammonia by *Zostera marina*. Marine Biology 72:109-112.

Thursby, G. and M. Harlin, 1984. Interaction of leaves and roots of *Ruppia maritima* in the uptake of phosphate, ammonia and nitrate. Marine Biology 83:61-67.

Twilley, R., W. Kemp, K. Staver, J. Court Stevenson, and W. Boynton, 1985. Nutrient enrichment of estuarine submersed vascular plant communities. 1. Algal growth and effects on production of plants and associated communities. Mar. Ecol. Progr. Ser., 23:179-191.

Twilley, R., G. Ejdung, P. Romare and W.M. Kemp. 1986. A comparative study of decomposition, oxygen consumption and nutrient release for selected aquatic plants occurring in an estuarine environment. Oikos, 47:190-198.

Wanless, H.R., 1981. Fining-upwards sedimentary sequences generated in seagrass beds. J. Sed. Petrol., 51:445-454.

Ward, L., W. Kemp, and W. Boynton, 1984. The influence of waves and seagrass communities on suspended articulates in an estuarine embayment. Marine Geology, 59:85-103.

Westlake, D.F., 1967. Some effects of low-velocity currents on the metabolism of aquatic macorphytes. J. Exp. Bot., 18:187–205.

Wetzel, R.G., 1964. A comparative study of the primary productivity of higher aquatic plants, periphyton, and phytoplankton in a large, shallow lake. Int. Reveu ges. Hydrobiol. 49:1–61.

Wetzel, R.G. and P. Penhale, 1979. Transport of carbon and excretion of dissolved organic carbon by leaves and roots/rhizomes in seagrasses and their epiphytes. Aquatic Botany 6:149–158.

Wetzel, R.G. and P. Penhale, 1983. Production ecology of seagrass communities in the lower Chesapeake Bay. Mar. Technol. Soc. J., 17(2):22–.

Wetzel, R.L., R. vanTine, and P.A. Penhale, 1982. Light and submerged aquatic vegetation in Chesapeake Bay: A synthesis of recent research. Report to US Environmental Protection Agency, Chesapeake Bay Program, Annapolis, MD.

Wiginton, J.R. and C. McMillan, 1979. Chlorophyll composition under controlled light conditions as related to the distribution of seagrasses in Texas and the U.S. Virgin Islands. Aquat. Bot., 6:171–184.

Williams, S.L., 1977. Seagrass productivity: The effect of light on carbon uptake. MS Thesis, University of Alaska, Fairbanks, 95pp.

Williams, S.L. and C.P. McRoy, 1982. Seagrass productivity: the effect of light on carbon uptake. Aquatic Botany, 12:321–344.

Wood, E.J.F., W.E. Odum and J.C. Zieman, 1969. Influence of seagrasses on the productivity of coastal lagoons, In Laguna Costeras. UN Simposio Mam. Simp. Intern. Lagunas Costeras. Nov. 1967, Mexico, DF, pp. 495–502.

Zieman, J.C., 1975. Quantitative and dynamic aspects of the ecology of turtlegrass, *Thalassia testudinum*. In L.E. Cronin (Ed.), Estuarine Research. Academic, New York, pp. 541–562.

Zieman, J.C. and R.G. Wetzel, 1980. Productivity in seagrasses: Methods and rates. In D.C. Phillips and C.P. McRoy (Eds.), Handbook of Seagrass Biology: An Ecosystem Perspective. Garland STPM, New York, pp. 87–118.

REDUCED CARBON AND ITS FATE IN THE ESTUARY

OFFPRINTS FROM: ESTUARINE ECOLOGY
Edited by John W. Day Jr., Charles A. S. Hall., Dr. W. Michael Kemp, and Alejandro Yáñez-Arancibia
Copyright © 1989 by John Wiley & Sons, Inc.

▬▬ 7

Microbial Ecology
and Organic Detritus
in Estuaries[1]

7.1 INTRODUCTION

Imagine what an estuary would be like if nutrients were not recycled, decomposition did not take place, or indigestible refractory detrital materials were not made "palatable" to large consumers. The activities of microorganisms dominate these processes, and thus are critical in controlling the function and structure of estuarine ecosystems. The organisms themselves and their activities are the subject of the first part of this chapter. We address who they are, where you find them, what they do, and what controls them. In the second part of the chapter we discuss organic detritus, its dynamics, its relation to microorganisms and its importance to the estuary.

Estuaries tend to have high levels of organic materials for two principal reasons. The first is the characteristic high rate of primary production, described in Chapters 4-6. The second reason is that annual production exceeds consumption in many coastal ecosystems, so that organic matter accumulates in estuarine sediments at a rate far greater than the input of oxygen that would be stoichiometrically necessary to convert it back to CO_2. Oxygen diffuses so slowly through submerged sediments or waterlogged soils that even sediments overlain by oxygen-rich water normally have an oxidized surface layer less than a few millimeters. Thus a key aspect of estuarine function is oxygen limitation, and this limitation results in a large anaerobic subsystem that underlies estuarine sediments in many areas (Fenchel and Riedl 1970). For example, the oxygen demand of 1 ml of disturbed bottom sediment in the Georgia coastal zone in the

---

[1]Co-authored by R. R. Christian.

summer was found to be equivalent to the total amount of dissolved oxygen in about 900 ml of overlying water (Frankenberg and Westerfield 1968).

In contrast, the organic matter that falls to the sediment surface in most terrestrial systems is oxidized rapidly and, therefore, the buildup of organic humus in undisturbed terrestrial areas is slow. In deep marine systems as well, little organic matter accumulates because most readily usable organic matter produced in the water column is consumed and oxidized completely before it ever reaches the bottom. Although the lack of oxygen contributes to the buildup of organic matter in sediments, biological activity does not stop. As we will discuss in this chapter, the anaerobic habitats of estuaries are sites for complex microbial interactions and often high rates of metabolism.

7.2 THE ECOLOGY OF ESTUARINE MICROORGANISMS

7.2.1 Introduction

Traditionally microorganisms have been divided into viruses, bacteria, fungi, protozoans, and algae, and members of all of these groups may be found in less than a cubic centimeter of mud (Fig. 7.1). The bacteria and blue-green "algae" (which also may be considered blue-green bacteria or cyanobacteria) are proca-

THE ECOLOGY OF MARINE MICROBENTHOS

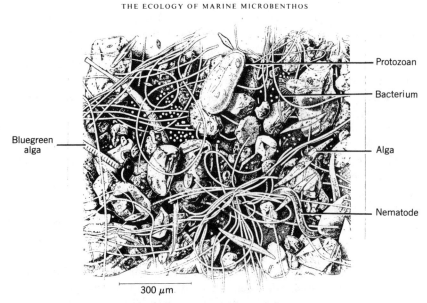

Figure 7.1 Typical microbial organisms that occur in estuaries including various bacteria, algae, nematodes, and protozoa (from Fenchel 1969).

ryotic in that they do not have a true nucleus and have distinctly different cellular structure compared with the nucleated or eucaryotic protozoans, fungi, and algae. On the basis of this major difference, bacteria and cyanobacteria have been included in the kingdom *Monera*. Other algae and protozoans are grouped as *Protista* by most taxonomists, with equal stature to fungi, plants, and animals among the eucaryotic kingdoms. Still other algae may be considered as plants. The viruses are not true cells, and their taxonomic position remains obscure. Representative sizes and morphologies of bacteria, cyanobacteria, protozoans, fungi, and viruses are shown in Fig. 7.2. As can be seen, each group has a

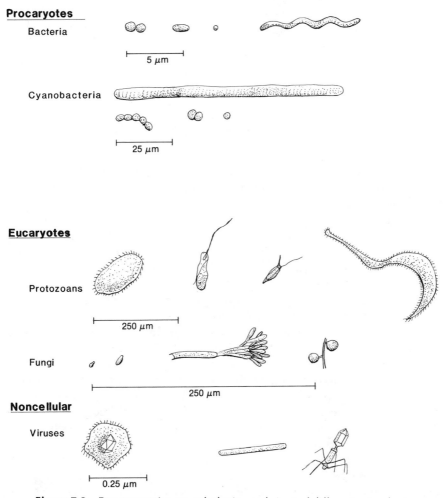

REPRESENTATIVE MORPHOLOGIES AND SIZES

Procaryotes

Bacteria

5 μm

Cyanobacteria

25 μm

Eucaryotes

Protozoans

250 μm

Fungi

250 μm

Noncellular

Viruses

0.25 μm

Figure 7.2 Representative morphologies and sizes of different microbes.

variety of morphologies, and the size of individuals can range over an order of magnitude for each group. Thus the "microbial community" of an estuary would generally include not only the organisms shown in Fig. 7.2 but at times small metazoans such as nematodes and harpacticoid copepods (the meiofauna) because they can be in the same size group. The meiofauna will not be considered here but is discussed in Chapter 9.

The direct identification of all microorganisms to species from water and sediment samples is often extremely difficult, or even impossible, for several reasons. First, these organisms are notoriously diverse; second, they are difficult to examine owing to their size; third, they are so ubiquitous that samples often become contaminated with airborne spores; and finally, they are phenotypically "plastic" in that their morphologies sometimes change under different conditions. Thus, microbial ecologists often classify groups of microbes by their functional attributes, rather than simply by their morphological appearance. In a sense this is a more ecological approach since it emphasizes the role these organisms play in the environment. We will stress these functional attributes in this chapter. When it is necessary to attempt to identify collections of microorganisms to species and to measure the density of each group in a sample, the following techniques are used.

7.2.2   Identification and Enumeration of Bacteria

Bacterial species are identified on the basis of morphological, cultural, staining, physiological, biochemical, and most recently molecular genetic characteristics. In most cases when bacteria are to be identified, the bacteria must be isolated from their habitat, grown in pure culture in the laboratory, and subjected to an array of tests. Few bacteria have morphologies unique enough to be identified to the species or genus level by direct microscopy, and there is considerable metabolic diversity among bacterial species. The major reference for bacterial taxonomy is *Bergey's Manual of Determinative Bacteriology* (Buchanan and Gibbons 1974). But for the estuarine ecologist the question often is more "what are the bacteria doing" rather than "what species of bacteria is that."

Bacteria are enumerated primarily by culture and microscopic techniques. The former measure "viable" bacteria by diluting a sample sequentially until individual colonies, presumably from individual cells, are formed. The results are referred to as viable counts. Any medium used to cultivate these microbes is selective, so that culture techniques invariably underestimate bacterial densities relative to microscopic counts. No one medium or incubation condition allows for the growth of all of the diverse physiological and taxonomic groups. For example, any samples incubated in the air will cause the exclusion of obligate anaerobes to whom oxygen is toxic.

Microscopic techniques do not require growing the bacteria, rather, cell densities are derived from total counts of a sample using appropriate staining (e.g., acridine orange in conjunction with epifluorescence microscopy). Ratios of total counts to viable counts range from $10:1$ to $10,000:1$ for a variety of aqueous environments. Thus, although many bacteria are present in an environment, very few may be culturable at a given time. The in situ relationships and activities of the nonculturable and culturable organisms is an important area of research.

Table 7.1 shows total bacterial densities estimated for some estuarine and coastal marine environments. Sediments and salt marsh soils generally harbor more bacteria per unit volume than does the water column. Within the water column, however, localized high densities may be found in the surface layer neuston or associated with decomposing macrophyte rafts. Several studies have demonstrated that the majority of bacteria in the water column may not be attached to particles (Wiebe and Pomeroy 1972, Marsh and Odum 1979, also see Christian and Wetzel 1978). This remains an active area of research, however, as some habitats do show that a large proportion of the bacteria are attached (Bell and Albright 1981). The large proportion of attached bacteria in the Humber estuary (Table 7.1) may be associated with an exceptionally high suspended solid load (Goulder 1976). Lastly, there appears to be higher bacterial densities within most estuaries studied than in the nearby coastal marine or river waters studied. Thus estuaries have a rich bacterial flora which reflects and complements generally high estuarine primary and secondary production.

7.2.3 Identification and Enumeration of Fungi

Fungi are identified largely on the basis of morphology and, in the case of yeast, also physiological characteristics. Determination of species often requires knowledge of the stages of sexual reproduction. No one universally accepted reference on fungal taxonomy comparable to *Bergey's Manual* for bacteria exists. Until recently, *Fungi in Oceans and Estuaries* by Johnson and Sparrow (1961) served as a major work in estuarine taxonomic studies. This has been superceded for the higher fungi by *Marine Mycology: The Higher Fungi* by Kohlmeyer and Kohlmeyer (1979). However, treatises on the various specific fungal taxa are often used as well.

The identification of fungal species and the enumeration of individual fungi in estuarine samples is as difficult as it is for bacteria. Contamination of samples by spores, differential growth on culture media, and the difficulty of distinguishing separate organisms in a mass of filamentous mycelia are some of the problems encountered. The complex life cycles of these organisms adds to the difficulty.

The number of fungal species associated with estuarine habitats is extremely large. For example, over 100 species of higher filamentous fungi occur just on the salt marsh grass genus *Spartina* (Gessner and Kohlmeyer 1976). Some of the fungal species are unique to estuaries, while others have a broader range of habitats. Both higher and lower (primitive) fungi, as well as both yeasts and molds, are found in estuaries. A list of some of the characteristics of fungi found in various estuarine habitats is given in Table 7.2. Most of these organisms have been implicated in decomposition, a major ecological role for fungi.

TABLE 7.1 Bacterial Densities in some Estuarine and Coastal Marine Environments as Determined by Fluorescence Microscopy.

Habitat	Location	Density (cells/ml)	Reference
Water	Sapelo Island, GA	10^6–10^7/ml	Wiebe and Pomeroy 1972
	Kaneohe Bay, HI	$\geq 10^3$/ml	Wiebe and Pomeroy 1972
	Continental Shelf, GA	10^3–10^5/ml	Wiebe and Pomeroy 1972
	Kiel Fjord, Germany	1.6–5.7×10^6/ml	Meyer-Reil 1977
	Kiel Bight, Germany	0.8–2.7×10^6/ml	Meyer-Reil 1977
	Newport River Estuary, NC	1.95–18.4×10^6/ml	Palumbo and Ferguson 1978
	Humber Estuary, UK	4.6×10^5–5.6×10^6/ml (attached)	Goulder 1976
		4.6×10^4–3.0×10^5/ml (free)	
	Three estuaries and coastal waters, Mass., USA	0.7–7.0×10^6/ml	Wright and Coffin 1983
Surface layer of water	Palo Alto Salt Marsh, CA	2.5×10^7/ml	Harvey and Young 1980
Subsurface water	Palo Alto Salt Marsh, CA	5.4×10^6/ml	Harvey and Young 1980
Spartina raft interstitial water	Sapelo Island, GA	2×10^7/ml	Wiebe and Pomeroy 1972
Sediment	Sapelo Island, GA	10^6–10^7/ml	Wiebe and Pomeroy 1972
	Petpaswick Inlet, Canada	1.2×10^8–1×10^{10}/g dry wt	Dale 1974
Salt marsh soil	Nemport River Estuary, NC	8.4–10.9×10^9/cm^3 (surface)	Rublee and Dornseif 1978
		2.2–2.6×10^9/cm^3 (20 cm)	

TABLE 7.2 Expected Microbial Community Structure of Estuarine Habitats

Habitat		Microbial Community Structure
Water column	Bacteria	Dominate numbers of microbes
		Pseudomonas and *Vibrio* species often isolated
		Aerobic and facultatively anaerobic bacteria most common
		Most are not attached to particles
	Fungi	Aquatic fungi and yeasts dominate active fungi
		Contaminating spores present
		Few fungi on particles
	Protozoans	Small forms are common
		Large forms found in floating wracks of plant material
Sediment and waterlogged soils	Bacteria	Found in very high densities
		Decrease in abundance with depth
		Complex mosaic of aerobes and anaerobes
		Many species found but species list differs between surface and subsurface
	Fungi	Low densities
		Active species primarily in surface aerobic zones
		Decreases in numbers and species rapidly with depth
		Spores found throughout sediments
	Protozoans	High densities
		Dominated by ciliates and foraminifera
		Decrease in numbers and species with depth
		Some species capable of anaerobic metabolism
Wetland macrophytes	Bacteria	Increase in numbers with senescence and death of plant
		Many aerobic and facultatively anaerobic species
	Fungi	Biomass increases with senescence and death of plant
		Dominate microbial biomass
	Protozoans	Dominated by few species dependent on plant type
		Few found

TABLE 7.2 Expected Microbial Community Structure of Estuarine Habitats (continued)

Habitat		Microbial Community Structure
Submerged seagrass	Bacteria	Numbers increase with senescence and death of plant
		Many aerobic and facultatively anaerobic species
	Fungi	Biomass increases with senescence and death of plant
		Biomass is generally low compared to bacterial biomass
		Species dependent on plant type
	Protozoans	Attached forms present
		Many transient planktonic species present

Fungi may occur in large densities in various estuarine habitats. The importance of fungi has been demonstrated by scanning electron and other microscopy, which shows that much of the microbial biomass in decaying material may be fungal hyphae (Gessner et al. 1972, Newell and Hicks 1982). Also, fungal propagules (any fungal structure which produces a colony on appropriate culture medium) may be quite numerous. For example, Chrzanowski and Stevenson (1980) found 10^4 propagules/g wet weight of intertidal mud, and Meyers and coworkers (1970, 1971) found as many as 9×10^4 yeasts/cm^3 in sediments, but less than 20/cm^3 in estuarine waters. Seshadri and Sieburth (1975) enumerated different genera of yeasts in various seaweeds. They found that densities of *Candida* spp. could exceed 10^4 cells/g dry weight of macroalgae during certain times of the year. At other times densities were less than 10^2/g. As with the other microbial groups, the abundance of fungi varies over orders of magnitude both within and between habitats.

7.2.4 Identification and Enumeration of Protozoa

The *ciliates* are the group of protozoans that have been studied most intensively with respect to their ecological roles in estuaries. Recently, flagellates have received considerable attention as well. Morphology is the primary distinguishing criterion for identification, and tedious microscopy is required for both identification and enumeration. Most protozoan taxonomists working with ciliates refer to the several treatises by Kahl (beginning in 1928). References for the taxonomies of other protozoan groups have been developed substantially by Sieburth in Sea Microbes (1979), which will stand for years to come as an excellent reference to marine microorganisms in general.

The microfauna of estuaries has been studied to a lesser extent than have either the bacteria or fungi. The most complete studies were done by T. Fenchel and appeared as a series of monographs in the journal *Ophelia* during the late 1960s (1967–1969). Within these papers, he meticulously describes the ecology of benthic ciliates: their distribution, species abundance, food preferences, and interactions with their physical and chemical environments.

The number of protozoans per volume of material estimated from different estuarine habitats spans orders of magnitude (Table 7.2). In the sediments studied by Fenchel (1967), ciliates were numerically dominant, yet in a *Spartina* raft floating in a Georgia estuary, Wiebe and Pomeroy (1972) did not find significant numbers of ciliates. Tintinnid ciliates, however, were found to be potentially important consumers of primary production in Long Island Sound (Capriulo and Carpenter 1983). Sherr and Sherr (1983) found heterotrophic microprotozoan densities in excess of 10^3 cells/ml in the waters of the Georgia estuary. Many of these were flagellates, and such organisms are receiving considerable attention from estuarine ecologists because of the roles these protozoans may play in the estuarine food web (Sherr and Sherr 1984). Physical and chemical factors strongly regulate the distribution of protozoans, as described in Section 7.4.

7.2.5   Identification and Enumeration of Viruses

Environmental virology is in its infancy. Identification of viruses requires electron microscopy, biochemical analyses, and information on host specificity. The general guidelines for viral identification are given in Bitton (1980). No generally accepted compendium of taxonomy for all viruses exists, however.

Enumeration of viruses requires the use of a specific host as a medium for viral *in vitro* (literally "in glass," or in a laboratory culture) growth. The hosts may be procaryotes, protists, fungi, animals, or plants. For some viruses the conditions for *in vitro* growth are unknown. Thus the simple question "How many viruses are in an estuary?" is almost impossible to answer. The viruses that infect bacteria, or bacteriophages, are perhaps the easiest to study. One study determined the occurrence of bacteriophages in a variety of sea water, sediment, and seafood samples (Baross et al. 1978). Bacteriophages whose hosts were *Vibrio* were isolated from 177 of 643 samples, and they occurred more frequently in seafood than in sediments or seawater. Their densities ranged from < 10 to $10^6/$ g of sample. Thus at least one type of virus is readily found in estuaries. Although this is not the only work on the subject, the amount of research in this area is scanty, and this field is wide open to estuarine microbial ecologists.

7.2.6   Determination of Microbial Community Structure by Biochemical Techniques

Thus far we have discussed microscopical and cultural methods of enumeration of microbes. In recent years quantification of microbial biomass has been done by a variety of biochemical methods. One of the first was the use of adenosine triphosphate (ATP) as an index of general microbial "living" biomass (Holm-Hanson and Booth 1966). If the larger organisms are filtered or picked out, the ATP presumably gives an index of the microbial biomass. The ATP concentrations in a variety of estuarine habitats have been determined. Karl (1980) reviewed ATP analyses and summarized the literature on concentrations from both sediments and water. The ATP concentrations in surface sediments and water-logged soils in estuaries ranged from 640 to 6400 ng/g of dry sediment. Concentrations decreased with depth and were generally larger in estuaries than in oceanic sediments or beach sands. Also, the ATP concentrations in estuarine waters were generally greater than in inflowing rivers or adjacent oceanic waters. The ATP concentrations in estuarine waters ranged from 100 to 1200 ng/L. Thus ATP concentrations in water are much lower than in sediments. Although there are numerous problems in converting ATP to biomass, the most used conversion factor is 250g C:1 g ATP. Thus the measurement of ATP can be used to estimate microbial carbon concentrations.

Other biochemical procedures are also being used to unravel the microbial community structure. D. C. White and his co-workers have developed or refined a number of techniques useful in discerning the biochemical composition and abundance of the microbial communities in estuaries. They have measured ATP and total adenylate nucleotide pool concentrations to estimate "living" biomass (Morrison et al. 1977), muramic acid, a cell-wall component of procaryotes, as a biomass index (King and White 1977); lipid phosphate, also as an index of biomass; poly(β-hydroxybutyrate) as an index of nutritional history; and lipid composition as an index of community structure (White et al. 1979, Bobbie and White 1980). These techniques have been used to separate bacterial, fungal, protozoan, and algal biomass and characterize their relative importance to the community. The development of these and other new methods affords the estuarine microbial ecologist a new potential to rephrase old questions and formulate new ones to understand the abundance and structure of the microbial community.

7.2.7 Habitat Comparisons

Table 7.2 summarizes the typical microbial community compositions for a few estuarine habitats. Bacteria may dominate the biomass of the three groups discussed: for the water column, for sediments, and for the populations that live on sea grasses. Fungal biomass may be the dominant type in some senescing and dead wetland macrophytes. Other macrophytes may have microbiota which are mostly bacterial, but may contain large numbers of yeast. Protozoan biomass may equal bacterial biomass in some sediments, but they tend to be less important in other habitats.

According to an old adage in microbial ecology, "Everything is everywhere" This concept, coupled with the problems of isolation and identification discussed in the previous sections, makes it difficult to assign species lists to the habitats. In each of the groups of microbes, thousands of species are recognized. Any one investigator may work on only one subgroup and only a relatively few species of the thousands that are there. For example, bacteriologists may identify only aerobic, heterotrophic bacteria, ignoring anaerobes and the autotrophic bacteria. Within the aerobic heterotrophs, *Pseudomonas* and *Vibrio* species are often identified as dominant in estuarine environments. But as mentioned previously, the numbers of organisms isolated may be less than 10% of the total. We know what genera are commonly cultured from estuarine habitats, but which species dominate numerically among the total densities remains to be determined. The same considerations apply to the fungi and protozoans, although the latter group need not be cultivated for identification.

A listing of all species is far beyond the scope of this chapter, and again we refer the interested reader to the treatise on marine microbes by Sieburth (1979) for further information. While we have barely cataloged estuarine microbial species here, some further information will be given in the context of microbial processes discussed in the next sections. Some of these processes are associated with particular genera or species of microbes, and where possible we list them.

7.3   PROCESSES ASSOCIATED WITH MICROORGANISMS

7.3.1   General Comments

We have addressed the questions "How many and what kinds are there?" and have shown how closely the answer depends upon the methodology. The next question we will address is, "What do they do?" The simplest answer is almost everything, and again the answer you get depends in part on the methods you use. Figure 7.3 summarizes various flows in an estuary and those flows that may be dominated by or unique to microbes. Conceivably every pathway could be dominated by microbial activities. In fact much of the processing of energy and matter in many if not most estuaries is done by microbes. For example, it has been estimated that half of the aerobic respiration and almost all anaerobic transformations of organic matter in salt marsh soils are the result of microbial metabolism (Hopkinson et al. 1978, Howarth and Hobbie 1982). The following is a summary of the ways in which microbes are associated with energy flow and nutrient cycling. In particular we will address the carbon, nitrogen, phosphorus, and sulfur cycles and the roles of microbes in each. The reader may refer to Chapter 3 for more detailed accounts of nutrient cycling as we cover many of the same processes emphasizing the importance of microbes.

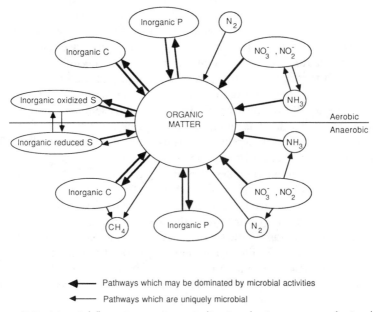

Figure 7.3   Material flows in an estuary indicating the importance of microbes.

7.3.2 Energy Flow and Carbon Cycling

Although we normally think of estuarine food chains as starting with grasses or phytoplankton and ending with large carnivores such as fish and birds, microbes may represent a major portion of both the first and last trophic levels within an estuary, and they may dominate flow in between. Primary productivity was discussed in Chapters 4-6, and it is clear that in many estuaries microalgae, including very small nannoplankton, are responsible for much of the primary production. Additionally, much if not most macrophytic production is not grazed directly, but is utilized after microbial transformation (Teal 1962, Day et al. 1973). As microalgae, seagrasses, or marsh or swamp macrophytes senesce and die, microbes invade the plant tissues and begin to transform the organic matter. As an example, when *Spartina alterniflora* shoots senesce, fungal hyphae and bacteria develop around and in the dead tissues and become a major component of the standing dead plant (Gessner et al. 1972). The result in the context of energy flow is that some of the energy originally fixed by the macrophyte is lost by respiration of the microbes, some is leached as dissolved organic matter into the water, some is incorporated into microbial biomass, and some may be transformed to other organic compounds not incorporated into microbial cells. Much of the organic matter of dead plant tissue is structural lignocellulose. This is not readily available to most animals who lack the appropriate gastrointestinal enzymes to hydrolyze this tough material. Once this organic matter has been transformed into microbial biomass, however, a larger portion of the associated energy is available to animal consumers. This is an underlying principle of the detritus food web to be discussed in Section 7.6. Many questions remain as to the importance of this principle *in situ*.

Dead animal tissues, feces, and pseudofeces are also substrates for microbial transformations. But microbes affect energy flow not only as primary producers and decomposers; microbes often use dissolved organic matter unavailable to the rest of the community. For example, amino acids dissolved in estuarine waters are rapidly consumed by microbes (Crawford et al. 1974). Thus microbes prevent the loss of some energy that would otherwise be lost as dissolved organic matter from the estuary and, since the microbes are eaten by other organisms, redirect it through the food web. Other roles of microbes in energy flow include their activities as grazers and pathogens. Protozoans may graze other microbes and serve as a trophic link to higher animal grazers or act to short circuit the flow of energy from higher organisms (Pomeroy 1984); this latter pathway is the so-called "microbial loop." Pathogens on the other hand may redirect energy flow by causing a decrease in the population size of an animal or plant. Also the trophic structure may be altered as debilitated hosts become prey to predators that normally cannot catch them.

Bacteria show a variety of metabolic pathways in which carbon and energy requirements differ from those of higher organisms. For this reason bacterial metabolism has been divided into four categories: photoautotrophy, photoheterotrophy, chemoautotrophy, and chemoheterotrophy (Table 7.3). The prefixes

TABLE 7.3 Categorization of Metabolism Based on Energy and Carbon Source

Category	Energy Source	Carbon Source	Examples
Photoautotrophy	Light	CO_2	Plants, algae, and many photosynthetic bacteria
Photoheterotrophy	Light	Organic Matter	Some purple and green photosynthetic bacteria
Chemoautotrophy	Reduced inorganic matter	CO_2	Nitrifying bacteria and thiobacilli
Chemoheterotrophy	Reduced organic (and sometimes inorganic matter)	Organic matter	Animals, protozoans, fungi, and many bacteria

photo and chemo refer to the source of energy of the organism; Photo refers to light energy and chemo to chemical energy. The "auto" and "hetero" refer to the source of carbon for the organism--inorganic and organic, respectively. The classical photosynthesizing autotrophs are thus photoautotrophs, and the classical heterotrophs are chemoheterotrophs. However, the other two categories are also represented in nature. For example, some photosynthetic bacteria are photoheterotrophs, and the bacteria responsible for most of the oxidation of ammonia to nitrate (nitrification) are chemoautotrophs.

As many of the sediments and water-logged soils of estuaries are anoxic, it is important to understand the nature of this anaerobic decomposition beyond what is discussed in Chapter 3. The four catabolic processes are fermentation, dissimilatory nitrogenous oxide reduction, dissimilatory sulfate reduction, and methanogenesis (methane production). Each of these processes may be considered to be associated with a "functional" population group, that is a group of species that collectively do a particular biochemical process. A diagram of their interactions with respect to carbon flow is given in Fig. 7.4 (adapted from Pomeroy et al. 1977). The complex array of organic compounds available for decomposition in general can be used only by the fermenters and dissimilatory nitrogenous oxide reducers. The dissimilatory sulfate reducers and methane producers

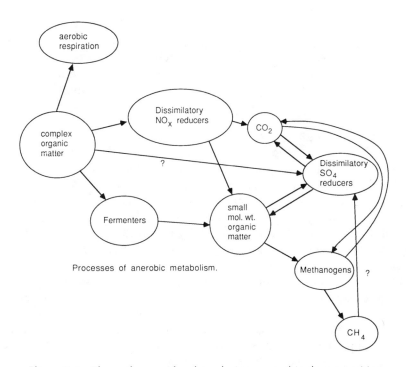

Figure 7.4 The pathways of carbon during anaerobic decomposition.

(methanogens) were once thought to have a more restricted diet, but some recent evidence exists that both may have broader diets than suspected previously. The metabolism of these latter two populations probably depends largely on the activities of the first two and primarily on the fermenters. The limitations on growth of any of these populations, however, may not be carbon but rather insufficient electron donors or receptors. For example, dissimilatory nitrogenous oxide reducers require NO_3 or NO_2, and dissimilatory sulfate reducers require SO_4, for terminal electron acceptors. The electron donor for methanogenesis may be H_2. Recently researchers have begun to understand the interactions between these functional populations and to hypothesize interesting modes of limitation which involve competition for electron donors and acceptors between functional populations as well as interference between populations through the accumulation of toxic metabolic end products (Martens and Berner 1974, Sorensen 1984).

Until recently the importance of microbial secondary production in estuaries could only be inferred. Methods were not available to provide reliable estimates of microbial growth *in situ* and hence microbial production. Now a number of techniques are available involving (1) the uptake of radioactive nucleic acid precursors, (2) density increase measurements in the absence of predators, and (3) measurements of the frequency of dividing cells as an index of growth rate (see Karl 1980 and Newell 1984 for reviews). From the results so far accumulated for estuarine waters it appears that bacterial productivity may range between 0.01 and 10 mg C/m^3 h. However, the rates in estuaries tend to exceed those in adjacent waters. Bacterial productivity in sediments has also been studied using radiotracer techniques. For example, in an estuarine seagrass bed in Australia, sediment bacterial production was about 1.5 times that for an equal area of water column above it (Moriarty et al. 1985). The factors regulating levels within this wide range remain to be studied.

7.3.3   Nitrogen Cycling

Nitrogen is a major limiting nutrient for primary production in estuaries (see Chapters 4–6), and all of the possible biological transformations of nitrogen are done by microorganisms. Several processes can be done only by microbes, while others may be dominated by the activities of microbes (see Fig. 7.5). The processes that can be done only by microbes include nitrification, dissimilatory nitrogenous oxide reduction, and nitrogen fixation (Fig. 7.5). The nitrogen cycle and the role of microorganisms in that cycle are often very confusing to the beginning (or even advanced) student. Some of the confusion can be lessened if it is recognized that some of the processes are used by microorganisms to get their own nitrogen, but other processes are done for the microorganism to get energy. Nitrification, the biological oxidation of ammonia to nitrite and then to nitrate, is principally a bacterial process used to gain energy by organisms, although some fungi may also do it. While some chemoheterotrophic microbes may nitrify, it appears that most nitrification in estuaries is by the activities of a group

Processes Uniquely microbial

Nitrification

$NH_3 \longrightarrow NO_2^- \longrightarrow NO_3^-$ (*Nitrosomonas, Nitrobacter*)

Dissimilatory nitrogenous oxide reduction

$NO_3^- \longrightarrow NO_2^- \longrightarrow N_2O$ (*Pseudomonas denitrificans*)

$\longrightarrow N_2$

$\longrightarrow NH_3$

Nitrogen fixation   (*Clostridium, Azobacter*)

$N_2 \longrightarrow NH_3$

Processes which may be dominated by microbial activities

Ammonification

$R\text{-}NH_2 \longrightarrow NH_3$

Ammonia immobilization

$NH_3 \longrightarrow R\text{-}NH_2$

Assimilatory nitrogenous oxide reduction

$NO_3^- \longrightarrow NO_2^- \longrightarrow NH_3$

Figure 7.5 Microbial processes associated with the nitrogen cycle. Representative microbial organisms which carry out particular reactions are indicated.

of chemoautotrophs which use reduced inorganic nitrogen for an energy source, since the oxidation releases energy. These are obligately aerobic organisms that use the energy from either the oxidation of ammonia to nitrite (e.g., *Nitrosomonas*) or nitrite to nitrate (e.g., *Nitrobacter*) to fix inorganic carbon for growth.

Dissimilatory nitrogenous oxide reduction is also undertaken predominantly by bacteria, where nitrate or nitrite is used as the terminal electron acceptor instead of oxygen. It is an anaerobic process, in contrast to the obligately aerobic nitrification. A variety of bacteria may reduce these nitrogenous oxides with four possible reduced nitrogen end products. Some bacterial processes reduce only nitrate to nitrite. Other species produce nitrous oxide (N_2O), diazo nitrogen or free nitrogen gas (N_2), or ammonia (NH_3). The first two are gaseous, and when a gas is produced the process is called *denitrification*. These gaseous end products represent a potential loss of nitrogen from the estuary, and as a result there has been considerable interest in the magnitude of denitrification in estuaries (Kaplan et al. 1979, Sorensen 1984). The ecological importance of denitrification and nitrogen limitation is covered in Chapters 3–6.

The principal way nitrogen gas is utilized by estuarine organisms is through the microbial process called *nitrogen fixation*. Only procaryotes contain the necessary enzyme systems for this process, although in some cases nitrogen fixation by the procaryotes may require symbiosis with a eucaryote, which often provides the required energy. Both the bacteria and the cyanobacteria include species capable of nitrogen fixation. The enzyme nitrogenase reduces atmospheric N_2 to ammonia, which may be incorporated into amino acids. The enzyme requires an anaerobic environment to be active, but this may be maintained in microenvironments within the cell. Thus both aerobic and anaerobic nitrogen fixation may occur in an estuary (Smith 1980).

Other transformations of nitrogen may be performed by macro- as well as microorganisms; these include assimilatory nitrogenous oxide reduction, ammonification, and ammonia immobilization. However, these processes tend still to be dominated by microorganisms. Assimilatory nitrogenous oxide reduction is the reduction of nitrate and/or nitrite to ammonia as a first step in incorporation into biomass. Ammonia immobilization is the conversion of ammonia nitrogen to organic nitrogen, and ammonification is the reverse process. The former two processes are generally associated with autotrophy, although nonautotrophic bacteria and fungi also possess these capabilities. The competition for ammonia between autotrophs and aerobic decomposing bacteria may sometimes limit primary production (Thayer 1974). Ammonification occurs during excretion by animals and during microbial mineralization of organic matter in the water column.

Thus microbes are responsible for introducing usable forms of nitrogen to the estuarine community via nitrogen fixation, assimilation of nitrogen into microbial biomass, and mineralization of nitrogen for autotrophic uptake. At the same time they may cause the loss of usable nitrogen through denitrification. Because nitrogen species have different abilities to adsorb to substrates and to be complexed, microbial transformations result in the sequestering of nitrogen within habitats or the flow of nitrogen from one habitat to another. Thus the roles of microbes in the nitrogen cycle of estuaries are varied, complex, and important.

7.3.4 Phosphorus Cycling

The phosphorus cycle in estuaries is also regulated in large part by the activities of microorganisms. Because phosphorus is so biologically active, the residence time of dissolved phosphate may be very short in estuarine waters (Pomeroy 1960). Inorganic dissolved phosphate may be biologically immobilized by both autotrophic macro- and microorganisms and by nonautotrophic microbes. Also, physical processes, especially within sediments, may remove phosphate from the water column (Welsh 1980 and Chapter 3). Release of inorganic phosphate into the water column may result from either biological or physical processes. It appears that bacteria tend more to immobilize, or fix, than to mineralize phosphate. Mineralization occurs during egestion and excretion by both protozoan and metozoan consumers.

Phosphate is taken up and released by both aerobic and anaerobic sediments, although more exchange occurs between water and anaerobic, as opposed to aerobic, sediments (see and Chapter 3). Also, more exchange occurs with disturbed than undisturbed sediments (Pomeroy et al. 1965). As oxygen slowly diffuses into sediments it is rapidly consumed by the benthic community. As the oxygen concentration is depleted with depth, dissimilatory sulfate reduction dominates, producing sulfide, which decreases the redox potential, causing a solubilization of inorganic phosphate (Fenchel and Riedl 1970). If the surface of the sediment remains aerobic, much of this phosphate is again made insoluble as it diffuses, or is bioturbated, into the aerobic zone. If the overlying waters are anoxic, however, the phosphate may enter the waters, stimulating photosynthesis (Webb and d'Elia 1980). Thus the availability of inorganic phosphate to estuarine phytoplankton depends upon direct and indirect microbial processes in both the water and sediment.

7.3.5 Sulfur Cycling

The activities of microorganisms in the sulfur cycle are similar in several ways to those in the nitrogen cycle. While some of the transformations of sulfur compounds may be carried out by both macro- and microorganisms, others are uniquely microbial processes (Fig. 7.6). For example, assimilatory sulfate reduction, the reduction and uptake of sulfate for later incorporation into biomass, can be performed by both plants and a variety of microbes. The reduction of sulfate as a terminal electron acceptor in respiration (dissimilatory sulfate reduction), however, can be done by only a small group of anaerobic bacteria. The most commonly found genus of these organisms is *Desulfovibrio*. The reduction of sulfate by these organisms is analogous to the reduction of oxygen by aerobes or the reduction of nitrogenous oxides by facultative anaerobes. In the largely anaerobic sediments and water-logged soils of estuaries, dissimilatory sulfate reduction is an extremely important process that passes energy from autotrophs to food chains based on reduced sulfur (Fenchel and Riedl 1970, Howarth and Hobbie 1982, Postgate 1984). This process may be important in anoxic waters. As stated previously in this chapter and Chapter 3, much of the anaerobic carbon and energy flow in estuaries, where it has been studied, is accounted for by this process. Also, the presence of reduced sulfur lowers the E_h in sediments, thus regulating the solubility of various ions and the distribution of plants and animals.

Just as reduced nitrogen serves as an energy source for some chemoautotrophs, reduced sulfur serves as a source for others. Anoxygenic photosynthesis (see Table 7.3) by green and purple sulfur bacteria uses reduced sulfur along with sunlight as an energy source to fix carbon dioxide. These organisms are common as colorful green and purple mats within surface sediments in estuaries and in shallow salt marsh pannes or potholes. Here they receive light even though they reside within an anaerobic microenvironment which allows them to derive sulfides from below. Nonphotosynthetic but chemoautotrophic bacteria get their carbon from inorganic sources and their energy from reduced com-

1. Dissimilatory sulfate reduction *(Desulfouibrio)*

   $SO_4^= \longrightarrow S^=$

   (using $SO_4^=$ as the terminal electron acceptor
   for anaerobic respiration)

2. Assimilatory sulfate reduction

   $SO_4^= \longrightarrow R\text{-}SH$

   (incorporation of S into organic matter)

3. Sulfur mineralization
   a. Sulfide mineralization (putrefaction)

      $R\text{-}SH \longrightarrow H_2S$

   b. oxidized sulfur mineralization

      R-oxidized S (eg. $SO_4^=$) $\longrightarrow SO_4^=$

4. Reduced sulfur oxidation   (photosynthetic and non-photosynthetic chemoautotrophy)

   $S^= \longrightarrow S \longrightarrow S_2O_3^- \longrightarrow SO_4^=$ *(Thiobacillus, Thiothrix Beggiatoa)*

5. Sulfur immobilization
   a. reduced sulfur immobilization

      $S^= \longrightarrow R\text{-}SH$ or $R_1\text{-}S\text{-}R_2$

   b. oxidized sulfur immobilization

      $SO_4^= \longrightarrow R\text{-}$ (oxidized sulfur)

6. Volatile organic sulfide formation

   $R_1\text{-}S\text{-}R_2 \longrightarrow$ Small molecular weight organic S compounds

Figure 7.6 Microbial transformations within the sulfur cycle indicating organisms associated with particular processes.

pounds, including reduced sulfur. These chemoautotrophs include species of the genera *Thiobacillus, Thiothrix,* and *Beggiatoa.*

Other portions of the sulfur cycle are mediated by microorganisms. Microbes may transform sulfur to the reduced organic sulfur compounds found in estuaries, and life in general, including the amino acids cysteine and methionine as well as complicated organic compounds with oxidized sulfur (Fitzgerald 1976). Volatile sulfur emitted from swamps, estuaries, and salt marshes, which gives them their special smell, includes many low- molecular weight organic compounds containing reduced sulfur as well as hydrogen sulfide. The origins of these compounds have not been investigated fully but may well be microbial.

7.3.6   Summary of Chemical Cycling

Carbon, nitrogen, phosphorus, and sulfur are the elements whose cycles have been most thoroughly studied in estuaries. As shown, each cycle depends greatly on the activities of microorganisms as do most other elemental cycles not discussed. In particular, metals undergo transformations associated with microbial activities. For example, manganese and cobalt precipitation is mediated by microbial metabolism in fjord waters (Tebo et al. 1984), and mercury is transferred from bacteria to ciliates to copepods in microcosms using estuarine species (Berk and Colwell 1981). A discussion of each is beyond the scope of this chapter, but the reader is referred to the following references for a discussion of some of these: Engler and Patrick (1975), Ehrlich (1978), and Leppard (1983). A more quantitative analysis of estuarine chemical cycling is presented in Chapter 3.

7.4 FACTORS CONTROLLING MICROBIAL ACTIVITIES

7.4.1 General Comments

As can be seen, microorganisms are responsible for a diverse assortment of important processes in estuaries. This diversity is far greater than that for macroorganism processes. While we know what processes do occur in estuarine habitats, and, in some cases, the general magnitude of a process, less is known of the manner in which processes are regulated *in situ*. Numerous factors may regulate individual processes, and different processes may be regulated by different sets of factors. For a simple example, light is a major and very general regulating factor of photoautrophic processes, but it may have little direct effect on chemoautotrophic processes. The following is a discussion of general regulating factors and a consideration of how they may control microbial processes. In particular we discuss light, temperature, water availability and flow, sediment texture, redox potential, nutrients, toxic substances, competition, and predation.

7.4.2 Physical Regulatory Factors

The physical environment of microorganisms includes a variety of potential regulating factors. The quality and quantity of light not only regulates photosynthetic processes directly, but may affect nonphotosynthetic processes indirectly. For example, the penetration of light into the water column or sediments partially determines the penetration of oxygen produced from oxygenic photosynthesis. Thus whether aerobic or anaerobic microbial processes dominate a habitat may in part be due to the indirect effects of light.

The rates at which microbial processes occur, and, indeed the structure of the microbial community, is dependent in large part on the environmental temperature. As expected from our general biological experience, increases in temperature often are accompanied by increases in process rates within the biokinetic zone (the temperature range of life). Temperature also may produce qualitative differences in processes. For example, one study found that most of the production of sulfide in one set of anaerobic sediments came from sulfate above 5–10°C, and from organic sulfur below these temperatures (Nedwell and Floodgate 1972). The latitudinal differences in climatic temperatures should alter the nature of the microbial community, but systematic, comparative studies of microbial processes in estuaries with different climates have yet to be carried out.

Water flow and availability are undoubtedly two of the most important and yet least studied factors that regulate the activities of microbes. The manner in which water flows through an estuary, its sources, and its residence times are important considerations in designing sampling programs and in predicting the cycling of elements within the estuary (see Chapter 2 and Imberger et al. 1983). For example, the degree to which organic matter is decomposed within an estuary is dependent largely upon its residence time within that estuary, which in turn is dependent upon the residence time of the water. Similarly the exchange of nutrients between the water column and sediments, and the degree of transformations by microbes in the sediments, is dependent on the frequency of tidal inundation and the velocity of the ambient water.

Water activity (or water potential) is a measure of the amount of water available for growth by organisms (Brown 1976). Water activity, and hence the availability of water to organisms, decreases with increased salinity and increased sorption to soils. Evaporation and transpiration remove water from intertidal soils, sediments, and other substrata for microbes including rocks and macrophyte shoots. These very basic processes that decrease water activity alter the structure of the microbial community and its rates of activity.

The texture of the substratum is also important. Sediments high in silt and clay content retain water more readily than do either those with high sand content or hard rock surfaces. As a result sandy and rocky intertidal habitats dry more rapidly when exposed to air. Also, sandy habitats tend to have less reserves of organic matter and inorganic nutrients than silt–clay habitats. As a result of all of these features coarse-textured intertidal sediments tend to have smaller populations of microbes than do fine-textured sediments (Fenchel 1967, Dale 1974). Finally, the smaller quantity of water held in sandy sediments allows oxygen to diffuse more readily than in fine textured sediments. This may increase the depth at which anaerobic activities replace aerobic activities.

7.4.3   Chemical Regulatory Factors

The quantity and quality of organic and inorganic nutrients regulate microbial activities in all habitats of an estuary. Considerable research has been done on the uptake of selected organic compounds by estuarine microbial communities (e.g., Crawford et al. 1974, Palumbo et al. 1983). Most of these studies have used radioisotopes to analyze the rate of uptake or turnover time of the compound (for methodological details see Wright 1973, Christian and Hall 1977, and Chapter 3). These studies have shown that readily utilizable (or *labile*) compounds such as amino acids and sugars, may turn over in a matter of hours in estuarine water and minutes in sediments. In contrast, the turnover times of relatively recalcitrant (or *refractory*) compounds such as cellulose and lignin may be months or years, and the breakdown of these substances is complex (MacCubbin and Hodson 1980, Benner et al. 1986a,b). A small portion of the organic matter in water or sediments is readily usable, while most is refractory. It is unclear at present whether microbial communities derive most of their nutrition from the small portion of labile organic matter or from the slow decomposition of the larger quantity of refractory organic matter.

Oxygen, carbon, nitrogen, phosphorus, and sulfur are the major elements in inorganic form that regulate microbial activities in estuaries. As discussed in Chapter 3 and earlier in this chapter, the presence or absence of oxygen determines which catabolic metabolisms serve in organic transformations and hence regulate the microbial community structure. As the oxygen concentration decreases within a habitat, the redox potential (E_h) becomes controlled more by the presence and state of elements other than oxygen.

Inorganic carbon, nitrogen, and phosphorus are required for production of autotrophic and often heterotrophic organisms. Since organic matter in estuaries tends to have a high ratio of carbon to nitrogen, growth requires an external source of nitrogen which may be in the form of inorganic nitrogen, and while sulfate is plentiful in most estuarine waters, it may be limiting for sulfate reduction in oligohaline estuaries and either deep in sediments or in microzones within sediments. Thus the chemical environment regulates microbes which in turn are important in regulating overall estuarine productivity.

7.4.4 Biological Regulatory Factors

In pure cultures, sediments, and water-logged soils, microbial growth is often inhibited by the buildup of toxic end products of microbial metabolism. Wherever water movement is slow, toxic end products may not be removed, as is the case in free-flowing water. These toxic end products include fermentation end products (e.g., fatty acids and alcohol), secondary metabolites, and sulfides. These substances may also be contributed from decaying organic matter (Wilson et al. 1986) and human activities. One current interest in environmental science is the effects of new man-made toxins on natural microbial communities. Pesticides and the by-products of industrial activity are examples of new toxic materials that may alter the normal nutrient cycling and energy flow in impacted estuaries.

Finally, interpopulation interactions control microbial activities as they do for larger macroorganisms. There is constant competition for resources between microbial species, and microbes may be both predators and prey. The competition between individual species of microbes or species-specific predator–prey relationships rarely have been studied, although there are a few marvelous cases (Lee 1980a,b). Again methodological constraints often have limited such studies.

7.5 HOW MICROBES CONTROL OTHER COMPONENTS OF THE ECOSYSTEM

7.5.1 General Comments

We have seen what kinds of microbes there are, what processes they are responsible for, and some controls on their activities. Throughout this chapter the importance of microbes to macroorganisms and to the ecosystem as a whole has been implicit. In this section we will explicitly discuss the question: "How do microbes control other components of an estuarine ecosystem?"

7.5.2 Productivity

First, microbes are critical in the determination of the rates of primary production because they may themselves be primary producers, because they make nutrients available through mineralization, and because they compete with primary producers for inorganic nutrients. The chemoautotrophic and anoxygenic photoautotrophic organisms that make organic carbon from inorganic carbon, and use reduced inorganic compounds for reducing power, are the "secondary" primary producers. Locally such production may be the most important source of organic matter, although normally oxygenic photosynthetic primary production is dominant at an ecosystem level.

Secondary productivity is also influenced greatly by microbial activities. Microbes are a food source for micro-, meio-, and macrofauna. Protozoans consume bacteria, algae, fungi, and other protozoans. Thus within the microbial community a food web exists (Lee 1980b). Each time one organism is eaten by another, energy is lost through respiration and organic carbon is converted to CO_2. The more trophic links after primary production within a microbial community the less energy and organic carbon are available to macroconsumers. But even with the losses associated with intramicrobial feeding, microbes make available organic matter to the macrofauna that would not otherwise be available. Much of the structural materials of plants is indigestible by macrofauna because most animals lack cellulolytic and lignolytic enzymes to use these compounds. Some microbes can transform these compounds into their own monomers and hence into microbial biomass available for animal consumption. This microbial conversion underlies the detritus food web discussed in Section 7.6. Plant biomass, however, is not the only material that is converted and in a sense "made useful" to the rest of the organisms in the ecosystem. The minerals and organic matter of animal bodies and feces is brought back into the mainstream of energy flow through microbes. Not only are the conversions of carbon important; as mentioned earlier, the energy of reduced inorganic matter can be converted to energy associated with biomass by chemoautotrophic and photoautotrophic bacteria. Thus energy and organic matter may be conserved for macrofauna, and eventually harvested by people. Truly the food webs of estuaries are far richer and more complex than we once thought.

7.5.3 Disease

The populations of both plants and animals may be regulated by the pathogenicity of microorganisms, and microbial pathogens may be responsible for subtle or drastic alterations in most populations of higher organisms. Two examples of major changes in estuarine higher organisms due to pathogens are the die-offs of American oyster populations because of protozoan pathogens (Sprague 1971) and the reductions in eelgrass in many estuaries of the northeastern United States in the first half of this century—believed to be caused by an aquatic fungus (Johnson and Sparrow 1961). These reductions had great effects on the ecology and economy of these regions. Thus the potential impact of infectious disease among estuarine organisms cannot be overemphasized. Diseases of estuarine fish, cultured fish, or fish that use estuaries for part of their life cycle are of particular importance to people (Colwell and Grimes 1984, Fryer and Rohovec 1984). Also, human diseases may be caused by estuarine microbes. For example, several species of the bacterial genus *Vibrio* inhabit estuaries and cause human diseases (Colwell 1984). The environmental conditions that would allow for the epidemic spread of disease are rarely known. Therefore, outbreaks of diseases may occur unpredictably and with sometimes devastating results, although these outbreaks are often associated with humanly caused perturbations.

7.5.4 Nutrient Cycling

Last, as can be seen by the multitude of chemical processes associated with microbes, nutrient cycling in estuaries is greatly influenced by the microbial community. Many transformations of nutrients are uniquely microbial, while the rates of others are dominated by microbial activities. The carbon, nitrogen, phosphorus, oxygen, and sulfur cycles are particularly regulated, both directly and indirectly, by microorganisms, as may be the cycling of certain metals.

7.6 ORGANIC DETRITUS

One of the most active areas of estuarine research and controversy over the past two decades concerns the role and dynamics of organic detritus in coastal systems. There is no doubt that organic detritus is a major component of most estuaries. But what are the sources of this material and how is it utilized by estuarine consumers. Organic detritus has been reported to be one of the most important food sources in estuaries and, when exported, in the coastal ocean. High fishery production has been related to organic detritus and a major part of energy flow in most estuaries seems to be via detrital pathways. In this section, we will address these issues, but first we will define organic detritus.

7.6.1   Organic Detritus—What Is It?

The term detritus originated from the Latin word detere, which means to disintegrate or diminish. Detritus in coastal systems has been defined in a variety of ways. Biodetritus was originally described by Odum and de la Cruz (1967) as dead particulate organic matter inhabited by decomposer microorganisms. Darnell (1967) referred to detritus as "all types of biogenic material which represent a potential energy source for consumer species." Others included in the detritus pool only nonliving particulate organic matter, and thus excluded bacteria. Wetzel et al. (1972) described as detritus all carbon lost from each trophic level in a nonpredatory pathway, that is, by egestion, excretion, secretion, or "nonviolent" mortality, plus allocthonous carbon input to the ecosystem. Mann (1972) defined detritus more broadly, including all nonliving organic matter with its associated microbial community. Still more definitions could be stated, but enough have been presented to make it clear that detritus is considered differently by different researchers. The student should always be aware of which definition is being considered. We subscribe to Mann's definition for the pragmatic reason that it is unrealistic and difficult for either a scientist or a consumer organism to distinguish between the nonliving organic matter and its associated microbiota.

Organic matter in aquatic systems is often classified into two components: dissolved organic matter (DOM) and particulate organic matter (POM). DOC, POC, and TOC are commonly used abbreviations that refer to dissolved, particulate, and total organic carbon, respectively. This distinction is somewhat arbitrary as it is based on the separation of those substances that either pass through filters (usually having a pore size of approximately 0.45 μm) or that are retained by these (standard) filters. The only functional significance of this particle size distinction is that the smallest particles retained by standard filters are about the size of many bacteria, corresponding to the smallest particles that can be retained by suspensionfeeding organisms or seen easily under a light microscope. Nevertheless, the presence of inorganic suspended matter (especially clay particles) obscures the distinction between DOM and POM, because DOM often adsorbs strongly to clay particles and is thus transformed to POM. Some of the agglomeration of DOM in turbulent aquatic systems is due to the physical effect of bubbles rising through the water column.

Two other commonly used terms referring to suspended matter in water bodies are seston and tripton. *Seston* refers to all suspended matter in the water column, both living and nonliving. *Tripton* is a subset of seston that includes only nonliving matter. *Plankton* is a subset of seston that includes the living organisms passively suspended in the water column and not attached to inanimate particles.

7.6.2   Detrital Sources

Organic carbon is added to an estuary in both dissolved and particulate forms. Input to the water column and surface sediments can occur via allochthonous input from riverine, marine, and terrestrial sources, from the autochthonous primary production of macrophyte leaves and stems, phytoplankton, epiphytes, and benthic algae, and from autochthonous secondary production. Inputs of carbon to subsurface sediments occur via the burial of incompletely decomposed carbon and by the below ground production of macrophyte material, which often is very significant.

The relative amounts of DOM versus POM added to estuarine systems are still largely unknown, because the leaching rate of DOM from macrophytes and phytoplankton is uncertain. This leaching rate may be as high as 1 g/m^2 day (Turner 1978), a number as high as many estimates of aquatic primary productivity. The turnover rate of DOM is not easily determined, for DOM represents both labile and refractory compounds. The labile portion appears to recycle rapidly, whereas the refractory portion is recycled very slowly. The labile DOM may be "packaged" and converted to POM as microorganisms incorporate it into their own biomass. Also, there is some evidence that macroheterotrophic organisms are capable of utilizing some dissolved organic matter directly, as well as contributing to the pool of DOM through excretion and egestion. Some aquatic autotrophs are capable of utilizing DOM at night, and these facultative heterotrophs include, for example, blue-green algae, eucaryotic algae, and possibly some floating aquatic plants such as duckweed in oligohaline areas. Thus there are many ways by which organic material gets recycled in estuaries.

7.6.3   Aerobic Detrital Decomposition

A variety of factors influence the decomposition of organic matter. We will illustrate this process by investigating the breakdown of macrophyte leaves from marsh grass, mangroves, and seagrasses. There is often an initial decrease in the nitrogen (protein) content as soluble organics rich in nitrogen are leached from the leaves following death. This is illustrated for *Spartina alterniflora* in Fig. 7.7. Colonization by fungi and bacteria soon begins to weaken fibrous tissue. As the plant structural materials weaken due to both biological and physical processes, plants are broken down into smaller pieces. Mechanical grinding of this tissue by amphipods, grass shrimp, and other macrofauna reduces the particle size and increases the surface area for further microbial colonization. As the detrital substrate is slowly consumed, more of the total biomass of the community becomes microbial and less the original plant material. The increase in protein shown in Fig. 7.7 reflects nitrogen uptake and incorporation into mibrobial biomass and production of humus-like materials.

The paradigm of detrital feeding which has evolved over the past two decades is that detrital material is ingested, the microbial community digested, the remaining detrital substrate "packaged" as fecal pellets, egested, recolonized by bacteria, and subsequently reingested by other consumers. During each cycle the dwindling unoxidized carbon is upgraded in quality as expressed by the C/N ratio until the organic substrate is exhausted. Repeated excretion, recolonization, and reingestion of fecal pellets enhances the nutritional quality of the re-

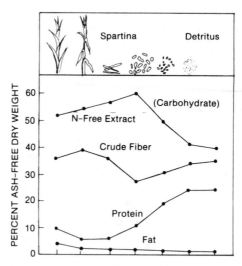

Figure 7.7 Decomposition of *Spartina alterniflora* illustrating changes in detrital material with decreasing particle size (from Odum and de la Cruz 1967, copyright © 1967 by the American Association for the Advancement of Science).

maining reduced carbon and speeds up its decomposition rate. Fecal pellets can be significant in estuaries. For example, exposed intertidal mud flats are often visibly littered with fecal pellets from polychaetes, crustaceans, and other benthic animals.

The primary factors that regulate the rate of aerobic detrital decomposition in estuaries are temperature, the presence or absence of water, particle size, detrital source, oxygen availability, faunal abundance, and seasonality. Each of these is treated below and illustrated in Figs. 7.8 and 7.9 (see Mann 1972, 1982; Tenore et al. 1982; Valiela 1984; Mitsch and Gosselink 1986 for a more complete treatment of this subject). All of these factors are interrelated and the impact of one is often determined by the condition of the others.

Decomposition rates of detritus fragments from different plant species and even from different parts of the same plant vary. Submergent seagrasses (such as *Thalassia testudinum* and *Zostera marina*) decompose more rapidly than the more fibrous emergent marsh plants (such as *Juncus* or *Spartina*), and leaves of most species decompose more readily than the more fibrous stems. Different proportions of fiber, lignin, and soft parts account for this phenomenon, which is illustrated in Fig. 7.8. Material also decomposes more slowly under dry conditions.

Water temperature strongly regulates the rate of organic decomposition. For example, oxygen consumption by the microbial community on decomposing *Spartina* detritus increases with increasing temperature, but the increase is much more rapid with smaller particle size (7.9A).

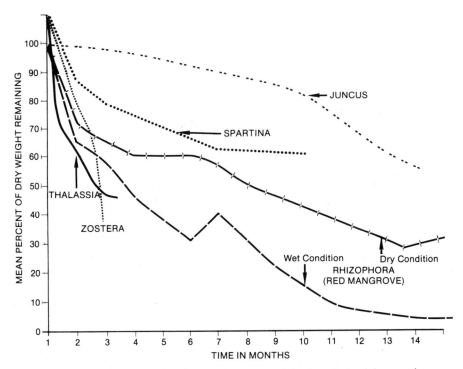

Figure 7.8 Comparison of the degradation rates of detritus derived from red mangrove under wet and dry conditions (from Heald 1969) and *Juncus* (from de la Cruz 1965), *Thalassia* (from Zieman 1975), *Zostera* (from Burkholder and Doheny 1968), and *Spartina* (from Odum and de la Cruz 1967).

The rate of decomposition of detrital particles is inversely related to their average size. This is reflected in a number of ways. Oxygen consumption by the microbial community on decaying *Spartina* (Fig. 7.9A) and *Thalassia* (Fig. 7.9D) detritus increases with decreasing particle size. The number of bacteria, flagellates, and ciliates is higher per volume on smaller particles (Fig. 7.9C) as is total microbial biomass (Fig. 7.9B). Obviously aerobic decomposition cannot take place in the absence of oxygen. The oxygen uptake of decomposing detritus in the laboratory increases with decreased particle size, as indicated above, and correlates with the pattern of microbial abundance.

The rate of mechanical breakdown of large fragments of macrophyte tissue is markedly increased by mechanical fragmentation during feeding, especially by amphipods. Passage of detritus through the gut of these macroconsumers and fragmentation while chewing enhance the particle's susceptibility to bacterial colonization. This increased growth of bacteria results in higher respiration. For example, when amphipods were added to *Thalassia* detritus, the rate of oxygen consumption increased more than could be explained by the respiration of the

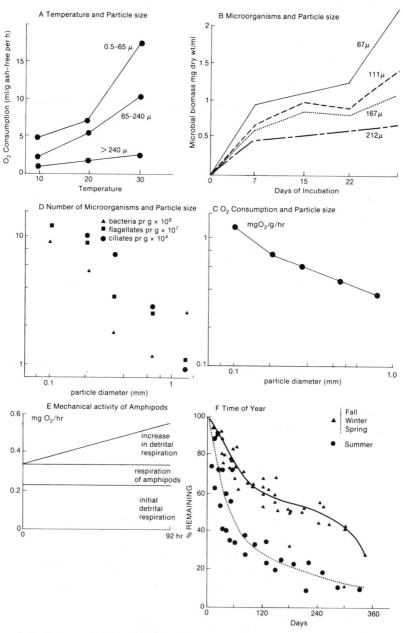

Figure 7.9 Factors affecting the decomposition of organic detritus. (a) Oxygen consumption of three different size fractions of Spartina detritus at 10, 20, and 30°C (from Odum and de la Cruz 1967). (b) Microbial biomass as a function of *Spartina* detrital particle size (from Gosselink and Kirby 1974). (c) Numbers of organisms and (d) Oxygen consumption of Thalassia detritus as a function of particle size (from Fenchel 1970). (e) Effect of amphipods on oxygen consumption by Thalassia detritus (from Fenchel 1970). (f) Weight loss in litter bag experiments begun at different times of year (from Montagna and Ruber 1980).

amphipods (Fig. 7.9E). This was due to stimulation of bacterial respiration or was a result of decreased particle size (Fenchel 1970). The importance of micro-consumers such as protozoans to decomposition is just beginning to be under-stood. Protozoans are known to readily graze bacteria that may be on detrital particles. This pathway of carbon flow may greatly affect the detrital food web.

An important variable determining the overall rate of aerobic detrital decom-position is the time of the year at which the macrophyte plant tissue is released into the estuarine system (Fig. 7.9F). Test bags of litter experimentally exposed to different estuarine conditions lost weight at greatly different rates depending on the season at which they were set out. This is probably a reflection of the effects of temperature on the activity and structure of the decomposer community.

Because they are taken up by microbes during the breakdown of detritus, nutrients may limit microbical growth and the rate of decomposition. This is illustrated for the decomposition of mangroves in Figure 7.10. At the riverine site with higher nutrients, the rate of decomposition and nutrient content of mangrove litter are higher than at the marine site where there are generally lower nutrient levels.

7.6.4 Anaerobic Detrital Decomposition

The breakdown of buried organic matter under anaerobic conditions is different in a number of ways from the aboveground process. This decomposition, essen-tially always in the absence of oxygen, represents a complex family of reactions of great significance to the estuarine environment (see Fig. 7.3). The organic matter that is deposited or produced (by plant roots, for example) in estuarine sediments supports the growth of aerobic decomposers that quickly use up the available free oxygen. Thus any aerobic decomposition that subsequently takes place is limited by the rate at which new oxygen diffuses into the bottom. The majority of decomposition below ground is via anaerobic processing by various microorganisms. In addition, some metazoan animals (e.g., nematodes) are fa-culative anaerobes and can exist for different lengths of time in anaerobic sedi-ments (Fenchel and Riedl 1970).

The complex transformations of organic matter in anaerobic sediments have been discussed previously in Chapter 3 and Section 7.3.2. The magnitude of anaerobic respiration is only just beginning to be measured and there are still questions about methods (eg. Howes et al. 1984). Howes et al. (1985) reported belowground metabolism in a Massachusetts salt marsh of about 850 g C/m^2 yr, among the highest measured values for marine sediments. Howes et al. (1984) concluded that over half of this metabolism was associated with sulfate reduc-tion There needs to be more measurement in a number of different areas before an accurate picture of below-ground metabolism can be developed. It is clear, however, that anaerobic activity is a major energetic pathway in coastal systems and that much of this activity is associated with reduced sulfur dynamics.

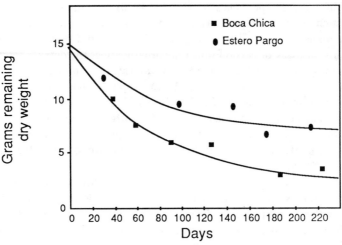

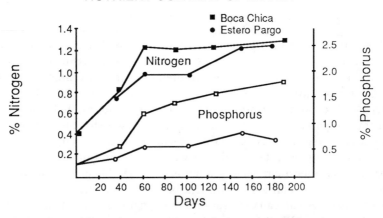

Figure 7.10 Rate of litter decomposition and nitrogen and phosphorus content of mangrove detritus at two sites in the Laguna de Terminos, Mexico. Estero Pargo is a high salinity, marine influenced site, and Boca Chica is a low salinity, riverine influenced site (from Day et al. 1982).

7.6.5 Organic Export

A central paradigm of estuarine ecology over the past two to three decades is that coastal wetlands in particular, and estuaries in general, tend to produce an annual excess of organic matter, some of which is exported seaward where it represents a major energetic pathway and supports coastal fisheries. This is the so-called "outwelling hypothesis" (Odum 1980). This idea has been extremely influential when used as a rationale for preserving estuaries, for it has been argued that estuaries are important in supplying food to coastal fish. Many states have passed laws to protect estuaries based on this hypothesis.

Since the enunciation of the outwelling hypothesis a great amount of research has been carried out and a great deal of controversy has been generated. This controversy is due to the use of different techniques, boundaries and approaches, the appropriateness of conclusions drawn from different lines of evidence, and the generality of the phenomena of outwelling. Because of the amount of research and the controversy, this has been one of the most exciting areas of estuarine research during the past two decades. And the excitement continues today because this question is yet to be resolved. In the remainder of this chapter we review various aspects of this issue.

A number of early studies used ecosystem carbon or energy budgets to calculate carbon or energy export. All sources of primary production were summed and measured, and respiration was subtracted from this value. "Excess" carbon or energy was assumed to be exported since estuarine waters are continually flushed by tides. The first example of such an energy budget is the classic work by John Teal (1962) on the energy budget of the salt marsh ecosystem at Sapelo Island, Georgia. The idea of outwelling was based on early work at the University of Georgia Marine Institute at Sapelo Island, and scientists at the laboratory continue to be among the most active in this area. Teal developed an energy-flow diagram for the salt marsh which indicated that almost half of the aboveground *Spartina* production was exported as organic detritus (Fig. 7.11). He concluded that "the tides remove 45% of the production before marsh consumers have a chance to use it and in so doing permit the estuaries to support an abundance of animals." Day et al. (1973) used this same approach to develop a budget for the Barataria Bay estuary in Louisiana (Fig. 7.12). They calculated significant export from the marsh to the bay and from the estuary to the Gulf of Mexico. A later budget for the entire Barataria Basin supports this conclusion (Day et al. 1982, Conner and Day 1987). The drawback of such studies is that export estimates are calculated by difference and there are no direct measurements of export.

A number of studies have attempted to directly measure the export of organic detritus. Many of these involved measurement of materials flux over one to several tidal cycles, and calculating net flux. Care must be taken in such analyses because there can be marked asymmetries in the flood and ebb discharges for coastal systems. For example, Kjerfve and Proehl (1979) reported that on three consecutive tidal cycles in a South Carolina salt marsh, there was a net export of water on two and a net import on one (Table 7.4). Nixon (1980) reviewed the literature on flux studies and found that, in general, most salt marsh systems exported organic detritus (Fig. 7.13). He then compared marsh production and export to open water phytoplankton production for a number of coastal systems in an effort to estimate the quantitative importance of marsh export (Fig. 7.14). He found that organic carbon exported from marshes varied from less than 5%

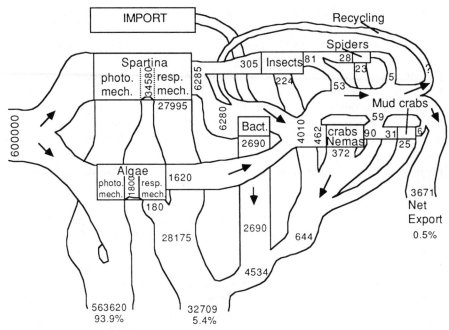

Figure 7.11 Energy flow in the salt marsh ecosystem at Sapelo Island, GA (from "Energy Flow in the Salt Marsh Ecosystem of Georgia" by J. Teal, Ecology 1962, *43*, 614–624; copyright © 1962, Ecological Society of America, reprinted by permission). Values in kcal/m²/yr.

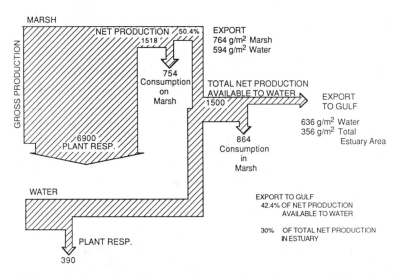

Figure 7.12 Organic budget of Barataria Bay, Louisiana (Day et al. 1973). Values in g organic matter/m²/yr.

TABLE 7.4 Comparison of Rising and Falling Tidal Range and Ebb and Flood Discharge Rates for Three Consecutive Tidal Cycles in the North Inlet, SC Salt Marsh Estuary[a]

	Tidal Cycle 1	Tidal Cycle 2	Tidal Cycle 3
Rising range (m)	1.81	2.41	1.64
Falling range (m)	2.05	1.99	2.27
Maximum flood discharge (m^3/s)	1392	1888	1218
Maximum ebb discharge (m^3/s)	-1599	-1571	-2135
Cumulative flood flow (10^6m^3)	17.97	24.84	15.19
Cumulative ebb flow (10^6m^3)	-22.11	-19.53	-30.47
Net discharge (m^3/s)	-92	118	-340

[a]After Kjerfve and Proehl (1979).

NET ANNUAL TIDAL FLUXES BETWEEN SALT MARSHES AND COASTAL MARSHES

Marsh	Salinity	DOC	POC	Reference
Great Sippewisset Cape Cod, Mass	28-33		E	1
Flax Pond Long Island, NY	26	O	E	2
Canary Creek Delaware Bay	10-28	E	E	3
Gott's Marsh Patuxent Rv., Md.	0-9		E	4
Ware Creek York River, VA	0-7	E	E	5
Carter Creek York River, VA	0-12	E	E	6
Dill's Creek Charleston Harbor, SC	10-23		E	7
North Inlet, SC		E	E	8
Barataria Bay, Louisiana	15-25	E	E	9

Figure 7.13 A summary of the net annual export (E), input (I),or lack of exchange (O) reported in the literature for dissolved (DOC) and particulate (POC) organic carbon for various tidal marshes along the Atlantic and Gulf coasts of the United States. Sources of information: (1) Valiela and Teal 1979, (2) Woodwell et al. 1979a and b, (3) Lotrich et al. 1979, (4) Heinle and Flemmer 1976, (5) and (6) Moore 1974, (7) Settlemyre and Gardner 1975, (8) Happ et al. 1977, and (9) Chrzanowski et al. 1982, 1983 (modified from Nixon 1980).

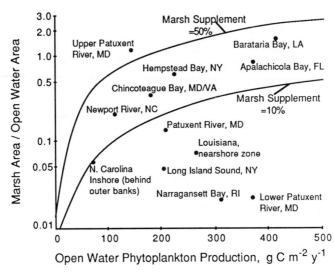

Figure 7.14 The ratio of vegetated marsh area to open water area in various estuarine ecosystems compared to annual phytoplankton production in the open water. The lines are drawn to show where organic carbon exports from the marshes would provide a supplement for the open waters equal to 10 and 50% of phytoplankton production, assuming an export of 100 g/C m² yr (from Nixon 1980).

to greater than 50% of phytoplankton production in estuarine and coastal waters. These calculations were based on the relative productivities and areas of marsh and open water. In a recent study, Hopkinson (1985) addressed the question of organic export from the point of view of the receiving water, that is, the nearshore coastal zone. He measured aquatic primary productivity and community respiration in nearshore waters off Sapelo Island, Georgia. He found that total respiration was 23% higher than *in situ* productivity. Seasonally, excess respiration corresponded with the times of high river flow and greatest marsh grass degradation; Hopkinson concluded that marsh export must be occurring. Finally, W. E. Odum (1984) suggested that organic detritus in estuaries occurs principally along two gradients: the salinity gradient and from the marsh to open water. Evidence indicates that organic carbon is highest in marsh creek and in river water, suggesting that these two areas are sources of organic matter.

Another line of evidence has been used in the debate over marsh export. This is the isotopic composition of food sources and consumers. Since this topic is also related to the question of the value of detritus as a food, we will address this in the next section.

7.6.6   The Detritus-Based Estuarine Food Web: Paradigm and Controversy

A central tenent of estuarine ecology for over two decades has been that organic detritus, derived mainly from vascular plants, is a major food source for estuarine consumers. This idea is closely linked to the concept of organic export because material exported from wetlands (and other areas such as seagrass beds) is an important source of organic matter. In this final section we address the question of organic detritus as a food source for estuarine consumers. Reviews of the role of organic detritus in estuarine systems are provided by Mann (1972, 1982), Nixon (1980), Valiela (1984), and Mitsch and Gosselink (1986).

The first evidence that organic detritus was an important component of estuarine trophic dynamics came from gut analysis. Examination of gut contents of estuarine animals showed that many contained considerable amounts of organic detritus. In a now classic study, Darnell (1961) analyzed the trophic spectrum of Lake Pontchatrain, Louisiana and found that organic detritus was one of the most important items in the gut of lower-level consumers (Fig. 7.15). The food value was not the dead organic matter substrate but the microbial community living on it (Darnell 1967). Organisms that consumed detritus were thought to digest this community and pass the organic substrate relatively unaffected. Newell (1965) reported that the nitrogen content of feces of the bivalve *Hydrobia ulvae* increased while in sea water but dropped after being reingested and passing through the gut (Fig. 7.16). The nitrogen increase was due to the growth of a microbial community as described in Section 7.6.3 and its depletion was due to the consumption of the microbes. The functioning of the detrital food web was summarized by W. E. Odum (1970) for a mangrove ecosystem in the Everglades. Mangrove leaves falling into the water were colonized by microbes. The resulting detritus was then consumed by an assortment of detritivores which utilized the microbial community and were in turn fed upon by higher consumers (Fig. 7.17).

This view of the detrital food chain was accepted as essentially correct through the mid 1970s. Then the development of a new analytical tool provided results which brought this idea into question. This new approach involved the measurement of the ratios of the naturally occurring isotopes of carbon (^{12}C and ^{13}C) in different estuarine producers and consumers. The basis of the isotope ratio technique is that different primary producers (phytoplankton, marsh grass, seagrass, etc.) take up the two isotopes in distinctly different ratios. The isotopic ratio is then thought to be conserved in organisms that consume a given plant. Thus the ratio can be used as a qualitative tracer of food pathways. This technique has been used to trace the fate of material exported from wetlands to estuarine waters. The form of the expression by which the ratio is calculated is as follows:

$$\delta^{13}C = \frac{^{13}C/^{12}C \text{ sample}}{^{13}C/^{12}C \text{ standard}} \times 1000$$

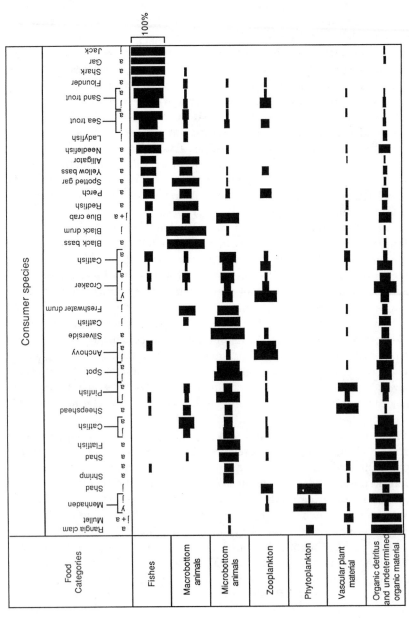

Figure 7.15 The trophic spectrum of Lake Pontchatrain, Louisiana, illustrating the importance of organic detritus (from "Trophic spectrum of an estuarine community based on studies of Lake Pontchartrain, Louisiana" by R. Darnell, Ecology 1961, 42, 553–568; copyright by the Ecological Society of America, reprinted by permission).

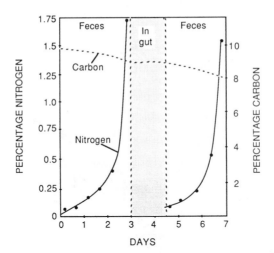

Figure 7.16 Changes in the carbon and nitrogen content of feces of *Hydrobia ulvae* during 3 days in sea water, during passage through the gut, and during a second period of exposure to sea water (from Newell 1965).

The $\delta^{13}C$ expresses the relative depletion of ^{13}C relative to ^{12}C in parts per thousand because ^{12}C is taken up perferentially since it is lighter. For example, the $\delta^{13}C$ for *Spartina* is about -12, which means that it is depleted by about 12 ppt ^{13}C relative to the standard.

In the late 1970s, a series of papers were published on the marshes at Sapelo Island, Georgia that questioned the validity of the detrital-based food chain (Haines 1976a,b, 1977, 1979, Haines and Dunstan 1976, Haines and Montague 1979). An example of these data is presented in Table 7.5. The $\delta^{13}C$ values of *Spartina*, mud diatoms, and phytoplankton are about -12, -16, and -21, respectively. If significant amounts of *Spartina* detritus were being exported and consumed, then one should be able to trace the *Spartina* $\delta^{13}C$. Few organisms in the marsh had $\delta^{13}C$ values close to *Spartina;* nor did suspended particulate matter in tidal creeks and shelf waters. Only the snail *Littorina irrorata* and the grass shrimp *Palaemonetes pugio* had values close to *Spartina*. Many of the organisms in the marsh had values similar to the algae that live on the surface of the marsh mud, and particulate suspended matter was between mud algae and phytoplankton (Table 7.5). It was concluded that the data did not support the idea that *Spartina* detritus was the major source of organic matter in the system as had been suggested.

Isotopic studies have also been carried out in other areas. In seagrass beds in Texas, results seemed to clearly indicate that seagrass material was a major dietary component in the Corpus Christi Bay-upper Laguna Madre system. The seagrass *Halodule wrightii* has a $\delta^{13}C$ of about -10, while ephiphytes growing on the plant have a $\delta^{13}C$ of about -16. Sedimentary organic carbon in the seagrass beds had $\delta^{13}C$ values between *Halodule* and its epiphytes. The values of

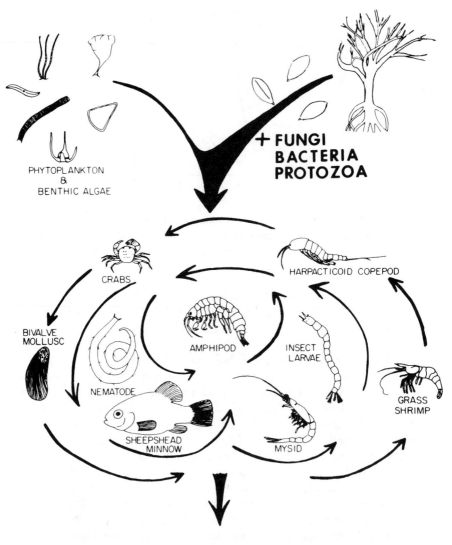

2ND CONSUMERS

Figure 7.17 A schematic diagram of the detrital food chain of the North River estuary in the Everglades National Park. Detritus consuming omnivorous organisms ingest small amounts of living algae along with large quantities of vascular plant detritus. The cyclical nature of the diagram depicts the utilization and reutilization of detritus particles in the form of fecal material (from Odum 1970).

TABLE 7.5   Carbon Isotope Composition in Marshes and Coastal Waters of Georgia[a]

	d^{13} C(%)
Marsh grass	
Spartina alterniflora Live	-12.7 to -13.6
Spartina alterniflora Dead	-12.3
Distichlis spicata	-13.1
Juncus roemerianus	-22.8
Salicornia virginica	-26.0
Marsh soil	
Soil surface (0–5 cm)	-16.0 to -22.6
Organic matter in soil (0–5 cm)	-13.2 to -13.4
Mud diatoms -16.2 to -17.9	
Marsh fauna	
Palaemonetes pugio	-13.6
Littorina irrorata	-14.7
Ischnodemus badius	-15.0
Grammonota trivittata	-15.2
Nassarius obsoletus	-15.9
Uca pugilator	-16.2
Uca pugilator	-16.3
Uca pugnax	-16.8
Uca pugnax	-17.8
Sesarma sp.	-19.1
Crassostrea virginica	-21.0
Phytoplankton	
Diatom bloom (*Skeletonema costatum*)	-22.1 to -22.7
Dinoflagellate bloom (*Kryptoperidinium* sp.)	-20.0
Green flagellate bloom	-26.3
Suspended particulate matter	
Estuary tidal creeks	-19.8 to -22.8
Shelf (0–10 km offshore)	-18.0 to -24.3
Shelf (20 km offshore)	-21.0 to -23.9

[a]From Haines 1976b, Haines and Dunstan 1975.

sedimentary organic carbon changed gradually toward that of phytoplankton with distance from the grass beds (Fig. 7.18). Organisms in the grass beds had δ^{13}C values in the range of *Halodule* and its epiphytes (Fry and Parker 1979).

Having such data in mind, it is critical to understand what the δ^{13}C technique can and cannot do. For example, the data in Table 7.5 show that the fiddler crab, Uca pugilator, had a δ^{13}C value of -16.2. One might conclude that this crab consumes mud diatoms, since diatoms have δ^{13}C values between -16.2 and -17.9. But it is also possible that the crabs' diet consisted of about 50% each of *Spartina* and *Juncus* detritus or 50% each of *Spartina* detritus and phytoplankton that had settled onto the marsh surface. Thus the only thing that δ^{13}C data can definitively provide is the overall isotopic composition of an organism's diet.

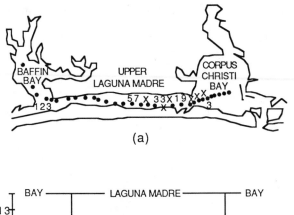

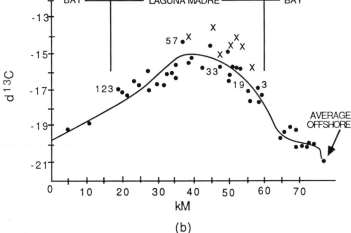

Figure 7.18 $\delta^{13}C$ sedimentary organic carbon for estuaries along the Texas coast. (a) The study area. Numbers refer to channel markers in the intracoastal waterway. x = sample site in seagrass bed; dot = sample from nonseagrass area. (b) ^{13}C values along the transect (from Fry et al. 1977).

These results indicate that there are a number of questions about the use of isotopic analysis. In an ecosystem such as an estuary with so many potential food sources, care must be taken in interpreting such data. Fry and Sherr (1984) reviewed the use of $\delta^{13}C$ measurements and came to the following conclusions.

1. When an organism consumes detritus, it may consume both the dead organic substrate (such as a fragment of *Spartina*) as well as the microbial community. And it is thought that this community is the real food of organic detritus. The microbial community may contain algae which as we have seen often have a different $\delta^{13}C$ value than the inert substrate. Bacteria and fungi may derive some of their food from a source other than the substrate (such as the algae) and thus have still a different $\delta^{13}C$ value. The substrate material may serve mainly as a carrier and decompose very slowly.

2. There may be considerable variability of isotopic ratio values within a functional food source. For example, phytoplankton from Georgia averaged -20 to -22, while those from the Gulf of Mexico ranged from -15 to -18 (Fry and Parker 1979).

3. There are indications that the $\delta^{13}C$ value may not be conserved and that there is further fractionation along a food chain (DeNiro and Epstein 1978, Fry 1977).

4. The isotopic ratio may not be constant for different tissues of a single organism. For example, Fry and Parker (1979) found that the $\delta^{13}C$ for lipid-free muscle of red snappers (*Lutjanus campechanus*) was -15.3 while that of total lipids was -20.9.

5. As stated earlier, the isotopic ratio is an average value of all food consumed. For example, an organism with a $\delta^{13}C$ of -15 could have eaten a single food source of -15, or equal amounts of two food sources with values of -10 and -20, respectively.

It has been suggested that mixing of different food sources might account for the unexpected $\delta^{13}C$ values of suspended particulate matter, such as those reported for Georgia estuaries. Howarth and Teal (1979) and Peterson et al. (1980) measured $\delta^{13}C$ values of photosynthetic sulfur bacteria of -30 to -40. Because these bacteria exist in anaerobic environments, they use reduced sulfur as an electron donor in photosynthesis (see Section 7.3.5). This reduced sulfur is produced during anaerobic metabolism by sulfate-reducing bacteria and leaches toward the surface of the marsh and creek banks where it can be used by photosynthetic sulfur bacteria. These bacteria may fix atmospheric CO_2 or recycled sediment carbon. The hypothesis is that this material could then be fed upon directly or exported to tidal creeks where it enters the food chain. The resulting $\delta^{13}C$ values of the consumers or suspended particulate matter would thus be a mixture of *Spartina*, bacteria, and phytoplankton. This pathway is ultimately driven indirectly by *Spartina* since the initial sulfate reduction takes place mainly during the decomposition of Spartina roots. Howarth (1984) suggested that chemoautotrophic bacterial production may represent a significant source of organic matter in some sediments and may be grazed by animals. On the other hand, Howes et al. (1985) estimated that export of DOC from a New England salt marsh was less than 5% (< 36 g C/m^2 yr) of total belowground carbon production.

Recently, studies using isotope ratios of sulfur and nitrogen in addition to carbon seem to allow the flows of organic matter and food-web relationships in coastal systems to be traced without the ambiguities of using a single isotope (Peterson et al. 1985). Peterson et al. studied the isotopic ratios of C, N, and S of the ribbed mussel *Geukensia demissa* in a New England salt marsh. The use of the three tracers allowed a separation of the data not possible with one isotope (Fig. 7.19). Mussels from deep within the marsh were closer to *Spartina* values, while those nearer to the bay were closer to phytoplankton, suggesting a mixing of the two food sources depending on the position of individual mussels within

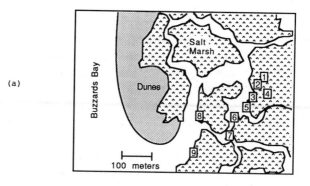

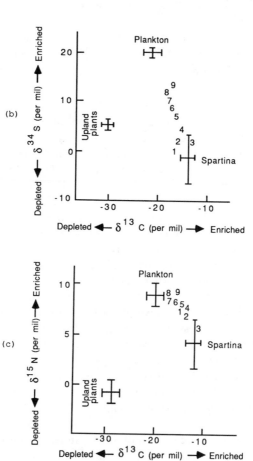

Figure 7.19 The sources of food for the ribbed mussel Geukensia demissa in the Great Sippewissett marsh as determined by isotopic analysis. (a) The study area showing sampling sites. (b) Carbon and sulfur isotopic ratios of Geukensia compared with phytoplankton, Spartina, and upland plants. (c) Similar results for nitrogen and carbon (from Peterson et al. 1985, copyright 1985 by the American Association for the Advancement of Science).

the marsh system. The multiple isotope approach was also used to analyze organic matter flow in the Sapelo Island salt marsh estuary (Peterson and Howarth 1987). The results were similar to those shown in Figure 7.19, and indicated that *Spartina* detritus and phytoplankton were about equally important to marsh and estuarine consumers.

In summary, by the early 1970s it appeared that estuarine ecologists could hold up the classical detritus food web paradigm as a significant advancement in our understanding of how estuaries worked. However, as can be seen from this section, problems arose in the story in that phytoplankton often appeared to have a very large role. Thus the system is much more complex than originally imagined. There still is considerable need to answer the various questions that continually arise from the further probing of this paradigm, even though we believe that the bulk of the evidence continues to support the fundamental role of the detrital food web in estuarine trophic dynamics.

REFERENCES

Baross, J.A., J. Liston, and R.Y. Morita, 1978. Incidence of *Vibrio parahaemolyticus* bacteriophages and other *Vibrio* bacteriophages in marine samples. Appl. Environ. Microbiol., 36:492-499.

Bell, E.R. and L.J. Albright, 1981. Attached and free-floating bacteria in the Fraser River Estuary, British Columbia, Canada. Mar. Ecol. Prog. Ser., 6:317-327.

Benner, R., M. Morgan, and R.E. Hodson, 1986a. Biogeochemical cycling of lignocellulosic carbon in marine and freshwater ecosystems: relative contributions of procaryotes and eucaroyotes. Limnol. Oceanogr., 31:89-100.

Benner, R., A.E. Maccubbin, and R.E. Hodson, 1986b. Temporal relationship between the decomposition and microbial degradation of lignocellulosic detritus in a Georgia salt marsh and the Okefenokee Swamp. Microb. Ecol., 12:291-298.

Berk, S.G. and R.R. Colwell, 1981. Transfer of mercury through a marine microbial food web. J. Exp. Mar. Biol. Ecol., 52:157-172.

Bitton, G., 1980. Introduction to Environmental Virology. Wiley, New York, 326 pp.

Bobbie, R.J. and D.C. White, 1980. Characterization of benthic microbial community structure by high-resolution gas chromatography of fatty acid methyl esters. Appl. Environ. Microbiol., 39:1212-1222.

Brown, A.D., 1976. Microbial water stress. Bacteriol. Rev., 40:803-846.

Buchanan, R.E. and N.E. Gibbons (Eds.), 1974. Bergey's Manual of Determinative Bacteriology. 8th ed. Williams and Wilkins, Baltimore, MD, 1246 pp.

Burkholder, P. and T. Doheny, 1968. The biology of eelgrass with special reference to Hempstead and South Oyster Bays, Nassau County, Long Island, New York. Lamont Geological Observatory, Contribution 1227, 120 pp.

Capriulo, G.M. and E.J. Carpenter, 1983. Abundance, species composition and feeding impact of tintinnid micro-zooplankton in central Long Island Sound. Mar. Ecol. Prog. Ser., 10:277-288.

Christian, R.R. and J.R. Hall, 1977. Experimental trends in sediment microbial heterotrophy: Radioisotopic techniques and analysis. In B. Coull (Ed.), Ecology of Marine Benthos. University of South Carolina Press, Columbia, pp. 67–88.

Christian, R.R. and R.L. Wetzel, 1978. Interaction between substrate, microbes and consumers of *Spartina* detritus in estuaries. In M.L. Wiley (Ed.), Estuarine Interactions. Academic, New York, pp. 93–113.

Chrzanowski. T.H. and L.H. Stevenson, 1980. Filamentous fungal propagation as potential indicators of sediment–detritus resuspension. Bot. Mar., 23:251–256.

Chrzanowski, T., L. Stevenson, and J. Spurrier, 1982. Transport of particulate organic carbon through the North Inlet ecosystem. Mar. Ecol. Prog. Ser., 7:231–245.

Chrzanowski, T., L. Stevenson, and J. Spurrier, 1983. Transport of dissolved organic carbon through a major creek of the North Inlet ecosystem. Mar. Ecol. Prog. Ser., 13:167–174.

Colwell, R.R. (Ed.), 1984. Vibrios in the Environment. Wiley, New York, 634 pp.

Colwell, R.R. and D.J. Grimes, 1984. *Vibrio* diseases of marine fish populations. Helgolander Meeresunters., 37:265–287.

Conner, W., and J. Day, (Eds.), 1987. The ecology of the Barataria Basin, Louisiana: an estuarine profile. U.S. Fish and Wildl. Ser., Biol. Rept. 85(7.13), 165 pp.

Crawford, C.C., J.F. Hobbie, and K.L. Webb, 1974. The utilization of dissolved free amino acids by estuarine microorganisms. Ecology, 55:551–563.

Dale, N.G., 1974. Bacteria in intertidal sediments: Factors related to their distribution. Limnol. Oceanogr., 19:509–518.

Darnell, R.M., 1961. Trophic spectrum of an estuarine community, based on studies of Lake Pontchatrain, Louisiana. Ecology, 42(3):553-568.

Darnell, R.M., 1967. The organic detritus problem. In G. Lauff (Ed.), Estuaries. American Association for the Advancement of Science, Publication No. 83, pp. 374–375.

Day, J.W., Jr., W.G. Smith, P.R. Wagner, and W.C. Stowe, 1973. Community structure and carbon budget of a salt marsh and shallow bay estuarine system in Louisiana. Center for Wetland Resources, Louisiana State University, Baton Rouge, Publ. No. LSU-SG-72-04, 79 pp.

Day, J., R. Day, M. Barreiro, F. Ley-Lou, and C. J. Madden, 1982. Primary production in the Laguna de Terminos, a tropical estuary in the southern Gulf of Mexico. Oceanol. Acta. No, SP:269–276.

de la Cruz, A., 1965. A study of particulate organic detritus in a Georgia salt marsh-estuarine system. PhD Thesis, University of Georgia, Athens.

De Niro, M. and S. Epstein, 1978. Influence of diet on the distribution of carbon isotopes in animals. Geochim. Cosmochim. Acta, 42:495–506.

Ehrlich, H.L., 1978. Inorganic energy sources for chemolithotrophic and mixotrophic bacteria. Geomicrobiol. J., 1:65–83.

Engler, R.M. and W.H. Patrick, Jr., 1975. Stability of sulfides of manganese, iron, zinc, copper and mercury in flooded and nonflooded soils. Soil Sci., 119:217–221.

Fenchel, T., 1967. The ecology of marine microbenthos. I. The quantitative importance of ciliates as compared with metazoans in various types of sediments. Ophelia, 4:121–137.

Fenchel, T., 1968. The ecology of marine microbenthos. III. The reproductive potential of ciliates. Ophelia, 5:123–136.

Fenchel, T., 1969. The ecology of marine microbenthos. IV. Structure and function of the benthic ecosystem, its chemical and physical factors and the microfauna communities with special reference to the ciliated protozoa. Ophelia, 6:1-182.

Fenchel, T., 1970. Studies on the decomposition of organic matter derived from turtle grass, *Thalassia testudinum.* Limnol. Oceanog., 15:14-20.

Fenchel, T.M. and R.J. Riedl, 1970. The sulfide system: A new biotic community underneath the oxidized layer of marine sand bottoms. Mar. Biol., 7:255-268.

Fitzgerald, J.W., 1976. Sulfate ester formation and hydrolysis: A potentially important yet often ignored aspect of the sulfur cycle of aerobic soils. Bacteriol. Rev., 40:698-721.

Frankenberg, D. and C.W. Westerfield, 1968. Oxygen demand and oxygen depletion capacity of sediments from Wassaw Sound, Georgia. Bull. Georgia Acad. Sci., 26:160-172.

Fry, B., 1977. Stable carbon isotope ratios—A tool for tracing food chains. MS Thesis. University of Texas, Austin, 126 pp.

Fry, B., and P. L. Parker. 1979. Animal diet in Texas seagrass meadows: $\delta^{13}C$ evidence for the importance of benthic plants. Estuarine Coastal Mar. Sci., 8:499-509.

Fry, B., and E. Sherr, 1984. $\delta^{13}C$ measurements as indicators of carbon flow in marine and freshwater ecosystems. Contrib. Mar. Sci., 27:13-47.

Fry, B., R. Scalan, and P. Parker, 1977. Stable carbon isotope evidence for two sources of organic matter in coastal sediments: Seagrasses and plankton. Geochim. Cosmochim. Acta, 41:1875-1877.

Fryer, J.L. and J.S. Rohovec, 1984. Principal bacterial diseases of cultured marine fish. Helgolander Meeresunters., 37:533-545.

Gessner, R.V. and J. Kohlmeyer, 1976. Geographical distribution and taxonomy of fungi from salt marsh *Spartina*. Can. J. Bot., 54:2023-2037.

Gessner, R.V., R.D. Goos, and J.McN. Sieburth, 1972. The fungal microcosm of the internodes of *Spartina alterniflora*. Mar. Biol., 16:269-273.

Gosselink, J. and C. Kirby, 1974. Decomposition of salt marsh grass, *Spartina alterniflora,* Loisel. Limnol. Oceanogr., 19:825-832.

Goulder, R., 1976. Relationships between suspended solids and standing crops and activities of bacteria in an estuary during a neap-spring-neap tidal cycle. Oecologia., 24:83-90.

Haines, E., 1976a. Relation between the stable carbon isotope composition of fiddler crabs, plants, and soils in a salt marsh. Limnol. Oceanogr., 21:880-883.

Haines, E., 1976b. Stable carbon isotope ratios in the biota, soils, and tidal water of a Georgia salt marsh. Estuarine Coast. Mar. Sci., 4:609-619.

Haines, E., 1977. The origins of detritus in a Georgia salt marsh. Oikos, 29:254-260.

Haines, E., 1979. Interactions between Georgia salt marshes and coastal waters: A changing paradigm. In R. Livingston (Ed.), Ecological Processes in Coastal and Marine Systems. Plenum, New York, pp. 35-46.

Haines, E., and W. Dunstan, 1975. The distribution and relation of particulate organic material and primary productivity. Estuarine Coast. Mar. Sci., 3:431-441.

Haines, E., and C. Montague, 1979. Food sources of estuarine invertebrates analyzed using $^{13}C/^{12}C$ ratios. Ecology, 60:48-56.

Happ, G., J. Gosselink, and J. Day, 1977. The seasonal distribution of organic carbon in a Louisiana estuary. Estuarine Coastal Mar. Sci., 5:695-705.

Harvey, R.W. and L.Y. Young, 1980. Enumeration of particle-bound and unattached respiring bacteria in the salt marsh environment. Appl. Environ. Microbiol., 40:156-160.

Heald, E., 1969. The production of organic detritus in a south Florida estuary. PhD Dissertation, University of Miami, Florida, 110 pp.

Heinle, D. and D. Flemmer, 1976. Flows of materials between poorly flooded tidal marshes and an estuary. Mar. Biol., 35:359-373.

Holm-Hansen, O. and C.R. Booth, 1966. The measurement of adenosine triphosphate in the ocean and its ecological significance. Limnol. Oceanogr., 11:510-519.

Hopkinson, C. S., 1985. Shallow water benthic and pelagic metabolism: Evidence of heterotrophy in the nearshore Georgia Bight. Mar. Biol., 87:19-32.

Hopkinson, C.S., J.W. Day, Jr., and B.T. Gael, 1978. Respiration studies in a Louisiana salt marsh. An. Centro Cienc. Mar Limnol. Univ. Nal. Autón. Mexicó, 5:225-238.

Howarth, R., 1984. The ecological significance of sulfur in the energy dynamics of salt marsh and coastal marine sediments. Biogeochemistry, 1:5-27.

Howarth, R. W. and J. E. Hobbie, 1982. The regulation of decomposition and heterotrophic microbial activity in salt marsh soils: A review. In V. Kennedy (Ed.), Estuarine Comparisons. Academic, New York, pp. 183-207.

Howarth, R.W. and J.M. Teal, 1979. Sulfate reduction in a New England salt marsh. Limnol. Oceanogr., 24:999-1013.

Howarth, R.W. and J.M Teal, 1980. Energy flow in a salt marsh ecosystem: The role of reduced inorganic sulfur compounds. Am. Nat., 116:862-872.

Howes, B., J. Dacey, and G. King, 1984. Carbon flow through oxygen and sulfate reduction pathways in salt marsh sediments. Limnol. Oceanogr., 29:1037-1051.

Howes, B., J. Dacey, and J. Teal, 1985. Annual carbon mineralization and belowground production of Spartina alterniflora in a New England salt marsh. Ecology, 66:595-605.

Imberger, J., T. Berman, R.R. Christian, E.B. Sherr, D.E. Whitney, L.R. Pomeroy, R.G. Wiegert, and W.J. Wiebe, 1983. The influence of water motion on the distribution and transport of materials in a salt marsh estuary. Limnol. Oceanogr., 28:201-214.

Johnson, T.W., Jr. and F.K. Sparrow, Jr., 1961. Fungi in Oceans and Estuaries. Hafner, New York, 668 pp.

Kahl, A., 1928. Die infusorien (ciliata) der oldesloer saltzwasserstelen. Arch. Hydrobiol., 19:50-123; 189-246.

Kaplan, W., I. Valiela, and J.M. Teal, 1979. Denitrification in a salt marsh ecosystem. Limnol. Oceanogr., 24:726-734.

Karl, D.M., 1980. Cellular nucleotide measurements and applications in microbial ecology. Microbiol. Rev., 44:739-796.

King, J.D. and D.C. White, 1977. Muramic acid as a measure of microbial biomass in estuarine and marine samples. Appl. Environ. Microbiol., 33:777-783.

Kjerfve, B. and J. Proehl, 1979. Velocity variability in a cross-section of a well-mixed estuary. J. Mar. Res., 37:409-418.

Kohlmeyer, J. and E. Kohlmeyer, 1979. Marine Mycology: The Higher Fungi. Academic, New York, 690 pp.

Lee, J.J., 1980a. Informational energy flow as an aspect of protozoan nutrition. J. Protozool., 27:5–9.

Lee, J.J., 1980b. A conceptual model of marine detrital decomposition and the organisms associated with the process. In M.R. Droop and H.W. Jannasch (Eds.), Advances in Aquatic Microbiology. Academic, New York, Vol. 2, pp. 257–291.

Leppard, G.G. (Ed.), 1983. Trace Element Speciation in Surface Waters and Its Ecological Implications. Plenum, New York, 320 pp.

Lotrich, V., W. Meredith, S. Weisberg, L. Hurd, and F. Daiber, 1979. Dissolved and particulate nutrient fluxes via tidal exchange between a salt marsh and lower Delaware Bay. The Fifth Biennial International Estuarine Resrearch Conference Abstracts, Jekyll Island, GA, October 7–12, 1979.

MacCubbin, A.E. and R.E. Hodson, 1980. Mineralization of detrital lignocelluloses by salt marsh sediment microflora. Appl. Environ. Microbiol., 40:735–740.

Mann, K. H., 1972. Macrophyte production and detritus food chains in coastal waters. Mem. 1st Ital. Idrobiol., 29(Suppl.): 353–383.

Mann, K. H., 1982. Ecology of Coastal Waters. Univ. Calif. Press, Berkeley, 322 pp.

Marinucci, A.C., J.E. Hobbie, and J.V.D. Helfrich, 1983. Effect of litter nitrogen on decomposition and microbial biomass in *Spartina alterniflora*. Microb. Ecol., 9:27–40.

Marsh, D.H. and W.E. Odum, 1979. Effect of suspension and sedimentation on the amount of microbial colonization of salt marsh microdetritus. Estuaries, 2:184–188.

Martens, C.S. and R.A. Berner, 1974. Methane production in the interstitial waters of sulfate-depleted marine sediments. Science, 185:1167–1169.

Meyer-Reil, L.-A., 1977. Bacterial growth rates and biomass production. In G. Reinheimer (Ed.), Microbial Ecology of a Brackish Water Environment. Springer-Verlag, New York, pp. 223–236.

Meyers, S.P., M.E. Nicholson, P. Miles, J.S. Rhee, and D.G. Ahearn, 1970. Mycological studies in Barataria Bay, Louisiana, and biodegradation of oyster grass, *Spartina alterniflora*. LSU Coastal Stud. Bull., 5:111–124.

Meyers, S.P., D.G. Ahearn, and P.C. Miles, 1971. Characterization of yeasts in Barataria Bay. Coastal Stud. Bull., 6:7–15.

Mitsch, W., and J. Gosselink, 1986. Wetlands. Van Nostrand Reinhold Co., New York, 539 pp.

Montagna, P. and E. Ruber, 1980. Decomposition of *Spartina alterniflora* in different seasons and habitats of a northern Massachusetts salt marsh, and a comparison with other Atlantic regions. Estuaries, 3(1):61–64.

Moore, K., 1974. Carbon transport in two York River, Virginia estuaries. M. S. Thesis, University of Virginia, Charlottesville, 102 pp.

Moriarty, D.J.W., P.I. Boon, J.A. Hansen, W.G. Hunt, I.R. Poiner, P.C. Pollard, G.W. Skyring, and D.C. White, 1985. Microbial biomass and productivity in sea grass beds. Geomicrobiol. J., 4:21–51.

Morrison S.J., J.D. King, R.J. Bobbie, R.E. Bechtold, and D.C. White, 1977. Evidence for microbial succession on allochthonous plant litter in Apalachicola Bay, Florida, USA. Mar. Biol., 41:229–240.

Nedwell, D.B. and G.D. Floodgate, 1972. Temperature induced changes in the formation of sulfide in a marine sediment. Mar. Biol., 14:15–24.

Newell, R., 1965. The role of detritus in the nutrition of two marine deposit feeders, the prosobranch *Hydrobia ulvae* and bivalve *Macoma balthica*. Proc. Zool. Soc. London, 144:25–45.

Newell, S.Y., 1984. Bacterial and fungal productivity in the marine environment: A contrastive overview. 1st International Colloquium on Marine Bacteriology. Colloq. Int. Cent. Natl. Rech. Sci. 331:133–139.

Newell, S.Y. and R.E. Hicks, 1982. Direct-count estimates of fungal and bacterial biovolume in dead leaves of smooth cordgrass (*Spartina alterniflora* Loisel). Estuaries, 4:246–260.

Nixon, Scott W., 1980. Between coastal marshes and coastal waters—A review of twenty years of speculation and research on the role of salt marshes in estuarine productivity and water chemistry. In P. Hamilton and K. MacDonald (Eds.), Estuarine and Wetland Processes. Plenum, New York, pp. 437–525.

Odum, E.P., 1961. The role of tidal marshes. N. Y. Conserv., June–July, p. 12.

Odum, W.E., 1970. Pathways of energy flow in a south Florida estuary. PhD Dissertation, University of Miami, Florida, 162 pp.

Odum, E.P., 1980. The status of three ecosystem-level hypotheses regarding salt marsh estuaries: tidal subsidy, outwelling, and detritus-based food chains. In V. Kennedy (Ed.), Estuarine Perspectives. Academic, New York, pp. 485–495.

Odum, W. E. 1984. Dual-gradient concept of detritus transport and processing in estuaries. Bull. Mar. Sci., 35:510–521.

Odum, E. P. and A. de la Cruz, 1967. Particulate organic detritus in a Georgia salt marsh-estuarine ecosystem. In G. Lauff (Ed.), Estuaries. American Association for the Advancement of Science, Publication No. 83. pp. 383–388.

Odum, W. E. and E. J. Heald, 1975. The detritus-based food web of an estuarine mangrove community. In L. E. Cronin (Ed.), Estuarine Research. Academic, New York, Vol. 1 pp. 265–286.

Palumbo, A.V. and R.L. Ferguson, 1978. Distribution of suspended bacteria in the Newport River estuary, North Carolina. Estuarine Coastal Mar. Sci., 7:521–529.

Palumbo, A.V., R.L. Ferguson, and P.A. Rublee, 1983. Efficient utilization of dissolved free amino acids by suspended marine bacteria. J. Exp. Mar. Biol. Ecol., 69:257–266.

Peterson, B., R. Howarth, and R. Garritt, 1985. Multiple stable isotopes used to trace the flow of organic matter in estuarine food webs. Science, 227:1361–1363.

Peterson, B.J., R.W. Howarth, F. Lipschultz, and D. Ashendorf, 1979. Salt marsh detritus: An alternative interpretation of stable carbon isotope ratios and the fate of *Spartina alterniflora*. EOS, 34:173–177.

Peterson, B., and R. Howarth, 1987. Sulfur, carbon, and nitrogen isotopes used to trace organic matter flow in the salt-marsh estuaries of Sapelo Island, Georgia. Limnol. Oceanogr., 32:1195–1213.

Peterson, B., R. Howarth, F. Lipschultz, and D. Ashendorf, 1980. Salt marsh detritus: An alternative interpretation of stable carbon isotope ratios and the fate of *Spartina alterniflora*. Oikos, 34:173–177.

Pomeroy, L.R., 1960. Residence time of dissolved phosphate in natural waters. Science, 131:1731-1732.

Pomeroy, L.R., 1984. Significance of microorganisms in carbon and energy flow in marine ecosystems. In M.J. Klug and C.A. Reddy (Eds.), Current Perspectives in Microbial Ecology. American Society for Microbiology, Washington, DC, pp. 405-411.

Pomeroy, L.R., E.E. Smith, and C.M. Grant, 1965. The exchange of phosphate between estuarine water and sediment. Limnol. Oceanogr., 10:167-172.

Pomeroy, L.R., K. Bancroft, J. Breed, R.R. Christian, D. Frankenberg, J.R. Hall, L.G. Maurer, W.J. Wiebe, R.G. Wiegert, and R.L. Wetzel, 1977. Flux of organic matter through a salt marsh. In M. Wiley (Ed.), Estuarine Processes, Academic Press, New York, Vol. II, pp. 270-279.

Postgate, J.R., 1984. The Sulphate-Reducing Bacteria. Cambridge University Press, United Kingdom, 208 pp.

Rowe, G.T., C.H. Clifford, K.L. Smith, Jr., and P.L. Hamilton, 1975. Benthic nutrient regeneration and its coupling to primary productivity in coastal waters. Nature, 255:215-217.

Rublee, P. and B.E. Dornseif, 1978. Direct counts of bacteria in the sediments of a North Carolina salt marsh. Estuaries, 1:188-191.

Seshadri, R. and J. McN. Sieburth, 1975. Seaweeds as a reservoir of *Candida* yeasts in inshore waters. Mar. Biol., 30:105-117.

Settlemyre, J. and L. Gardner, 1975. A field study of chemical budgets for a small tidal creek—Charleston Harbor, S.C. In T.M. Church (Ed.), Marine Chemistry in the Coastal Environment. ACS Symposium Series No. 18, pp. 152-175.

Sherr, B. and E. Sherr, 1983. Enumeration of heterotrophic microprotozoa by epifluorescence microscopy. Estuarine Coastal Shelf Sci., 16:1-7.

Sherr, B. and E. Sherr, 1984. Role of heterotrophic protozoa in carbon and energy flow in aquatic ecosystems. In M.J. Klug and C.A. Reddy (Eds.), Current Perspectives in Microbial Ecology. American Society for Microbiology, Washington, DC, pp. 412-423.

Sieburth, J. McN., 1979. Sea Microbes. Oxford University Press, New York, 491 pp.

Smith, D.W., 1980. An evaluation of marsh nitrogen fixation. In V.S. Kennedy (Ed.), Estuarine Perspectives. Academic, New York, pp. 135-142.

Sorensen, J., 1984. Seasonal variation and control of oxygen, nitrate, and sulfate respiration in coastal marine sediments. In M.J. Klug and C.A. Reddy (Eds.), Current Perspectives in Microbial Ecology. American Society for Microbiology, Washington, DC, pp. 447-453.

Sprague, V., 1971. Diseases of oysters. Ann. Rev. Microbiol., 25:211-230.

Teal, J.M., 1962. Energy flow in the salt marsh ecosystem of Georgia. Ecology, 43:614-624.

Tebo, B.M., K.H. Nealson, S. Emerson, and L. Jacobs, 1984. Microbial mediation of Mn(II) and Co(II) precipitation at O_2/H_2S interfaces in two anoxic fjords. Limnol. Oceanogr., 29:1247-1258.

Tenore, K.R., L. Cammen, S.E.G. Findlay, and N. Phillips, 1982. Perspectives of research on detritus: Do factors controlling availability of detritus to macroconsumers depend on its source? J. Mar. Res., 40:473-490.

Thayer, G.W., 1974. Identity and regulation of nutients limiting phytoplankton in the shallow estuaries near Beaufort, N.C. Oecologia (Berlin) 14:75-92.

Turner, R.E., 1978. Community plankton respiration in a salt marsh estuary and the importance of macrophytic leachates. Limnol. Oceanogr., 23:422-451.

Valiela, I., 1984. Marine Ecological Processes. Springer-Verlag, New York, 546 pp.

Valiela, I. and J.M. Teal, 1979. The nitrogen budget of a salt marsh ecosystem. Nature, 280:652-656.

Webb, K.L. and C.F. d'Elia, 1980. Nitrogen and oxygen redistribution during a spring neap tidal cycle in a temperate estuary. Science, 207:983-985.

Welsh, B.L., 1980. Comparative nutrient dynamics of a marsh–mudflat ecosystem. Estuarine Coastal Mar. Sci., 10:143-164.

Wetzel, R.G., P.H. Rich, M.C. Miller, and H.L. Allen, 1972. Metabolism of dissolved and particulate detrital carbon in a temperate hard-water lake, in *Detritus and its Role in Aquatic Ecosystems,* Melchorri-Santalini, U. Hopton, J. Eds., Memoir Inst. Italiano Idriobiol., (Supp. 29), p. 185.

White, D.C., R.J. Bobbie, J.D. King, J. Nickels, and P. Amoe, 1979. Lipid analysis of sediments for microbial biomass and community structure. In C.D. Litchfield and P.L. Seyfried (Eds.), Methodology for Biomass Determinations and Microbial Activities in Sediments. ASTM STP 673. American Society for Testing and Materials, Philadelphia, PA, pp. 87-103.

Wiebe, W.J. and L.R. Pomeroy, 1972. Microorganisms and their association with aggregates and detritus in the sea: A microscopic study. Mem. 1st. Ital. Idrobiol., 29(Suppl.): 325-352.

Wilson, J.O., R. Buchsbaum, I. Valiela, and T. Swain, 1986. Decomposition in salt marsh ecosystems: Phenolic dynamics during decay of litter of *Spartina alterniflora.* Mar. Ecol. Prog. Ser. 29:177-187.

Wolaver, T.G., R.L. Wetzel, J.C. Zieman, and K.L. Webb. 1980. Nutrient interactions between salt marsh, mudflats and estuarine water. In V.S. Kennedy (Ed.), Estuarine Perspectives. Academic, New York, pp. 123-133.

Woodwell, G.M., C.A.S. Hall, D.E. Whitney, and R.A. Houghton, 1979a. The flax pond ecosystem study: Exchanges of inorganic nitrogen between an estuarine marsh and Long Island Sound. Ecology, 60(4): 695-702.

Woodwell, G.M., R.A. Houghton, C.A.S. Hall, D.E. Whitney, R.A. Moll, and D.W. Juers. 1979b. The flax pond ecosystem study: The annual metabolism and nutrient budgets of a salt marsh. In R.L. Jeffries and A.J. Davy (Eds.), Ecological Processes in Coastal Environments. Blackwell, Melbourne, Australia pp. 491-511.

Wright, R.T., 1973. Some difficulties in using ^{14}C-organic solutes to measure heterotrophic bacterial activity. In L.H. Stevenson and R.R. Colwell (Eds.), Estuarine Microbial Ecology, University of South Carolina Press, Columbia, pp. 199-217.

Wright, R.T. and R.B. Coffin, 1983. Planktonic bacteria in estuaries and coastal waters of northern Massachusetts: Spatial and temporal distribution. Mar. Ecol. Prog. Ser., 11:205-216.

Zieman, J., 1975. Quantitative and dynamic aspects of the ecology of turtle grass, *Thalassia testudinum.* In L. E. Cronin (Ed.), Estuarine Research, Academic, New York, Vol. 1, pp. 541-562.

ESTUARINE CONSUMERS

OFFPRINTS FROM: ESTUARINE ECOLOGY
Edited by John W. Day Jr., Charles A. S. Hall., Dr. W. Michael Kemp, and Alejandro Yáñez-Arancibia
Copyright © 1989 by John Wiley & Sons, Inc.

▬ 8

Zooplankton, the Drifting Consumers

Zooplankton are the small, floating or weakly swimming animals found in the waters of all estuaries. They are defined as those animals that swim too weakly to avoid the influence of water currents. Together with the phytoplankton and the bacterioplankton they constitute the plankton community. Although many zooplankters (as individuals are called) are visible to the naked eye as tiny specks in a water sample, observation is much more enjoyable and informative through a microscope. Such microscopic study of a sample from a typical estuarine zooplankton tow (i.e., those organisms captured when a zooplankton net is pulled through the water) reveals a diverse group of organisms. Some of them look like minature versions of larger animals such as fish or shrimp. Others resemble nothing at all in the macroscopic animal world. There are a few macroscopic members of the zooplankton community, like jelly fishes, which at times can be extremely abundant.

In this chapter we take a closer look at this miniature animal world. What are the species that comprise the zooplankton? Which are most common? Where and when are they most abundant? How fast do they grow and what role do they play in the estuarine ecosystem? These are some of the questions that we will seek to answer as we make our way (or perhaps gently float would be a more appropriate expression) through the world of estuarine zooplankton.

8.1 ZOOPLANKTON COMPOSITION

Zooplankton can be divided into two broad categories based on life history: *holoplankton* and *meroplanton*. As the name suggests, holoplankton spend their

311

entire life as members of the zooplankton. Meroplankton spend only part of their lives in the plankton as larval stages. A third group, the tycoplankton, is sometimes mentioned. These are organisms accidently swept from the bottom but generally of little importance. The division of the zooplankton into these two general groups is logical and, as we shall see, has ecological significance. The holoplankton always live in the very variable pelagic estuarine environment and have evolved rapid growth rates, broad physiological tolerances, and curious behavioral patterns that allow them to survive in this changeable environment. Individual members of the meroplankton spend a brief but very specific time in the plankton. They often appear during certain periods of the year when productivity is high and/or conditions are good for survival and growth.

In practically every estuary studied, and for most seasons, calanoid copepods comprise the bulk of the numbers of net holoplankton. Meroplanktonic larval stages as a group are often the next most abundant, and the rest of the holoplankton are generally a minor component except for the periodic occurrences of huge "blooms" of jelly fish. The meroplankton is much more diverse than the holoplankton because of the large number of otherwise benthic or pelagic species which spend their larval and/or juvenile stages in the plankton. Some common estuarine zooplankton are shown in Fig. 8.1. We shall now take a more detailed look at zooplankton composition. We will first dicuss net plankton (zooplankton captured in a net with a mesh size of about 200 mm) and then consider the smaller microzooplankton.

8.1.1   Holoplankton

Copepods of the genus *Acartia,* especially *A. tonsa* and *A. clausi,* are not only almost always the most abundant species in the zooplankton, but they are also the most widespread. *Acartia* ranges from nearly fresh to hypersaline waters, from 0 to 40°C, from clear to turbid, shallow to deep, and polar to tropical conditions. They can comprise 80–90% of the total numbers of the plankton. The following list of estuary types where *Acartia* is abundant shows how widespread this genus is:

1. Medium salinity estuaries including Long Island Sound (Deevey 1956), Delaware Bay (Deevey 1952), Chesapeake Bay (Heinle 1966) and the North River estuary in North Carolina (Fulton 1984).
2. Hypersaline estuaries like the Laguna Madre in Texas (Simmons 1957).
3. Blue water estuaries such as St. Andrew Bay, Florida (Hopkins 1966).
4. Cool coastal waters of California (Easterly 1928).
5. Arctic estuaries like the Eskimo Lakes–Liverpool Bay system in Canada (Evans and Granger 1980).
6. Shallow, turbid, low salinity estuaries of the Mississippi delta (Darnell 1961, Cuzon du Rest 1963, Gillespie 1971).

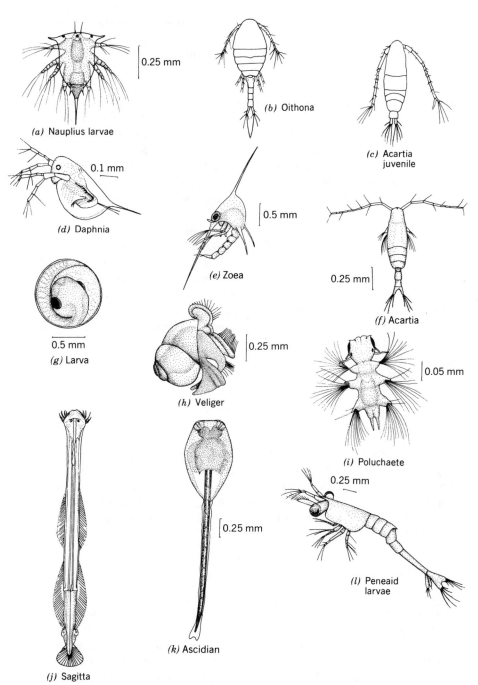

0.25 mm

(a) Nauplius larvae

(b) Oithona

(c) Acartia juvenile

0.1 mm

(d) Daphnia

0.5 mm

(e) Zoea

0.25 mm

(f) Acartia

0.5 mm

(g) Larva

0.25 mm

(h) Veliger

0.05 mm

(i) Poluchaete

0.25 mm

(j) Sagitta

0.25 mm

(k) Ascidian

0.25 mm

(l) Peneaid larvae

Figure 8.1 Common members of the estuarine zooplankton.

7. A number of tropical estuaries such as the Goa estuary in India (Goswami and Selvakumar 1977), the Laguna de Terminos, Mexico (Gomez-Aguirre 1974), Biscayne Bay, Florida (Woodmansee 1958), and the Caroni mangrove dominated system in Trinidad (Bacon 1971).

Along the Gulf of Mexico and much of the Atlantic coast, *Acartia tonsa* is most abundant. During winter in estuaries north of Cape Hatteras, North Carolina, *A. clausi* tends to replace *A. tonsa* (Riley 1967). This replacement may become more pronounced in higher latitudes, as *A. tonsa* is dominant in spring as well as winter in Narragansett Bay, Rhode Island (Martin 1968). *Acaitia clausi* is the dominant copepod in a Canadian arctic estuary while *A. tonsa* is absent (Evans and Granger 1980). Other copepod genera commonly reported from estuaries are *Temora, Paracalanus, Oithona, Labidocera, Centropages, Undinula,* and *Eurytemora.*

Generally, copepod larvae are more abundant than adult stages although adults may be more numerous during the late fall and winter months in higher latitudes. This has been reported for Raritan Bay, New Jersey (Fig 8.2) as well as for the Patuxent River estuary in Chesapeake Bay (Heinle 1966). Peak larval density was in the summer for both of these areas, although it was in spring in warmer Barataria Bay, Louisiana (Gillespie 1971).

The remainder of the holoplankton is composed mainly of noncopepod crustaceans and chaetognaths (arrow worms). The most abundant members of the crustaceans are small shrimplike creatures called carideans and mysids (Fig 8.1). *Sagitta* is a genus of chaetognath found in estuaries in many parts of the world (Fig 8.1).

8.1.2 Meroplankton

Meroplanktonic larvae are a diverse group of organisms with representatives of many different phyla. Most common are immature forms of benthic invertebrates and chordates (tunicates); eggs, larvae, and juveniles of adult nekton (shrimp, crabs, and fish), and the sexual stages of hydrozoan and scyphozoan coelenterates (jelly fishes) (Fig 8.1). A listing of some of the more common meroplanktonic zooplanton is presented in Table 8.1.

8.1.3 Microzooplankton

Microplankton are much more abundant than net zooplankton. Because these organisms are too small to be collected with standard zooplankton nets, it is only recently that the importance of microzooplankton in estuaries has become evident. These organisms can be very small metazoan larval forms such as those of *Acartia,* or they may be a number of different protozoans or other unicellular organisms. Unicellular microzooplankton include tintinnid ciliates, nonloricate ciliates (i.e., those which do not possess a lorica or shell as do the tintinnids), and various types of heterotrophic flagellates. The relative densities for macro

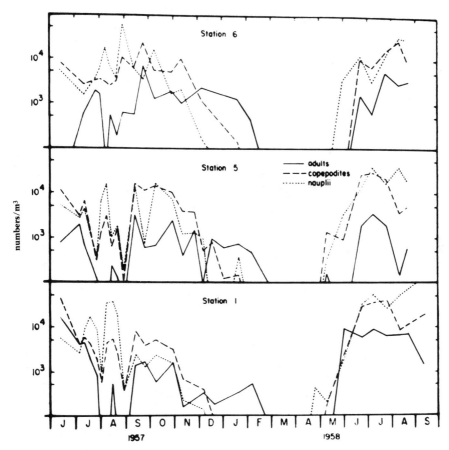

Figure 8.2 Seasonal abundance of *Acartia tonsa* adults, immature copepodites, and nauplii at three stations in Raritan Bay, New Jersey (from Jefferies 1962).

and microzooplankton in Cord Sound, Florida (Fig 8.3) indicate that the microzooplankton can be two orders of magnitude more numerous than the macroplankton. For example, tintinnids had an annual mean density of 121,000 individuals per cubic meter as compared with 2933/m^3 for *Acartia tonsa*, the dominant member of the macrozooplankton. Several other authors have reported microzooplankton composition in estuaries. In Long Island Sound, Capriulo and Carpenter (1980) noted that tintinnid and total microzooplankton numbers varied widely, with tintinnids ranging from 1000 to 9600 cells/l and total numbers ranging from 1000 to 10500. In a later study of Long Island Sound, 28 tintinnid species were identified with densities ranging from 260 to 12600 cells/l. In Terrebonne Bay, Louisiana, the following densities (in cells/l) were reported: tintinnids, 540–1400; nonloricate ciliates, 3160–20360; other ciliates, 420–3500; and zooflagellates, up to 18000 (Gifford and Dagg 1988). Smetacek (1981) described

TABLE 8.1   Common Members of Estuarine Meroplankton[a]

Group	Common Members	Larval Stages
Benthic invertebrates	Tunicates	
	Ciona sp.	
	Polychaetes	Trochophore
	Nereis	
	Pomatoceros	
	Notomastus	
	Coelenterates	Planula, Medusa
	Aurelia	
	Cyanea	
	Barnacles	Nauplius, Cyprid
	Balanus	
	Molluscs	Veliger
	Oysters	
	Ostrea, Crassostrea	
	Mussels	
	Mytilus	
	Clams	
	Mercenaria, Rangia	
	Snail	
	Littorina, Neritina	
	Bryozoan	Cyphonautes
	Echinoderms	Pleuteus
	Crabs	Zoea, Megalops
	Sesarma	
	Uca	
	Callinectes	
	Shrimp	
	Peneaus	
Vertebrates	Anchovies	Eggs, Larva,
	Anchoa	Juveniles
	Croaker	
	Micropogonias	
	Menhaden	
	Brevoortia	
	Mullet	
	Mugil	
	Plaice	
	Pleuronectes	
	Mackerel	
	Scomber	
	Cod	
	Gadus	
	Sole	
	Solea	

[a]See figure 8.1 for examples.

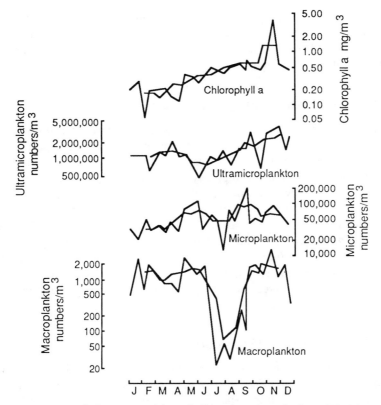

Figure 8.3 Seasonal changes in chlorophyll a, ultramicroplankton (20–64 mm), microzooplankton (64–200 mm), and macroplankton (>200 mm) in Card Sound, Florida (from Reeve and Cosper, 1973 as reproduced in Reeve 1975).

the annual cycle of protozooplankton (hetertrophic flagellates and ciliates) in Kiel Bight, Germany. There were spring and fall peaks with a minimum in the summer. Peak numbers reached 28000 cells/l in the spring and 20000 cells/l in the fall, with the spring peak coinciding with the phytoplankton peak. Nonloricate ciliates dominated the biomass and tintinnids were of little importance. These studies show that microzooplankton densities are generally significantly higher than macrozooplankton, that numbers vary widely, and that the relative importance of different groups of the microzooplankton varies among different estuaries.

There is, therefore, a continuum of size classes of organisms which may be considered as zooplankton. The largest are the gelatinous jellyfishes and ctenophores which are weakly swimming. Ichthyoplankton (such as larvae of anchovies and striped bass) and some small planktivorous fish on the order of 0.5–1.0 cm can be considered at least partially planktonic. Macrozooplankton

(>200 mm) include animals such as adult copepods, chaetognaths, and mero-plankton, while microzooplankton (20-200 mm) include copepod nauplii and ciliates. Finally, heterotrophic nannoplankton (<20 mm), composed of hetero-trophic flagellates and small ciliates, are the smallest class.

8.1.4 Salinity Effects on Species Distribution

The discussion thus far has dealt with zooplankton of medium salinity waters of estuaries. As the salinity becomes fresher or more saline, the species of zoo-plankton change. An extreme example is the Margaree River in the Gulf of St. Lawrence, which is drained completely at low tide because of the extreme tidal range. It has virtually no zooplankton characteristic of estuaries. During high water, a marine assemblage characterized by the marine genera *Calanus, Po-don,* and *Evadne,* is present. At low water, the estuary is fresh and there is a freshwater group with freshwater cladocerans (water fleas) such as *Bosmina, Daphnia,* and *Holopedium* and freshwater copepods such as *Cyclops* and *Diap-tomus* (Haertel and Osterberg 1967). While this case is unusual, these two groups of organisms are representative of those that occur at the extremes of the estuarine salinity gradient.

8.1.5 Examples from Six Estuaries

The information on zooplankton composition discussed above is illustrated for a number of different estuaries in Table 8.2. In the Patuxent River, when a large mesh net was used, adult *Acartia* sp. was the dominant organism. When nets with smaller mesh sizes were used, however, immature copepods (mostly of the genus *Acartia*) were often the most common. The use of nets with a smaller mesh also resulted in higher densities, reflecting the capture of smaller microzooplankton.

8.2 TEMPORAL AND SPATIAL PATTERNS

If we sampled zooplankton in a typical medium-salinity estuary at different loca-tions and depths over an annual cycle, we would find populations of most of the species discussed in Section 8.1. The temporal and spatial composition and den-sity of the community would vary greatly, however. In this section we will discuss these different patterns.

8.2.1 Seasonal Abundance

In the open sea (especially in higher latitudes) there are generally distinct sea-sonal zooplankton peaks. This results from a number of factors. First, the phy-toplankton usually experience distinct spring and fall peaks related to nutrient availability and the seasonal stability of the water column. Since these phyto-

TABLE 8.2 Zooplankton Composition in Six Different Estuaries[a]

Estuary	Patuxent River, Maryland (1)[b]	North Inlet, South Carolina (2)[b]	Sandy Hook, New Jersey (3)[b]	Cord Sound, Florida (4)[b]	Potomac River, Virginia (5)[b]	Eskimo Bay, Canada (6)[b]
Net mesh size/μm	370	153	203	200	150	73
Average annual density/m^{3c}	1425	9258	8052	3765	20,191	121,000
Percent Composition[c]						
Acartia adults	61	19.7	32	75	13.4	4
Immature copepods		17.8	28.6		66.6	41.4
Other copepods	36.3	29.8	17.4	15.8	7	11.8
Meroplankton	1.2	24.2	8.8	7.9	11.2	2.7
Other	1.5	8.2	16.2	1.9	2	41.1

[a]Note that with smaller mesh sizes both the density and composition change. At smaller meshes more immature forms are captured. In the case of Eskimo Bay, many small ciliates were taken.

[b](1) Herman et al. (1968); (2) Lonsdale and Coull (1977); (3) Sage and Herman (1972); (4) Reeve 1975; (5) Sage et al. (1976); (6) Evans and Granger (1980);

[c]With the exception of Eskimo Bay, which is for August.

plankton are practically the only food source for herbivorous zooplankton, the zooplankton tend to follow the seasonal phytoplankton pattern closely. Additionally, because the seasonal recruitment of larvae into the zooplankton has much less effect on population numbers, marine zooplankton are dominanted by holoplankton to a much greater degree than is the plankton of estuaries.

Seasonal abundance of zooplankton in estuaries is much more variable, however, and it is difficult to make generalizations. There are several factors which cause this. Meroplankton are much more important in estuaries and the larvae of different species are recruited into the water column at many different times of the year. There are a variety of different food sources, and estuarine zooplankton are much less dependent on phytoplankton alone than are oceanic species. In addition, estuarine phytoplankton are much less likely to show the spring–fall peak than those of the open sea, partly because most estuaries are shallow and do not stratify in the summer as does the temperate open sea.

Perhaps the most general statement we can make about seasonal changes in zooplankton numbers is that they fluctuate rapidly throughout much of the year although in higher latitudes winter levels generally are lowest. These fluctuations are a result of variable larval recruitment into the population, variable food sources, and physical processes which may bring in or remove both larvae and adults. Nevertheless, many individual species or groups of species show very clear patterns that repeat year after year as that particular species keys in on patterns of environmental variability that are not always clear to the scientific observer.

Although there are no clear general patterns of zooplankton abundance in estuaries, some regional seasonal patterns have been described. For example, zooplankton population fluctuations in high latitude estuaries have a clear seasonal cycle with one or several peaks in midsummer and very low numbers during the winter. This is clearly shown for the Eskimo Lakes–Liverpool Bay estuary in the Canadian Arctic (Fig. 8.4). Note the importance of polychaete and barnacle (cirripedes) larvae to the two summer biomass peaks.

Seasonal abundance of zooplankton in the temperate zone is usually more variable. While there is generally a winter minimum, consisting of adults, a number of workers have also reported summer minima. Both of these conditions occur in Raritan Bay, New Jersey (Fig. 8.2). Sometimes there is a spring peak. In the Patuxent River, for example, adult *Acartia tonsa* attained the highest population densities (about 9000 individuals per cubic meter) in the spring, a time when this species accounted for over 80% of the population (Heinle 1966). A spring peak and summer minima have also been reported along the Louisiana coast (Gillespie 1971, Cuzon du Rest 1963).

The most obvious difference between tropical estuaries and higher latitude ones is the lack of a low seasonal population during the winter. This is true for the Laguna de Terminos, Mexico (Gomez-Aguirre 1974) and Biscayne Bay, Florida (Woodmansee 1958, Reeve 1975). In Card Sound, which is part of Biscayne Bay, there was a distinct summer minimum for the macrozooplankton,

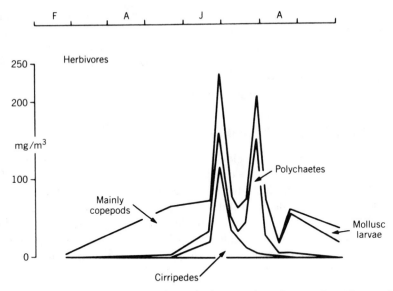

Figure 8.4 Seasonal fluctuations of zooplankton in the Eskimo Lakes–Liverpool Bay estuary in the Canadian Arctic in 1972 (from Evans and Granger 1980).

but this pattern was not seen in microzooplankton (Fig 8.3). A summer minimum was present, but less pronounced, in Biscayne Bay. In Laguna de Terminos, there was a minimum in May and June at the end of the dry season. Higher values occurred in February and in September during periods of relatively high river flow. In a mangrove estuary in Trinidad, Bacon (1971) also found the highest zooplankton populations following periods of rainfall and the lowest during the dry season. Finally, it should be noted that abundance and productivity are not necessarily closely related, so that there may be clearer annual patterns of production than there is for abundance, although few studies have been done.

8.2.2   Daily Vertical Variation

Many estuarine zooplankton exhibit diurnal vertical migration. Organisms such as copepods, cladocerans, chaetognaths, and many larvae react positively to low light intensities and are found near the surface at sunset (Perkins 1974). This general reaction may allow for nighttime feeding in the relative safety of darkness, which reduces predation. For some species the response is much more subtle; for example, the naupliar larvae of a number of barnacles exhibit a photonegative swimming response at low salinities, which in many estuaries will take them into deeper, more saline waters which are nearer their physiological optimum. For example, in the Patuxent River, Maryland, both nauplii and adults of *Acartia tonsa* were more abundant in deeper waters (Heinle 1966). In general, daily vertical movements combined with tidal water mass movements may allow zooplankton populations to maintain their position in the estuary within a given salinity range. This is illustrated in Fig. 8.5 for a hypothetical estuary. Since there is often a net surface outflow and a net inflow along the bottom, zooplankton can maintain their position by vertical migration. It may also allow larvae to migrate over long distances using tidal currents.

8.2.3   Spatial Variability within the Estuary

Because of such factors as complex water mass movements, vertical migration, larval influx, and predation, the distribution of zooplankton in an estuary often is "patchy." This is well illustrated for the Patuxent River where there was high variability for *A. tonsa* between stations (Fig. 8.6). This patchiness also may be due to different species compositions in different parts of the estuary. Jeffries (1967) indicated that different categories of the holoplanktonic copepods are variably abundant in different parts of the estuary (Fig 8.7), indicating that different "patch-producing" processes occur for different species.

8.3   PHYSIOLOGICAL TOLERANCE

Most estuarine zooplankton have evolved broad physiological tolerances to ensure survival in the highly variable conditions of estuaries. *Acartia tonsa,* for example, has a wide salinity and temperature range. Gillespie (1971) collected this species throughout the temperature (5–35°C) and salinity (0.3 to 30 ppt) ranges encountered in Barataria Bay, Louisiana. In the Laguna Madre, Texas, *Acartia* occurred from 10 to 80 ppt, the ctenophores *Beroe ovata* from 10 to 80 ppt, and *Mnemiopsis macradyi* from 10 to 75 ppt, and the copepod *Metis japonica* from 25 to 80 ppt (Simmons 1957)

The following information from Perkins (1974) gives a general indication of the wide range of physiological tolerances of zooplankton. The jelly fish *Aurelia* can survive from 6 to 35 ppt. The eggs and larvae of *Nereis* are resistant to low salinity and anerobic conditions; for example, the larvae of *N. diversicolor* tolerate salinities of 12 to 35 ppt. Many barnacle larvae have the ability to resist salinity change over a wide temperature range. Oyster larvae develop optimally from 17 to 30°C and 12 to 17 ppt, but can survive well beyond this range. The larvae of many molluscs can tolerate substantial silt levels in the water. By contrast the range of tolerance of oceanic species of zooplankton to environmental variation such as mentioned above is very low.

8.4   GROWTH RATE AND PRODUCTION

As we have mentioned before, peak abundance and peak production are not always closely connected in time. This is principally because predation may re-

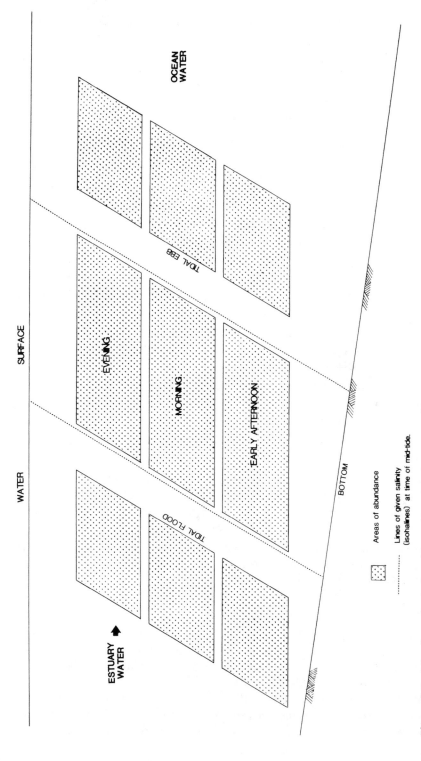

Figure 8.5 Nine hypothetical positions that might be assumed by an estuarine zooplankton population influenced by tidal phase and time of day while remaining within a given salinity range (from Frolander 1964, J. Water Pollution Control Federation).

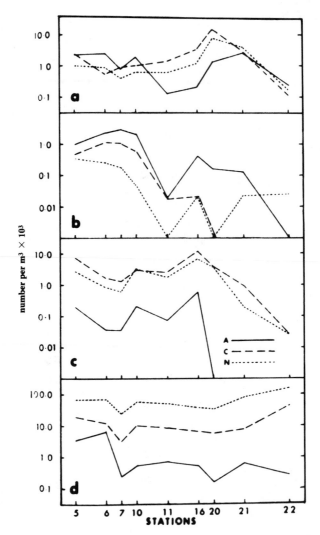

Figure 8.6 Distribution of *Acartia tonsa* in the Patuxent River estuary showing "patchiness" between stations. A, adults, C, copepodites, N, nauplii (from Heinle 1966, used with permission of the Estuarine Research Federation).

move much of the production achieved. Thus one important reason for understanding secondary production is to assess its support of higher trophic levels such as fish. The growth rate and secondary production of zooplankton is dependent on a number of factors, the most important being temperature and food supply. A number of studies have estimated production of estuarine zooplankton and analyzed contributing factors. Heinle (1966) studied production of *Acartia tonsa* in the Patuxent River, Maryland. Growth of this copepod from

NET CIRCULATION PATTERN

SALINITY DISTRIBUTION

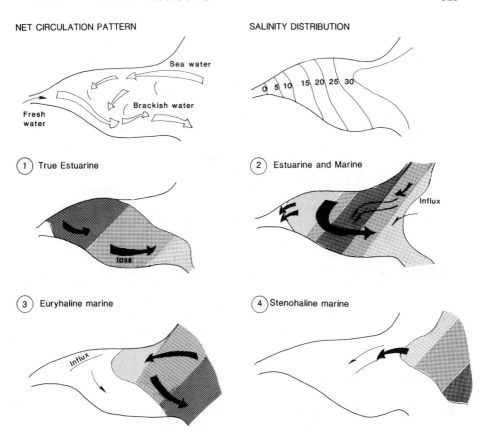

Figure 8.7 Stylized distributions of four categories of holoplanktonic copepods in a hypothetical estuary. Darkened arrows indicate the drift of animals produced in areas shown by diagonal lines; the lines are closely spaced in the centers of propagation. Relative development in an estuary is a function of salinity distribution and net circulation (reprinted from Jefferies 1967, used with permission).

egg to eggs of the next generation required 7, 9, and 13 days at 29.5, 22.4, and 15.5°C, respectively, indicating the strong temperature-dependence of growth. Based on measured growth rates and biomass, Heinle estimated that production for *A. tonsa* during a month period in the summer of 1964 was 0.19 g dry weight/m^2 day. Similar temperature dependence has been shown for a number of meroplanktonic larvae (Perkins 1974).

One indicator of the combined effect of temperature and food on growth is the number of generations a species passes through in 1 year. In most arctic waters, a single generation in a year is the rule. *Acartia clausi,* however, passed through two generations in the Eskimo Lakes–Liverpool Bay estuary in the Canadian arctic (Evans and Granger 1980). The higher growth rate was attributed to warmer (5–12°C) waters in the estuary during the summer, much higher than the near-zero temperatures in the adjacent ocean. *Acartia clausi* also passes through two generations per year in waters near Martha's Vineyard, Massachusetts (Deevey 1948), where the water temperature is similar to that reported for the abovementioned Canadian estuary, and as many as five to six in the English Channel, where the water temperature is somewhat higher (Digby 1950). In tropical Biscayne Bay, Florida, Woodmansee (1958) estimated that *A. tonsa* passed through 11 generations per year. The growth rates reported for microzooplankton are considerably higher than those reported for macrozooplankton. Sherr and Sherr (1983) reported that 2–20-μm zooflagellates in a Georgia estuary had doubling times between 9.7 and 18.2 hours, which is in the range of 8–24 hours for heterotrophic flagellates grown in cultures with varying food densities (Sorokin 1981). In feeding experiments on five tintinnids from coastal waters of the southern California Bight, Heinbokel (1978) found that ingestion and growth rates increased with food concentration up to a maximum similar to growth and uptake curves described in earlier chapters. Maximum hourly ingestion was 10–20% of body weight, doubling times were between 12–24 hours, and growth efficiency exceeded 50% much of the time. Similarly, phagotrophic microflagellates from Kaneohi Bay, Hawaii, consumed about 4.7 times their body weight per day and grew at 1.4 to 1.9 doublings per day (Landry et al. 1984).

8.5   TROPHIC RELATIONSHIPS

Most estuarine net zooplankton are thought to be herbivores, grazing on phytoplankton, and herbivorous zooplankton include most of the holoplankton and many of the meroplankton. The proportion of the available phytoplankton grazed varies widely, however. Heinle (1966) estimated that at least half of the planktonic primary production in the Patuxent River was consumed by *A. tonsa* during the summer months. In contrast, Williams et al. (1968) suggested that food consumption by zooplankton in a shallow, highly turbid estuary in North Carolina was only 2–9% of net photosynthesis by phytoplankton. A later study in the same estuary suggested that macrozooplankton grazing was considerably higher, about 45% (Fulton 1984). In Flax Pond, N.Y., Carlson (1978) estimated that zooplankton consumed 5–13% of the phytoplankton standing crop. Such variable observations indicate that zooplankton are probably of variable importance in regulating phytoplankton populations.

Microzooplankton seem to be much more important grazers than macrozooplankton on phytoplankton primarily because of the much higher density of phytoplankton cells in the nano-size range. The data in table 8.3 show that from 13 to 88% of phytoplankton production or standing crop can be grazed by microzooplankton. In Pacific coastal waters of Washington, the major consumers of phytoplankton were copepod nauplii and tintinnids, while the nonloricate cilliates which comprised 80–90% of the numerical abundance of microzooplankton appeared to contribute little to phytoplankton mortality (Landry and Hassett

TABLE 8.3   Proportion of Nano-Phytoplankton Consumed by Microzooplankton in Different Coastal Systems.

Location	% of phytoplankton consumed	References
Washington coastal waters	6–24% biomass 17–52% daily production	Landry and Hassett 1982
Long Island Sound New York	27% annual aquatic primary production	Capriulo and Carpenter 1983
Long Island Sound New York	max of 41% standing crop per day	Carpenter 1980
Kaneohi Bay	29–37% of standing crop	Landry et al. 1984
Buffan Bay Canada	37–88% potential daily production	Paranjape 1987
Celtic Sea	13–42% of standing crop	Burkill et al. 1987

1982). Microzooplankton also appear to be important consumers of bacterio-plankton. Lessard and Swift (1985) concluded that flagellates and ciliates may be relatively important bacterial consumers. Sherr et al. (1986) found that small protozoa (< 20 μm) appeared to consume 40–45% of bacterioplankton in estua-rine waters near Sapelo Island, Georgia. Microzooplankton can be an important food source for macrozooplankton as Robertson (1983) found that zoea of *Uca* and *Acartia tonsa* fed heavily on tintinnids.

A number of workers have suggested that suspended, organic detritus is an important secondary food source for estuarine macrozooplankton. In Louisiana, large amounts of organic detritus are often collected in zooplankton tows (Gilles-pie 1971, Cuzon du Rest 1963). In addition peak zooplankton populations occur in the spring, a time when phytoplankton biomass is low (Day et al. 1982) and suspended organic matter is high (Happ et al. 1977). Heinle and Flemer (1975) found that the production of algae in the Patuxent River was much less than the requirements of a population of the copepod Eurytemora (*Eurytemora affinis*), and concluded that *E. affinis* must consume detritus to meet part of its energy requirement. Heinle et al. (1977) fed a variety of detrital foods derived from marsh plants to two species of estuarine copepods. The copepods did not survive well or produce eggs when feeding on detritus with small amounts of microbiota, but did well when a rich and abundant microbiota was present. Ciliated protozo-ans appeared to be particularly important in the quality of detrital food for cope-pods. In a similar study, Roman (1984) measured the ingenstion, survivorship, and growth of *A. tonsa* when fed on mixtures of the diatom, *Thalassiosira weissflogii,* and detritus from the seagrass, *Thalassia testudinum.* Copepods fed on detritus survived better than controls in filtered seawater but not as well as those fed on diatoms. Addition of detritus to low and intermediate diatom con-centrations enhanced survival over experiments with diatoms alone. These results suggest that in estuaries with relatively high levels of detritus, the more abundant detritus might supply most of the carbon, nitrogen, and calories to support zooplankton growth while phytoplankton supply essential amino acids, fatty acids, and vitamins. Based on these results it appears that organic detritus may at times be an important food source for the zooplankton.

Zooplankton serve as food for a variety of estuarine consumers. Some of the zooplankton are themselves carnivorous, so that smaller zooplankton may be food for larger ones. Completely or partially carnivorous zooplankton include some copepods, such as *Labidocera aestiva,* meroplankton such as decapod and fish larvae, and jelly fishes and ctenophores. Some zooplankton that are normally considered herbivores exhibit at times carnivorous feeding behavior. For example, Lonsdale et al. (1979) showed that *Acartia tonsa* fed at significantly higher rates on nauplii of other species. Feeding on nauplii allows adult copepods to feed indirectly on the very small nanoplankton which they cannot filter directly. It also provides them with a higher quality food.

It has been noted by a number of authors that an increase in tentaculate ctenophores (and sometimes jelly fishes) is often accompanied by decreases in copepods. This has been found in shallow bays of Long Island Sound (Barlow 1955), Narragansett Bay (Deason and Smayda 1982), Delaware Bay (Cronin et al. 1962), the Patuxent River (Herman et al. 1968), the Mississippi Sound (Philips et al. 1969), and Barataria Bay (Gillespie 1971). Philips et al. concluded that ctenophores and jelly fishes constituted the most important group of predators on zooplankton because of their periodic extreme local abundance and their voracious feeding habits. Deason and Smayda (1982) studied ctenophore–zooplankton–phytoplankton interactions in Narragansett Bay, Rhode Island during 1972-1977. They found that in four of the years, the beginning of the pulse by the ctenophore, *Mnemiopsis leidyi,* was accompanied by a rapid decline in zooplankton density and a summer phytoplankton bloom. Yearly variations in the density of the diatom, *Skeletonema costatum,* were related to the size of the ctenophore pulse. Deason and Smayda concluded that the ctenophores regulated both zooplankton and phytoplankton populations. The control on phytoplankton is both indirect through grazing on zooplankton and direct by nutrient excretion.

Several studies have indicated that zooplankton production was insufficient to meet ctenophore nutrition. Carlson (1978) concluded that in Flax Pond crustaceans and phytoplankton were sufficient to support only 55% of estimated ctenophore food needs during the summer. The only other potential food source which, when combined with phytoplankton and zooplankton, was sufficient to meet ctenophore energy demands was suspended organic detritus. Carlson suggested that a combination of the three food types was utilized. Heinle (1974) also concluded, from an analysis of published data, that total biomass of zooplankton in the Patuxent River was inadequate to meet the minimum energy demands of ctenophores and jelly fish for part of the year. Phytoplankton stocks were more than adequate, however. Heinle concluded that the most efficient feeding strategy for ctenophores and jelly fish would be nonselective filter feeding.

These conclusions are complicated by the fact that jelly fish eat ctenophores (Cargo and Shultz 1966). In addition, some ctenophores eat other ctenophores. For example, *Beroe cucumis* is known to feed on *Pleurobrachia* (Raymont 1963). Fraser (1962) reported that when *Pleurobrachia* was abundant the rest of the plankton was not; however, if *Beroe* was numerous, it ate *Pleurobrachia* and the plankton thrived. From the evidence presented here it is obvious that ctenophores are important predators on zooplankton and that organic detritus is probably also an important food source. But the precise nature of their nutritional value is yet to be worked out.

Other important feeders on zooplankton include many of the smaller pelagic forage fish such as anchovies, silversides, and shads, as well as the young of many fishes. Philips et al. (1969) noted that ctenophores and jelly fishes are fed on by several fishes, crabs, and shore birds.

8.6   ECOLOGICAL RELATIONSHIPS

In this section we want to summarize the information on zooplankton and discuss two questions. What are the factors that control zooplankton abundance, composition, and growth rate? What is the role of zooplankton in the overall estuarine ecosystem?

8.6.1   Factors Controlling Zooplankton

Temperature, food supply, and predation have been identified as the main factors controlling zooplankton populations in general. In addition, salinity obviously is important for estuarine species because of the range of values encountered. We will discuss each of these separately.

The information discussed earlier in this chapter shows that the growth rate of zooplankton is temperature-dependent, resulting in a higher number of generations per year in warmer waters. Thus seasonal population fluctuations are partially related to temperature, especially in temperate and arctic regions. These seasonal changes also result from larval recruitment which is partially temperature-dependent. In contrast, temperature appears to play a relatively minor role in determining species composition of estuarine zooplankton except by determining relative species growth rates. Most species are eurythermal and tolerate broad temperature ranges. There are some species changes (i.e., *A. clausi* for *A. tonsa* in colder waters), but most species have a broad range.

In contrast to most marine zooplankton, herbivorous estuarine zooplankton are often not considered to be food limited. The studies that have been undertaken indicate that they generally consume no more than 50%, and often much less, of phytoplankton production. In addition, estuarine zooplankton standing crop fluctuations often do not follow phytoplankton standing crop changes, as is the case in Fig. 8.3, where chlorophyll a is a measure of phytoplankton standing crop. Recent evidence suggests, however, that at low chlorophyll concentrations, zooplankton may be food limited (Mullin 1988). The ready availability of organic detritus as a food in estuaries makes the potential food resources available to herbivores even greater. Carnivorous zooplankton (i.e., ctenophores), however, may at times be food-limited.

Predation appears to be a major force affecting the standing crop of herbivorous zooplankton. A number of studies (see Section 8.5) have shown that when predators on macrozooplankton (such as ctenophores) are abundant, standing crop of the prey zooplankton decreases. In addition, two studies estimated that zooplankton standing crop is insufficient to meet energy demands of planktivores. Smetacek (1981) found that predation by macroplankton was an important factor regulating the size of protozooplankton populations in Kiel Bight, Germany.

Salinity affects the overall composition of the zooplankton community and may affect individual species at different stages of their life cycle. Although most estuarine zooplankton species are euryhaline, many studies have shown that individual zooplankton species have optimum salinity ranges, and that they do not grow well and may not survive outside these ranges (see Section 8.3). The tolerances of all the individual species collectively seem to produce an optimum for the community in general. For example, in Barataria Bay the highest zooplankton volumes occurred in the range of 5–20 ppt, a salinity range which characterizes the bay for most of the year. Thus, in summary, temperature, salinity, food, and grazing have been identified as being important in regulating zooplankton abundance.

8.6.2 Ecological Role of Zooplankton

Zooplankton play several important roles in estuarine ecosystems. They serve as an important link between phytoplankton primary production and many important estuarine carnivores, including many commercial fish, and they can regulate phytoplankton populations through grazing. A large number of benthic and nektonic adults spend part of their life in the zooplankton, and as such the plankton stage influences the distribution and abundance of adult populations. Zooplankton appear important in nutrient cycling in at least some estuaries and coastal waters. These roles are developed below.

As we noted above, the amount of net phytoplankton production consumed by zooplankton is variable, ranging from less than 5% to greater than 50%. Thus at times zooplankton can be the main consumers of phytoplankton. This especially seems true for microzooplankton grazing on nanoplankton. Zooplankton are an important food for a variety of estuarine consumers, including ctenophores, some meroplanktonic larvae, a number of important forage fish, and some benthic organisms such as sponges and molluscs (Reeve 1975, see also Section 8.5). Microzooplankton, such as tintimids, may be an important link between nanoplankton, bacterioplankton, and the macrozooplankton. Thus zooplankton are an important link in the grazing food chain of estuaries. They may also be important in transferring energy from one ecosystem to another. Carlson (1978) presented an example of an entire ecosystem "feeding" on zooplankton. He measured the flux of zooplankton washed into and out of Flax

Pond with the tides. On an annual basis, the salt marsh "consumed" zooplankton, as more moved into Flax Pond than moved out. Carlson suggested that grazing by the abundant plankton-feeding fish community inside the pond was responsible for the net "consumption."

A number of authors have suggested that zooplankton grazing is an important factor controlling the density, species composition, and size distribution of phytoplankton (Martin 1970, Poulet 1978, Ryther and Sanders 1980, Lynch and Shapiro 1981, Deason and Smayda 1982). If grazing does determine phytoplankton species composition, however, it would require that zooplankton feed selectively. There is some controversy, however, as to whether zooplankton are opportunistic feeders (where zooplankton feed on the most abundant food) or whether there is size-specific feeding. Several factors could be responsible for selective grazing on particular types of zooplankton, including differences in size, morphology, and chemical composition of phytoplankton, the structure of the grazer's mouth parts or the relationship between the size of the grazer and the size of the food. While it is almost certainly true that grazing sometimes structures phytoplankton communities, it is not known if this is a general phenomena.

Another interesting question about the estuarine zooplankton community is the existence of a wide variety of nonplanktonic organisms that spend a part of their life cycle as zooplankton (Table 8.2). There are differing opinions as to why so many organisms should have planktonic stages.

Some hold that it is a dispersive phase concerned only with ensuring a widespread distribution of species, others that it is a means by which the young organism can take advantage of large supplies of "baby food," e.g. nanoplankton which is so important to some larvae. Still others hold that by first releasing and then feeding upon large numbers of these larvae the benthos is extending its food supply. There is no doubt that whichever of these postulates is true, larvae are very abundant at certain times of the year (Perkins 1974).

Earlier we showed that some members of the zooplankton community could maintain position within a section of estuary by vertical migration. Sandifer (1975) studied the distribution of several larval decapod crustaceans in the lower Chesapeake Bay. He found that larvae of species which were most dependent on estuarine existence were more abundant in the lower layer of the water column where there is a net upstream transport and thus tended to be retained within the estuary. This process is called larval retention. For these species, larval retention seemed to be the primary mechanism for recruitment of adult estuarine populations. No distributional adaptation for retention was observed for species not restricted to estuarine habitats. The major mechanism by which the estuarine populations of such species are restocked is probably immigration of juveniles or adults. The more dependent a given species is on the estuarine habitats, the more likely it is to exhibit recruitment by larval retention.

Another way in which zooplankton may be important in the processes of the estuary as a whole is their role in nutrient cycling. Because of their high densities

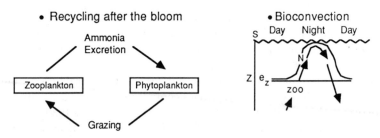

Figure 8.8 Two possible ways that zooplankton may be important in the remineralization and transport of nutrients (from Harris 1959).

and feeding rates, zooplankton can remineralize large amounts of inorganic nutrients. In addition, they may be important in moving nutrients from deeper waters to the surface during vertical migrations. Based on studies of phytoplankton–nutrient interaction in Long Island Sound by a group of scientists at Bingham School of Oceanography, Harris (1959) suggested a model of the role of zooplankton in nutrient cycling.

He observed that ammonia and nitrate were equally good substrates for primary production, and that zooplankton and bacteria were good sources of ammonia. Harris concluded that ammonia production was a function of the grazing rate of phytoplankton by herbivores, and hence that new plant growth was accelerated by zooplankton feeding. Harris argued that this system operated in all of the oligotrophic areas of the oceans and the large changes in phytoplankton abundance was largely the result of the input of nutrients by way of vertical mixing, and not by ammonium release from zooplankton. Hence for most oligotrophic areas, changes in numbers of phytoplankton in time and space could best be described as monotonous. Harris also implicated the zooplankton in the vertical transport of nutrients. He recognized that during daylight the phytoplankton might be temporarily nutrient deficient. However, at night, zooplankton migrating upward to feed in surface layers would excrete nitrogen as ammonia, thereby recharging the euphotic zone with nigrogen. Harris named this process appropriately "bioconvection" (Fig. 8.8). Thus we see that the production and consumption processes of estuaries are very tightly linked. Later work suggests that grazing by microzooplankton on nanophytoplankton and bacterioplankton may be very important in nitrogen regeneration (Sherr et al. 1986).

REFERENCES

Achuthankutty, C.T., M.J. George, and S.C. Goswami, 1977. Larval ingression of penaeid prawns in the estuaries of Goa. Proceedings of the Symposium on Warm Water Zooplankton. Publication of the National Institute of Oceanography, Goa, UNESCO, pp. 412–424.

Bacon, P.R., 1971. Plankton studies in a Caribbean estuarine environment. Caribb. J. Sci., 11(1–2):81–90.

Barlow, J.P., 1952. Maintenance and dispersal of the endemic zooplankton population of a tidal estuary, Great Pond, Falmouth, Massachusetts. PhD Thesis, Harvard University, Cambridge, MA.

Barlow, J.P., 1955. Physical and biological processes determining the distribution of zooplankton in a tidal estuary. Biol. Bull., 109:211-225.

Burkill, P., R. Mantoura, C. Llewellyn, and N. Owens, 1987. Microzooplankton and selectivity of phytoplankton in coastal waters. Mar. Biol. 93:581-590.

Calef, G.W. and G.D. Grice, 1967. Influence of the Amazon River outflow on the ecology of the western tropical Atlantic. 2. Zooplankton abundance, Copepod distribution, with remarks on the fauna of low-salinity areas. J. Mar. Res., 25:84-96.

Caperon, J., 1975. A trophic level ecosystem model analysis of the plankton community in a shallow water, subtropical estuarine embayment. In E. Cronin (Ed.), Estuarine Research: Chemistry, Biology and the Estuarine System. Academic, New York, Vol. 1, pp. 691-709.

Capriulo, G, and E. Carpenter, 1980. Grazing by 35-102 μm microzooplankton in Long Island Sound. Mar. Biol., 56:319-326.

Capriulo, G, and E. Carpenter, 1983. Abundance, species composition and feeding impact of tintinnid-zooplankton in central Long Island Sound. Mar. Ecol. Prog. Ser., 10:277-288.

Cargo, D.G. and L.P. Schultz, 1966. Notes on the biology of the sea nettle, *Chrysaora quinquecirrha,* in Chesapeake Bay. Chesapeake Sci., 7(2):95-100.

Carlson, D.M., 1978. The ecological role of zooplankton in a Long Island salt marsh. Estuaries, 1(2):85-92.

Carricker, M.R., 1951. Ecological observations on the distribution of oyster larvae in New Jersey estuaries. Ecol. Monogr., 21:19-38.

Chandramohan, P. and T.S.S. Rao, 1972. Tidal cycle studies in relation to zooplankton distribution in Godavari estuary. Proc. Indian Acad. Sci., 75(1):23-31.

Cronin L.E., J.C. Daiber, and E.M. Hulburt, 1962. Quantitative seasonal aspects of zooplankton in the Delaware River estuary. Chesapeake Sci., 3:63-93.

Cuzon du Rest, R.P., 1963. Distribution of the zooplankton in the salt marshes of southeastern Louisiana. Publ. Inst. Mar. Sci., Univ. Texas, 9:132 155.

Day, J.W., Jr., C.S. Hopkinson, and W.H. Conner, 1982. An analysis of environmental factors regulating community metabolism and fisheries production in a Louisiana estuary. In V.S. Kennedy, (Ed.), Estuarine comparisons. Academic Press, New York, pp. 121-136.

Darnell, R.M., 1961. Trophic spectrum of an estuarine community based on studies of Lake Pontchartrain, Louisiana. Ecology, 42(2):553-568.

Deason, E.E. and T.J. Smayda, 1982. Ctenophore-zooplankton-phytoplankton interactions in Narragansett Bay, Rhode Island, USA, during 1972-1977. J. Plankton Res., 4(2):203-217.

Deevey, G.B., 1948. The zooplankton of Tisbury Great Pond. Bull. Bingham Oceanogr. Coll., 12(1):1-44.

Deevey, G.B., 1952. A survey of the zooplankton of Block Island Sound, 1943-1946. Bull. Bingham Oceanogr. Coll., 13(3):65-119.

Deevey, G.B., 1956. Oceanography of Long Island Sound. V. Zooplankton. Bull. Bingham Oceanogr. Coll., 15:114-155.

Digby, P.S., 1950. The biology of the small planktonic copepods off Plymonth. J. Mar. Biol. Ass., U.K., 29:393-438.

Dhawan, R.M., 1970. Plankton and hydrobiological features at Kandla in the Gulf of Kutch during 1960-1963. Indian J. Fish., 17(1-3):122-131.

Easterly, C.O., 1928. The periodic occurrence of copepods in the marine plankton of two successive years at La Jolla, California. Bull. Scripps Inst. Oceanogr, Tech., 1:247-345.

Evans, M.S. and E.H. Granger, 1980. Zooplankton in a Canadian Arctic estuary. In V. S. Kennedy (Ed.), Estuarine Perspectives. Academic, New York, pp. 199-210.

Fraser, J.H., 1962. The role of ctenophores and salps in zooplankton production and standing crop. Rapp. P.-V. Reun., Cons. Int. Explor. Mer, 153:121-123.

Frolander, H.F., 1964. Biological and chemical features of tidal estuaries. J. Water Poll. Contr. Fed. 36(8):1037-1048.

Fulton, R., 1984. Distribution and community structure of estuarine copepods. Estuaries, 7:38-50.

Gifford, D.J. and M.J. Dagg, 1988. Feeding of the estuarine copepod *Acartia tonsa* Dana: carnivory versus herbivory in natural microplankton assemblages. Bull. Mar. Sci., 43:(in press).

Gillespie, M.C., 1971. Analysis and treatment of zooplankton of estuarine waters of Louisiana. Cooperative Gulf of Mexico Estuarine Inventory and Study, Louisiana Phase IV., Biology. Louisiana Wildlife and Fisheries Commission, pp. 108-175.

Gomez-Aguirre, S., 1974. Recomocimientos estacionales de hidrologia y plancton en la Laguna de Terminos, Campeche, Mexico. An. Cent. Cienc. Mar Limnol. Nal. Auton. Mexico 1(1):61-82.

Goswami, S.C. and R.A. Selvakumar, 1977. Plankton studies in the estuarine system of Goa. Proceedings of the Symposium on Warm Water Zooplankton. Special Publication of the National Institute of Oceanography, Goa, UNESCO, pp. 226-241.

Haertel, L. and C. Osterberg, 1967. Ecology of zooplankton, benthos, and fishes in the Columbia River estuary. Ecology, 48(3):459-472.

Happ, G., J.G. Gosselink, and J.W. Day, Jr., 1977. The seasonal distribution of organic carbon in a Louisiana estuary. Estuarine Coastal Mar. Sci., 5:695-705.

Harris, E., 1959. The nitrogen cycle in Long Island Sound. Bull. Bingham Oceanogr. Collect., 17:31.

Heinbokel, J., 1978. Studies on the functional role of tintinnids in the southern California Bight. I. Grazing and growth rates in laboratory cultures. Mar. Biol., 47:177-189.

Heinle, D.R., 1966. Production of a calanoid copepod *Acartia tonsa*, in the Patuxent River Estuary. Chesapeake Sci., 7(2):59-74.

Heinle, D.R., 1974. An alternate grazing hypothesis for the Patuxent estuary. Chesapeake Sci., 15(3):146-150.

Heinle, D.R. and D. Flemer, 1975. Carbon requirements of a population of the estuarine copepod *Eurytemora affinis*. Mar. Biol., 31:235-247.

Heinle, D.R., R.P. Harris, J.F. Ustach, and D.A. Flemer, 1976. Detritus as food for estuarine copepods. Mar. Biol., 40:341-353.

Herman, S.S. and J.R. Beers, 1969. The ecology of inshore plankton population in Bermuda. Part II. Seasonal abundance and composition of the zooplankton. Bull. Mar. Sci., 19:483-503.

Herman, S.S., J.A. Mihursky, and A.J. McErlean, 1968. Zooplankton and environmenal characteristics of the Patuxent River Estuary. 1963-1965. Chesapeake Sci., 9(2):67-82.

Hopkins, T.L., 1966. Plankton of the St. Andrew Bay system of Florida. Publ. Inst. Mar. Sci. Univ. Texas, 11:12-64.

Hopper, A.F., 1960. The resistance of marine zooplankton of the Caribbean and South Atlantic to changes in salinity. Limnol. Oceanogr., 5:43-47.

Jeffries, H.P., 1962. Succession of two *Acartia* species in estuaries. Limnol. Oceanogr., 7(3):

Jeffries, H.P., 1967. Saturation of estuarine zooplankton by congeneric associates. In G.H. Lauff (Ed.), Estuaries. Amer. Assoc. Adv. Sci. Spec. Publ., 83:500-508.

Kaliamurthy, M., 1975. Observations on the plankton ecology of Pulicat Lake. Indian J. Fish., 22:86-95.

Lance, J., 1963. The salinity tolerance of some estuarine planktonic copepods. Limnol. Oceanogr., 8:440-449.

Landry, M., and R. Hassett, 1982. Estimating the grazing impact of marine micro-zooplankton. Mar. Biol., 67:283-288.

Landry, M., L. Hass, and V. Fagerness, 1984. Dynamics of microbial plankton communities: experiments in Kaneohe Bay, Hawaii. Mar. Ecol. Prog. Ser., 16:127-133.

Lessard, E., and E. Swift, 1985. Species-specific grazing rates of heterotrophic dinoflagellates in oceanic waters, measured with dual-label radioisotope technique. Mar. Biol., 87:289-296.

Lewis, R.M. and W.C. Mann, 1971. Occurrence and abundance of larval Atlantic Menhaden, *Brevoortia tyrannus* at two North Carolina inlets with notes on associated species. Trans. Am. Fish. Soc., 100(2):296-301.

Lonsdale, D.J. and B.C. Coull. 1977. Composition and seasonality of zooplankton of North Inlet, South Carolina. Chesapeake Sci., 18:272-283.

Lonsdale, D.C., D. Heinle, and C. Siegfried, 1979. Carniverous feeding behavior of the adult calanoid copepod *Acartia tonsa* Dana. J. Exp. Mar. Biol. Ecol., 36:235-248.

Lynch, M. and J. Shapiro, 1981. Predation, enrichment and phytoplankton community structure. Limnol. Oceanogr., 26(1):86-102.

Madhupratap, M., T.S.S. Rao, and P. Haridas, 1977. Secondary production in the Cochin backwaters, a tropical monsoonal estuary. Proceedings of the Symposium on Warm Water Zooplankton. Special Publication of the National Institute of Oceanography, Goa, UNESCO, pp. 515-519.

Manrique, F.A., 1977. Seasonal variation of zooplankton in the Gulf of California. Proceedings of the Symposium on Warm Water Zooplankton. Special Publication of the National Instute of Oceanography, Goa, UNESCO, pp. 242-249.

Mansueti, A.J. and J.D. Hardy, Jr., 1967. Development of fishes of the Chesapeake Bay region, and atlas of egg, larval, and juvenile stages, Pt. I. Natural Resources Institute, University of Maryland, 202 pp.

Martin, J.H., 1968. Phytoplankton-zooplankton relationships in Narragansett Bay. III. Seasonal changes in zooplankton excretion rates in relation to phytoplankton abundance. Limnol. Oceanogr., 13(1):63-71.

Martin, J.H., 1970. Phytoplankton-zooplankton relationships in Narragansett Bay. IV. The seasonal importance of grazing. Limnol. Oceanogr., 15:414-418.

Martinez-Guerrero, A., 1978. Distribucion y varacion estacional del zooplankton en cinco lagunas costeras del estado de Guerrero. Am. Centr. Cienc. Mar. Limnol. Univ. Nat. Auton. Mexico, 5(1):201-214.

Mohan, P. Ch., 1977. Seasonal distribution of copepods in the Godavari estuary. Proceedings of the Symposium on Warm Water Zooplankton. Special Publication of the National Institute of Oceanography, Goa, UNESCO, pp. 330-336.

Mullin, M.M., 1988. Production and distribution of nauplii and recruitment variability—putting the pieces together. In B.J. Rothschild (Ed.), Toward a Theory on Biological-Physical Interactions in the World Ocean, Kluwer Academic Publishers, pp. 297-320.

Paranjape, M., 1987. Grazing by microzooplankton in the eastern Canadian arctic in summer. Mar. Ecol. Prog. Ser., 40:239-246.

Perkins, E.J., 1974. The Biology of Estuaries and Coastal Waters. Academic, London, 678 pp.

Peters, D.S., 1971. Planktonic copepod (Crustacia: Harpacticoida) distibution and regulating factors in the Pamlico River Estuary. ASB Bull., 18(2):50.

Philips, R.J., W.D. Burke, and E.J. Keener, 1969. Observations on the trophic significance of jelly fishes in Mississippi Sound with quantitative data on the associative behavior of small fishes with medusae. Trans. Am. Fish. Soc., 98(4):703-712.

Poulet, S., 1978. Comparison between five naturally coexisting species of marine copepods feeding on naturally occurring particulate matter. Limnol. Oceanogr., 23(6):1126-1143.

Prasad, R.R., 1969. Zooplankton biomass in the Arabian sea and the Bay of Bengal with a discussion on the fisheries of the regions. Proc. Natl. Inst. Sci. India, 35(5):399-437.

Rao, T.S.S., 1977. Salinity and distribution of brackish warm water zooplankton in Indian Estuaries. Proceedings of the Symposium on Warm Water Zooplankton. Special Publication of the National Institute of Oceanography, Goa, UNESCO, pp. 196-204.

Rasim, S.Z., 1977. Contribution of zooplankton in the food chains of some warm water environments. Proceedings of the Symposium on Warm Water Zooplankton. Special Publication of the National Institute of Oceanography, Goa, UNESCO, pp. 700-708.

Raymont, J.E., 1963. Plankton and Productivity in the Oceans. Pergamon Press, New York, 660 pp.

Reeve, M.R., 1964. Studies on the seasonal variation of the zooplankton in a marine subtropical inshore environment. Bull. Mar. Sci., 14:103-122.

Reeve, M.R., 1970. Seasonal changes in the zooplankton of south Biscayne Bay and some problems of assessing the effects on the zooplankton of natural and artificial thermal and other fluctuations. Bull. Mar. Sci., 20:894-921.

Reeve, M.R., 1975. The ecological significance of the zooplankton in the shallow subtropical waters of South Florida. In E. Cronin (Ed.), Estuarine Research: Chemistry, Biology and the Estuarine System. Academic, New York, Vol. 1, pp. 352-371.

Reeve, M.R. and E. Cosper, 1973. The plankton and other seston in Card Sound, Soutrh Florida, in 1971. Univ. Miami Tech. Rept., UM-RSMAS-73007. 24 pp. (Unpublished manuscript)

Riley, G.A., 1967. The plankton of estuaries. In G.H. Lauff (Ed.), Estuaries. Amer. Assoc. Adv. Sci. Spec. Publ., 83:316-326.

Robertson, J., 1983. Predation by estuarine zooplankton on tintinnid ciliates. Est. Coast. Shelf Sci., 16:27-36.

Roman, M. R. 1984. Utilization of detritus by the copepod, *Acartia tonsa.* Limnol. Oceanogr. 29(5):949-959.

Ryther, J. and J. Sanders, 1980. Experimental evidence of zooplankton control of the species composition and size distribution of marine phytoplankton. Mar. Ecol. Prog. Ser., 3:279-283.

Sage, L.E. and S.S. Herman, 1972. Zooplankton of the Sandy Hook area, N.J. Chesapeake Sci., 13(1):29-39.

Sage, L.E., J.M. Summerfield, and M.M. Olson. 1976. Zooplankton of the Potomac Estuary. The Potomac Estuary: Biological Resources, Trends and Options. Interstate Commission on the Potomac River Basin/Maryland Power Plant Siting Program.

Sandifer, P.A., 1975. The role of pelagic larvae in recruitment to populations of adult decapod crustaceans in the York River Estuary and adjacent lower Chesapeake Bay, Virginia. Estuarine Coastal Mar. Sci., 3:269-279.

Sherr, B., and E. Sherr, 1983. Enumeration of heterotrophic microprotozoa by epifluorescence microscopy. Est. Coast. Shelf Sci., 16:1-7.

Sherr, B., E. Sherr, T. Andrew, R. Fallon, and S. Newel, 1986. Trophic interactions between heterotrophic protozoa and bacterioplankton in estuarine water analyzed with selective metabolic inhibitors. Mar. Ecol. Prog. Ser., 32:169-179.

Simmons, E.G., 1957. An ecological survey of the upper Laguna Madre of Texas. Publ. Inst. Mar. Sci. Univ. Texas, 4(2):156-200.

Smetacek, V., 1981. The annual cycle of protozooplankton in the Kiel Bight. Mar. Biol., 63:1-11.

Sorokin, Y., 1981. Microheterotrophic organisms in marine ecosystems. In A. Longhurst (Ed.), Analysis of Marine Ecosystems. Academic Press, New York, pp. 293-342.

Stoecker, D., A. Michaels, and L. Davis, 1987. Large proportion of marine planktonic ciliates found to contain functional chloroplasts. Nature, 326:790-792.

Thompson, P.K.M. and D.C.V. Easterson, 1977. Dynamics of cyclopoid population in a tropical estuary. Proceedings of the Symposium on Warm Water Zooplankton. Special Publication of the National Institute of Oceanography, Goa, UNESCO, pp. 486-496.

Wickstead, J.H., 1958. A survey of the larger zooplankton of Singapore Straits. J. Cons. Int. Explor. Mar., 23:340-353.

Wiley, M.L., T.S.Y. Koo, and L.E. Cronin, 1973. Finfish productivity in coastal marshes and estuaries. In R.H. Chabreck (Ed.), Proceedings of the 2nd Coastal Marsh and Estuary Managment Symposium. Louisiana State University Division of Continuing Education, Baton Rouge, pp. 139-150.

Williams, A.B., 1971. A ten-year study of meroplankton in North Carolina estuaries: Annual occurrence of some brachyuran developmental stages. Chesapeake Sci., 12(2):53-61.

Williams, R.B., M.B. Murdoch, and L.K. Thomas, 1968. Standing crop and importance of zooplankton in a system of shallow estuaries. Chesapeake Sci., 9(1):42-51.

Wood, L. and W.J. Hargis, Jr., 1971. Transport of bivalve larvae in a tidal estuary. Fourth European Marine Biology Symposium, pp. 29-44.

Woodmansee, A., 1958. The seasonal diistribution of the zooplankton of Chicken Key in Biscayne Bay, Fla. Ecology, 39(2):247-262.

Yentsch, C.S., 1980. Phytoplankton growth in the sea: A coalescence of disciplines. In P. Falkowski (Ed.), Primary Productivity in the Sea. Plenum, New York, pp. 17-32.

OFFPRINTS FROM: ESTUARINE ECOLOGY
Edited by John W. Day Jr., Charles A. S. Hall., Dr. W. Michael Kemp, and Alejandro Yáñez-Arancibia
Copyright © 1989 by John Wiley & Sons, Inc.

■ **9**

The Estuarine Bottom and Benthic Subsystem

9.1 INTRODUCTION

The bottom substrate of estuaries provides a residence for many sessile, burrowing, crawling, and even swimming organisms, a storehouse of organic matter and inorganic nutrients, and a site for many vital chemical exchanges and physical interactions. One might even conclude that the primary attribute of estuaries that clearly distinguishes them from deep-water marine systems is that estuaries have bottoms that interact strongly with sunlit surface waters. The bottom of an estuary regulates or modifies most physical, chemical, geological, and biological processes throughout the entire estuarine system via what could be called a *benthic effect*. In earlier chapters we considered various aspects of the chemistry, plant life, and microbial ecology of the bottom. The primary objective of this chapter is to familiarize the reader with benthic animals and consider in more detail benthic processes, including the benthic effect. We first introduce the reader to some basic terms and descriptive material and then describe some prominent benthic organisms found in estuaries. Finally we describe the various processes that together comprise the benthic effect.

This chapter is intended to provide a broad overview of benthic organisms and processes in estuaries. It is far from exhaustive in that the extant literature on benthic organisms in coastal ecosystems is enormous. Carriker (1967) and Coull (1973) review benthic organisms and processes. More recently Wolff (1983) reviewed estuarine benthic ecology. An excellent broad, process-oriented discussion of the benthic community dynamics in coastal waters is presented by Mann (1982). Parsons et al. (1977) presented an overview of marine benthic ecology. Rhoads (1974) discussed marine benthic organisms and processes of muddy bottoms. Intertidal flats are reviewed by Whitlatch (1982) and Peterson and Peterson (1979), open bay bottoms by Armstrong (1987), and oyster reefs by Bahr and Lanier (1981).

Benthic is an adjective of Greek origin, the root of which originally alluded to depths of the sea. Benthic is frequently applied to a wide range of subjects including organisms, sediments, processes, ecosystems, and even ecologists who specialize in aquatic bottom communities (cf., Positions Wanted columns in technical journals). The noun *benthos* is generally intended to include the entire bottom community and its immediate physical environment, all of which together have been termed the *benthic boundary layer* (McCave 1976).

Just as estuaries are broadly defined to span entire coastal zones, so the benthic boundary layer in an estuary encompasses a wide range of physicochemical conditions. For example, estuarine bottoms can include depths from about 200 m or more in deep estuaries such as fjords, to the highest intertidal level (or even splash zone) at the shore.

The environmental extremes that must be endured by benthic organisms are greatest in the high intertidal zone. Dessication and extreme ranges of temperature, salinity, dissolved oxygen, and current velocity produce physiological and physical stresses on intertidal benthic organisms in many estuaries and tolerance limits of organisms are often taxed. Environmental variability is less in deeper water, so intertidal and shallow subtidal environments are generally much more stressful than deep benthic environments.

Benthic organisms comprise a broad assemblage of diverse forms that are related only by their distribution in space, rather than by phylogeny or exclusive functional attributes. Nevertheless, the fact that they spend part or all of their lives in intimate association with the bottom results in certain unifying consequences, both for the animals and for the estuary. Benthic animals are directly or indirectly involved in most physical and chemical processes that occur in estuaries. These processes sometimes compliment and sometimes contradict each other. For example, some animals clarify the water by filtering particulate matter, while others increase turbidity by stirring up sediments. All benthic heterotrophs regenerate nutrients that can stimulate primary production, and nearly all serve as food for birds and for the large numbers of demersal nekton that characterize these shallow water systems. Humans also feed avidly on certain benthic organisms, as demonstrated by the large harvests and economic value of oyster, mussel, and clam fisheries in many coastal areas. Some benthic animals filter the water for food and thus compete with swimming filter feeders; however, bottom dwellers also release enormous numbers of eggs and larvae every year that contribute to the pool of floating food.

Some benthic animals "soften" their environment by biodepositing blankets of fecal matter, while others build solid reefs. Most benthic animals remove oxygen from the bottom zone, but some irrigate and oxygenate the sediments by pumping water into them. Many benthic animals scavenge toxic materials and pathogenic organisms from the water column and concentrate these materials in their tissues. This process can in turn result in the concentration of toxic materials in the animals that feed in the bottom. Each of these benthic processes is discussed in more detail below. But let us first examine a typical estuarine bottom and its residents by burrowing into it, raising a plume of sediment as we do.

9.2   THE BENTHIC ENVIRONMENT AND COMMUNITY STRUCTURE

The bottom of an estuary is often obscured (even to a diver) by turbid waters. When it is visible, such as on exposed intertidal mud or sand flats or under clear water conditions, the bottom often appears barren to the eye. In reality it is extremely active and alive. If one were able to collect a chunk of undisturbed bottom material from a typical estuary, and immobilize in space all of the living organisms while removing all of the sediments, the organisms would form a "biological lattice" that would conform closely to the shape of the original sample. This living network, with its particular mix of kinds and numbers of organisms as they are associated and oriented at a moment in time is referred to as the *benthic community structure.* Obviously this structure is not static, but it changes much more slowly than the nektonic and planktonic community structures in the overlying water column. Thus if one were to examine a benthic sample collected in the same area a few weeks later it would appear very similar to the original.

If our idealized bottom sample were about 10×10 cm on the surface and 10 cm deep it would probably contain only one or two (if any) relatively large animals (1–10 cm in length) such as clams. Dozens of intermediate sized (1–10 mm) animals may be present (e.g., small polychate worms), but the smallest animals just visible to the naked eye would far outnumber all the larger forms, and most of these would probably be nematodes. Microscopic organisms (bacteria and protozoa), however, would far outnumber everything else. We know much less, however, about these organisms, for often when a benthic grab sample is collected, it is sieved through a screen, so that the smallest organisms are lost. Partly for this reason, information about larger benthic organisms was developed much earlier than for smaller organisms. Sieving also destroys the three-dimensional distribution and orientation of the organisms, so much of the information contained in the original sample of bottom is lost.

Within a given estuary a rough spatial distribution pattern of large (macrobenthic) organisms is apparent. Shallow sandy-mud to muddy areas with significant current speed are often dominated by suspension feeding animals. Examples include the soft-shelled clam (*Mya arenaria*) and other small clams such as the stout razor clam (*Ensis directus*). Finer sediments in more sheltered areas are likely to be colonized by deposit-feeding animals such as mud snails (*Nassarius vibex*) and mud crabs (*Panopeus herbstii*). Along tidal streams in salt marsh and mangrove-dominated estuaries, an eroding bank may be lined with a fringe reef of oysters (*Crassostrea virginica*). The upper oligohaline zone of warmer estuaries is colonized by the brackish water clam (*Rangia cuneata*) and chironomid insect larvae, while downstream higher-salinity habitats may be occupied by hard clam beds (*Mercenaria mercenaria*).

Members of the fouling or epibenthic community occur on hard surfaces such as pilings. These include barnacles (*Balanus* sp.), oysters, mussels, hydroids, cephalochordates (e.g., *Molgula manhattensis*), tiny moss animals or bryozoans, sponges, and many small amphipods, polychate worms, flatworms, and other motile forms. This diverse community extends high up into the intertidal zone, and the elevation of the mean high-water level at any estuarine location is indicated approximately by the elevation of the highest barnacle scars on a piling. By the same token, the mean low-water level is often indicated by the highest dense growth of sponges, bryozoans, and hydroids. Figure 9.1 illustrates many of these patterns of distribution as well as different benthic habitats in a hypothetical estuary.

Benthic organisms are often classified into nontaxonomic functional categories according to a variety of general characteristics, especially size, orientation, and feeding type. Some of these categories, their corresponding characteristics, and typical examples are shown in Table 9.1. We will refer to these groups and terms throughout this chapter.

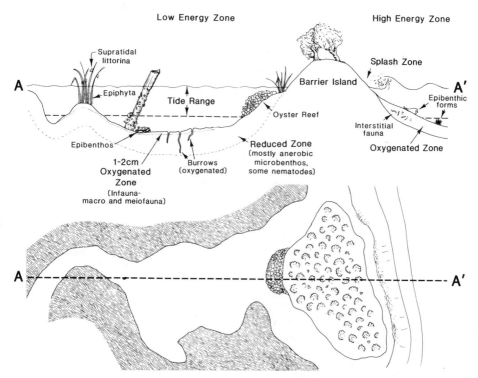

Figure 9.1 Benthic habitats and distribution of some major types of benthic organisms in an idealized estuary.

TABLE 9.1   Functional Groups of Estuarine Benthic Organisms, Their Characteristics and Typical Examples

Name	Functional Characteristics	Examples
Adult Size		
Macrobenthic (megabenthic) animals, macrofauna, macro metazoa (large multicellular benthic animals)	Large enough to be retained on screen with pore size of 500 μm (0.5 mm)	Most molluscs, many polychaetes, decapods and other crustacea, nemerteans
Meiobenthic animals, meiofauna, micrometazoa, (small multicellular benthic animals)	Smaller than macrobenthic forms but retainable on screen with pore size of either 67 μm or 44 μm	Nematodes, harpacticoid copepods, many tubellaria, several minor phyla
Microbenthic organisms	Smaller than Meiobenthic forms	Protozoa (e.g., ciliates, foraminifera)
Microhabitat		
Epibenthic animals, epifauna, epipelic animals, fouling animals	Surface living, either on bottom or on elevated or floating surfaces (including intertidal surfaces)	Oysters, barnacles, sponges, hydroids, some polychaetes, tunicates, echinoderms (most suspension feeders)
Infauna	Living beneath sediment surface in tubes or burrows	Most bivalves, many polychaetes, nematodes (most benthic animals)
Interstitial fauna (psammon)	Living between sediment particles, usually in high-energy sandy zones	Beach meiofauna, tardigrades
Feeding Type		
Suspension-feeding benthic animals	Feed by non-selectively trapping and concentrating food from water column using various organs such as gills, palps, lophophores, mucous secreting glands, and cilia	Sponges, bryozoa, many bivalves, some polychaetes, some crustacea (e.g., barnacles) (many epibenthic and some tube-dwelling and burrowing forms)

TABLE 9.1 Functional Groups of Estuarine Benthic Organisms, Their Characteristics and Typical Examples (continued)

Name	Functional Characteristics	Examples
Feeding Type		
Filter-feeding benthic animals	A subset of suspension feeders that feed by passing water through filtering apparatus, retaining particles by size characteristics	Porifera, tunicates, many bivalves
Non selective deposit feeders	Feed by ingesting sediments and assimilating living and dead organic material contained therein	A wide range of macro- and meiobenthic animals (e.g., gastropods such as hydrobiidae, many polychaetes)
Selective deposit feeders	Selectively ingest organically enriched sediments such as diatom films	Some nematodes, sand dollars, fiddler crabs
Raporial feeders and predators	Ingest individual particles of food, living or dead, either from sediments or from the water column	Some polychaetes, some decapods, star fish gastropod ''drills,'' nematodes, turbellaria
Parasites and commensals	Usually specialized forms that reside in or on benthic animals and suck body fluids or ''borrow'' food from gills	Parasitic flatworms and copepods, pea crabs in oysters
Sediment Preference		
Soft-bottom forms	Silt, silty clay, clayey silt, muck	Infauna, deposit feeders
Sandy-bottom forms	Sand, sandy silt	Suspension feeders, interstitial fauna
Hard-bottom forms	Rocky intertidal, clay pans	Epifauna

9.3   BENTHIC FAUNA OF ESTUARIES

There are relatively few species of benthic animals that are limited strictly to estuarine zones. Freshwater benthic animals frequently are found in oligohaline zones and many "marine" benthic animals occur in euryhaline zones. A commonly cited "rule" of estuaries is that the variety of organisms (also known as the species richness) of the benthic community typically declines as one progresses from ocean waters upstream into lower salinities, often reaching a minimum between 4 and 6 ppt (Remane and Schlieper 1971; Wolff 1973, 1983; Gainey and Greenburg 1977), although some researchers believe that this "rule" has not been demonstrated adequately (e.g., Abele and Walters 1979). On the other hand, although estuaries may contain relatively few benthic species, the abundance of total organisms in a unit area of the estuarine bottom is normally very high, exceeding the average density of organisms in freshwater and marine ecosystems. Figure 9.2 illustrates diagrammatically this relationship between salinity and benthic species diversity and abundance. Thus the diversity is lower in estuaries, but the abundance of organisms is much higher (Table 9.2), owing to higher food availability as well as other factors.

The most common nontaxonomic distinction drawn between groups of benthic animals is based on "life style," including habitat preference and mode of

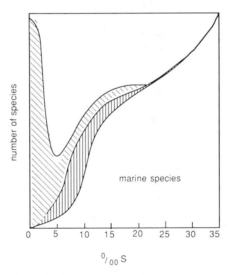

Figure 9.2   Number of species in relation to salinity. Obliquely hatched: fresh water species. Vertically hatched: brackish-water species. White: marine species (after Remane and Schlieper 1971).

TABLE 9.2 Comparison Between Numbers and Weight of Benthic Animals from Selected Marine, Estuarine, and Freshwater Habitats in Britain[a]

	Number of Species	Number of Animals/m^2	Mean Weight of Animals (g flesh dry wt/m^2)
Marine beach			
Exposed	8	450	0.58
Moderately exposed	12	600	1.13
Sheltered	19	1,600	1.9
Marine sublittoral	40	1,000	3.98
Estuarine beach			
Lower reaches	18	18,000	21.3
Upper reaches	4	100,000	27.9
Freshwater loch	54	58,000	11.4

[a]From McClusky (1980).

feeding (Table 9.1). Thus benthic research projects often concentrate on (1) epifauna, especially sessile "fouling" animals, (2) infauna or soft-sediment animals, or (3) motile animals that crawl over the bottom and dig into it for food or protection. In addition, studies of benthic animals are often limited to either large or small organisms (macrofauna vs. meiofauna) because the detailed examination of each group demands considerable effort and taxonomic skill and the use of different methods. Accordingly, the following section is divided into four parts: epifauna, macroinfauna, meiofauna, and motile benthos. Microbenthos (protozoa, fungae, and bacteria) and organic detritus were discussed in Chapter 7, but we will consider them in somewhat more detail in this chapter.

9.3.1 Epifauna

Epifauna includes the creatures that grow on or around structures, and can be subdivided into those organisms that live on the bottom and the fouling community, named because it has been for centuries the bane of navies, maritime fleets, fishermen, and pleasure boaters. The annual cost worldwide of removing epifauna from ship hulls, repairing damage caused by these animals, and providing extra fuel due to frictional losses (not to mention the environmental costs of the use of antifouling chemicals) is very high. For example, a six-month accumulation of fouling organisms can reduce a vessel's cruising speed by 10% and require 40% more operating fuel.

The magnitude of this fouling problem is indicative of the very high abundance of planktonic larvae that are seeking colonizable surfaces. Whereas the densities of many organisms are limited by available food supplies, epifauna are typically limited by space. Research on the successional patterns of epifaunal colonization of surfaces in coastal intertidal and subtidal communities has led to some now-classic ecological studies (e.g., Paine 1974).

Typically, the estuarine epifaunal community is dominated by barnacles, hydroids, mussels and oysters, sea squirts, bryozoans, sponges, and tube-building animals. These sessile forms attract, in turn, such slow-moving organisms as gastropods, polyclad flatworms, sea urchins, amphipods, isopods, and polychaetes, resulting in dense and often colorful communities. People who fish from piers often see members of the epifaunal community being preyed on by such midlevel nektonic consumers as the sheepshead (*Arcosargus probatocephalus*) and the blue crab (*Callinectes sapidus*). Although coastal epifauna are commonly associated with rocks and human artifacts such as boats and piers, some epifaunal organisms build their own colonizing surfaces. These are the reef builders, particularly oysters and mussels. One of the most typical epifauna communities of estuaries is found on oyster reefs (Fig. 9.3). Some epibenthic organisms which occur on intertidal flats are shown in Fig. 9.4.

Several characteristics of epibenthic existence, including reef formation, are important. These are gregarious behavior, suspension feeding, and the integra-

Figure. 9.3 An example of an epibiotic community inhabiting an oyster reef: the common eastern oyster, *Crassostrea virginica;* the hooked mussel, *Branchidontes reourvus;* the anemone, *Aiptasiomorpha texaensis;* the stone crab, *Menippe mercenaria;* the barnicle, *Balanus eburneus;* and the serpulid worm, *Eupomatus dianthus* (reprinted from *Beachcomber's Guide to Gulf Coast Marine Life* by Nick Fotheringham and Susan Brunemeister, with permission from Gulf Publishing, Houston, Texas; copyright © 1980, all rights reserved).

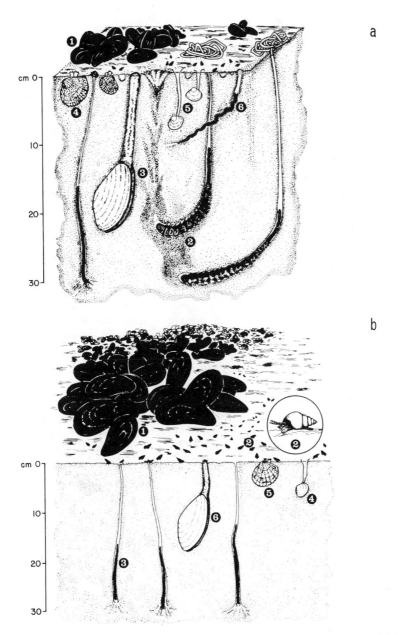

Figure 9.4 Macrofauna assemblages from the Dutch Wadden Sea. (a) Intertidal flats: (1) *Mytilus edulis;* (2) *Arenicola marina;* (3) *Mya arenaria;* (4) *Cerastoderma edule;* (5) *Macoma balthica;* (6) *Nereis diversicolor;* and (7) *Heteromastus filiformis.* (b) Subtidal areas: (1) *Mytilus edulis;* (2) *Hydrobia ulvae;* (3) *Heteromastus filiformis;* (4) *Macoma balthica;* (5) *Cerastoderma edule;* and (6) *Mya arenaria* (from de Wilde and Beukema 1974).

tion of conditions over time. A sessile adult life-style normally requires gregarious behavior on the part of larvae, so that successful reproduction can occur. For example, mature oyster and barnacle larvae settle preferentially near other members of their respective species by responding to chemical cues or pheromones. Some elegant research by Crisp and Meadows (1962) documented this phenomenon, and pilings covered with barnacles of the same species attest to its significance, as do oyster reefs of almost solid oysters.

Suspension feeding is a primary means of gathering food by sessile epibenthic animals, and the members of the epibenthic community tend to be suspension feeders. Suspension feeders must pump and filter a large quantity of water to obtain sufficient food of the proper quality. For example, a single adult oyster may actively pump (by ciliary action) several liters of water per hour across its gills. Therefore dense populations of suspension feeders can become food limited in estuarine areas that lack sufficient circulation, such as at the heads of tidal creeks.

The processing of large amounts of water by suspension feeders often results in the concentration of more than food. For example, some shellfish actively concentrate pathogenic organisms such as coliform bacteria, hepatitus viruses, heavy metals such as cadmium and zinc, and chlorinated hydrocarbons. Productive oyster beds have been closed in many estuaries for health reasons, and nonhuman shellfish predators may also be affected by this phenomenon.

Another implication of a sessile, suspension feeding existence is that the communities integrate over time various water-quality parameters. For example, the specific composition of the epibenthic community reflects the average salinity, temperature, and oxygen concentration over the previous months or years. This fact makes the epibenthic community a useful tool for monitoring water quality in areas where a cultural perturbation may have occured or may be contemplated. For example, experimental collecting plates have been exposed to ambient conditions in areas being tested, and the resulting epibenthic community that colonizes the plates used diagnostically to document changes in water quality.

To summarize, epifauna in estuaries are often most conspicuous and significant in intertidal areas and on man-made structures. Population densities of so-called "fouling" animals tend to be limited by the quantity of hard surfaces available for settling. Epifauna include the reef builders, notably oysters and mussels in estuaries, as well as the colonizers of reefs and other hard surfaces. Epifauna are primarily suspension feeders or filter feeders, and they depend on natural estuarine currents to augment the feeding currents they generate themselves. Suspension feeders have been shown to remove an amount of seston up to eight times their weight every day in coastal environments (Tenore 1977). This is especially important in Spanish and Japanese estuaries, where the growth of extensive raft cultures of oysters and mussels can actually become limited owing to diminished local food availability.

Epifauna reduce turbidity by water filtration, they regenerate ammonia and phosphorus, and in the form of reefs they can modify local currents and sedimentation patterns. They also serve as important sources of food for birds, nekton, and people.

9.3.1.1 The oyster—A Classic Example of an Epifaunal Estuarine Animal.
The oyster is an excellent example of an animal that is highly adapted to estuarine existence (see Fig. 9.3); and members of the family Ostreidae occur in estuaries worldwide from 44 S to 64 N latitude (Galtsoff 1964). Members of the genus Ostrea and Crassostrea are particularly well suited to estuarine existence because they can tolerate wide ranges of temperature (0–40°C), salinity (4–45 ppt), turbidity, and oxygen tension, and because they can generate their own firm substrate.

The eastern oyster (*Crassostrea virginica*) ranges along the Atlantic coast from Nova Scotia to Venezuela, and all around the Gulf coast. In some parts of its range, where tidal conditions are favorable—salinity is relatively high and winter air temperature is not too low—this oyster builds massive intertidal reefs (Fig. 9.5). These reefs serve as "islands" of hard substrate in otherwise soft sediments, they help to prevent marsh erosion, baffle water currents, regenerate nutrients, and feed terrestrial and aquatic predators.

The distribution of estuarine oyster reefs is organized at several levels of reso-

Figure 9.5 This view of the intertidal zone at Sapelo Island, Georgia shows the position of oyster reefs relative to the surrounding marshes and mudflats. Photo by Leonard Bahr.

lution. At the broadest level, overall reef distribution in a salt marsh estuary reflects the tidal regime, the pattern of sediment deposition, and current patterns. At the individual reef level each reef tends to become oriented in a way that maximizes its overall exposure to currents. This occurs because of the differential growth rates of individual oysters. At the most detailed level of resolution, individual oysters in a densely populated reef grow vertically (rather than the more horizontal growth of uncrowded oysters). They also tend to grow at right angles to the prevailing current patterns, thereby maximizing their frictional influence on water flow. Detailed discussions of oyster biology and of oyster reef ecology can be found in Galtsoff (1964), Bahr (1976), Dame (1976), and Bahr and Lanier (1981).

9.3.2 Macroinfauna

Macroinfauna are the relatively large organisms that reside beneath the sediment surface, invisible in undisturbed bottoms except for occasional burrow openings or siphon tubes (see Fig. 9.4). Thus seemingly barren mudflats or subtidal estuarine bottoms may conceal a teeming community of macrobenthic organisms of various sizes and taxonomic categories, including the commercially important edible clams that have been enjoyed by seafood lovers since prehistoric times.

Macroinfauna as a group are the most widely studied benthic organisms. In many benthic studies bottom samples are collected by dropping from a boat a heavy metal grab sampler attached to a cable with a triggering device, retrieving it with a chunk of the bottom, then washing the sediment sample through a sieve on board. The mesh size has traditionally been either 1.0 or 2.0 mm, although presently investigators are using 0.5 mm as the lower limit for macrofauna. Animals remaining on sieves are then preserved for subsequent identification, measuring, weighing, and enumeration. This kind of sampling is extremely labor intensive, but large numbers of such studies have been carried out in coastal and deep waters around the world. Great variability among samples is not unusual, and replicate sampling is usually necessary to ensure statistical validity. Nevertheless, patterns have emerged among macrobenthic communities in different areas.

Polychaete worms, such as *Neanthes* sp., and bivalves typically dominate the macroinfaunal community, both in terms of numbers and biomass. Bottom samples may also contain a variety of other groups, however, including small hydrobid snails, nemertean worms, echinoderms such as sea cucumbers, isopods, and other small crustaceans.

A broad classification of macroinfauna includes some animals that also could be considered epibenthic. These organisms live close to the sediment-water interface and are sometimes only partially covered by the soft flocculant surface layer of sediment that is typical of many estuarine zones. Examples include many gastropods, flatworms, isopods, amphipods, polychaetes, and anthozoa. An example of a macroinfaunal community in the Dutch Wadden Sea is shown

in Fig. 9.4 (see also Fig. 9.18). The total biomass of this macrobenthic community averages about 27 g ash-free dry mass/m^2 with maximum values of about 40
g/m^2, which is high for animals in most environments. These organisms are responsible for a high degree of reworking and oxidation of the sediments. The
piles of excavated material deposited on the sediment surface by the polychaete
Arenicola marina (as shown in Fig. 9.4) often contain reduced sediment material
although the walls of the burrows are oxidized.

The specific composition and distribution of the macroinfaunal community
in any given area is a function of the response of individual species to such factors as sediment characteristics, salinity regime, position in the intertidal zone,
and oxygen levels. This is illustrated in Fig. 9.6 for several species in the Rhine–
Meuse estuary in the Netherlands (from Wolff 1973). The polychaete worm *Boc-
cardia ligerica* occurs in subtidal lower salinity waters from about 2–8 ppt and
substrates ranging from peat to clay to muddy sands. The bivalve *Macoma
balthica* is more widely distributed in both brackish and high-salinity parts of the
estuary. It was found in both intertidal and subtidal areas on a wide variety of
substrates. The polychaete *Nereis diversicolor* is also widespread in the estuaries, but does not occur in the North Sea. It occurs mainly subtidally in lower-
salinity areas, but intertidally in more marine areas. It prefers muddy to sandy-
muddy sediments. The polychaete *Ophelia borealis* was found only offshore and
in high-salinity parts of the estuary in medium sands. Remane and Schlieper
(1971) showed that a number of macrobenthic estuarine species were distributed
according to salinity, and also that the maximum length decreased with decreasing salinity (Fig. 9.7)

We are not able at this time to define the functional roles of most benthic
invertebrates (e.g., their exact food requirements) and so we must depend on
statistical tests to determine the significance of species distributions and cooc-
currences. A large portion of the benthic literature is devoted to the development
and use of elegant statistical methods to distinguish among different communities based on the similarities (or dissimilarities) of their species compositions.
Boesch (1977) gives a concise summary of some of the basic methods used.

There are several theories concerning the dominant members of the macroinfaunal community in estuarine and marine waters. In the *parallel bottom community hypothesis,* Gunnar Thorson (1957) proposed that the macrobenthic
community in geographically distinct water bodies of similar depth and bottom
composition would be dominated by phylogenetically (and presumably function-
ally) similar organisms (e.g., members of the same genus). In other words, Thorson suggested that different coastal and deep-water systems in temperate latitudes, where bottom sediments and depths were similar, would be populated by
similar macrobenthic communities dominated by members of the same genus.
He identified some of these communities and named them after the dominant
organism (e.g., *Macoma, Tellina,* and *Venus* communities). There is, however,
evidence for increasing diversity in bottom communities toward the tropics (Fig.
9.8), which makes it difficult to apply this concept generally. Coull and Herman
(1970) reported a similar parallel structure in some meiobenthic communities.

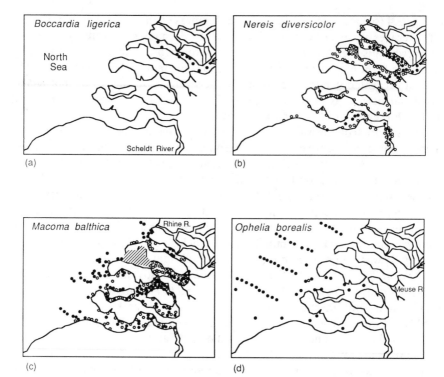

Figure 9.6 Distribution of some benthic organisms from the estuarine area of the southwest Netherlands in the Rhine, Meuse, and Scheldt Rivers. Dots are subtidal, circles are intertidal diagonal line are both subtidal and intertidal (after Wolff 1973). Published by permission of the Riyksmuseum van Natuurlijke Histoire, Leiden.

Benthic ecologists have been especially interested in community level questions for many years. One view is that a benthic community is analgous to an organism, with its tissues and organs comprised of dominant species populations. In this view a community is relatively concrete and definable (e.g, the oyster reef community in the southeastern United States). The opposing argument is that a (benthic) community is a loose, random association of populations of various species that happen to share space but have few or no obligate interactions. The reality of most communities probably falls nearer the latter view for few communities have distinct boundaries and most are ambiguous with respect to their species composition. A concise discussion of this argument is presented by Mills (1969).

Howard Sanders (1968) developed what is known as the *time-stability hypothesis* to explain the development of high diversity in many benthic communities. According to this hypothesis, the composition of macrobenthic communities in high-energy or changeable stressed areas (e.g., boreal estuaries), is

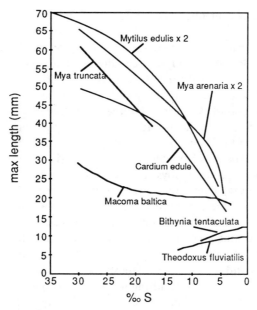

Figure 9.7 Reduction of maximal length of some molluscs with diminishing salinity in a transect from the North Sea to the Baltic Sea (after Remane and Schlieper 1971).

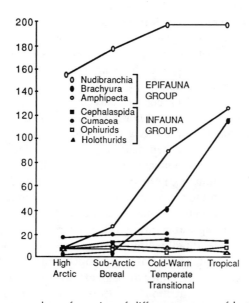

Figure 9.8 Average number of species of different groups of bottom invertebrates from equally large coastal areas in different latitudes (redrawn from Thorson 1957).

primarily physically controlled and tends to be dominated by opportunistic or r species. Such species are characterized by short life spans, high gamete production, and the ability to colonize new areas rapidly. Conversely, Sanders hypothesized that under more stable physical conditions such as shallow tropical areas, density-dependent biological controls such as competition, predation, and food limitation would lead to a community with proportionately more conservative, specialized, longer-lived K species. He theorized that relatively greater biotic regulation that occurs with the passage of time, in any setting, would yield stable communities over time, hence time-stability. This model has been challenged recently (e.g., see Abele and Walters 1979) but, consistent with Sander's theory, estuaries are in general more physically controlled than either marine or freshwater systems, and typically show lower species richness.

Coastal macrobenthic communities tend to be dominated by either nonselective deposit feeders or by suspension feeding organisms, but the dominant organisms of both feeding types are rarely observed together. Several theories have been put forth to explain this fact. According to the *trophic comensalism hypothesis* (Rhoads and Young 1970) deposit feeders, where they are abundant, destabilize bottom sediments, resulting in sediment suspension by normal water currents. This is shown in Fig. 9.9 for Buzzard's Bay, Massachusetts, where areas supporting higher levels of deposit-feeding benthos are also characterized by turbid waters above the bottom. This increase in suspended sediments clogs the filtering apparatus of suspension feeders and inhibits their feeding. In addition, many suspension feeders, especially large ones, tend to be relatively immobile and unable to move upward to maintain their feeding position vis-a-vis a rapidly sedimenting bottom. A related theory that has been proposed is that suspension feeders, which were formerly dominant in ancient benthic ecosystems, have been gradually displaced in evolutionary time by the diversifying deposit feeding organisms (or "biological bulldozers" as they have been called; Thayer 1979). Such animals, including holothurians (sea cucumbers), echinoids, and malacostracan crustacea, turn over sediments very rapidly and disrupt the habitat of suspension feeders. This process of burrowing into bedded sediments and disturbing them is known as bioturbation.

To summarize, macroinfauna as a group includes the larger animals that spend their adult lives buried beneath the sediment surface. In coastal areas, various polychaete worms and bivalve molluscs typically dominate the macroinfauna. Most of these animals can be grouped into two broad feeding types: suspension feeders that tend to predominate in sandier sediments and deposit feeders that favor siltier sediments. Members of the former group feed and eliminate wastes by either pumping water through their burrows, where it is filtered and pumped out, or by extending feeding structures (siphons, modified gills, etc.) above the bottom through which water is pumped and filtered. Deposit feeders ingest organic-rich sediments either through extensible siphons or by active burrowing. They derive their nutritional needs from living organisms and organic detritus. In this manner they "bulldoze," flush, and aerate the sediment and

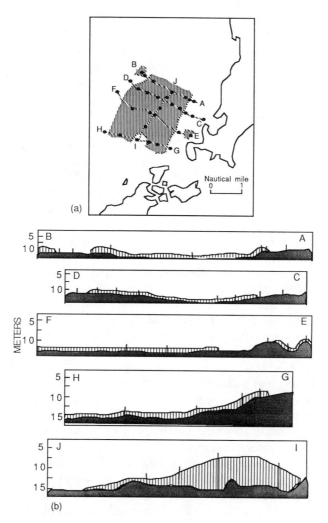

Figure 9.9 (a) Distribution of deposit-feeding benthos community in Buzzards Bay, Massachusetts, in a silty clay deposit. (b) Distribution of cloud of turbidity above the area (after Rhoads 1973).

lower its bulk density and stability (Rhoads and Young 1970). Estuarine macroinfauna contribute significantly to biodeposition, they regenerate inorganic nutrients, they can destabilize sediments and irrigate them with feeding currents, they prey on meiofauna, microfauna, and larval macroinfauna, and they serve as an important source of food energy for each other, for demersal nekton, and for human beings.

9.3.3 Meiofauna

The traditional method of benthic sampling in which a sample of bottom sediment is washed through a sieve has already been described. Because this technique was the principal one used to study benthic communities, small organisms were little studied for many years. Consequently, the scientific literature on meiobenthos is markedly limited relative to that on macroinfauna. Two important earlier works on meiofauna are by McIntyre (1969) and Remane and Schlieper (1971). Much of the following section summarizes information from these papers as well as from Coull and Bell (1979) and Fenchel (1978). These papers reflect the relatively recent surge of interest in ecological or functional aspects of meiofauna. Yet many open questions remain about the distribution, abundance, food habits, predators, and overall function of benthic organisms in coastal ecosystems. This statement is especially true for the meiofauna, which have been studied little, but which seem more important as they are studied more.

Meiofauna in estuaries and other ecosystems can be divided into two groups, temporary and permanent forms. The former include juvenile macroinfaunal organisms such as small gastropods that may, at times, be very dense. These are temporary in the sense that if they survive long enough they grow out of the meiofauna size range. Permanent meiofauna include Rotifera, Gastrotricha, Kinorhyncha, Nematoda, Archiannelida, Tardigrada, Copepoda, Ostracoda, Mystacocarida, and Halacarida, many groups of Turbellaria and Oligochaeta, some Polychaeta, and a few specialized members of Hydrozoa, Nemertina, Bryozoa, Gastropoda, Aplacophora, Holothuroidea, and Tunicata. McIntyre (1969) defines true meiofauna as "a group of small metazoans mostly passing a 0.5 mm mesh, which by their size, number, generation time, and adaptation can conveniently be considered separately from the larger members of the benthos." The *microbenthos,* by contrast, includes bacteria, flagellates, diatoms, and ciliates. A number of important meio- and microbenthic organisms are illustrated in Fig. 9.10 and 9.11.

Meiofauna have been distinguished from benthic macroinfauna primarily on the basis of size and, although there is some size overlap between macro and meiofauna, the 0.5-mm cutoff is fairly effective at separating the adults of both groups. This separation, based on a traditional sieve size, was fortuitous because, when researchers began looking at meiofauna in detail, it was discovered that although they are metazoan animals, they have a different life-style as a group than do the macroinfauna.

Meiofauna are, as a group, more conservative than macroinfauna in the sense that they expend proportionately less energy on reproduction, because they produce relatively few but larger gametes, and because some reproduce parthenogenetically under certain conditions. Whereas many macroinfauna release gametes freely into the water column, where fertilization takes place, some meiofauna require copulation and even nurture the developing zyotes during de-

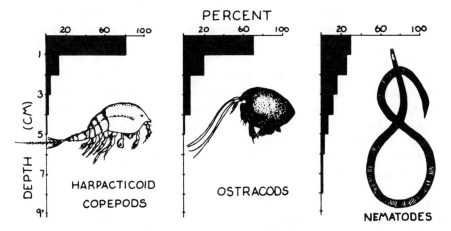

Figure 9.10 Examples of several meiobenthic organisms indicating depth distribution (from Whitlatch 1982).

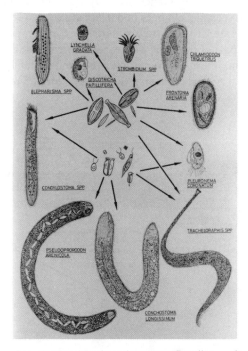

Figure 9.11 Examples of microbenthos: bacteria, flagellates, diatoms, and herbivorous ciliates in estuarine surface sands (from Fenchel 1969).

velopment. Meiofauna do tend to not have larvae that spend time drifting in the water column as is the case with meroplanktonic macroinfaunal larvae.

Meiofaunal organisms, like macroinfauna, are strongly affected by sediment characteristics. Two broad groups of meiofauna have been distinguished: burrowing mud bottom forms, and interstitial sandy-bottom forms. The former group burrows through sediments, displacing particles as they move, and their body forms tend to be streamlined, making burrowing easier. Interstitial meiofauna reside within the spaces between sand grains. In general, interstitial communities tend to be more diverse than burrowing communities. The high permeability of sandy beaches and their high wave energies ensures the rapid exchange of water and renewal of organic matter and oxygen into the subsurface sediments (Fenchel and Riedl 1970). Thus the meiofaunal community penetrates deeply into the sediments in such areas, sometimes over a meter. In muddy areas, on the other hand, meiofauna are generally found in the upper few centimeters, as indicated for Barataria Bay, Louisiana in Fig. 9.12 (see also Fig. 9.10). Some meiofaunal organisms can tolerate anoxic conditions for extended periods, which allows their presence in reduced sediments. This is indicated for a number of meiofauna and microfauna in Fig. 9.13.

Temperature appears to influence strongly the meiofaunal community, in that the pronounced seasonal changes in density are related strongly to temperature. In north temperate latitudes such as northern Europe, peak densities occur during the warmest part of the year, whereas in subtropical latitudes (e.g., Florida estuaries), the maximum occurs in November and December. Standing density (biomass) over an annual cycle may vary by a factor of 5 or more. The stand-

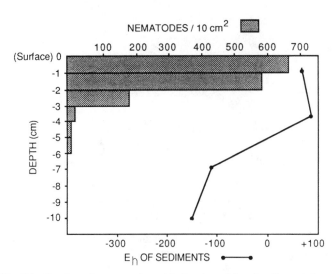

Figure 9.12 Distribution of nematodes with depth and E_h of sediments in salt marshes of Barataria Bay, Louisiana (from Sikora and Sikora 1982).

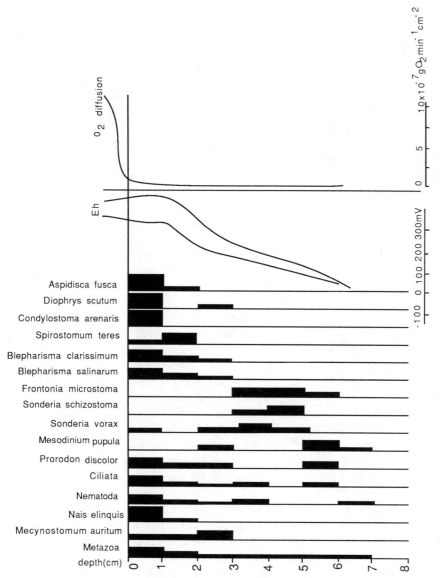

Figure 9.13 Vertical distribution of meio- and microfauna in relation to sediment depth, E_h, and O_2 availability in the intertidal zone of Askö Island, Sweden, Baltic Sea (after Fenchel and Jansson 1966).

ing biomass of meiofauna is normally lower than that of the macroinfauna but the density, metabolic rate, and production of the smaller animals is proportionately much higher (see Table 9.3). Meiofaunal density tends to be highest in intertidal areas of estuaries, and gradually declines in a seaward direction. This probably reflects the declining availability of organic matter in the sediments in deeper waters.

Coull and Bell (1977) reported that meiofaunal density averaged over all conditions for which it has been examined approximates 10^6 organisms/m^2 and standing crop biomass from 1 to 2 g/m^2. This means that the average individual weighs less than one-millionth of a gram. The highest reported densities of 26 $\times$ 10^6 organisms/m^2 are from intertidal mudflats and, in general, detritus-rich sediments contain higher populations than clean sands. Nematodes and harpacticoid copepods tend to be the two dominant taxonomic groups.

The degree to which meiofauna are consumed by larger predators has been one of the most controversial aspects of their function. McIntyre (1969) concluded that not many predators feed on these small organisms and that their functional importance is generally limited to remineralization of organic matter. He implied that in a sense the meiofauna represent an energetic "dead end" in which only decomposers use meiofaunal tissue. This premise was based on sandy-sediment interstitial forms, however, many of which live out of the reach of large predators, rather than on or at the sediment–water interface. More recent evidence suggests a major trophic role for meiofauna, especially nematodes, in energy flux though estuarine food webs, especially in silty, less sandy areas (Coull and Bell 1977, Sikora 1977, Sikora and Sikora 1982). Moreover, because many meiofauna extend down into the reduced zone (Figs. 9.12 and 9.13), they seem to be a major pathway for food flow from the reduced zone back to the aerobic zone. Over 15 years ago Fenchel (1969) showed that anaerobic bacteria were an important component in the diet of ciliates (Fig. 9.14). Because belowground production can be very high (as discussed in Chapter 7), this pathway may be very important. Montagna (1984) used radiotracers to quantify meiobenthic grazing rates on sediment bacteria and benthic diatoms in a South Carolina estuary. He found that, on the average, 3% of bacteria and 1% of diatoms were removed per hour and that the growth rate of the microbial community was sufficient to maintain it in steady state under this grazing pressure. Thus meiofaunal grazing probably represents a significant stimulatory effect on the microbial community.

To summarize, true meiofauna in estuaries are the extremely abundant small metazoan animals living mostly in the upper layers of bottom sediments. They are small enough to pass through a 0.5-mm sieve and they weigh roughly about one-millionth of a gram. Meiofauna are almost as diverse in their feeding habits and "life styles" as the macroinfauna—some are predatory and others are deposit feeders, but none are sessile suspension feeders. Meiofaunal biomass turns over much more rapidly than macroinfaunal tissue, with generation times commonly 1 month or less. As a group the estuarine meiofauna probably obtain much of their energy from microbial organisms. They in turn appear to contrib-

TABLE 9.3 Comparative Estimates of Population Densities, Biomass, and Energetic Parameters for Macrofauna and Meiofauna in an Estuarine Mudflat in Cornwall, UK[a]

| | Number/m^2 | Biomass (g C/m^2) | (g C/m^2 yr) | | | | P/B |
			Production	Respiration	Assimilation	Consumption	
Total macroinfauna (including 18 species or related groups of both large and small forms	423,825	6.8	12.3	37.8	50.1	107.8	1.8
True meiofauna (including Nematodes, Copepods, Ostrocods, *Protohydra leuckarti*, and Kinorhynchs)	12,902,689	1.2	13.4	26.0	39.5	58.5	11.1

[a]From Warwick et al. (1979).

COMPOSITION OF THE FOOD OF THE
CILIATE POPULATION IN THE SEDIMENTS
OF THE NIVA BAY (SUMMER)

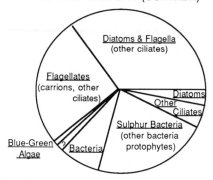

Figure 9.14 The relative importance of different food items for the total ciliate population in the sediments of Niva Bay, Denmark (from Fenchel 1969).

ute a significant portion of the energy requirements of deposit-feeding macroinfauna and nekton. The most abundant estuarine meiofauna in all habitats other than high-energy beaches are the nematodes.

9.3.4 Motile Benthos

This group of organisms is perhaps the least well defined of the major categories of benthic forms. It includes both vertebrates and invertebrates, and organisms that lead double lives, sometimes swimming and sometimes burrowing. In estuaries, the major invertebrate group of motile benthos is the relatively large heterogenous assemblage of crustacea known as decapods. These include most estuarine crabs and shrimp (including penaeid shrimp), although the commercially important shrimp and blue crabs (*Callinectes sapidus*) are usually considered nektonic species. Other invertebrates that belong to the motile benthos category are some echinoderms, such as estuarine brittle stars, sea urchins, and starfish, and gastropods such as the drills which, along with the starfish, feed on oyster populations. Chordates are represented by the tiny coastal sand-burrowing lancelets, such as *Amphioxus,* and such small bottom-living fish as blennies and naked gobies, which probably are more accurately classified as benthos than nekton.

The ecological processes undertaken by the motile benthos include active burrowing into sediments (bioturbation), predation on macrobenthos (both epifauna and infauna), deposit feeding (including predation on meiobenthos and microbenthos), scavenging dead organisms, serving as prey for demersal nekton, and nutrient regeneration.

9.4 BIOMASS AND SECONDARY PRODUCTION OF THE BENTHIC COMMUNITY

Benthic biomass and secondary production is high in estuaries when compared with other aquatic ecosystems and with the estuarine water column. Generally high primary production and allochthonous organic matter input ensure an abundance of food. The shallowness and active water movements of most estuaries means that this food is widely distributed and readily available to benthic consumers.

Total macrobenthic biomass varies considerably, depending on such factors as substrate, temperature, tidal flushing, and depth. Table 9.4 presents biomass and production data for benthic species from a number of different areas. In general, suspension feeders have the highest biomass. The maximum biomass is attained by reef-building organisms. For example, biomass values for the oyster *Crassostera virginica* of 970 g/m^2 (ash-free weight) and 165 g/m^2 have been reported for Georgia (Bahr 1976) and South Carolina (Dame 1976), respectively. The maximum biomass for mussel (*Mytilus edulis*) beds in Great Britian ranged from dry flesh weight of 400 to 1420 g/m^2 (Dame 1976). Obviously such dense aggregations depend on a large area of estuary for food supply. Even though they are much more abundant, the biomass of meiobenthic organisms is generally less than that of macrobenthic organisms because of the small average size. However, production may be equivalent, owing to the high turnover of the meiobenthos compared with the macrobenthos. For example, in a mudflat in Cornwall, United Kingdom the production to biomass ratios (P/B) for macroinfauna and meiofauna were 1.8 and 11.1, respectively (Table 9.3). This is also demonstrated in Fig. 9.15, which shows that animals with short life spans have high P/B ratios.

There are seasonal and spatial patterns in benthic biomass and production in temperate estuaries. Biomass and production tend to be higher in shallower water, as is demonstrated for a number of estuaries in Table 9.5. This is probably due to the higher availability of food, more active water movement, and a preponderence of suspension feeders. Day et al. (1973) demonstrated that biomass of larger macrobenthic organisms in a Louisiana salt marsh was significantly higher near the water's edge (Fig. 9.16). In temperate latitudes there is often a distinct seasonality of biomass and metabolism. This is demonstrated for changes in benthic biomass for an estuary in The Netherlands (Fig. 9.17a) and for respiration of an oyster reef in Georgia (Fig. 9.17b). These seasonal changes are due to temperature and seasonal food availability.

9.5 THE BENTHIC EFFECT

In previous sections, we discussed the major groups of benthic organisms that reside in estuaries and the roles that they play. We now attempt to synthesize and summarize this information into a discussion of the overall "benthic effect,"

TABLE 9.4 Biomass and Production Values for Some Estuarine Macrobenthic Species Found in Investigations of Large Areas[a]

Area Investigates	Reference	Species	Feeding Type	Biomass	Production
Long Island Sound USA, subtidal, about 1000 km²	Sanders (1956)	*Nephtys incisa*	Deposit feeder	4.3	9.3
		Cistenoides gouldii	Deposit feeder	0.9	1.7
		Pandora gouldiana	Suspension feeder	3.1	6.1
Conway Bay, Wales, intertidal, 19 ha	Hughes (1970)	*Yoldia limatula*	Deposit feeder	1.4	3.2
		Scrobicularia plana	Deposit feeder	3.8–40.8	3–13
Petpeswick Inlet, Canada, intertidal, about 5 km²	Burke and Mann (1974)	*Mya arenaria*	Suspension feeder		11.6
		Macoma balthica	Deposit feeder		1.9
		Littorina saxatilis	Grazer	0.1–0.8	3.3
		Mytilus edulis	Suspension feeder	2.7–15.2	
		Melampus lineatus	Grazer	0.8	
		Nassarius obsoletus	Grazer	0.9	
Southampton Water, England, intertidal, 60 ha	Hibbert (1976)	*Cerastoderma edule*	Suspension feeder		29–71
		Mercenaria mercenaria	Suspension feeder		4–14
Grevelingen Estuary, The Netherlands, intertidal and subtidal, 140 km²	Wolff and De Wolff (1977)	*Cerastoderma edule*	Suspension feeder	18.7	10–120
		Macoma balthica	Deposit feeder	1.0	0.3–7.9
		Arenicola marina	Deposit feeder	1.8	3.3–6.3
		Hydrobia ulvae	Grazer	2.2	7.2–12.8
Sapelo Island, USA, Intertidal Oyster Reef	Bahr and Lanier (1981)	*Crassostrea Virginioa*	Suspension feeder	970	

[a]Adapted from Wolff 1983, biomass in gAFDW m⁻², production in gAFDW m⁻² yr⁻¹.

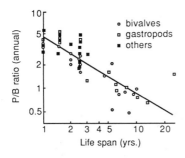

Figure 9.15 The relationship of annual population production to biomass ratios to life span for a number of different estuarine benthic animals (from Mann 1982 as redrawn from Robertson 1979).

TABLE 9.5   Production, Biomass, and P/B Ratio for Total Benthic Communities in Various Locations[a]

Depth (m)	Location	P (g C/m²yr)	B (g C/m²)	P/B	Reference
0	Estuary, The Netherlands	16.5	10	1.6	Wolff and de Wolff (1977)
0	Estuary, Cornwall, UK	5.3	5.3	1.0	Warwick and Price (1975)
17	Severn Estuary, UK	10.0	17.0	0.6	Warwick et al. (1978)
18	Long Island Sound, USA	12.0	4.8	2.5	Sanders (1956)
46	Baltic Sea	2.7	1.7	1.6	Cederwall (1977)
80	North Sea	0.7	1.7	0.4	Buchanan and Warwick (1974)

[a]From Mann 1982.

emphasizing that the bottom subsystem of an estuary affects markedly the entire system. The benthic effect in estuaries, or the functional role of the benthic boundary layer, can be divided conveniently into three interdependent sets of processes. These are (1) organismal - sediment relations, (2) benthic community metabolism and nutrient recycling, and (3) mediation of energy flow by the benthic subsystem. These three sets of processes will now be described briefly.

9.5.1   Organismal–Sediment Relations

This set of processes basically includes the effect of estuarine bottom sediment characteristics on benthic organismal distribution and, conversely, the effect of benthic organisms on sediment characteristics.

It is hardly surprising that the organisms living in intimate association with bottom sediments are strongly dependent on the characteristics of those sediments. Important descriptors of sediment "quality" in a given area include: (1) average grain size; (2) percent composition of silt, sand, and clay; (3) organic content; (4) carbonate content; and (5) bulk density. Bulk density is important

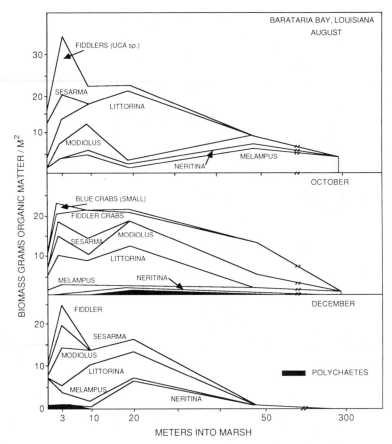

Figure 9.16 Distribution of large macroinfauna from a *Spartina alterniflora* marsh of Barataria Bay, Louisiana in August, Octrober, and December 1972 (from Day et al. 1973).

for a number of reasons. For example, if undisturbed (bedded) bottom sediments are mixed (e.g., by a hydraulic suction dredge) they become homogenized into a frothy liquid known as fluidized mud. This substance has a lower bulk density than the original sediment, and is correspondingly more easily disturbed. It will also not support the weight of many common macrobenthic organisms.

The preferences of some major groups of benthic organisms for certain sediment types has already been mentioned. Suspension-feeding organisms often tend to favor firmer (sandier) substrates than do deposit feeders; interstitial meiofauna inhabit sandy areas, while burrowing meiofauna inhabit silty mud; and some organisms require high levels of organic matter. The organic content of the sediment also affects its rate of oxygen depletion in the sediments. When a

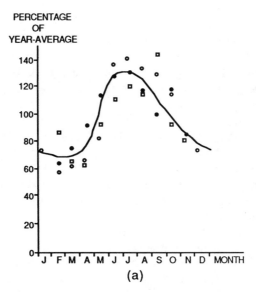

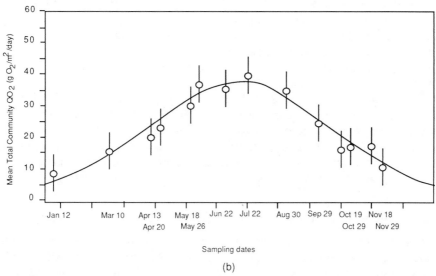

Figure 9.17 (a) Relative biomass of shallow-living animals in tidal flats of the Wadden Sea, The Netheralnds, expressed as mean percentages of average annual biomas (after Beukema 1974). (b) Annual pattern of respiration of an intertidal oyster reef in Georgia (from Energetic aspects of the intertidal oyster reef community at Sapelo Island, Georgia (U.S.A.) by L. Bahr, Ecology, 57: 121–131; copyright © 1976 by the Ecological Society of America, reprinted by permission).

reduced zone develops beneath the sediment surface, organismal distribution is affected strongly (see Figs. 9.12 and 9.13).

The physical influence of the local current and wave regime in different parts of an estuary accounts for much of the observed differences in sediment characteristics, and in turn for the pattern of organism distribution. Mean sediment grain size tends to be large in high-energy areas such as tidal channels, and small in quiet, low-energy areas that trap fine sediment.

Organisms living on or in the bottom alter the sediment quality in several ways: (1) bioturbation; (2) organic carbon depletion; (3) the production of binding agents such as shells and mucous; (4) biodeposition; and (5) oxygenation of anaerobic sediments. Some of these are illustrated in Fig. 9.18. Some of these effects are destabilizing (1), and some are stabilizing (3). Laboratory experiments by Rhoads et al. (1978) have demonstrated these antagonistic affects by measuring the resistance to erosion of test sediments exposed to varying current speeds. Bacteria and some larger macroorganisms produce mucopolysaccharides that cement surface particles together, increase their functional grain size, and make them somewhat more resistant to erosion. Fecal pellets produced by some crustacea and polychaetes do the same thii.g. Mollusc shells form a kind of matrix that also increases erosion resistance. Oyster and mussel reefs provide the extreme example of this effect. These reefs actually trap suspended sediments and augment deposition rates.

The effects of biodeposition (the active buildup of bottom deposits by the production of macroinfaunal feces and pseudofeces) can be extremely important in estuaries. For example, oysters at typical densities in planted oyster beds have been estimated to biodeposit sediment at a rate of about 60 kg/m^2 yr (Lund 1957). Large organisms that feed deep in the sediments but deposit feces, psudeofeces, and excavated sediment material on the sediment surface have been called "conveyor-belt" species by Rhoads (1974, Fig. 9.18a and b, see also Fig. 9.4 which shows surface deposition). Rhoads speculated that organic matter brought up from the anaerobic zone was an important food source during times of low organic deposition to organisms living at the sediment surface.

9.5.2 Benthic Community Metabolism and Nutrient Recycling

The metabolic rate of the benthic system is the sum of the combined respiration rates of all living organisms in the bottom, as well as chemical oxidation. This rate represents the metabolic cost associated with all biological processes, that is, decomposition, maintenance, feeding, growth, and reproduction (for a comprehensive review of benthic metabolism see Pamatmat, 1977). A comparison of the relative metabolic rates of a variety of benthic systems, from freshwater lakes and coral reefs to deep ocean bottoms, shows a range of values spanning five orders of magnitude from 0.7 to over 7000 mg O_2/m^2 day. Estuarine benthic systems are found toward the upper end of the scale.

Respiration is a catabolic process in which (reduced) organic matter is at least partially oxidized. This process not only releases inorganic carbon but also min-

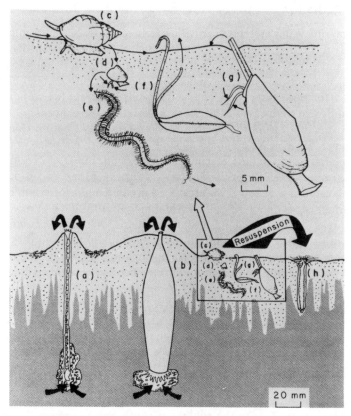

Figure 9.18 Methods of mixing and recycling of sediment by deposit feeders: (a) maldanid polychaete, (b) holothurian, (c) gastropod (*Nassarius*), (d) bivalve (*Nucula* sp.), (e) errant polychaete, (f) tellinid bivalve (*Macoma* sp.), (g) bivalve (*Yoldia* sp.), (h) anemone (*Cerianthus* sp.). Oxidized mud, lightly stippled; reduced mud, gray. Species a and b are conveyor-belt species, pumping reduced sediment from below the RPD layer to the oxidized surface, cycling within the oxidized surface is done by species c–g; arrows show routes of sediment ingestion and egestion of feces (from Rhoads 1974).

eralizes nitrogen and phosphorus, the basic growth nutrients for primary production. It is becoming apparent that one of the most important ways that the benthic community influences other components of the estuarine ecosystem is by the mineralization and release of these plant nutrients. In addition, whereas in the past the microbial population in the sediments was thought to be mainly important for remineralization, the macroinfauna and meiofauna are now believed by some to be also important in that role. The role of the benthic systems in remineralization has been discussed in Chapters 3, 4, and 7.

9.5.3   Mediation of Energy Flow by the Benthic Boundary Layer

In deep marine water systems energy flow between surface waters and the benthos tends to be unidirectional; from the surface to the bottom. By contrast, material and energy flows between the bottom and the overlying water column are highly interactive. There are major food pathways into and out of the benthos. Data for two estuaries in The Netherlands illustrate the variable importance of different pathways (Table 9.6). In both the Grevelingen and Ems estuaries, detritus input from the North Sea is important as a benthic food source. Benthic microalgae make up about 10% of total in both estuaries, while phytoplankton is important in the Grevelingen estuary while land runoff is high for the Ems. The importance of the different sources varies for these two estuaries, as it will for all estuaries. Mann (1982) reviewed organic input for a number of systems. Surface algae on an intertidal system may fix 100–200 g C/m^2 yr, but for subtidal areas algal production is usually less than 100 g C/m^2 yr and decreases rapidly with depth. External inputs from phytoplankton and other sources ranged from about 30 to 300 g C/m^2 yr. In shallow areas 30–40% of the carbon supply in the water column may be used by the benthos, but this is much smaller in deeper waters.

A number of studies have indicated that benthic feeding may control phytoplankton biomass in overlying waters. Cloern (1982) reported that in south San Francisco Bay, phytoplankton biomass remained low from May through December in this system with expansive shallows, although light and nutrient conditions were sufficient to sustain high growth rates. Transport process and zooplankton grazing exerted little influence on phytoplankton biomass. Cloern found that suspension-feeding bivalves were sufficiently abundant to filter a volume of water equivalent to the volume of south San Francisco Bay daily. He concluded that feeding by benthos was the major factor controlling phyto-

TABLE 9.6   Proportion of Benthic Food Sources in Two Estuaries in the Netherlands.

	% of Total Food Available	
Food Source	Grevelingen Estuary[1]	Ems Estuary[2]
Detritus from saltmarshes	0	<1
Detritus from seagrass beds	1.5–6.7	0
Detritus from North Sea	~50	46[3]
Detritus from land runoff	<1	41
Benthic microalgae	7.8–12.8	11.5
Phytoplankton	41	~1

[1]From Wolff (1977).
[2]From Van Es (1977).
[3]Includes input from River Ems.

plankton biomass during summer and fall. Officer et al. (1982) also analyzed the situation in south San Francisco Bay and likewise concluded that benthic filter feeding limited phytoplankton growth even though the area receives heavy nutrient loading from sewage effluent. They suggest that benthic feeding was a natural eutrophication control. Nichols (1985) suggested that benthic filter feeding, especially by the bivalve *Mya arenaria* was responsible for low phytoplankton biomass in northern San Francisco Bay during the drought of 1976–1977. Apparently, increasing salinity as a result of the drought allowed a large increase in the bivalve population. Cohen et al. (1984) concluded that a 40–60% reduction in phytoplankton abundance a segment of the Potomac River, Maryland during 1980–1981 was due to filtration by the introduced Asiatic clam *Corbicula fluminea*. Carlson et al. (1984) came to similar conclusions in a study of the impact of a small tidal mudflat on the plankton in overlying waters. Extensive culture of some bivalves also has been implicated in depletion of ambient concentrations of phytoplankton (Cadee and Hegeman 1974).

Benthic secondary production supports a high degree of feeding by organisms in the water column, including many invertebrates, demersal nekton, and wading and diving birds. Experiments designed to measure the effect of nekton predation on benthic organisms in estuaries tend to show dramatic differences between control and experimental areas where predators are excluded. For example, Virnstein (1977, 1979) found large increases in density and diversity of benthic organisms when fishes and crabs were excluded from shallow subtidal sand communities in Chesapeake Bay. Birds have also been shown to be very important feeders of benthic organisms (Botton 1984, Quammen 1984). Similar results have been found from exclosure studies in salt marshes (Kneib and Stiven 1982), salt marsh pools (Ward and Fitzgerald 1983), and seagrass beds (Nelson 1981, Summerson and Peterson 1984). All of these studies imply very active feeding on benthic organisms by nekton and birds. In Chapters 10 and 11, we will consider in more detail the role of the bottom communities in providing food to nekton and wildlife.

Another important way that the benthic systems affects the overlying waters is via nutrient regeneration. As we have discussed in several earlier chapters (3, 4, and 7) benthic regeneration may be an important source of nutrients supporting phytoplankton production in overlying estuarine waters. In a review of the literature on this subject, Nixon (1981) reported that benthic regeneration could supply, at times, over 100% of N and P needed to support measured phytoplankton production in a variety of estuaries (see Chapters 3 and 4). In addition, Nixon speculated that the relative rates of release of N and P to the water column was largely responsible for the fact that nitrogen normally limits phytoplankton in coastal waters. This results from the fact that in anerobic estuarine sediments, significant amounts of N are loss via the denitrification pathway, resulting in a low N:P ratio of regenerated nutrients. This was discussed in detail in Chapter 3, but here it is important as an example of the way one part of an ecosystem can profoundly effect another.

REFERENCES

Abele, L.G. and K. Walters, 1979. Marine Benthic Diversity: A Critique and Alternative Explanation. J. Biogeoyr., 6:115–126.

Armstrong, N., 1987. The ecology of open-bay bottoms of Texas: A community profile. U. S. Fish Wildl. Serv., Washington, Biol. Rept. 85(7.12), 104 pp.

Bahr, L., 1976. Energetic aspects of the intertidal oyster reef community at Sapelo Island, Georgia (U.S.A.). Ecology, 57(1):121–131.

Bahr, L. and W. Lanier, 1981. The intertidal oyster community of the South Atlantic coast: A community profile. U. S. Fish and Wildlife Service, Office of Biological Services, Washington D.C., FWS/OBS-81/15, 105 pp.

Baillie, B.W. and B.L. Welsh, 1980. The effect of tidal resuspension on the distribution of intertidal epipelic algae in an estuary. Estuarine Coastal Mar. Sci., 10:165–180.

Beukema, J., 1974. Seasaonal changes in the biomass of the macrobenthos of a tidal flat in the Dutch Wadden Sea. Neth. J. Sea Res., 8:94–107.

Birman, I.B., 1969. Distributions and growth of young sockeye salmon in the sea. Vopr. Ikhtiol. T.9, Vyp., 5158:859–877. English translation in Problems of ichthyology, Am. Fish. Soc., 9(5):651–666.

Boesch, D.F., 1977. Application of Numerical Classification in Ecological Investigations of Water Pollution. Ecol. Res. Ser., EPA-600/3-77-033, 113 pp.

Botton, M.L., 1984. Effects of laughing gull and shoreboird predation on the intertidal fauna at Cape May, New Jersey. Estuarine Coastal Shelf Sci., 18:209–220.

Buchanan, J. and R. Warwick, 1974. An estimate of benthic macrofaunal production in the offshore mud of the Northumberland coast. J. Mar. Assoc. U. K., 54:197–222.

Burke, M.V. and K.H., Mann, 1974. Productivity and production: Biomass ratios of bivalve and gastropod populations in an eastern Canadian estuary. J. Fish. Res. Board Can., 31:167–177.

Cadee, G.C. and J. Hegeman, 1974. Primary production of phytoplankton in the Dutch Wadden Sea. Neth. J. Sea Res., 8:240–259.

Carlson, D.J., D.W. Townsend, A.L. Hillyard, and J.F. Eaton, 1984. Effect of an intertidal mudflat on plankton of the overlying water column. Can. J. Fish. Aquat. Sci., 41:1523–1528.

Carriker, M.R., 1967. Ecology of estuarine benthic invertebrates: A perspective. In G. Lauff (Ed.), Estuaries. AAAS Publication No. 83, Washington, D.C., pp. 442–487.

Cederwall, H., 1977. Annual macrofauna production of a soft bottom in the Northern Baltic proper. In B.F. Keegan, P.O. Ceidigh, and P.J.S. Boaden (Eds.), Biology of Benthic Organisms: Proceedings of the 11th European Symposium on Marine Biology. Pergamon, Oxford, pp. 155–164.

Cloern, J.E., 1982. Does the benthos control phytoplankton biomass in south San Fransicso bay? Mar. Ecol. Prog. Ser., 9:191–202.

Cohen, R., P. Dresler, E. Phillips and R. Cory, 1984. The effect of the Asiatic clam, Corbicula fluminea, on phytoplankton of the Potomac River, Maryland. Limnol. Oceanogr., 29:170–180.

Coull, B.C., 1973. Estuarine meiofauna: a review. In L.H. Stevenson and R. R. Colwell (Eds.), Estuarine Microbial Ecology. University of South Carolina, Columbia, South Carolina, pp. 499–512.

Coull, B.C., (Ed.), 1977. Ecology of the Marine Benthos. University of South Carolina Press, Columbia, 467 pp.

Coull, B.C. and S.S. Bell, 1979. Perspectives of marine meiofaunal ecology. In R.J. Livingston (Ed.), Ecological processes in coastal and marine systems. Marine Science Series, Plenum Press, New York, Vol. 10, 548 pp.

Coull, B.C. and S.S. Herman, 1970. Zoogeography and parallel level-bottom communities of the meiobenthic harpacticoida (Crustacea, Copepoda) of Bermuda. Oecologia (Berlin), 5:392–400.

Crisp, D.J. and P.S. Meadows, 1962. The chemical basis of gregariousness in Cirripedia. Proc. R. Soc. Biol., 156:500–520.

Dame, R., 1976. Energy flow in an intertidal oyster population. Estuarine Coastal Mar. Sci., 4:243–283.

Day, J., W. Smith, P. Wagner, and W. Stowe, 1973. Community structure and carbon budget of a salt marsh and shallow bay estuarine system in Louisiana. Center for Wetland Resources, Louisiana State University, Baton Rouge, Publication No. LSU-SG-72-04, 79 pp.

de Wilde, P. and J. Beukema, 1984. The role of the zoobenthos in the consumption of organic matter in the Dutch Wadden Sea. Netherlands Institute for Sea Research, Publication Series No. 10, pp.145–158.

Fenchel, T. M., 1969. The ecology of marine microbenthos. IV. Structure and function of the benthic ecosystem, its chemical and physical factors and the microfauna communities with special reference to the ciliated protozoa. Ophelia, 6:1–182.

Fenchel, T. M., 1978. The ecology of micro and meiobenthos. Ann. Rev. 9:99–121.

Fenchel, T. M. and B.-O. Jansson, 1966. On the vertical distribution of the microfauna in the sediments of a brackish water beach. Ophelia, 3:161–177.

Fenchel, T.M. and R.J. Riedl, 1970. The sulfide system: a new biotic community underneath the oxidized layer of marine sand bottom. Mar. Biol., 7:225–268.

Fotheringham, N. and S. Brunenmeister, 1975. Common Marine Invertebrates of the Northwestern Gulf Coast. Gulf Publishing, Houston. 197 pp.

Gainey, L. F., Jr. and M. J. Greenberg, 1977. Physiological basis of the species abundance–salinity relationship in molluscs. Mar. Biol., 40:41–49.

Galtsoff, P.S., 1964. The American oyster *Crassostrea virginica* (Gmelin). U.S. Fish Wildl. Serv. Fish. Bull., 64:1–480.

Hibbert, C. J., 1976. Biomass and production of a bivalve community on an intertidal mud-flat. J. Exp. Mar. Biol. Ecol., 25:249–261.

Hughes, R.N., 1970. An energy budget for a tidal-flat population of the bivalve *Scobicularia plana* (Da Costa). J. Anim. Ecol., 39:357–381.

Kneib, R.T. and A.E. Stiven, 1982. Benthic invertebrate responses to size and density manipulations of the common mummichog, *Fundulus heteroclitus* in an intertidal salt marsh. Ecology, 63(5):1518–1532.

Lund, E.J., 1957. Self-silting by the oyster and its significance for sedimentation geology. Publ. Inst. Mar. Sci. Univ. Tex., 4(2):320 327.

Mann, K., 1982. Ecology of Coastal Waters: A Systems Approach. University of California Press, Berkley, 322 pp.

Margalef, R., 1971. Ecological Correlations and the Relationship Between Primary Productivity and Community Structure. Instituto de Investigaciones Pesqueras, Spain.

McCave, I. N. (Ed.), 1976. The Benthic Boundary Layer. Plenum, New York, 323 pp.

McClusky, D.S., 1981. The Estuarine Ecosystem. Halsted, New York, 145 pp.

McIntyre, A.D., 1969. Ecology of marine meiobenthos. Biol. Rev., 44:245-290.

Mills, E.L., 1969. The community concept in marine zoology, with comments on continua and instability in some marine communities: A review. J. Fish. Res. Board Can., 26:1415-1428.

Montagna, P., 1984. In situ measurement of meiobenthic grazing rates on sediment bacteria and edaphic diatoms. Mar. Ecol. Prog. Ser., 18:119-130.

Nelson, W.G., (1981). Experimental studies of decapod and fish predation on seagrass macrobenthos. Mar. Ecol. Prog. Ser., 5:141-149.

Newell, R. C., 1979. Biology of intertidal animals. Marine Ecological Surveys, Taversham, Kent, U.K., 781 pp.

Nichols, F., 1985. Increased benthic grazing: An alternative explanation for low phytoplankton biomass in Northern San Francisco Bay during the 1975-1977 drought. Estuarine, Coastal Shelf Sci., 21:379-388.

Nixon, S. W., 1981. Remineralization and nutrient cycling in coastal marine ecosystems. In B. Neilson and L. Cronin (Eds.), Estuaries and Nutrients. Humana, Clifton, NJ, pp. 111-138.

Officer, C.B., T.J. Smayda, and R. Mann, 1982. Benthic filter feeding: A natural eutrophication control. Mar. Ecol. Prog. Ser., 9:203-210.

Paine, R., 1974. Intertidal community structure: Experimental studies on the relationship between a dominant competitor and its principal predator. Oecologia (Berlin), 15:93-120.

Pamatmat, M.M., 1977. Benthic community metabolism: A review and assessment of present status and outlook. In B. Coull (Ed.), Ecology of Marine Benthos. Univ. South Carolina Press, Columbia, pp. 89-111.

Parsons, T., M. Takahashi, and B. Hargrave, 1977. Biological Oceanographic Processes, 2nd ed. Pergamon, Oxford.

Peterson, C., and N. Peterson, 1979. The ecology of intertidal flats of North Carolina: A community profile. U.S. Fish and Wildlife Service, Office of Biological Services, Rept. FWS/OBS/-79/39, 73 pp.

Quammen, M.L., 1984. Predation by shorebirds, fish, and crabs on invertebrates in intertidal mudflats: An experimental test. Ecology, 65(2):529-537.

Remane, A. and C. Schlieper, 1971. Biology of Brackish Water. Wiley, New York, 372 pp.

Rhoads, D. C., 1973. The influence of deposit-feeding organisms on sediment stability and community trophic structure. Am. J. Sci., 273:1-22.

Rhoads, D. C., 1974. Organism–sediment relations on the muddy sea floor. Oceanogr. Mar. Biol., Annu. Rev., 12:263-300.

Rhoads, D.C. and D.K. Young, 1970. The influence of deposit-feeding organisms on sediment stability and community trophic structure. J. Mar. Res., 28(2):150-178.

Rhoads, D.C., P.L. McCall, and J.Y. Yingst, 1978. Disturbance and production on the estuarine seafloor. Am. Sci., 66:577-587.

Robertson, A.I., 1979. The relationship between annual production: biomass ratios and life spans for marine macrobenthos. Oecologia (Berlin), 38:193-202.

Sanders, H.L., 1956. Oceanography of Long Island Sound, 1952-1954. X. Biology and marine bottom communites. Bull. Bingham Oceanogr. Coll., 15:345-414.

Sanders, H.L., 1968. Marine benthic diversity: a comparative study. Am. Nat., 102:243-282.

Sikora, W.B., 1977. The ecology of *Paleomonetes pugio* in a southeastern salt marsh ecosystem with particular emphasis on production and trophic relationships. Ph.D. Dissertation. University of South Carolina, Columbia, 122 pp.

Sikora, W. and J. Sikora, 1982. Ecological implications of the vertical distribution of meiofauna in salt marsh sediments. In V. Kennedy (Ed.), Estuarine Comparisons. Academic, New York, pp. 269-282.

Summerson, H.C. and C.H. Peterson, 1984. Role of predation in organizing benthic communities of a temperate-zone seagrass bed. Mar. Ecol. Prog. Ser., 15:63-77.

Tenore, K.R., 1977. Food chain pathways in detrital feeding benthic communities: A review, with new observations on sediment resuspention and detrital recycling. In B. C. Coull (Ed.), Ecology of the Marine Benthos. University of South Carolina Press, Columbia, pp. 37-53.

Thayer, C. W., 1979. Biological bulldozers and the evolution of marine benthic communities. Science, 203:458-461.

Thorson, G., 1957. Bottom communities. Mem. Geol. Soc. Am., 67(1):461-534.

Van Es, F., 1977. A preliminary carbon budget for a part of the Ems estuary: The Dollard. Helgol. Wiss. Meeresunters., 30:283-294.

Vernberg, W. and J. Vernberg, 1972. Environmental Physiology of Marine Mammals. Springer-Verlag, New York, 346 pp.

Virnstein, R.W., 1977. The importance of predation by crabs and fishes on benthic infauna in Chesapeake Bay. Ecology, 58:199-1217.

Virnstein, R.W., 1979. Predation on estuarine infauna: Response patterns of component species. Estuaries, 2(2):69-86.

Ward, G. and G.J. Fitzgerald, 1982. Fish predation on the macrobenthos of tidal salt marsh pools. Can. J. Zool., 61:1358-1361.

Warwick, R.M. and R. Price, 1975. Macrofauna production on an estuarine mudflat. J. Mar. Biol. Assoc. U.K., 55:1-18.

Warwick, R.M., C.L. George, and J.R. Davies, 1978. Annual macrofauna production in a *Venus* community. Estuarine Coastal Mar. Sci., 7:215-241.

Warwick, R., I. Joint, and P. Radford, 1979. Secondary production of the benthos in an estuarine environment. In R. Jefferies and A. Davy (Eds.), Ecological Processes in Coastal Environments, Blackwell, Oxford, pp. 429-450.

Whitlatch, R., 1982. The ecology of New England tidal flats: A community profile. U.S. Fish and Wildlife Service, Biological Services Program, Washington, D.C., FWS/OBS-81-01, 125 pp.

Ward, G. and G.J. Fitzgerald, 1983. Fish predation on the macrobenthos of tidal salt marsh pools. Can. J. Zool., 61:1358-1361.

Wolff, W. J., 1973. The estuary as a habitat. An analysis of data on the soft-bottom macrofauna of the estuarine area of the rivers Rhine, Meuse, and Scheldt. Museum of Natural History, Leiden, The Netherlands, Zoological Treatise No. 126, 242 pp.

Wolff, W., 1977. A benthic food budget for the Grevelinger Estuary, the Netherlands, and a consideration of the mechanisms causing high benthic secondary production in estuaries. In B. Coull (Ed.), Ecology of Marine Benthos. Univ. South Carolina Press, Columbia, pp. 267–280.

Wolff, W. J., 1983. Estuarine benthos. In B. H. Ketchum (Ed.), Ecosystems of the World, Estuaries and Enclosed Seas. Elsevier, New York, pp. 151–182.

Wolff, W.J. and L. de Wolff, 1977. Biomass and production of zoobenthos in the Gravelingen Estuary, The Netherlands. Estuar. coast. mar. Sci., 5:1–24.

▬ 10

Nekton, the Free-Swimming Consumers[1]

A casual examination of commercial fish landings attests to the high levels of biomass and production for fish and other nekton (free-swimming consumers) in estuaries as compared with other environments (Fig. 10.1). The biomass of nekton in estuaries is commonly among the greatest biomass of higher trophic levels found in natural ecosystems anywhere in the world (Woodwell et al. 1973, Haedrich and Hall 1976). But before we go farther we must define nekton more carefully. *Nekton* are actively swimming pelagic organisms comprised mostly of fishes, but often squid, scallops, crabs, lobsters, shrimp, seals, and porpoises as well.

Because of these ecologically interesting observation, and especially because of the large commercial and recreational value of fish, scientists expend considerable effort to analyze the interrelationship of nekton and estuaries. These studies show us that nekton interact with estuaries in ways far more complex than we had once thought. The role of estuaries in fish production, both measured and assumed, has been a powerful contributor to the scientific rationale for protecting estuaries from human impact. This role emphasizes the necessity of understanding the environments of fish (and other nekton), as well as the fish themselves.

The relationship of nekton to estuaries is a fascinating story. It is full of subtleties and complexities, which require the study of morphological, physiological, and behavioral adaptations, as well as nekton life history and estuarine ecology. This chapter begins with a description of the taxonomic composition of estuarine nekton, then considers estuarine adaptations with respect to a

[1]Co-authored by L. A. Deegan.

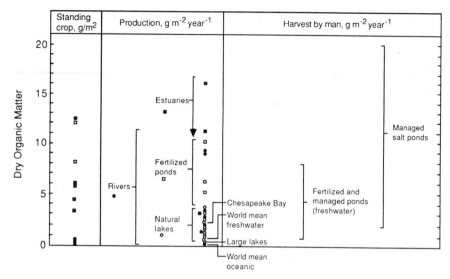

Figure 10.1 Standing crop, production, and yield of various aquatic ecosystems. Live weight is approximately 5 times that of dry organic matter (from Woodwell et al. 1973).

nektonic existence in general and then with respect to estuarine nekton in particular. We then develop an overview of the patterns by which nekton use estuaries emphasizing the importance of estuarine nekton migration and including detailed life histories of selected estuarine fish (because most nekton are fish we use these terms interchangeably). Finally, we consider the general role of nekton in estuarine communities and food chains. A number of reviews of estuarine nekton have been published (Springer and Woodburn 1960, McHugh 1967, Day et al. 1981, Haedrich 1983, Yáñez-Arancibia 1975, 1978, 1986, Yáñez-Arancibia and Sánchez-Gil 1988). One of the most recent comprehensive treatments on estuarine nekton ecology is by Yáñez-Arancibia (1985).

10.1 TAXONOMIC COMPOSITION OF ESTUARINE NEKTON

Although the particular species vary among estuaries, the types of nekton and nektonic life histories found in different parts of the world are frequently very similar. Almost all estuarine nekton species (and most of the biomass) are fish (McHugh, 1967). The rest are 1) mammals such as seals, porpoises, and whales and 2) a taxonomically diverse assemblage of invertebrates.

There are various ways to study nekton community structure, and each indicates something different about the community. The simplest is the species list, which indicates, in the most general way, the kinds of fishes that use estuaries.

The total number of species captured in most estuaries is moderate compared with nearby marine or freshwater systems, and usually between 8 and 15 species constitute 90% by number of the fish captured (Table 10.1).

Several authors have pointed out that there are more fish species in tropical and subtropical waters than in comparable temperate zone waters (Gunter 1945, Richard 1963, Leon 1972, Wagner 1973, Lowe-McConnell 1975, Gerking 1978, Moore 1978, Yáñez-Arancibia et al. 1980, 1982, 1985). This finding seems to apply in general, although some large high-latitude estuaries, such as Narragansett Bay, also have a large number of species (Table 10.1). The abundances in Table 10.1 also reflect the amount and season of sampling effort and gear used in the different habitats. For example, scientists who study marsh creeks using sienes will find more shallow-water fish than scientists who use a trawl in open bay areas. Fish abundances are also influenced by the tide, the moon stage, the presence or absence of underwater vegetation, the bottom type, and whether samples were taken in the day or at night.

Although the exact species and dominance rank changes from estuary to estuary, the dominant fishes usually come from only a few taxonomic groups. Important families for *temperate* systems are the Anguillidae (freshwater eels), Clupeidae (herring-like fish), Engraulidae (anchovies), Ariidae (salt water catfish), Cyprinodontidae (killifish), Gadidae (cods), Gasterosteridae (stickleback), Serranidae (basses), Sciaenidae (sea trout, drums, croakers), and Pleuronectidae (flounders) (McCleave et al. 1984). Important families in the *tropics* are Clupeidae, Engraulidae, Ariidae, Synodontidae (lizard fish), Mugilidae (mullets), Polynemidae (threadfins), Sciaenidae (drums), Gobiidae (gobies), Cichlidae (Tilapia-like fish), Dasyatidae (rays), Tetraodontidae (puffers), Gerreidae (mojarras), Pomadasyidae (grunts), and various flounder families such as Bothidae, Soleidae and Cynoglossidae (Yáñez-Arancibia 1985, 1986). In contrast, *boreal* estuaries have the simplest faunas and are dominated by Salmonidae (salmon and trout), Osmeridae (smelt and caplin), Gasterosteidae (sticklebacks), Ammodytidae (sandlance), and Cottidae (sculpins) and their relatives (Dadswell et al. 1987, Gross et al. 1988). In the southern hemisphere the Salmonidae are replaced by their ecological analogs the Galaxioidei.

Species composition transitions from one region to the next are gradual with species changes within families, then whole families become less important until they are replaced by another family. For example, the clupeiform fishes are important in all estuaries, but the herrings dominate in temperate and boreal estuaries, while the anchovies dominate in the tropics. But, even though the dominant families may change with latitude, the distribution of some species is widespread. The striped mullet (*Mugil cephalus*) occurs worldwide in tropical and subtropical estuaries. The arctic charr and the stickleback are circumglobal in cold northern estuaries, while *Galaxias maculatus* is widespread in southern cold estuaries. In temperate waters along the Atlantic coast of North America, menhaden, alewifes, silversides, and marsh minnows are found from Newfoundland to the Gulf of Mexico.

Crustacea are the most important invertebrate members of the nekton. The

TABLE 10.1 Examples of the Nekton Community in Nine Gulf of Mexico and Atlantic Ocean Estuaries.[ab]

	Tropical	Subtropical			South Temperate			North Temperate	
	Laguna de Terminos, Mexico	Barataria Bay, LA	Lake Pontchartrain, LA	Apalachicola Bay, FL	Coastal Georgia	Chesapeake Bay, MD	Delaware Bay, DE	Narragansett Bay, RI	Flax Pond, NY
SHALLOW WATER FISHES									
Killifish—Cyprinodontidae									
Sheepshead minnow, Cyprinodon variegatus	0.1	<0.1	2.6	<0.1	<0.1	<0.1	<0.1	<0.1	<0.1
Gulf killifish, Fundulus grandis		<0.1	1.5						
Fundulus heteroclitus		25			<0.1	<0.1	<0.1	<0.1	11
Striped killifish, Fundulus majalis		12							8
Livebearers—Poeciliidae									
Molly, Poeciliopsis spp.	1.0								
Silversides—Atherinidae									
Inland silverside, Menidia beryllina		0.4	9.8						
Atlantic silverside, Menidia menidia							<0.1	17	
Sticklebacks-Gasteristeidae									
Fourspine Stickleback, Apeltes quadracus									0.4
PELAGIC FISHES									
Herring—Clupeidae									
Blueback herring, Alosa aestivalis						9.7		1.0	

Species									
Alewife, *Alosa pseudoharengus*					0.1	4.6	0.2	0.4	0.2
Atlantic menhaden, *Brevoortia tyrannus*					1.7	1.5	0.2	0.2	3.0
Gulf menhaden, *Brevoortia patronus*		13.4	14.5	0.2					
Sardine, *Sardinella macrophthalmus*	6.3								
Anchovies—Engraulidae									
Striped anchovy, *Anchoa hepsetus*	17.9	0.03	0.1	0.2	0.1	0.5	0.2	0.1	
Bay anchovy, *Anchoa mitchilli*	8.7	79.6	35.2	41.3	4.6	77.4	0.1		0.1
Bigeye anchovy, *Anchoa lamprotaenia*	4.0								
Anchoveta, *Centengraulis edentulus*	1.4								
Harengula jaguana	1.4								
BOTTOM-ORIENTED FISH									
Catfish—Ariidae									
Hardhead catfish, *Arius melanopus*	9.3								
Arius felis	3.8	0.1	1.8	1.2	5.2				
Gafftopsail catfish, *Bagre marinus*	7.9	0.3							
Codfish—Gadidae									
Spotted hake, *Urophycis regius*					1.8	3.3	0.9	3.0	
Sivler hake, *Merluccius bilinearis*						0.1		4.0	

TABLE 10.1 Examples of the Nekton Community in Nine Gulf of Mexico and Atlantic Ocean Estuaries. Continued

	Tropical	Subtropical			South Temperate			North Temperate	
	Laguna de Terminos, Mexico	Barataria Bay, LA	Lake Pontchartrain, LA	Apalachicola Bay, FL	Coastal Georgia	Chesapeake Bay, MD	Delaware Bay, DE	Narragansett Bay, RI	Flax Pond, NY
Temperate basses—Percichthyidae									
Striped bass, *Morone saxatilis*						0.4			<0.1
White perch, *Morone americana*						0.7			
Seabasses—Serranidae									
Rock sea bass, *Centropristis philadelphica*									<0.1
Drums—Sciaenidae									
Silver perch, *Bairdiella chrysoura*	7.0		0.1	0.9	3.6	2.1	1.3		
Spot, *Leiostomus xanthurus*		0.7	2.2	3.1	3.4		0.9		
Atlantic croaker, *Micropogonias undulatus*	1.2	10.2	8.2	31.1	2.9	0.1	0.2		
Sand seatrout, *Cynoscion arenarius*	0.5	0.1	0.9	9.1					
Spotted seatrout, *Cynoscion nebulosus*	1.0		0.5						
Weakfish, *Cynoscion regalis*									
Southern kingfish, *Menticirrhus americanus*				1.9	0.4				
Star drum, *Stellifer lanceolatus*					4.6	33.0	4.3	8.0	
Mojarras—Gerreidae	0.8				46.1				

Silver jenny,									
Eucinostomus gula	15.0								
Mojarra,									
Diapterus rhombeus	2.5								
Jacks—Carangidae									
Pacific bumper,									
Chloroscombrus spp.	0.3			2.3					
Porgies—Sparidae									
Sheepshead,									
Archosargus probatocephalus	0.2		0.1	0.1					
Sea Bream,									
Archosargus rhomboidalis	11.8								
Pinfish,									
Lagodon rhomboides			0.1						
Grunt—Pomadasys									
White Grunt,									
Haemulon plumieri	1.4								
Pigfish,									
Orthopristis chrysoptera	11.9								
Mullet—Mugilidae									
Striped mullet,									
Mugil cephalus	0.1	1.1			0.1	0.4			<0.1
White mullet,									
Mugil curema	0.2								
Lefteye-Flounder—Bothidae									
Bay Whiff,									
Citharichthys spilopterus	0.7		0.2						
Summer flounder,									
Paralichthys dentatus						0.7	0.1	14.0	
Windowpane,									
Scophthalmus aquosus						4.2		14.0	0.2

TABLE 10.1 Examples of the Nekton Community in Nine Gulf of Mexico and Atlantic Ocean Estuaries. Continued

	Tropical	Subtropical			South Temperate			North Temperate	
	Laguna de Terminos, Mexico	Barataria Bay, LA	Lake Pontchartrain, LA	Apalachicola Bay, FL	Coastal Georgia	Chesapeake Bay, MD	Delaware Bay, DE	Narragansett Bay, RI	Flax Pond, NY
Righteye-Flounder—Pleuronectidae									
Winter flounder, *Pseudopleuronectes americanus*						1.3		36.0	41
Sole—Soleidae									
Hogchoker, *Trinectes maculatus*			0.6	0.6	0.9	19.1	0.1	0.1	<0.1
Tonguefish—Cynoglossidae Blackcheek tonguefish, *Symphurus plagiusa*				1.9	7.2		0.1		
Puffer—Tetraodontidae Checkered Puffer *Sphoeroides testudineus*	5.3								
NUMBER OF SPECIES IN STUDY	134	106	85	76	70	69	62	99	20
Number of dominant species[c]	31	7	9	8	10	6	6	7	6
Percentage of total abundance accounted for by dominant species	90	98.7	87.0	91.9	81.1	61.7	98.8	80.0	93

[a]Numbers in the table represent the percentage of the total number for some selected species of individuals caught in the study. Studies used different gears to catch fish; however, each study is representative of the estuary.

[b]Sources: Laguna de Terminos, Mexico (Yáñez-Arancibia et al. 1980, 1985a), Barataria Bay, Louisiana (Day et al. 1973, Chambers 1980) Lake Pontchartrain, Louisiana (Thompson and Verret 1980), Apalachicola Bay, Florida (Livingston 1976, 1985), Coastal Georgia (Dahlberg and Odum 1970), Chesapeake Bay, Maryland (McEarlean et al. 1973), Delaware Bay, Delaware (Maurer and Tinsman 1980), Narragansett Bay, Rhode Island (Nixon and Ovaitt 1973, Oviatt and Nixon 1973), Flax Pond, New York (Woodwell and Pecan 1973)

[c]Not all dominant species are represented in the table.

decapod crustacea are the most widespread and are divided into two suborders: Reptantia, the creeping forms, and Natantia, the swimmers. Most Reptantia are not nektonic, but a few species have evolved as very good swimmers. For example, the blue crab (*Callinectes sapidus*) of the Atlantic and Gulf coasts of the United States and Mexico has developed the capacity to swim by a modification of the fifth pair of thoracic legs to form paddle-like swimming organs. The legs and carapace are slender, and light in weight, and have few bulky spines and protuberances. These modifications allow blue crabs to swim off the bottom for extended periods, and even to perform extensive seasonal migrations. Many members of the subclass Natantia which are active swimmers, may also crawl on or bury in, the substrate. Important members of this group are the shrimps, some of which, like the penaeid shrimps, are of great commercial importance.

10.1.1   Functional or Ecological Classification

Fishes also may be classified according to their way of life or ecology. Within estuaries we can recognize three major groups: the shallow-water, the pelagic, and the bottom-oriented (epibenthic) fishes (Fig. 10.2, Table 10.2).

The shallow-water fishes (or *littoral fishes* when near the shore) that inhabit estuarine edges, marshes, grassbeds, and tide pools are usually quite small (adult size less than 10 cm). Most do not exhibit migratory behavior. The near-bottom schools of fish observed along the beach or marsh edge are usually killifishes (*Fundulus* sp. or *Cyprinodon* sp.). Schools of silversides (*Menidia* sp.), found near the water surface in open areas are also common. Pipefish (*Syngnathus* sp.), which are odd-looking pencil-shaped fish related to seahorses, inhabit grassbeds. All of these fish feed primarily on copepods, amphipods, and other small animals. Killifish feed primarily on the bottom, while silversides pick crustaceans out of the water column.

Pelagic species are those that swim freely throughout the water column, usually in schools near the surface. Pelagic fishes usually exhibit strong migration behavior and tend to be either plankton feeders or higher carnivores. Some plankton-feeding pelagic species have specialized at using food at the lowest trophic levels (phytoplankton or detritus), thereby tapping vast food reserves for themselves. These fishes including menhaden (*Brevoortia* sp.), herring (*Alosa* sp.), anchovies (*Anchoa* sp.), smelt (*Osmerus* sp.), and sardines (*Sardinella* sp.) (Table 10.2, Fig. 10.2), are often extremely abundant and form the basis for many coastal fisheries. Herring and menhaden use modified gills to filter copepods, cladocerins, and algal species out of the water column. Anchovies, smelt, and sardines prey on small crustaceans such as copepods, amphipods and mysid shrimp and on fish larvae. Higher carnivorous pelagic fishes include the jacks (Carangidae), bluefish (*Pomatomus saltatrix*), salmon (*Salmo* sp. or *Oncorhyncus* sp.), striped bass (*Morone saxatilis*), and ladyfish (*Elops* sp.). They often feed primarily on other pelagic species, such as herring or menhaden.

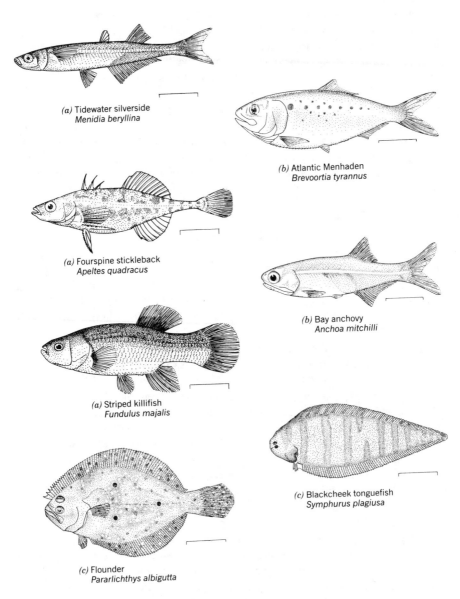

(a) Tidewater silverside
Menidia beryllina

(b) Atlantic Menhaden
Brevoortia tyrannus

(a) Fourspine stickleback
Apeltes quadracus

(b) Bay anchovy
Anchoa mitchilli

(a) Striped killifish
Fundulus majalis

(c) Blackcheek tonguefish
Symphurus plagiusa

(c) Flounder
Pararlichthys albigutta

Figure 10.2 Representative examples of fishes found in estuaries. (a) Shallow water fishes. (b) Pelagic fishes. (c) Benthic flatfish. (d) Benthic demersal midlevel carnivores. (e) Benthic omnivore, catfish. (f) Pelagic bottom feeder, mullet. (g) Benthic carnivore, shark.

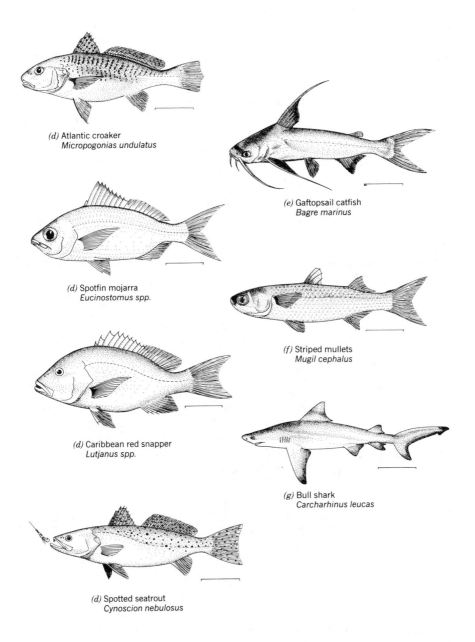

(d) Atlantic croaker
Micropogonias undulatus

(e) Gaftopsail catfish
Bagre marinus

(d) Spotfin mojarra
Eucinostomus spp.

(f) Striped mullets
Mugil cephalus

(d) Caribbean red snapper
Lutjanus spp.

(g) Bull shark
Carcharhinus leucas

(d) Spotted seatrout
Cynoscion nebulosus

Figure 10.2   (Continued)

The bottom-oriented fish (*epibenthic* or *demersal*) live on or near the bottom throughout the estuary, but frequently feed and swim in the water column close to the bottom (Fig. 10.2). This is the most diverse group of fish found in estuaries, probably because of the variety of substrates and the strong biotic and abiotic interactions associated with the bottom such as reproductive stratagies, migration patterns, and availability of food resources (Deegan and Day 1985, 1986, Yáñez-Arancibia and Sánchez-Gil 1988, Weinstein and Heck 1979). Within the bottom-oriented fish three forms are usually present: catfish, flatfish, and the croakers, cods, and sea trouts.

Catfishes, of which the seacats (*Arius* sp., *Bagre* sp.) are typical, are similar in appearance (Fig. 10.2). They usually have distinctive whiskerlike barbels, smooth scaleless bodies, and sharp barbed spines at the margins of their pectoral fins. All species move along the bottom searching for food with "taste buds" located on their barbels. The barbels play an important role in searching for food since visability is generally poor. Catfish are omnivorous bottom feeders which grab at any form of food including worms, small fish, and dead material (Deegan and Thompson 1985, Yáñez-Arancibia et al. 1986, Lara-Domínguez et al. 1981, Yáñez-Arancibia and Lara-Domínguez 1988).

Flatfishes are immediately recognizable by their flattened shape and their asymetrical eyes on the dark-colored top sides of their bodies (Fig. 10.2). Most flatfishes begin life with normally arranged eyes. With growth, metamorphosis occurs and the eye of the side that will be on the bottom migrates to the other side and a rearrangement of internal organs also occurs. Most species prefer soft muddy bottoms where they lie buried in sediment when at rest. The hogchoker (*Trinectes* sp.), baywhiff (*Citharichthys* sp.) and blackcheek tonguefish (*Symphurus* sp.) are small flounders with wide distribution. The summer (*Paralichthys* sp.) and winter (*Pseudopleuronectes* sp.) flounders are larger, with a more northern distribution, and are prized by sport and commercial fishermen. The smaller flounders eat small crustaceans, worms, and molluscs; the larger flounders also consume larger shrimps, crabs, and fish (Haedrich and Hall 1976, Musick et al. 1985).

The most diverse of the bottom fishes are croakers, cods, mullets, and sea trouts. Within these fishes there are two feeding types. The first are bottom feeders, similar to catfish, with down-turned mouths and often barbels on the lower jaw. These species eat mostly benthic invertebrates including small crustaceans, annelid worms, and small molluscs. Three widely distributed members of this group along the Atlantic coast of North America are the croaker (*Micropogonias* sp.), spot (*Leiostomus* sp.), and silver perch (*Bairdiella* sp.). Cods (*Gadus* sp.) and hake (*Urophyscis* sp.) are common members of this group in northern estuaries in North America and Europe, while mullet (*Mugil* sp.) are more typical in tropical and subtropical estuaries. These fish usually congregate in loose monospecific schools and forage along the bottom. Some species change their bottom preference from muddy to firmer substrates as they grow older. The second feeding type is the "mobile predator." In this group top carnivores, which are only loosely associated with the bottom, feed on more motile prey such as penaeid

TABLE 10.2 Secondary Production (g/m² yr) of Selected Fish Species by Habitat

Common Name	Scientific Name	Productivity	References[a]
SHALLOW WATER SPECIES			
Mummichog	*Fundulus heteroclitus*	12.5–64.0	1,2,3
Saltwater killifish	*Fundulus majalis*	2.1–6.3	1
Atlantic silversides	*Menidia menidia*	8.8–22.0	1
PELAGIC SPECIES			
Atlantic menhaden	*Brevoortia tyrannus*	3.7–5.7	1
Gulf menhaden	*Brevoortia patronus*	13.5	4
Sardine	*Lile stolifera*	3.8	5
Anchovy	*Anchoa panamensis*	9.3	5
Jenny	*Diapterus peruvianus*	1.2	5
Alewife	*Alosa pseudoharengus*	0.1–0.4	1
BOTTOM-ORIENTED SPECIES			
Croaker	*Micropogonias undulatus*	23.4	4
Mullet	*Mugil curema*	9.4	5
Catfish	*Galeichthys caerulescens*	2.7	5
Seatrout	*Cynoscion xanthulus*	3.8	5
Flounder	*Pseudopleuronectes americanus*	22.4–41.4	1
Sole	*Achirus mazatlanus*	0.8	5
Tautog	*Tautog onitis*	0–6.6	1
American eel	*Anguilla rostrata*	5.7–10.5	1
Scup	*Stenotomus chrysops*	0.3–1.9	1
Cunner	*Tautogolabrus adspersus*	0.6	1

[a] 1 Hall and Woodwell (unpublished data)
2 Meredith and Lotrich 1979
3 Valiela et al. 1977
4 Deegan and Thompson, 1985
5 Warburton 1979

shrimp and pelagic fishes. Typical estuarine species are the sea trouts (*Cynoscion* sp.) and sharks.

10.2 ADAPTATIONS TO NEKTONIC AND ESTUARINE EXISTENCE

10.2.1 Nektonic Adaptations

The principal morphological and physiological adaptations for truly nektonic organisms are the existence and position of swimming organs (fins), a smooth streamlined body, and a specific gravity reasonably close to water (Nikolsky 1963). Another important requirement for a nektonic existence is the ability to extract oxygen at a relatively rapid rate from the surrounding water in order to support the large energy requirements of swimming. Finally, most pelagic organisms have well-developed sensory organs that are well suited to an active nektonic existence.

Most fishes have achieved these requirements. For example, most are streamlined and able to control their depth through varying their specific gravity by changing the amount of gas in the swim bladder. Fishes have gills well adapted for rapid oxygen exchange, which permit active and sustained movement. Fish have developed a sensory organ called the lateral line, which is very sensitive to sound waves and to changes in water density. Some have also developed chin barbels which help locate food. Nektonic shrimp and crabs, although less streamlined than fish, tend to be more so than their benthic counterparts.

10.2.2   Estuarine Adaptations

Nekton obviously have general adaptations that allow them to survive in water; however, there are specific adaptations that allow them to flourish in estuaries. One of the most fundamental and intriguing biological questions that can be posed is "how is it possible for one group of animals to thrive under conditions that would be intolerable for another group?" This is particularly interesting when the environment is apparently hostile or stressful. Estuaries are very dynamic and the rapidly changing physical and chemical environment imposes great energy demands on fish, so that most species simply cannot survive there. In fact, the number of species and the number of families found only in estuaries for their entire lives is low, emphasizing that few kinds of fish have evolved to remain in estuaries their entire lives. There are, however, a larger number of fish species that spend at least part of their lives in estuaries. This leads to an intriguing question that we will discuss. If the estuarine environment is so energetically demanding for fish, why have so many groups of fish evolved a life history requiring that some or all of their lives be spent in an estuary? And why are these groups so often very abundant?

There are three possible outcomes when an animal encounters stressful conditions, depending on its adaptive capacity: (1) it can migrate to a more favorable environment; (2) it can adapt, adjust, and survive; (3) if conditions are too rigorous, the animal dies. The dynamic interaction of an animal and various components of its environment is represented in Fig. 10.3a. For each species only a certain portion of the total range of each abiotic environmental factor is compatible with life (Vernberg and Vernberg 1976). Within the relatively large range within which an organism can survive there is a smaller range where the organism can prosper, that is, where the organisms can have a positive energy balance and can grow and reproduce (Fig. 10.3b). Different life stages, especially the juvenile, may be adapted to very different environmental conditions compared with adults. Thus the concept of adaptations is complex and dynamic, especially for estuarine nekton where young and adults live in very different environments. These differences may avoid competition, optimize growth, or reduce predation.

Before we can answer the question of why so many fish use estuaries for part of their lives, it is necessary to examine specific environmental demands and the

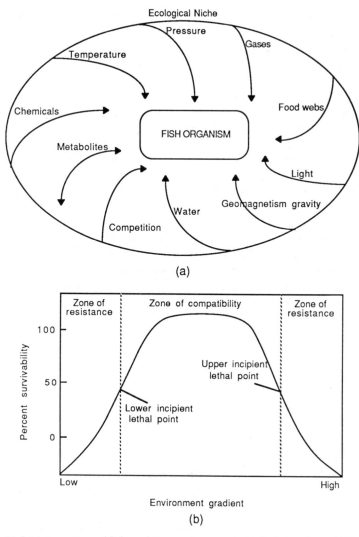

Figure 10.3 Interaction of fish and the environment. (a) Relationship of fish to environmental factors. (b) Zones of resistance and compatibility of an organism in response to an environmental gradient (from Vernberg and Vernberg 1976).

organism's response in more detail. Probably the most difficult problem faced by estuarine nekton is osmoregulation—maintaining nearly constant internal osmotic conditions in a very changeable external osmotic environment. The relatively impermeable skin, scales, and coat of mucus characteristic of estuarine nekton minimize ion and water exchange associated with changes in salinity (Vernberg and Vernberg 1976). Fish also adjust physiologically by the transport of specific ions across the gills, by drinking water, or by controlling the amount of water passed into the urine. Finally, behavioral mechanisms help fish try to avoid extreme situations. Through active movements fish avoid large variations outside their physiological tolerances in salinity, temperature, dissolved oxygen, and suspended silt. For example, many nektonic species move up and down the estuary in response to changes in salinity.

Estuarine species may be divided into tolerance categories with respect to several parameters at once, usually temperature and salinity. This particular relationship is shown as Fig. 10.4, where lines circumscribe different areas of tolerance (Muus 1967). Some species require high salinities and are never found in the riverine reaches of estuaries. This kind of fish can be either polar (1), temperate (3), or tropical (2), depending on its temperature tolerance. Some species possess a wide range of salinity tolerance (4, 5, or 6), but are restricted by their range of temperature tolerances to polar (4), temperate (5), or tropical (6) areas. There are few species in nature adapted to withstand extreme variation in both temperature and salinity (7).

Temperature and salinity may operate synergistically. Reduced or fluctuating salinity in combination with varying temperature offers special physiological problems for osmoregulation for most species. For example, plaice (a flatfish) is euryhaline at low temperatures and eurythermal at high salinities. However, they do not thrive in a low-salinity, warm location because they cannot survive the combination of low salinity and high temperature. For the temperate zone it perhaps may be considered a general rule that an increase in water temperature leads to a reduced ability to withstand wide variations in salinity (Muus, 1967),

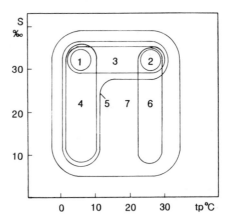

Figure 10.4 Estuarine fishes may be divided into tolerance categories in response to two environmental parameters, for example, temperature and salinity (after Muss 1967). (1) High salinity, low temperature requirements, not tolerant of much variation in either. (2) High salinity, high temperature, not tolerant of much variation. (3) Narrow salinity tolerance, high temperature tolerance. (4 or 6) High salinity tolerance, but restricted to either low temperature (4) or high temperature (6). (5) At low temperatures can tolerate high salinity variation, or at high temperatures can tolerate low salinity variation. (7) Wide tolerence for both temperature and salinity. See text for further explanation.

possibly because of the effect of warm temperatures on enzymes that regulate osmoregulation.

10.3   NEKTONIC FOOD WEBS

Nekton are important in estuarine food webs because they are the dominant top and midlevel carnivores, and because they often regulate, through predatory pressure, lower trophic levels. And, of course, many humans are extremely interested in fish for aesthetic, culinary, commercial, and recreational reasons.

Many different taxa appear in fish stomachs and there is considerable spatial and temporal variation in food eaten even for the same species (Fig. 10.5; Darnell 1961, de Sylva 1975, Levine 1980, Yáñez-Arancibia 1978, 1981, Livingston 1980, 1982, 1984, 1985). The complexity of food sources found in fish stom-

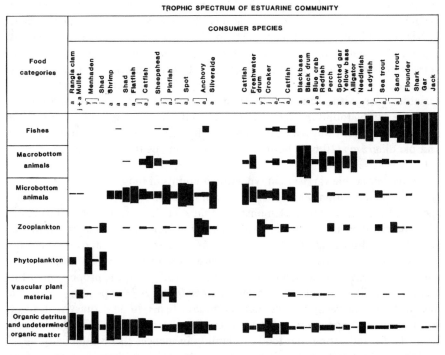

Figure 10.5   Trophic spectrum of an estuarine community based on data from Lake Pontchartrain, Louisiana. Note that most species eat a wide variety of prey items, and that most species show shifts in food types between juveniles and adults (from "Trophic spectrum of an estuarine community, based on studies of Lake Pontchartrain, Louisiana" by R. Darnell, Ecology, 1961, 42: 553–568; copyright © 1961 by the Ecological Society of America, reprinted by permission).

achs reflects changes in food preferences and sources as fish grow (ontogenetic changes) and the opportunistic nature of most fish species; often the diet of a single species comprises more than 20 different food types. The whole trophic structure does not comprise specific trophic levels as fish eat food from a variety of sources (Yáñez-Arancibia et al. 1986).

Ontogenetic changes in diet are typical of most fish in estuaries. For example, the stomach contents of croaker (*Micropogonias undulatus*) in Apalachicola Bay, Florida, show a great variation with size of fish, indicating ontogentic changes in diet (Sheridan and Livingston 1979, Fig. 10.6*a*). Fish between 10 and 70 mm eat mostly (>60%) polychaetes, detritus, and insect larvae, as well as a diversity of other minor items such as amphipods, mysids, harpacticoid copepods, and calanoid copepods. For larger fish between 100 and 150 mm, the number of food items decreases and shifts to include polychaetes, shrimps, chironomids, juvenile fishes, and a small but variable amount of detritus.

Stomach contents of the seabream (*Archosargus rhomboidalis*) in Terminos Lagoon also show considerable variation with fish growth, indicating changes in diet (Chavance et al. 1986, Fig. 10.6*b*). Young fish (30–80 mm) eat mostly small crustaceans (35% of dry weight), and occasionally polychaetes. Plant material (fragments of *Thalassia* and filamentous algae) is a minor part of the diet. Fishes from 80 to 160 mm feed mostly on plants (unicellular and filamentous algae and *Thalassia*). Animal food items are scarce but diverse (microfauna, polychaetes, and small fishes). Large fish (160–200 mm) eat predominantly crustaceans (e.g., shrimps and tanaids). The proportion of detritus in the diet is variable, even within an alimentary stage. Some additional information on Sparidae can be found in Blaber (1974). The information presented in Fig. 10.6 shows two different ways of expressing food habit data. Cluster analysis (10.6*a*) and pie diagrams (10.6*b*); both show dietary composition by different sizes of fish.

The considerable variation in types and amounts of foods consumed by a species at a given location, and the similarity of major food types eaten by different species at a given location, demonstrate that diet composition of omnivores is often determined mostly by food availability. For example, Yáñez-Arancibia (1976) studied food habits of the mullet, *Mugil curema,* in several coastal lagoons on the west coast of Mexico. Detritus was usually 50% of the food of adults at all seasons in all lagoons studied (Fig. 10.7). But the proportion of the diet that was filamentous algae varied between 0 and 28% depending on season and location. Interestingly, the most abundant fishes in an estuary tend to be omnivorous and opportunistic at all sizes (Odum and Heald 1975, Miller and Dunn 1980), indicating that food availability influences fish productivity.

Fishes differ greatly in the character of the food they consume; however, they show a basic dependence on phytoplankton and detritus through both the pelagic and benthic pathways. The pelagic pathway begins with phytoplankton, and goes to copepods, decapods, and mysids, to small fishes like anchovy and herring, then to large predators like sea trout. The benthic pathway begins with detritus and other organic matter, which is consumed by benthic copepods and

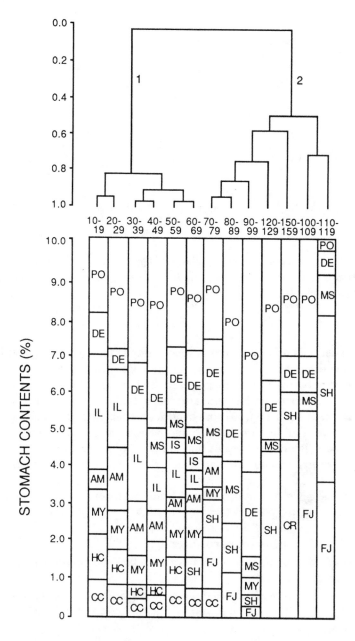

CODES INDICATE FOOD ITEMS:

PO = polychaetes   DE = detritus
IL = insect larvae   AM = amphipods
MY = mysids   HC = harpacticoid copepods
CC = calanoid copepods   SH = shrimp
FJ = juvenile fishes   MS = miscellaneous
CR = chironomids

(a)

Figure 10.6

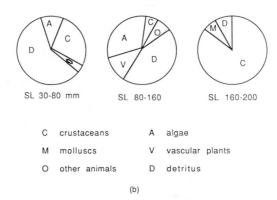

SL 30-80 mm   SL 80-160   SL 160-200

C crustaceans   A algae

M molluscs   V vascular plants

O other animals   D detritus

(b)

Figure 10.6 Ontogenetic changes in feeding of (a) Atlantic croaker *Micropogonias un-dulatus* in Apalachicola Bay, Florida. Numbers below the dendogram indicate the size range (in mm) of each feeding category (from Sheridan and Livingston 1979), and (b) Seabream, *Archosargus rhomboidalis* in Terminos Lagoon, Mexico, SL = standard length (from Chavance et al. 1986).

polychaetes as well as filter feeding organisms; and then these are eaten by small benthic dwelling fish, which are eaten by large predators like trout. These pathways are closely linked because many species eat both pelagic and benthic organisms, and the top carnivore is often the same fish in both pathways (Sibert et al. 1978). Because many fish feed from both benthic and pelagic pathways, they are the main organisms that link the benthic and pelagic energy flow. This culminates in the production of fish species that are often of interest to people—the top carnivores, like trout and salmon (Healy 1979, 1982, Naiman and Sibert 1979).

In summary the general characteristics of feeding relationships among estuarine fishes are:

1. Flexibility of feeding in time and space.
2. Sharing of the common pool of most abundant food resources among many species.
3. The taking of food from different levels of the food web by each species.
4. The changing of the diet with growth, food availability, and locality within the estuary.
5. The use of both the pelagic and benthic pathways by a given species.

10.3.1 Adaptations for Feeding in Estuarine Nekton

Even though many estuarine fish eat many food types, most possess adaptations that increase the probability of successfully handling and ingesting a particular group of prey. Differences in the size and position of mouth, kind and position of

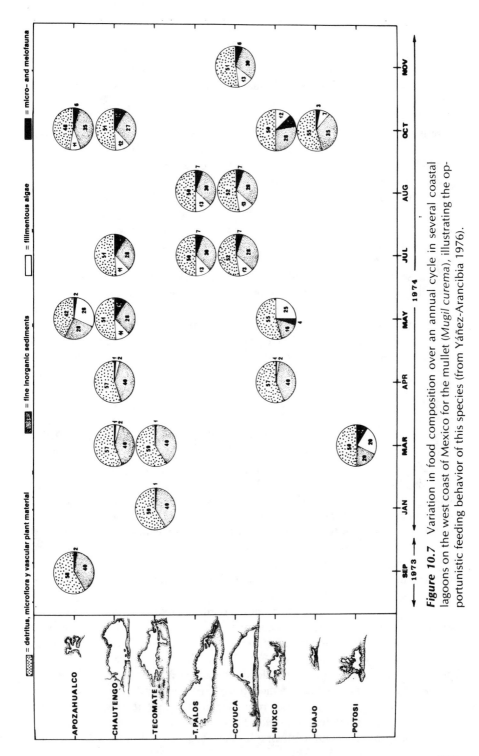

Figure 10.7 Variation in food composition over an annual cycle in several coastal lagoons on the west coast of Mexico for the mullet (*Mugil curema*), illustrating the opportunistic feeding behavior of this species (from Yáñez-Arancibia 1976).

397

teeth and branchial arches, shape and length of intestines all have important consequences for food capture and use (Hyatt 1979).

Because a large mouth intuitively seems to be a good way to increase the probability of prey capture, we may wonder why all fish do not have huge mouths. One answer is that selective pressures acting to favor particular shapes or positions of any organ often conflict. In some cases, one selective pressure has been more important than another, resulting in a mouth design that has important implications for food acquisition. To eat a wide range of prey sizes, a mouth should be large. However, if the mouth is located at the front of the head, which serves as the bow to a streamlined body, that part should be small and pointy. Fish compromise by changing the location of the mouth and the size in accordance with how they eat. Common first order consumers, such as mojarras (*Gerres* sp., *Eucinostomus* sp., *Eugerres* sp.), in estuaries often have extremely conspicuous modifications of the jaw bones so that the mouth can be protruded in order to feed on small benthic organisms and on the leaf surfaces of plants such as seagrasses (Cyrus and Blaber 1982, 1983, Aguirre-Léon and Yáñez-Arancibia 1986). Fish with dorsal mouths, such as silversides (Fig. 10.8*a*), often suck in floating insects from the water surface. Top predators such as trout, which usually pursue other fish species, have a large, terminal mouth, while demersal fish such as hake (*Urophyscis* sp.) have ventral mouths. Some fish, such as croaker, which use both the pelagic and benthic pathways equally, have compromised and have semiventral mouths (Fig. 10.8*a*, see also Chao and Musick 1977).

Although food is collected by mouth, the real processing takes place in the throat or pharynx, where the pharyngeal bones are located. Often a wide range of dental development is associated in a predictable way with the types of food eaten. The number, size, and structure of teeth on these bones differs according to food type most commonly processed (Fig.10.8*b*, Hyatt 1979).

At the most fundamental level it is generally true that active predators have strong jaws with sharp teeth. The surfaces of the pharyngeal plate of phytoplankton eaters (such as shad) are covered with rows of fine recurved teeth so that when the two sets slide together the algae are combed backward. Fish eaters, such as trout, tend to have sharply pointed teeth that point backward. These teeth grip and force backward fish held in the mouth. Mollusc eaters, such as black drum, possess massive bones with a number of large flat "molars" which crack the shells of the prey.

Modification of the branchial arches and gill rakers, which aid in food selection and processing, has received much attention (Hyatt 1979). The presence of numerous, long, thin and closely spaced gill rakers indicates a fish species that filters plankton out of the water (Fig.10.8*c*). The appearance in a single fish species of elaborate gill-raker modifications during development and accompanying dietary shifts has been demonstrated. For example, June and Carlson (1971) discovered that the change from zooplankton to a phytoplankton diet in Atlantic menhaden (*Brevoortia tyrannus*) is accompanied by an increase in the number, length, and complexity of gill rakers (Fig. 10.8*c*). Similarly the initia-

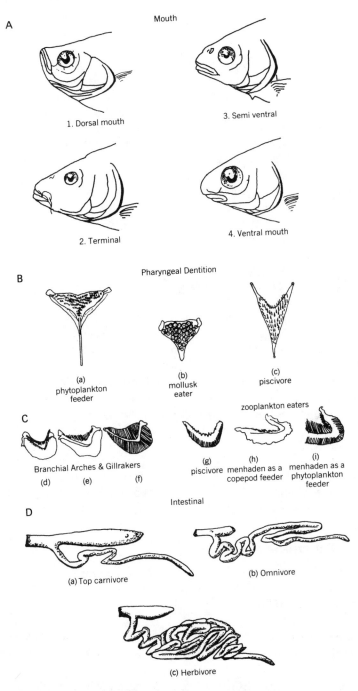

A

Mouth

1. Dorsal mouth

3. Semi ventral

2. Terminal

4. Ventral mouth

B Pharyngeal Dentition

(a)
phytoplankton
feeder

(b)
mollusk
eater

(c)
piscivore

zooplankton eaters

C

Branchial Arches & Gillrakers

(d)   (e)   (f)

(g)
piscivore

(h)
menhaden as a
copepod feeder

(i)
menhaden as a
phytoplankton
feeder

Intestinal

D

(a) Top carnivore

(b) Omnivore

(c) Herbivore

Figure 10.8 Adaptations for feeding: (A) Position and size of mouth; (B) variation in pharygal dentation for feeding (from Hyatt 1979); (C) variation in gill rakers for plankton feeding (from Hyatt 1979); (D) changes in intestinal shape and length with food type.

tion of phytoplankton feeding by the anchovy (*Engraulis anchoveta*) is correlated with the formation of elaborate gill rakers.

Once the food has been captured and consumed, the ability of the fish to utilize the food is dependent on the digestive process. In general, the length and complexity of the gut increases from top carnivore to herbivore (Fig. 10.8*d*). This is a response to the digestibility of the food item. Top carnivores generally consume fish or invertebrates which are primarily protein and are easily digested and assimilated. Plant tissue or detritus is a structural complex food made of difficult to digest carbohydrates, lignen and cellulose. For this reason, herbivores have long, complex guts which increase the time the food spends in the intestine. This results in a longer time period for enzymes to break down the more complex structures. Many herbivores also have highly acidic guts, which cause a chemical breakdown, and gizzards that grind the food into small particles before it enters the intestine.

10.4 NEKTON LIFE HISTORIES

Different species of nekton have evolved various life-history "strategies" for living in estuaries. Many species are considered "estuarine-dependent," that is requiring estuaries for a part of their life history. This pattern often results in specific life-history patterns that are bewilderingly and fascinatingly complex. Almost certainly the benefits from such life histories are related to the high primary and secondary productivity of estuarine waters. Presumably the food energy gained by those species that utilize estuaries more than offsets the energy losses to the population in physiological adaptation, migration, and high mortality rates.

We next consider in overview some of the basic patterns of reproduction and migration by which nekton utilize estuaries, develop the life histories of several species in some detail, and then discuss the general concept of the estuary as a "nursery ground" for these species.

10.4.1 Patterns of Migration

Particular nekton often spend different stages of their life in widely varying locations. There are a number of terms used to describe general patterns of nekton migrations (Myers 1949):

A. Potamodromous—fish whose migrations occur wholly within fresh water, such as the landlocked kokanee (sockeye) salmon or suckers (catostomids); see Hall (1972).

B. Oceanodromous—fish that live and migrate wholly in the sea (such as most tunas).

C. Diadromous—fish that migrate between the sea and fresh water. All species of diadromous fish must pass through estuaries on their migrations, and most species spend a considerable amount of time there. These generally are divided into three classes:

1. Anadromous. These fishes spend most of their lives in the sea and migrate to fresh water for breeding (e.g., salmon, shad, and sea-lamprey). Semi-anadromous fish do not travel all the way to fresh water, but spawn in low-salinity estuarine water.

2. Catadromous. These fishes spend most of their lives in fresh water and migrate to the sea for breeding. A well-known example is the American eel.

3. Amphidromous. These fishes migrate from fresh water to the sea, or vice versa, not for the purpose of breeding, but regularly at other stages in their life cycle, often for feeding excursions.

Because all of the diadromous migrations involve use of estuaries, but for different ecological reasons, McHugh (1967) modified this classification to include the reasons, such as spawning location, feeding, and salinity tolerance. These can be summarized as six ways fish utilize estuaries (see Fig. 10.9):

1. Freshwater fishes that occasionally enter brackish water.

2. Truly estuarine species that spend their entire lives in estuaries.

3. Estuarine-marine species that use the estuary primarily as a nursery ground, usually spawning and spending much of their adult life at sea, but often returning seasonally to estuaries.

4. Marine species that pay regular seasonal visits to estuaries, usually as adults looking for food.

5. Anadromous and catadromous species in transit.

6. Occasional visitors, which appear irregularly, and apparently accidently.

These ways represent a continuum and some fish have life-history patterns intermediate between several of these types (Fig. 10.9).

The development of patterns of reproduction and spawning are important characteristics of a species' life history, and we will address the ways that fish use estuaries for reproduction first. Later, we will integrate the use of estuaries as feeding grounds with reproduction to give an overall picture of estuarine fish community dynamics.

10.4.2   Patterns of Reproduction

There are three major migration patterns by which nekton use estuarine systems for reproduction and juvenile feeding (Fig. 10.10):

1. Saltwater spawning, followed by immigration of the larvae into an estuary.

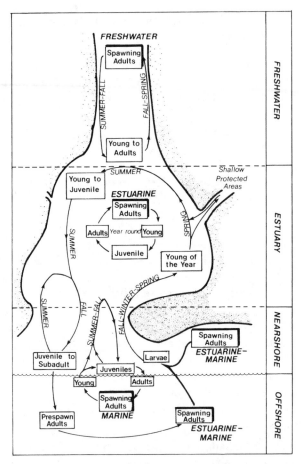

Figure 10.9 Diagram of temporal and spatial use of estuaries by estuarine, marine, freshwater, and estuarine-dependent marine species (from Deegan and Thompson 1985).

2. Estuarine spawning, in which the larvae remain for the most part within an estuary.
3. Freshwater spawning, followed by the downstream drift or swimming of larvae and juvenile nekton into an estuary.

The patterns for some species are intermediate or are a combination of these basic patterns. Usually a species exhibits only one of these patterns. Rarely, different populations of a species may exhibit different patterns.

In Atlantic coast estuaries of the United States, the juveniles are derived proportionately more from saltwater spawners while on the Pacific coast they tend to be derived from freshwater spawners. The young fish in tropical estuaries

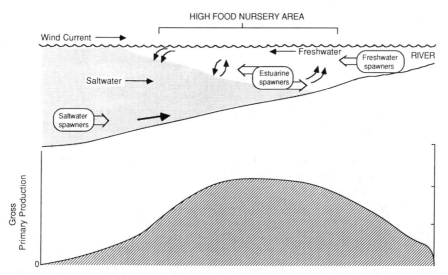

Figure 10.10 A representation of the use of an estuary by fish which spawn in freshwater, the estuary, and the sea (from Hall 1977). In many estuaries, the less-dense fresh water flows seaward above the salt water. The salt water, in turn, flows upstream below the fresh water to replace other salt water that is entrained into the surface waters. Primary production is often highest in the central part of the estuary and the three types of spawners have evolved different strategies to exploit the high productivity.

seem to come primarily from the saltwater spawners. The extent to which boreal estuaries serve as nursery areas is not well documented except for salmon; however, there seems to be a mixture of freshwater- and saltwater- spawned juveniles.

In the next section we consider more specifically the three patterns mentioned above, and give examples of how particular species fit the general patterns. Specifics for many species can be found in Bigelow and Shroeder (1953), Springer and Woodburn (1960), Smith et al. (1966), Douglas and Stroud (1971), Cronin and Manzueti (1971), Copeland and Birkhead (1972), Kjelson et al. (1973), Haedrich and Hall (1976), Herke (1977a, b), Ogren and Brusher (1977), Yáñez-Arancibia (1985) and Tyler (1971).

10.4.2.1 Saltwater Spawners. Probably the most common nekton life history cycle that involves the use of estuaries is that of the saltwater spawner. In the past these have often been called "estuarine dependent". These species usually spawn in nearshore coastal waters. Then the larvae and/or eggs move into estuaries on coastal currents. The juveniles spend a few weeks to several years in an estuary before moving offshore to return to adult feeding grounds.

Estuarine-dependent stocks of fish have developed spawning strategies which, when coupled with average estuarine circulation patterns, maximize the number of larval fish reaching zones of high primary and secondary production. For example, by staying near the bottom, passively drifting larvae often move into an estuary on the deeper landward-moving bottom currents of the typical two-layered circulation pattern (Fig.10.10). In other estuaries, wind-driven surface currents transport pelagic eggs and larvae into the estuary (Parrish et al. 1981). In addition, some organisms have evolved elaborate behavioral patterns geared to day–night and tidal cycles that increase the chances of their entering estuaries even though they are exposed to very complex currents.

Menhaden (*Brevoortia* spp.). This is one of the most abundant estuarine fish species along the Atlantic and Gulf coasts of the United States (Table 10.1). Menhaden are planktonic filter feeders and are relatively low in the food chain. Adult menhaden are usually found in offshore coastal waters of relatively high salinity. They are abundant and commercially important from southern New England to Texas. This abundance is reflected in the Louisiana fishery, which exceeds 500×10^6 kg annually and supports the largest commercial catch (in number and weight) in the contiguous United States. Adult menhaden spawn offshore and the young drift with the tides and currents, presumably seeking estuarine environments (Reintjes and Pacheco, 1966; Fig. 10.11). Larval entrance into the estuary on the Atlantic Coast is related to wind-driven surface currents. Fish enter the estuary when they are 15–20 mm in length, move immediately into the shallow marsh areas until midsummer, then move into the open bay areas until fall, when they migrate out to the ocean (Deegan 1985). In some years the juveniles overwinter in estuaries.

Bluefish (*Pomatomus saltatrix*). Bluefish vary slightly from the general saltwater pattern in that they usually appear in New York and New England estuaries as juveniles, not larvae, which have clearly been maturing some since their birth in oceanic or coastal waters (Fig. 10.12). It is very evident when these small active predators enter estuaries, for they are constantly hungry and chasing after smaller fish. When they reach about 10 cm they are called "snapper blues" because of their fierce nature. The snapper blues stay in estuaries until the fall when they migrate out of the estuary and south along the Atlantic coast. Adult bluefish are a coastal migratory species highly prized as a sport and food fish, especially in the northeast.

Mullet (*Mugil* spp.). Throughout tropical and subtropical estuaries of the world, the mullet is an important forage and food fish. *Mugil curema* is found throughout much of the tropics (Yáñez-Arancibia, 1976) and *M. cephalus* is abundant in both tropical and subtropical latitudes (Lenanton and Hodgkin 1985), and have life cycles similar to that of the bluefish. Juvenile mullets enter the estuaries in large schools, during the rainy season, which is July to September–October in much of Mexico (Fig. 10.13). They remain there for about 12 months, feeding on detritus and filamentous algae until they reach sexual maturity. The adults leave the estuarine systems and enter the sea to spawn in Novem-

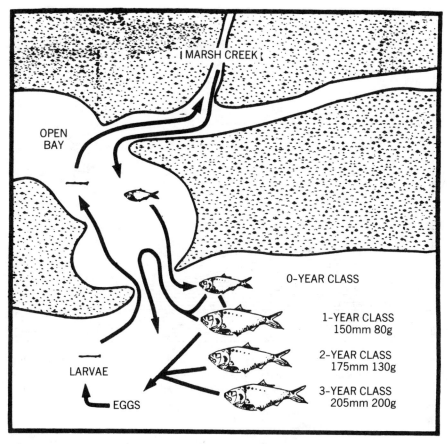

Figure 10.11 Life history of menhaden (*Brevoortia patronus*) in Louisiana (from Deegan 1985). 1, 2, and 3-year old fish are captured in the commercial fishery offshore.

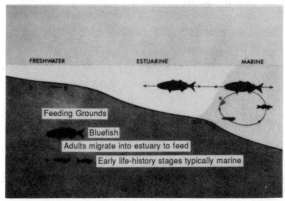

Figure 10.12 Life history of bluefish, *Pomatomus saltatrix* (from Cronin and Manzuetti 1971).

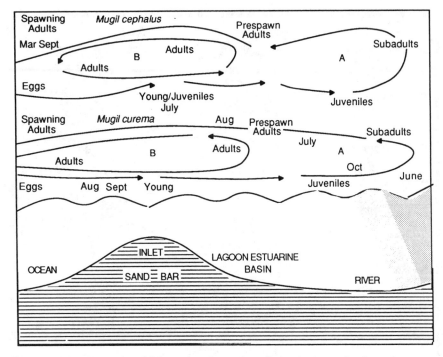

Figure 10.13 Generalized life cycle of *Mugil cephalus* in Australia (from Lenanton and Hodgkin 1985) and *M. curema* in Mexico (from Yáñez-Arancibia 1976). Cycles (A) represent the reproductive life history from eggs to adults, and cycles (B) represent adult movements for feeding.

ber to January. Once again, the following fall, the lagoon system is invaded by large schools of small individuals, which are the product of the spawning of the previous year.

Shrimps (*Penaeidae*). Shellfish, as well as finfish, often have complex life cycles utilizing offshore spawning and estuaries as nursery grounds (Kutkuhn 1966). For example, in the Gulf of Mexico, three species of shrimp are important—the brown (*Penaeus aztecus*), the white (*Penaeus setiferus*), and the pink (*Penaeus duoraram*). All three have similar life-history cycles that differ principally in seasonal timing and the degree to which the larvae use estuaries (Fig. 10.14). Shrimp eggs are spawned in the Gulf of Mexico at different distances from shore, depending on the species. The eggs hatch rapidly and proceed through a number of larval stages while drifting toward the estuaries. During the next 2–4 months in the estuary, the shrimp grow rapidly, then migrate to the gulf to complete their life cycle. Although details differ, this pattern holds for most Penaeidae of the world.

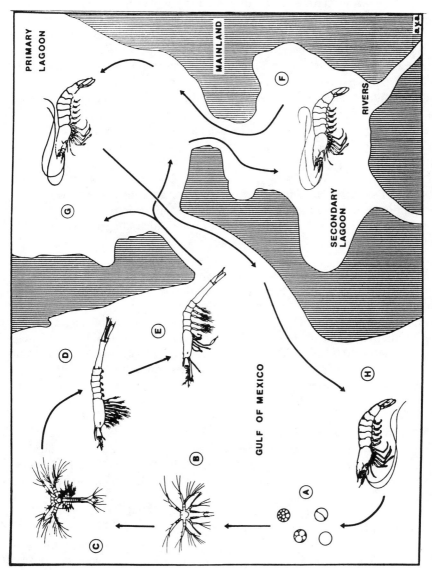

Figure 10.14 Generalized life history of shrimp (*Penaeus* spp.) from Yáñez-Arancibia 1986.

Blue Crab (*Callinectes sapidus*). Among those species exceptionally well fitted for the estuarine environment from tropical to temperate waters is the blue crab. Blue crabs spawn in nearshore ocean waters to produce planktonic zoea larvae similar to shrimp larvae (Cronin and Manzueti 1971). The megalops, or second-stage larvae, settle to the bottom, and individuals in subsequent postlarval stages move into the estuaries in bottom currents. The juvenile crabs semihibernate during cold weather in the bottom of estuaries and continue to shed their exoskeletons and grow, especially when the weather warms again. Mating occurs in the estuary at middle-to-low salinities, and the females move out of the estuary to the offshore spawning grounds.

Other abundant species that are saltwater spawners include croaker, spotted sea trout, striped sea robin, scup, and some flounders. Although it is clear that juveniles of many species use estuaries as a nursery, it is instructive to mention again that it is not clear how many could develop into adults without entering estuaries.

10.4.2.2 Estuarine Spawners. Estuarine spawners either spend their entire life in estuaries or move into estuaries to spawn. Many estuarine spawners, such as the tomcod, have adhesive, nonbouyant eggs which cling to vegetation or rocks so that the eggs are not swept to sea.

Winter flounder (*Pseudopleuronectes americanus*). In New England some winter flounders move into estuaries and lay large clusters of adhesive, nonbuoyant eggs during winter and early spring in the inland parts of estuaries (Pearcy 1962, Fiske et al. 1966). This species also has a clear pattern of migration between estuaries and nearshore coastal waters (Musick et al. 1985). After hatching, the rest of their life cycle is similar to that of saltwater spawner. Interestingly, not all winter flounder spawn in estuaries. Some remain offshore and spawn in nearshore areas. Some of these larvae then move into estuaries to grow.

Killifish (*Fundulus* spp.). Killifish, which probably spend their entire life cycle in one estuary, spawn in spring when large schools crowd into small tidal creeks. The males become very brightly colored and avidly pursue the females. The large eggs are laid in shallow water where they stick to rocks and plants on the bottom.

Silversides (*Menidia* spp.). The silversides, another very common estuarine fish, wait until late spring and summer to spawn over sandy bottoms and near the base of *Spartina* plants. The abundant eggs adhere with long sticky filaments to bottom sediments or to *Spartina* leaves. Silverside eggs are very resistant to drying, so that even when the tide drops the eggs on the *Spartina* leaves survive.

Sticklebacks (*Gasterosteus* spp.). Sticklebacks do not rely on great numbers of eggs to insure survival. Instead, the male stickleback builds a small nest of plant material during spring and early summer. After an elaborate courtship, a few eggs are spawned within the nest. The male guards them until hatching and even for some time thereafter. Some very famous behavior studies were done on the mating behavior of sticklebacks.

Hogchoker (*Trinectes maculatus*). The hogchoker is a common flatfish that completes its life cycle entirely within one estuary. Eggs are spawned in saline waters near the mouth of the estuary, and the larvae migrate back to the head waters of the estuary. For the next 4–5 years the fish move further downstream, while retreating to the fresh areas less and less each winter.

Sea catfishes. The life history of *Arius melanopus* in Terminos Lagoon is somewhat similar to that of the hogchoker. This fish spawns in very low-salinity waters and moves into higher-salinity waters as it grows; but it always remains within the lagoon (Fig. 10.15, Lara-Domínguez et al. 1981, Yáñez-Arancibia and Lara-Domínguez 1988). This contrasts with the other two species of sea catfish which are found in Terminos Lagoon. *Arius felis* and *Bagre marinus* spend part of their life cycles in nearshore coastal waters, but are estuarine dependent (Fig. 10.15). Catfish in general produce very large eggs and often brood the eggs in their mouths. The fry are large, well-developed juveniles at hatching.

Another interesting example of an estuarine spawner is *Cichlasoma urophthalmus,* a Cichlidae with a freshwater origin, which is now completely adapted to reproduce and spawn in estuarine conditions (salinities from 25–35 ppt), especially in *Rhizophora* and *Thalassia* habitats (Caso et al. 1986).

10.4.2.3 Freshwater Spawners. Among estuarine fishes, freshwater spawners are fishes that spawn in fresh water and spend at least part of their life cycle in estuaries. Among the best known freshwater spawners are the anadromous species, such as salmon (Foerster 1968, Healy 1982, Manzer and Shepherd 1962, Royce et al. 1968, Dadswell et al. 1987). They are conspicuous when they migrate, are often commercially important, and their struggle up rivers have captured the imagination of many observers.

Striped Bass (*Morone saxatilis*). Striped bass are large, anadromous fish that spend much of their life cycles directly in or near estuarine waters (Fig. 10.16); they are rarely found farther than 10 km from the shore. The most important spawning grounds for migratory striped bass on the east coast are the Hudson River, New York and the rivers flowing into Chesapeake Bay. The essential features of the life cycle are as follows: the fish are spawned in May and June in fresh water just above saltwater influence. The eggs and larvae spend about two weeks near the bottom of the river. After 2 weeks or so the young bass are found throughout the water column and drift downstream with the water current as they develop. As the fish become strong enough to swim feebly, they exhibit a diel pattern of migration, swimming to the bottom during the day and

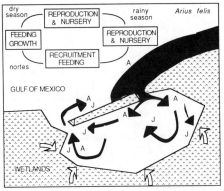

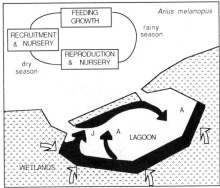

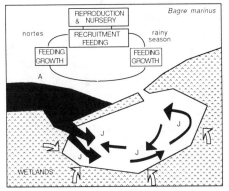

Figure 10.15 Life cycles of three species of sea catfishes in Terminos Lagoon, Mexico. *Arius felis* spawns in high salinity waters of the nearshore Gulf as well as the lagoon during the rainy season and juveniles move into the central lagoon at the end of the rainy season when winter storms ("nortes") begin. During the dry season they are found in the nearshore zone. *Arius melanopus* spends its entire life cycle within the lagoon. It spawns in low salinity areas near river mouths at the end of the rainy season and juveniles and adults move into the high salinity grass beds for feeding and growth during the dry season. *Bagre marinus* spawns in riverine-influenced nearshore waters of the Gulf at the end of the dry season and juveniles move into low salinity areas of the lagoon for feeding and growth during the rainy and norte season. White arrows indicate river discharge, J = juveniles, A = adults (from Lara-Dominguez et al. 1981 and Yáñez-Arancibia and Lara-Dominguez 1988).

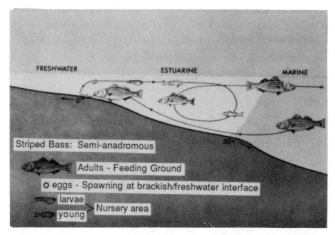

Figure 10.16 Life history of striped bass, *Morone saxatilis* (from Cronin and Manzuetti 1971).

to the surface at night. As the young fish drift downstream into the influence of the salt wedge, they are swept seaward during the night, when they are in the relatively fresh surface water, and upstream during the day, when they are found nearer the bottom. This allows them to remain in one place. Later, they are able to maintain their position by swimming against the current. When they are able to swim, the majority of the juveniles are found in shallow regions of low salinity. This basic pattern of upstream spawning and downstream drift is not always observable at all locations, however. For example, Setzler-Hamilton et al. (1980) found that larval fish were most abundant slightly upstream from maximum egg concentrations in the Potomac estuary.

Salmons (*Onchoryncus* spp. and *Salmo* spp.). The best-known migratory fishes in northern areas are the salmons, including Atlantic salmon (*Salmo salar*) and the six species of Pacific salmon (*Onchorhyncus* spp.). These fish are all anadromous. What is not as well appreciated is the key role that estuaries and other nearshore waters play in the early life cycle of many stocks of salmon. Currently, estuarine dependence is better documented for Pacific than for Atlantic salmon (Simenstad et al. 1982).

Salmon are among the most wide-ranging migratory animals known, for individual salmon characteristically move thousands of kilometers during their life (Harden-Jones 1968, Dadswell et al. 1987). Pacific salmon move north and south with the seasons, at the rate of thousands of kilometers per season, and apparently these migration patterns are tied to seasonal variations in primary and secondary productivity patterns (Fig. 10.17). When mature, they return to the rivers, often to within a few meters of the area where they were spawned, after swimming upstream hundreds to thousands of kilometers from their mid-Pacific feeding grounds.

Most salmon spawn in strictly fresh water, and pink and chum salmon often spawn at the upper reaches of estuaries just above saltwater influence. Probably

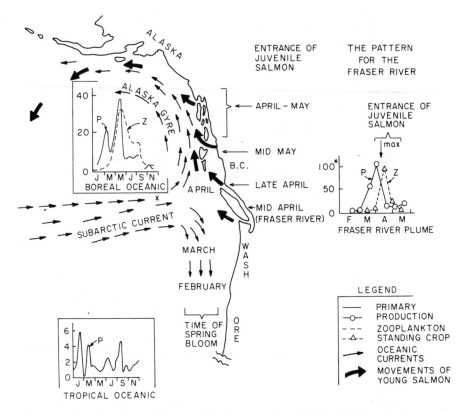

Figure 10.17 Overview of the spatial and temporal variability of primary and secondary productivity in the North Pacific Ocean and their relation to salmon migrations during their first year at sea. The pattern of abundance of primary producers (P) in tropical oceans is not strongly seasonal. In contrast, there tend to be strong coastal and oceanic spring blooms in temperate and boreal environments which are followed by blooms of zooplankton. Small salmon tend to enter estuaries and the coastal ocean to coincide with the zooplankton peak, which is progressively later to the north. Many small salmon move northward so that they tend to stay with the peak of zooplankton (derived in part from Royce et al. 1968 and Le Brasseur et al. 1969).

the largest ecological differences among the five different species of Pacific salmon occur in the first year of life. Sockeye salmon initially spend 1–4 years in a pelagic lake existence, eating zooplankton (Foerster 1968); coho spend 1 year in streams or lake shores, where they feed principally on insects drifting with the current or on the water surface (Mundie 1969); chinook salmon spend 90 days to a year in larger rivers; pink and chum salmon move downstream shortly after emerging from the redds (spawning nests) and generally are found in brackish waters within a few weeks.

The movements of young salmon in the first year or so after they leave fresh water is the least well-understood component of the entire life cycle. Apparently most young fish spend at least several months in estuaries or nearshore waters. Young Asian cohos spend at least several months in nearshore waters, and in New England, transplanted cohos remained in the estuary up to 9 months after release. Conditions in the estuary were important in determining year class strength (Deegan 1981). There is also considerable evidence from the Pacific coast of North America of the importance of estuaries. Manzer and Shepard (1962) report that "a substantial number of pinks spend up to several months living and growing in the inshore waters before moving to the high seas," and Manzer (1968) writes of "astronomical numbers" of young salmon in coastal and estuarine British Columbia in the late spring. But sockeye salmon migrate north soon after they enter estuaries. The food habits of young salmon in estuaries are considered in Le Brasseur et al. (1969), Sibert et al. (1978), and Naiman and Siebert (1979).

What is not known as well is what proportions of a population stay in estuaries or migrate northward immediately. Levy and Northcote (1982) found that young chinook salmon used the mouth of the Fraser River well into the summer. After 1–7 years in the sea, mature salmon return to the coast, pass through estuaries, and migrate back to the rivers where they were spawned to complete the life cycle.

Other Anadromous Species. Other examples of anadromous species are members of the herring family, including alewife (*Alosa psuedoharengus*) and blueback herring (*Alosa aestivalis*), and the shads (hickory shad, *Alosa mediocris,* and American shad, *Alosa sapidissima*). All are found in coastal areas as adults. Alewife populations spawn in freshwater ponds and the young spend the summer in those ponds before moving into estuaries (Durbin et al. 1979). Blueback herring spawn at the upper reaches of estuarine influence and grow up in estuaries. The American shad spawn in fresh water, and the young move down to estuaries relatively quickly to feed during their first summer (Fig. 10.18). The next 3–4 years are spent in the open ocean.

10.4.3   The Use of the Estuary as a Nursery

Estuarine fish communities are often dominated by the juveniles of species which spawn somewhere else and move into the estuary as larvae or juveniles (Ross and Epperly 1985, Deegan and Day 1985, 1986). It is very interesting to sample ichthyoplankton over a yearly cycle, because waves of larvae appear, even though there are no signs of adults. For example, Louisiana Bays are devoid of adult menhaden in winter, but in January and February high densities of larval menhaden suddenly appear. The young menhaden stay until about November or December when they depart for offshore. Similarly, masses of tiny menhaden, scup, and bluefish appear suddenly in Flax Pond, New York in July and August, again with little evidence of the adults. Observations like these have been made over and over again in most estuaries studied. As a result, important

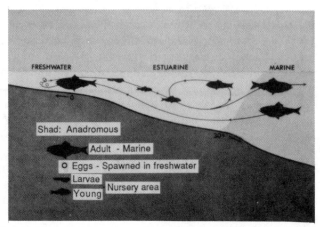

Figure 10.18   Life history of American shad, *Alosa sapidisima* (from Cronin and Manzuetti 1971).

concepts that describe how nekton use estuaries are those of the "estuarine nursery ground," and the related concept of "estuarine dependence."

10.4.3.1   The Concept of Estuarine Dependence.   The widespread use of estuaries by larvae and juveniles of so many species has led to the concept of "estuarine dependence," implying that the estuary is required for some part of the life cycle of these organisms. Some people have questioned whether species really "require" estuaries, because over geologic time any particular estuary is short lived (less than several thousand years) (Walford 1966, Schubel and Hirschberg 1978). Nevertheless, even if a particular estuary is short lived, estuaries have always been found at the edge of the sea and many fish have evolved life histories to use them. We are certain that many common commercially important species currently use estuaries as their primary nursery area, although some species may also use other locations which are influenced by estuaries such as the shelf (Herke 1977a, b, Lenanton 1982, Lenanton and Hodgkin 1985, Sánchez-Gil and Yáñez-Arancibia 1986). Still, it is important to understand that relatively few species are absolutely estuarine dependent (Lenanton and Potter, 1987, McDowall 1976).

Estuarine Nursery Areas.   Because attributes of nursery areas are difficult to define, nursery areas are empirically determined by estimates of the abundance of larvae and juveniles. Within estuaries there are apparently three primary nursery areas: wetlands (salt marshes and mangroves), including the shallow marsh fringe areas and mudflats, the low salinity area at the head of the estuary, and grass beds.

Several workers (Weinstein 1979, 1985, Bozeman and Dean 1980, Shenker and Dean 1979) have demonstrated that shallow tidal creeks and marsh shoals harbor dense populations of juvenile marine species such as spot (*Leiostomus xanthurus*), mullet (*Mugil* sp.), and flounder (*Paralichthys* sp.), while adult predatory fish were rare. Some of these studies showed that young fish actively seek the creek headwaters, essentially filling the creek from its headwaters during recruitment. The period of residence in these creeks is lengthy, with recruitment in the Carolinas and the Gulf of Mexico usually occurring in the winter (Bozeman and Dean 1980) and either a mass exodus occurring in the following fall (Weinstein 1979) or slowly throughout the late summer and fall, with the larger fish moving downstream first (Herke 1977a, Dunham 1972). The marshes are very productive areas and even though many of the fish are not themselves detritivores, they may benefit indirectly from the productivity of detrital food chains.

The low-salinity open-water portion of many estuaries is a region of exceptional value to fish (Horn and Allen 1976, Warburton 1978, Daniels 1979, Amezcua Linares and Yáñez-Arancibia 1980, Yáñez-Arancibia et al. 1980, Yáñez-Arancibia 1985). This region receives fish eggs, larvae, and young from freshwater spawners, semi-anadromous and anadromous fish, estuarine spawners, and even some larvae spawned in the lower estuary or ocean, and this habitat acts as a control on distributional ecology (Deegan and Thompson 1985, Ross and Epperly 1985, Weinstein 1985). Its high value is not obvious, however, since these small stages of fish are not visible to anyone except those who employ the highly specialized collecting gear required to reveal the diversity and abundance of young fish and their food. These rich fish nurseries merit special care and protection; it is an unfortunate coincidence that many cities are located near regions close to the head of navigable deep water.

Seagrass meadows are another distinct and important nursery area for species such as spot, bluecrab, pinfish, and sea trout and a number of other species (Thayer et al. 1976, Adams 1976a, b, Heck and Orth 1980, Yáñez-Arancibia and Lara-Domínguez 1983). Larvae occupy seagrass beds seasonally, similar to tidal creeks, and juveniles have intensive trophic relationships (Adams 1976b, Carr and Adams 1973). There is much more information on use of seagrasses as nurseries (Adams 1976b, Brook 1977, Thayer et al. 1976, Weinstein and Heck 1979, Livingston 1985) than is available for mangrove swamps (Odum and Heald 1975, Beumer 1978, Yáñez-Arancibia 1978, Alvarez et al. 1986, Thayer et al. 1987).

The distribution of juvenile fishes within primary nursery areas has been related to a variety of factors. Physiochemical parameters, which affect individual tolerances, apparently govern broad spatial distributions within the estuary, while species interactions seem to fine tune spatial distributions. Factors that affect distribution in a broad sense include temperature (Joseph 1973, Yáñez-Arancibia et al. 1982), salinity (Gunter 1961, Yáñez-Arancibia et al. 1985b), turbidity (Blaber and Blaber 1980, Yáñez-Arancibia 1985c), calm water (Blaber and Whitfield 1977), food availability (May 1974, Houde 1978, Lasker 1975, Whitfield 1980. Livingston 1982, Yáñez-Arancibia et al. 1986), and predation pressure (Blaber and Blaber 1980). Some factors, such as salinity or turbidity, may also influence distribution secondarily by controlling the distribution of predators (Joseph 1973, Blaber and Blaber 1980).

In summary, there are three major requirements for a nursery area: (1) physiologically suitable with respect to temperature, salinity, and other physiochemical parameters; (2) abundant suitable food with a minimum of competition at critical trophic levels; (3) a degree of protection from predators (Joseph 1973).

Mechanisms Used to Locate Nursery Areas. Fishes seem to occupy specific locations within the estuary; however, the mechanisms used by fish to find these locations are not well understood. Larvae apparently select a specific location by behavioral and physiological responses to interactions among depth, location, and tide direction. The locating or retention mechanisms are probably species-specific, and involve three major elements and their interactions (Bousfield 1955): (1) utilization of the nontidal (i.e., net "salt wedge" currents—seaward in the upper layer and landward along the bottom); (2) diel changes in vertical position; and (3) changing behavioral patterns with respect to tidal direction. These ideas were developed based on larval stages of invertebrates, but can be applied to fish.

Weinstein et al. (1980) showed that different adaptations using these three elements resulted in species using different areas as nursery grounds. Several important differences in behavioral response controlled the ultimate residence in the two primary nursery areas of spot, croaker, and flounder (Fig. 10.19). Both spot and flounder responded to ebb tidal currents by "settling out" of the water column, and to flood currents by active movements in the water column. This helped them penetrate further into the estuary and into tidal creeks. Migration into the marsh creeks is also aided by staying near the surface on night flood tides, when large numbers of individuals would be carried into the shoal areas. Once in the marshes the tendency to settle out on ebb tide allows some to remain. Conversely, by tending to remain more bottom oriented at all times, Atlantic croaker accumulate in greater numbers in the deeper waters.

Changes in behavioral response with growth of the fish accentuate location selection. Species that exhibit a strong ebb/flood response when younger will travel further. Once the preferred region is reached a decreased ebb/flood response will aid in maintaining position. Pearcy (1962) found that small flounders changed their depth distribution pattern between night and day and this, combined with salt-wedge water movements, concentrated them in the estuaries.

In addition to using the salt-wedge and tidal currents to enter estuaries, some species have evolved to use periodic weather-induced current patterns (Pauly 1985). In the Gulf of Mexico, where tidal and salt-wedge currents are slight, the spawning of sand sea trout in the nearshore Gulf in winter coincides with periods of highest frequency of onshore winds (Shlossman and Chittenden 1981). These periodic winds cause landward surface currents which bring the larvae into the estuary. Off the Pacific coast of North America coastal spawning species with pelagic eggs also spawn in the winter when wind drift is onshore (Parrish et al. 1981). A similar correlation of Atlantic menhaden year-class strength with wind-driven surface layer transport led Nelson et al. (1977) to conclude this mecha-

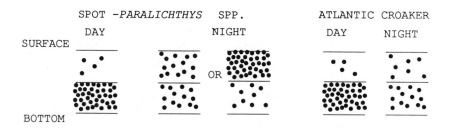

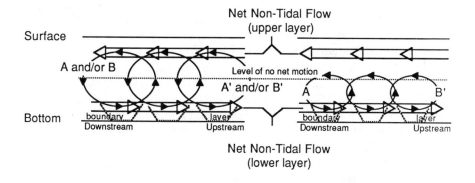

A - Tidal response (movement toward bottom on ebb)
A' - Tidal response (movement toward surface on flood)
B - Photoperiod response (Bottom orientation during day)
B' - Photoperiod response (Surface orientation at night)

Figure 10.19 Conceptual diagram of the mechanisms of retention of larvae in estuaries based on response to photoperiod and tidal currents. The pattern for spot (*Leiostomus xanthurus*) and flounder (*Paralichthys* spp.) is a high concentration in the bottom during the day and either dispersed through the water column or concentrated in surface waters at night. The croaker (*Micropogonias undulatus*) is concentrated in bottom waters during the day but more are found in the surface waters at night (adapted from Weinstein et al. 1980).

nism was a more satisfactory explanation than the classic salt-wedge bottom-layer transport model for this species.

10.5 COMMUNITY ASPECTS OF NEKTON

The dynamic nature of estuaries and the migratory nature of much of the nekton inhabiting estuaries means that the species composition of the fish community found in the estuary is highly variable over time. The study, in various ways, of the diversity and abundance of the species present is commonly called the study of community structure, and is of considerable theoretical and applied interest.

There are at least four reasons for the characteristically large variations in the fish community structure of estuaries. First, many species migrate in response to the seasons. Second, many species utilize estuaries for feeding in response to seasonal events, such as river flooding. Third, many species utilize estuaries seasonally for spawning and as nursery grounds for young fish. Fourth, absolute abundances of any given species vary from one year to the next. The use of estuaries by different species is dynamic and varies from estuary to estuary, species to species, and year to year, and even among different individuals of the same species. The admixture of these different patterns has produced a very dynamic community structure of the fishes that frequent estuaries. Selected references on the community aspects of nekton are Allen and Horn (1975), Bechtel and Copeland (1970), Cairn and Dean (1976), Chambers (1980), Dahlberg and Odum (1970), Deegan and Thompson (1985), Haedrich and Haedrich (1974), Harima and Mundy (1974), Hillman et al. (1977), Hoese et al. (1968), Hoff and Ibarra (1977), Livingston (1976), Moore et al. (1970), Sabins and Truesdale (1974), Subrahamanyan and Drake (1975), Turner and Johnson (1973), Wagner (1973), Yáñez-Arancibia et al. (1982), and Yáñez-Arancibia (1985).

In this section, we will first discuss how fish use estuaries temporally and spatially within one year, and then discuss factors that influence community structure between years. This essentially goes from the factors we know the most about to the factors we know the least about.

10.5.1   Temporal and Spatial Use within a Year

Fishes come in, leave, and locate themselves within the estuaries with the seasons in response to changes in environmental conditions. The spatial pattern of fish diversity changes as each species moves with its own seasonal sequence. In tropical and subtropical estuaries we find different species using the same location for different portions of the year, resulting in little to no change in diversity over the seasons. In temperate estuaries, where few species remain in the winter, diversity peaks in the spring or summer. The complexity of fish movement may produce a regular or occasional presence of over a hundred species at one place over the course of a year. Yet the interaction of individual species' salinity and temperature tolerances meld together to produce a general pattern of estuarine use. This pattern has recognizable spatial and temporal characteristics.

Earlier we divided the nekton into several main groups with respect to their salinity tolerance and life-history characteristics: estuarine, freshwater, estuarine-marine (estuarine dependent), and marine (nonestuarine-dependent) (Fig. 10.9). When we look at the sequence of abundance of these four groups, a general pattern emerges. Freshwater nekton use the low-salinity portion of the upper estuary extensively during the late fall, winter, and spring when freshwater discharge is greatest and salinity is lowest. From early winter to late spring rising salinities cause the retreat of most of the freshwater community back to the upper, completely freshwater portions of the estuary. Estuarine and estuarine-dependent marine species dominate the catch during spring and summer seasons. Warm temperatures and increased salinities are accompanied by occasional summertime excursions of nonestuarine-dependent marine species into the most saline portions of the basin. At the same time a gradual offshore emigration of juvenile estuarine-dependent marine nekton is occurring. In the fall, most of the remaining estuarine-dependent marine species move offshore to overwinter. During the fall and winter, the freshwater community again expands into low-salinity regions and begins another annual cycle.

The seasonal pattern described in Fig. 10.9 is more pronounced in more northern estuaries, because many fish often leave the estuary altogether. Temperature has a strong effect on fish distribution. For example, we caught no fish in experimental nets in Flax Pond, New York during winter sampling. Because shallow, salty water may cool to less than $-2°C$, below the temperature at which most fishes' blood will freeze, there appears to be strong selective pressure against fishes overwintering in shallow, cold estuaries in the northern regions. Some fish (winter flounder, smelt, and even cod) do overwinter in estuaries, but only in deep portions near the seaward edges where the water is warmer. Yet large numbers of striped bass overwinter in Haverstraw Bay, Hudson River, where the deep, relatively fresh water will neither freeze nor become colder than the freezing temperature of the fish's blood (Boyle 1969).

The annual cycle in the occcurrence and abundance of nekton fauna that seems so much a part of estuaries is an important mechanism for resource partitioning. Food may be abundant, but it is not inexhaustible, especially when animals concentrate in specific locations like tidal creeks. Food abundance is affected by seasonal changes in physiochemical conditions and predation. For many species the times of entering and leaving estuaries is very distinct, and there are some arguments that the different species are programmed to avoid intense competition. In Louisiana estuaries, even though fish use the estuary year-round, Deegan and Thompson (1985) found that within major groups (i.e., drums and flatfishes) where feeding habits are most similar, peak occurences of species did not overlap greatly (Fig. 10.20). Muus (1967) examined in detail the times of arrival, growth, and the autumn emigration for the dominant crustacean and flounder species in a Danish estuary (Fig. 10.21). The species arrive in approximately the following chronologic order: (1) spring stock of *Crangon crangon* (A); (2) recently metamorphosed *Plathicthys flesus* and mature *Paralichthys microps;* (3) young of *P. microps;* (4) young of *Crangon* (B); (5) young of *Crangon* (C); (6) young of *C. maenas;* (7) young of *Crangon* (D). The lead in growth which the earliest arriving species or generations gain over the later arrivals causes the individual populations to remain at all times in different size groups and thus, to at least some degree, at different trophic levels. A relatively brief overlapping in food utilized by both the rising flounder stock and the spring

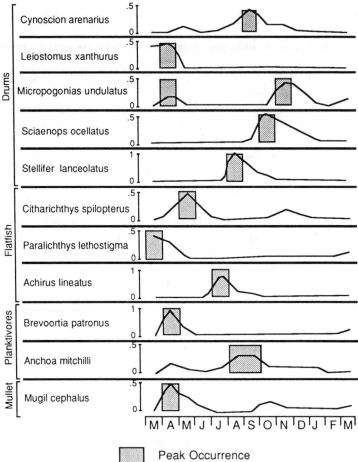

Figure 10.20 Seasonal occurrence of different species in the tidal creek nursery area of the Atchafalaya Delta, Louisiana (from Deegan and Thompson 1985). Vertical scale is the fraction of the yearly total numerical abundance caught during that month.

stock of *Crangon* (A) coincides with the spring peak in abundance of their principal food, harpacticod copepods.

The immigration sequence and the trophic sequence form a pattern that through the whole summer seems to make the exploitation of the food animals in some cases optimal for the consumers, as there is relatively little direct competition. Muus (1967) found that the food animals living in the uppermost layer of the substrate (such as the harpacticod copepods and amphipods) generally were

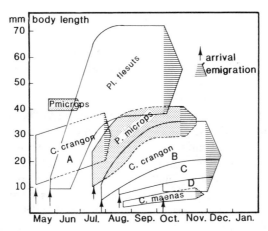

Figure 10.21 Occurrence and growth of different crustacean and flatfish species in a Danish estuary showing the different arrival and emigration times and growth rates of the different species. See text for explanation (from Muus 1967). A, B, C, and D represent different waves of immigration of *Crangon*.

"grazed" down to a certain relatively low level which is maintained through the summer in spite of a high potential of reproduction and growth of these organisms. Any time there was a lessening of the pressure on the part of the consumers, such as following a major emigration of their predators, local blooms in the stock of these benthic species resulted.

We imagine that this time-sharing results in the nekton "carrying capacity" of the estuary being fully realized during the year, contributing to the high nekton productivity characteristic of these systems. Nevertheless, as a general tendency the majority of exploitation of estuaries by nekton occurs during the times of highest primary and secondary production.

10.5.2 Factors Controlling the Year-to-Year Abundance of Estuarine Fish

It is of considerable importance for both scientists and managers of fish stocks to understand and predict how many individuals of a species will be present, and hence available for harvest, in a given year. Because of the obvious relationship between environment conditions and survivorship, and the role of the estuary as a nursery ground, many scientists have tried to explain the changes in abundance of fish based on changes in estuarine conditions. This approach, based on the original concepts of Hjort (1916), assumes that the survival of the young during the critical first days to months of life determines population size. The basic idea is that whatever influences feeding rates or food availability, such as temperature or the physical factors that supply nutrients to phytoplankton, will control the abundance of fish. A very important review of this general approach is given in Caddy and Sharp (1986).

This approach appears particularly useful in estuaries because of the large importance of seasonal and year-to-year variations in temperature, salinity, and river flow. For example, Sutcliffe (1973) found that the commercial catch of halibut (*Hippoglossus* spp.) and lobster (*Homarus americanus*) in the St. Lawrence estuary is strongly influenced by the discharge of the St. Lawrence River. According to Sutcliffe's theory, years with heavy spring discharge lead to higher primary production and conditions under which a higher proportion of small fish survive. Similar relations between river discharge and Texas estuarine-dependent shrimp were found by Chapman (1966). Another possible explanation for these correlations is that high river discharge increases the amount of nursery area in the correct salinity range, thus increasing yields. Further information on this "ecosystem" approach to fisheries prediction and management can be found in Cushing (1975) and Pauly and Murphy (1982) and in Chapter 12. Ideally, future research will combine more explicitly population dynamics with an increasingly sophisticated analysis of how ecosystem processes affect survival (Yáñez-Arancibia and Pauly 1986, Longhurst and Pauly 1987). This topic is covered in more detail in Chapter 12.

10.6   SECONDARY PRODUCTION OF NEKTON

One reason estuaries produce so much fish is because the individual species that occupy the estuary have high production rates. Estimates of fish secondary productivity are few because the complex migration pattern makes it difficult to use many of the standard methods (Winberg 1971). In cases where detailed studies have been done on individual species, these species are very productive compared with freshwater or marine species (Table 10.2). In part this is because many of the species are in estuaries during their juvenile period, an age at which productivity is usually highest.

Because there are few data on nekton secondary production in estuaries, data on catch per unit effort or standing crop are frequently used to compare fish productivity. For example, Yáñez-Arancibia (1978) reported that nekton standing crop in coastal lagoons with ephemeral inlets on the Mexican Pacific ranged from 246 to 667 kg wet wt/ha depending on salinity and season. By comparison, the standing crop range in Terminos lagoon with permanently open inlets was 6–49 kg wet wt/ha (Yáñez-Arancibia et al. 1980). Other standing crop data reported are for the northwest Gulf of Mexico (56–316 kg wet wt/ha, Haedrich and Hall 1976), the Philippines (213 kg wet wt/ha, Pauly and Mines 1982), and for tropical coastal ecosystems in general (300–600 kg wet wt/ha, Marten and Polovina 1982).

It is difficult to make comparisons of total fish community secondary productivity because there are few studies and differences in methods used often obscure general trends. Apparently, there is no clear pattern of distribution of standing crop and fish productivity, possibly because of the time–space scale of different studies and the size of the system studied. It was first assumed, based on fisheries yield, that tropical estuaries should be more productive than temperate estuaries. The high value reported for Flax Pond (Table 10.3) may be due to the small size and nature of the area; it is essentially a tidal creek of Long Island Sound. Much more work is needed before we can make good inter-estuarine comparisons of productivity rates. This is an important topic for further research.

10.7 THE ROLE OF FISHES IN ESTUARINE ECOSYSTEMS

Although fishes are normally studied from the perspective of the fish themselves it also is legitimate to inquire about the effect of the fishes on other components of the ecosystems where they are found, including the system as a whole. This

TABLE 10.3 Estimates of Total Fish Community Productivity (g/m²/yr) in Selected Temperate, Subtropical and Tropical Estuaries

Location	Fish Production	Reference
TEMPERATE		
Italy	9.0–17.0[a]	DeAngelis 1960
Chesapeake Bay, MD	9.0[a]	Mansueti 1961
Wadden Sea, Netherlands	10.01	Postma and Rauck 1979
Flax Pond, NY	108–146[b]	Hall and Woodwell, unpublished data
Southern North Sea	5.2[a]	Korringa 1967
SUBTROPICAL		
Texas coastal lagoons	12.1–57.6[b]	Jones et al. 1963 Hellier 1962
Barataria Bay, LA	35.0–72.8[b]	Wagner 1973 Day et al. 1973
Mexican Pacific Coast	34.5[b]	Warburton 1979
TROPICAL		
India	5.8–124[a]	Pakrasi et al. 1964
Phillipines	47.0–50.[a]	Rabanal 1961
Cuban lagoons	22.0–27.6[b]	Holcik 1970
Mexican Pacific lagoons	24.6–66.7[b]	Yáñez-Arancibia 1978
Terminos Lagoon, Mexico	20.0[b]	Yáñez-Arancibia and Lara Dominguez 1983

[a]based on information from fisheries yield.
[b]based on summation of production estimates of selected component species.

holostic view of nekton and estuaries can be found in several works (Yáñez-Arancibia and Nugent 1977, Deegan and Thompson 1985, Weinstein 1985 and a number of other chapters in Yáñez-Arancibia 1985).

The first and most obvious way that nekton affect their environment is by cropping and often depleting food organisms. Experiments excluding fish from benthic areas have shown large changes in the numbers and biomass of the benthos, supporting the concept that fish cropping is important in determining community structure and biomass (Virnstein, 1977, 1978, Holland et al. 1980). Fish predation has been shown to alter the size structure and population abundance of freshwater and marine zooplankton (Brook 1977, Durbin 1979, Blaxter and Hunter 1982). Unfortunately, this question has not been looked at in estuarine pelagic regions to our knowledge.

Fishes and other nekton may control other trophic levels through grazing but the ultimate effect depends in part on the particular trophic level of the fish, and the trophic levels of the populations the fish eats (Day 1967). Top carnivores may "control" (through predation) the abundance of midlevel carnivores, which in turn may control the abundance of herbivores and so on. Maciolek (1980) developed a trophic level index for each species to indicate this importance in the food web. Nekton that may not originally appear important serve as links in food chains to fish that are important commercially or for recreation. Fish serve as a link between lower trophic levels and higher ones that are often of greater interest to humans including, of course, the situation where people are the top predator and eat the fish, but also including piscivorous birds, mammals (such as seals), and other fish.

In a few documented cases fish have important impacts on ecosystem functions, such as primary production or nutrient transport, even where their biomass is relatively small. Such a relation has been shown for nutrient-poor freshwater salmon nurseries where phosphorus may be "returned" in the bones of dead postspawning fish (Donaldson 1967, Krokhin 1975). It is more difficult to postulate such a relation for estuaries, which tend not to be nutrient-poor, but it may exist (Durbin et al. 1979). Some workers have suggesed that flux through juvenile fish populations may be a major biological process in the cycling of trace metals in highly productive coastal plain estuaries (Cross et al. 1975). Fish also may be important in regenerating locally-obtained nutrients by excreting sufficient nutrients to affect phytoplankton (Oviatt et al. 1972).

SUMMARY

Those who study estuarine nekton are impressed with the intricacies of the adaptations of individual fish and whole fish communities to an estuarine existence. Estuaries and lagoons are physiologically demanding, relatively unpredictable, and in many senses inhospitable environments, yet, as a rule, they teem with nekton. Tiny larval and juvenile fish are especially abundant and diverse, despite their seeming fragility and the very complex life histories required to get them there. The best explanation for this apparently contradictory situation is that estuaries and lagoons are regions of great productivity. Whatever physiological and behavioral costs that the nekton pay appears well recompensed by the higher survivability of the young in the food-rich estuarine environments. The high areal productivity tends to be concentrated in relatively shallow waters, making exploitation by nekton easy. Anadromy is much more common in higher latitudes while catadromy is more common in lower latitudes, and Gross et al. (1988), recently hypothesized that this was due to the relative differences in the primary productivity of oceanic and fresh waters. In both types of migration, fish pass through and use the resources of estuaries. In using the resources of estuaries and in migrating through them, fish transform energy from primary sources, exchange energy with neighboring ecosystems, constitute a form of energy storage, and function as agents of community regulation.

The use of these environments appears to be finely tuned to seasonal events that produce periods of greater and lesser food availability. In Barataria Bay, where spring occurs earlier, most fish enter estuaries starting in February and March (Deegan and Thompson 1985). In Terminos Lagoon, most young fish enter the lagoon primarily from September to November during the period of high river flow and high productivity (Yáñez-Arancibia et al. 1980). At Flax Pond most young fish do not enter the estuaries until about July, reflecting the later spawning season and the delayed primary productivity peak in that environment. In all cases, fish show a number of complex life history stratagies and adaptive responses. Additionally, some studies have shown that the seasonal use of estuaries by different nekton species is such that there is relatively little overlap in food usage. All of these patterns are hints of the intricacies by which natural selection has adjusted different species to their complex, demanding estuarine environment.

Experimental ecology with fishes is difficult because of the variability of the estuarine ecosystem and especially of fish populations, and the difficulty of conducting experimental work on fishes *in situ*. Because of their value, there is also a marked tendency to study commercially important species, especially from the fishery point of view. It is becoming apparent that to effectively manage fishery species, an understanding of the overall ecosystem and the role of nekton is necessary. It is only through such comprehensive study that an understanding of the factors which affect fishery yield and the impacts of human activities can be developed (Weinstein 1982).

REFERENCES

Adams, S., 1976a. The ecology of eelgrass, *Zostera marina* (L.) fish communities. I. Structural analysis. J. Exp. Mar. Biol. Ecol., 22:269-291.

Adams, S., 1976b. Feeding ecology of eelgrass fish communities. Trans. Amer. Fish. Soc., 105:514-519.

Aguirre-León, A. and A. Yáñez-Arancibia, 1986. The "mojarras" from Terminos Lagoon: Taxonomy, biology, ecology and trophic dynamic (Pisces: Gerreidae). An. Inst. Cienc. del Mar y Limnol. Univ. Nal. Autón. México, 13:369–444.

Allen, L.G. and M.H. Horn, 1975. Abundance, diversity and seasonality of fishes in Colorado Lagoon, Alamitos Bay, California. Estuarine Coastal Mar. Sci., 3:371–380.

Alvarez Rubio, M., F. Amezcua, and A. Yáñez-Arancibia, 1986. Ecology and structure of fish communities in the Teacapán-Agua Brava estuarine system, Nayarit (Central Pacific coast of Mexico). An. Inst. Cienc. del Mar y Limnol. Univ. Nal. Autón. México, 13:185–242.

Amezcua Linares, F. and A. Yáñez-Arancibia, 1980. Ecology of fluvial–lagoon systems associated with Terminos Lagoon: The habitat and structure of fish communities. An. Centro del Cienc. Mar Limnol. Univ. Nal. Auton. México, 7(1):69–118.

Bechtel, T.J. and B.J. Copeland, 1970. Fish species diversity indices as indicators of pollution in Galveston Bay, Texas. Contrib. Mar. Sci., 15:103–132.

Beumer, J.P., 1978. Feeding ecology of four fishes from a mangrove creek in North Queensland, Australia. J. Fish Biol., 12:475–490.

Bigelow, H.B. and W.C. Schroeder. 1953. Fishes of the Gulf of Maine. Fish. Bull., 53:1–575.

Blaber, S.J.M., 1974. Field studies of the diet of *Rhabdosargus holubi* (Steindachner) (Teleostei Sparidae). J. Zool., Lond. 173:407–417.

Blaber, S.J.M. and T.G. Blaber, 1980. Factors affecting the distribution of juvenile estuarine and inshore fish. J. Fish Biol., 17:143–162.

Blaber, S.J.M. and A.K. Whitfield, 1977. The biology of the burrowing goby *Croilia mossambica* Smith (Teleostei Gobiidae). Env. Biol. Fish., 1:197–204.

Blaxter, H.H.S. and J.R. Hunter, 1980. The biology of clupeoid fishes. Adv. Mar. Biol., 20:1–223.

Bousfield, E.L., 1955. Ecological control of the occurrence of barnacles in the Miramichi estuary. Nat. Mus. Can. Bull., 137:1–69 pp.

Boyle, R. 1969. The Hudson River: A Natural and Unnatural History, Norton, New York, 304 pp.

Bozeman, E.L. and J.M. Dean, 1980. The abundance of estuarine larval and juvenile fish in a South Carolina creek. Estuaries, 3:89–97.

Brook, I., 1977. Trophic relationships in a seagrass community (*Thalassia testudinum*) in Card Sound, Florida. Fish diet in relation to macrobenthic and cryptic faunal abundance. Trans. Am. Fish. Soc., 106(3):219–229.

Caddy, J.F. and G. P. Sharp, 1986. An Ecological Framework for Marine Fishery Investigations. FAO Fisheries Tech. Paper 283. FAO, Rome, 152 p.

Cairn, R.L. and J.M. Dean, 1976. Annual occurrences, abundance and diversity of fish in a South Carolina intertidal creek. Mar. Biol., 36:369–379.

Carr, W., and C. Adams, 1973. Food habits of juvenile marine fishes occupying seagrass beds in the estuarine zone near Crystal River, Florida. Trans. Amer. Fish. Soc., 102:511–540.

Caso Chávez, M., A. Yáñez-Arancibia, and A. Lara-Domínguez, 1986. Biology, ecology and population dynamics of *Cichlasoma urophthalmus* (Gunther) (Pisces: Cichlidae) in habitats of *Thalassia testudinum* and *Rhizophora mangle* (Terminos Lagoon, southern Gulf of Mexico). Biotica, 11:79–112.

Chambers, D.G., 1980. An analysis of nekton communities in the upper Barataria Basin, Louisiana. MS Thesis, Louisiana State University, Baton Rouge, 286 pp.

Chao, L.N. and J.P. Musick, 1977. Life history, feeding habits, and functional morphology of juvenile sciaenid fishes in the York River Estuary, Virginia. Fish. Bull., 75(4):657-702.

Chapman, C., 1966. The Texas basins project. In R. Smith, A. Swartz, and W. Massmann (Eds.), Symposium on Estuarine Fisheries. Am. Fish. Soc. Spec. Publ. No. 3:83-92.

Chavance, P., D. Flores, A. Yáñez-Arancibia, and F. Amezcua, 1984. Ecology, biology and population dynamics of *Bairdiella chrysoura* in Terminos Lagoon, southern Gulf of Mexico (Pisces: Sciaenidae). An. Inst. Cienc. del Mar y Limnol. Univ. Nal. Autón. México, 11:123-162.

Chavance, P., A. Yáñez-Arancibia, D. Flores, A. Lara-Domínguez and F. Amezcua, 1986. Ecology, biology and population dynamics of *Archosargus rhomboidalis* (Pisces: Sparidae) in a tropical lagoon system, southern Gulf of Mexico. An. Inst. Cienc. del Mar y Limnol. Univ. Nal. Autón. México, 13:11-30.

Copeland, B.J. and W.S. Birkhead, 1972. Some ecological studies of the lower Cape Fear River estuary, ocean outfall and Dutchman Creek, 1971. First Annual Report to Carolina Power and Light Co., Raleigh, NC, Vol. 71, pp. 1-105.

Cronin, L.E. and A.J. Manzuetti, 1971. The biology of the estuary. A Symposium on the Biological Significance of Estuaries. Sport Fishing Institute, Washington, D.C., pp. 14-39.

Cross, F.H., H.N. Willis, L.H. Hardy, N.Y. Jones, and J.M. Lewis. 1975. Role of juvenile fish in cycling of Mn, Fe, Cu, and Zn in a coastal plain estuary. In L.E. Cronin (Ed.), Estuarine Research. Academic, New York, Vol. I, pp. 45-63.

Cushing, D.H., 1975. Marine Ecology and Fisheries. Alden Press, Oxford, 278 pp.

Cyrus, D., and S. Blaber, 1982. Mouthpart structure and function and the feeding mechanisms of *Gerres* (Teleostei). S. Afr. J. Zool., 17:117-121.

Cyrus, D., and S. Blaber, 1983. The food and feeding ecology of Gerridae (Bleeker, 1859) in estuaries of Natal. J. Fish Biol., 22:373-394.

Dadswell, M., R. Klauda, C. Moffitt, R. Saunders, R. Rulifson, and J. Cooper, 1987. Common Stratagies of Anadromous and Catadromous Fishes. Am. Fish. Soc. Symp. 1, Baltimore, Maryland, 562 pp.

Dahlberg, M.D. and E.P. Odum, 1970. Annual cycle of species occurrence, abundance and diversity in Georgia estuarine populations. Am. Midl. Nat., 83:382-392.

Daniels, K., 1979. Habitat designation based on cluster analysis of Ichthyofauna. In J.W. Day, Jr., D.D. Culley, R.E. Turner, and A.J. Mumphrey (Eds.), Proceedings of the 3rd Coastal Marsh and Estuary Management Symposium. Louisiana State University Division of Continuing Education, Baton Rouge, pp. 317-324.

Darnell, R.M., 1961. Trophic spectrum of an estuarine community, based on studies of Lake Pontchartrain, Louisiana. Ecology, 42(3):553-568.

Day, J.H., 1967. The biology of Kynsna Estuary, South Africa. In G.H. Lauff (Ed.), Estuaries. Amer. Assoc. Adv. Sci. Spec. Publ. 83: pp. 397-407.

Day, J.H., S. Blaber and J. Wallace, 1981. Estuarine Fishes. In J. H. Day (Ed.), Estuarine Ecology with Particular Reference to Southern Africa. A. A. Balkema, Rotterdam, pp. 197-221.

Day, J.W., W. Smith, P. Wagner, and W. Stowe, 1973. Community structure and carbon budget of a salt marsh and shallow bay estuarine system in Louisiana. Publ. No. LSU-56-72-04. Center for Wetland Resources, Louisiana State Univ., Baton Rouge, La., 79 pp.

DeAngelis, R. 1960. Brackish-water lagoons and their exploitation. Stud. Rev. gen Fish. Coun. Mediterr. 12.

Deegan, L., 1981. Increased estuarine survival of juvenile coho salmon vaccinated against *Vibrio anguillarum.* Trans. Am. Fish Soc., 110:656-659.

Deegan, L., 1985. The population ecology and nutrient transport of gulf menhaden in Fourleague Bay, Louisiana. Ph.D. Dissertation, Louisiana State University, Baton Rouge, 134 pp.

Deegan, L., and J. W. Day, 1985. Estuarine fish habitat requirements. In B. Copeland, K. Hart, N. Davis, and S. Friday (Eds.), Research for Managing the Nation's Estuaries. UNC Sea Grant College Publ. UNC-4-08, North Carolina State University, Raleigh, pp. 315-336.

Deegan, L., and J. W. Day, 1986. Coastal fishery habitat requirements. In A. Yáñez-Arancibia and D. Pauly (Eds.), Recruitment Processes in Tropical Coastal Demersal Communities. Ocean Science in Relation to Living Resources (OSLR), International Recruitment Project (IREP). IOC-FAO-UNESCO Workshop OSLR/IREP Project. Vol. 44. UNESCO, Paris. pp. 44-52

Deegan, L.A. and B.A. Thompson, 1985. The ecology of fish communities in the Mississippi River Deltaic Plain. In A. Yáñez-Arancibia (Ed.), Fish Community Ecology in Estuaries and Coastal Lagoons: Towards an Ecosystem Integration. Editorial Universitaria, UNAM-PUAL-ICML, Mexico, D.F., pp. 35-56.

de Sylva, D.P., 1975. Nektonic food webs in estuaries. In L.E. Cronin (Ed.), Estuarine Research. Academic, New York, Vol. 1: pp. 420-447.

Donaldson, J.R., 1967. Phosphorus budget of Iliamna Lake, Alaska, as related to the cyclic abundance of sockeye salmon. PhD Thesis, University of Washington, Seattle.

Douglas, P.A. and R.H. Stroud (Eds.), 1971. Symposium on the biological significance of estuaries. Sport Fishing Institute, Washington, D.C., 144 pp.

Dunham, F., 1972. A study of commercially important estuarine dependent industrial fishes. La. Wildlife Fish. Comm. Tech. Bull., 4:1-63.

Durbin, A.G., 1979. Food selection by plankton-feeding fishes. In H. Clepper (Ed.), Predator— Prey Systems in Fisheries Management. Sport Fishing Institute, Washington D.C., pp. 203-218.

Durbin, A.G., S.W. Nixon, and C.A. Oviatt, 1979. Effects of the spawning migration of the alewife, *Alosa pseudoharengus,* on freshwater ecosystems. Ecology, 60:8-17.

Fiske, J.D., C.E. Watson, and P.G. Coates, 1966. A study of the marine resources of Pleasant Bay. Monograph Series No. 5, Mass. Div. Marine Fisheries.

Foerster, R.E., 1968. The sockeye salmon, *Oncorhynchus nerka.* Fisheries Research Board of Canada, Bulletin No. 162.

Fry, F.E.J., 1971. The effect of environmental factors on the physiology of fish. In W.S. Hoar and D.J. Randall (Eds.), Fish Physiology, Vol. VI, Academic, New York.

Gerking, S.D. (Ed.), 1978. The Biological Basis of Freshwater Fish Production. Blackwell, Oxford, 539 pp.

Gross, M., R. Coleman, and R. MacDowall, 1988. Aquatic productivity and the evolution of diadromous fish migration. Science, 239:1291-1293.

Gunter, G., 1945. Studies on marine fishes of Texas. Publ. Inst. Mar. Sci. Univ. Texas, 1(1):1-190.

Gunter, G., 1961. Some relationships of estuarine organisms to salinity. Limnol. Oceanogr., 6:182 -190.

Haedrich, R.L., 1983. Estuarine fishes. In B. Ketchum (Ed.), Estuaries and Enclosed Seas, Ecosystems of the World, Vol. 26. Elsevier, Amsterdam, pp. 183-207.

Haedrich, R.L., and S.O. Haedrich, 1974. A seasonal survey of the fishes in the Mystic River, a polluted estuary in downtown Boston, Massachusetts. Estuarine Coastal Mar. Sci., 2:59-73.

Haedrich, R.L. and C.A.S. Hall, 1976. Fishes and estuaries. Oceanus, 19(5):55-63.

Hall, C., 1972. Migration and metabolism in a temperate stream ecosystem. Ecology, 53:585-604.

Hall, C., 1977. Models and the decision making process. In C. Hall and J. Day (Eds.), Ecosystem Modeling in Theory and Practice. Wiley Interscience, New York, pp. 346-364.

Harden-Jones, F.R., 1968. Fish Migration. Edward Arnold, London, 326 pp.

Harima, H. and P.R. Mundy, 1974. Diversity indices applied to the fish biofacies of a small stream. Trans. Am. Fish. Soc., 103:457-461.

Healy, M.C., 1979. Detritus and juvenile salmon production in the Nanaimo estuary: I. Production and feeding rates of juvenile chum salmon (*Oncorhynchus keta*). J. Fish. Res. Board Can., 36:488-496.

Healy, M.C., 1982. Juvenile Pacific salmon in estuaries: The life support system. In V.S. Kennedy (Ed.), Estuarine Comparisons. Academic, New York, pp. 315-341.

Heck, K.L. and R.J. Orth, 1980. Seagrass habitats: The role of habitat complexity, competition and predation in structuring associated fish and motile invertebrate assemblages. In V.S. Kennedy (Ed.), Estuarine Perspectives. Academic, New York, pp. 449-464.

Hellier, T.R., 1962. Fish production and biomass studies in relation to photosynthesis in the Laguna Madre of Texas. Publ. Inst. Mar. Sci. Univ. Texas, 8:212-215.

Herke, W.H., 1977a. Use of natural and semiimpounded Louisiana tidal marshes as nursuries for fishes and crustaceans. PhD Thesis, Louisiana State University, Baton Rouge, 264 pp.

Herke, W.H., 1977b. Life history concepts of motile estuarine-dependent species should be re-evaluated. Tech. Report, School of Wildlife, Forestry, and Fisheries, Louisiana State University, Baton Rouge, 97 pp.

Hillman, R.E., N.W. Davies, and J. Wennemer, 1977. Abundance, diversity and stability in shore zone fish communities in an area of Long Island Sound affected by the thermal discharge of a nuclear power station. Estuarine Coastal Mar. Sci., 5:355-381.

Hjort, J. 1916. Fluctuations in the great fisheries of Northern Europe viewed in the light of biological research. Rap. P.-V. Cons. Int. Explor. Mer. 20:1-228.

Hoese, H.D., B.J. Copeland, F.N. Moseley, and E.E. Lane, 1968. Fauna of Aransas pass inlet, Texas. III. Diel and seasonal variations in trawlable organisms of the adjacent area. Tex. J. Sci., 20:33-60.

Hoff, G.J. and R.M. Ibarra, 1977. Factors affecting the seasonal abundance, composition and diversity of fishes in Southeastern New England Estuary. Estuar. Coast. Mar. Sci., 5:665-678.

Holcik, J., 1970. Standing crop, abundance, production, and some ecological aspects of fish population in some waters of Cuba. Vestn. Cs. Spol. Zool. (Acta Zoc. Zool. Bohemuslov.), 34: 184-201.

Holland, A.F., N.K. Mountford, M.H. Hiegel, K.R. Kaumeyer, and J.A. Mihursky, 1980. Influence of predation on infaunal abundance in upper Chesapeake Bay, USA. Mar. Biol., 57(3):221-236.

Horn, M.H. and L.G. Allen, 1976. Number of species and faunal resemblance of marine fishes in California Bays and estuaries. Bull. South. Cal. Acad. Sci., 75(2):159-170.

Houde, E.D., 1978. Critical food concentrations for larvae of three species of subtropical marine fishes. Bull. Mar. Sci., 28:395-411.

Hyatt, K.D., 1979. Feeding strategy. In W.S. Hoar, D.J. Randall, and J.R. Brett (Eds.), Bioenergetics and Growth. Academic, New York, Vol. VIII, pp. 71-119.

Jones, R., W. Ogletree, J. Thompson, and W. Flennilsen, 1963. Helicopter borne purse net for population sampling of shallow marine bays. Publ. Inst. Mar. Sci. Univ. Texas, 9:1-6.

Joseph, E.B., 1973. Analysis of a nursery ground. In A.L. Pacheco (Ed.), Proceedings of a workshop on egg, larval and juvenile stages of fish in Atlantic coast estuaries. Technical Publication No. 1, NMFS, Highland, NJ, pp. 118-121.

June, F.C. and F.T. Carlson, 1971. Food of young Atlantic menhaden, *Brevoortia tyrannus*, in relation to metamorphosis. Fish. Bull., 68(3):493-511.

Kjelson, M.A., G.N. Johnson and R.L. Watson, 1973. Biomass and densities of the Newport Estuary, North Carolina. In T.R. Rice (Ed.), Annual Report to the Atomic Energy Commission. US Department of Commerce, National Marine Fisheries Service, Beaufort, NC, pp. 169-182.

Korringa, P., 1967. Estuarine fisheries in Europe as affected by man's multiple activities. In G. Lauff (Ed.), Estuaries. Amer. Assoc. Adv. Sci. Spec. Publ. 83:608-666.

Krokhin, E.M., 1975. Transport of nutrients by salmon migrating from the sea into lakes. In A.D. Hasler (Ed.), Coupling of Land and Water Systems. Springer-Verlag, New York, pp. 153-156.

Kutkuhn, J.H., 1966. The role of estuaries in the development and perpetuation of commercial shrimp resources. In R.F. Smith, A.H. Swartz, and W.H. Massmann (Eds.), A Symposium on Estuarine Fisheries. Amer. Fish. Soc. Spec. Publ. 3, pp.16-36.

Lara-Domínguez, A., A. Yáñez-Arancibia, and F. Amezcua, 1981. Biology and ecology of *Arius melanopus* (Gunther) in Terminos Lagoon, southern Gulf of Mexico (Pisces: Ariidae). An. Inst. Cienc. del Mar y Limnol. Univ. Nal. Auton. Mexico, 8(1):260-285.

Lasker, R., 1975. Field criteria for survival of anchovy larvae: The relation between inshore chlorophyll maximum layers and successful first feeding. Fish. Bull., 73:453-462.

Laurence, G.C., 1977. A bioenergetic model for the analysis of feeding and suvival potential of winter flounder *Psuedopleuronectes americanus* larvae during the period from first hatching to metamorphosis. Fish. Bull., 75:529-546.

Le Brasseur, R.J., O. Kennedy, and T.R. Parsons, 1969. Production studies in the Strait of Georgia. Part 3. Observations on the food of larval and juvenile fish in the Fraser River plume, February to May, 1967. J. Exp. Mar. Biol. Ecol., 3:51–61.

Lenanton, R., 1982. Alternative non-estuarine nursery habitats for some commercially and recreationally inportant fish species of southwestern Australia. Austr. J. Mar. Freshw. Res., 33:881–900.

Lenanton, R. and E. Hodgkin, 1985. Life history stratagies in some temperate Australian estuaries. In A. Yáñez-Arancibia (Ed.), Fish Community Ecology in Estuaries and Coastal Lagoons: Towards an Ecosystem Integration. Editorial Universitaria, UNAM-PUAL-ICML, Mexico, D.F., pp. 267–284.

Lenanton, R., and I. Potter, 1987. Contribution of estuaries to commercial fisheries in temperate Western Australia and the concept of estuarine dependence. Estuaries, 10:28–35.

Leon, E.P., 1972. Ecologia de la ictiofauna del Golfo de Nicoya, Costa Rica, un estuario tropical. Rev. Biol. Trop., 21(1):5–30.

Levine, S.J., 1980. Gut contents of forty-four Lake Pontchartrain fish species, 1977–1978. In J.H. Stone (Ed.), Environmental Analysis of Lake Pontchartrain Louisiana, its Surrounding Wetlands, and Selected Land Uses. Coastal Ecology Laboratory, Center for Wetland Resources, Louisiana State Univ., Baton Rouge. Tech. Rept., pp. 899–1030.

Levy, D., and T. Northcote, 1982. Juvenile salmon residency in a marsh area of the Fraser River estuary. Can. J. Fish. Aq. Sci., 39:270–276.

Livingston, R.J., 1976. Diurnal and seasonal fluctuations of organisms in a North Florida estuary. Estuarine Coastal Mar. Sci., 4:373–400.

Livingston, R.J., 1980. Ontogenentic trophic relationships and stress in coastal seagrass systems in Florida. In V. Kennedy (Ed.), Estuarine Perspectives. Academic Press, New York, pp. 423–435.

Livingston, R.J., 1982. Trophic organization in a coastal seagrass system. Mar. Ecol. Prog. Ser., 7:1–12.

Livingston, R.J., 1984. Trophic response of fish to habitat variability in coastal seagrass systems. Ecology, 65:1258–1275.

Livingston, R.J., 1985. Organization of fishes in coastal seagrass systems: The response to stress. In A. Yáñez-Arancibia (Ed.), Fish Community Ecology in Estuaries and Coastal Lagoons: Towards an Ecosystem Integration. Editorial Universitaria, UNAM-PUAL-ICML, Mexico, D.F., pp. 367–382.

Longhurst, A., and D. Pauly, 1987. Ecology of Tropical Oceans. Academic Press, New York, 408 pp.

Lowe-McConnell, R.H., 1975. Fish Communities in Tropical Freshwaters. Longman, New York, 337 pp.

Maciolek, J.A., 1980. Consumer trophic relations in a tropical insular estuary. Bull. Mar. Sci., 31(3)702–711.

Manzer, J.I. 1968. Food of Pacific salmon and steelhead trout in the Northeast Pacific Ocean. J. Fish. Res. Board Can., 25(5):1055–1059.

Manzer, J.I. and M.P. Shepherd, 1962. Marine survival, distribution and migration of pink salmon (O. gorbuscha) off the British Columbia coast. Symposium on Pink Salmon. Institute of Fisheries, University of British Columbia, pp. 113–122.

Marten, G., and J. Polovina, 1982. A comparative study of fish yields from various tropical ecosystems. In D. Pauly and G. Murphy (Eds.), Theory and Management of Tropical Fisheries. ICLARM Conference Proceedings 9, Manila, Philippines, pp. 255–258.

Maurer, D. and J.C. Tinsman, 1980. Demersal fish in Delaware coastal waters. J. Nat. Hist., 14:65–77.

May, R.C., 1974. Larval mortality in marine fishes and the critical period concept. In J.H.S. Blaxter (Ed.), The Early Life History of Fish. Springer-Verlag, Berlin, pp. 3–19.

McCleave, J., G. Arnold, J. Dodson, and W. Neill (Eds.), 1984. Mechanisms of Migration in Fishes. NATO Conference Series, Ser. IV: Marine Sciences, 14:574 pp.

McDowall, R.M., 1976. The role of estuaries in the life cycles of fishes in New Zealand. Proc. New Zealand Ecol. Soc., 23:27–32.

McErlean, A.J., S.G. O'Connor, J.A. Mihursky, and C. Gibson, 1973. Abundance, diversity and seasonal patterns of estuarine fish populations. Estuar. Coast. Mar. Sci., 1:19–36.

McHugh, J.L., 1967. Estuarine nekton. In G.H. Lauff (Ed.), Estuaries. Amer. Assoc. Adv. Sci. Spec. Publ. 83, pp. 581–619.

Meredith, W. and V. Lotrich, 1979. Production dynamics of a tidal creek population of *Fundulus heteroclitus* (Linnaeus). Estuar. Coast. Mar. Sci., 8:99–118.

Miller, J., 1965. A trawl survey of the shallow gulf fishes near Port Aransas, Texas. Publ. Inst. Mar. Sci. Univ. Texas, 10:80–107.

Miller, J. and M.L. Dunn, 1980. Feeding strategies and patterns of movements in juvenile estuarine species. In V.S. Kennedy (Ed.), Estuarine Perspectives. Academic, New York, pp. 437–448.

Moore, D., H.A. Brusher, and L. Trent, 1970. Relative abundance, seasonal distribution and species composition of demersal fishes off Lousiana and Texas, 1962–1964. Contrib. Mar. Sci., 15:45–70.

Moore, R., 1978. Variations in the diversity of summer estuarine fish populations in Aransas Bay, Texas, 1966–1973. Estuar. Coast. Mar. Sci., 6:495–501.

Mundie, J.H., 1969. Ecological implications of the diet of juvenile coho in streams. In T.G. Northcote (Ed.), Symposium on Salmon and Trout in Streams. Inst. of Fisheries, University of B.C., Vancouver, pp. 133–152.

Musick J., J. Colvocoresses, and E. Foell, 1985. Seasonality and the distribution, availability and composition of fish assemblages in Chesapeake Bight. In A. Yáñez-Arancibia (Ed.), Fish Community Ecology in Estuaries and Coastal Lagoons: Towards an Ecosystem Integration. Editorial Universitaria, UNAM-PUAL-ICML, Mexico, D.F., pp. 451–474.

Muus, B.J., 1967. The fauna of Danish estuaries and lagoons. Middelson Danmarks Fisheri-og Havundersogelser. Ny Serie 5:1–316.

Myers, G.S., 1949. Usage of anadromous, catadromous, and allied terms for migratory fishes. Copeia, 89–97.

Naiman, R.J. and J.R. Sibert, 1979. Detritus and juvenile salmon production in the Nanaimo estuary. III. Importance of detrital carbon to the estuarine ecosystem. J. Fish. Res. Board. Can., 36:504–520.

Nelson, W.R., M.C. Ingham, and W.E. Schaaf, 1977. Larval transport and year-class strength of Atlantic menhaden, *Brevoortia tyrannus*. Fish. Bull., 75(1):23–41.

Nikolsky, G.V., 1963. The Ecology of Fishes. Academic Press, New York, 352 pp.

Nixon, S., 1982. Nutrient dynamics, primary production and fishery yields of lagoons. In P. Lasserre and H. Postma (Eds.), Coastal Lagoons. Oceanologica Acta, Vol. Spec. 5:357-371.

Nixon, S.W. and C.A. Oviatt, 1973. Ecology of a New England salt marsh. Ecol. Monogr., 43:463-498.

Odum, W.E. and E.J. Heald, 1975. The detritus based food web of an estuarine mangrove community. In L.E. Cronin (Ed.), Estuarine Research. Academic, New York, Vol. 1, pp. 265-286.

Ogren, L.H. and H.A. Brusher, 1977. The distribution and abundance of fishes caught with a trawl in the St. Andrews Bay System, Florida. Northeast Gulf Sci., 1:83-105.

Oviatt, C., and S. Nixon, 1973. The demersal fish of Narragansett Bay: An analysis of community structure, distribution and abundance. Estuarine Coastal Mar. Sci., 1:361-378.

Oviatt, C.A., A.L. Gall, and S.W. Nixon, 1972. Environmental effects of Atlantic menhaden on surrounding waters. Chesapeake Sci., 13:321-323.

Pakrasi, B.B., Das, P.R., and T. Hakurta, S. 1964. Culture of Brackish-water fishes in impoundments in West Bengal. Publications of the Indo-Pacific Fisheries Council No. 2.

Parrish, R.H., C.S. Nelson, A. Bakun, 1981. Transport mechanisms and reproductive success of fishes in the California current. Biol. Oceanogr., 1(2):175-203.

Pauly, D., 1985. Ecology of coastal and estuarine fishes in Southeast Asia: A Philippine case study. In A. Yáñez-Arancibia (Ed.), Fish Community Ecology in Estuaries and Coastal Lagoons: Towards an Ecosystem Integration. Editorial Universitaria, UNAM-PUAL-ICML, Mexico, D.F., pp. 499-514.

Pauly, D., and A. Mines, (Eds.), 1982. Small-scale fisheries of San Miguel Bay, Philippines: Biology and stock assesment. ICLARM Tech. Rept. 7. Manila, Philippines, 124 pp.

Pauly, D., and G. Murphy, (Eds.), 1982. Theory and Management of Tropical Fisheries. ICLARM Conference Proceedings 9. Manila, Philippines, 360 pp.

Pearcy, W.G., 1962. Ecology of an estuarine population of Winter flounder (*Pseudopleuronectes americanus*). Bull. Bingham Oceanogr. Coll., 18:39-64.

Postma, H., and G. Rauck, 1979. The fishery in the Wadden Sea. In N. Dankers, W. Wolff, and J. Zijlstra (Eds.), Fishes and Fisheries of the Wadden Sea. A. A. Balkema, Rotterdam, pp. 139-157.

Reintjes, J.W. and A.T. Pacheco, 1966. The relationship of menhaden to estuaries. Am. Fish Soc. Spec. Pub., 3:50-58.

Rabanal, H.R., 1961. Status and progress of *Chanos* fisheries in the Philippines. Occasional paper 61/8, Indo-Pacific Fisheries Council.

Richard, S.W., 1963. The demersal fish populations of Long Island Sound. Bull. Bingham Oceanogr. Coll., 18:1-101.

Ross, S., and S. Epperly, 1985. Utilization of shallow estuarine nursery areas by fishes in Pamlico Sound and adjacent tributaries. In A. Yáñez-Arancibia (Ed.), Fish Community Ecology in Estuaries and Coastal Lagoons: Towards an Ecosystem Integration. Editorial Universitaria, UNAM-PUAL-ICML, Mexico, D.F., pp. 207-232.

Royce, W.F., L.S. Smith, and A.C. Hart, 1968. Models of oceanic migrations of Pacific salmon and comments on guidance mechanisms. U.S. Fish Wildlife Serv., Fish. Bull., 66(3):441–462.

Sabins, D.S. and F.M. Truesdale, 1974. Diel and seasonal occurrence of fishes in a Louisiana tidal pass. Proceedings of the 28th Annual Conference of the Southern Association of Game and Fish Commission, pp. 161–172.

Sánchez-Gil, P., and A. Yáñez-Arancibia, 1986. Discussion on recruitment relationships in lagoon-estuarine environments of fishes from the southern Gulf of Mexico. In A. Yáñez-Arancibia and D. Pauly (Eds.), Recruitment Processes in Tropical Coastal Demersal Communities. Ocean Science in Relation to Living Resources (OSLR), International Recruitment Project (IREP). IOC-FAO-UNESCO Workshop OSLR/IREP Project. Vol. 44. UNESCO, Paris, pp. 215–228.

Schubel, J.R. and D.J. Hirschberg, 1978. Estuarine graveyards, climatic change, and the importance of the estuarine environment. In M.W. Wiley (Ed.), Estuarine Interactions. Academic, New York, pp. 285–303.

Setzler-Hamilton, E., J. Mihursky, W. Boynton, K. Wood, G. Drewry, and T. Polgar, 1980. Striped bass spawning and eggs and larval stages. In H. Clepper (Ed.), Marine Recreation Fisheries 5. Sport Fishing Institute, Washington, pp. 89–100.

Shenker, J.M. and J.M. Dean, 1980. The utilization of an intertidal, salt marsh creek by larval and juvenile fishes: Abundance, diversity, and temporal variation. Estuaries, 2:154–163.

Sheridan, P. and R.J. Livingston, 1979. Cyclic trophic relationships of fishes in an unpolluted, river-dominated estuary in North Florida. In R. Livington (Ed.), Ecological Processes in Coastal and Marine Systems. Plenum, New York, 143–161.

Shlossman, P.A. and M.E. Chittenden, Jr., 1981. Reproduction, movements, and population dynamics of the sand seatrout, *Cynoscion nebulosus*. Fish. Bull., 79(4):649–689.

Sibert, J.R., T.J. Brown, M.C. Healey, B.A. Kas, and R.J. Naiman, 1978. Detritus-based food webs: Exploitation by juvenile chum salmon (*Oncorhyncus keta*). Science, 196:649–650.

Simenstad, C.A., K.L. Tresh, and E.O. Salo, 1982. The role of Puget sound and Washington coastal estuaries in the life history of Pacific salmon: The unappreciated function. In V.S. Kennedy (Ed.), Estuarine Comparisons. Academic, New York, pp. 343–364.

Smith, R.F., A.H. Swartz, and W.H. Massmann, (Eds.), 1966. A Symposium on Estuarine Fisheries. Amer. Fish. Soc. Spec. Pub. No. 3, 154 pp.

Springer, V.G. and K.D. Woodburn, 1960. An ecological study of the fishes of the Tampa Bay area. Prof. Pap. Ser. Mar. Lab. Fla., 1:1–104.

Subrahmanyan, C.B. and S.H. Drake, 1975. Studies on the animal communities in two North Florida salt marshes. Part. I. Fish communities. Bull. Mar. Sci., 25(4):445–465.

Sutcliffe, W.H., Jr., 1973. Correlations between seasonal river discharge and local landings of American Lobster (*Homarus americanus*) and Atlantic halibut (*Hippoglossus hippoglossus*) in the Gulf of St. Lawrence. J. Fish. Res. Board Can., 30:856–859.

Talbot, G.B., 1966. Estuarine environmental requirements and limiting factors for striped bass. In R.F. Smith, A.H. Swartz, and W.H. Massmann (Eds.), A Symposium on Estuarine Fisheries. Amer. Fish. Soc. Spec. Pub. No. 3, pp. 37–49.

Thayer, G.W., S. Marshall Adams, and M.W. Lacroix, 1976. Structural and functional aspects of a recently established *Zostera marina* community. In L.E. Cronin (Ed.), Estuarine Research. Chemistry, Biology and the Estuarine Systems. Academic, New York, pp. 518–540.

Thayer, G.W., D.R. Colby and W.F. Hettler, Jr. 1987. Utilization of the red mangrove prop root habitat by fishes in South Florida. Mar. Ecol. Prog. Series 35:25–38.

Thompson, B.A. and J.S. Verret, 1980. Nekton of Lake Pontchartrain, Louisiana, and its surrounding wetlands. In J.H. Stone (Ed.), Environmental Atlas of Lake Pontchartrain, Louisiana, its Surrounding Wetlands, and Selected Land Uses. Coastal Ecology Laboratory, Center for Wetland Resources, Louisiana State University, Baton Rouge. pp.

Turner, W.R. and G.N. Johnson, 1973. Distribution and relative abundance of fishes in Newport River, North Carolina. NOAA Technical Report, Washington, NMFS-666, 23 pp.

Tyler, A.V., 1971. Periodic and resident components in communities of Atlantic fishes. J. Fish. Res. Board Can., 28:935–946.

Valiela, I., J. Wright, J. Teal, and S.B. Volkman, 1977. Growth, production and energy transformations in the salt marsh killifish, *Fundulus heteroclitus*. Mar. Biol., 40:135–144.

Vernberg, W.B. and F.J. Vernberg, 1976. Physiological adaptations of estuarine animals. Oceanus, 19(5):48–54.

Virnstein, R., 1977. The importance of predation by crabs and fishes on benthic infauna in Chesapeake Bay. Ecology, 58:1199–1217.

Virnstein, R., 1978. Predator caging experiments in soft sediments: Caution advised. In M. Wiley (Ed.), Estuarine Interactions. Academic Press, New York, pp. 261–273.

Wagner, P., 1973. Seasonal biomass, abundance, and distribution of estuarine dependent fishes in the Caminada Bay system of Louisiana. PhD Dissertation. Louisiana State University, Baton Rouge, 193 pp.

Walford, L.A., 1966. The estuary as a habitat for fishery organisms. In R.F. Smith, A. Swartz, and W. Massman (Eds.), A Symposium on Estuarine Fishes. Amer. Fish. Soc. Spec. Publ. No. 3, p. 15.

Warburton, K., 1978. Community structure, abundance and diversity of fish in a Mexican Coastal lagoon system. Estuar. Coast. Mar. Sci., 7:497–579.

Warburton, K., 1979. Growth and production of some important species of fish in a Mexican coastal lagoon system. J. Fish. Biol., 14:449–464.

Weinstein, M.P., 1979. Shallow marsh habitats as primary nurseries for fish and shellfish, Cape Fear River, North Carolina. Fish. Bull., 77:339–357.

Weinstein, M.P., 1982. Commentary: A need for more experimental work in estuarine fish ecology. Northeast Gulf Sci., 5:59–64.

Weinstein, M.P., 1985. Distributional ecology of fishes inhabiting warm-temperate and tropical estuaries: Community relationships and implications. In A. Yáñez-Arancibia (Ed.), Fish Community Ecology in Estuaries and Coastal Lagoons: Towards an Ecosystem Integration. Editorial Universitaria, UNAM-PUAL-ICML, Mexico, D.F., pp. 285–310.

Weinstein, M.P. and K. Heck, 1979. Ichthyofauna of seagrass meadows along the Caribbean coast of Panama and in the Gulf of Mexico: Composition, structure and community ecology. Mar. Biol. 50:97–108.

Weinstein, M.P., S.L. Weiss, R.G. Hodson, and L.R. Gerry, 1980. Retention of taxa of post larval fishes in an intensively flushed tidal estuary, Cape Fear River, North Carolina. Fish. Bull., 78:419-436.

Whitfield, A.K., 1980. Distribution of fishes in Mhlanga Estuary in relation to food resources. S. Afr. J. Zool., 15:159-165.

Winberg, G., 1971. Methods for the Estimation of Production in Aquatic Animals. Academic Press, New York.

Woodwell, G.M., and E. Pecan, 1973. Flax Pond: An estuarine marsh. Brookhaven National Laboratory Publ. BNL-50397, Brookhaven, New York, 7 pp.

Woodwell, G.M., P.H. Rich and C.A.S. Hall, 1973. Carbon and estuaries. In G.M. Woodwell and E. Pecan (Eds.), Carbon and the Biosphere. Brookhaven Symposium in Biology, Upton, New York, pp. 221-240.

Yáñez-Arancibia, A., 1975. On the studies of fishes in coastal lagoons: Scientific note. An. Centro. Cienc. del Mar y Limnol. Univ. Nal. Auton. Mexico, 2:53-60.

Yáñez-Arancibia, A., 1976. Observaciones sobre *Mugil curema* Valenciennes, en areas naturales de crianza, Mexico. Alimentacion, madurez, crecimiento y relaciones ecologicas. An. Centro. Cienc. del Mar y Limnol. Univ. Nal. Autón. México, 3:92-124.

Yáñez-Arancibia, A., 1978. Taxonomy, ecology and structure of fish communities in coastal lagoons with ephemeral inlets on the Pacific Coast of Mexico. Centro. Cienc. del Mar y Limnol. Univ. Nal. Autón. México, Publ. Esp., 2:1-306.

Yáñez-Arancibia, A., 1981. Ecological studies in Puerto Real Inlet, Terminos Lagoon, Mexico: Discussion on trophic structure of fish communities in *Thalassia testudinum* banks. In P. Lasserre, H. Postma, J. Costlow, and M. Steyaert (Eds.), Coastal Lagoon Research Present and Future. Tech. Paper Mar. Sci., UNESCO, 33:191-232.

Yáñez-Arancibia, A., (Ed.), 1985. Fish Community Ecology in Estuaries and Coastal Lagoons: Towards an Ecosystem Integration. Editorial Universitaria, UNAM-PUAL-ICML, Mexico, D.F., 654 pp.

Yáñez-Arancibia, A., 1986. Ecología de la Zona Costera: Analisis de Siete Topicos. Editorial AGT, Mexico, D.F., 200 pp.

Yáñez-Arancibia, A., and A.L. Lara-Domínguez, 1983. Environmental dynamic of Estero Pargo Inlet and structure of fish communities in daily and seasonal changes in *Rhizophora mangle/Thalassia testudinum* habitats (Terminos Lagoon, southern Gulf of Mexico). An. Inst. Cienc. del Mar. y Limnol. Univ. Nal. Autón. México, 10:85-116.

Yáñez-Arancibia, A., and A.L. Lara-Domínguez, 1988. Ecology of three catfish species in a tropical coastal ecosystem (Southern Gulf of Mexico). Mar. Ecol. Prog. Ser., *in press*.

Yáñez-Arancibia, A., and R.S. Nugent, 1977. The ecological role of fishes in estuaries and coastal lagoons. An. Centro. Cienc. del Mar. y Limnol. Univ. Nal. Autón. México, 4:107-114.

Yáñez-Arancibia, A., and D. Pauly (Eds.), 1986. Recruitment Processes in Tropical Coastal Demersal Communities. Proc. IOC-FAO-UNESCO Workshop. OSLR/IREP Project. UNESCO, Paris, Vol. 44, 324 pp.

Yáñez-Arancibia, A., and P. Sánchez-Gil, 1988. Ecología de los Recursos Demersales Marinos: Fundamentos en Costas Tropicales. Editorial AGT, Mexico, D. F., 230 pp.

Yáñez-Arancibia, A., F. Amezcua, and J.W. Day, 1980. Fish community structure and function in Terminos Lagoon, a tropical estuary in the Southern Gulf of Mexico. In V. Kennedy (Ed.), Estuarine Perspectives. Academic Press, New York, pp. 465-482.

Yáñez-Arancibia, A., A.L. Lara-Domínguez, P. Sánchez-Gil, I. Vargas, P. Chavance, A. Aguirre, S. Diaz, and F. Amezcua, 1982. Ecosystem dynamics and nichthemeral and seasonal programming of fish community structure in a tropical estuarine inlet, Mexico. In P. Lasserre and H. Postma (Eds.), Coastal Lagoons. Oceanologica Acta, Vol. Spec. 5:431-440.

Yáñez-Arancibia, A., A.L. Lara-Domínguez, A. Aguirre, S. Diaz, F. Amezcua, D. Flores and P. Chavance, 1985a. Ecology of dominant fish populations in tropical estuaries: Environmental factors regulating biological stratagies and production. In A. Yáñez-Arancibia, (Ed.), Fish Community Ecology in Estuaries and Coastal Lagoons: Towards an Ecosystem Integration. Editorial Universitaria, UNAM-PUAL-ICML, Mexico, D.F., pp. 311-366.

Yáñez-Arancibia, A., A.L. Lara-Domínguez, H. Alvarez Guillen, 1985b. Fish community ecology and dynamics in estuarine inlets. In A. Yáñez-Arancibia, (Ed.), Fish Community Ecology in Estuaries and Coastal Lagoons: Towards an Ecosystem Integration. Editorial Universitaria, UNAM-PUAL-ICML, Mexico, D.F., pp. 127-168.

Yáñez-Arancibia, A., A.L. Lara-Domínguez, P. Sánchez-Gil, I. Vargas, Ma. C. García, H. Alvarez Guillen, M. Tapia, D. Flores and F. Amezcua, 1985c. Ecology and evaluation of fish community in coastal ecosystems: Estuary–shelf interrelationships in the southern Gulf of Mexico. In A. Yáñez-Arancibia, (Ed.), Fish Community Ecology in Estuaries and Coastal Lagoons: Towards an Ecosystem Integration. Editorial Universitaria, UNAM-PUAL-ICML, Mexico, D.F., pp. 475-498.

Yáñez-Arancibia, A., A.L. Lara-Domínguez, A. Aguirre-Leon, and S. Diaz-Ruiz, 1986. Feeding ecology of tropical estuarine fishes in relation to recruitment processes. In A. Yáñez-Arancibia and D. Pauly (Eds.), Recruitment Processes in Tropical Coastal Demersal Communities. Ocean Science in Relation to Living Resources (OSLR), International Recruitment Project (IREP). IOC-FAO-UNESCO Workshop OSLR/IREP Project. Vol. 44. UNESCO, Paris.

OFFPRINTS FROM: ESTUARINE ECOLOGY
Edited by John W. Day Jr., Charles A. S. Hall., Dr. W. Michael Kemp, and Alejandro Yáñez-Arancibia
Copyright © 1989 by John Wiley & Sons, Inc.

▬▬ 11

The Role Of Wildlife in Estuarine Ecosystems[1]

Wildlife, in this chapter, means the higher vertebrates—mammals, birds, reptiles, and amphibians. They are the animals most often noticed by casual visitors to estuaries. Shorebirds pecking at the mudflats, a flight of ibis over the mangroves at twilight, the tantalizing voices of clapper rails in the cordgrass, muskrats whose lodges dot the bulrush stands, a cow grazing salt hay, or snapping turtles drifting down the creek with the receding tide—how do these animals interact with their environment? Although larger animals generally are believed to have less impact on tidal wetlands and shallows ecosystems than the more numerous smaller animals, wildlife can be abundant and ecologically important at certain times and places. Wildlife is also a significant link between estuaries and human society. In this chapter we discuss the responses of wildlife individuals and populations to the dynamic estuarine habitat, and we show that concentrations of wildlife sometimes have remarkable effects on estuarine sediments, vegetation, and animal communities.

11.1 WILDLIFE DIVERSITY

Estuarine wildlife is taxonomically diverse. Among the more important groups of mammals are the rodents, carnivores, cetaceans, and ungulates; of birds, the herons, waterfowl, hawks, rails, gulls, shorebirds, and songbirds; and of reptiles, the crocodiles and turtles. Many frogs and salamanders are known to enter estuarine habitats (Neill 1958), but few are abundant there, because of difficul-

[1]By E. Kiviat.

438

ties with osmoregulation due to the permeable amphibian skin, and to the need of many species for still fresh water for spawning.

Body size ranges from the 5 g Suisun shrew to the 14 metric ton gray whale. Different species eat leaves, roots, seeds, invertebrates, fish, other wildlife, carrion, and some are omnivores eating a wide variety of foods. They are associated with wooded swamps, marshes, mudflats, and shallow waters, where they live part of the time or permanently. Some species tolerate salty water or great tidal fluctuation and other species do not. Most wildlife species found in estuaries are also found in other habitats (freshwater, marine, or terrestrial); only a few species, like the diamondback terrapin, are estuarine "endemics." An example of a tidal marsh food web (Fig. 11.1) shows several kinds of birds and mammals representative of estuarine wildlife.

11.2   TEMPORAL AND SPATIAL DISTRIBUTION

Animal species have different geographic ranges and habitat affinities related to the availability of resources and the stress of adverse conditions. Estuarine wildlife distributions are shaped by landforms, climate, salinity, tides, vegetation, other animals, and human activities. Individuals of some species live their entire life history in estuaries (e.g., snapping turtle, and muskrat), and other species are part time (or permeant) users of estuarine habitats. The permeants enter from the sea (bottle-nosed dolphin) or from land (raccoon). Permeants need particular combinations of habitats. For example the endangered light-footed clapper rail of southern California tidal marshes needs mudflats for feeding next to California cordgrass stands for shelter and nesting (Anon. 1979). If either of these habitats is altered, the rails no longer use a marsh. Animals need food (for energy and for macro- and micronutrients), shelter (for nesting and hiding), special resources such as display stations or symbiotic species, and sometimes freshwater. When needed resources are plentiful, a species may attain high density by immigration or reproduction. Daiber (1982) treats the distribution of wildlife in relation to estuarine variables.

11.2.1   Seasonal Patterns of Distribution

Climate and the seasonal availability of resources affect the ways estuaries are used by wildlife species as feeding, reproduction, and migration areas. Wildlife may move seasonally between inland habitats and coastal habitats, between estuarine and marine habitats, or between high latitudes and low latitudes. Few resident winter-active species occur in northern estuaries because of extreme cold, storms, shifting tidal ice, and restricted access to food. Hard freezes may cause mass mortality in species that winter in wetlands that are normally ice-free. Many species that breed on beaches or near inland waters, however, winter in milder tidal wetlands to exploit abundant food such as benthic invertebrates. Tidemarsh pools may be ice-free earlier in spring and later in fall compared to

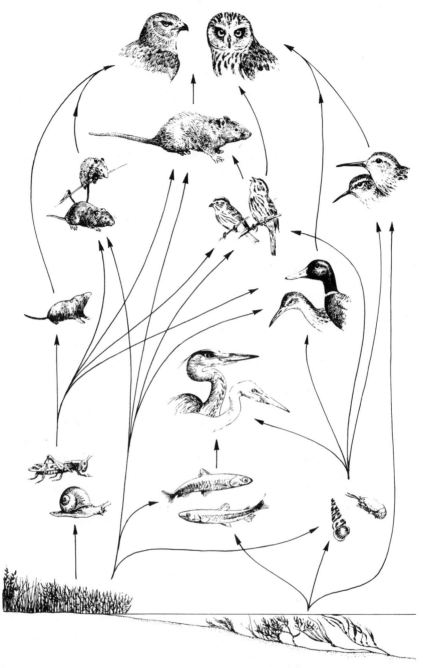

Figure 11.1. Partial food web of a tidal marsh, San Pablo Bay north of San Francisco. Wildlife species illustrated are northern harrier, short-eared owl, Norway rat, salt-marsh harvest mouse, California vole, song sparrow, savannah sparrow, sandpipers, Suisun shrew, mallard, clapper rail, great blue heron and great egret. From New York State Conservationist, based on information in Johnston (1956a, b, 1957).

inland ponds, and the pools are heavily used by migrating water birds that range as far north as open water is available (e.g., Seymour and Titman 1979). Over an annual cycle the pattern of wildlife distribution in any particular estuary is a composite of the different species using the area. This is illustrated for bird use of a Louisiana estuary in Fig. 11.2, where there is a high standing crop of birds all year but different species are important at different times.

Nektonic wildlife may move seasonally between marine and estuarine waters, to exploit changing food resources or favorable temperatures. Manatees, for example, escape potentially fatal cold spells by wintering in deep freshwater springs or power plant thermal plumes in Florida, sometimes in large herds (Hartman 1979). The harbor porpoises studied by Neave and Wright (1968) moved from the Atlantic Ocean into the Bay of Fundy to bear their young, evidently attracted by calmer waters, more favorable salinity, and abundant food.

Many species of birds and mammals migrate along estuaries or marine shores, using the coastlines for orientation and stopping to rest and feed in wetlands or other sheltered habitats. During coastwise movements, migratory wildlife and humans come into contact, and these migrations are often exploited by hunters and watchers of wildlife. Three of the birds for which coast-oriented flight has been reported are: the greater flamingo along the Mediterranean shore (Johnson 1975), the roseate spoonbill of the southeastern United States (Allen 1942), and the peregrine falcon of eastern North America (Slack and Slack 1981).

The high productivity of estuaries often provides sources of energy critically needed by small birds for long-distance migrations. Fall-migrating sora rail and red-winged blackbirds pass through the Chesapeake Bay when seeds are at peak availability in the marshes (Meanley 1961, 1965). Also, estuarine wetlands and shallows are "staging" areas where many bird species concentrate after the

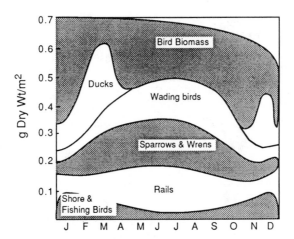

Figure 11.2. Seasonal pattern of population composition and biomass of birds in a Louisiana salt marsh estuary (from Day et al. 1973).

breeding season for feeding, molting, or roosting with relative safety from predators. Eider duck "molt-migrations" may be as long as 2500 km and involve tens of thousands of birds that congregate on food-rich arctic bays during the flightless period of the postbreeding molt (Salomonsen 1968).

11.2.2 Distribution Patterns Related to Salinity

Salinity patterns affect wildlife in a variety of ways. A few highly mobile and tolerant species with broad diets, such as the bald eagle, seem relatively unresponsive to salinity. Some species, such as the silver leaf monkey studied by Lim Boon Hock and Sasekumar (1979) or many small birds, can remain aloft in canopy microhabitats of estuarine forests and have little contact with brackish water. Most estuarine animals, however, show distributions or behaviors that are related to salinity patterns (Table 11.1). Mammal community composition in Louisiana coastal marshes shows species sorting along salinity gradients (Fig. 11.3). Muskrats are most common in brackish marshes (dominated by saltmeadow cordgrass), while nutria are most common in fresh marshes. Some marine birds and mammals (like marine fish) intrude various distances up-estuary depending upon their tolerances for reduced salinity; incursions of marine animals into East Coast estuaries occur with rising salinity in summer and fall. Freshwater species occur various distances down-estuary depending upon their tolerances for increased salinity. The crab-eating frog of Thailand spawns after rains freshen brackish pools; even though the frog can tolerate 20% seawater, larval development is favored by lower salinity (Gordon and Tucker 1965). Some taxa have "ecological equivalents" in higher and lower salinity environments: examples are clapper rail and king rail (Meanley 1969); diamondback terrapin and map turtle; American crocodile and American alligator.

Although many wildlife species migrate seasonally in response to changing

TABLE 11.1 Salinity Patterns and Wildlife Responses

Salinity Patterns	Effects/Responses
Spatial gradients	Sorting by: Species
	Population density
	Population class
	Social organization
	Diet
	Morphology
Spatial mosaics	Selection to fulfill needs
(habitat juxtaposition)	
Seasonal change	Migration or incursion
	Reproduction
Infrequent extremes	
Increase (intrusion)	Movement, mortality
Decrease (freshening)	Movement, mortality

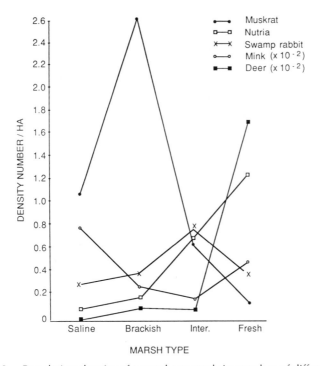

Figure 11.3. Population density of several mammals in marshes of different salinities on the Louisiana coast (from Abernethy 1987).

salinity, more sedentary animals may be vulnerable to infrequent events that cause rapid and extreme changes in salinity. Severe droughts or storms with on-shore winds can raise salinity severely and rapidly, killing animals unable to flee. Muskrat mortality occurred in a Chesapeake Bay brackish marsh during a se-vere salinity incursion (Dozier 1947). Likewise, suddenly reduced salinity can be a problem; dugongs in Australian coastal waters may die after heavy rains be-cause of the death of their seagrass food (Anderson 1979).

Population density may vary with salinity, or different age and sex classes of a population may use habitats with different salinities. Juvenile American croco-diles cannot tolerate full strength seawater and need estuarine nursery habitats (Ellis 1981) as do the hatchlings of the Asian river turtle which cross high-salinity waters from their beach nests to reach low salinity nurseries (Dunson and Moll 1980). On St. Catherine's Island, Georgia, American alligator juveniles and adult females live in fresh ponds whereas adult males live mainly in saline tidal marsh creeks (Meyer 1975).

Diet often differs with salinity–not surprisingly, since prey organisms often have more narrow salinity tolerances than higher vertebrates. The sora rail eats seeds when in the less brackish marshes, and insects when in the more brackish marshes of the Housatonic River estuary of Connecticut (Webster 1964). Muskrats in fresh nontidal habitats in Maryland use about 30 food plants, none individually important in the diet; in brackish tidal habitats, muskrats eat only nine species of plants, of which two comprise 80% of the diet (Willner et al. 1975).

A species may use a mosaic of habitats of different salinities in combination to satisfy different needs. Feral ponies on Assateague Island, Virginia graze in the salt marsh and wade in the bay for respite from biting flies, but require fresh drinking water from forest ponds (Keiper 1979).

11.2.3 Tide Effects on Wildlife

Changing water levels affect access to resources and the safety of estuarine wildlife (Table 11.2). Animals tend to enter shallows and wetlands from land at low tide, and from deeper water at high tide. Protection from predators or food availability can be so strongly determined by the tides that tidal cycles often outweigh diel cycles as determinants of behavior. Tidal fluctuation similarly is a concern to observers of wildlife. The tidal variable compounds sampling problems, but also creates opportunities. At high water, the wetlands are accessible by boat, and wildlife such as snakes and rails may be driven to high ground or exposed to view; at low water, humans can wade and normally submerged species like turtles may be visible.

Many animals feed only when the tide is at a certain stage or feed in different habitats at different stages of the tide. This behavior is best known among "terrestrial" species that feed at lower tide stages when food resources are exposed or concentrated. Low tide feeding has been reported for water snakes, herons,

TABLE 11.2 Tidal Effects on Wildlife with Selected Examples

Highwater level	
Positive effects	Allows "aquatic" species to enter intertidal zone
	Affords protection from predators, heat, dessication
	Assists and orients emergence of "aquatic" species onto land
Negative effects	Drowns or destroys nests, eggs, young
	Forces animals from cover and exposes them to predators, heat, etc.; drives inland or onto roads
	Covers or kills food, damages vegetation
Low water level	
Positive effects	Allows "terrestrial" species to enter intertidal zone
	Exposes, concentrates or traps food (prey)
Negative effects	Strands aquatic animals on mud or in tidepools
	Exposes animals to predators, weather
Tidal current	Transports animals
	Brings or concentrates food (prey)

brant, rails, shorebirds, belted kingfisher, raccoon, feral pigs, and many other taxa. Bottle-nosed dolphins in Georgia work in pairs at low tide to round up fish and trap them on the banks of marsh creeks (Hoese 1971). The population implications of tidal behavior are illustrated by the American oystercatcher, most common where the shore exposed at low tide is widest, less common where the tide range is small (Tomkins 1947).

Aquatic species that enter shallower water at high tide include the green turtle and dugong (Anderson and Birtles 1978) and the harbor seal (Scheffer and Slipp 1944). Although the harbor seal exploits changing water levels to use different haul-out areas (Scheffer and Slipp 1944), other marine mammals feeding inshore may be trapped by ebbing tides (Geraci 1978). Snapping turtles in a tidal marsh follow the ebbing tide down, often seeking shelter from heat by burying themselves in the mud or entering muskrat burrows, and return to the intertidal zone with the rising tide (Fig. 11.4; Kiviat 1980). Diamondback terrapins (Burger and Montevecchi 1975) emerge from the marsh onto land to nest at high tide to be exposed to the heat for shorter periods and to locate their nests above potential inundation.

Extremely high tides ("flood tides") often harm wildlife by damaging food or

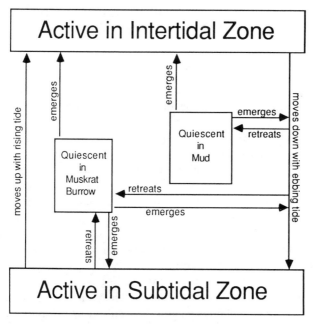

Figure 11.4. Snapping turtle tide-related behavior in a Hudson River fresh-tidal marsh. Turtles follow the ebbing tide down creeks and across mudflats, moving in and out of shelters (muskrat burrows, vegetation, debris, mud), then move back up in the intertidal zone as the tide rises.

cover, by drowning nests and young, or by driving animals from cover and making them vulnerable to predation. Destruction of nests and mortality of eggs or young due to flood tides has been described for a number of species ranging from the American alligator in Louisiana (Fleming et al. 1976) to the Suisun shrew in California (Johnston and Rudd 1957). Tides that cover marsh vegetation and drive animals to high ground expose song sparrows (Johnston 1956b) and California voles to predation by marsh hawks and short-eared owls in California, and have forced king rails with their broods onto Louisiana highways (Meanley 1969).

The nesting behavior of some birds is adapted to monthly extreme high tides. Sharp-tailed sparrows in Nova Scotia (Bleakney 1972) and saltmarsh song sparrows in California (Johnston 1956a, b) time their nesting cycles to avoid nest-threatening flood tides. Although Georgia marsh wrens may lose 21% of their eggs to high water, they do not time nesting to the lunar cycle; instead, a long nesting season and the ready ability to renest prevent limitation of production in most years (Kale 1965). Among species of birds that nest on or near the ground (e. g., gulls and terns), nest site selection and nest construction are often strongly influenced by high tide levels.

The role of tidal currents in the lives of estuarine wildlife is less well known, but intriguing. Allen (1947) described nighttime feeding by roseate spoonbills on shrimp and small fish that, in turn, followed plankton on a thermal current in a Texas lagoon, and Lauro (1980) noted that foraging Bonaparte's gulls rode on tidal currents that entered a lagoon and concentrated planktonic prey.

11.2.4 Vegetation and Wildlife Distributions

Estuarine vegetation comprises plankton, attached micro and macroalgae, submerged vascular plants including seagrasses, emergent vascular plants such as cordgrasses, and trees such as mangroves. Vascular plants are especially important to wildlife. The high content of structural materials (cellulose, lignin, silica) that makes many estuarine vascular plants resistant to decay also makes them abrasive and difficult to eat but useful for shelter from the elements.

On first inspection, estuarine wetlands may appear vast and uniform. But spatial patterns, or seasonal and year-to-year changes in species composition, height, form and texture of plants, and presence of litter or standing dead vegetation are characteristics that affect wildlife. Fire, storms, ice movements, sedimentation, ditching, diking, and other natural or anthropogenic events can change vegetation and thus the habitat.

A majority of saline tidal marshes in the northeastern United States has been ditched in a grid pattern for mosquito control. The sediment removed has generally been piled alongside the ditches, and the resulting spoil banks often support narrow strips of woody vegetation contrasting with the surrounding grassy marsh. Post (1974) documented different seaside sparrow social organization and space use for nesting and feeding in a ditched marsh with the shrub marsh-elder than in an unditched marsh without marsh-elder. And clapper rails nested on mosquito ditch spoil banks only if shrubs were absent, because predatory crows used shrubs for hunting perches (Shisler and Schulze 1977). Mosquito ditch spoils, with or without woody vegetation, provide flood-safe nesting sites for many birds.

Although vertebrates in coastal areas often tend to have broad habitat affinities, a few wildlife species depend upon a single plant species to a great degree. A change in the abundance of such a plant can have profound effects upon associated animals in vegetationally simple estuarine communities. The brant of the eastern United States were unusual in their specialization on a single food plant, eelgrass. The disease that decimated eelgrass beds in the Northeast caused massive mortality of brant, a change to sea lettuce in the survivors' food habits, and even a shift in migration routes (Clough 1976).

Little is known about animal tolerance to abrasion by vegetation. In northeastern marshes, sharp-tailed sparrows nest and forage in dense saltmeadow cordgrass, whereas seaside sparrows forage in more open areas. The sharptail suffers more feather abrasion from the dense grass and is unusual among songbirds in having two complete molts per year while the seaside sparrow has only one complete and one partial molt (Hill 1968, Woolfenden 1968). Sharptails, moreover, have fewer feather lice because of the extra molt (Post and Enders 1970).

The affinities of animals to structural and/or taxonomic elements in vegetation extend to fallen or dead plants. Snags, driftwood, wrack, litter, and lodged (fallen-over) herbs are important habitat components used by small animals for escape cover, nesting, and foraging. These microhabitats may also stay cool and store fresh moisture. The "cowlicks" of lodged saltmeadow cordgrass are a distinctive feature of the New England high salt marsh and important shelter for meadow voles (Howell 1984) and small birds, and the island glass lizard of the Southeast hides under palmetto leaves in tide wrack (Neill 1958). On New Jersey marshes, laughing gulls tend to nest on saltwater cordgrass wrack while common terns and black skimmers nest on eelgrass wrack (Burger et al. 1978).

11.3 POPULATIONS AND PRODUCTION

Wildlife populations tend to increase and decrease in response to the availability of resources and the intensity of stressors in the dynamic estuarine environment. These changes occur through the responses of individuals (migration, dispersal, aggregation), or through responses at the population level (reproduction, mortality).

11.3.1 Reproduction, Mobility, and Aggregation

Species vary in their manner of adjusting population to environment. The 1 kg muskrat is a "boom-and-bust" species in the Louisiana coastal marshes, regulated by fur trapping or by damage by the muskrats to their own vegetation habitat. A strong tendency to disperse, and a high reproductive rate, facilitate rapid population growth in suitable localities. Louisiana muskrats may breed at 6 months of age, may breed in any month of the year, and females average 5–6 litters per year of about 4 young each (Errington 1963). Live biomass is in the range 0.1–12 g/m^2 (1–123 kg/ha) (Lynch et al. 1947).

At the other end of the spectrum is another herbivore, the manatee, an endangered mammal weighing up to 590 kg. The female takes 6–8 years to mature and has a single calf every 2–3 years. Although there are only 1000 manatees in Florida in winter, as many as 141 have been counted in the warm water effluent of the Riviera Beach power plant, and in another area, Kings Bay, live biomass may reach 12.5 g/m^2 (125 kg/ha) (Campbell and Powell 1976, Anon. 1978, Hartman 1979). While both muskrat and manatee can concentrate their numbers where conditions are suitable, the muskrat does so by rapid compensatory reproduction and dispersal in different habitat types (Palmisano 1973), and the manatee by long life and long-distance migration.

Wildlife populations that are both sedentary and stable are apparently unusual in temperate estuaries. The saltmarsh song sparrow of California's San Pablo Bay is neither migratory nor cyclic in numbers. Sparrow territories are only 350–650 m^2 in size, and are closely tied to the patterns of pickleweed, coyote bush, and waterways in the marsh; dispersal is very limited and creeks over 50 m wide are barriers to dispersal (Josselyn 1983). Sparrow numbers remained constant seasonally and from year to year, at a density around 0.005/m^2 (50/ha) (Johnston 1956a, b). The marsh wren also maintains a constant density from year to year despite large changes in production. Kale (1965) suggested,

> perhaps the vast expanse of coastal Spartina marsh, which extends from the Carolina coast to northern Florida, acts as a huge reservoir or buffer system for the animal populations living in it. Low reproductive success in one part of the marsh may be balanced by higher production elsewhere.

Populations of permeant species may be regulated by conditions outside the estuary. On the Georgia coast, two largely terrestrial mammals may move into the saline marshes to feed when insufficient food is available in the forests. Raccoons fed on saltwater cordgrass more during a winter of high population density and acorn shortage; cordgrass seemed a low-quality substitute food (Hudson 1978, Harman and Stains 1979). Feral pigs fed more on saltwater cordgrass rhizomes and other marsh foods in summer when acorns and palmetto berries were not available. Dispersed feeding behavior and starvation was common in summer, compared to defense of fruiting trees in winter (Graves and Graves 1977).

11.3.2   Secondary Productivity

There have been few detailed studies of energy flow through estuarine animals grazing higher plants. Such studies (e.g., Smalley 1960) have typically shown that secondary producers get only a small proportion (5–10% or less) of marsh primary production. With regard to vertebrates, the findings of Nienhuis and van Ierland (1978) that 5 bird species (mainly mute swan) and an isopod consumed only 4% of living eelgrass production in a brackish lake in the Netherlands are perhaps typical of low rates of grazing by herbivores. On the other hand, marsh carnivores may consume a larger proportion of available herbivore or detritivore production; Milne and Dunnet (1972), for example, found that birds and fish consumed virtually all of the net production of a mussel bed. Most of these studies have been done in saline flats, cordgrass marshes, or mangrove swamps where the vascular plants have strong defenses against grazing. In fresher habitats, herbivores such as the muskrat at times harvest considerably higher percentages of the vegetation. Unfortunately, quantitative data are not available on these relationships.

Probably the most thorough study of consumption by an estuarine wildlife species is Kale's (1965) research on the marsh wren in the tidal marshes of Georgia. The marsh wren exploits the tidal marsh productivity with extraordinary efficiency, gleaning insects, spiders, and snails from the cordgrass. The grazing food chain supplies 85% of the wren's energy intake and the detritus food chain 12%. A wren family needs about 3500 kcal for the 140 day breeding season, or about 20% of the estimated standing crop of insects and spiders per day on an average 100 m^2 territory! Kale thought that the elongate creekbank territories of tall saltwater cordgrass filter moving insects from unused habitat in the remainder of the marsh, to support this high predation demand. Not surprisingly, Kale suggested that the marsh wren "may be a major factor in control of the secondary consumers among the arthropods of the grazing food chain."

The productivity data in Table 11.3 represent wildlife species of various sizes and diets. The seal is energetically the most efficient, consuming only three times its weight per year (C/B) and also having the highest production/consumption ratio. The energetic efficiency of the harbor seal was attributed to the high energy content of its diet and to the seal's large size and insulating coat of fat by Boulva and McLaren (1979). These estimates possibly exaggerated the caloric content of seal food and underrated food consumption in the wild (see Ashwell-Erickson and Elsner 1982), however, even if seal consumption were twice as great, it would still be in marked contrast to the other species in Table 11.3. The coot consumes 38 times its weight per year, about 10 times as much as the seal, and the wren and shrew consume an order of magnitude more. Nonetheless, the shrew seems a far more efficient producer (P/C) than the wren and the coot, although the absence of a value for excretion casts some question on these numbers.

11.4   FACTORS REGULATING WILDLIFE

Besides the chance events mentioned, competition, predation, and human influences contribute to regulation of wildlife populations. Fluctuating estuarine conditions (salinity, water levels, temperature) prevent some animals from using

TABLE 11.3   Secondary Productivity of Some Estuarine Wildlife Populations.

Biomass (B) kcal/m²	Consumption (C) kcal/m²/yr	Respiration kcal/m²/yr	Excretion kcal/m²/yr	Production (P) kcal/m²/yr
Red-knobbed coot, Swartvlei (brackish lake), South Africa (a)				
0.52	19.5			0.05
C/B = 38	P/B = 0.093	P/C = 0.0025		
Marsh Wren, Sapelo Island (saline marsh), Georgia (b)				
0.52	126	88	38	0.5
C/B = 241	P/B = 0.95	P/C = 0.0040		
Suisun shrew, San Pablo Bay (saline marsh), California (c)				
0.074	26.1	25.8		0.28
C/B = 355	P/B = 3.8	P/C = 0.011		
Harbor seal, The Wash (shallow bay), Britain (d)				
2.59	8.23			0.47
C/B = 3.2	P/B = 0.18	P/C = 0.057		

(a) Food = subtidal plants, 90% pondweed (Fairall 1981).

(b) Food = invertebrates on plants, mainly insects (Kale 1965).

(c) Food = benthic invertebrates (Newman 1970). Excretion is not mentioned although production + respiration = consumption.

(d) Food = mainly fish. Population density and diet at The Wash from Bonner (1972) and energy parameters from Boulva and McLaren (1979).

estuarine habitats and thus may reduce predation and competition for some wildlife species in the estuarine environment. Lessened predation and competition allow species tolerant of the estuarine conditions to reach higher population densities. These concentrations of wildlife are able to exploit rich food resources but are vulnerable to natural disasters, pollution, and other stressors. And, in these wildlife concentrations, predation and competition do occur, sometimes with great intensity.

11.4.1   Competition

Although food may be abundant in estuaries, it is not inexhaustible. This is especially true when animals concentrate in winter at rich but spatiotemporally limited food sources. Evidence of intraspecific competition (spacing behavior, territoriality, aggression, food depletion, weight loss, etc.) has been reported in a number of estuarine species including whooping crane (Fig. 11.5; Allen 1952), brant (Charman 1979), and several shorebirds (e.g., Burger et al. 1977, Bryant 1979, Myers 1980).

Interspecific competition also occurs in estuaries, usually where high densities of animals are harvesting concentrated food resources. Competition has ̣een reported between the introduced mute swan and native waterfowl feeding

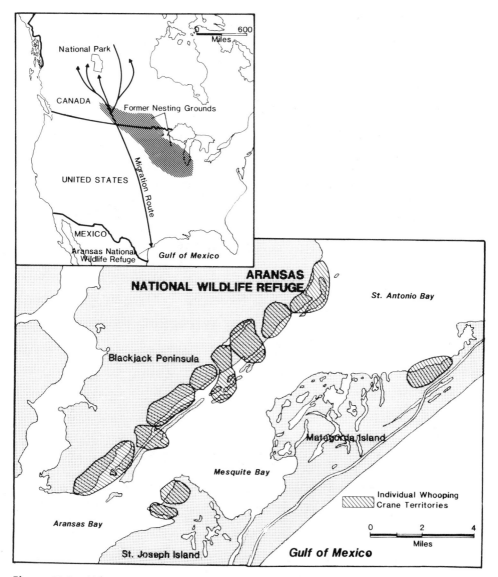

Figure 11.5. Whooping crane winter territories on the Texas coast (adapted from Allen 1959).

on submerged vascular plants (Reese 1975), between muskrat and snow goose eating emergent plant underground parts (Lynch et al. 1947), between sora and red-winged blackbird preying on emergent plant seeds (Meanley 1965). Competition for resources other than food may also occur, for example, competition among birds for safe, high nest sites.

11.4.2   Predation

Even though broad expanses of fluctuating water, dense vegetation, and soft substrates discourage some predators from successful foraging in estuarine habitats, concentrations of wildlife at rich food sources in turn may attract concerted predation. The loss of large numbers of individuals to predators can occur, although this does not always imply population control. Burger (1976) found that raccoon and fox ate eggs in 60% of diamondback terrapin nests, Page and Whitacre (1975) observed hawks and owls take 8–21% of 5 species of wintering sandpipers, and Kale (1965) reported marsh wrens lost 39–81% of their eggs to predators (15–56% to the marsh rice rat alone). Kale considered egg predation of only local importance to the wrens because the wren population was stable during the 3 year study (Fig. 11.6).

In general, extensive wetlands offer some protection from both terrestrial and aquatic predators for which the habitat is too wet or too dry, respectively. Tidal fluctuation enhances this screening effect, and some predators are probably also discouraged from successful foraging by dense vegetation or soft substrates in tidal wetlands. Two interesting examples involve the raccoon and flood tides. Prolonged high water in Louisiana marshes reduced raccoon predation on alligator nests (Fleming et al. 1976); and roseate spoonbills had higher nesting success in the occasional year after a hurricane when raccoons were apparently extirpated from the mangrove islet rookeries in south Florida (Allen 1947). In another instance of protection by water, the salt marsh song sparrow was spared Norway rat predation during a rainy year when the rats moved shoreward into a different plant community (Johnston 1956b).

Johnston also noted that brood parasitism by the brown-headed cowbird (a kind of predation on nestling songbirds) was low in tidal marshes. Why this should be so is not obvious; perhaps the cowbird is adapted to a life in trees and on the dry ground, and unable to find food or the nests of its hosts in wet, dense, marsh vegetation. Further indication that songbirds can escape predation if they can tolerate the tidal marsh environment is provided by Meanley and Webb (1963) who recorded a 57% nest success in Chesapeake Bay marsh-nesting red-winged blackbirds, high for open-nest songbirds (Meanley and Webb 1963).

11.4.3   Human Influences

Coastal areas are strongly affected by human activities, including industry, fishing and hunting, housing, tourism, transportation, structural alterations, and pollution. Wildlife is subject to disturbance, direct mortality, habitat degradation or destruction, and toxic substances. The larger, longer-lived, conspicuous animals that are high on food chains and have lower reproductive rates are most vulnerable because they have high space requirements and the capability to accumulate persistent poisons. Consequently, declines, endangerment, and extirpation of coastal wildlife have occurred, and many species are becoming rarer. Among these are the manatee, many whales and dolphins, harbor seal, sea otter,

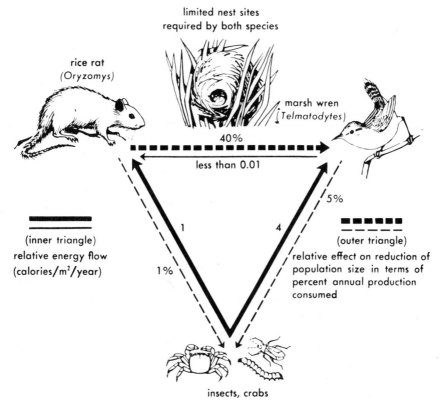

Figure 11.6. Relationship of the rice rat and marsh wren in a Georgia salt marsh. The inner triangle shows estimated energy flow from prey to predator; the outer triangle estimated effect of predator (rat) on production of prey. The disproportionate effect of rat on wren is due to predation on eggs and usurpation of nests of the wren (from E. P. Odum, 1963, Ecology, Holt, Rinehart & Winston, New York; based on data of H. Sharp, H. Kale, and E. P. Odum).

brown pelican, some herons, some waterfowl and shorebirds, many raptors (including the bald eagle, osprey, and peregrine falcon), most sea turtles, and most crocodilians.

Estuaries tend to funnel and concentrate persistent poisons of cultural origin. Many of these substances are associated with fine suspended material and accumulate in areas of rapid deposition in some wetlands and shallows. Large and long-lived fish-eating animals are among those most affected by poisons such as chlorinated hydrocarbons. For example, a 90% decline in osprey populations from 1940 to 1970 in the New York to Boston area was correlated with levels of DDT metabolites in food and eggs and with eggshell thinning. A partial recovery has followed reduced use of DDT (Spitzer and Poole 1980). A 37% incidence of birth defects in one Washington population of harbor seals in 1972 was associated with PCB pollution (Newby 1978). Snapping turtles in the tidal Hudson River have up to 8000 ppm PCB in their fat, 26 ppm dieldrin in fat, and 26 ppm cadmium in liver tissue (Stone et al. 1980). The effects of these body burdens on the turtles are not yet known.

Estuarine habitats are continually changed by natural agency, but dredging, filling, diking, and ditching of tidal wetlands have added a new, massive impact which severely affects some wildlife. Two-thirds of the historic cordgrass marshes in the southern California range of the light-footed clapper rail have been destroyed, and restriction of tidal flow has further affected available habitat (Anon. 1979, Zedler 1982). Overall bird diversity and abundance are greater in impounded and ditched marshes than in natural marshes in New Jersey, but natural marshes are required by clapper rail, seaside sparrow, and sharp-tailed sparrow (Burger 1982). In contrast to this example, North Carolina heronries on dredge spoil contain 92% of all the nests and are larger than heronries on natural ground (Parnell and Soots 1978). Although human impacts are certainly beneficial to some species, it is often the case that animals specially adapted to stressful habitats have narrower niches and are adversely affected by environmental alterations. Diversity of habitats per se is not a useful management tool; rather, the niche requirements of individual species must be considered.

Vandalism and other human predation and disturbance can also have serious impact upon wildlife populations. Manatees are killed by motorboats (half the mortality in Florida), crushed in boat locks, and killed by vandals (Campbell and Powell 1976). More than 90% of terns and black skimmers in Virginia nested on barrier beaches, but in more human-populous estuarine New Jersey only 9% nested on beaches because of disturbance by bathers, pets, and vehicles (Erwin 1980). Cultural development on shores forced beach and scrub-nesting herons, shorebirds, terns, and gulls to nest in marshes in New Jersey (Burger and Shisler 1979). The aggregate impact of all general shoreline development on water birds has not been calculated to my knowledge, but is probally the overwhelming negative impact on estuarine wildlife populations.

In summary, the distribution and abundance of wildlife in estuaries is in continual flux as physicochemical factors fluctuate around stressful levels and food resources vary. Many of these phenomena are discussed in greater detail by Daiber (1982) with specific reference to tidal marshes. What is important to remember for the moment is that the numbers, and therefore the biomass, production, and role in the ecosystem, of wildlife in estuarine communities are constantly changing.

11.5   TROPHIC RELATIONSHIPS

Estuarine wildlife species eat four classes of food: plants, invertebrates, fish, and other wildlife. Many species do not specialize on a single food class—the raccoon eats all four types, and even the manatee, an apparently strict herbivore, gets some of its protein from accidentally ingested invertebrates. Also, food produced in the estuary may be consumed at other locations, such as turtle eggs on land or migratory fish in the open sea, and food produced on land such as seeds or insects may be consumed in the estuary.

11.5.1 Plant Feeders

Living vascular plant material is the main type of plant food eaten by wildlife. A few wildlife species eat the larger algae (e.g., green turtle, brant, manatee, dugong) but often this is the result of a lack of available vascular vegetation. Microalgae and dead plant material are rarely consumed in quantity by wildlife, although they are very important foods for many invertebrates and fish. Estuarine vascular plants include intertidal (emergent) plants and subtidal (submerged and floating) plants. Many of the more important estuarine plants, such as the cordgrasses, seagrasses, and mangroves, resist grazing by their high content of structural cellulose, lignin, or silica. Herbivorous animals select "softer" species or eat young shoots, stem bases, and underground parts or seeds which are more palatable and nutritious, contain less structural material, and are often less encrusted with sediment or small organisms than are mature leaves and stems. Live biomass values for herbivores range up to 12.5 g/m^2 (125 kg/ha) at extreme concentrations, and food consumption rates can be as high as 33% of body weight per day (for muskrat, O'Neil 1949:64) or 0.4-4 $g/m^2/d$ (4-40 kg/ha/day) wet weight.

11.5.2 Invertebrate Feeders

Wildlife species catch flying insects over marshes and shallows (e.g., swallows, some terns, bats), glean invertebrates from plants above water (anole lizard, marsh wren, many other small birds), pick, probe, or excavate for invertebrates on and in the substrate (shorebirds, seaside sparrow, gray whale, sea otter), and select or filter zooplankton in the water (black tern, baleen whales). The marsh wren makes novel use of small snails as gizzard stones in lieu of mineral grit in Georgia salt marshes (Kale 1965). Estuarine invertebrates are often an abundant, productive, and nutritious food supply and there may be much competition within and among wildlife species that eat invertebrates. Food consumption rates vary from 4 to 5% of body weight per day for baleen whales to 100% for wintering shorebirds.

11.5.3 Fish Feeders

Many larger species are wholly or partly fish eaters, among them crocodiles, snapping turtles, osprey, river otters, and harbor seals. Osprey fly as far as 15 km from their nests to catch fish in estuaries (Prevost 1979). Herons and other wading birds aggregate at immense concentrations of top minnows and killifish as shallow waters recede from the irregularly flooded black mangrove swamps of south Florida, consummating a highly productive food chain that begins with particulate detritus and mosquito larvae (Heald et al. 1974). Snapping turtles are "cold- blooded" and efficient users of energy from fish and other organisms, and in the Hudson River possibly eat as little as 1–2 times their own body weight in an entire 100-day feeding season (Kiviat 1980). Food consumption rates vary from about 1 to 2% body weight per day for snapping turtle, to 5% for harbor seal, to as much as 29% for young brown pelicans. This high food requirement of young pelicans was dramatized by reduced reproductive success during a year of red tide fish kills in south Florida (Schreiber 1979).

Nile crocodiles in the St. Lucia estuary of South Africa migrate and concentrate with the seasonal seaward spawning migration of striped mullet (Whitfield and Blaber 1979). The crocodiles feed cooperatively where the immense schools of mullet funnel through channels as narrow as 500 m. Crocodile counts rose from 3 before to 60+ after the arrival of the mullet. A 2.5 m captive crocodile consumed 1100 g wet weight of mullet per day, and a 4.8 m crocodile consumed 8000–26000 g/day depending upon the weather, indicating crocodiles consumed almost 4 million g of fish (about 0.8 g wet weight of fish per m^2 of the 5-km^2 estuary) during the 5-week mullet spawning season in the year of study. What fraction of mullet production is harvested by the crocodiles is not known, but in any case it must be remembered that neither predator nor prey spends the entire year in the estuary. This sort of mobility, so typical of estuarine wildlife, means that area-based estimates of production and consumption are extremely difficult to obtain and usually fraught with qualifications.

11.5.4   Predators of Other Wildlife

Some of the larger wildlife species are predators on other higher vertebrates. American alligator, short-eared owl, and mink are examples.

11.6   ECOLOGICAL ROLE OF WILDLIFE

Animals affect their environment by eating, excreting, building, and trampling (Chapman 1976). These activities influence other populations, communities, sediments, and nutrient and energy flows, and can contribute to the linking of different ecosystems. The importance of animal effects depends on population density, which can be highly variable. A rapid increase in the number of resident muskrats or wintering shorebirds can cause striking changes in a marsh or mudflat ecosystem. In the succeeding paragraphs I discuss the ways that concentrated wildlife activities can affect community and ecosystem processes in estuaries.

Wildlife feeding can influence food organism populations or communities. Moderate grazing, for example, can increase the productivity and nutrient content of the grazed plants. Other effects include change in density and community composition of food species, increasing or decreasing the availability of food to other consumers, dispersal of propagules, and detritus production. Because estuarine vegetation tends to be resistant to grazing and many habitats do not support a large biomass of vertebrate grazers, the situations where intensive grazing occurs are all the more striking.

Herbivores often feed selectively, and thus differentially reduce abundance of the selected taxa, age classes, or plant parts. Space thus created in a community may be filled by the increase of another species or invasion of a new species. At low levels, wildlife grazing and associated activities generally have little effect on ecosystems. At moderate levels, wildlife disturbances to soil and vegetation often make gaps in monotonous stands of intertidal or subtidal plants. These openings may remain bare for a time or be colonized by secondary plant species, increasing species diversity and community (patch) diversity and making the habitat structurally more complex. At very high levels, wildlife use can reduce structural complexity because of massive mortality and morbidity of the eaten and damaged plants. Extremely intense feeding by mammals or birds that removes virtually an entire marsh plant community is called an "eat-out." Such temporary removal of the primary producer component may constitute a drastic loss of structure at the local level, but can be seen as an increase in diversity at the landscape level because the damage creates a unique temporary habitat.

In addition to the role in structuring habitats, grazing animals affect the fate of vascular plant production. Plant material is either untouched, harvested (cut or broken) but unused, incorporated into nests, eaten but structural material defecated, or eaten and largely digested. Uneaten food, undigested materials in dung, and old nest material all contribute to the stock of estuarine detritus. This animal-conditioned detritus may be physically or chemically different than plant material broken down by other means. Intensive animal grazing can increase or decrease the amount of marsh litter which the tides can redistribute within the marsh or export to adjacent open waters (Smith and Odum 1981). Thus, major fluctuation in numbers of grazers is a "switch" that determines the amount of plant production going into different food chains. Although researchers have speculated on the contribution by wildlife to detritus processing (e.g., Smith and Odum 1981, Howell 1984), there is little information on the fate of plant materials harvested by larger animals.

Animals can influence plant demography not only by consumption of shoots or mature plants, but also by consumption or transportation of seeds and seedlings. Predation of marsh plant seeds by animals may slow recruitment to areas left bare by overgrazing, or by the normal fall death of annuals (Lynch et al. 1947, Whigham and Simpson 1977). The competition by dabbling ducks, rails, and blackbirds for wild-rice seeds in the northern United States is believed to influence wild-rice population dynamics. Dispersal of seeds or vegetative propagules by animals is also important, especially in low salinity habitats where many plant species compete for space. Harvested but uneaten food, material from disintegrating nests, and undigested plant materials in dung may be dead or still alive. Living plant materials cut by animals and transported by animals or water may strand and grow at new locations.

Estuarine sediments are generally anaerobic just beneath the surface, and may be bound by a dense plant turf. Animal treading, burrowing, and foraging mix the sediments, exposing anaerobic layers to water and air, enhancing decomposition, releasing nutrients, loosening and resuspending materials, and diversifying microtopography (see for example Fig. 11.7). Furthermore, wildlife activities often help prevent filling of marsh pools with sediment and vegetation.

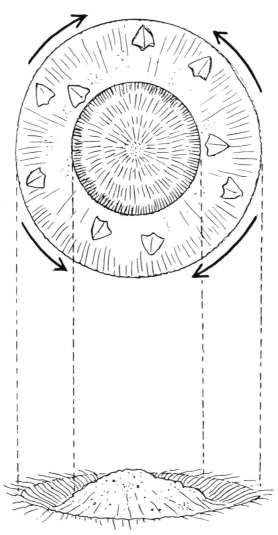

Figure 11.7. A ''rond'' or stamping mound (diameter about 38 cm) made by a flamingo sifting small food organisms from the sediment with its bill, Inagua, Bahamas (from R. P. Allen, 1956, The Flamingos: Their Life History and Survival, Research Report 5, National Audubon Society).

Animals can also influence nutrient cycling in estuaries. Organic matter, nutrients, and microbes are shifted within or between ecosystems when a large biomass of animals feeds in one area and defecates in another. Even when materials are digested where eaten, nutrient transformations occur in the gut and excreta may release inorganic nutrients rapidly. Concentrated excretion, usually by birds that roost or nest socially, can create toxic levels of ammonia, killing algae or vascular plants.

In estuaries, wildlife food may be distributed irregularly in dense patches, abundant but difficult to reach. There are many commensal relationships in which one species exploits food made available by the activities of another species. Many birds catch fish that have been driven out of cover, into shallows, or nearer the surface by other birds or larger fish. More complex relationships occur where one bird species steals captured prey from another; many examples of piracy (kleptoparasitism) have been reported from estuarine birds. In a review of piracy, Brockman and Barnard (1979) stated that it is common where prey is abundant, and foraging predators easily seen by pirates. Analogous commensalisms occur in which herbivores avail themselves of plant material harvested by larger, stronger, or deeper-diving animals. Lynch et al. (1947) noted that snow goose rooting brings up food for dabbling ducks, while Kirby and Obrecht (1980) recorded an interesting example of brant eating eelgrass brought to the surface by human shellfish harvesters.

Another type of commensalism involves the exploitation by one species of safe nest sites created by another species. Scarcity of abovewater nest sites in tidal marshes may limit some populations. Many mammals and birds at times use elevated nests built by marsh rice rats and songbirds, lodges of muskrats (Kiviat 1978), and blinds built by duck hunters (e.g., Reese 1972). In a complex example of shelter commensalism, eastern kingsnakes and their marsh rice rat prey both survive winter flood tides in air-trapping refuges gnawed by the rats in waxmyrtle root crowns (Lazell 1979). Fleming et al. (1978) mentioned another three-way relationship: "During dry summers, when preferred foods are not as available, raccoons spend more time searching for fish around open water areas in the vicinity of alligator nests, thereby increasing the likelihood of nest predation." How often are such complex (and probably common) interspecies relationships considered when predicting the impact of management practices?

11.6.1   Some Examples of Animal Effects

A few cases of significant influences of wildlife upon vegetation, sediments, water quality, and nutrient cycling in estuaries will illustrate the generalizations made above. Although the large spatiotemporal concentrations of animal activity discussed here can certainly have dramatic effects, it is important to remember that many of the cases reported are extremes. Perhaps by illustrating the more dramatic kinds of modifications caused by wildlife, it will alert us to the more subtle roles in estuarine ecosystems played by the majority of wildlife populations.

11.6.2   Large Reptiles

The American alligator, generally considered a freshwater species, is also a typical inhabitant of brackish and in some instances quite saline wetlands of Georgia, Florida, and Louisiana. Alligators interact with wetland ecosystems as a powerful predator, and by building nest mounds and creating and maintaining trails and wallows (alligator ponds) that often hold water during droughts. Alligator ponds serve as dry-season refuges for fish, turtles, and other aquatic animals and their bird and mammal predators. Nest mounds are often the highest ground in wetlands, and are used by plants and animals seeking dry spots to grow, bask, or lay eggs. Thus alligators enhance microtopographic diversity in generally flat landscapes by creating both raised and lowered substrates, and these divergent features in turn provide habitats for organisms that otherwise might not survive.

Craighead (1968) observed a number of specific ways that south Florida alligators influence sediments and vegetation. Alligators help create and maintain moats around tree islands in low salinity mangrove estuaries. In freshwater sawgrass marshes alligators tear up vegetation and build nest mounds 0.6-0.9 m above water level and 1.2-2.4 m across. These nests become compacted from long use, are fire resistant, and a numerous and characteristic feature of the sawgrass community. Soon after abandonment by alligators, the nests are colonized by ferns and trees, and form the cores of future islands. When saltwater invades (after drainage, drought, and fire), the only sawgrass left is atop the old alligator nests, now surrounded by scrub mangroves. When water levels are falling in the scrub mangroves, alligators migrate across the soft mud forming troughs that are often 15 cm deep and 60 cm wide. Some of these trails erode and become bypasses of clogged creeks; others become strands of red mangrove or eventually other woody vegetation. During summer floods, wandering male alligators help keep small mangrove creeks open by tearing out red mangrove proproots. Slight rims around alligator ponds are survival sites for invading flora after vegetation destruction by hurricanes because vegetation on the pond rims is above the evaporating saline storm-tide waters.

11.6.3   Waterfowl and Other Gregarious Birds

Geese often congregate in large flocks and graze intensively on aboveground or underground parts of marsh plants. Snow geese may pull up and discard 10 times the material actually eaten (Lynch et al. 1947). Aboveground grazing by snow geese in an Arctic salt marsh and barnacle geese in a Dutch salt marsh removes large portions of aboveground production but causes major increases in production and nitrogen content of vegetation (Cargill 1981, Ydenberg and Prins 1981). However, underground grazing (rooting) by snow geese in three North Carolina marsh communities reduced aerial plant cover and net underground production and removed 50 to 64% of underground biomass (Smith and Odum 1981). The heavily damaged North Carolina communities recovered, apparently from seeds.

Substantial areas of subtidal vascular vegetation, also, may be heavily cropped or even denuded by black swan, canvasback duck, and certain other waterfowl species (e.g., Phillips 1974). Although subtidal grazing by birds has apparently not been studied in detail, it might prove similar to underwater grazing by a large herbivorous reptile, the green turtle. In one of the most thorough studies of underwater grazing by a large vertebrate, Bjorndal (1982) found that Caribbean green turtles consistently recropped certain areas of turtle-grass, leaving adjacent stands untouched. "Grazing plot" regrowth was more productive, digestible, and nutritious.

Small birds in cool climates, because of their high metabolic rates, require large amounts of high-energy food. Aggregations of shorebirds (sandpipers, plovers, etc.) during fall migration or in winter on mudflats and sandflats have been shown in a number of studies to intensively crop and regulate populations and communities of benthic macroinvertebrate prey such as mollusks and annelid worms (as discussed in Chap 8). These predator–prey relationships are characterized by dense patches of predators and prey, predation behavior related to tidal fluctuations and prey distribution, complex resource subdivision involving size, bill and leg length and feeding technique of predators, and size, burrowing depth, and behavior of prey (Fig. 11.8). Not infrequently, consumption of large fractions of prey production and competition among and within predator species occur.

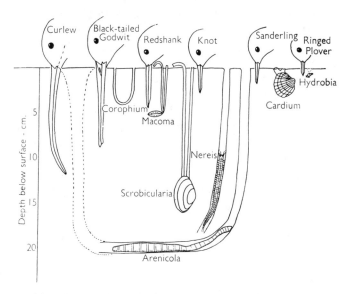

Figure 11.8.   Shorebird bill lengths in relation to burrow depths of invertebrate prey species, Great Britain. Waders catch *Arenicola* when it ascends the tail shaft to defecate (from J. Green, 1968, The Biology of Estuarine Animals, University of Washington, Seattle, p. 309).

A good example was provided by Milne and Dunnet (1972) from the Ythan of Scotland. A gross production of mussels of 1341 kcal/m^2/yr was virtually all accounted for by a combination of winter metabolism, human harvest (18%), and predation by eider (21%), gulls (9%), and oystercatcher (7%). In another study by Drinnan (1957), a flock of 30,000 oystercatchers on a British estuary from September to March consumed 22% of the intertidal 100/m^2 cockle population; total cockle mortality was 74% with human harvest and predatory fish accounting for the rest of the loss. Even transient shorebirds can cause a large decline of their benthic prey as Schneider (1978) found on Massachusetts intertidal flats during the July-September southward migration. In both Schneider's and Drinnan's studies, the birds selected the large, abundant prey species. Thus predators, like herbivores, can reduce entire communities or change the balance among species of food organisms.

Several examples show the local role of concentrated bird excretion in estuaries. A 3000-nest heronry brought an estimated 3-4 metric tons (wet) of feces to a marsh island in a Georgia river; Shanholtzer (1974) noted that the fecal nitrogen could have a fertilizing effect on the cordgrass. A mangrove stand fertilized by a wading bird rookery in south Florida had higher productivity but also higher consumption of leaves by insects (Onuf et al. 1977). Densities of 100–4000 seabirds generated 20 metric tons of nutrient and mollusk-shell rich feces per km^2 one summer in the St. Lawrence estuary of Canada. Yet the seabird contribution to nutrient regeneration to the surface waters was dwarfed by nutrients from land drainage and mixing of rich deep water layers. Bedard et al. (1980) concluded that where birds are concentrated, their nitrogen contributions may be locally significant during the June–July period of surface water nitrogen depletion. Dung can be particularly important in small sheltered habitats, such as the brackish Baltic Sea rockpools where ammonia from gull and eider dung inhibits development of algae (Ganning and Wulff 1969). Similar to the effects of grazing on plant communities, local productivity and diversity in estuarine systems appear to be enhanced by moderate additions of bird dung, but degraded by extremely concentrated excretion. Generally, however, nutrient cycling in estuaries is dominated by physical, microbial, and anthropic factors.

Waterfowl concentrations cause higher fecal coliform counts in surface water and sediment in Chesapeake Bay, potentially restricting shellfishing. No enteric bacterial pathogens, however, were detected in healthy migrant tundra swans and Canada geese by Hussong et al. (1978).

11.6.4 Rodents

Very high populations of muskrats and/or snow geese in Gulf Coast brackish marshes cause eat-outs that cover many hectares. Annual plants may quickly cover these denuded areas, and perennials return in one to several years from seeds and rhizome fragments. Lighter levels of goose and muskrat disturbance and fire prevent the formation of stands of dense perennial graminoids little used by game animals, and the resulting clearings are used by wildlife seeking seeds, invertebrates, and small fish for food (O'Neil 1949, Lynch et al. 1947).

Muskrat and snow goose eat-outs may lower the ground level. Lynch et al. (1947) observed that "Small ponds are created by geese, muskrats, peat fires, alligators, hurricanes, and by human agencies." The soil in eat-outs may be broken to depths of 12-20 cm by geese and up to 50 cm by muskrats, sometimes creating a "sea of mud" with virtually no live plants. Soil-binding roots are lost, and tidal flow erodes channels into eat-out areas; storm tides may wash out much sediment and detritus. Or soil and debris from the broken marsh floor may be bouyed by decomposition gases to form a floating mat.

Low-salinity marshes where eat-outs have not occurred are nonetheless often honeycombed with intact and collapsed underground and surface muskrat runways, connecting feeding areas in vegetation to lodges and creeks. The burrows increase the extent of the sediment surface, presumably increasing chemical activity per hectare of marsh. Runways increase water circulation and exchange (Garbisch 1977), and create hummocky microtopography. Muskrat lodge clearings are slight depressions, due to erosion of sediment by tides from the muskrat-trampled and burrowed marsh floor; the lodges themselves are raised substrates that are used by other animals or plants. A muskrat lodge contains 0.04-0.7+ m^3 of cut above and belowground plant material which is dispersed on the marsh by floods after lodge abandonment.

Nutria (larger than muskrats) at peak populations up to $0.0007/m^2$ (7/ha) in Louisiana make many clearings in the vegetation, harvesting aboveground or underground plant parts depending on the water level. They produce holes 15 cm deep and 15-20 cm across, with some areas of concentrated digging as large as 0.4 ha. The nutria eat little of what they harvest, often leaving the tops of dug-up plants. Vegetation density may be reduced as much as 80% in clearings 15 m across. Recovery occurs the following summer, but small stands of reed and cattail may be eliminated, and species composition changes as opportunistic plants invade openings (Harris and Webert 1962).

Many marsh plants, including reed, cattails, sweetflag, and arrowheads, propagate from vegetative parts cut or dug by muskrat or nutria (e.g., Harris and Webert 1962, Kiviat observations). This is probably an important means of dispersal for plants like sweetflag and reed that rarely produce viable seeds. Nutria evidently disperse beggarticks seeds, and stuck seeds can damage fur and skin, reducing pelt value (Kinler and Chabreck 1979).

11.6.5 Livestock

Cattle are grazed on the landward portions of tidal marshes in many parts of the world, and other livestock including sheep, as well as feral stock (horses, pigs, etc.) also graze tidal marshes in places. Cattle grazing reduces aboveground standing crop, nitrogen content, and litter in grass-glasswort marsh in Georgia (Reimold et al. 1975), and saltgrass occurs only in lightly grazed areas (see Shanholtzer 1974). Sheep grazing of high British salt marsh causes invasion of a short grass palatable to sheep and other wildlife, and sheep compaction of the soil offsets deposition and stabilizes the community (Ranwell 1972, p. 209, Pl. 6). Feral ponies on Assateague Island, Maryland, wear conspicuous paths bare of vegetation on the high salt marshes, and the feral horses and cattle of the Camargue, France, are said to help keep pools open in the marshes (Silvester 1975). Manure from cattle on New Jersey marshes elevated coliform bacteria counts in adjacent shellfish harvesting areas and grazing was discontinued (Reimold et al. 1975).

11.7 SIGNIFICANCE OF ESTUARINE WILDLIFE TO HUMAN SOCIETY

In the wild, estuarine wildlife is valuable for food, hides, recreation, education, art, and science. Some taxa (especially carnivores, marine mammals, the larger birds, and reptiles) are star attractions on television and in zoos. But some birds and mammals compete with humans for fish or shellfish stocks. Also, a few animals can cause human death or injury (although the dangers of wildlife attacks have often been overrated, and in most cases these species are less common now than formerly). Treatment of a species as a problem in one area or by one segment of society, and as an esthetic or material resource at another place or time, suggests opportunities for more creative wildlife management.

11.7.1 Reptiles

Turtle meat and eggs and turtle shells are harvested around the world. Also some turtles (e.g., the leatherback and the loggerhead) experience significant mortality in commercial fishing operations, and the sandy nesting habitats of many species have been lost or degraded by tourist use, bright lights, and increases in egg predators such as the feral pig. Most populations of sea turtles are currently endangered due to these factors. Turtle "farming" (captive propagation for food) is practiced in some estuaries. The diamondback terrapin, once overharvested for food from East Coast saline marshes, declined and then recovered in many areas. Snapping turtles (generally abundant although they may be depleted locally) are harvested both for home use and for commerce. Maryland's Chesapeake Bay coast provided 2.9 metric tons of terrapin and 16.6 of snapper in 1964, well below peak catches of 198 and 77 metric tons in 1957 (Schwartz 1967).

Crocodilian hides are important items of commerce (legal and illegal). The American alligator, still considered in danger in much of its range, recently increased enough under strict protection in southwestern Louisiana coastal marshes to allow a regulated harvest. In 1973, 0.24 to 1.36 alligators were taken per square kilometer in various marsh types, the hides worth $92 each (Chabreck 1979). Some other crocodilians have not been so fortunate, and most species have undergone declines or endangerment. Crocodiles in estuaries are known for attacks on humans in Asia and Oceania, and venomous snakes are dangerous in some estuaries (the water moccasin scarcely so in the southeastern United States).

11.7.2   Birds

Ducks and geese are the primary estuarine game birds. Rails are hunted locally in the United States and other birds are hunted overseas. In 1961–1970, 3 million ducks and geese were harvested in the "Water Resource Regions associated with estuarine areas" (not just on estuaries). This was 44% of the total United States diving duck harvest, 27% of dabbling ducks, and 33% of the geese (Lynch et al. 1976). Before the present century's protective laws, market hunting for food consumed far greater numbers of waterfowl (as well as shorebird species that are now protected). Egrets and spoonbills also were killed for their feathers. "Egging" for food decimated many rookeries of colonially nesting coastal birds. Many estuarine bird species declined, some of which have recovered (at least partly).

That some birds and bird products can be harvested under sensible management, without population declines, is well illustrated by the gathering of eider duck down, harmless to the birds or their production, an important industry in Iceland and the Solviet Union (Johnsgard 1976). The scientific management of waterfowl for sport hunting has made great progress in North America, although there are still problems to be solved, notably including the loss of wetland habitat (tidal and nontidal) in breeding, wintering, and migration stopover areas, the toxicity of lead shot accumulated in surface sediments and ingested by feeding ducks and other birds, and the decline of the black duck in the eastern United States due at least partly to genetic swamping by the mallard.

States with tidal coasts had 5 million birdwatchers in 1970 who spent an estimated 300 million recreation days watching birds (Lynch et al. 1976). Estuaries are very exciting for birders because of the large regular faunas and the potential for storm-blown or wandering accidental species. Awareness of the population declines of bald eagle, osprey, peregrine falcon, and brown pelican in the 1950s-1960s was significantly stimulated by concerns of estuarine birdwatchers, and led to research on pesticide toxicity and stricter pesticide regulations to protect wildlife and humans alike.

11.7.3   Mammals

Mammals are important for fur, meat, and other purposes. The most important furbearer is the muskrat. In 1971, 1.58 million ha of Louisiana coast marshes produced about 2 million muskrat pelts worth $3 million; the brackish marshes, the best muskrat habitat, produced an average maximum of 16 pelts/ha/yr ($0.0016/m^2$/yr) (Palmisano 1973). Raccoon, nutria, mink, and river otter are harvested for fur from United States estuaries, and muskrat and raccoon meat is marketed locally. There is a limited harvest of valuable polar bear fur, and tourists visit Churchill, Manitoba, on the Hudson Bay, to see the concentrated and highly visible bears (Davids 1978).

Many seals and cetaceans, especially the smaller species, enter estuarine habitats where they may be harvested commercially or for native use. Products include meat, pet food, furs, and oil. Killing of marine mammals is highly controversial because of past or present declines in most cetacean and seal stocks, and the availability of substitute products. Highly developed sociality, vocalization, play, migration, and intelligence of whales and dolphins receive intense popular and scientific interest. The Washington and British Columbia estuarine population of the strikingly patterned and highly social killer whale, for example, has fascinated people for centuries, and plays a large role in regional art, literature, and tourism.

Livestock are often grazed on the higher areas of tidal marshes. Georgia salt marshes are nearly as valuable for beef production as the adjacent upland pastures, and this use of marshes provides a rationale for protecting them from more damaging uses (Reimold et al. 1975). However, cattle may compete with other estuarine wildlife (Lynch et al. 1947).

The larger seals, walrus, brown bear, and polar bear are some of the occasionally dangerous mammals encountered in far northern estuaries, and other potentially dangerous large mammals occur in some tropical estuaries.

11.8 CONCLUSIONS

Although higher vertebrates often are not important in the energy flow or nutrient cycles of estuaries, it is clear that estuarine wildlife may be important locally or episodically as consumers, regulators of vegetation and sediment structure, maintainers of habitats, diversifiers, food chain "switches," linkers of ecosystems, and providers of shelter. Animals with high reproductive rates like the muskrat respond to the rapidly changing estuarine environment with population pulses. Species with low reproductive rates like sea mammals respond to fluctuating levels and locations of resources with individual mobility and aggregation. Competition for food within and between some species shows that large estuarine food resources are not necessarily limitless; substantial population reductions or even "eat-outs" of marsh or seagrass vegetation or benthic invertebrates occur under certain conditions of concentrated feeding. Many wildlife species are less abundant now than formerly, due to human influences; the roles of these species were once that much greater in estuarine ecosystems. Nonetheless, wildlife roles may be more important in some estuarine habitats than is generally assumed.

Wildlife mirrors the highly productive and rapidly changing estuarine ecosystem. In the words of Milne and Dunnet (1972):

The most conspicuous feature of the fauna of the estuary is the high level of flux—in daily and tidal cycles of feeding and movement; in seasonal patterns of abundance, different for each of the many species, especially the highly mobile predators; and in energy flow due to the marked seasonal patterns of growth, reproduction and predation. Despite this high level of flux, the large populations of a few highly productive species of invertebrates support, year after year, up to 75 species of predating birds and fish, each with its own characteristic pattern and level of seasonal abundance, feeding behaviour, diet, and food requirements. The system calls to mind a transit camp, with a well-organised catering department designed to supply the needs of a fluctuating and very diverse clientele, and adaptable enough for the establishment to stay in business!

This characterization of Scotland's Ythan estuary, with slight taxonomic differences, may well apply to many temperate estuaries, and indeed estuaries of other climatic zones.

Concentrations of wildlife in estuaries not only potentially affect ecosystem function, but also make the animals themselves vulnerable to natural disasters and toxic pollution. Larger carnivores, particularly fish-eaters at the top of estuarine food chains, can be used as monitors of environmental pollution funneling into and through estuaries. Population dynamics, behavior, and tissue burdens of chemicals can indicate danger levels, perhaps before humans are adversely affected. Furthermore, as Palmisano (1973) said, "Vigorous plant communities which support optimum populations of fur bearing animals and waterfowl are an excellent index to the overall 'health' or well being of the entire estuarine ecosystem." In this respect, hunting, trapping, fishing, and birdwatching are cheap and effective techniques for monitoring environmental quality.

Estuarine wildlife also has a large cultural importance–not only as food, sport, and fur, but as objects of study and enjoyment. Because they appeal to people, these animals can be used to focus attention on environmental problems and the management and stewardship of estuarine ecosystems.

11.8 ACKNOWLEDGMENTS

I thank Karen Bjorndal, Susan M. Cargill, Stewart I. Fefer, Paul A. Johnsgard, William T. Maple, Terrell C. Newby, James R. Newman, Alan Poole, Thomas J. Smith, III, Dick T. Stalling, and others for providing unpublished material and references, Paul R. Spitzer for reading a draft and discussing many ideas, Joshua L. Royte for reading a draft, and the American Littoral Society for financial support. This chapter is Bard College Field Station–Hudsonia Contribution 33.

REFERENCES

Abernethy, R.K., 1987. Wildlife. In W. Conner and J. Day (Eds.), The Ecology of the Barataria Basin: An Estuarine Profile. U.S. Fish. Wildl. Ser., Biol. Rep. 85(7.13), pp. 96–109.

Allen, R. P., 1942. The Roseate Spoonbill. Natl. Audubon Soc. Res. Rep., 2. New York.

Allen, R. P., 1947. The Flame Birds. Dodd, Mead, New York. 233 pp.

Allen, R. P., 1952. The Whooping Crane. Nat. Audubon Soc. Res. Rep. 3. New York.

Anderson, P. K., 1979. Dugong behavior: on being a marine mammalian grazer. Biologist, 61(4):113–144.

Anderson, P. K. and A. Birtles, 1978. Behaviour and ecology of the dugong, *Dugong dugon* (Sirenia): observations in Shoalwater and Cleveland Bays, Queensland. Australian Wildlife Research, (5):1–23.

Anon., 1978. Service steps up manatee recovery efforts. Endangered Species Technical Bulletin, 3(2):4–5.

Anon., 1979. Recovery planned for light-footed clapper rail, woundfin, eastern brown pelican. Endangered Species Technical Bulletin, 4(8):1, 5–6.

Ashwell-Erickson, S. and R. Elsner, 1982. The energy cost of free existence for Bering Sea harbor and spotted seals. In D. W. Hood and J. A. Calder (Eds.), The Eastern Bering Sea Shelf: Oceanography and Resources, Univ. Washington Press, 2:869–899.

Bedard, J., J. C. Therriault, and J. Berube, 1980. Assessment of the importance of nutrient recycling by seabirds in the St. Lawrence estuary. Can. J. of Fisheries and Aquatic Sciences, 37(4):583–588.

Bjorndal, K. A., 1982. The consequences of herbivory for the life history pattern of the Caribbean green turtle, *Chelonia mydas*. In K. A. Bjorndal (Ed.), Biology and Conservation of Sea Turtles; Proceedings of the World Conference on Sea Turtle Conservation, Washington, DC, 1979. Smithsonian Institution Press, Washington, DC.

Bleakney, J. S., 1972. Ecological implications of annual variation in tidal extremes. Ecology, 53(5):933–938.

Bonner, W. N., 1972. The grey seal and common seal in European waters. Oceanog. and Mar. Biol., 10:461–507.

Boulva, J. and I. A. McLaren, 1979. Biology of the harbor seal, *Phoca vitulina,* in eastern Canada. Dept. of Fisheries and Oceans, Ottawa, Canada, Bulletin 200, 24 pp.

Brockmann, H. J. and C. J. Barnard, 1979. Kleptoparasitism in birds. Animal Behaviour, 27(2):487–514.

Bryant, D. M., 1979. Effects of prey density and site character on estuary usage by overwintering waders (Charadrii). Estuarine Coastal Mar. Sci., 9:369–384.

Burger, J., 1976. Behavior of hatchling diamondback terrapins (*Malaclemys terrapin*) in the field. Copeia, 1976(4):742–748.

Burger, J., M. A. Howe, D. C. Hahn, and J. Chase, 1977. Effects of tide cycles on habitat selection and habitat partitioning by migrating shorebirds. Auk, 94(4):743–758.

Burger, J. and W. A. Montevecchi, 1975. Nest site selection in the terrapin *Malaclemys terrapin.* Copeia, (1):113–119.

Burger, J. and J. K. Shisler. 1979. The immediate effects of ditching a salt marsh on nesting herring gulls *Larus argentatus*. Biol. Conserv., 15:85–103.

Burger, J., J. Shisler, and F. Lesser. 1978. The effects of ditching salt marshes on nesting birds. Proceedings of the Colonial Waterbird Group: 27–37.

Burger, J., J. Shisler, and F. H. Lesser, 1982. Avian utilisation on six salt marshes in New Jersey. Biol. Conserv., 23:187–212.

Campbell, H. W. and J. A. Powell, 1976. Endangered species: the manatee. Florida Naturalist, April, 15–20.

Cargill, S. M., 1981. The effects of grazing by lesser snow geese on the vegetation of an arctic salt marsh. M.Sc. thesis, Botany Department, University of Toronto, Toronto, Ontario. 191 pp.

Chabreck, R. H., 1979. Wildlife harvest in wetlands of the United States. In P. E. Greeson et al. (Eds.), Wetland Functions and Values: the State of Our Understanding. American Water Resources Association, Minneapolis, MN, pp. 618-631.

Chapman, V. J., 1976. Coastal Vegetation. 2nd ed. Pergamon Press, Oxford, 292 pp.

Charman, K., 1979. Feeding ecology and energetics of the dark-bellied brent goose (*Branta bernicla bernicla*) in Essex and Kent. In R. L. Jeffries and A. J. Davy (Eds.), Ecological Processes in Coastal Environments. Blackwell Scientific Publications, Oxford, pp. 451-465.

Clough, T. R., 1976. The little sea goose. Cape Naturalist, 5(2):23-29.

Craighead, F. C., Sr., 1968. The role of the alligator in shaping plant communities and maintaining wildlife in the southern Everglades. Florida Naturalist, 41(1-2):3-7, 69-74, 94.

Daiber, F. C., 1982. Animals of the Tidal Marsh. Van Nostrand Reinhold Co., New York, 422 pp.

Davids, R. C., 1978. Polar bears aren't pets, but this town is learning how to live with them. Smithsonian, 8(11):70-79.

Day, J., W. Smith, P. Wagner, W. Stowe, 1973. Community structure and carbon budget of a salt marsh and shallow bay estuarine system in Louisiana. Center for Wetland Resources, Louisiana State University, Baton Rouge, Publication No. LSU-SG-72-04, 80 pp.

Dozier, H. L., 1947. Salinity as a factor in Atlantic coast tidewater muskrat production. North American Wildlife Conference, 12:398-420.

Drinnan, R. E., 1957. The winter feeding of the oyster catcher (*Haematopus ostralegus*) on the edible cockle (*Cardium edule*). J. of Anim. Ecol., 26:441-469.

Dunson, W. A. and E. O. Moll, 1980. Osmoregulation in sea waters of hatchling Emydid turtles, *Callagur borneoensis*, from a Malaysian sea beach. J. of Herpetology, 14:31-36.

Ellis, T. M., 1981. Tolerance of sea water by the American crocodile, *Crocodylus acutus*. J. of Herpetology, 15(2):187-192.

Errington, P. L., 1963. Muskrat populations. Iowa State Univ. Press, Ames, 665 pp.

Erwin, R. M., 1980. Breeding habitat use by colonially nesting waterbirds in two mid-Atlantic US regions under different regimes of human disturbance. Biol. Conserv., 18:39-51.

Fairall, N., 1981. A study of the bioenergetics of the red-knobbed coot *Fulica cristata* on a South African estuarine lake. S. Af. J. Wildlife Research, 11(1):1-4.

Fleming, D. M., A. W. Palmisano, and T. Joanen, 1978. Food habits of coastal marsh raccoons with observations of alligator nest predation. Proceedings of the Annual Conference of the Southeastern Fish and Wildlife Agencies, Jackson, Mississippi, 30:348-357.

Ganning, B. and F. Wulff, 1969. The effects of bird droppings on chemical and biological dynamics in brackish water rock pools. Oikos, 20:274-286.

Garbisch, E. W., Jr., 1977. Recent and planned marsh establishment work throughout the contiguous United States: a survey and basic guidelines. U. S. Army Corps of

Engineers, Dredged Material Research Program, Contract Report D-77-3, Wash. DC, 42 pp.

Geraci, J. R., 1978. The enigma of marine mammal strandings. Oceanus, 21(2):38–47.

Gordon, M. S. and V. A. Tucker, 1965. Osmotic regulation in the tadpoles of the crab-eating frog (*Rana cancrivora*). J. Experimental Biology, 42:437–445.

Graves, H. B. and K. L. Graves, 1977. Some observations on biobehavioral adaptations of swine. In G. W. Wood (Ed.), Research and Management of Wild Hog Populations. Belle W. Baruch Forest Science Institute of Clemson University, Georgetown, South Carolina, pp. 103–110.

Harman, D. M. and H. J. Stains, 1979. The raccoon (*Procyon lotor*) on St. Catherine's Island, Georgia. 5. Winter, spring and summer food habits. American Museum Novitates, 2679.

Harris, V. T. and F. Webert, 1962. Nutria feeding activity and its effect on marsh vegetation in southwestern Louisiana. US Fish and Wildlife Service Special Scientific Report-Wildlife 64, 53 pp.

Hartman, D. S., 1979. Ecology and behavior of the manatee (*Trichechus manatus*) in Florida. American Society of Mammalogists Special Publication 5, 153 pp.

Heald, E. J., W. E. Odum, and D. C. Tabb, 1974. Mangroves in the estuarine food chain. In P. J. Gleason, (Ed.), Environments of South Florida: Present and Past. Miami Geological Society Memoir 2, pp. 182–189.

Hill, N. P., 1968. *Ammospiza caudacuta caudacuta* (Gmelin); eastern sharp-tailed sparrow. In A. C. Bent (Ed.), Life Histories of North American Cardinals, Grosbeaks, Buntings, Towhees, Finches, Sparrows and Allies. Dover, New York, pp. 795–812.

Hoese, H. D., 1971. Dolphin feeding out of water in a salt marsh. J. of Mammalogy, 52(1):222–223.

Howell, P. T., 1984. Use of salt marshes by meadow voles. Estuaries, 7:165–170.

Hudson, E. M., 1978. The raccoon (*Procyon lotor*) on St. Catherines Island, Georgia. 2. Relative abundance in different forest types as a function of population density. American Museum Novitates 2648, 15 pp.

Hussong, D., J. M. Damare, R. J. Limpert, J. L. Sladen, R. M. Weiner, and R. R. Colwell, 1979. Microbial impact of Canada geese (*Branta canadensis*) and whistling swans (*Cygnus columbianus columbianus*) on aquatic ecosystems. App. Environ. Microbiology, 37(1):14–20.

Johnsgard, P. A., 1976. Flight of the sea ducks. Natural History, 85(7):68–73.

Johnson, A. R., 1975. Camargue flamingos. In J. Kear and N. Duplaix-Hall (Eds.), International Flamingo Symposium, Slimbridge, England, 1973. T. and A. D. Poyser, Berkhamsted, England, pp. 17–25.

Johnston, R. F., 1956a. Population structure in salt marsh song sparrows, Part I. Environment and annual cycle. Condor 58:24–44.

Johnston, R. F., 1956b. Population structure in salt marsh song sparrows, Part II. Density, age structure, and maintenance. Condor, 58:254–272.

Johnston, R. F. and R. L. Rudd, 1957. Breeding of the salt marsh shrew. J. of Mammalogy, 38:157–163.

Josselyn, M., 1983. The ecology of San Francisco Bay tidal marshes: a community profile. U. S. Fish and Wildlife Service FWS/OBS-83/23, 102 pp.

Kale, H. W., II., 1965. Ecology and bioenergetics of the long-billed marsh wren *Telma-

todytes palustris griseus (Brewster) in Georgia salt marshes. Nuttall Ornithological Club: Cambridge, Massachusetts, 141 pp.

Keiper, R. R., 1979. The behavior, ecology, and social organization of the feral ponies of Assateague Island. Proceedings of the First Conference on Scientific Research in the National Parks, November 9-12, 1976, New Orleans, Louisiana. National Park Service Transactions and Proceedings Series, 1(5):369-371.

Kinler, N. W. and R. H. Chabreck, 1979. Nutria pelt damage from *Bidens laevis*. Proceedings of the Annual Conference of the Southeast Association of Fish and Wildlife Agencies, 32:369-377.

Kirby, R. E. and H. H. Obrecht, III., 1980. Atlantic brant—human commensalism on eelgrass beds in New Jersey. Wildfowl, 31:158-160.

Kiviat, E., 1978. Vertebrate use of muskrat lodges and burrows. Estuaries, 1:196-200.

Kiviat, E., 1980. A Hudson River tidemarsh snapping turtle population. Trans. Northeast Section, Wildlife Society, 37:158-168.

Lauro, A. J., 1980. The winter ecology of Bonaparte's gull on the south shore of Long Island. Linnaean Newsletter, 34(1):1-3.

Lazell, J. D., 1979. Deployment, dispersal, and adaptive strategies of land vertebrates on Atlantic and Gulf barrier islands. Proceedings of the First Conference on Scientific Research in the National Parks, November 9-12, 1976, New Orleans, Louisiana. National Park Service Transactions and Proceedings Series, 1(5):415-419.

Lim Boon Hock and A. Sasekumar, 1979. A preliminary study on the feeding biology of mangrove forest primates, Kuala Selangor. Malayan Nature J., 33(2):105-112.

Lynch, J. J., T. O'Neil, and D. W. Lay, 1947. Management significance of damage by geese and muskrats to Gulf coast marshes. J. Wildlife Management, 11(1):50-76.

Lynch, M. P., B. L. Laird, N. B. Theberge, and J. C. Jones (Eds.), 1976. An assessment of estuarine and nearshore marine environments. Special Report in Applied Marine Science and Ocean Engineering 93 (revised), Virginia Institute of Marine Science, Gloucester Point, VA. 132 pp.

Meanley, B., 1961. Late-summer food of red-winged blackbirds in a fresh tidal-river marsh. Wilson Bulletin, 73(1):36-40.

Meanley, B., 1965. Early-fall food and habitat of the sora in the Patuxent River Marsh, Maryland. Chesapeake Sci. 6(4):235-237.

Meanley, B., 1969. Natural history of the king rail. North American Fauna 67, 117 pp.

Meanley, B. and J. S. Webb, 1963. Nesting ecology and reproductive rate of the red-winged blackbird in tidal marshes of the upper Chesapeake Bay region. Chesapeake Sci., 4(2):90-100.

Meyer, G. R., 1975. Alligator ecology and population structure on Georgia Sea Islands. Abstracts of the American Society of Ichthyologists and Herpetologists 55th Annual Meeting, 8-14 June 1975:54, Williamsburg, VA.

Milne, H. and G. M. Dunnet, 1972. Standing crop, productivity and trophic relations of the fauna of the Ythan estuary. In R. S. K. Barnes and J. Green (Eds.), The Estuarine Environment. Applied Science, London, pp. 86-106.

Myers, J. P., 1980. Sanderlings *Calidris alba* at Bodega Bay: facts, inferences and shameless speculations. Wader Study Group Bulletin, (30):26-32.

Neave, D. J. and B. S. Wright, 1968. Seasonal migrations of the harbor porpoise (*Phocoena phocoena*) and other Cetacea in the Bay of Fundy. J. Mammalogy, 49:259-264.

Neill, W. T., 1958. The occurrence of amphibians and reptiles in saltwater areas, and a bibliography. Bull. Mar. Sci. Gulf Caribb., 8(1):1–97.

Newby, T. C., 1978. Pacific harbor seal. In D. Haley (Ed.), Marine Mammals of Eastern North Pacific and Arctic Waters. Pacific Search Press, pp. 185–191.

Newman, J. R., 1970. Energy flow of a secondary consumer (*Sorex sinuosus*) in a salt marsh community. Ph.D. thesis, University of California, Davis. 101 pp.

Nienhuis, P. H. and E. T. Van Ierland, 1978. Consumption of eelgrass, *Zostera marina*, by birds and invertebrates during the growing season in Lake Grevelingen (SW Netherlands). Netherlands J. Sea Research, 12(2):180–194.

O'Neil, T., 1949. The muskrat in the Louisiana coastal marshes: a study of the ecological, geological, biological, tidal, and climatic factors governing the production and management of the muskrat industry in Louisiana. Louisiana Department of Wild Life and Fisheries, New Orleans, 152 pp.

Onuf, C. P., J. M. Teal and I. Valiela, 1977. Interactions of nutrients, plant growth and herbivory in a mangrove ecosystem. Ecology, 58(3):514–526.

Page, G. and D. F. Whitacre, 1975. Raptor predation on wintering shorebirds. Condor, 77(1):73–83.

Palmisano, A. W., 1973. Habitat preference of waterfowl and fur animals in the northern Gulf Coast marshes. In R. H. Chabreck (Ed.), Proceedings of the Coastal Marsh and Estuary Management Symposium, Louisiana State University, Baton Rouge, 17-18 July 1972, pp. 163-190

Parnell, J. F. and R. F. Soots, Jr., 1978. The use of dredge islands by wading birds. Wading Birds, Research Report, Nat. Audubon Soc., 7:105–111.

Phillips, R. C., 1974. Temperate grass flats. In H. T. Odum, B. J. Copeland, and E. A. McMahan (Eds.), Coastal Ecological Systems of the United States, Vol. 2. Conservation Foundation, Washington, DC., pp. 244–299.

Post, W., 1974. Functional analysis of space related behavior in the seaside sparrow. Ecology, 55:564–575.

Post, W. and F. Enders, 1970. The occurence of Mallophaga on two bird species occupying the same habitat. Ibis, 112:539–540.

Prevost, Y., 1979. Osprey-bald eagle interactions at a common foraging site. Auk, 96:413–414.

Ranwell, D., 1972. Ecology of salt marshes and sand dunes. Chapman and Hall, London, 258 pp.

Reese, J. G., 1972. A Chesapeake barn owl population. Auk, 89:106–114.

Reese, J. G., 1975. Productivity and management of feral mute swans in Chesapeake Bay. J. of Wildlife Management, 39(2):280–286.

Reimold, R. J., R. A. Linthurst and P. L. Wolf, 1975. Effects of grazing on a salt marsh. Biol. Conserv., 8:105–125.

Salomonsen, F., 1968. The moult migration. Wildfowl, 19:5–24.

Scheffer, V. B. and J. W. Slipp, 1944. The harbor seal in Washington State. American Midland Naturalist, 32:373–416.

Schneider, D., 1978. Equalisation of prey numbers by migratory shorebirds. Nature, 271(5643):353–354.

Schreiber, R. W., 1979. Reproductive performance of the eastern brown pelican, *Pele-*

canus occidentalis. Natural History Museum of Los Angeles County, Los Angeles, California, Contributions in Science Number 317, 43 pp.

Schwartz, F. J., 1967. Maryland turtles. University of Maryland. 35 pp.

Seymour, N. R. and R. D. Titman, 1979. Behaviour of unpaired male black ducks (*Anas rubripes*) during the breeding season in a Nova Scotia tidal marsh. Can. J. Zoology, 57(12):2421-2428.

Shanholtzer, G. F., 1974. Relationship of vertebrates to salt marsh plants. In R. J. Reimold, (Ed.), Ecology of Halophytes. Academic Press, New York, pp. 463-473.

Shisler, J. K. and T. L. Schulze, 1977?. Some aspects of open marsh water management procedures on clapper rail production. Trans. of the Northeast Section, Wildlife Society, 33:101-104.

Silvester, H., 1975 (1976 English translation). Horses of the Camargue. Penguin, New York.

Slack, R. S. and C. B. Slack, 1981. Fall migration of peregrine falcons along the Rhode Island coast. J. of Field Ornithology, 52:60-61.

Smalley, A. E., 1960. Energy flow of a salt marsh grasshopper population. Ecology, 41:672-677.

Smith, T. J., III, and W. E. Odum, 1981. The effects of grazing by snow geese on coastal salt marshes. Ecology, 62(1):98-106.

Spitzer, P. and A. Poole, 1980. Coastal ospreys between New York City and Boston: a decade of reproductive recovery 1969-1979. American Birds, 34(3):234-241.

Stone, W. B., E. Kiviat, and S. A. Butkas, 1980. Toxicants in snapping turtles. N. Y. Fish and Game Journal, 27:39-50.

Tomkins, I. R., 1947. The oyster-catcher of the Atlantic Coast of North America and its relation to oysters. Wilson Bulletin, 59(4):204-208.

Webster, C. G., 1964. Fall foods of soras from two habitats in Connecticut. J. of Wildlife Management, 28:163-165.

Whigham, D. and R. Simpson, 1977. Growth, mortality and biomass partitioning in freshwater tidal wetland populations of wild rice (*Zizania aquatica* var. *aquatica*). Bull. Torrey Botanical Club, 104(4):347-351.

Whitfield, A. K. and S. J. M. Blaber, 1979. Predation on striped mullet (*Mugil cephalus*) by *Crocodylus niloticus* at St. Lucia, South Africa. Copeia, (2):266-269.

Willner, G. R., J. A. Chapman and J. R. Goldsberry, 1975. A study and review of muskrat food habits with special reference to Maryland. Publications in Wildlife Ecology 1, Maryland Wildlife Administration, Annapolis, 25 pp.

Woolfenden, G. E., 1968. *Ammospiza maritima maritima* (Wilson); northern seaside sparrow. In A. C. Bent (Ed.), Life histories of North American Cardinals, Grosbeaks, Buntings, Towhees, Finches, Sparrows and Allies. Dover, New York, pp. 819-831.

Ydenberg, R. C. and H. H. T. Prins, 1981. Spring grazing and the manipulation of food quality by barnacle geese. J. Applied Ecology, 18:443-453.

Zedler, J. B., 1982. The ecology of southern California coastal salt marshes: a community profile. U.S. Fish and Wildlife Service FWS/OBS-81/54. 110 pp.

SCIENTIFIC NAMES OF ORGANISMS MENTIONED IN CHAPTER 11

Plants

Arrowheads	*Sagittaria spp.*
Beggarticks	*Bidens laevis*
Cattail	*Typha spp.*
Cordgrass, saltmeadow	*Spartina patens*
Cordgrass, saltwater	*Spartina alterniflora*
Cordgrass, California	*Spartina foliosa*
Coyotebush	*Baccharis pilularis*
Eelgrass	*Zostera marina*
Marsh-elder	*Iva frutescens*
Palmetto	*Sabal palmetto*
Pickleweed	*Salicornia*
Pondweed	*Potamogeton pectinatus*
Reed	*Phragmites australis*
Sweetflag	*Acorus calamus*
Wax-myrtle	*Myrica cerifera*
Wild-rice	*Zizania aquatica*

Invertebrates

Cockle	*Cardium edule*
Lice, feather	Mallophaga
Mussel	*Mytilus edulis*

Lower Vertebrates

Mullet, striped	*Mugil cephalus*
Frog, crab-eating	*Rana cancrivora*
Alligator, American	*Alligator mississippiensis*
Crocodile, American	*Crocodylus acutus*
Crocodile, Nile	*Crocodylus niloticus*
Leatherback	*Dermochelys coriacea*
Lizard, island glass	*Ophisaurus compressus*
Loggerhead	*Caretta caretta*
Moccasin, water	*Agkistrodon piscivorus*
Snake, water	*Nerodia*
Terrapin, diamondback	*Malaclemys terrapin*
Turtle, Asian river	*Callagur borneoensis*
Turtle, green	*Chelonia mydas*
Turtle, map	*Graptemys geographica*
Turtle, snapping	*Chelydra serpentina*

Birds

Blackbird, red-winged	*Agelaius phoeniceus*
Brant	*Branta bernicla*
Canvasback	*Aythya valisineria*
Coot, red-knobbed	*Fulica cristata*
Cowbird, brown-headed	*Molothrus ater*
Crane, whooping	*Grus americana*
Crow	*Corvus sp.*
Duck, black	*Anas rubripes*
Eagle, bald	*Haliaeetus leucocephalus*
Egret, great	*Casmerodius albus*
Eider	*Somateria spp.*
Falcon, peregrine	*Falco peregrinus*
Flamingo, greater	*Phoenicopterus ruber*
Goose, barnacle	*Branta leucopsis*
Goose, snow	*Chen caerulescens*
Gull, Bonaparte's	*Larus philadelphia*
Gull, laughing	*Larus atricilla*
Harrier, northern	*Circus cyaneus*
Heron, great blue	*Ardea herodias*
Kingfisher, belted	*Ceryle alcyon*
Mallard	*Anas platyrhynchos*
Osprey	*Pandion haliaetus*
Owl, short-eared	*Asio flammeus*
Oystercatcher	*Haematopus ostralegus*
Oystercatcher, American	*Haematopus palliatus*
Pelican, brown	*Pelecanus occidentalis*
Rail, clapper	*Rallus longirostris*
Rail, king	*Rallus elegans*
Skimmer, black	*Rynchops niger*
Sora	*Porzana carolina*
Sparrow, savannah	*Passerculus sandwichensis*
Sparrow, seaside	*Ammodramus maritimus*
Sparrow, sharp-tailed	*Ammodramus caudacutus*
Sparrow, song	*Melospiza melodia*
Spoonbill, roseate	*Ajaia ajaja*
Swan, black	*Cygnus atratus*
Swan, mute	*Cygnus olor*
Tern, common	*Sterna hirundo*
Wren, marsh	*Cistothorus palustris*

Mammals

Bear, brown	*Ursus arctos*
Bear, polar	*Ursus maritimus*
Cattle	*Bos taurus*
Deer, white-tailed	*Odocoileus virginianus*
Dolphin, bottle-nosed	*Tursiops truncatus*
Dugong	*Dugong dugon*
Fox	*Vulpes vulpes and Urocyon cinereoargenteus*
Manatee	*Trichechus manatus*
Mink	*Mustela vison*
Monkey, silver leaf	*Presbytis cristatus*
Mouse, salt-marsh harvest	*Reithrodontomys raviventris*
Muskrat	*Ondatra zibethicus*
Nutria	*Myocastor coypus*
Otter, river	*Lutra canadensis*
Otter, sea	*Enhydra lutris*
Pig, feral	*Sus scrofa*
Pony, feral	*Equus caballus*
Porpoise, harbor	*Phocoena phocoena*
Rabbit, swamp	*Sylvilagus aquaticus*
Raccoon	*Procyon lotor*
Rat, marsh rice	*Oryzomys palustris*
Rat, Norway	*Rattus norvegicus*
Seal, harbor	*Phoca vitulina*
Sheep	*Ovis aries*
Shrew, Suisun	*Sorex sinuosus*
Tern, black	*Chlidonias niger*
Vole, California	*Microtus californicus*
Vole, meadow	*Microtus pennsylvanicus*
Walrus	*Odobenus rosmarus*
Whale, gray	*Eschrichtius robustus*
Whale, killer	*Orcinus orca*

HUMANS AND ESTUARIES

OFFPRINTS FROM: ESTUARINE ECOLOGY
Edited by John W. Day Jr., Charles A. S. Hall., Dr. W. Michael Kemp, and Alejandro Yáñez-Arancibia
Copyright © 1989 by John Wiley & Sons, Inc.

▬ 12

Estuarine Fisheries[1]

For many people the most interesting thing about estuaries is that they are fishy, meaning that those people relate directly to the fact that the rich estuarine fish production provides them with opportunities to catch fish for fun or for a living, or to eat unique and delicious food. In many estuarine regions the commerce and culture are dominated by fishing and related activities, and, for example, in Louisiana alone there are nearly 15,000 shrimp boats, and the fisheries provide the basis for a several hundred million dollar annual industry. Other important coastal fishery areas include Chesapeake Bay, the Ganges-Bramaputra delta area, and the Campeche Sound. We know many people who simply would not consider living anywhere but on the coast so that they can continue to sport fish for estuarine fish. It is no accident that many of the world's great population centers developed on or close to estuaries, in part because of their abundant food resource.

The word fisheries refers to the fish, fishermen, boats, canneries, markets, and so forth associated with the catching, processing, and marketing of sport and commercial fish and shellfish. Modern fisheries differ from modern agriculture and animal husbandry in that, for the most part, they rely upon the natural environment, more or less unmodified by people, for production. But fishing still modifies the natural environment considerably, for as certain species are caught, or overcaught, species composition changes, there is a reduction in predatory pressure on certain items of fish food, and there may be an increase in other fish which are not fished.

In earlier times, much of the world fishing pressure was directed toward fish

[1]This chapter is derived in part from Hall et al. 1980, Chapter 18, used by permission.

and shellfish in estuaries and nearshore coastal areas, where relatively large resources could be harvested with a relatively small investment of human energy or capital. Today commercial fishing has become a much more sophisticated and capital-intensive process. It is normally done with nets of some kind or, less commonly, with long strings of baited fishhooks, and a modern fishing fleet is very energy-intensive. Figure 12.1 shows some common types of fishing gear. Today most fisheries, like most agriculture, require very large quantities of fossil fuel.

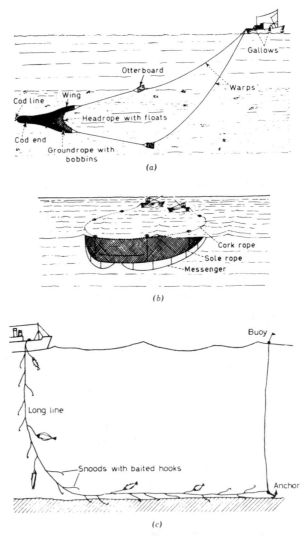

Figure 12.1 Common types of fishing gear (From Tait, 1968). a. Trawl, b. pursp seine, c. long time.

Even today, with the rapid development of distant water fishing fleets by several nations, much of the world's marine fish catch still comes from coastal waters (although often from the coast of another nation), and many of the productive marine fishing grounds are in or near estuaries or lagoons, or at least in shallow coastal environments. Although the very largest fisheries of the world are oceanic (i.e., cod on the Grand Banks of Newfoundland, the anchovies of the Humboldt current off Peru, and herring in the North Sea), in general estuarine fisheries are more important than oceanic fisheries. In addition many oceanic fisheries are comprised of a wide variety of vertebrate and invertebrate species (Tables 12.1 and 12.2) whose life histories are tied to that of the estuary and adjacent inshore waters. And, of course, the extremely valuable catches of anadromous species, such as salmon, often occur in estuaries as they move to and from feeding and spawning grounds. Estuarine and estuarine-related fisheries are also higher per unit area than offshore fisheries. As we discussed in Chapter 10, estuarine-related species have often been called estuarine-dependent.

By comparison with fisheries of the temperate and high latitudes, tropical fisheries are poorly understood. Longhurst and Pauly (1987) reported that it is difficult to accurately determine tropical fishery production. The tropical ocean includes almost 50% of the total oceanic and about 30% of total continental shelf areas, but produces only about 16% of global marine fish production. This is an enigma because the tropical zone includes several of the largest river deltas and coastal lagoon systems of the world. We will address this issue in a preliminary way in this chapter.

The importance of estuarine-related species in marine commercial and recreational fisheries varies widely by latitude and region. McHugh (1977a, b, c, 1980, 1984) estimated that in recent years total fish and shellfish landing for the United States were about 3.0 million metric tons, of which about 2.0 million were considered estuarine-dependent. Although McHugh's definition of estuarine dependent is perhaps overly generous, it is clear that estuaries are responsible in some way for at least half of the commercial landings each year. That proportion depends upon the region. On the Atlantic coast estuarine species are proportionally more important as one moves from north to south, while on the Pacific coast the converse is true. In the northern Gulf of Mexico 98% (by weight) of the commercial catch was considered estuarine-dependent (which we will call estuarine-related) by McHugh (1980, 1984). Similarly, Lindall and Saloman (1977) determined that for the states bordering the Gulf of Mexico, about 90% of the marine commercial catch and about 70% of the recreational fishery catch were estuarine-related. In the southern Gulf of Mexico, there is a similar pattern, where more than 90% of the commercial catch from the states of Campeche and Tabasco are estuarine-related (Yáñez-Arancibia and Aguirre-Léon 1988). As might be expected, the importance of estuarine environments to fisheries in general is greatest in regions of major estuarine development, both in cold and warm latitudes, and it comes as no surprise that greatest fish yield in the United States comes from Louisiana, the state (with the exception of Alaska) with the largest area of estuaries, lagoons, and coastal marshes.

TABLE 12.1 Species in Official Fishery Statistics of the United States (Lyles, 1965) Identified for the Purposes of the This Chapter as Estuarine-Dependent

Common Names	Scientific Names
Alewives	*Alosa pseudoharengus, A. aestivalis*
Catfish	*Ictalurus* spp.
Croaker	*Micropogon undulatus*
Drums	*Pogonias cromis, Sciaenops ocellata*
Eel	*Anguilla rostrata*
Flounders	*Pseudopleuronectes americanus, Paralichthys* spp., *Platichthys stellatus*
Garfish	*Lepisosteus* spp.
Gizzard shad	*Dorosoma cepedianum*
Hickory shad	*Alosa mediocris*
Hogchoker	*Trinectes maculatus*
Menhaden	*Brevoortia* spp.
Salmon	*Oncorhynchus* spp., *Salmo salar, S. gairdneri*
Scup or porgy	*Calamus* spp., *Stenotomus* spp.
Sea bass (Atlantic)	*Centropristes striatus*
Sea robin	*Prionotus* spp.
Sea trout or weakfish	*Cynoscion* spp.
Shad	*Alosa sapidissima*
Silversides	*Menidia* spp.
Smelt	Families Atherinidae and Osmeidae
Spot	*Leiostomus xanthurus*
Striped bass	*Morone saxatilis*
Sturgeon	*Acipenser* spp., *Scaphirhynchus platorhynchus*
Swellfish	*Sphaeroides maculatus*
Tautog	*Tautoga onitis*
Tenpounder	*Elops saurus*
White perch	*Morone americanus*
Yellow perch	*Perca flavescens*
Crabs	*Callinectes sapidus, Cancer magister, Carcinus maenas*
Horseshoe crab	*Limulus* spp.
Shrimp	Penaeus spp., Xiphopenaeus spp.
Clams	*Cardium corbis, Saxidomus nuttalli, Protothaca staminea, Mercenaria mercenaria, Mya arenaria*
Mussels	*Mytilus* spp.
Oysters	*Crassostrea* spp., *Ostrea lurida*
Periwinkles	*Littorina* spp.
Bay scallop	*Aequipecten irradians*
Terrapin	*Malaclemys* spp.
Turtles	Various species
Bloodworms	Family Glyceridae
Sandworms	*Nereis* spp.

TABLE 12.2   The 12 Most Important Kinds of Commercial fish and Shellfish Landed in the United States in 1963

By Weight (in Thousands of kg)			By Value (in Thousands of Dollars)		
Rank	Kind of Fish	Weight	Rank	Kind of Fish	Value
1	Menhaden*	825,362	1	Shrimp*	$70,044
2	Tuna	146,190	2	Salmon*	49,012
3	Salmon*	133,717	3	Salmon*	40,170
4	Crabs*	114,697	4	Oysters*	27,105
5	Shrimp*	109,308	5	Menhaden	22,386
6	Sea herring	88,000	6	Crabs*	21,354
7	Flounders*	80,362	7	Lobsters	18,567
8	Ocean perch	59,940	8	Flounders*	15,411
9	Haddock	56,350	9	Clams*	14,202
10	Jack mackerel	43,565	10	Haddock	11,705
11	Whiting	42,110	11	Scallops*	10,334
12	Clams*	28,819	12	Halibut	6,972
	Totals	1,728,427			$307,262

*Strongly estuarine dependent

Estuaries may also influence offshore fisheries. Moore et al. (1970), Chittenden and McEachran (1976), Sánchez-Gil et al. (1981), and Soberón-Chávez and Yáñez-Arancibia (1985) provide evidence that the standing crop and population levels of individual demersal fish species in continental shelf regions in the Gulf of Mexico are influenced by bathimetry, sediments, littoral vegetation, and epicontinental waters, all of which are influenced in turn by adjacent estuaries. The relationships between estuaries and continental shelf fishery sometimes can be quite complex. Darnell and Soniat (1979) described the estuary-pass-shelf complex as an interactive system whose internal dynamics are controlled, in large measure, by driving forces external to the system, such as river discharges and tides.

12.1   REGIONAL AND TEMPORAL VARIATIONS IN FISHERIES

There are significant variations in fishery yields from different coastal areas, and there are also significant differences in yield from any specific estuary or region from one year to another. A number of reasons have been suggested to explain these variations. These include (1) area of habitat, especially wetlands, (2) climatic factors such as river discharge and precipitation, and (3) food availability. In this section we will address those factors that may regulate fisheries. One procedure that has been used to unravel the relative importance of different factors is correlation of different parameters, either singly or in combination, with fishery yield.

12.1.1   Regional Variation in Coastal Fisheries

It has been observed for many years that coastal areas with large estuaries, broad wetlands, and large rivers tend to support high fishery yields (Walme 1972). For example, over 20 years ago, Gunter (1967, 1969) speculated that fisheries production in the Gulf of Mexico was related to estuarine area and river discharge. He called the area around the Mississippi Delta the "fertile fisheries crescent" because of the importance of the fishery. Over the past two to three decades, a body of evidence has developed which gives much more scientific support to this idea. Turner (1977, 1979) showed a strong correlation between wetland area and fisheries yield, both worldwide and in the Gulf of Mexico. He demonstrated a strong correlation between local intertidal wetland area and shrimp catch for many areas of the world (Fig. 12.2*a*). These data also indicate that the catch per unit area for shrimp is higher nearer the equator. For the northern Gulf of Mexico, total shrimp yield was correlated with intertidal area (Fig. 12.2*b*). This pattern of estuarine-relatedness does not always hold for coastal fisheries. For example, in the southern Gulf of Mexico, demersal fisheries are clearly estuarine-related while in the Gulf of Guinea on the tropical West African coast, this is less so. Both areas, however, are among the most important fishery zones in the intertropical belt (Yáñez-Arancibia et al. 1985a, Longhurst and Pauly 1987).

The area of saline wetlands can also affect the species composition of the catch. For example, Turner found that the proportion of the total shrimp catch that was brown shrimp (a species that uses marsh tidal channels as a nursery) in the subestuaries of the Mississippi deltaic plain was related to the amount of salt marsh in each subestuary (Fig. 12.3). It has been argued that this strong correlation between wetland areas and fish harvest does not always hold. Nixon (1980) compared commercial landings along the Atlantic and Gulf coasts of the United States with the ratio of marsh area to open water area. He found that, in general, coastal areas with a greater proportion of marsh had higher landings. But he also found that Chesapeake Bay had a high fishery yield per unit area but a low marsh to water ratio (Fig. 12.4). The fishery in Chesapeake Bay seems to be based more on the pelagic zone, although there are also large areas of submerged aquatic plants that, if included as wetlands, might produce a similar finding to the wetland-water correlations.

Why should wetland area be related to fisheries yield? In Chapter 10 we presented evidence that tidal creeks and salt marshes provide excellent habitat for the young of many important fishery species. In the Barataria Basin, the biomass of nekton was 7 to 12 times greater in tidal creeks and near the marsh edge than in open bay waters, and most of this high biomass was young fish (Day et al. 1982). Young nekton seem to seek out these areas and, during certain parts of the year, they are much more abundant in marshes and tidal creeks than they

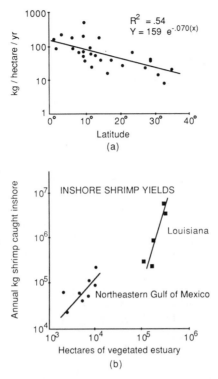

Figure 12.2 (a) The relationship between commercial yields of penaeid shrimp per area of intertidal land versus latitude. (b) The relationship between the average annual yield of shrimp caught inshore (heads-off) and the area of vegetated estuary for several estuarine systems of the northeastern Gulf of Mexico and for different hydrological units in the Mississippi River Delta estuary (from Turner 1977).

ever are in open waters of estuaries. These habitats seem to provide high quality habitat in terms of food availability, protection from predators, calm water, and favorable physiological ranges of temperature, salinity, and turbidity (Boesch and Turner 1984).

The mean annual volume of river discharge is also correlated with regional variations in fish harvest. The Gulf of Mexico is an excellent geographical area to study this relationship because of the wide range of river discharges and fishery production. Moore et al. (1970) presented data on the abundance of estuarine-related demersal fish off the Louisiana and Texas coasts. They found that fish abundance was highest near the Mississippi River and decreased with distance from the river (Fig. 12.5). This distribution pattern is probably also related to the broad expanse of wetlands in the Mississippi deltaic plain which serves as habitat for most of the species. For the Texas coast, Chapman (1966) showed that estuaries with higher average river discharge had higher average

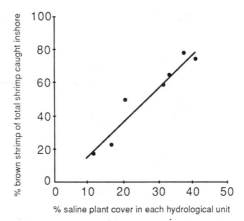

Figure 12.3 The relationship between the percentage of brown shrimp of the total shrimp caught for each hydrological unit in the Mississippi River Delta estuary and the percentage of the marsh vegetation which is saline marsh (from Turner 1977).

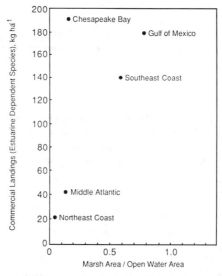

Figure 12.4 The correlation between the ratio of local intertidal wetland area to open water, and estuarine-related fish and shellfish catch for different regions of the eastern and southern United States (from Nixon 1980).

fish yields per unit area (Fig 12.6*a*) and that fisheries harvest was higher in wet years (12.6*b*). Yáñez-Arancibia et al. (1985b) and Soberón-Chávez et al. (1986) studied the relationship between river discharge, recruitment relationships, and fish capture in the southern Gulf of Mexico. They found that fish capture per unit area of lagoons and estuaries was correlated with river discharge (Fig. 12.7).

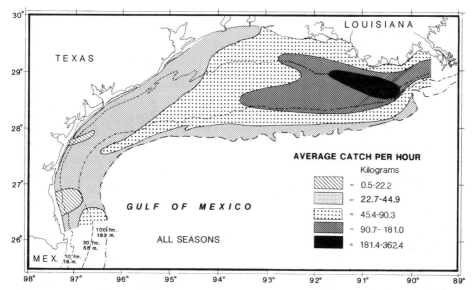

Figure 12.5   Relative abundance (by weight) of demersal fishes from 1962 to 1964, off the coast of Louisiana and Texas. In general fish catch is greater in the eastern part of this region off the Mississippi Delta where freshwater discharge and estuarine wetland and water area are much greater (from Moore et al. 1970).

The relation of fish yield and river discharge may be due to a number of factors. In Chapters 3 and 4, we reviewed findings that show that riverine inputs stimulate aquatic primary production and reminerialization. Rivers also carry suspended sediments to estuarine systems. The deposition of these sediments creates shallow habitats where intertidal wetlands can develop, as indicated for the Gulf of Mexico by the analysis of Deegan et al. (1986). Such wetlands then can support high production of fishery species. Of course the astute reader will realize that the development of salt marshes also is partly dependent upon river volume, so that part of the reason that fisheries yield is correlated with both marsh and river discharge is that they are correlated with each other.

Food availability also helps to explain regional differences in fisheries yield and food availability is often dependent upon both marsh production and river discharge. Bahr et al. (1982) analyzed trophic dynamics and energy flow in various parts of the Mississippi delta and concluded that primary production inputs were quantitatively related to fishery yield. Nixon (1982) found a relationship between aquatic primary production and fisheries yield in a number of different coastal systems (Fig. 12.8). This suggests that food availability may limit secondary production. An intriguing result of Nixon's analysis is that estuarine areas are more efficient in converting primary production into fish production than are other water bodies. On the average, each unit of estuarine primary production supported 10 times more fishery yield than did a comparable level of pri-

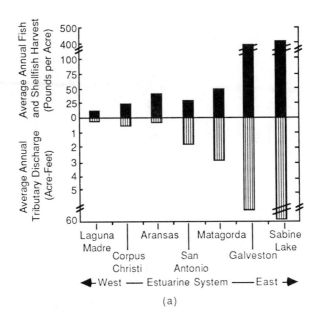

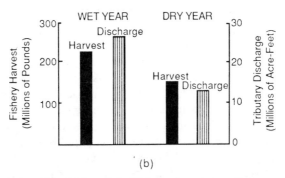

Figure 12.6 Relationship of fish and shellfish catch and river discharge for (a) different regions of the Texas coast, and (b) for all of Texas for a wet year and a dry year (reproduced from Chapman 1966, used by permission).

mary production in large lakes. The reasons for this surprising finding are not clear. If the estuarine fish species were lower on the food chain this could explain such a difference, but it is not clear that this is the case. Large areas of intertidal vegetation, tidal creeks, and grassbeds may allow a larger standing crop of nekton so that primary production is efficiently utilized. Or, as Nixon suggests, the shallowness of estuaries may allow a more efficient exploitation of available resources by both primary producers and fish.

In summary, the available information suggests that wetlands and river dis-

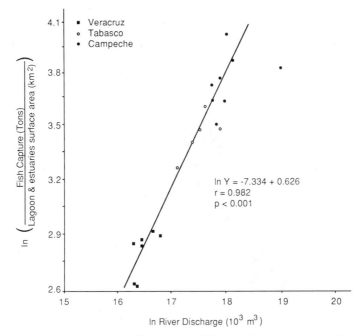

Figure 12.7 Correlation of river discharge and fish catch per unit area of coastal lagoons and estuaries in the Mexican states of Veracruz, Tabasco, and Campeche in the southern Gulf of Mexico. The data are from the years 1973 to 1985 (from Soberón-Chávez and Yáñez-Arancibia 1985).

charge enhance fisheries, but that estuaries with relatively low wetland areas can also support high fisheries if they have other shallow regions of high productivity. Whatever the reasons, it is clear that the interactions among habitat, river discharge, primary production, and fisheries is very complex and more study is needed to understand fully these interactions.

12.1.2   Year to Year Variations in Coastal Fisheries

There are distinct year to year variations in fish yield for specific estuaries and for entire regions. Many investigations have indicated that such variations are correlated with river discharge. For example, Chapman (1966) found that total fish harvest along the Texas coast was higher during wet years (Fig. 12.6*b*). Similarly, Yáñez-Arancibia et al. (1985b) showed that fish capture for individual states bordering the Gulf of Mexico in Mexico was related to river discharge (Fig. 12.7). Such relationships have been reported for individual species as well as for total catch. Sutcliffe (1972, 1973, 1976) found correlations between the discharge of the St. Lawrence River and catches of soft shell clam, halibut, haddock, and lobster (Fig. 12.9). Sutcliffe also warned that change or diversions in

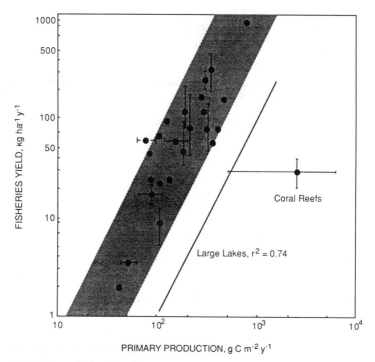

PRIMARY PRODUCTION, g C m^{-2} y^{-1}

Figure 12.8 The relationship between aquatic primary productivity and fisheries yields for a number of different lagoons and estuaries from different parts of the world (solid circles), large lakes, and coral reefs. Note that fisheries yield per unit of primary production is much higher for coastal lagoons and estuaries than for coral reefs or large lakes (from Nixon 1982).

drainage systems could reduce fish yield. Finally, the seasonality of river flow may be crucial. Herrgesell et al. (1981) reported that river discharge in June and July was strongly correlated with the abundance of striped bass in the Sacramento-San Joquin delta, California (Fig. 12.10). The similarity of these findings over a wide latitudinal range suggests that river discharge is generally important for fisheries production.

In summary, the results of a number of studies show that estuarine and coastal systems are important fishery regions. Factors such as intertidal wetland area, river discharge, and food availability are important in determining the levels of fisheries. The specific patterns by which different species use estuaries were discussed earlier in Charpter 10, but it is clear that we have much to learn about the reasons which lead to high fish prodcution and important fisheries. The relationship of fish production and fisheries to ecosystem variability is reviewed by Yáñez-Arancibia and Pauly (1986) and Yáñez-Arancibia and Sánchez-Gil (1986, 1988). Our next question is to consider the ways that people exploit fish and, ideally, the ways this exploitation can be optimized.

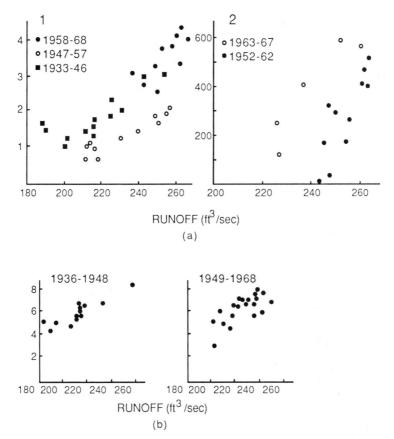

Figure 12.9 The correlation between discharge of the St. Lawrence River and (a) the catch of halibut and, (b) the catch of lobsters (from Sutcliffe 1972).

12.2 THE CATCHING OF FISH

Where fish are abundant, as in coastal and upwelling regions, the most desirable fish species tend to be exploited very heavily, so that on average an adult fish is about as likely to be caught in a fish net as to die of old age or predation. This is especially true in productive fisheries grounds that are near human population concentrations, such as is the case for fish of many estuaries. Often, as new fisheries are developed, such as for Gulf menhaden, the catch for the total fishery will increase dramatically as successful fishing techniques and new markets are developed (Fig. 12.11). Often, however, a fishery will decline severely or even collapse after time, presumably mostly as a result of overfishing that depletes spawing stock, but perhaps often simply as a result of poorly understood natural factors (McHugh 1976, Hennemuth et al. 1980, Longhurst and Pauly 1987).

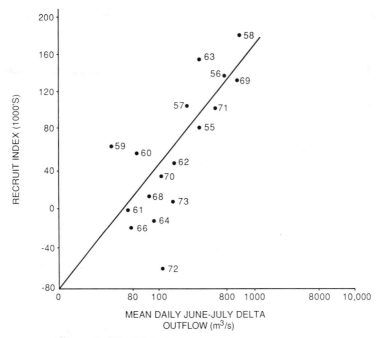

Figure 12.10 Relationship between the index of abundance of three year old striped bass and mean daily freshwater discharge from the Sacromento-San Joaquin Delta during June and July, three years earlier. Numbers adjacent to points indicate year-classes (from Stevens 1977 and Herrgesell et al. 1980).

Interestingly, the landings (by weight) each year for the total United States fisheries has remained about constant for the past 30 years, despite wild fluctuations in the landings for individual species (Brown and Lugo 1981). Even though the catch has remained relatively constant during this time period, the total effort invested each year in catching fish has increased a great deal (Fig. 12.12a), so that the catch per effort (see below) has declined considerably Of particular importance is the observation that increasing amounts of energy are being used to get about the same yield of fish (12.12b). In other words, we are now catching about the same amount of fish with a greater imput of human effort, and especially, capital equipment and fuel.

The problem is compounded as new technology, such as sonar, makes each boat a more efficient exploiter of fish. This is a common problem in resource economics—although it may still make sense for any individual fisherman to enter the fishery (because he/she can make a living or a profit at it) it does not make sense for the fisheries as a whole, at least from the perspective of the efficiency of use of capital equipment, energy, or the resource itself. So two chronic problems in fisheries, and in resource management in general, are chronic over-

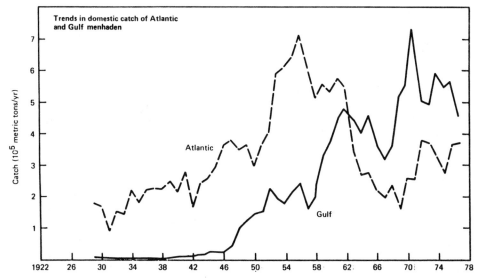

Figure 12.11 Total domestic catch of Atlantic and Gulf menhaden from 1930 to 1978. Note that the fishery for the Atlantic menhaden, which began much earlier than that for the Gulf menhaden, peaked in 1958 and subsequently declined. The fishery for Gulf menhaden, which began after World War II, has yet to suffer such a marked decline. Note also the considerable interannual variability which is typical of most fisheries (from Brown and Lugo 1981).

harvesting, resulting in a reduction in the catch that might be taken with skilled regulation, and overcapitalization, resulting in a wastage of fuel and other resources.

12.3 FISHERIES MANAGEMENT

Fisheries management can mean many things, including fish culture in hatcheries or artificial ponds, removal of predatory or competing fishes, and, especially, regulation of catch through various limits on time that can be spent fishing, quantities of fish that can be kept, or gear that can be used. The need for management of fish was at first a hotly contested issue, both in the United States and in Great Britain. Nielsen (1976) and Sissenwine et al. (1978) have documented some of the controversy that surrounded the development of the concept of regulation and management in the 19th century and the changes that have taken place in management philosophy since. A particularly lively debate in Great Britain initially resulted in the abolishment of all laws restricting fishing, based principally on the concept that natural mortality was much larger than fishing mortality. This view was reversed however, at a formal debate held at an

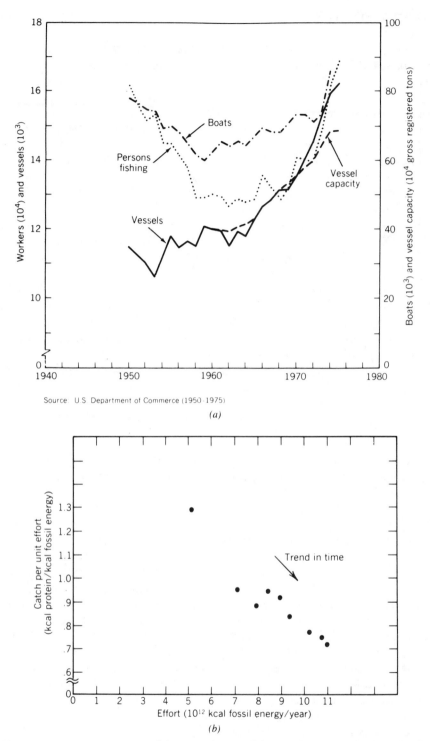

Source: U.S. Department of Commerce (1950-1975)

(a)

(b)

Figure 12.12 Basic statistics of the United States fishing industry, (a) trends in the domestic fishing fleet working on boats, on vessels, and onshore, and (b) catch per unit of energy invested, 1950 to 1980 (from Brown and Lugo 1981).

International Fisheries exhibition in London in 1883 where fisheries scientists who favored regulation and the concept that fish were, in some sense, exhaustable, won the debate and set the stage for later regulation of the industry.

In the United States the need for mangement was first noted at the federal level when a number of fisheries scientists, among them Spencer Baird, convinced the United States Congress to establish the U.S. Fisheries Commission. Since there were not very comprehensive or accurate records kept at that time on the catch of various fisheries it is difficult to get good documentation on the perceived decline in fisheries noted at that time or even whether things are much worse (or better) now (see Nixon 1982).

The initial thrust in management was the *a priori* logical step of constructing hatcheries to supplement natural reproduction. It soon became apparent that either the hatcheries had little effect, especially for marine fish, or (more frequently) that it was impossible to determine whether a given fish even came from a hatchery. Increasingly managers turned to catch regulation, especially through setting the length of seasons, to attempt to manage and replenish supposedly depleted fish stocks.

12.3.1 The Evolution of Procedures for Estimating Desirable Levels of Catch

An important concept in the development of a theoretical rationale for management was the development and use of the catch per unit effort (CPUE) concept, that is, how many fish were caught per fisherman per hour, or per some other unit of effort. Although the concept was familiar (certainly it is the most familiar component to an individual fisherman) the usefulness of the idea was not generally realized until it became obvious that the catch per effort for North Sea fishes had increased following the lull in fishing activities associated with World War I. This was the first clear evidence that a reduction in fishing effort could bring about an increase in yield, and demonstrated clearly that fishing effort was in fact affecting fish populations. Over time two basic, and to some degree antithetical schools of thought, have dominated fisheries management: first, that factors intrinsic to fish populations dominated subsequent fish reproduction and availability (the density-dependent population dynamics approach) and second, that factors external to the fish population dominated reproduction and availability (the ecosystem approach).

12.3.2 The Population Dynamics Approach

Basic fisheries management concepts were initially developed, although not especially utilized, in Russia in the 1930s (e.g. Baranov 1918, Borisov 1960). The beginning of a more formalized approach to what actually does happen to a fish population was developed by Russell (1942). Russell's basic equation formalized changes in stock numbers as

$$P_2 = P_1 + (R' + G') - (M + F)$$

where P_1 is the stock in a given year, P_2 is the stock in the next year, G' is the annual addition to the stock biomass from growth, R' is addition due to recruitment of a new age class, M is loss due to natural mortality, and F is loss due to fishing mortality. Although Russell's equation gave an explicit approach to understanding the components that caused stocks to change it was not especially useful in actually helping estimate any of these parameters beyond that of the already measurable fishing mortality, nor did it give any particular rationale as to what level of fishing mortality would be optimum for fish or fishermen. At best it could be said that, in general, fishing pressure was too intense for any particular fishermen to have as good a catch as he once had, and that some important fish stocks were becoming increasingly difficult to catch.

The only protection that heavily exploited fish had was that at some point (often too late) it became uneconomical to fish for them. Much of the theoretical research over the past 50 years in fisheries has been attempts to develop a good rationale for determining catch rates, and to use these for convincing fishermen, legislators, and even other investigators that only so many fish should be caught. There was at first not a clear rationale within fisheries science itself for determining the best level of fishing intensity. Interestingly some experimental and theoretical developments within the emerging science of ecology did offer hope for deriving what was needed. The next paragraphs document these developments, which will be followed by later sections on their application to fisheries.

In general the new approach taken was mathematical and related to the population dynamics of the fish. It was often based on the most easily obtained information—the number of fish caught by the fisheries each year (this data was easy to get because the fishermen did all the sampling work)—generally with the assumption that catch per effort was proportional to the number of adult fish, which is known as stock. The approach was mathematical because clearly the problem had a quantitative component and because there was at that time the model of research in physics which showed how successful certain mathematical approaches could be in predicting scientific phenomenon. The mathematical approach was seductive in part because mathematics was doable and gave concrete numerical predictions, while the behavior of real biological organisms was, in general, very difficult to understand and predict. This mathematical approach was further encouraged by the remarkable early success of some equations, especially the logistic, in predicting population growth rates and levels for certain laboratory studies. Unfortunately, as we shall see, some of these approaches have proven not only weak but perhaps even misleading in trying to understand and manage real fish. Although their heuristic value is clear, and almost surprisingly they were sometimes quite useful in giving a rationale for conservation, the uncritical use of this approach was at least occasionally detrimental to real fish stocks (Hall 1988, Hall et al. 1986).

12.3.3 The Use of the Logistic Equation in Fisheries Management

Very elegant and influential concepts in fisheries management were those of Beverton and Holt (1957) and especially Ricker (1954, 1975). Ricker used the logistic equation concept and the relation of the number of adults (stock) and the number of young produced for the next generation (recruits) to devise a rather clever scheme for managing fisheries. Ricker assumed that year to year variations in spawning success were due principally to density-dependent effects, and that any density-independent effects (e.g., weather) would be smoothed out for species that spawned more than once before they died.

In theory a fish population would grow rapidly when it was well below its "carrying capacity" but much less so as it approached that carrying capacity. As a result, the number of recruits would be strongly dependent upon the number of spawning adults. When the stock was low, the total number of young produced would be small (since the number of spawners was small, point a on Fig. 12.13) but the per capita survival of the young would be high, due to the lack of population damping from density-dependent factors. If the population was larger, the number of young produced would be larger (point b). However, if the population gets much larger, density compensation becomes more important, and although the number of young spawned increases, the survivability of each individual decreases. At some point along this curve only as many young are produced and survive as are necessary to maintain a stable population over time (Fig. 12.13, point d, assuming adults spawn only once). If larger numbers of adults are spawning, then density compensation will cause high juvenile mortality and reduce the recruitment so that the population will actually decrease (point e). The concept in the "Ricker curve" approach to management was to increment natural mortality with fishing mortality, keeping the population at the maximum

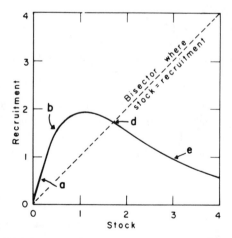

Figure 12.13 Ricker Curve or stock recruitment theory. As the number of spawners (stock) increases, then the number of young produced will also increase until density compensation effects are sufficient to decrease per capita survival of the young. At some point, increasing the number of spawners actually decreases the total production of offsrping (after Hall et al. 1986).

yield point, in a sense resulting in having your cake (increasing recruitment) while eating it too (catching the fish). The original data base given to construct this relation (British Columbia sockeye salmon) was thought to fit the relation and some additional studies gave a more specific assessment of how density-dependent factors would operate (e.g. Johnson, 1965). The concept was widely used as a means of regulating fishing pressure for many species. Increasingly sophisticated corrections were made in the basic model to include age structure, fishing mortality, and so on (Ricker 1954, 1975). Although we later criticize the Ricker curve approach to management, it should be pointed out that the approach was in a certain sense extremely logical and Ricker himself has been among the most persistent and intelligent critics of the uncritical application of the theory.

12.3.4 Does the Logistic Equation Represent Nature?

It is not especially clear whether or not the Ricker method has worked as a general procedure for managing fish (see Valiela 1984, Hall et al. 1986). In a recent symposium on fish and fisheries, a keynote speaker said "At this time we must acknowledge that stock-recruitment models have failed us, for there is rarely any consistent relation between stock and recruitment. The question is, what should we replace it with" (Laurence 1981). Although it may be true that the theory the Ricker model was based on is not proven, the theory did have the positive effect of giving a rationale for preventing excessive overfishing and, perhaps, avoiding the type of severe overfishing that appears to have caused the collapse of certain fisheries. In other cases, it may have actually hurt fisheries (Hall 1988).

The use of the logistic equation approach seems to be particularly unsuitable for tropical fisheries. This is partially because nekton dynamics are much more complicated in the tropics. For instance, rates of growth, mortality, and food consumption are generally higher, spawning is more frequent, fish longevity is shorter, and life histories, use of different habitats, and recruitment processes are often more complicated (Longhurst and Pauly 1987, Yáñez-Arancibia and Pauly 1986, Yáñez-Arancibia and Sánchez-Gil 1988). In general, it seems that recruitment is a principal determinant of abundance variability in many stocks, and recruitment is highly dependent on environmental factors and biological interactions (Yáñez-Arancibia and Pauly 1986).

12.3.5 Schaefer Curves

Since it was rather difficult to determine the particular relation between stock and recruitment that would optimize the number of fish caught and/or the production of progeny, other means of determining optimum fishing effort have been sought. An interesting and reasonably successful approach was that of Schaefer (1961, 1957a,b), who relied upon information from the fishery itself to determine the optimum catch in a given year. This approach too uses the logistic curve in part for its justification, although the empirical nature of the anlysis greatly restricts the importance of the logistic curve for final results.

Schaefer, working initially with Pacific yellowfin tuna, determined for each year of the fishery the amount of effort (i.e. boat-days spent fishing) and the reported catch of the boats. From this information the catch per unit effort (CPUE) and the total catch could be plotted as a function of effort (Fig. 12.14). Schaefer found that as the fishery developed the catch per effort declined, presumably due to depletion of the stock. In other words, the first boats out found it easy to catch fish for there were many fish to be caught, but in later years as more boats joined the fleet the catch per effort declined (Fig. 12.14a). The total catch is equal to the catch per effort times the effort, and at first this increased with increasing effort but eventually peaked and declined as the decline in catch per effort became more important than the increase in effort. The data analyzed by Schaefer fit the model rather well except that there was insufficient information about the behavior of the fishery on the right hand side of the curve. In addition, problems may occur when the average boat size or the type of gear used changes (as when the Pacific tuna fleet changed from using rods and chum to using purse seines) so that intercalibrations between boats and gear must be made. Probably in the absence of any other justification the Schaefer approach is as good as any for managing fish, especially if enough data is available to see if the data fit the model. In theory, as in the Ricker curve, a reduction in stock will increase production (according to the logistic concept) so that a moderate level of fishing should produce sustained high yields. In practice, for both the Ricker and the Schaefer approach the highest yields should be at an intermediate fishing intensity.

Given a well-behaved fish population, that is, one that plots nicely on a

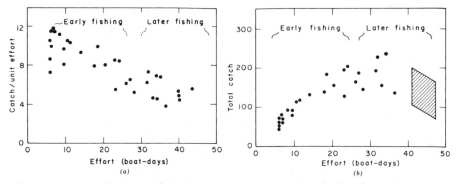

Figure 12.14 Schaefer analysis showing (a) a continuous decline in catch per unit effort with increased effort, and (b) a rising catch with initial increase in effort followed by an asymptotic and, perhaps, eventual decline in catch. In many fisheries total catch declines with greater effort as represented by the shaded area. Dots are data for Pacific yellow-fin tuna fisheries, 1950s–1960s (from Hall et al. 1986).

Schaefer plot, one can make decisions about what point would optimize the fishery according to some particular criteria. A common objective is that of the "maximum sustained yield" (MSY), that is, the point at which the greatest sustained catch can be made (Fig. 12.14 *b*). This has served as a management objective in many fisheries for a number of decades, the idea being that the best objective for fisheries should be to produce as many fish as possible. At this time, however, the concept of maximum sustained yield is being questioned from many quarters (e.g. Nielson 1975, Brown and Lugo 1981, Clark 1976, 1985). There are other possible management objectives. For example, the best economic return on investment (either in terms of dollars or energy) would be at a fishing level considerably less than the MSY, where the quantity of fish caught per unit of effort is highest. On the other hand Pacific halibut have been deliberately overfished for years because it is cheaper for the province of British Columbia, Canada, to allow this than to pay unemployment funds to fishermen. One result of this policy, of course, is that it requires about twice the effort to catch a halibut compared to more restrictive regulations. Finally, conservative catch restrictions might be considered useful simply from a conservation view or in order to protect recreational fisheries (e.g. Nielson 1975). At any rate, there is not much evidence that many fish stocks exhibit the "Schaefer-type" behavior (Hall et al. 1986)

In the tropics, it is practically impossible to use the concept of maximum sustained yield. This is because tropical fisheries are almost always based on multispecies stocks which are composed of mainly short-lived species with very complex biological and environmental interactions (Pauly and Murphy 1982, Mercer 1982, Doubleday and Rivard 1981, Yáñez-Arancibia and Sánchez-Gil 1986, 1988, Longhurst and Pauly 1987, Smith et al. 1983). This suggests that fishery management for high latitude, as well as for tropical fish stocks should be based on an "optimum" and not necessarily a "maximum" sustained yield approach. Thus, both biological recruitment (to the population) and fishery recruitment (to the net) have to be considered. This approach must include both ecosystem and population considerations, and we will address this in the next section.

12.3.6 Toward an Integration of Ecosystem and Population-Level Information

Given the failure of straightforward Ricker analyses and the obvious importance of density-independent factors such as river discharge and habitat, it became necessary to develop a more comprehensive approach to the relation of stock and recruitment. Attempts to integrate information about the relation between environmental conditions and the survival of young fish are found in Cushing (1975), Pauly and Murphy (1982), and Longhurst and Pauly (1987). Although Cushing did not clearly establish the mechanisms by which environmental conditions would be translated into year to year differences in fish recruitment, nor did it give any particularly better prescription for management than had been available previously, it provided an excellent beginning synthesis of ecosystem and population approaches. The later works address the environmental variability as one of the main factors affecting interannual variability of many fish stocks.

More recent and sophisticated research, however, has shown that density-independent factors can act in more subtle ways than was once thought, ways that nevertheless may make a great deal of difference to the fish populations. In fact, there appears to be an emerging consensus among many fisheries researchers that the key to understanding and predicting fish stocks for any given year is to determine the events that produce high or low survival during the critical days, weeks, or months after the fish are born, or the recruitment into the population as was mentioned earlier. For example, Laurence and Rogers (1976) have shown that not just the growth but also the survival rate of young haddock is critically a function of food supply. Lasker (1975, 1978) showed similar relations for Pacific coast species; the higher the concentrations of plankton in the water the greater the survival rate of young sardines. In Terminos Lagoon, Lara-Dominguez and Yáñez-Arancibia (1986) and Yáñez-Arancibia and Sánchez-Gil (1986, 1988) reported that environmental conditions of salinity, turbidity, and temperature in tidal inlets were critical in determining migratory patterns of a number of fish species. In general, it is important for young fishes to grow out of the stages in which they are very vulnerable to predation as rapidly as possible, and environmental conditions such as food availability and habitat greatly affect growth rates. In addition, of course, the many interesting correlations in Figures 12.2 to 12.10 suggest strongly that environmental factors strongly influence the abundance of fishes. The question then becomes whether or not we can predict the factors that determine such things as plankton abundance and habitat area, and which environmental factors contribute most strongly to fish survival and growth.

12.3.7 How Are Fisheries in Fact Managed?

Although we have presented a number of theories as to how we might manage a fishery, many fisheries are not managed at all. Anyone who wants to fish does so, and catches as many fish as possible. As a result many fisheries are strongly cyclic as fisheries develop, overcapitalize, overfish, and decline (Fig. 12.15). Sometimes the fish recover after the fishermen go elsewhere and sometimes they do not. One philosophy is that as the fishery becomes unprofitable because of overfishing it will retard further increases in fishing effort—although by that time it may be too late. One would think that a more stable fishery might be preferable, and that this could be achieved by thorough restrictions on fishing effort as has been done often in Canada where the fishing industry is often more highly regulated. Such regulations have also sometimes worked in the United States (as in the tuna fisheries), when the fisherman agree to be regulated. Unfortunately even those Canadian fisheries that are tightly regulated may be overfished and decline, such as the Pacific halibut and the Pacific salmon. Whether this is due to the failure of the concept of regulation or whether the general polit-

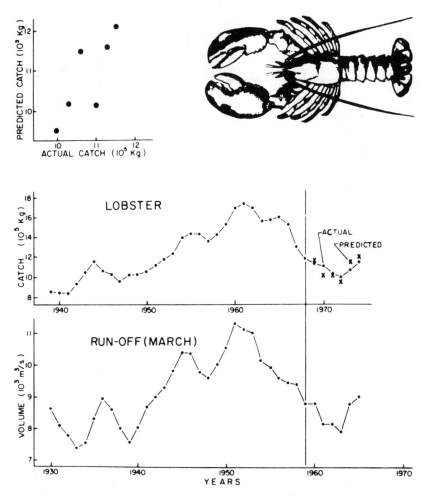

Figure 12.15 Annual regional lobster catch and March discharge of the St. Lawrence River 10 years earlier. The change in the size of the catch reflects the earlier changes in freshwater discharge and accompaning injection of more or less nurient-rich salt water into the fish nursery area (after Sutcliffe 1976).

ical failure of fisheries scientists to get as strict regulations as they would prefer is not clear (see McHugh 1966, 1984).

Whatever the management rationale, or lack thereof, it is clear that fish yields per unit of fossil energy used have declined a great deal (e.g. Fig. 12.12). Meanwhile most of the world's fisheries are becoming relentlessly industrialized. This probably should be the most important component of fisheries analysis but it seems to have escaped the attention of most analysts.

12.4   THE NEW CHALLENGE TO THE FISH MANAGER

Given the partial or complete failure of many traditional fisheries management schemes, such as the unmodified Ricker analysis, the difficulties in applying theoretical population methodology to successful fisheries management, and the difficulty of predicting the physical factors that may influence year-class success, what options are available for management? Although it is impossible to give a simple prescription, there are a number of promising approaches that can be used, with caution, for various fisheries. These approaches may be complimentary or occasionally contradictory to standard population concepts, but one important thing is to use, as much as possible, data from the fishery itself to help determine the best approach.

The first approach, already mentioned, is the use of the Schaefer curve approach (e.g. Fig. 12.14) to examine the impact of effort on catch and to help determine what level of regulation would be optimal for whatever economic, social or environmental goals are deemed most desirable. This approach can work only for well-developed fisheries that have both a relatively lengthy data record, including information from periods of very different fishing intensity, and "well-behaved" fish, that is fish that plot relatively nicely on the axis given in Figure 12.14 (but see caveats in Roff and Fairbairn 1980). In addition to providing means for achieving standard management objectives (e.g. determining maximum sustained yield) this approach also is useful for determining fishing strategies relative to energy criteria. Since the energy use and level of effort are normally closely related, point b on Fig. 12.13 would be the maximum fish return per unit fossil energy investment, and point d would be the point of maximum yield. Clearly fishing at point d would be a wasteful use of energy—for as many fish could be caught at about one third the energy investment at point b. Unfortunately that appears to happen fairly often.

A second approach is to replace the standard "stock-recruitment" approach with a "larval fish-recruitment" approach (Laurence 1981). This approach recognizes that environmental conditions that determine survival of small fish are more important than stock abundance for estimating the number of fish that can be fished for, and substitutes a program of estimating larval or juvenile fish abundance directly for one of estimating abundance of spawning stock. This method is used routinely to predict and manage George's Bank (New England) cod and haddock but is not used, to our knowledge, for any estuarine species yet. At present it is too early to know whether this approach will work in general although it has shown some success for, for example, predicting the year-class strength of California sardines (Lasker 1975, 1978).

A third modern approach to prediction that has management implications is based on a concept originally suggested by Hjort (1916) and recently developed in some detail by Sutcliffe and his associates (Sutcliffe 1972, 1973, Sutcliffe et al. 1976). This approach is based on an assessment of the year to year functioning of the entire ecosystem rather than on population characteristics alone and has been introduced earlier in this chapter. Sutcliff's hypothesis is that periods of heavy freshwater discharge into the Gulf of St. Laurence estuary should be associated with higher inputs of nutrients (both from the land-derived drainage and in river-driven "inwelling" of deeper salt waters to the estuarine nursery regions—resulting in high levels of survival for the young of various species. In fact there has been a very strong correlation between river discharge and both fish catch and Sutcliffe's prediction of fish catch, based on earlier year's river discharge (as in Fig. 12.15). Similarly, Lara-Dominguez and Yáñez-Arancibia (1986) showed that survival and recruitment of three sea catfish species in Terminos Lagoon, Mexico, were correlated with salinity, temperature, turbidity, and river discharge, so that it was possible to predict future population levels and suggest appropriate levels of fishing.

Just as the year-to-year functioning of an ecosystem may determine a specific fishery over time, the status of the habitat may determine fishery levels from place to place. As demonstrated earlier in this chapter (Section 12.1), the area of intertidal wetlands seems to be important in supporting fisheries. Therefore, another management approach is to protect habitat. Many laws have been passed to protect wetlands based, in part, on the idea that they were important to fisheries.

Another example of the use of a systems approach for successfully managing an estuarine-related fish stock is given in LeBrasseur et al. (1979) for sockeye salmon originating from Great Central Lake, Vancouver Island, British Columbia. This is a particularly interesting case because Canadian salmon have been intensively managed according to population concepts for decades in such a way as should increase the catch, while in fact the catch has been decreasing.

Sockeye salmon spawn in small streams running into lakes, or occasionally along lake shores, in the fall. The young emerge from the spawning bed the next spring and move more or less immediately into the open lake, where they spend about a year feeding on zooplankton. The following spring they migrate down rivers to estuaries and eventually to the sea, where they undergo extensive migrations (see Fig. 10.17 and Royce 1968).

LeBrasseur and his colleagues knew that, in general, the larger the salmon were when they went to sea the higher the probability they would return to spawn several years later, and that in general the lakes where they grew up were deficient in the element phosphorus, the lack of which decreased the production of the phytoplankton in the lake and hence the growth of the salmon. Some investigators thought that part of this phosphorus deficiency was due to the fishing pressure on the adult sockeye salmon—that although (according to stock-recruitment models) enough fish escaped the fishery to produced a suitable number of spawning adults the large catch deprived the lake of a large part of one very important source of phosphorus—the dead bodies of spawned out adults. In other words, the fish themselves brought phosphorus (in their bones) "uphill" from the sea. LeBrassuer et al. (1979) suggested that this "missing" phosphorus could be resupplied by adding commercial phosphorus to the lake, and such an experiment was undertaken in Great Central Lake. The results have been extremely encouraging, for the commercial catch has increased from about 50,000 to about 245,000 fish per year, even while allowing more spawners to escape the fishery. The economic return on investment was about 2.8 to 1, even though a large portion of that budget went into the salaries of scientists. It is clear, however, that about 200,000 2-3 kg salmon, worth at that time about \$4/kg (\$2,000,000 worth of salmon) could be produced each year for less than \$30,000 worth of fertilizer. Presumably the energy return on investment would show a similar 100 to 1 return on investment, although the energy costs of catching the fish (which are not large, as they swim right into a net at the river mouth) would have to be included. In this case a systems approach that used information about the interaction of fish and their environment was more successful than the population approach for managing salmon, for not only had it increased the catch but it had also increased the stock. All such approaches require careful thought and experimentation, however, for as other lakes were fertilized in an attempt to duplicate the success of the Great Central Lake experiment at least one of the lakes produced only millions of commercially useless sculpins and few additional salmon. But other lakes were successfully fertilized and it is hoped that this approach will be able to reverse the long term downward trend of salmon for at least some salmon stocks. Fertilization also has been attempted in estuaries with positive, but rather expensive results.

A fourth approach, one that can be combined with others, is the use of what has come to be known as "adaptive management" (Holling 1978). The term is defined somewhat vaguely on purpose, but refers to a general set of procedures for dealing with environmental uncertainty by updating decision making as increased information becomes available about the resource itself, since it is the most recent information that is most useful in understanding the resource. An example of the use of this idea is in the setting of fishing seasons. Instead of making fixed decisions about the length of a salmon fishing season, as is traditionally the case, a deliberate flexibility is built in. If more fish come in than expected from predictive formulae (such as Ricker analyses), a larger catch is allowed. If, on the other hand, the run is much smaller than anticipated, the fishing season can be made more restrictive. Modern communications systems and computers makes this relatively easy. This approach has the advantage of utilizing/protecting the resource much better, but has the disadvantage of being difficult for fishermen, since it is difficult to plan.

It is still too early to tell whether any or all of the possibilities described above will work generally or even for a given specific fishery. At a minimum most of these procedures share with the Ricker-type analysis the basic virtue of at least giving some kind of good excuse to avoid overfishing—which all too often has been ecologically and economically disastrous. In the meantime we have learned from the failures of other types of analyses to be flexible and not be too closely tied to theories that may or may not hold for the species, or ecosystem, or time period that we are managing.

Another difficult problem is that there is not presently a well-developed and empirically tested body of theory relating to how one might optimize the catch from a fishery with a widely varied recruitment. If, for example, we can predict the strength of a year-class either from the abundance of larval fish or from environmental factors (e.g. Figs. 12.2 to 12.10) we still do not know whether it is in our best interest to fish the strong year-class especially hard (since there are many, thus perhaps a surplus) or not as hard (since the abundance of fish might contribute more effectively to building up future stocks). Even if we could decide, there would be sociological problems with implementing whatever was decided because fishermen do not like to have their boats sitting idly at the dock in the off-years. It is possible that a very complicated management scheme might be devised that would trade off fishing for one species versus another, depending upon the abundance or lack of abundance of each species, so that the fishermen always had something to fish for.

12.4.1   The Remaining Social Problem

Unfortunately, even if we arrive at a more predictive science in fisheries owing to increasingly sophisticated knowledge of the relations of stock, environment, fisheries, effort, and catch, it is still difficult both to decide what level is optimal for fishing and, especially, to implement whatever regulatory conclusions might be reached. If, for example, a fishery shows a reliable and consistent Schaefer relation (Fig. 12.14) there is not a consistent view as to whether the fishery should be managed for maximum sustained yield, for maximum economic return on investment, or for highest return on energy (or dollars) invested. Some economists have even suggested that we catch all the fish right away and take the proceeds and invest them (Clark 1976, 1985). Few ecologists would agree with that idea. From our perspective it seems clearly desirable to manage for the left hand side of Fig. 12.14*b*; at least compared to the right hand side of Fig. 12.14*b* we would be catching the same number of fish with only (roughly) one quarter the energy invested and, if nothing else, fish might become cheaper although that in turn would create the confusing situation of increasing the demand! From the perspective of an individual fisherman, however, it would be very undesirable to be shut out of one's means for a livelihood, and it might be undesirable for society as a whole to have to either provide unemployment compensation, suffer the consequences of failing to provide that compensation, or even employing that worker in some other activity that might be even more fuel-intensive while providing, again, little or no social benefit. One possible solution is to deliberately decrease the capital and fuel used by fishermen—in other words to deliberately make fishermen less efficient, such as has been done for the oyster fishery in upper Chesapeake Bay. This would increase the labor used per fish while decreasing the fuel used per fish, presumably a desirable social objective— but it is extremely difficult to convince fishermen that they should become less efficient. However, we believe that it is likely that there will be less fuel available in the future and this will certainly affect fisheries (Hall et al, 1986).

In conclusion, it seems obvious that there will not be one simple answer to the problems that plague the fishing industry, and that will increasingly plague the industry as the price of fuel goes up in future decades. But good flexible managment that is not tied to outmoded theory will be very useful. In addition we are hopeful that the merging of ecosystem level concepts (such as the factors that produce strong year-classes), population concepts (such as stock-recruitment relations), and energy analysis will give us a stronger basis to make management decisions than we have had in the past. But probably we will never be able to eliminate the ambiguities and conflicts of differing social objectives.

REFERENCE

Bahr, L., J.W. Day, and J. Stone, 1982. Energy cost-accounting of Louisiana fishery production. Estuaries, 5: 209–215.

Baranov, F.I., 1918. On the question of the biological basis of fisheries. Nauchn. Issled. Ikhtiologicheskii Inst., Izv., 1(1):81–128.

Beverton, R. and S. Holt, 1957. On the dynamics of exploited fish populations. Fishery Invest. (London) Serv., 2(19): 1–533.

Boesch, D. and R. Turner, 1984. Dependence of fishery species on salt marshes: The role of food and refuge. Estuaries, 7: 460–468.

Borisov, P.G., 1960. Fisheries Research in Russia. A Historical Survey. U.S. Dept. of Commerce, Office of Technical Services, Washington, D.C.

Brown, S. and A.E. Lugo, 1981. Management and Status of U.S. Commercial Marine Fisheries. Council on Environmental Quality, Washington, D.C.

Chapman, C. R., 1966. The Texas basins project. In R. Smith, A. Swartz, and W. Massmann (Eds.), Symposium on Estuarine Fisheries. Am. Fish. Society Spec. Publ. No. 3: 83–92.

Chittenden, M. E. and J. D. McEachran, 1976. Compositon, ecology and dynamics of demersal fish communities in the Northwestern Gulf of Mexico. Texas A & M University Press, Sea Grant Publ. 76(208): 1–104.

Clark, C., 1976. Mathematical Bioeconomics: The Optimal Management of Renewable Resources. Wiley-Interscience, New York.

Clark, C., 1985. Bioeconomic Modeling and Fisheries Management. Wiley Interscience, New York.

Cushing, D., 1975. Marine Ecology and Fisheries. Cambridge University Press, Cambridge, 278 pp.

Darnell, R. M. and T. M. Soniatt, 1979. The estuary/continental shelf as an interactive system. In R. J. Livingston (Ed.), Ecological Precesses in Coastal and Marine Systems. Plenum Press, New York, pp. 489–525.

Darnell, R. M., W. Pequegnat, B. Jane, F. Benson, and R. Defenbaugh, 1976. Impacts of construction activities on wetlands of the United States. Environmental Protection Agency, Environ. Res. Laboratory, Office of Research and Development, Corvallis, Oregon, Report EPA-600/3-76045.

Day, J.W., C. Hopkinson, and W. Conner, 1982. An analysis of environmental factors regulating community metabolism and fisheries production in a Louisiana estuary. In V. Kennedy (Ed.), Estuarine Comparisons. Academic Press, New York, pp. 121–136.

Deegan, L., J.W. Day, J. Gosselink, A. Yáñez-Arancibia, G. Soberón-Chávez, and P.

Sánchez-Gil, 1986. Relationships among physical characteristics, vegetation distribution, and fisheries yield in Gulf of Mexico estuaries. In D. Wolff (Ed.), Estuarine Variability. Academic Press, New York, pp. 83-100.

Doubleday, W. and D. Rivard (Eds.), 1981. Bottom Trawls Surveys. Can. Spec. Publ. Fish. Aquat. Sci., 58: 1-273.

Gunter, G., 1967. Some relationships of estuaries to the fisheries of the Gulf of Mexico. In G. H. Lauff (Ed.), Estuaries. Am. Assoc. Adv. Sci. Spec. Publ., 83: 621-638.

Gunter, G., 1969. Fisheries in coastal lagoons. In A. Ayala-Castañares and F. B. Phleger (Eds.), Coastal Lagoons, a Symposium. UNAM-UNESCO. Editorial Universitaria, Mexico D.F., pp. 663-670.

Hall, C., 1972. Migration and metabolism in a temperate stream ecosystem. Ecology, 53: 585-604.

Hall, C., 1988. An assesment of several of the historically most influential theoretical models used in ecology and of the data provided in their support. Ecological Modelling, 43:5-31.

Hall, C., C. Cleveland, and R. Kaufmann, 1986. Fisheries. In Energy and Resource Quality: The Ecology of the Economic Process. Wiley, New York, pp. 437-459.

Hennemuth, R.C., J.E. Palmer, and B.E. Brown, 1980. A statistical description of recruitment in eighteen selected fish stocks. Norw. Atl. Fish. Sci., 1:101-111.

Herrgesell, P., D. Kohlhorst, L. Miller, and D. Stevens, 1981. Effects of freshwater flow on fishery resources in the Sacramento-San Joquin estuary. In R. Cross and D. Williams (Eds.), Proceedings of the National Symposium on Freshwater Inflow to Estuaries. USFWS, Washington DC. Publ. No. FWS/OBS-81/04, pp. 71-108.

Hjort, J., 1916. Fluctuation in the great fisheries of Northern Europe viewed in the light of biological research. Rapp. P.-V. COns. Int. Explor. Mer., 20:1-228.

Holling, C.S., 1978. Adaptive Environmental Assessment and Management. Wiley, New York.

Johnson, W. E., 1965. On mechanisms of self-regulation of population abundance in *Onchorhynchus nerka,* Mitt. Inernat. Ver. Limnol., 13:66-87.

Lara-Domínguez, A. L. and A. Yáñez-Arancibia, 1986. Recruitment in tropical sea catfishes. In A. Yáñez-Arancibia and D. Pauly (Eds.), Recruitment Processes in Tropical Coastal Demersal Communities. Ocean Science in Relation to Living Resources (OSLR), International Recruitment Project (IREP). IOC-FAO-UNESCO Workshop OSLR/IREP Project. Vol. 44, UNESCO Paris.

Lasker, R., 1975. Field criteria for survival of anchovy larvae: The relation between the onshore chlorophyll layers and successful feeding. Fish. Bull., 71: 453-462.

Lasker, R., 1978. The relation between oceanographic conditions and larval anchovy food in the California current: Identification of factors contributing to recruitment failure. Rapp. P.-V. Réun., Cons. Int. Explor. Mer, 173: 212-230.

Laurence, G.C., 1981. Overview. Modelling—an esoteric or potenially utilitarian approach to understanding larval fish dynamics. Rapp. P.-V. Reun. Cons. Int. Explor. Mer., 178:3-6.

Laurence, G.C. and C.A. Rogers, 1976. Effects of temperature and salinity on comparative embryo development and mortality of Atlantic cod (*Gadus morhau* L.) and haddock (*Melanogrammus aeglefinus* L.). J. Cons. Int. Explor. Mer., 36:220-228.

LeBrasseur, R., C. D. McAllister, and T. Parson, 1979. Addition of nutrients to a lake leads to greatly increased catch of salmon. Environ. Conserv., 6: 187-190.

Lindall, W. N. and C. H. Saloman, 1977. Alteration and destruction of estuaries affecting fishery resources of the Gulf of Mexico. Mar. Fish. Rev., 39: 1-7.

Longhurst, A. and D. Pauly, 1987. Ecology of Tropical Oceans. Academic Press, New York, 408 pp.

Manzer, J.I., 1964. Preliminary observations on the vertical distribution of Pacific salmon (genus *Oncorrhynchus*) in the Gulf of Alaska. J. Fish Res. Bd. Can., 21(5):891-903.

McHugh, J. L., 1966. Management of estuarine fisheries. In R. F. Smith, A. M. Swartz, and W. H. Massmann (Eds.), A Symposium on Estuarine Fisheries. Am. Fish. Soc. Spec. Publ. No. 3: 133-154.

McHugh, J. L., 1976. Effects of climatic change on fisheries. National Climate Program Act. New York Sea Grant Institute, pp. 3-8.

McHugh, J. L., 1977a. Estuarine fisheries: Are they doomed? In M. L. Wiley (Ed.), Estuarine Processes, Uses, Stress and Adaptation to the Estuary. Academic Press, New York, Vol 1, pp. 15-28.

McHugh, J. L., 1977b. Fisheries and fishery resource of New York Bight. NOAA Tech. Rept. NMFS, 401: 1-50.

McHugh, J. L., 1977c. Limiting factors affecting commercial fisheries in the middle Atlantic estuarine area. Proc. Estuarine Pollution Control Assessment Conference. U.S. Environ. Protection Agency Washington, D C. New York Sea Grant Institute, 1: 149-169.

McHugh, J. L., 1980. Coastal fisheries. In R.T. Lackey and L.A. Nielsen (Eds.), Fisheries Management. Blackwell Scientific Publ., Oxford, pp. 323-346.

McHugh, J. L., 1984. Fishery Management. Lecture Notes on Coastal and Estuarine Studies. Springer Verlag, Berlin, 207 pp.

Mercer, M. (Ed.), 1982. Multispecies approaches to fishery management advice. Can. Spec. Publ. Fish. Aquat. Sci., 59: 1-169.

Moore, D., H. A. Brusher, and L. Trent, 1970. Relative abundance, seasonal distribution, and species composition of demersal fishes off Louisiana and Texas, 1962-1964. Contr. Mar. Sci., 15: 45-70.

Nielsen, L.A., 1976. The evolution of fisheries management philosophy. Mar. Fish. Rev., 38:15-23.

Nixon, S. W., 1980. Between coastal marshes and coastal waters—a review of twenty years of speculation and research on the role of salt marshes in estuarine productivity and water chemistry. In P. Hamilton and K. Macdonald (Eds.), Estuarine and Wetland Processes. Plenum Press, New York, pp. 437-525.

Nixon, S. W., 1982. Nutrient dynamics, primary productivity, and fisheries yields of lagoons. In P. Lasserre and H. Postma (Eds.) , Oceanologica Acta. Spec. Vol. 5 :357-371

Pauly, D. and G. Murphy (Eds.), 1982. Theory and Management of Tropical Fisheries. ICLARM Conference Proceeding 9. Manila, Philippines, 360 pp.

Ricker, W. E., 1954. Stock and Recruitment. J. Fish. Res. Board Canada, 11:559-623.

Ricker, W. E., 1975. Composition and Interpretation of Biological Statistics of Fish Populations. Bull. Fish. Res. Board Canada, Spec. Vol. 191:1-382.

Roff, D.A. and D.J. Fairbairn, 1980. An evaluation of Gulland's method for fitting the Schaefer model. Can. J. Fish. Aq. Sci., 37:1229–1235.

Royce, W.F., L. Smith, and A.C. Hartt, 1968. Models of oceanic migration of Pacific salmon and comments on guidance mechanisms. USFWS Fish Bull. 66(3):441–462.

Sáchez-Gil, P., A. Yáñez-Arancibia, and F. Amezcua Linares, 1981. Diversity, distribution and abundance of species and populations of demersal fishes in the Campeche Sound (Summer 1978). An. Inst. Cienc. del Mar y Limnol., Univ. Nal Autón. México, 8 (1):209–240.

Schaefer, M.B., 1957a. Fishery dynamics and present status of the Yellowfin Tuna population of the Eastern Tropical Pacific Ocean. Bull. Inter-Am. Trop. Tuna Comm., 2(6):247–285.

Schaefer, M.B., 1957b. A study of the dynamics of the fishery for Yellowfin Tuna in the Eastern Tropical Pacific Ocean. Bull. Inter-Am. Trop. Tuna Comm., 2:245–285.

Schaefer, M., 1961. Report on the investigations of the IATTC for the year 1959. Annu. Rep. Inter.-Am. Trop. Tuna Comm., 1959, pp. 39–156.

Sissenwine, M. P., B. E. Brown, and J. Brennan-Hoskins, 1978. Brief history of the art of fish production models and some applications to fisheries of the Northeastern United States. Center for Ocean Studies (reprint. Proceedings from a workshop Climate and Fisheries).

Smith, I. R. , D. Pauly, and A. Mines, 1983. Small-scale Fisheries of San Miguel Bay, Philippines: Options for Management and Research. ICLARM Technical Report 11. Manila, Philippines, 80 pp.

Smith, R. F., A. H. Swartz, and W. H. Massmann (Eds.), 1966. A Symposium on Estuarine Fisheries. Am. Fish. Soc., Spec. Publ. No. 3:1–154.

Soberón-Chávez, G., and A. Yáñez-Arancibia, 1985. Ecological control of the demersal fishes: Environmental variability of the coastal zone and the influence in the natural production of fishery resources. In A. Yáñez-Arancibia (Ed.), Recursos Pesqueros Potenciales de México: La Pesca Acompañante del Camarón. Progr. Univ. Alimentos; Inst. Cienc. del Mar y Limnol.; Inst. Nal de Pesca. Editorial Universitaria, UNAM, México D. F., pp. 399–486.

Soberón-Chávez, G., A. Yáñez-Arancibia, P. Sánchez-Gil, J.W. Day, and L.A. Deegan, 1986. Relationships between physical/biological characteristics and fishery recruitment in tropical coastal ecosystems. In A. Yáñez-Arancibia and D. Pauly (Eds.), Recruitment Processes in Tropical Coastal Demersal Communities. Ocean Science in Relation to Living Resources (OSLR), International Recruitment Project (IREP). IOC-FAO-UNESCO Workshop OSLR/IREP Project. Vol 44 , UNESCO Paris.

Stone, J. H., J. W. Day, L. M. Bahr, and R. H. Muller, 1978. The impact of possible climatic changes on estuarine ecosystems. In M. L. Wiley (Ed.), Estuarine Interaction. Academic Press, New York, pp. 305–322.

Sutcliffe, W. H., 1972. Some relations of land drainage, nutrients, particulate material, and fish catch in two eastern Canadian bays. J. Fish. Res. Board Canada, 29(4):357–362.

Sutcliffe, W.H., 1973. Correlations between seasonal river discharge and local landings of American lobster (*Homerus americanus*) and Atlantic halibut (*Hippolossus hippoglossus*) in the Gulf of St. Lawrence. J. Fish. Res. Board. Can., 30(6):856–859.

Sutcliffe, W.H., 1976. Fish production and its relationship to climate and oceanographic variation. In M.P. Latremouille (Ed.), Biennial Review, 1975/76. Bedford Institute of Oceanography, Dartmouth, Nova Scotia, Canada, p. 100.

Tait, R.V., 1968. Elements of Marine Ecology. Plenum Press, New York.

Turner, R. E., 1977. Intertidal vegetation and commercial yields of Penaeid shrimps. Trans. Am. Fish. Soc., 106(5):411-416.

Turner, R. E., 1979. Louisiana's coastal fisheries and changing environmental conditions. In J.W. Day, D. Culley, R.E. Turner, and A. Munphrey (Eds.), Proc. Third Coastal Marsh and Estuary Management Symposium. Louisiana State University, Division of Continuing Education, Baton Rouge La., pp. 363-372.

Valiela, I., 1984. Marine Ecological Processes. Springer Verlag, New York, 548 pp.

Walme, P. R. , 1972. The importance of estuaries to commercial fisheries. In R. S. K. Barnes and J. Green (Eds.), The Estuarine Environment. Applied Science Publ., London, pp. 107-118.

Yáñez-Arancibia, A. and A. Aguirre-León, 1988. Fisheries in the Terminos Lagoon region. In A. Yáñez-Arancibia and J.W. Day (Eds.) Ecology of Coastal Ecosystems in the Southern Gulf of Mexico: The Terminos Lagoon Region. Inst. Cienc. del Mar y Limnol. UNAM, Coast. Ecol. Inst. LSU. Editorial Universitaria, México D. F., pp. 431-452.

Yáñez-Arancibia, A. and D. Pauly (Eds.), 1986. Recruitment Processes in Tropical Coastal Demersal Communities. Proc. IOC-FAO-UNESCO Workshop. OSLR/IREP Project, UNESCO Paris, Vol 44, 350 pp.

Yáñez-Arancibia, A. and P. Sánchez-Gil, 1986. The Demersal Fishes of the Southern Gulf of Mexico Shelf. 1. Environmental Characterization, Ecology, and Evaluation of Species, Populations and Communities. Inst. Cienc. del Mar y Limnol. Univ. Nal. Autón. México, Spec. Publ. 9:1-230.

Yáñez-Arancibia, A. and P. Sánchez-Gil, 1988. Ecología de los Recursos Demersales Marinos: Fundamentos en Costas Tropicales. Editorial AGT, México D. F., 230 pp.

Yáñez-Arancibia, A., P. Sánchez-Gil, M. Tapia García, and M. C. García-Abad, 1985a. Ecology, community structure, and evaluation of tropical demersal fishes in the southern Gulf of Mexico. Cahiers Biol. Mar, 26 (2):137-163.

Yáñez-Arancibia, A., G. Soberón-Chavez, and P. Sánchez-Gil, 1985b. Ecology of control mechanisms of natural fish production in the coastal zone. In A. Yáñez-Arancibia (Ed.), Fish Community Ecology in Estuaries and Coastal Lagoons: Towards an Ecosystem Integration. Editorial Universitaria, UNAM-PUALICML, Mexico D. F., pp. 571-594.

OFFPRINTS FROM: ESTUARINE ECOLOGY
Edited by John W. Day Jr., Charles A. S. Hall., Dr. W. Michael Kemp, and Alejandro Yáñez-Arancibia
Copyright © 1989 by John Wiley & Sons, Inc.

▬ 13

Human Impact in Estuaries

Humans have lived in or near and prospered from estuaries for tens of thousands of years. Many "cradles of civilizations" were located near estuaries of the Tigris-Euphrates, Nile, Indus, Usumacinta and Yangtze Rivers. Initially, the abundance of food invited human settlements. Later, river mouths became important sites for commerce and today many of the world's largest cities border major estuarine systems, including New York, London, Cairo, Calcutta, and Shanghai. From the beginning, human activities resulted in alterations in the natural state of estuaries. Early examples include construction of mounds for homesites and harvest of fish and shellfish. Human impacts have continued through the centuries, so that today there are almost no estuarine systems completely in their natural state. The rate and degree of human impact have accelerated over the past two centuries as a result of increasing population, industrial growth, and the development of new technologies such as modern dredges and powerful pumps. Because the effects of different kinds of impacts can build slowly over time and can be synergistic, W. E. Odum (1970) called the effects of human activity the "insidious alteration of the estuarine environment." In a synthesis of coastal ecological systems of the United States (H. T. Odum et al. 1974), the effects of a number of specific types of impacts are discussed from the perspective of new energy inputs altering older natural energy flows.

In this chapter we discuss specific ways that human activities affect estuarine ecosystems. Over the past several decades there has been a great deal of scientific study of human impacts in estuaries. A complete review of this literature would take considerably more space than this entire volume. In this chapter, therefore, we want to do only a few things. First we present a generic classification scheme which organizes impacts into a few major types. We then give examples of each type of impact for a number of different estuarine systems. In doing so we accomplish two things: we demonstrate the responses to different kinds of impacts and we show how human impacts affect different aspects of the structure and function of estuarine ecosystems such as primary production, nutrient cycling, and community structure. A number of texts have dealt with various aspects of human impacts in coastal systems and the reader may want to consult these for more detailed treatments (Olson and Burgess 1967, H.T. Odum et al. 1974, Hall and Day 1977, Gerlach 1981, Neilson and Cronin 1981).

13.1   A CLASSIFICATION OF HUMAN IMPACTS IN ESTUARIES

We identify four general categories of impacts on estuarine ecosystems: enrichment with excessive levels of organic material, inorganic nutrients, or heat; physical alterations; introduction of toxic materials; and direct changes in community structure through harvest or introduction of exotic species. Table 13.1 outlines this classification and gives examples of each type of impact.

Enrichment is the addition of generally naturally occurring substances or heat at levels that are not toxic but that lead to changes in the structure and metabolism of the ecosystem. Eutrophication is a type of enrichment which occurs as a result of the addition of high levels of inorganic nutrients. The addition of excess heat is generally called thermal pollution or calefaction. *Physical alterations* are direct changes in the physical structure or dynamics of an estuary. Physical alterations are mainly of two related types: hydrologic changes and reclamation. In this chapter we define hydrologic changes as those that alter water movement, but not to the extent that the system is completely destroyed (i.e., the system retains a wetland or estuarine character). Reclamation is the conversion of an estuarine system to dry land by drainage and/or filling. As it implies, the introduction of *toxic materials* is the introduction of materials that are toxic to organisms, either acutely or chronically. Toxins can be naturally occurring materials such as heavy metals (which are in concentrations much higher than that which naturally occurs) or exotic organic compounds such as pesticides or byproducts of industrial activity. *Harvest or introduction of exotic species* leads to direct changes in species composition. These usually lead to changes in the relative abundance of different species, but if harvest pressure is great enough for a sustained period, species may be driven to extinction in a local area. In the remaining sections of this chapter, each of these types of impacts is discussed in more detail and several examples of each are given to illustrate the kinds changes that can occur.

13.2   ENRICHMENT

Progressive enrichment of estuarine waters with inorganic nutrients, organic matter, or heat leads to changes in the structure and processes of estuarine ecosystems.

TABLE 13.1 Classification of Human Impacts on Coastal Ecosystems

Impact Type	Examples
Physical Changes	
Hydrologic changes	
Channelization of streams, canals for oil exploration, dredging, drainage, and navigation	Petroleum production in Mississippi Delta, Harbor dredging
Impoundments	
Reclamation	Polders in the Netherlands
Enrichment	
Eutrophication	Algal blooms resulting from agricultural runoff
Organic enrichment	Fish processing wastes
Thermal pollution	Power plants
Toxins	
Heavy metals, pesticides, and other exotic organics	DDT, PCB's, Mercury
Direct Changes in Species Composition	
Harvest and overharvest	Overfishing
Introduction of exotic species	Striped bass on US west coast, nutria in Louisiana

13.2.1 Nutrient Enrichment and Eutrophication

Nutrient enrichment can lead to excessive algal growth, increased metabolism, and changes in community structure, a condition known as eutrophication. There have been many studies of eutrophication in coastal waters (a number of examples are cited in Neilson and Cronin 1981). Jaworski (1981) discusses the sources of nutrients and the scale of eutrophication problems in estuaries. The following examples will serve to illustrate the effects of excessive nutrient enrichment in estuaries.

Information available for the past several decades shows the effect of increasing nutrient levels in upper Chesapeake Bay. During this time concentrations of both nitrate and phosphorus have increased dramatically in the Patuxent River, a tributary of the bay (Fig. 13.1*a* and *b*), leading to increased phytoplankton chlorophyll *a* (Fig. 13.1*c*). The decrease in dissolved oxygen in bottom waters (Fig. 13.1*d*) is almost certainly the result of the decomposition of both sinking algal cells and organic matter from sewage inputs and other sources. Eutrophic conditions, such as exist in the Patuxent River, are common in the tributaries of

HISTORICAL TRENDS IN PATUXENT RIVER

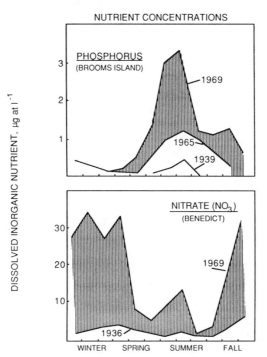

Figure 13.1 Historical trends for a number of parameters in the Patuxent River demonstrating the progressive eutrophication and decline in oxygen in bottom waters, (a) phorphorus and (b) nitrate (from Mihursky and Boynton 1978), (c) chlorophyll a at Benedict, and (d) bottom water dissolved oxygen levels in June and August (from Heinle et al. 1980).

Chesapeake Bay. Widespread anoxic bottom waters also occur in the Baltic and have been attributed to similar causes (Jansson and Wulff 1977).

A number of studies have documented the degree and causes of eutrophication in Barataria Basin, Louisiana. Chlorophyll *a* levels in the lakes of the midbasin during May 1977 indicate the level of eutrophication (Fig. 13.2). Chlorophyll levels in Lake Cataouatche are much higher than in Lake Salvador or Little Lake, due to upland runoff from the New Orleans area. Productivity in Lake Cataouatche is over twice as high as Lake Salvador (Hopkinson and Day 1979). Under natural conditions, runoff from the natural levee uplands along the Mississippi River flowed through wetlands before entering water bodies. Such overland flow has been shown to effectively cleanse upland runoff (Kemp and Day 1984). Now, however, canals carry the runoff directly to water bodies, leading to eutrophication. This condition is common in the basin and Gael and Hopkinson (1979) showed that the water quality of different subwatersheds within the basin

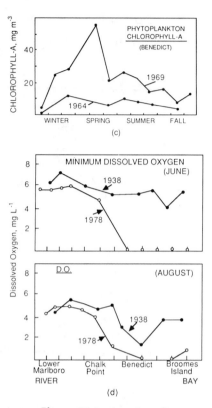

Figure 13.1   (continued)

was correlated with the density of artificial drainage canals. Areas with more artificial canals had poorer water quality. Eutrophic conditions similar to those in the Barataria Basin are widespread in estuarine waters of the Mississippi Delta. In North Carolina, Kuenzler and Craig (1986) reported similar causes for eutrophication in the Chowan River estuary, where increasing fertilizer runoff and wetland drainge were related to decreased water quality.

Since the 1960s, there has been a major loss of submerged aquatic vegetation (SAV) in Chesapeake Bay (Bayley et al. 1978), perhaps linked to the conditions described above. Because it is widely recognized that SAV plays an important role in the ecology of coastal waters, a considerable amount of study has focused on this problem. A hierarchial research design consisting of field research and experiments in ponds, microcosms, and bioassay tanks was used to study the problem (Kemp et al. 1980, 1983, Twilley et al. 1985, Fig. 13.3). Three factors were emphasized in the study: runoff of agricultural herbicides, erosional inputs of fine-grained sediments, and nutrient enrichment and associated algal growth. They found that normal herbicide concentrations (< 5 ppb) had little measurable impact on plants. Reduced light levels caused by a combination of sus-

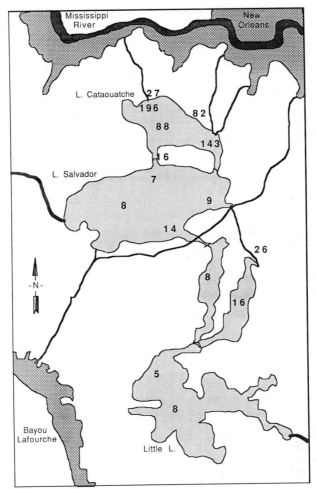

Figure 13.2 Chlorophyll a concentration in the waters of the mid Barataria Basin, Louisiana in May 1977 in milligrams per cubic meter. Lake Cataouatche, which receives runoff from the New Orleans area, is eutrophic (from Hopkinson and Day 1979). White areas are wetlands and cross-hatched areas are uplands.

pended sediments, phytoplankton chlorophyll *a*, and epiphytic growth lead to a decline in SAV biomass (Fig. 13.4*a*) The results of the different experiments were synthesized into an ecosystem model which indicated that the relative importance of the three factors to SAV decline was nutrients > sediments > herbicides (Fig. 13.4*b*). It was concluded that reductions of sediment erosion and nutrient inputs would be necessary if the SAV decline were to be reversed. In a case similar to that in Chesapeake Bay, declines in SAV in Cockburn Bay, Aus-

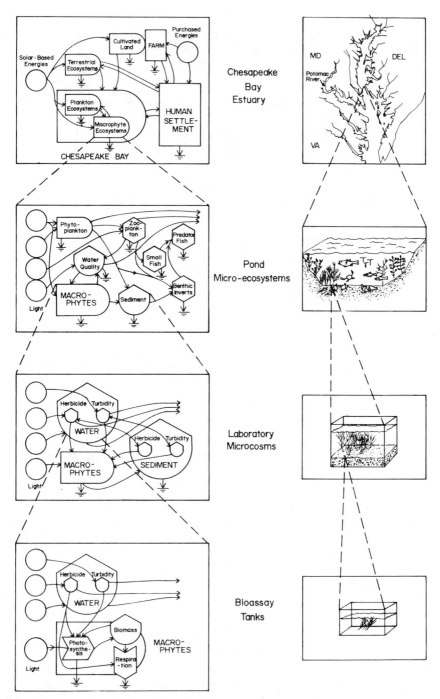

Figure 13.3 Conceptual scheme illustrating the hierarchical design of research on submerged aquatic vegetation and associated ecosystems of Chesapeake Bay. The illustrations on the right show various scales of research focus, and model diagrams on the left represent principal parts and processes of systems that correspond with the hierarchical level being studied (from Kemp et al. 1980).

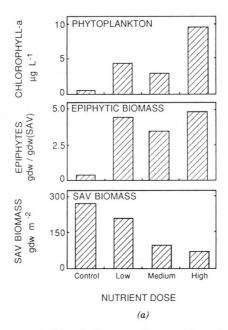

Figure 13.4a Summary of phytoplankton stocks (as chlorophyll a), weight of epiphytic material, and submerged aquatic vegetation biomass in August 1981, for experimental ponds treated with four levels of nutrient enrichment after 8 weeks (from Kemp et al. 1983).

tralia, were attributed to increased nutrient levels and industrial pollution (Cambridge and McComb 1984).

13.2.2   Addition of Excessive Levels of Organic Matter

The enrichment of coastal waters with excessive levels of organic matter results from a variety of different sources and leads to a number of changes (Weiss and Wilkes 1974). The source of high levels of organic matter is normally sewage waste water, but high levels can also result from such things as seafood processing wastes and industrial effluents. These wastes lead to bacterial contamination and lowered dissolved oxygen concentrations. There are often very large changes in community structure and metabolism that result. Inorganic nutrients from mineralization of the organic matter or which are a part of the wastes can stimulate dense algal blooms and lead to another source of excessive organic matter. Therefore, the impacts of excessive nutrients and organic matter are often similar.

One of the earliest, and now classic, examples of organic enrichment in a coastal system occurred in the Great South Bay complex, New York (Ryther 1954, Barlow et al. 1963, Weiss and Wilkes 1974). Beginning around 1940 there

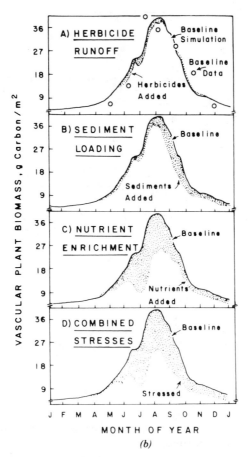

Figure 13.4b Results of numerical simulations of submerged vascular plant biomass over an annual cycle under conditions of (A) maximum herbicide runoff, (B) doubled sediment loading, (C) doubled nutrient enrichment, and (D) a combination of these three stresses. In all cases the upper line (shown for comparative purposes) represents the baseline conditions which are compared to means of field observations in the upper panel (from Kemp et al. 1983).

was a decline in oyster and fish production from the bay, which coincided with the expansion of duck farms along the tributaries of the bay. It was found that the duck wastes fertilized the water and resulted in dense algal blooms of the very small algae *Nanochloris* sp. and *Stichococcus* sp. that reached densities of greater than 10^6 organisms per ml. These alage differed greatly from the normal phytoplankton of the area. The oyster industry declined because oysters need to consume a mixed algal population. Although the oysters fed on the small forms, they were an incomplete food source, and the oysters declined.

When an area is enriched with organic matter, the structure of the benthic community can change dramatically. Organisms that burrow into anaerobic sediments have to be able to oxygenate their burrows by pumping oxygenated water through. With increasing organic loading of an area, from sewage pollution for example, the burrowing organisms are eliminated as the anaerobic zone moves closer to the sediment surface. In grossly polluted areas only worms such as *Capitella* can survive, and they may do very well by consuming organic matter at the sediment surface (Mann 1982). Figure 13.5 illustrates this phenomenon for Loch Eil in Scotland.

13.2.3 Thermal Additions

One of the most commonly described impacts of power generation is most often called thermal pollution, although calefaction or thermal loading may be more appropriate (Hall et al. 1978). Under certain conditions, thermal effluent can selectively eliminate large segments of a healthy aquatic ecosystem; however, most often the impacts are less pronounced. Impacts on individuals include interference with physiological processes, behavioral changes, enhancement of disease, and impacts from changing gas solubilities. For example, in winter fishes may become thermally marooned in the warm water around power plants. These fish are then susceptible to the shutdown of the plant. Clark and Brownell (1973) reported a kill of about 100,000–200,000 menhaden from cold shock when a power plant in New Jersey shut down in January 1972.

Thermal additions can also lead to changes on whole aquatic communities and ecosystems. In their review of the subject, Hall et al. (1978) reported that physical, chemical, physiological, and behavorial changes may combine to affect

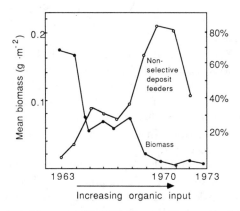

Figure 13.5 Changes in biomass of individual organisms and in the proportion of non-selective deposit-feeders in the benthos of Loch Eil as a result of increasing organic input, 1963–1973 (from Mann 1982, as modified from Pearson and Rosenberg 1978).

entire aquatic systems by changing primary and secondary production, community respiration, species composition, biomass, and nutrient dynamics. For example, *Thalassia testudinum* beds in South Biscayne Bay, Florida, disappeared when exposed to temperatures 5°C above ambient. The changes can come very abruptly, for temperature rises of 2–3°C resulted in increased overall animal biomass, while areas 3–4°C above normal had lower standing crops (Thorhaug et al. 1973). Zeiman (1970) reported that thermal loading lowered productivity of seagrasses and decreased the abundance and diversity of phytoplankton in the same area. From a total systems perspective, tropical and subtropical systems seem to be more susceptible to thermal increases because many organisms are living near to their thermal maximum. Zieman and Wood (1975) proposed that temperatures consistently above 30–32°C are likely to cause substantial mortality of entire communities in tropical communities.

13.3   PHYSICAL ALTERATIONS

13.3.1   Local Alterations

Physical alterations within coastal systems include such activities as filling and draining of wetlands, construction of deep navigation channels through shallow water bodies, bulkheading, and canal dredging through wetlands. Two major types of impacts resulting from these activities are habitat destruction and hydrologic alteration. For example, canals and deep navigation channels can alter circulation, allow saltwater intrusion, and promote the development of anoxic waters in the bottoms of channels.

One of the major physical alterations of coastal systems is the direct destruction of wetlands. A number of both natural and cultural factors lead to wetland loss (Table 13.2), but in general cultural factors are much more important. Wetlands along the U.S. coast in areas with high population densities have generally suffered the greatest proportional loss (Fig. 13.6), a reflection of the pressure for development in these areas.

The coast of the Netherlands and the Mississippi Delta serve as two examples where human activities have resulted in dramatic regional changes in coastal systems. In the Netherlands the changes have proceeded deliberately to provide protection from the sea and land for urban development and agriculture. In the Mississippi Delta many of the changes have followed as the indirect and cumulative impacts of human activities. In both cases, large areas of coastal ecosystems have been altered and destroyed.

For over 1000 years the Dutch have systematically reclaimed their coastline to provide protection and space for a dense population (Fig. 13.7). Much of the coast once could be considered as an extended estuary of the Rhine River complex. Alterations to this system have proceeded in a number of ways. Practically all coastal marshlands have been converted to polders, which is the Dutch word for a diked and drained area. Initially, diked areas were drained at low tide and

TABLE 13.2 Activities and Processes Causing Wetland Loss[a]

Cultural
  Direct
    Dredging
    Spoil disposal
    Land fill
    Waste disposal
    Impounding and draining (e.g., for agriculture)
    Marsh buggies and other wetland transportation vehicles
  Indirect
    Sediment diversion (e.g., dams, deep channels)
    Hydrologic alterations (e.g., by canals, spoil banks)
    Subsidence due to extraction of groundwater, oil, gas, sulphur, and other
      minerals
Natural
  Subsidence (apparent water level rise)
    Isostatic adjustments (e.g., crustal downwarping or uplift)
    Differential consolidation of sediments due to textural variability
    Consolidation of sediments due to weight of other features (e.g., natural or
      artificial levees, buildings)
    Eustasy
    Droughts
    Hurricanes and other storms
    Erosion
    Biotic effects (e.g., muskrat and goose eat-outs)

[a]From Gosselink and Baumann 1980.

prevented from flooding by gates. With the development of efficient windmills in the 16th century, polders were pumped and reclamation became much more widespread. Before the development of modern fossil-fueled pumps, there were on the order of 10,000 windmills in the Netherlands. Large areas of salt marsh and intertidal mudflats have been reclaimed along the coast of the Wadden Sea. This was done by building enclosures of about 1 ha surrounded by low brush fences in the intertidal zone. The fences had small openings which allowed sediment-laden water to enter the enclosure on the rising tide. The brush fences calmed the water and suspended material settled out and marsh vegetation began to colonize the area. The surface slowly built up to the level of the high tide. At that time, a dike was constructed in front of the area and the reclaimed area was used for agriculture. Such reclamation in the Dutch Wadden Sea has now ceased, but this technique is now being used to create new salt marshes in an effort to partially replace those lost earlier.

    In two instances, embayments or arms of the sea have been diked. In the 1930s the Zuider Sea was separated from the sea by a dike and converted to a freshwater lake, the Ijsselmeer. As would be expected, marine fisheries from the

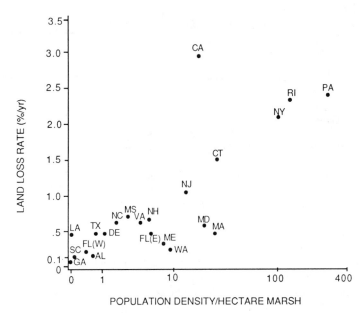

Figure 13.6 Relationship of coastal wetland loss (1954–1974) to population density for coastal counties in the United States (from Gosselink and Baumann 1980).

area declined greatly. Freshwater fisheries have increased, but not to the level that existed for the saltwater species (Table 13.3) Subsequently, several large polders were reclaimed from former Zuider Sea bottoms (see Fig. 13.7).

Two of the mouths of the Rhine River have also been diked (Fig. 13.7). One has been converted to a freshwater lake (Lake Haringvliet, Ferguson and Wolff 1984) and the other to a nontidal brackish lake (Lake Grevelingen, Nienhuis and Huis en 't Veld 1984). Conversion to a freshwater lake obviously destroyed all marine habitat in the former estuary. In addition, the largest area of fresh-water tidal ecosystems in Europe was nearly eliminated. When the Grevelingen estuary was converted to a nontidal brackish lake, there were mass mortalities of benthic organisms due to anoxic conditions resulting from the lack of tidal flushing. The closure also led to major changes in the organic carbon budget of the area (Fig. 13.8). With the closure of the estuary, the single most important source of organic carbon (input from the North Sea) was eliminated. Production by sea grasses increased because of better water clarity, and phytoplankton production has also increased due to increasing eutrophication of the area.

In the Mississippi Delta dramatic changes have taken place, not because of deliberate planning, but because of the lack of it. Nearly 100 km^2 per year of coastal wetlands have disappeared over the past several years as a result of a disasterous interaction of human actions with natural processes. The Mississippi Delta was formed by the successive building of a number of major delta lobes as

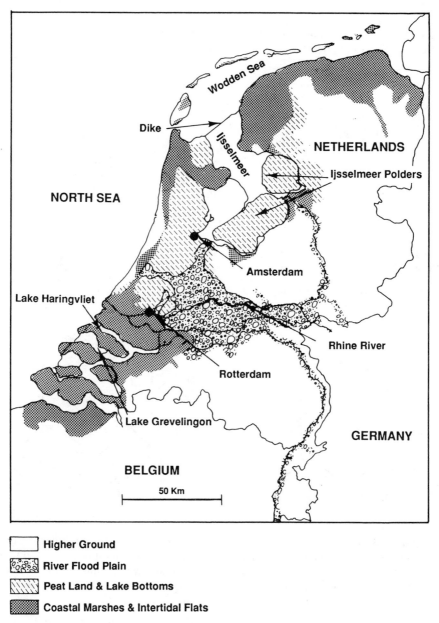

Higher Ground

River Flood Plain

Peat Land & Lake Bottoms

Coastal Marshes & Intertidal Flats

Figure 13.7 Alteration of coastal ecosystems in the Netherlands. Large areas of coastal marshes and intertidal flats have been reclaimed along the Wadden Sea. The former Zuider Sea was separated from the Wadden Sea by a dike and converted into the freshwater Lake Ijssel. Subsequently several large polders were created from the lake. Two arms of the Rhine–Meuse estuary have been significantly altered. The Haringvliet estuary was converted into a freshwater lake and the Grevelingen estuary is now a nontidal brackish lake.

TABLE 13.3   Changes in Fishery Yields from the Zuider Sea Area after Dike Construction Converted the Sea to a Freshwater Lake[a]

	Herring	Anchovy	Flounder	Smelt	Eel	Freshwater Species
1930			3647	1285	838	7
1931		3598	2321	1349	941	8
1932	10,000	378	1273	476	1048	14
1933	12	0	1265	337	2125	11
1934	0	0	1124	447	2688	25
1935	0	0	232	317	1907	32
1936	0	0	48	271	2405	60
1937	0	0	43	130	3595	145
1938	0	0	25	209	2588	243
1939	0	0	27	24	2108	2920
1940	0	0	45	7	3205	1674
1941	0	0	63	73	4563	1782

[a]All figures are in tons per year (from Wolff and Zijlstra 1982).

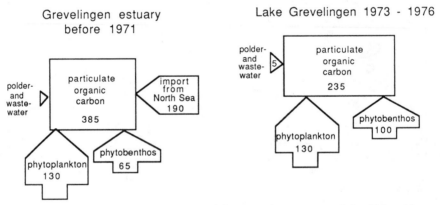

Figure 13.8 Organic carbon budgets of the Grevelingen area of the Rhine–Meuse delta when it was still an estuary with free tidal action and after it was conerted to a nontidal brackish lake. Units are gCm^{-2} yr^{-1} (reprinted with permission from Water Science and Technology, Vol. 16, Nienhuis and Huis en 't Veld, Grevelingen: From an estuary to a saline lake, Copyright 1984, Pergamon Journals, Ltd.).

the river changed course every 500–1000 years (Frazier 1967). The entire deltaic region is subsiding at a rate of about 1 cm per year because of such processes as compaction, consolidation, and dewatering of sediments deposited by the river. Therefore, the deposition of new sediments is critically important in allowing wetlands to maintain surface elevation in this subsiding environment. These sediments come from two sources: the Mississippi River and resuspended bay bottom sediments (Baumann et al. 1984). Historically this occurred both at the mouth of the river and over much of coastal Louisiana by overbank flooding. The riverine sediments are deposited mainly during the spring flood. Resuspended sediments are deposited primarily during high-energy events such as winter frontal passages and tropical storms.

A number of human impacts have altered the natural cycle in the delta. One of the most important is that the river has been leveed (diked) essentially to its mouth. Thus input of riverine sediments has basically ceased for most of the coastal zone. The wetlands themselves have also been altered dramatically. Large areas have been impounded. Most of the earlier impoundments were reclaimed for agriculture, but these projects mostly failed owing to subsidence, soil oxidation, and high rainfall. Most can be identified today as large retangular water bodies in the coastal marshes. Perhaps the most damaging impact in the wetlands has been the construction of over 15,000 km of canals for drainage and navigation, and mainly for petroleum exploration and production (Fig. 13.9). These canals destroy wetlands directly, but cumulatively they have led to changes in regional hydrology. Because they are straight and deep, canals preferentially capture flow and natural channels disappear (Craig et al. 1979, 1980). These canals speed water movement and have allowed salt water to flow into fresher areas, resulting in the death of freshwater wetlands. Finally, the spoil banks that border these canals are barriers to overland sheet flow of water and alter wetland hydrology (Swenson and Turner 1987). Thus the spoil banks impede water exchange, sediment deposition, and movement of nekton. Since sediments resuspended by winds are important for marsh surface accretion, canals with associated spoil banks are an important factor contributing to land loss. This has been demonstrated by a number of studies which show a strong correlation between canal density and land loss (Craig et al. 1979, 1980; Scaife et al. 1983; Deegan et al. 1984; Fig. 13.9). It is clear that unless action is taken to reintroduce riverine sediments and control canal construction, most of the wetlands of the Mississippi Delta will disappear within a century.

13.3.2 Upstream Alterations

Upstream changes in rivers can have pronounced effects on the estuaries into which they discharge. Construction of dams, diversion of fresh water, and groundwater withdrawals lower the amount of fresh water, nutrients, and suspended sediment input. We have documented in a number of places in this book the importance of these inputs to estuarine productivity (see Chapters 2, 4, 10, and 12). Dams also impede or block the movement of migratory organisms, and by changing the timing of water discharge they may interfere with migratory fish life histories that are finely tuned to those discharges. On the other hand, channelization of streams causes more rapid pulses of water to coastal systems. Construction of impoundments on the Mississippi River system has resulted in about a 50% decrease in suspended load (Meade and Parker, 1984), undoubtedly aggravating the land loss problem in the delta while these sediments fill up the upstream reservoirs. Freshwater diversions from the Colorado River in the western United States are causing hypersaline conditions and deterioration of the delta of the river. Because most of the water use occurs in the United States but the coastal problems are felt in Mexico, this issue has been an important point of contention and discussion between the two countries. For the Gordon River near Naples, Florida, Littlejohn (1977) showed that clearing freshwater cypress swamps and increasing groundwater withdrawals would lead to saltwater intrusion.

The construction of the Aswan High Dam is an excellent case study of the impact of dam contruction on a coastal system. A comparison of pre- and post-construction conditions illustrates the impacts (George 1972). Phosphorus concentrations in the eastern Mediterranean average 0.1 μM, but near the mouth of the Nile 6.5 μM has been measured. The density of phytoplankton cells in Egyptian coastal waters, which averaged about 35,000 cells per liter during low-flow period, reached 2,400,000 cells per liter during peak flood. As a result of the dam construction the input of water, suspended sediments, and nutrients has decreased dramatically. George states that this marked "the dawn of a new nutrient regime for the southeastern Mediterranean." The Egyptian fishery harvest dropped from 30,600 metric tons per year prior to the dam to 12,600 after construction, primarily owing to the loss of the sardine fishery at the mouth of the Nile (George 1972). Because of the loss of sediments, the shoreline of the Nile delta is now undergoing retreat (Kassas 1972). Recently Stanley (1988) reported that the eastern part of the delta was undergoing subsidence of about 0.5 cm/yr. This rapid subsidence combined with reduction of sediment imput due to the Aswan Dam and rising sea level is likely to lead to flooding of a large part of the delta plain by the end of next century.

13.4   TOXINS

Toxic materials include such compounds as pesticides, heavy metals, petroleum products, and exotic by-products of industrial activity. These materials can be acutely toxic, or more commonly, they can cause chronic or sublethal effects. Toxins can also bioaccumulate in food chains. One well-known and moving example in which humans were directly affected is the so-called Minamata disease which resulted when a chemical company discharged mercuric wastes into Minamata Bay, Japan. The wastes were concentrated by fish that were consumed by local inhabitants. Numerous cases of disease, death, and birth defects occurred before the discharge ceased. Smith and Smith (1975) published a series of moving photographs which are a powerful testimony to the need for proper stewardship of coastal ecosystems. H.T. Odum et al. (1974) also present a number of examples of the effects of toxins in coastal sysems.

The environmental impacts of petroleum extraction, processing, and transport in the coastal zone has been a concern for many years. The National Academy of Sciences (1975) estimated that about six million metric tons of oil enters

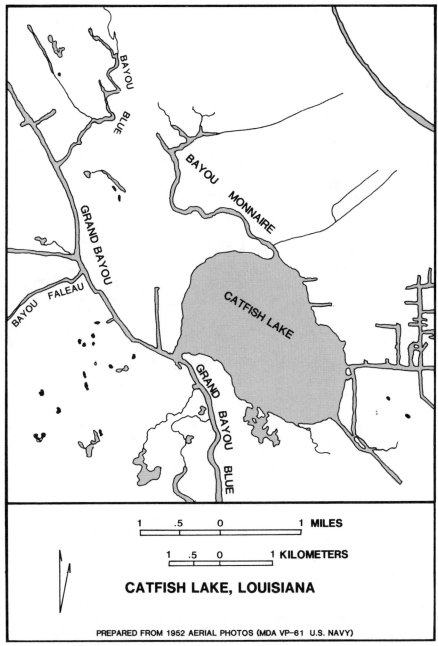

1 .5 0 1 MILES

1 .5 0 1 KILOMETERS

CATFISH LAKE, LOUISIANA

PREPARED FROM 1952 AERIAL PHOTOS (MDA VP-61 U.S. NAVY)

Figure 13.9 Changes in the salt marsh surrounding Catfish Lake, Louisiana, between 1952 and 1979. Numerous canals were dug for petroleum exploration and production. The shorter canals are for access to drilling sites and the long straight canal cutting diagonally across the bottom of the 1979 map is for a pipeline. Note spoil banks around several of the canals (prepared from 1952 aerial photos, MDA VP-61 U. S. Navy, and USGS Golden Meadow and Bay Courant Quadrangles 1964, photorevised 1979, court-sey Eric Swenson).

529

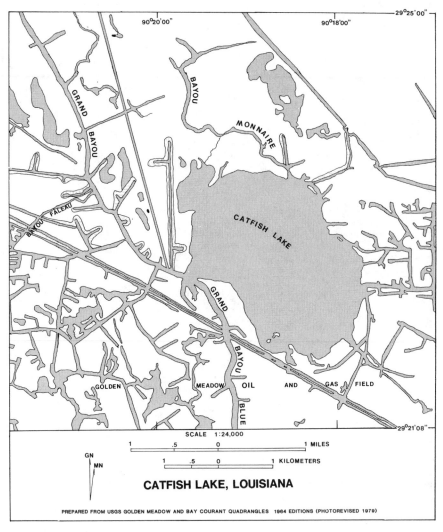

Figure 13.9 (continued)

the marine environment each year, much of it into coastal waters. Hall et al. (1978) reviewed the literature on the environmental impacts of this oil. These included mortality, growth inhibition, reduced reproduction, shifts in species importance, and tainted flesh in fish and shellfish. Hood et al. (1975) found that chronic oil pollution in a Louisiana salt marsh led to a shift in the microbial flora from dominance by cellulose-using forms toward a greater proportion of hydro-carbonoclastic bacteria and fungae. In a recent review of the ecological effects of oil spills, Teal and Howarth (1984) stated these generalizations: "oil regularly reaches sediments after a spill; oil in anoxic sediments is persistent; oil regularly contaminates zooplankton and benthic invertebrates; fish are also contaminated, but to a lesser extent; and oil contamination decreases the abundance and diversity of benthic communities".

One phenomenon which often characterizes persistent toxins is that of biological concentration of a substance as it moves up through a food web. This process has been called bioaccumulation or biomagnification. There are many examples of this for persistent pesticides. One classic example is for DDT in a salt marsh system on the shore of Long Island Sound, New York. Woodwell et al. (1967) measured the concentration of DDT and several breakdown products in the water, soil, and biota of the estuary. The DDT concentrations increased with trophic level by more than 5 orders of magnitude (Table 13.4). Concentrations ranged from 0.00005 ppm in water to 75.5 ppm in ring-billed gulls. The highest concentrations were close to being acutely toxic. Bans on the use of such persistent pesticides in many parts of the world have decreased the incidence of the problem, but this example vividly illustrates the process of biomagnification. Meanwhile, although DDT use in the United States has declined a great deal, DDT production has increased and it is still widely used in many other parts of the world.

Industrialization has led to the pollution of many estuaries. An example is the Rhine–Meuse estuary discussed earlier (Fig. 13.10). In Lake Haringvliet, which receives direct input of river water, heavy metal levels in the sediments are nearly as high as, and sometimes higher than, Rhine River sediments. In the southern part of this delta area the Schelde River, which drains the port of Antwerp, also has high levels of heavy metals. In other parts of the system, heavy metal levels are relatively low.

An example of the indirect impact of industrial effluents on a coastal ecosystem was described by Clements and Livingston (1983) and Livingston (1984). They compared the food habits of fishes inhabiting seagrass beds in an estuary in Florida which was polluted by pulp mill effluent with those of fish in an unpolluted estuary. The effluent did not affect the fish directly, but changed the environment where the fish lived. In the polluted estuary, major grassbeds were eliminated and overall benthic productivity was reduced, while there was an increase in nutrient concentrations and phytoplankton productivity. The dominant food habits in the unpolluted estuary were characterized by benthic, detrital-based feeders. In the estuary receiving pulp mill waste, grassbed fish were replaced by plankton and macrofauna feeders. Seasonally, there was a progression of various opportunistic feeders. Though many of the same species were present in both areas and diversities were not significantly different, the trophic diversity was lower in the polluted system, with species feeding on a less varied selection of food.

TABLE 13.4   DDT Residues (DDT + DDE + DDD) in Samples from Carmans River Estuary and Vicinity, Long Island, New York[a]

Sample	DDT Residues (ppm)	Percent of Residue as		
		DDT	DDE	DDD
Water	0.00005			
Plankton, mostly zooplankton	0.040	25	75	Trace
Cladophora gracilis	0.083	56	28	16
Shrimp	0.16	16	58	26
Opsanus tau, oyster toadfish (immature)	0.17	None	100	Trace
Menidia menidia, Atlantic silverside	0.23	17	48	35
Crickets	0.23	62	19	19
Nassarius obsoletus, mud snail	0.26	18	39	43
Gasterosteus aculeatus, threespine stickleback	0.26	24	51	25
Anguilla rostrata, American eel (immature)	0.28	29	43	28
Flying insects, mostly Diptera	0.30	16	44	40
Spartina patens, shoots	0.33	58	26	16
Mercenaria mercenaria, hard clam	0.42	71	17	12
Cyprinodon variegatus, sheepshead minnow	0.94	12	20	68
Anas rubripes, black duck	1.07	43	46	11
Fundulus heteroclitus, mummichog	1.24	58	18	24
Paralichthys dentatus, summer flounder	1.28	28	44	28
Esox niger, chain pickerel	1.33	34	26	40
Larus argentatus, herring gull, brain	1.48	24	61	15
Strongylura marina, Atlantic needlefish	2.07	21	28	51
Spartina patens, roots	2.80	31	57	12
Sterna hirundo, common tern	3.15	17	67	16
Sterna hirundo, common tern	3.42	21	58	21
Butorides virescens, green heron (immature, found dead)	3.51	20	57	23
Larus argentatus, herring gull (immature)	3.52	18	73	9
Butorides virescens, green heron	3.57	8	70	22
Larus argentatus, herring gull, brain	4.56	22	67	11
Sterna albifrons, least tern	4.75	14	71	15
Sterna hirundo, common tern	5.17	17	55	28
Larus argentatus, herring gull (immature)	5.43	18	71	11
Larus argentatus, herring gull (immature)	5.53	25	62	13
Sterna albifrons, least tern	6.40	17	68	15
Sterna hirundo, common tern (five abandoned eggs)	7.13	23	50	27
Larus argentatus, herring gull	7.53	19	70	11
Larus argentatus, herring gull	9.60	22	71	7
Pandion haliaetus, osprey (one abandones egg)	13.8	15	64	21
Larus argentatus, herring gull	18.5	30	56	14
Mergus serrator, red-breasted merganser (1964)	22.8	28	65	7
Phalacrocorax auritus, souble-cested cormorant (immature)	26.4	12	75	13
Larus delawarensis, ring-billed gull (immature)	75.5	15	71	14

[a]In parts per million wet weight of the whole organism, with the proportions of DDT, DDE, and DDD expressed as a percentage of the total (from Woodwell et al. 1967).

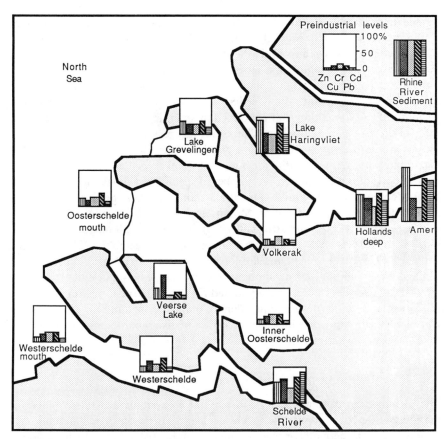

Figure 13.10 Distribution of heavy metals in sediments of the Rhine–Meuse delta area. The levels are given as percentages of those occurring in sediments of the Rhine River. Preindustrial era levels of heavy metals were estimated from concentrations in sediments over which the Rhine River flowed in the 17th century (after Solomons personal communication).

13.5 CHANGES IN BIOTIC STRUCTURE DUE TO HARVEST AND INTRODUCTION OF NEW SPECIES

13.5.1 Harvest

As we demonstrated in the last chapter, one of the great attractions of estuaries is that they often support a high degree of fishing effort. If an individual species is exploited too heavily or overfished, there can be pronounced changes in the composition of the estuarine community. In the last chapter we gave a number of examples of the effects of depletion of the stocks of individual species. When a specific species is reduced, its competitors and food supply may increase.

One kind of industrial activity in the coastal zone which can be considered as a kind of accidental harvest is the trapping of fish and plankton in the cooling water intake of power plants and other facilities. This has been termed entrainment and can lead to significant mortality because of the enormous amounts of water which can pass through a plant. In fact, Nugent (1971) compared an electric power plant to a giant "filter-feeder" which in 2–3 weeks can ingest (entrain) a volume of water equal to that contained in an entire estuary. Because the majority of the estuarine fauna have planktonic larvae and many important fishery species are both estuarine-dependent and have planktonic life stages, entrainment holds enormous potential for both ecological as well as economic damage. How important is entrainment? A number of specific examples will illustrate the point. Between 7 and 160 million menhaden and river herring were lost daily at the Brayton Point power plant on Mount Hope Bay, Massachusetts during the summer of 1971 (Clark and Brownell 1973). Thirty-six million young fish were killed in 16 days at a power plant in Connecticut in November 1971 (Clark and Brownell 1973). If power plants are located in ecologically critical areas of an estuary, the potential for entrainment is great. For example, Hall (1977) estimated that a series of plants once planned for the mid-Hudson River would use in 18 days an amount of water equivalent to that contained in a 50-km section of the mid-Hudson and drifting eggs or larvae of fish would have about a 75% probability of entrainment.

13.5.2   Introduction of New Species

The introduction of new species into coastal ecosystems has taken place for many centuries both on purpose and by accident. Purposeful introductions have mainly been commercially or recreationally valuable fish and shellfish, although some species have been introduced for utilitarian reasons such as weed control. Most accidental introductions of new species into coastal and estuarine waters have been on the hulls or in the ballast water of ships. Some species were purposely imported and then accidently released. We will now discuss each of these in more detail.

Moyle (1986) reviewed fish introductions into North America. The transplantation of fishes has a long history. The Romans took carp from the Danube River to Italy and Scandinavians transplanted salmonids in the twelfth century. By the 1870s, Pacific salmon were regularly brought to the Atlantic coast. The introduction of new species, not only of fish but other aquatic organisms as well (Carlton 1974), continues to the present. Moyle reported that there were few introduced fish species in east and Gulf coast estuaries, while they were common in west coast estuaries, and at times were the most abundant species. He attributed this to the relatively depauperate fish fauna in west coast estuaries, the much larger area of estuaries on the east and Gulf coasts, and the relative "youth" of estuaries on the west coast. For example, half of the 42 fish species collected by Moyle et al. (1986) from the Sacramento-San Joaquin estuary were introduced. The most abundant species, the striped bass, was introduced. The importance of introduced species seems to decline in more northerly coastal systems as well as in small isolated systems. In a small southern California estuary, 19% of 32 species were introduced (Allen 1982) as compared to 6% of 31 species in a large British Columbia estuary (Levy et al. 1979).

In the Suisun Marsh in the Sacramento-San Joaquin delta, Herbold (1987) noted feeding differences between native and introduced fishes. The small opossom shrimp (*Neomysis mercedis*) seems to be a major food item for most of the fishes of the area. When the shrimp migrates from the area in the fall or its density is reduced by predation, native fishes switch to other food items while the introduced species continue to feed largely on the shrimp. Consequently, the fullness of their stomachs declines, while this does not happen for the native fishes. Moyle et al. (1986) report that the native species tend to form a very stable assemblage that becomes increasingly likely to change as new species are introduced. Because the introduced species are less well adapted to local conditions, their population dynamics may be more variable. This may explain why fisheries managers often have such difficulty maintaining adequate populations of introduced species such as striped bass. In general, however, Moyle (1986) concluded that communities with introduced species seem to be structurally similar to estuarine fish communities without introduced species.

Many species of vertebrates and invertebrates have been accidently introduced into coastal and estuarine systems as fouling organisms on the hulls and pipes as well as in ballast water of ships. Carlton (1974, 1985) lists numerous species of such organisms, representing practically all major plant and animal groups. Carlton (1985) suggests that ballast water may be particularly important in the transport of many adult and juvenile organisms, as it has been shown that numerous organisms can survive passage through ship's pumps and for relatively long periods in ballast tanks. Carlton (1985) suggests that transport via ballast water is perhaps the major synanthropic dispersal mechanism operating for marine species in the world today. He also suggests that a number of coastal species which are considered cosmopolitan, in fact, may have been introduced before careful biological surveys were carried out.

Two introduced species which have become important in coastal areas around the Gulf of Mexico are the nutria (*Myocastor coypu*) and the water hyacynth (*Eichhornia crassipes*). The nutria, a native South American mammal, was introduced into Louisiana in the 1930s for fur production and weed control (O'Neil 1949, Lowery 1974). Subsequently, the nutria spread rapidly and its population grew, and by the late 1950s the total population was estimated at over 20 million animals (Lowery 1974). It is now the single most important species in the trapping industry in Louisiana. Nutria may also be contributing to the coastal wetland loss problem in Louisiana. Because they cause extensive "eat-outs" of existing marsh and feed heavily on new shoots, they contribute to marsh destruction and regrowth. For example, 250 nutrias were introduced to the Mississippi River delta in 1951 and the population in the delta increased so rapidly that the marsh in areas of the delta was eliminated by 1957. More recently, it has become apparent that nutria are an important factor preventing the regrowth of cypress forests because they feed heavily on seedlings (Conner 1988). The nutria is thus a case where a single species can be both beneficial (in terms of the fur harvest) and detrimental (contributing to land loss). The water hyacynth was introduced into Louisiana late last century as an ornamental at an international exibition held at New Orleans. It was accidently released and has spread widely since. It is now a pest species in many tidal freshwater areas obstructing waterways and some-times leading to low oxygen conditions. Millions of dollars have been spent try-ing to control this plant.

13.6 CONCLUSIONS

Thus far in the chapter, we have discussed impacts individually so as to indicate clearly their causes and consequences. It should be clear at this point that there are serious problems in many, if not most, coastal systems. What we have not stressed so far, but what is probably obvious, is that many coastal systems are characterized by multiple stresses. The level of ecological damage is many sys-tems is staggering, and if steps are not taken, more ecological resources with considerable economic value will be lost. We will come back to the question of economics later, but first we will discuss a number of examples estuarine systems with multiple impacts.

Nichols et al. (1986) provide an excellent summary of changes in the San Francisco Bay estuary. Extensive hydraulic mining in the drainage basin in the second half of last century greatly altered streams feeding into the bay system and deposited considerable sediments in the bay. Of the original 2200 km^2 of tidal marsh, only about 125 km^2 of undiked marsh remains today. Due to exten-sive use of freshwater for irrigation and domestic consumption, fresh water in-flow to the bay system has been reduced by about 60%. This disruption of flow has affected migratory fish populations. Considerable numbers of young fish are drawn into irrigation pumps and siphons and the abundance of striped bass, for example, has declined to 25% of that of the mid-1960s. Wastes from industry, municipalities, and agriculture flow into the bay and historical fishery levels have declined.

Data presented for the Mississippi Delta, Chesapeake Bay, and the Rhine Delta show similar impacts. In these areas there have been large reductions in habitat, widespread eutrophication, pollution by toxic materials, and decreases in fisheries. For example, almost all coastal wetlands in the Rhine Delta area have been destroyed, there have been significant reductions of both wetlands and submerged vegetation in Chesapeake Bay, and the rate of wetland loss in the Mississippi Delta can only be described as catastrophic. Unfortunately, this pic-ture of pervasive alteration of the estuarine environment is all too common around the world. Although there is much concern and activity, the situation may not be improving much, and in the developing world, the pace of degrada-tion seems to be accelerating.

Given the high productivity and economically valuable resources of estuarine systems, why has such environmental degradation been permitted and why is it still permitted? The answers to these questions are varied and complex. On one hand, the lack of understanding of how estuarine systems functioned, such as the role of wetlands and seagrasses in supporting fisheries, limited rational decision making. On the other, relentless pressure for development combined with a narrow economic view led to an undervaluing of estuarine resources (and natural resources in general). Thus, large areas of wetlands have been "reclaimed" for agricultural, industrial, and urban use. Much of this has ceased in developed countries, but in the developing world many coastal habitats are still being destroyed. An example of this in the tropics is the widespread destruction of mangroves for the construction of shrimp ponds. There is an immediate economic gain in terms of shrimp harvest, but the costs of mangrove destruction include declines in natural fisheries and decreases in water quality. In addition, most of the shrimp are sold on international markets but the availability of high quality protein (from natural fisheries) to local populations decreases. The failure to balance short-term benefits against long-term sustained resource use is a common problem in most parts of the world.

There has been a lack of appreciation of just how severe human impacts can be and a lack of understanding of the cumulative and synergistic nature of environmental impacts. Thus in Chesapeake Bay, many inputs of nitrogen and phosphorus have led to a serious eutrophication problem. And in Louisiana, the cumulative impact of thousands of canals has been devastating. On a worldwide basis, the burning of fossil fuels has caused an increase in carbon dioxide in the atmosphere which many believe will lead to global warming and sea level rise. This would flood most of the coastal wetlands of the world such as suggested for the Nile Delta by Stanley (1988).

At the base of many of these problems is a failure to appreciate the total value of natural resources such as occur in coastal systems. It is not difficult to understand the value of estuarine systems in terms of fisheries which have direct economic benefits. But natural systems do much more that benefits human society. Examples of natural work services are flood control, maintenance of chemical cycles, alleviating water quality problems, and providing general homeostasis. Natural energy flows have always been the basis for economic health, but the current dependence on fossil energies tends to mask their value. It has become increasingly clear that most conventional economic analysis neglects the high value of natural systems and deliberately "discounts" the environment in many ways (Dohan 1977, Hall et al. 1986, Hall 1988). Some calculations find that the value of marshland in the natural state is as high as $20,000 per ha (Farber and Costanza 1987).

Finally, a great problem overall is the continued increase in population numbers and affluence of our own species. As the number and wealth of people increase their demand for resources—and the secondary impacts associated with that demand—cause ever increasing impacts on all environments. In the developed world many environmental laws have meant that impacts are less than they might be, and some estuaries are genuinely getting cleaner. In much of the developing world, however, environmental protection is viewed as a luxury, even though many more people there depend on estuaries for their direct economic well-being. Globally estuaries are preferred sites for human habitation, and hence are very heavily impacted. There is as yet no general plan for alleviating these problems and conserving these important resources. There is much for the readers of this book to do.

REFERENCES

Allen, L., 1982. Seasonal abundance, composition, and productivity of the littoral fish assemblages in Upper Newport Bay, California. Fishery Bull., 80:769-790.

Barlow, J., C. Lorenzen, and R. Myren, 1963. Eutrophication of a tidal estuary. Limnnol. Oceanogr., 8(2):251-262.

Baumann, R., J. Day, and C. Miller, 1984. Mississippi deltaic wetland survival: sedimentation vs. coastal submergence. Science, 224:1093-1095.

Bayley, S., V. Stotts, P. Springer, and J. Steenis, 1978. Changes in submerged aquatic macrophyte populations at the head of Chesapeake Bay, 1958-1975. Estuaries, 1:73-84.

Cambridge, M. and A. McComb, 1984. The loss of seagrasses in Cockburn Sound, Western Australia. I. The time course and magnitude of seagrass decline in relation to industrial development. Aq. Bot., 20:229-243.

Carlton, J., 1974. Introduction of intertidal invertebrates. In R. Smith and J. Carlton (Eds.), Light's Manual of Intertidal Invertebrates of the Central California Coast. Univ. California Press, Berkeley, pp. 17-25.

Carlton, J., 1985. Transoceanic and interoceanic dispersal of coastal marine organisms: The biology of ballast water. Oceanogr. Mar. Biol. Ann. Rev., pp. 313-371.

Clark, J. and W. Brownell, 1973. Electric Power Plants in the Coastal Zone: Environmental Issues. American Littoral Society Special Publication No. 7, pp. VI-15 and V-14 American Littoral Society, Highlands, NJ, 146 pp.

Clements, W. and R. Livingston, 1983. Overlap and pollution-induced variability in the feeding habits of filefish (Pices: Monacanthidae) from Apalachee Bay, Florida. Copeia, 2:331-338.

Conner, W., 1988. Natural and artificial regeneration of bald cypress in the Barataria and Verret basins of Louisiana. PhD Diss., La. State Univ., Baton Rouge, 148 pp.

Craig, N., R. Turner, and J. Day, 1979. Land loss in coastal Louisiana (U.S.A.). J. Environ. Manage., 3:133-144.

Craig, N., R. Turner, and J. Day, 1980. Wetland losses and their consequences in coastal Louisiana. Z. Geomorph. N. F. (Berlin), Suppl.-Bd., 34:225-241.

Deegan, L., H. Kennedy, and C. Neill, 1984. Natural factors and human modifications contributing to marsh loss in Louisiana's Mississippi River deltaic plain. Environ. Manage., 8:519-528.

Dohan, M., 1977. Economic values and natural ecosystems, In C. Hall and J. Day (Eds.), Ecosystem Modeling in Theory and Practice. Wiley-Interscience, New York, pp. 134-171.

Farber, S. and R. Costanza, 1987. The economic value of wetlands systems, J. Envir. Manage., 24:41-51.

Ferguson, H. A. and W.J. Wolff, 1984. The Haringvliet project: The development of the Rhine-Meuse estuary from tidal inlet to stagnant freshwater lake. Water Sci. Technol., 16:11-26.

Frazier, D, 1967. Recent deltaic deposits of the Mississippi River: their development and chronology. Trans. Gulf Coast Assoc. Geol. Soc., 17:287-315.

Gael, B. and C. Hopkinson, 1979. Drainage density, land-use, and eutrophication in Barataria Basin, Louisiana. In J. Day, D. Culley, R. Turner, and A. Mumphrey (Eds.), Proceedings of the Third Coastal Marsh and Estuary Management Symposium. Division of Continuing Education, Louisiana State University, Baton Rouge, pp. 147-163.

George, C., 1972. The role of the Aswan High Dam in changing the fisheries of the southeastern Mediterranean. In M. Farvar and J. Milton (Eds.), The Careless Technology. The Natural History Press, Garden City, NY, pp. 159-178.

Gerlach, S., 1981. Marine Pollution. Springer-Verlag, New York, 218 pp.

Gosselink, J. and R. Baumann, 1980. Wetland inventories: Wetland loss along the United States coast. Z. Geomorph. N. F. (Berlin). Suppl.-Bd., 34:173-187.

Hall, C., 1977. Models and the decision making process: The Hudson River power plant case. In C. Hall and J. Day (Eds.), Ecosystem Modeling in Theory and Practice. Wiley-Interscience, New York, pp. 345-364.

Hall, C., 1988. The failure of conventional econmics in the developing world. In Wali, M. (Ed). The rehabalitation of disturbed ecosystems, Springer-Verlag, New York. (in press)

Hall, C. and J. Day, 1977. Ecosystem Modeling in Theory and Practice. Wiley-Interscience, New York, 684 pp.

Hall, C., R. Howarth, B. Moore, and C. Vorosmarty, 1978. Environmental impacts of industrial energy systems in the coastal zone. Ann. Rev. Energy, 3:395-475.

Hall, C., C. Cleveland, and R. Kaufmann, 1986. Fisheries. In Energy and Resource Quality: The Ecology of the Economic Process. Wiley, New York, pp. 437-459.

Heinle, D., C. F. D'Elia, J. L. Taft, J. S. Wilson, M. Cole-Jones, A. B. Caplins, and L. E. Cronin, 1980. Historic review of water quality and climatic data from Chesapeake Bay, with emphasis on effects of enrichment. University of Maryland, Center for Environmental and Estuarine Studies, Ref. No. 80-15-CBL. Solomons, Maryland.

Herbold, B., 1987. Resource partioning with a non-coevolved assemblage of fishes. Ph.D. Dissertation, Univ. California, Davis.

Hood, M., W. Bishop, F. Bishop, S. Meyers, and T. Whelan, 1975. Microbial indicators of oil-rich salt marsh sediments. Appl. Microbiol., 30:982-987.

Hopkinson, C. and J. Day, 1979. Aquatic productivity and water quality at the upland-estuary interface in Barataria Basin, Louisiana. In R. Livingston (Ed.), Ecological Processes in Coastal and Marine Systems. Plenum, New York, pp. 291-314.

Jansson, B. and F. Wulff, 1977. Baltic ecosystem modeling. In C. Hall and J. Day (Eds.) Ecosystem Modeling in Theory and Practice. Wiley-Interscience, New York, pp. 324-343.

Jaworski, N., 1981. Sources of nutrients and the scale of eutrophication problems in estuaries. In B. Neilson and L. Cronin (Eds.), Estuaries and Nutrients. Humana, Clifton, NJ, pp. 83–110.

Kassas, M., 1972. Impact of river control schemes on the shoreline of the Nile Delta. In M. Farvar and J. Milton (Eds.), The Careless Technology. The Natural History Press, Garden City, NY, pp. 179–188.

Kemp, G. and J. Day, 1984. Nutrient dynamics in a Louisiana swamp receiving agricultural runoff. In K. Ewel and H. Odum (Eds.), Cypress Swamps. University of Florida Press, Gainesville, pp. 286–293.

Kemp, M., M. Lewis, J. Cunningham, J. Stevenson, and W. Boynton, 1980. Microcosms, macrophytes, and hierarchies: Environmental research in the Chesapeake Bay.In J. Giesy (Ed.), Microcosms in Ecological Research. U.S. Technical Information Center, U.S. Department of Energy Symposium Series 52 (CONF-781101), pp. 911–936.

Kemp, M., W. Boynton, R. Twilley, J. Stevenson, and J. Means, 1983. The decline of submerged aquatic vegetation in upper Chesapeake Bay: Summary of results concerning possible casues. Mar. Technol. Soc. J., 17:78–89.

Kuenzler, E., and N. Craig, 1986. Land use and nutrient yields of the Chowan River watershed. In D. Correll (Ed.), Watershed Research Perspectives. Smithsonian Institution Press, Washington, pp. 77–107.

Levy, D., T. Northcote, and G. Birch, 1979. Juvenile salmon utilization of tidal channels in the Fraser River Estuary, British Columbia. Westwater Research Center University, British Columbia, 20 pp.

Littlejohn, C., 1977. An analysis of the role of natural wetlands in regional water management. In C. Hall and J. Day (Eds.), Ecosystem Modeling in Theory and Practice. Wiley Interscience, New York, pp. 451–476.

Livingston, R., 1984. Trophic response of fishes to habitat variability in coastal seagrass systems. Ecology, 65:1258–1275.

Lowery, G., 1974. The Mammals of Louisiana and Its Adjacent Waters. Louisiana State Univ. Press, Baton Rouge, 565 pp.

Mann, K., 1982. Ecology of Coastal Waters A Systems Approach. University of California Press, Berkeley, 322 pp.

Meade, R. and R. Parker, 1984. Sediments in rivers of the United States. National Water Supply Summary. U.S. Geol. Survey Water-Supply Paper 2275.

Mihursky, J. and W. Boynton, 1978. A review of the Patuxent River data base. Maryland Department of Natural Resources, Power Plant Siting Program. Annapolis, Maryland.

Moyle, P., 1986. Fish introductions into North America: Patterns and ecological impact. In H. Mooney and J. Drake (Eds.), Ecology of Biological Invasions of North America and Hawaii. Springer-Verlag, New York, pp. 27–43.

Moyle, P., R. Daniels, B. Herbold, and D. Baltz, 1986. Patterns in distribution and abundance of a noncoevolved assemblage of estuarine fishes in California. Fishery Bulletin, 84:105–117.

National Academy of Sciences, 1975. Petroleum in the Marine Environment. National Academy of Sciences, Washington, D.C., 107 pp.

Neilson, B. and L. Cronin (Eds.), 1981. Estuaries and Nutrients. Humana, Clifton, NJ, 643 pp.

Nienhuis, P. H. and J. C. Huis in 't Veld, 1984. Grevelingen: From an estuary to a saline lake. Water Sci. Technol., 16:27–50.

Nugent, R., 1971. Elevated temperatures and electric power plants. Trans. Am. Fish. Soc., 99:848–849.

Odum, H. T., B. J. Copeland, and E. A. McMahan, 1974. Coastal Ecological Systems of the United States. The Conservation Foundation, Washington, D.C., Vol. III, 453 pp.

Odum, W. E., 1970. Insidious alteration of the estuarine environment. Trans. Am. Fish. Soc., 99:836–847.

Olsen, T. and F. Burgess (Eds.), 1967. Pollution and Marine Ecology. Wiley-Interscience, New York, 364 pp.

O'Neil, T., 1949. The muskrat in the Louisiana coastal marshes. La. Dept. Wildlife Fisheries, New Orleans, 152 pp.

Pearson, T. and R. Rosenberg, 1978. Macrobenthic succession in relation to organic enrichment and pollution of the marine environment. Oceanogr. Mar. Biol. Ann. Rev., 16:229–311.

Ryther, J.H., 1954. The ecology of phytoplankton blooms in Moriches Bay and Great South Bay Long Island, N.Y., Biol. Bull., 106:198–209.

Salomons, W., personal communication. Delft Hydraulics Laboratory, Haven, the Netherlands.

Scaife, W., R. Turner, and R. Costanza, 1983. Coastal Louisiana recent land loss and canal impacts. Environ. Manage., 7:433–442.

Smith, W. E. and A. Smith, 1975. Minamata. Holt, Rinehart and Winston, New York, 192 pp.

Stanley, D., 1988. Subsidence in the northeastern Nile Delta: Rapid rates, possible causes, and consequences. Science, 240:497–500.

Swenson, E. and R. Turner, 1987. Spoil banks: effects on a coastal marsh water-level regime. Estuarine, Coastal and Shelf Science, 24:599–609.

Teal J. and R. Howarth, 1984. Oil spill studies: a review of ecological effects. Environ. Manage., 8(1):27–44.

Thorhaug, A., D. Seger, and M. Roessler, 1973. Impact of a power plant on a subtropical estuarine environment. Mar. Pollut. Bull., 4:166–169.

Twilley, R., W. Kemp, K. Staver, J. Stevenson, and W. Boynton, 1985. Nutrient enrichment of estuarine submersed vascular plant communities. 1. Algal growth and effects on production of plants and associated communities. Mar. Ecol. Prog. Ser., 23:179–191.

Weiss, C. and F. Wilkes, 1974. Estuarine ecosystems that receive sewage wastes. In H. T. Odum, B. J. Copeland, and E. McMahan (Eds.), Coastal Ecological Systems of the United States. The Conservation Foundation, Washington, D.C. Vol. III, pp. 71–111.

Wolff, W. J. and J.J. Zijlstra, 1982. Effects of reclamation of tidal flats and marshes in the Netherlands on fishes and fisheries. In Polders of the World. International Institute for Land Reclamation and Improvement. Wageningen, The Netherlands, Vol. 3, pp. 57–67.

Woodwell, G., C. Wurster, and P. Isaacson, 1967. DDT residues in an east coast estuary: A case of biological concentration of a persistent insecticide. Science, 156:821–824.

Zieman, J., 1970. The Effects of Thermal Effluent Stress on the Seagrasses and Macroalgae in the Vicinity of Turkey Point, Biscayne Bay, Florida. PhD Dissertation, University of Miami, Coral Gables, FL, 160 pp.

Zieman, J. and E. Wood, 1975. Effects of thermal pollution on tropical-type estuaries, with emphasis on Biscayne Bay, Florida. In E. Wood and R. Johannes (Eds.), Tropical Marine Pollution. Elsevier, New York, pp. 75-98.